MARRIAGE AND FAMILY

Marriage and Family
A Foundation for Personal Decisions

KENNETH C. W. KAMMEYER

The University of Maryland

ALLYN AND BACON, INC.

Boston • London • Sydney • Toronto

Managing editor: Bill Barke
Series editor: Judy Shaw
Production coordinator: Peter Petraitis
Copy editor: Steve Dyer
Cover coordinator: Linda Dickinson
Cover designer: Vanessa Piñiero
Text designer: Megan Brook
Photo research: Christy Rosso/Leslie Galton

Library of Congress Cataloging-in-Publication Data
Kammeyer, Kenneth C. W.
    Marriage and family.

    Bibliography: p.
    Includes index.
    1. Family life education. 2. Family. 3. Marriage.
I. Title.
HQ10.K26 1987   306.8   85–19193
ISBN 0-205-08624-1

Printed in the United States of America

10 9 8 7 6 5 4 3   91 90 89 88

Photo/cartoon credits

Chapter 1

PHOTO 1.1 p. 1—© Kent Reno/Jeroboam, Inc. PHOTO 1.2 p. 5—UPI/Bettmann Newsphotos. CARTOON 1.1 p. 8—Drawing by Levin; © 1983 The New Yorker Magazine, Inc. PHOTO 1.3 p. 9—Gayle Levee. PHOTO 1.4 p. 14—© Stanley Rowin/The Picture Cube. PHOTO 1.5 p. 20—Douglas Kirkland/Sygma.

Chapter 2

PHOTO 2.1 p. 27—© Kent Reno/Jeroboam, Inc. PHOTO 2.2 p. 30—© Martin J. Dain/Magnum Photos, Inc. CARTOON 2.1 p. 34—Drawing by

(*continued on page following Subject Index*)

Lorenz; © 1984 The New Yorker Magazine, Inc. PHOTO 2.3 p. 36—UPI/Bettmann Newsphotos. PHOTO 2.4 p. 42—© Mikki Ansin/Taurus Photos, Inc. CARTOON 2.2 p. 45—Reprinted by permission: Tribune Media Services. PHOTO 2.5 p. 48—© Michael Abramson Liaison Agency.

Chapter 3

PHOTO 3.1 p. 63—A. Devaney. PHOTO 3.2 p. 66—Valentines from the collection of Jean P. Favalora, Gloucester, MA Photo: Christy L. Rosso. PHOTO 3.3 p. 71—Bridgeman/Art Resource Roman de la Rose, 1487–95, Dreamer Enters the Garden, British Library, London, England.

I am dedicating this book to my mother,
Lucinda Kammeyer Wedeking,
a strong and loving force in my life,
and to the memory of my father,
Emil Kammeyer,
for whom the same is true.

Brief Contents

Contents

Preface

College courses on marriage and the family often reflect two very different domains. Marriage and the family is first a field of study, with a rich and varied scholarly literature; it is also a very intimate and personal part of our lives. As teachers of these courses, it often happens that the topic of a particular class (love, husband-wife relations, sexual relationships, parent-child relations, separation and divorce) is at the same time a matter of great importance in our personal lives. The same is true of students, as many have reported, either in class or after class. This overlapping connection between the scholarly content of marriage and family courses and our personal involvement with the same issues can sometimes be a problem, but it also provides us with a special teaching opportunity. It is an opportunity that I have tried to take advantage of in this book.

The book is written in such a way that it provides both the scholarly foundations of the field of marriage and the family and the opportunity to relate these to personal decisions in our own lives. Each chapter presents the scholarly research, the theory, the conceptual insights, and the relevant statistics for the topic under consideration. At the end of each chapter, I have (with the advice and assistance of many other people) selected an issue that grows out of, or is related to, the topic of the chapter. As an example, the topic of Chapter 7 is entering marriage; the issue at the end of that chapter is, "Should couples have marriage contracts?" The philosophy of the book is that this contemporary issue can be discussed much more meaningfully after one is familiar with the history, cross-cultural variations, research, theory, and other important ideas on the topic. To take Chapter 7 as a specific case again, it may be important to know that in the nineteenth century most Irish farm families carefully worked out marriage contracts with other families before allowing their children to marry. Their contracts were different in many ways from the marriage contracts being considered by couples today, but this historical case may still be instructive when we consider whether a marriage contract is appropriate for our own circumstances.

Since Chapter 1 is an illustrative introduction to the remaining chapters of the book, it is not necessary to present an elaborate description of the chapter contents here. However, I can make a few statements that will clarify my decisions about how the book was written and organized. First, I am a strong believer in the usefulness of theory. A number of theories, or concepts and ideas derived from theories, are presented throughout the book. These theories (and they are not just sociological theories) are not presented in a cluster at the beginning of the book. Instead, I place them where they will clarify or enhance particular discussions. I do not present the theories at a single place out of consideration for the students. My students generally find mass introductions to be unclear, irrelevant, and forgettable. In class, the students seem much more receptive to theory when I can give them an immediate application, so I have followed that procedure in the writing of this book.

A second feature of this book is the way research is handled. I believe in the importance of research just as much as theory, but I do not believe in textbooks that present every last study on an issue. I have a definite preference for recent research over older research, unless the aim is to identify a trend or pattern over time. If the objective is simply to provide supportive evidence for a generalization, I will select one, two, or three pieces of research that provide the support. A study conducted in 1938 or 1963, even a well-done study, will not be used or cited just to demonstrate a comprehensive command of the literature.

It will also be apparent that I prefer to augment and supplement quantitative research findings whenever possible with the words of real people. Many concepts, ideas, and generalizations come alive when we can see them reflected in the realities of peoples' lives.

But the key to this book is the presentation of issues at the end of each chapter. Because marriage and family life has such a strong personal connection, I have chosen to make the issues at the ends of the chapters personal issues. Depending on the ages and experiences of the students, these are issues that they either have faced, are facing, or may face in the future. For each issue I have tried to present the pros and cons, or the alternative views, as fairly as possible. I do not claim to have made every possible argument that can be made. I see these statements as starting points for students, who can continue by offering their own particular ideas.

Perhaps a few words are needed on the mechanics of using these issues in college classes. Their use depends on a number of things, but especially important are personal teaching styles and class size. For those whose teaching style is heavily oriented toward student discussions, the issues provide fifteen ready-made discussion topics. Depending on the time period of the class, the discussions may cover an entire period or only part of a period, where they may serve as a change of pace. For instructors who do not wish to devote so much time to class discussions, the students can be polled at the beginning of the semester to see which issues are of greatest interest to them.

With regard to class size, I have often led discussions covering these and similar issues in classes with over one hundred students. To be sure, in large and very large classes not every student has the opportunity to voice his or her views fully. But this is not unlike any class where students make contributions. There are usually some students who are the "talkers," while others are the "listeners." The fact that some students do not speak out does not mean they are uninvolved in the discussion. I have had many occasions when after a particularly persuasive statement or argument by one student, other students in the class who feel their views have been expressed will applaud or otherwise express their concurrence. These students are no less involved in the discussion than the speaker. Also, I have often observed students who, though they said nothing during the class discussion, remained in the halls after class, in little knots of two or three students, discussing the issues vigorously.

It is also possible for these issues to be used as a basis for short, personal-position papers, if writing is an important element of a course. These are just a few thoughts on how the issues may be used, for certainly individual instructors will have or develop their own ways. As an additional convenience, the instructor's manual will provide more detailed descriptions of how the issues can be used.

ACKNOWLEDGMENTS

Among the many people who have encouraged and helped me in the publication of this book, I want especially to thank Al Levitt, who, as the Allyn and Bacon sociology editor, put himself on the line for me. I will not forget his confidence in me and his courage. While on the subject of editors, I wish also to praise the qualities of Judy Shaw, who assumed her new position when this project was well under way. As the new editor, she could have given it less than her full attention. Had she done so it would have been understandable, but she did quite the opposite. She was interested in the book, she was supportive, she was assiduous in making me commit myself to firm deadlines, and tolerant when I failed to meet them. She obviously has the makings of a great editor.

Among my professional colleagues, I owe my greatest debt to George Ritzer. The fundamental philosophy of this book can be traced back directly to his work on the issues, debates, and controversies in sociology. But, most importantly, George is the person I go to first when I need a clear judgment, straight advice, or simply to vent my professional frustrations. Several other of my colleagues at the University of Maryland are especially helpful when I need specific information, advice, a clarification, and so on. These include Barbara Altman, Glen Harper, Janet Hunt, Anne Imamura, Jennie McIntyre, Barbara Meeker, and Harriet Presser; Helen Ginn, my coauthor on another book, has been very understanding, and willing to take more than her share of that load when she understood that I was overwhelmed. I appreciate this special contribution.

Many colleagues around the country have read parts of the manuscript and have given me the benefit of their ideas, reactions, and knowledge. I cannot say that every report along the way has made me happy, and I have made some terrific mental ripostes to some of their criticisms, but in the long run I have been influenced by all reviewers. I wish to acknowledge now these many helpful colleagues:

John Ehle
Northern Virginia Community College

Connie Shehan
University of Florida

Jane Hall
Western Carolina University

Sandra Hanson
Case Western Reserve University

Karen Shroeder
University of Rhode Island

Judy Dowell
Western Carolina University

Ben Aquire
Texas A & M

Hugh Floyd
University of New Orleans

Karen Loscocco
SUNY—Albany

Carol Whitehurst
Humboldt State University

Gary Hansen
University of Southern Mississippi

Janice Stroud
University of California

Hilda Lineweaver
Shippensburg University

Tom Craven
St. Louis Community College at Meramec

David Kessel
Louisiana State University

Roger Little
University of Illinois

Rita Sackitt
Stonybrook, N.Y.

David Olday
Moorhead State University

Kay Paisley
University of Kentucky

Brent Miller
Utah State University

Ross Klein
Iowa State

Sherrill Richarz
Washington State University

Nancy Greenwood
North Dakota State University

Connie Aarons
University of Southern California

Marilyn Ihinger-Tallman
Washington State University

One of the reviewers, Connie Shehan, requires a special note of thanks, because she turned out to be a contributor more than a reviewer. Her reviews revealed that she was especially sensitive to both the style and the objectives of the book. On the basis of her review of a number of chapters, I asked if she would help me in writing the issues. With the help of the telephone, the postal service, and express package delivery systems, we carried on a dialogue about the issues. One of us would write a draft, and the other would react. I owe a great deal to Connie, because I know that she often put aside her own work to help me meet my deadlines.

One of the advantages of living in the Washington, D.C. area is the easy availability of information and statistics. But the particular advantage I wish to note is that the information comes not from an impersonal bureaucracy but from real people who are also friends. I especially want to mention three people in this regard, Lars Johanson, Paul Placek, and Barbara Wilson, but there are many others I have called on over the years, and I thank them all.

Two people, Maggie Brasted and Colleen O'Toole, served as research assistants in the course of the writing, and they both saved me many hours of work. These are two talented young people, and I wish them the best.

Two more people with Allyn and Bacon deserve my thanks. Peter Petraitis and I have not met, but as the person in charge of production he has kept things moving in a very professional way. I hope that we will have the opportunity to meet face-to-face before this project is complete. The second person is also a person I have not met, but feel very positive about—the copy editor, Steve Dyer. He is impressive in his attention to detail, and it is a great comfort to know that he has saved me so often from my misunderstandings, erroneous presumptions, careless writing, and on and on.

Before getting my own word processor, a number of friends in the Sociology Department did much typing from my longhand script. They always took a great interest, both in what I was writing about and in my deadlines. I want to thank Dorothy Bowers, Jane Deiter, Gladys Graham, Gerry Todd, Cass O'Toole, Bernadette Lasobic, Beverly Solomon, and Agnes Zane for their help through the years.

This book was started before Sonia became my wife, but not before she started influencing my thinking about the matters discussed here. In one way or another since we have been together, she and I have lived through quite an array of the issues covered (some good, some not so good). But the actual writing of this book will always be associated in my mind with the first three years of our marriage, and I would like to say here that they have been wonderful years. The only thing lacking has been enough time together. Perhaps with the completion of this work, we will have that too.

K.C.W.K.

1

Introduction to Marriage and Family Life
Facts, Theories, and Issues

There are plenty of critics of marriage and family life. There are cynics and skeptics, and those who predict the decline or death of marriage and the family. There are also the blamers, who are ready to hold the family responsible for any trend or problem in the society, from increasing premarital pregnancy to unemployment. But in spite of all this negativism, the family survives, and marriage continues to be popular. Even among many of the people who see its imperfections and shortcomings, the family is still the preferred way of life.

We might ask, along with one of the clearer and sharper analysts of the family, "Can family be all bad if the urge to have a family and be a family is so strong?" (Pogrebin, 1983, p. 25). The answer, according to this same writer, can be found in a series of metaphors.

> *If the family were a container, it would be a nest, an enduring nest, loosely woven, expansive, and open.*
>
> *If the family were a fruit, it would be an orange, a circle of sections, held together but separable—each segment distinct.*
>
> *If the family were a boat, it would be a canoe that makes no progress unless everyone paddles.*
>
> *If the family were a sport, it would be baseball: a long, slow, nonviolent game that is never over until the last out.*
>
> *If the family were a building, it would be an old, but solid structure that contains human history, and appeals to those who see the carved moldings under all the plaster, the wide plank floors under the linoleum, the possibilities. . . . (Pogrebin, 1983, pp. 25–26)*

These images are the goals and the ideals of family life. They are the advantages and the qualities that engage us and keep us coming back to the family as a preferred way of life, despite the critical and negative evaluations that are commonplace.

But let us not be too idealistic, for it is not always easy to accomplish these goals and ideals. There are both problems and complications that must be faced if we are to have the positive qualities of marriage and family life. Even as you begin this book, you are not unaware of many of these problems and complications. Some of you may already be married, or even divorced. All of you have probably discussed and thought about the many issues and decisions that are a part of marriage and family life. The primary purpose of this book is to help you as you continue to evaluate and assess these issues.

Each chapter of this book is designed to include three elements. First, there are *facts* and various kinds of *information* to increase your knowledge of the subject. Second, there are *insights* and *theories* that you can use to understand the nature and workings of marriage and family life. Third, there are presentations of *issues* and *controversies* that give you the opportunity to think about and make judgments and decisions in your own life.

I want to emphasize here, and will illustrate in the following sections, that I do not take a narrow view of either facts and information or insights and theories. Facts and information often come in the form of statistics and the quantitative results of social research, but, facts and information can also be in the form of historical materials, cross-cultural descriptions, and qualitative research findings. Similarly, when I refer to insights and theories, the sources will be wide-ranging and varied. Theories will come from sociology, psychology, and other fields of study. But, in addition, many different kinds of writers and thinkers will provide a number of other insights about marriage relationships and family life. Social commentators, biographers, novelists, philosophers, and many others often have important and insightful things to tell us about marriage and family relationships and experiences. Their contributions will be brought to the discussion whenever they help give a better understanding of the subject.

The issues and controversies will follow each of the chapters in this book. I am guided in this placement by the idea that any controversial issue can be approached more rationally and effectively after establishing a solid foundation of facts, information, insights and theories. To illustrate this approach, consider Chapter 7, which is devoted to the process of entering marriage. The body of the chapter examines a variety of facts and ideas about entering marriage, including historical and cross-cultural examples and a consideration of our own contemporary practices. Following this presentation an issue is considered that many people discuss today when they enter marriage: should a couple write a personal marriage contract, spelling out the couple's objectives, rights, and obligations, in advance? There are arguments for and against personal marriage contracts. I will provide what I hope will be a fair and balanced presentation of the arguments on both sides of the issue. It will then be up to you to consider, evaluate, and add to these arguments. This will be easier *after* you have gained a fuller understanding of the topic generally.

To give you a clearer sense of the approach of this book, the three major elements that shape each chapter will now be examined in more detail. Through illustrations and examples, you will see a sampling of facts and information, insights and theories, and issues and controversies.

FACTS AND INFORMATION

There are many kinds of facts and information about marriages and families. A fundamental type of fact is *statistics*. Statistics are facts that have been put into numerical form. While statistics are often necessary, most of us do not want a steady diet of statistical data. Statistics are best when they are both useful and interesting, though perhaps, on occasion, we have to settle for one or the other.

Statistics

One example of statistics is vital statistics, such as the median age of people in the United States at the time of their first marriage. For men the median age is 25.4; for women it is 23.0. These statistics tell us something about the age at which people in this society are most likely to marry and can be useful because they can be related to decisions in our personal lives. It might be interesting to know if one is marrying earlier or later than the median age in the United States. It might also be interesting to know if age at marriage is related to anything else, such as marital happiness or divorce. It can be useful to know that people who marry at a later age are generally less likely to divorce.

To pursue the matter of age at first marriage, it could be interesting to know something about the historical data. At what age do you think people married in the United States in the 1890s, or around 1900? You might have an idea, but is it correct? The statistical fact is that people were about the same age when they entered marriage at the beginning of the twentieth century as they are now. Men, on the average, married when they were older than twenty-six, and women were only a few years younger. In Figure 1.1 we show the median ages at first marriage for selected years, beginning in 1890. Statistics of this sort, especially when they differ from our preconceptions, can give us a little better perspective on our own times. It is true that we are marrying later today than we did a decade or so ago, but now we marry at about the same ages as our great-grandparents.

At the beginning of the twentieth century, men commonly married in their middle or late twenties; women in their early twenties.

Quantitative Studies

Statistics are only a small part of the range of facts and information. There are also the results and conclusions of surveys, studies, polls, and experiments. These are generally lumped together under the heading *social and psychological research*. It is difficult to find any area of marriage and family life that has not been the subject of some research. Unfortunately, that does not mean that the answers to all questions are known. Even though studies of marital happiness

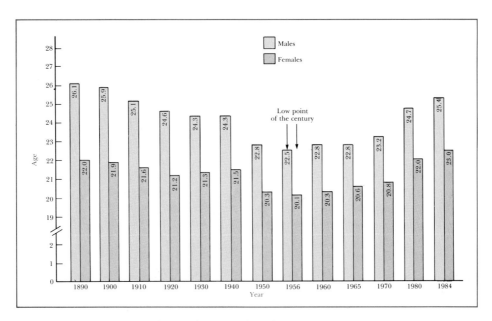

Figure 1.1 *Median age at first marriage, (selected years 1890–1984). (Source:* U.S. Bureau of the Census, *Current Population Report,* Series P. 20, No. 399, 1985.

have been conducted for at least fifty years, no researcher can yet say exactly how to have a happy marriage.

Most social and psychological research provides partial answers to some questions but leaves many other questions unresolved. Often, research studies will raise as many new questions as they answer. For example, we will see in a later chapter that married couples in general express less satisfaction with their marital relationships during the period of their lives when they have young children. But it is not clear exactly what reduces marital quality during this period of marriage. Further research can attempt to answer this question, but even without all the answers we can use this research information to focus our thinking and discussions. We can ask, what is *likely* to be happening in a relationship between a husband and wife when their children are young? Are there problems that stem from time pressures on both husbands and wives? Are there problems because many couples are struggling with economic matters? Although research may not provide all the answers, it can sensitize us to some of the problem areas of married life.

In this book the results of social research will be used primarily for the purpose of sensitizing and alerting us to the problems and realities of marriage and family life. We will be selective rather than comprehensive. The criteria for presenting research results will be that they must give us a better understanding of various parts of marriage and family life and at the same time be interesting.

Qualitative Research

Although some research results will be statistical, there are many areas of research that do not lend themselves to statistical and quantitative approaches. Even if they do, the research may have been done in a qualitative fashion so there are no statistical data. Sometimes these are the best kinds of research because they give us a more vivid picture of what social life is really like. Lillian Rubin (1976), for example, has written a book describing her interviews with young husbands and wives in the lower and working classes of American society. Rubin reveals many aspects of the lives of these young married couples, primarily through the words they used to answer her interview questions. For example, Rubin quotes the words of a thirty-year-old woman who married when she was eighteen:

> *Things were very bad after we got married. I think he used to feel like I didn't do anything but scream at him all the time. And I suppose that was true.*
>
> *We were very young and really immature, and we weren't ready for marriage and the problems you have to face right away. We both felt tied down, but he was worse about it than me. He had all his high school buddies in the neighborhood, and when he'd get bored, he'd just go out and hang out with them.*
>
> *I used to get jealous because I thought he wanted more than just me, and I thought I should be plenty for him. So I'd get mad and scream at him on top of my lungs, and he'd just withdraw. The more I screamed, the more he'd withdraw, until finally I'd go kind of crazy. Then he'd leave and not come back until two or three in the morning sometimes. That made me even madder, especially because I couldn't go anyplace. At first I had this big belly, what with being pregnant. Then when the baby was born, who would take care of her if I went out, too? So I felt like I was stuck in the house when he was out having a good time. (Rubin, 1976, pp. 78–79)*

Her husband is quoted as follows:

> *I didn't know how to handle her when we were first married. I couldn't understand what she was screaming about all the time. I guess I used to think she was possessive and too jealous, like she wanted to own me. . . .*
>
> *She still gets mad if I go out with the guys too often. But it's not the same now. I guess she trusts me more. I've been working at the same job for seven years now, and the money comes in regular. And you know, it makes a difference with the kids being a little older, and we can do things together again sometimes. (Rubin, 1976, p. 79)*

These thoughts and words of real people show clearly how difficult the adjustment to marriage can be, especially for those who marry when they are very

'Frankly, Harold, you're beginning to bore everyone with your statistics.'

young. Small wonder that divorce occurs so much more frequently for those who marry younger.

There are two additional kinds of social research that will be used widely throughout this book to broaden and deepen understanding and knowledge of marriage and family matters. These are *cross-cultural* and *historical* studies. Historical studies relating to marriage and family have been gaining in significance in recent years. Cross-cultural studies have been a mainstay of marriage and family studies for many years.

Cross-cultural Studies

Anthropologists have made great contributions to our knowledge about marriage and the family with studies of the ways of life of people around the world. Their reports, called *ethnographies*, often describe the cultural patterns of little-known societies. These ethnographic accounts of unusual ways of life have intrigued and fascinated readers for years. There are many lessons to be learned from cross-cultural studies, but certainly one of the most important is that marriage and family life, and all that is connected with them, can be conducted in an amazing variety of ways. For example, among the Nandi, a people who live in Kenya, it is possible for a married woman to take a young wife (Oboler, 1980). This is *not*, as we might initially assume, a case of a lesbian relationship. Indeed, the woman who takes a wife does not have a sexual relationship with her bride even though she will behave in almost all other ways like a male husband. Why, then, would a woman take a wife? The answer lies in the fact that she and her husband have been childless (or more specifically, they have not had a son). By taking a wife, a woman can yet have a son who will be able to inherit the family property and wealth. It works in this way. The young wife of the "female-husband" will have a lover who will visit her, and they will have sexual relations. When the young wife has a child, the female-husband will claim it as hers. If the child is a male, he will be eligible to inherit the family property and wealth. The biological father will not have rights to such a child, nor will he have any responsibilities for it.

This strikingly unusual case, coming from anthropological research, illustrates some of the variety that can be found in the ways marriage and family

Nandi women who marry each other.

systems are organized. But there is more to be learned from this case than an expanded view of cultural differences.

Another point to be derived from this case is that marriage often has an important *economic dimension.* It is clear that an economic consideration is the primary motivation for a Nandi woman when she marries a young female. A woman who has not borne a son and wishes to pass on her wealth to a male heir can achieve this economic objective by marrying a young female who will likely give her a son.

It is nearly impossible to exaggerate the importance of economic considerations in marriage. This is especially the case if one takes a broad historical and cross-cultural view. In society after society, from one historical period to another, marriages are made with a sharp eye on the economic implications of the marital union. Marriage has very often had as its primary purpose the transmission of wealth, power, and property to the next generation.

Later, when we examine in more detail the process of selecting marriage mates, we will see more examples of how widespread economic considerations are for marriage. In particular, we will also see how bargaining for the best possible marriage partner is a prominent feature of selecting a marriage mate. That point is also illustrated in the case of the young women among the Nandi who become the wives of older women. For these women the choice to marry an older woman instead of having the customary marriage to a man is an important decision. The young women who make this choice justify, or perhaps rationalize, their behavior in a number of ways. To begin with, they often have some characteristic that makes them less desirable as wives. Perhaps they have a physical or mental shortcoming, or they might already have a child or be pregnant by a man who refuses to marry them. Under these circumstances their bargaining power for a husband is diminished. That being the case, these young women often say that "it is better to be married by a wealthy woman than by a poor man" (Oboler, 1980, p. 76). For them, it is a better bargain.

The value of a marriage bargain can also be enhanced by noneconomic factors. In the case of the young women of the Nandi, some say they prefer to be married to a woman because such a marriage will give them greater social and sexual freedom. Female-husbands are much less likely than male husbands to question their wives' comings and goings. Female-husbands are less likely to be jealous and restrictive with their wives. Furthermore, female-husbands are thought to be more sympathetic and less demanding. Having been wives themselves, they can be more understanding about the wife's role. In even more concrete terms, female-husbands are less likely than male husbands to beat their wives (Oboler, 1980).

All of these considerations, although they are somewhat alien to most of us, are nonetheless understandable. We can also recognize that in our own marriage system there is bargaining involved. We may not bargain so explicitly for economic advantages, but economic considerations are not totally outside our awareness. Sexual and social freedoms are not likely to be prime considerations for us in selecting a marriage mate. However, other kinds of considerations will be found in our marriage bargaining. In a later chapter we will examine things that are important to us as we make the decision to marry.

Before leaving the cross-cultural example of the Nandi, there is one more point to be noted about women who become husbands. When these women take wives, they become more like men in their rights, prerogatives, and responsibilities. In sociological terms, their *gender role* changes. Gender roles are defined as the rights, duties, and behaviors associated with one's gender status, or sex. Gender roles are learned, and it is often assumed that once learned they remain relatively stable through life. Yet in the case of the Nandi, a woman who marries a young female in middle age or later suddenly changes her gender role. One such woman told an anthropological investigator, "When a visitor comes, I sit with him outside, and converse with him. My wife brings out maize-porridge, vegetables and milk. When we have finished eating I say, 'Wife, come and take the dishes,' Then I go for a walk with the visitor" (Oboler, 1980, p. 77). In general, female-husbands among the Nandi will avoid doing work that is customarily done by women. Even though they have spent a lifetime cooking, washing eating utensils, carrying water, collecting firewood, sweeping, plastering houses, and washing clothes, these "female tasks" suddenly become inappropriate and unacceptable. In theory female husbands also take on "men's work," which includes plowing, clearing bush, digging ditches, fencing, house-frame building, thatching, and slaughtering cattle for meat. However, since these women are often of advanced age they may not actually carry out many of these heavy tasks. They will, however, be responsible for hiring men who do these jobs for their households.

The main point to note is how easy it is to change deeply embedded gender roles. When the members of an entire society can create a marriage institution that completely reverses gender role expectations, it is clear that roles are not inextricably tied to one's biological gender. Gender roles are socially created and can therefore be socially changed or modified.

While the Nandi illustration reveals how gender role expectations can change, we must note in the interests of ethnographic accuracy that the transition among the Nandi is not total. The Nandi women who take wives do not become like men in every single respect. They do not quite achieve the same high status as men. If, for example, such a woman still has a male husband who is living, she may continue to provide services for him. "She will not wash her own clothes because in relation to her wife she is a man (husband); but she can still wash clothes for her male husband because in relation to him she is a wife and therefore a woman" (Oboler, 1980, p. 84). Perhaps it is for this reason that Nandi women who take wives never quite achieve the same high status as men. As one Nandi man put it, "They are more nearly equal to men than other women, but men are always ahead of them" (Oboler, 1980, p. 86).

Historical Studies of Marriage and Family

Much of historical research deals with the elite groups of a society (royalty, or political and military leaders) and with major military and political events. Increasingly, however, there is an interest in social histories that deal with the lives of everyday people. These often include historical details of marriage and family life in different time periods. Just as with cross-cultural research, historical research provides knowledge and information that broadens our perspectives on marriage and the family.

Perhaps the most important contribution of historical research is the way it allows us to see social changes in institutions and ideas. With respect to marriage and family life, historical research often shows us how things that now seem natural, normal, and unchanging have not always been as they are now.

An example of this can be found in the names and titles of women when they marry. Women entering marriage today often have to make a decision about what their name will be after marriage and how they wish to be addressed. The conventional form in the United States has been for a woman who is marrying to call herself *Mrs.* and then to take the name of her husband (e.g., Mrs. Carl Williams). Today, if a Mary Jones marries a Carl Williams there are quite a number of alternatives to the conventional form: Mrs. Mary Williams, Mrs. Carl Jones Williams, Mrs. Mary Jones Williams, Ms. Mary Williams, Ms. Mary Jones Williams, or Ms. Mary Jones. These are only some of the many possible options. However, women who are marrying often find it difficult to break away from what seems to be a deeply embedded tradition of using their husbands' names.

This tradition, however, is not as old as one might assume (Stannard, 1977). The title *Mrs.* is an abbreviation of *Mistress*, which was originally a title given only to women of high rank. Gradually, the term was applied to women of all social classes. But *Mrs.* did not necessarily refer to a woman who was married. In the middle of the seventeenth century in England, any mature woman, whether married or not, was appropriately called *Mrs.*

The title *Miss* also has relatively recent historical origins. This term was first used in the seventeenth century, but it did not refer to a woman who was single; rather, it was a slur on her character. A *Miss* was a woman of "loose morals" (Stannard, 1977, p. 6). It was not until about the 1730s that the term *Miss* was generally taken to mean an unmarried woman (including, of course, respectable women). Since the terms *Mrs.* and *Miss* are of relatively recent origin, and their usage has clearly changed over time, the adoption of the title *Ms.*, which seems contrived to some people, seems much less radical.

Even more recent as a convention is the use of a woman's husband's first and last name for her name, as in Mrs. John Jones. In the United States it was not until the 1840s that it became an established custom for a woman to use the first name of her husband. At the time of the first U.S. presidents, it would have been considered strange for a woman to refer to herself as Mrs. George Washington or Mrs. Thomas Jefferson. Stannard (1977) observes that such a usage would have sounded as strange to the people living then as Miss John Jones would sound to us today. When some women did begin to call themselves by their husband's first name, it was thought by many to be a kind of uppity snobbishness.

One other historical note on the titles and names of married women is that questioning the traditional ways is not new to this century. Many feminists of the nineteenth century spoke out vigorously against the practice of women having to take their husbands' names, first or last. Lucy Stone, an early feminist in the United States, married Henry R. Blackwell in 1855, and after using the name Lucy Stone Blackwell for a brief period she announced that henceforth she should only be referred to as Lucy Stone (Stannard, 1977). Lucy Stone was just one of many nineteenth-century feminists who retained their first and last names, although many added husbands' last names as well. Thus, we see that the contemporary practice of a woman keeping her family name, or combining it with her husband's last name, is not without precedent in the United States.

Even this brief review of some of the history of married names and titles gives us a little broader perspective on what often seems an unprecedented contemporary issue. Throughout this book historical facts will be used to give a broader view of current issues and controversies.

INSIGHTS AND THEORIES

While all types of facts and information will be important for our consideration of marriage and the family, our knowledge need not be limited to these "hard facts." Many people have given a great deal of thought to the nature and significance of all aspects of marriage and family life, and whenever possible we will take advantage of their insights and ideas. These can range from deep insights into the essence of human relations and family life to the creation of new theories, concepts or terms that sensitize us to what is happening in our own lives.

Often, an apt illustration or an unusual way of looking at some situation will help us to see reality more clearly. For example, in a short book of essays by Dorothy Samuel (1976) is the following thought-provoking idea about a "perfect marriage." Usually, the label *perfect marriage* is applied to couples who follow the ideal cultural patterns. This might be the case where one person has gone into a business or profession and achieved some financial success, while the other half of this perfect marriage is pleased with the partner's successful career and is happily supportive in many ways. This other half of the perfect marriage enjoys taking care of and improving the home, cooking meals, and caring for children, if there are children. This partner will, when necessary, take a job to help the family's finances but really prefers being in the home. This perfect marriage would be socially approved because the two partners are thought to be "a well-functioning unit." Each gets satisfaction from a primary task and responsibility, and at the same time each complements and supports the other. This is a perfect marriage—unless it is the wife who has the successful career and the husband who prefers to take care of the home.

How clearly this illustration brings to our attention the way in which we often think in terms of the traditional male and female roles. We also see, from our own reaction, how it may not be as easy to accept that the couple has a perfect marriage once we learn that the traditional husband and wife roles have been reversed. Samuel describes an actual couple of her acquaintance where a husband and wife had reversed their roles. They experienced various social pressures and had to devise defenses against them. They had to draw a curtain of mystery around their lives in order to protect their "perfect marriage." Because they lived in a large city, they were anonymous enough to keep their arrangement more or less secret. While the wife was having a successful business career, they told friends and acquaintances that her husband was in "rentals." This was a partial truth, because they did rent out some rooms in their home. Later, when he was somewhat older, they simply said he was retired. That small "white lie" satisfied their friends and acquaintances, yet the irony of the situation cannot be missed. Here was a couple with all the elements of a perfect mar-

A few couples prefer to reverse the tasks traditionally assigned to males and females, but a complete reversal usually requires some social defenses.

riage, except that the woman was doing what husbands are traditionally expected to do and the man was doing what wives are traditionally expected to do. This illustration came from the observation of a keen social observer rather than from a social researcher or social theorist, but that does not diminish in the least its instructiveness.

Theory as a Source of Insights

Social scientists develop theories as a way of making social life more understandable. This book is not specifically devoted to theories of marriage and the family, but it will take full advantage of theoretical formulations and conceptual insights whenever they can be useful. The best theories are often very useful because they are applicable to a wide variety of concrete situations. This view is contrary to the notions of many people who think of theories as lofty abstractions, far removed from reality. While that is sometimes the case, many times theories give us the keys we need to understand complex and confusing phenomena. One test for a *good* theory is whether or not it helps us to understand our own personal situations or problems.

Consider, for example, a problem that confronts most of us at one time or another: jealousy. Jealousy is an unpleasant emotion, one that we wish we did not feel when it besets us. In its most common form, an individual feels jealousy when there are threats to the continuation of a romantic relationship. The threat usually comes from a third person who is perceived as being attractive to one's partner.

Quite a number of theories have been advanced to explain jealousy. One theory explains it in terms of relationships we have in infancy, in particular the highly emotional relationship we have with our parents. This relationship is so important to us as children that we are threatened by its loss or potential loss. According to this theory of jealousy, the loss of an intimate relationship in later life can bring back some of the earlier feelings we had as infants and children, when we feared losing a parent's love (Skolnick, 1983). This theory would make jealousy a nearly universal phenomenon, since most people have intimate attachments to a parent when they are infants. But such a theory does not easily account for variations in the intensity of jealousy from one person to the next.

Another widely accepted theory of jealousy is more helpful in explaining variations from one person to the next. This theory holds that jealous reactions are closely linked to a person's feelings of self-worth, self-esteem, or self-image. It is part of a more general theory of personality that gives central importance to a person's feelings about herself or himself (Rosenberg, 1979). As it applies to jealousy, a person who has a negative self-image or low self-esteem will be more dependent on a romantic or love relationship and thus will be more susceptible to reactions of jealousy (Blood and Blood, 1978; Fullerton, 1977). This theory of jealousy locates the causes of jealousy in the personality or psychological shortcomings of an individual. In the extreme case, according to this theory, a person with a perfect positive self-image will not be threatened even when a love partner is clearly attracted to another person. There may not be a person with such a perfect self-image, but when this theory is extended to its logical extreme, it would seem that some people would never be jealous. While this theory of jealousy can help to explain why some people seem to have a greater tendency to be jealous than others, it does not account for differences in the same individual from one occasion to another.

You might have noticed in your own behavior that you can have very different degrees of jealous reactions. This suggests that in one romantic relationship a person can have feelings of jealousy at the slightest threat from a third person, but in another romantic relationship almost nothing can make that same person feel jealous. It is even possible that these different levels of jealousy can occur in relation to the same romantic partner at different times in the relationship. This indicates that jealous reactions can come from something in the relationship itself as much as from the personality of the individual. The idea that jealousy is a product of the nature of a relationship is the essential point of a theory of jealousy advanced by White (1977).

White's theory of jealousy rests on the idea that in any romantic relationship between two people, one person may be more involved than the other. *Being involved* refers in this context to how many rewards one is getting from a relationship. These rewards can be material things or services, but in a romantic relationship the rewards are more likely to be love, affection, improved self-esteem, sexual satisfaction, social prestige, and social status. The rewards that two romantic partners get from their relationship can be roughly equal, but frequently one person receives more rewards, and is thus more involved, than the other. When that is the case, the person receiving relatively more rewards is also more likely to be jealous than the person receiving relatively fewer rewards. In the words of White's theory of jealousy, a person who is more involved in a romantic relationship than his or her partner is more likely to be jealous. Research results provide enough support for this theory to take it into account when we consider the jealous reactions in ourselves or others (White, 1977). This theoretical perspective focuses more on the nature of the relationship between two people and less on an individual's alleged shortcomings. It views jealousy not as some kind of sickness, pathology, or character weakness, but more as a natural outcome of certain features of a relationship between two people. In White's words, "Jealousy may not be a flaw of personality as much as a relatively normal consequence of imbalances of [involvement and] power (White, 1977, p. 16).

This brief consideration of some theories of jealousy does not answer all questions about the subject, but it does illustrate how theories can be useful for understanding practical problems in our own lives. Furthermore, it is not necessary to select one of the theories as the total or final explanation. Each can contribute something to our understanding. A jealous reaction according to the first theory may be a nearly universal human reaction because of the similarity of our experiences in infancy and childhood. The second theory suggests that differences in self-image and self-esteem can affect our, or others', susceptibility to jealousy. And the final theory can explain why we might have such very different jealousy reactions from one relationship to another, or even over time in a changing relationship with one person.

This discussion of the practicality and usefulness of theory gives only a partial glimpse of just how important theory can be as a source of greater understanding into our own personal situations or problems. Jealousy is only one small example of an everyday occurrence that can be analyzed with greater sensitivity once we apply theoretical concepts and insights. This will be the purpose of introducing theory throughout this book.

ISSUES AND CONTROVERSIES

Earlier we noted that there are many controversies and issues connected with marriage and family life. These issues and controversies come from many sources, but the foremost cause is what sociologists call *social* and *cultural change*. Very simply, social change means that the people of a society make a change in their *patterns* of doing something (we will deal with cultural change in a moment). A major historical example is the change from argicultural production to industrial production as the dominant economic activity.

A family-related example of social change is a change in the way a marriage mate is chosen. In Japan, well into the twentieth century, almost all marriages were *arranged marriages* (Blood, 1967). Marriage mates were selected by the parents or families of young people. When parents arranged marriages for their children, the two young people often did not even know each other until the marriage had been arranged. Today there are still arranged marriages in Japan, but more and more marriages are the result of two people meeting and falling in love. The change from arranged marriages to *love marriages* in Japanese society is the source of an important issue faced by many Japanese young people. Should they follow the traditional way and let their parents choose a marriage partner for them, or should they let feelings of attraction and love guide their action?

Cultural change, which usually accompanies social change, is more closely connected with the *values* and *beliefs* people have. For example, a group of people might change their views about the importance of traditional ways of doing things. They might come to believe that the traditional ways of doing things are foolish, old-fashioned, or even stupid. The social change in the Japanese manner of selecting a marriage mate has very likely been accompanied by some kind of cultural change in the value that young Japanese place on tradition. For many, the traditional ways are no longer as highly valued as the more "modern" ways of the West.

Social and cultural change, as the Japanese illustration shows, are so closely intertwined that it is usually impossible to say that one is a cause and the other effect. But we can say, as we did at the outset, that social and cultural changes are important sources of issues and even controversies relating to marriage and family life. We can see more clearly how this occurs by examining some of the recent social and cultural changes in life in the United States.

Social and Cultural Change in the United States

Social and cultural changes can occur gradually, almost imperceptibly, or they can occur quickly with great intensity and drama. For example, the military overthrow of a government or a political revolution are examples of rapid social change. Changes under these circumstances can literally be made overnight. But there are other revolutions that are not quite so intense and rapid. These are often called social revolutions. Most social observers agree that the United States in recent times has experienced a social revolution, which came from a variety of interrelated social movements beginning in the 1960s and continuing into the 1970s. These movements have included, most notably, the civil rights movement, the women's movement, the student movement, the peace movement, and the gay-rights movement. Often these movements featured demonstrations and sometimes acts of civil disobedience in order to call attention to various problems of the society. As a society, we are still adjusting and reacting to many of the changes that came as a result of these events.

But even as this dramatic social revolution was occurring, there were also quieter more gradual changes. Ongoing economic and technological developments were also making changes necessary. To see this more clearly, let us take a concrete example of what has been happening to affect just one part of married life. Twenty-five years ago the customary and accepted way of life for an average married couple in the United States was for the husband to work at a job and the wife to work in the home. In those times a woman might work because the family needed or wanted the extra income, or in some cases because the woman wished to pursue an interesting career. But the woman's career or occupation was usually seen as secondary to the man's. Today, due to a variety of social and cultural changes, this is not the case. At the economic level it is often a virtual necessity for both a husband and a wife to be employed if the couple wishes to have a home, children, vacations, college education for the children, and the rest of the "standard American dream." Furthermore, as a result of changing ideas about women's roles, in large part brought about by the women's movement, many married couples are trying to bring the wife's work or career to an equal footing with the husband's.

These changes in both economic conditions and social attitudes have raised many new issues for married couples. When both work, how is housework and child care to be divided between husband and wife? If one spouse's job calls for moving to a new area, how should the other spouse's job affect the decision? If one spouse must move, is it possible to have what is called a *commuter, two-household* or *long-distance* marriage? If a husband and wife do live in different places, what kinds of social relationships can each have during those times when they are separated? These are just a few of the most important issues facing many American couples today as a result of recent changes in working patterns.

Although social and cultural changes are a fundamental and prime source of issues and controversies, there are other sources as well. There are, for example, technological developments that bring about new issues and controversies. There are also scientific debates and controversies that have important implications for the family. And there are philosophical, political, and ideological debates that foster issues and controversies about marriage and family life. While all of these could reasonably be subsumed under the general heading of social and cultural change, a brief consideration of each will help us to see how issues and controversies can arise. We will begin with some examples of how changing technology can raise new, controversial issues.

Changing Technology as a Source of Issues and Controversies

Technology is defined as a procedure or mechanism that makes it easier and simpler to accomplish an objective. As an example, modern birth control or contraceptive methods are technologies that make it easier to avoid conceiving a baby when having sexual intercourse. When new birth control technologies came into existence in the nineteenth century, they caused a great furor, because many people viewed contraception as immoral and sinful. Even medical descriptions of birth control methods were viewed as obscene. In both England and the United States it was illegal to sell such materials or send them through the mails (Chandrasekhar, 1981). In contemporary times, much of the debate over birth control and contraceptives has subsided, and the focus of controversy has shifted to abortion.

The clearest contemporary examples of technology as the source of issues and controversies stem from modern techniques relating to conception and childbearing. In recent years medical researchers have been successful in producing babies through artificial insemination. This has led to the use of surrogate mothers, i.e., women who become artificially inseminated with the sperm of a man whose wife is unable to bear children. There have also been instances of a male donor providing sperm for a woman (married or single) to become pregnant. And there have been a few successful instances of test-tube babies, where the conception takes place outside the woman's body, and the impregnated ovum is then implanted in the uterus.

All these technological innovations have raised significant issues and controversies. The Catholic Church has issued a blanket disapproval of all these

"Making babies" isn't what it used to be. The new technologies of reproduction are raising new issues controversies about and childbearing.

new methods of conception as being contrary to the moral precepts of the Church. But aside from the moral and theological issues, there are also a number of legal problems that can arise from this new technology. There have been reported instances of surrogate mothers who decided midway through pregnancy that they did not wish to give up the baby they were carrying. This raises the legal question, "Whose baby is it?" Does it belong to the father who provided the sperm, or to the surrogate mother who provided the ovum and nourished the fetus? In Chapter 9 we will consider these and other issues connected with modern reproductive technology.

Scientific Sources of Issues and Controversies

Scientific debates are ideally settled by research and experimentation, but in reality there are many scientific issues that provoke great amounts of argumentation and debate. This is especially true of the "large" or fundamental scientific questions. For example, there have been many scientific debates and arguments over a period of many years about whether a person's basic personality is shaped by genetic inheritance or by the way he or she has been reared. This is called the *nature versus nurture* debate. Obviously, it is a debate that has great significance for marriage and family life. If people are what they are because of their genetic inheritance, one would have to take this into account when marrying and planning for children. On the other hand, if the way in which a child is brought up determines what the child becomes, then much more of one's focus would have to be on child rearing practices. Clearly, the debate has practical consequences for our personal decision making.

In recent years, the long-standing debate about nature versus nurture has taken a new form with a new name. The current debate focuses on a theory called *sociobiology*. The fundamental idea of sociobiology is that human behavior is shaped by genetic inheritance, through the mechanism of evolution. The basic argument is that the human behaviors most beneficial for survival are those that are most likely to have been transmitted genetically in the human species.

One brief example here, in the area of sexual behavior, can illustrate the sociobiological perspective. It is widely believed that men have a greater desire for sexual variety than women. Women are thought to be more limited in their sexual desires and to be satisfied with one partner. In the past, mens' allegedly higher interest in sexual variety was attributed rather simply to greater sex drive. But sociobiologists offer a different explanation.

Sociobiologists begin with the assumption that a primary human objective is to have one's genes passed on to offspring. Women have only one egg each month that can be fertilized, and through which their genes can be passed on. By contrast, men's genes are passed on through sperm, of which there are an estimated 400 billion during a lifetime. A woman's genes are more likely to survive if the man who impregnates her also assists and supports her and the child. A man's genes are more likely to survive if he can impregnate as many women as possible. To be most successful, he has only to give the women as much support as is necessary to ensure the early survival of the offspring. Thus, sociobiologists argue that, as a result of the long evolutionary process, men are predisposed through their genes to want to have as many sexual relationships as possible. Women, on the other hand, are predisposed through their genes to want to "tie down" one man, and to achieve this they must use enticement and pressures (Trivers, 1972).

Many sociologists are very critical of this sociobiological explanation of differences between males and females. They are more likely to see male and female sexual behavior as shaped by the social systems in which people live rather than as a genetic inheritance of the species.

The resulting debate among scientists has often made its way into the public press and mass media. What started as a debate among scientists is now an issue being debated by the public at large. Obviously, which view one accepts will greatly influence one's own personal relationships and experiences.

Philosophical, Political, and Ideological Sources of Issues and Controversies

In a heterogeneous and changing society such as ours, there is a confusing array of philosophies, political views, and ideologies. There are humanists, fundamentalists, right-wingers, left-wingers, conservatives, liberals, feminists, and traditionalists, to name just a few. People who identify with these various labels range from those who have well-worked-out philosophies to those who simply respond automatically to key words. Almost any issue relating to marriage and the family has the potential for triggering reactions in different philosophical, political, and ideological sectors. Much of what one reads in the daily press or in magazines, or hears on radio and television, comes from spokespersons for these various views. Often what they have to say on the important issues of the time is interesting because the views are expressed with special force and conviction. We need not always share their beliefs in order to derive some meaning from them. In this book we will try, as we consider various issues and controversies, to bring in a lively assortment of viewpoints. The wider the range and the more vigorously these views are expressed, the more clearly we may be able to see what our own views are.

It is a major objective of this book to give everyone the chance to consider, evaluate, and develop personal views on the controversies and issues that surround marriage and family life. We have mentioned only a few of the many contemporary issues and controversies, primarily to see how they grow out of social, cultural, and technological change, scientific debates, and competing philosophies, ideologies, and politics. Even this brief look shows that there are many important and hotly contested issues related to marriage and family life occurring in our society today. These are the issues that need to be discussed by anyone considering marriage, or, for that matter, by anyone who is already in a marriage. In raising these issues I will try to present the arguments for and against the various alternatives in an impartial manner. It is not the aim to make final decisions for you, or to select the "best" solution to these issues or controversies. That, of course, cannot be done for others. As individuals we must make our own decisions, since in the last analysis they will be based on our personal values, attitudes, beliefs, and opinions.

A FINAL NOTE ON THE FAMILY
AND SOCIAL CHANGE

We noted at the beginning of this chapter that the family is often alleged to be the cause of various social trends and societal problems. Certainly it is plausible to look at the family as a potential source of social problems and societal trends, but there is a nearly opposite view that also needs to be expressed. The family can also be seen as the institution that is changed by other institutions, because it is frequently the family that must adapt to changing conditions (Vincent, 1966).

The case we considered earlier, in which both husband and wife are economically employed, can be seen as an example of the family adapting to changing economic conditions. The economy is such that two wage earners are nearly a necessity for many households. Indeed, economic necessity has long been an important factor in the decision of women to enter the work force. Research studies in past years have shown repeatedly that the strongest factor determining whether or not a married woman was employed was her husband's income. The lower her husband's income, the more likely she was to work (Gordon and Kammeyer, 1980). Over the last twenty years an increasingly higher percentage of married women has entered the labor force, and one explanation for that pattern is that when the economy does not provide sufficient economic means through the husband's income alone, it is necessary for the family to adapt by having the wife enter the labor force. Beginning twenty to thirty years ago, many Americans did adapt to the economic system's shortcomings, even at great hardship. Then, as now in American society, day-care and child-care facilities were not in abundance, and women who worked had great difficulties finding someone to care for their children. Furthermore, women, even when they were employed, were still expected to carry out most of the household and after-work child-rearing tasks. (That expectation might have diminished somewhat in recent years, but women who work are still often expected to carry the major domestic burdens.) Finally, women who by economic necessity entered the labor force, especially twenty to thirty years ago, were acting directly against the socially praised role of mother and homemaker. Women who worked outside the home often wondered and worried about whether they were making the right choice when they left their children with baby-sitters and relatives. Much discussion and research centered around the question of whether or not children of working mothers were in some way damaged thereby. In a modified form, the same discussions are going on today, as women, and sometimes men, consider how much time they should take from their work to be with their young children.

This simple illustration is only one example of the way in which families have to adapt to changing external conditions. There are numerous historical examples of family systems, as well as individual families, changing in an effort to accommodate to changing external conditions. When family systems go through these adaptive changes, we as individuals often face them as personal dilemmas and problems. The decisions we have to make are often made difficult because there are no clear and expected courses of action coming from existing social norms and cultural values.

With the completion of this illustrative introduction to the book, we are now ready to move into the major topics of marriage and family life. We will begin in the next chapter with a consideration of gender roles, which continue to have a pervasive influence on the relationships between men and women, within marriage and in nearly every other sphere of life.

Themes

1. Marriage and family life is the object of much criticism, but it continues to be the preferred way of life for most people.

2. There are many kinds of facts and information about marriages and families, including statistics, research results, cross-cultural studies, and historical accounts.

3. Cross-cultural studies of marriage and the family broaden our perspectives by showing how differently things can be done from one society to another.

4. Historical studies often reveal how social and cultural changes have occurred, and how features of marriage and family life that now seem natural and unchanging have not always been as they are now.

5. Theories coming from sociology and psychology often provide the keys to understanding complex and confusing phenomena, including our own personal situations and problems.

6. Issues and controversies connected with marriage and family life are often produced by social and cultural changes.

7. Technological innovations can also produce issues and controversies related to marriage and family life.

8. Other issues and controversies grow out of scientific debates and philosophical, political, and ideological differences.

9. The family is an institution that often must adapt to changes that have occurred in other institutions.

Facts

1. The median age at first marriage for men is 25.4; for women it is 23.0.

2. People who marry at a later age are generally less likely to divorce.

3. At the beginning of the twentieth century, men, on the average, married when they were older than twenty-six; women were only a few years younger.

4. Married couples in general express less satisfaction with their marital relationships when they have young children.

5. Among the Nandi, who live in Kenya, a married woman may take a wife so that the family can have an heir for its property.

6. Marriage often has an important economic dimension.

7. Before the seventeenth century, the title *Mrs.* was only given to women of high rank; later it was used by all social classes, and in the mid-seventeenth century applied to women who were both married and single.

8. In the seventeenth century the title *Miss* was used to refer to women of "loose morals."

9. It was not until the 1840s in the United States that it became an established custom for a married woman to use the first and last names of her husband, e.g., Mrs. John Jones.

10. There are at least three theories of jealousy. One finds the origins of jealousy in the feelings that infants and children have about losing their parents' love; a second finds jealousy to be rooted in negative self-image and low self-esteem; and a third suggests that jealousy grows out of the nature of the relationship between two people.

11. In Japan, well into the twentieth century, almost all marriages were arranged marriages.

12. In the nineteenth century medical descriptions of birth control methods were considered obscene, and it was illegal to send such writings through the mails.

13. Women's genes can only be passed on through the one egg she produces each month. Men can pass on their genes through any of the 400 billion sperm they can produce in a lifetime.

14. Past research has shown that a married woman is more likely to be employed if her husband's income is low.

Major Concepts

arranged marriage: Marriage mates are selected by the parents or families of young people.

commuter marriage: Husbands and wives living in different places; usually produced by different job requirements of either husband or wife.

cross-cultural studies Studies of the ways of life of people in other societies with different cultures that allow us to make comparisons across cultures.

cultural change: Changes in the values and beliefs of people in a particular society.

ethnographies: Accounts of the ways of life among the people who live in other societies with different cultures; usually produced by anthropologists.

gender role: The rights, duties, and behaviors associated with one's gender status or sex.

historical studies: Studies of the lives and events of people who have lived in earlier times.

jealousy: An emotion that is experienced when there are threats to a romantic relationship from a third person.

long-distance marriage: (*See* **commuter marriage.**)

nature versus nurture debate: The long-standing argument about whether a person's basic personality is shaped by genetic inheritance or by the way he or she has been reared.

self-image: The feelings one has about oneself.

social change: Changes in the patterns of doing something in a particular society by its people.

sociobiology: The idea that human behavior is shaped by genetic inheritance, through the mechanism of evolution.

statistics: Facts that are put into numerical form.

surrogate mothers: Women who become artificially inseminated and bear children for other people.

technology: A procedure or mechanism that makes it easier and simpler to accomplish an objective.

two-household marriages: (*See* **commuter marriage**)

2

Gender Roles
Change and Persistence

The behaviors traditionally expected of males and females are changing, and yet these expectations continue to influence our behavior greatly. These expected behaviors, called *gender roles,* are both persistent and pervasive. As an illustrative example, consider the case of Lucy Irvine, a young English-woman of twenty-six who recently spent a year as a castaway on a tiny island in the Pacific ocean north of Australia.

Lucy Irvine and a man she simply calls "G" had themselves deposited on an island that had barely enough water and food to survive. Their life threatening experiences are recounted in Irvine's (1983) book, *Castaway.* Reading Irvine's story, it is interesting to observe how quickly some of the trappings of English culture were dropped. For example, it was only a short while in this intensely hot climate before both were spending their days nude, or nearly so. These two people had been strangers before they embarked on their adventure, and though they had been forced to marry by the Australian government, it was a marriage in name only. Yet nudity in each other's presence was easily accepted. At one point during the year, two young Australian men paid an unexpected visit to the island. Lucy welcomed them in her usual costume, and it was not until some time after they had arrived that "G" urged her to "put on some knickers." Apparently, something as thoroughly learned as wearing clothing in the presence of strangers of the opposite sex can be unlearned or forgotten.

But there were some other learned behaviors that seemed not to be so easily forgotten. In her book, Irvine describes how she planned and prepared all the meals and made the tea, which she served to "G." There is no doubt that cooking and cleaning were left to Lucy in this two-person society. Of course, such an arrangement might simply have been part of a division of labor, in which "G" was doing the heavier, more difficult tasks. But that was clearly not the case, since "G" had some health problems that kept him around the campsite most of the time. As a result, Lucy did more than her share of the fishing, carrying firewood, and foraging the island for other types of food. Much of the time she took over these and other tasks exclusively. One might suppose that "G," in turn, would have taken over the cooking and cleaning, but there is no evidence that this occurred. Almost incredibly, Lucy Irvine seems not to have noticed that she continued to take nearly sole responsibility for planning and preparing the food and cleaning up afterward. She further reports how she tried to make new and varied meals from their exceedingly limited food supply. She also consciously provided nurturing and special little attentions for her companion in order to keep his spirits up. She avoided raising topics that she knew would upset and frustrate him. In short, she was fulfilling a number of expectations that are attached to the traditional feminine role.

The interesting sociological lesson that comes out of this real-life adventure story is the way in which the behaviors expected of a woman were so deeply ingrained that they could not be eradicated. Even on an isolated island, where other customs were easily discarded, the behaviors connected with gender were extremely persistent.

In this chapter we will consider how gender roles are learned and how they come to have such widespread influence on the behavior of men and women. It is important to have a clear understanding of gender roles, for they play a part in premarital sex, dating behavior, cohabitation, and almost all aspects of married life.

There is general agreement that the persistence of gender roles comes from the early training children receive from their parents. Parents teach boys and girls what is expected of them, and these early lessons are not easily abandoned, even in adulthood. At the end of this chapter, after we have examined the nature and impact of gender roles, we will consider the following question: Should we raise our children androgynously? (Androgynous child rearing means that boys and girls are raised in exactly the same way, with the same behaviors expected of both genders.)

The word *role* is familiar. We talk about the president's role, the role of the teacher, the news commentator's role, and so on. Yet when we use the word *role* in our everyday conversation, we may not be using it in quite the same way as sociologists or psychologists do. Among these specialists, *role* is a key concept in a theory of human behavior called *role theory* (Heiss, 1981). Since this theory has several applications to marriage and family life, we will examine it briefly here, before going on to consider gender roles specifically.

ROLE THEORY

A *role* is defined formally as "a prescription for interpersonal behavior associated with socially recognized categories of persons" (Heiss, 1976, p. 3). This definition requires a little explanation. Consider first the phrase "socially recognized categories of persons." Another name for a socially recognized category is a *status*.

In our society, males, females, the president, teachers, and news commentators are all socially recognized categories, or statuses. But to be the president, a teacher, or a news commentator would require some special effort before one attains the status. These are therefore referred to as *achieved statuses*. But to be a male or a female only requires that one be born. As soon as a person is born, in fact, this status is immediately noted. ("It's a girl!") Since nothing has to be done to achieve this status, it is called an *ascribed status*.

Whenever there are socially recognized statuses, whether achieved or ascribed, there are prescriptions for how the people filling these statuses should behave. Actually, there are usually prescriptions that indicate what people should or must do, and proscriptions for what they should not or must not do. While some prescriptions and proscriptions are strongly enforced (the president must not break into profanity while giving a public speech), it would be erroneous to suggest that there is rigidity or inflexibility in roles. The roles for most statuses are not rigid rules; they are closer to expectations. For example, we expect police officers to be firm but also friendly (or at least courteous). If one police officer is not, it would not be an extraordinary breach of conduct, but it might be something one would remark about to a friend. Roles are not so rigid that every person in a particular status will behave like everyone else in that status, but many roles are strong enough to produce a general pattern of behavior among people who hold the same status.

The example of the police officer's role reveals another aspect of roles. Roles are informal and socially understood. Most people have never read a police training manual, where it may say that officers should be firm, but friendly (or words to that effect). Nevertheless, most people probably do share an expectation about how police officers are to behave. Somewhere, somehow, in the course of growing up and living in this society they have learned what kind of behavior is expected of people who are in the status of police officer. The same is true with most roles.

There are role expectations about police officers and about males and females. Would a female officer be likely to assist a male of the same age crossing the street?

The principal elements of role theory can be summarized with the following statements:

- People can be identified as belonging to socially defined categories or statuses.
- There are socially held expectations about how people in those statuses will behave.
- These expectations are generally known and accepted by the people who fill the statuses, and by most other people.
- These mutually understood and accepted expectations shape and influence individual behavior and the interaction between people.
- While role expectations provide general guidelines for behavior, there is room for individual differences and variations.
- Finally, a point not made previously, social roles are not fixed. They can vary from one society to another and from one time to another.

With these principles in mind, we can now take a closer look at gender roles.

GENDER ROLES

Gender, as we have noted above, comes with being born; but, of course, we do not expect any special social behavior from infants. However, even at very early ages, parents often believe that their infants display certain personality traits that are characteristic of males and females. In this regard gender roles are quite different from most other roles. Returning to the example of police officers, it might be assumed that many police officers would have personality traits such as bravery or self-confidence, but the association is very loose. With gender the connection between being male or female and having distinctive personality traits is believed by many people to be much closer. These presumed personality traits of the sexes are often referred to as stereotypes, because there is a tendency to attach them to all males and females without regard to individual exceptions and variations. These stereotyped personality traits are an important aspect of gender roles, because they often relate directly to expectations of what men and women should and should not do.

Stereotyped Personality Traits

Females are often stereotyped as emotional, caring, and nurturant, whereas males are thought to be unemotional, detached, and aloof. Males are believed to be less affected by things that touch the feelings of females. Males are thought to be more aggressive, and females are seen as more passive. Even though the exceptions to these stereotypes are all around, the belief in them persists among many people. Often these personality differences are thought to reside in the biological makeup of males and females.

These stereotyped beliefs are apparent in much that we see and hear. They are often part of our thinking, about ourselves as well as others. Consider the following poignant statement by a young man describing an experience with his girlfriend.

> *There was an occasion when I went to Susan's one night, a happy man, and left feeling like a disheartened boy. She wanted to know why I didn't make a move on her and why I wasn't aggressive . . . I know I'm not as aggressive as other men are or as I "should be" but I told her that it shouldn't matter. . . . I took her in my arms and asked her if she knew I loved her, and she said she didn't know. I know she said it in disgust, but it really hurt me. I began to cry. Man, I just about ran out of the door because I didn't want her to see me cry. I was not a man: I wasn't aggressive and I didn't hide my emotions and I really felt bad. (Forisha, 1978, p. 160)*

It is clear from this young man's reactions to his own behavior how deeply embedded are the stereotyped views of male personality traits. He shows shame and dismay at his own characteristics and behavior. He failed by not being as aggressive as men are supposed to be, and he compounded the sin by displaying his emotions in front of his girlfriend.

Women, of course, are often equally trapped by the stereotypes about female personality traits. When they want to express aggressiveness, they might have to restrain themselves because it would be viewed as unfeminine.

There are a number of other personality traits that are thought to be associated with being either male or female. That is, there are still other stereotypes about the sexes. Women are thought to be followers rather than leaders, more sympathetic, sensitive, compassionate, and concerned about others, more inclined toward artistic and aesthetic activities, less inclined toward mathematics, science, and even intellectuality. Women are often thought to be more moral, more religious, or, in some cultures, "purer" than men. Men are thought to be better leaders, more objective, aggressive, independent, active, dominant, competitive, logical, scientific, calculating, tough, strong, and unsentimental.

The stereotyped personality traits traditionally attributed to males and females can be grouped into two major categories: instrumental and expressive. *Instrumental personality traits* are the achievement- and action-oriented traits associated with being male. *Expressive personality traits* emphasize emotional support and comfort, and are associated with being female.

Broverman and her colleagues (1972) have slightly different terms to describe these stereotyped personality traits. They use the terms *competency* for males and *warmth-expressiveness* for females. These basic dimensions of personality assume that males have the advantage in the general area of doing things. Males are assigned the traits that give them an edge in the world of achievement and action. By contrast, women are thought to be more able to provide emotional support and comfort by virtue of their alleged female traits. They are assigned the expressive tasks because that is where their talents are supposed to lie. In concrete terms, the boys are the football players, and the girls are the cheerleaders. The boys' role calls for them to go out to face the outside world (the other school's team), while the girls' role requires them to provide the emotional support.

Later in life, men are still expected to take the action and accomplish the major tasks, while women are often expected to take care of the emotional and supportive tasks. But now we have moved beyond personality traits, to the expected behaviors that follow quite naturally from those supposed personality traits of males and females.

Expected Behaviors Of Males And Females

The prescriptions for male and female behavior, according to the traditional gender roles, fit the assumed personality traits like a glove fits a hand. The expected behaviors of the traditional gender roles, like the personality traits, can be categorized as *instrumental* and *expressive.* Expected instrumental behaviors are behaviors that accomplish something. Expected expressive behaviors are behaviors that give comfort, meet emotional needs, and provide supportive services.

The importance of traditional gender role expectations will be found nowhere more intensely than in marriage and family life. However, in the economic and occupational world, as well as in many other spheres of life, gender role differences are also clearly in evidence. Women in the family are traditionally expected to perform supportive tasks while being, to a considerable degree, submissive and subordinate. Men are expected to provide for and in some cases defend the family. Men are expected to make contact with the world outside the family. Their job is to have a job. They must cope well enough with the world of work and business to provide for the needs of the family. If there is a threat to the family from the outside world, the male is the one who must deal with that threat, whether it is physical, economic, or otherwise.

People's traditional views about feminine and masculine roles have been undergoing some changes in recent years. Since the women's movement came into prominence in the 1960s, there has at least been a heightened sensitivity to the importance and impact of traditional gender roles. But our views on masculinity and femininity have been deeply etched by our learning experiences. Most of us have learned and accepted many of the basic elements of traditional gender roles. Sometimes, even when we try to change, the basic gender stereotypes shape our thinking and influence our behavior. In order to see how and

"I am cooking for Daddy, honey, but don't forget that sometimes he cooks for me. We do it because we love each other."

why we typically learn and accept stereotyped views of the sexes and traditional gender roles, we must examine the process of gender role learning.

LEARNING GENDER ROLES

Many people in recent years have made very genuine efforts to break away from traditional gender role thinking. Some have been successful to a considerable degree, but many will admit that thinking and behaving in gender-neutral ways are very difficult. The difficulty stems largely from the fact that we learn gender role expectations early in our lives. Moreover, this early learning is reinforced again and again in our daily lives. The ways in which we learn gender roles has been the subject of much theorizing and research. While there are several competing theories of how gender roles are learned, most experts agree that several interrelated processes are involved. We will begin our consideration of these processes by examining a basic theory of social learning and several related concepts.

Social Learning Theory

Many psychologists and some sociologists subscribe to a basic theory of how humans (and other animals as well) learn their behavior. In simple terms, humans learn by responding to their environment (Skinner, 1938; Homans, 1961). This theory is sometimes called *behaviorism*, because the emphasis is on a person's behavior rather than on any internal states of mind (motives, intentions, or attitudes, for example). The behavioristic theory of social learning holds that initially a person or other organism will simply behave in some way. This might be thought of as random behavior. If the environment of that person or organism, an environment that might include another person, rewards that behavior, then it will be reinforced. Reinforced behavior is likely to be repeated.

In classic behavioristic experiments with animals or birds, behavior is often rewarded with food. When food reinforces a particular behavior, animals will often repeat that behavior. If the same behavior is reinforced again, it will likely be repeated once more. Trained seals will do all sorts of amazing tricks as long as their trainers keep handing out pieces of fish. With humans the rewards that might reinforce behavior will probably not be food (though there have been experiments in which the behavior of children has been modified with the use of candy). Humans often feel rewarded for their behavior if another person responds positively either with words or with other actions.

When social learning theory is applied to learning gender roles, the hypothesis is that children, even very small children, are rewarded for behaviors that are consistent with the appropriate gender role. If a two-year-old boy falls and skins his knee, his parent might say, "Oh, you are such a brave little man, you won't cry. Will you? If you don't cry, we will let the puppy in the house." If parents respond one way to boys and another way to girls, and if their responses reinforce the expected gender role behaviors, then male and female behavior is likely to be shaped and modified accordingly.

While everyday observations would lead us to believe that such gender role reinforcement does go on, it has not been easy to document this reinforcement in scientifically controlled observational studies (Maccoby and Jacklin, 1974). What is demonstrable is that parents often have clearly defined beliefs about how boys and girls should behave. They do very often provide toys and clothes that are consistent with their expectations and beliefs about how children of each sex should behave. Thus, girls who receive dolls and frilly dresses have "feminine" behavior reinforced, just by receiving those things. Similarly, boys are reinforced when they receive trucks, trains, and tool chests, so they can engage in "masculine" activities. This kind of parental reinforcement is closely re-

The models for being astronauts are available for girls as well as for boys. (Astronaut Anna Fisher and daughter Kristin)

lated to a second process by which gender roles are learned. This process is called *modeling*.

Modeling

Children observe their parents (as well as others, such as sisters and brothers) and often imitate what they see. One hypothesis of gender role learning focuses on how this imitation serves to establish the male and female gender roles in children. Girls see what their mothers (and other females) do and try to model their behavior accordingly. Boys model themselves after the behavior of their fathers and other males. Obviously, this hypothesis depends on the child observing and being motivated to imitate the gender-appropriate behavior. If children do not attend to and imitate people of the same sex, then gender role learning of this type will not occur. The modeling hypothesis is particularly problematic with regard to boys, since in our society they are in the presence of women more than men. This is clearly the case in the childhood years, when modeling behavior is thought to be most important.

Much like the social learning hypothesis just discussed, the modeling hypothesis can often be observed in everyday life, and yet empirical, scientific support for it has been mixed. Quite a number of experimental and observational studies have been carried out, and many have failed to demonstrate that direct modeling (of same-sex parents, for example) is a strong determinant of gender-appropriate behavior (Maccoby and Jacklin, 1974; Stockard and Johnson, 1980; Frieze et al., 1978). Despite the lack of strong or consistent evidence for modeling, the unarguable fact still exists that gender role models are found, both within the family and in the broader society. These roles are obviously adopted by most children at a fairly early age. Furthermore, some studies have shown that children do imitate behavior that is consistent with the traditional gender role expectations (Fehrenbach et al., 1979; Perry and Bussey, 1979).

Research studies, and much everyday observation, indicates clearly that children do learn what is "gender-appropriate" behavior. Equally important, it appears that children are generally highly motivated to follow the appropriate behavior. The social learning hypothesis explains part of their motivation; they are rewarded for following the expected gender role and perhaps negatively sanctioned if they do not. But, do children only follow the culturally prescribed gender roles because of rewards and punishments, or is there something else that accounts for their general acceptance of the traditional male and female gender roles? There is a widely accepted theoretical perspective that says there is something else. This perspective advances the view that the children themselves are active participants in seeking out the behaviors and values that are consistent with traditional gender roles. This theoretical perspective is called *cognitive development theory.*

Cognitive Development Theory

This theory of gender role learning rests on the idea that children have ever-increasing levels of ability in their reasoning and thinking, that is, in their cognitive development. This view of the cognitive development of children was originally advanced by the psychologist Jean Piaget. The theory of cognitive development has been adapted and expanded by psychologist Lawrence Kohlberg (1966) to explain how children become active participants in learning the gender roles of their culture.

The first step in this learning process is for children to learn that there are two gender categories—male and female (boys and girls, mommies and daddies, etc.) Having learned that, and parents are usually quite insistent that their children make the distinction early in life, the next step is for them to learn which category they belong to. Most children have learned their gender by about age three. At this age, they can also usually determine the gender of others. They use one or two visual cues such as style of dress, hair length, or facial hair to make the distinction. This can cause them to make some mistakes at first, as when a male has long hair, but as their cognitive ability improves they use more complicated standards and are right most of the time.

Even though young children learn their own gender at an early age, it is not until sometime later that they recognize their gender places them in a general category of humans (e.g., females). Again, as they develop cognitive ability, children recognize that girls, mommies, aunts, saleswomen, and others belong to a single category of people and that they themselves are, or are not, a part of this category. By age four or five most children have achieved this level of understanding.

According to Kohlberg, there is another important step in this cognitive development process of children. At about age six, children come to understand that the gender one belongs to is a constant. It is not something that a person can change by taking some action such as wearing different clothing. From the

child's view at this age, gender is a fixed and stable category, and he or she belongs to one or the other of the two sexes. Kohlberg argues that this is a critically
important understanding, because once learned, gender gives the child a very
powerful and significant category for organizing behavior, attitudes, and values. From this point in their development, children take an active part in adopting and accepting the gender roles of the culture in which they live. Let us see
how that occurs.

Children are faced with a complex world, which they must deal with and
manage in some way. They must understand and be able to predict how the
world works and be able to act effectively in that world. To do this, they need
organizing schemes (e.g., some things are safe, some things are dangerous;
some things are good, some things are bad). Part of every person's world, perhaps the most complicated part, will be other people. Children, as well as
adults, need organizing schemes to interpret what other people are doing and
to predict what they might do. Gender is one potentially useful scheme for understanding and predicting behavior. In many ways, through words and actions, parents convey that message to their children. And, as we have noted,
what parents are most likely to convey are the cultural stereotypes about gender. There is a substantial amount of evidence that even young children do understand the cultural stereotypes about gender roles and use them to predict
what people will do. By the age of four gender role stereotypes have emerged as
a key organizing factor when children are asked to predict behavior (Frieze et
al., 1978).

But predicting what other people will do is only one task of children as they
learn how to get along in a complex world. The other task is learning how *they*
should act. As we have noted, the social learning hypothesis and the modeling
hypothesis give children some basis for behaving along traditional gender role
lines. Parents and others are likely to reward behavior that is thought to be gender appropriate and not reward, or punish, behavior that is not. And parents or
others also provide models for children to imitate; but as we now see more
clearly, modeling takes on its full significance only when children recognize
their own gender and that they are part of a larger gender category. It is at this
point that cognitive development theory goes beyond social learning and modeling, because it suggests that children *actively seek out* and *adopt* those things
that are consistent with prevailing gender roles.

In concrete terms, a boy will learn that certain things are associated with
being a boy (or a male). For example, active and rough-and-tumble games might
be associated with boys. Having learned this, a boy will seek out and place a
positive value on things and activities that fit this part of the "boy's role." A football or wrestling with other boys will be accepted, because these are both consistent with the active and rough-and-tumble things associated with being a
boy. A sewing basket and cutting out doll dresses will not be. These will be
called "girls' things."

The most distinctive feature of the cognitive development theory of gender role learning is that it does not make the child a passive recipient of the culturally prescribed roles. The child is an active participant in adopting and accepting the gender role expectations of the culture. It is important to note that cognitive development theory does not contradict or negate the mechanisms of social learning or modeling. To use a physical metaphor, the social learning and modeling hypotheses are the equivalent of pushing a car to get it started and moving in a certain direction; cognitive development theory is equivalent to a driver taking over and actively keeping it moving.

In the remainder of this chapter we will examine how the traditional gender roles, once learned, have an impact on our lives. The objective will be limited in that not all the ways gender roles impact on marriage and family life will be covered here. Some things, such as power and decision making in marriage, or work in the home and in the labor force, are greatly influenced by the prevailing gender roles. These and several other issues will be covered in later chapters where they can receive the fuller treatment they deserve. Here, the aim will be to highlight the importance of gender roles by focusing on a few selected issues. To provide some structure for the issues we will begin with some seemingly trivial aspects of social life and move toward the most significant. We will start with touching, talking, standing, sitting, speaking, and the use of language. Then we will proceed to the political world, occupations and economics, and the treatment of the sexes in the mass media.

THE IMPACT OF TRADITIONAL GENDER ROLES

Before looking at some of the specific areas where gender roles have an impact on behavior, there are a few general statements that can be made about the overall effects of traditional roles found in American society:

1. Gender roles, as they are traditionally defined, place women in subordinate and less valued positions than men.

2. The traditional feminine gender role calls for women to make more sacrifices than men. Another way of putting this is that men have more latitude, a wider range of options, than do women (Goode, 1982).

3. Traditional gender roles work to the disadvantage of women in most spheres of life, but especially in what is called the "public world" beyond the family.

There are some who argue that traditional gender roles are just as disadvantageous for men as they are for women. Men, they say, are constrained and controlled by the masculine role, much as women are by the feminine role. In some specific areas of life that may be true, as when males are found to respond more negatively to being unemployed than do women (David and Brannon, 1976; Goldberg, 1976). Even occupational success can carry with it the burdens of stress and anxiety for many men. However, with the majority of women now in the labor force, and many of them in equally stressful jobs, the burdens of work can be found among both sexes. We thus return to the position we started with, namely that women are especially disadvantaged by traditional gender roles. This can be seen even in such seemingly inconsequential things as the way people talk and the way they touch each other.

Touching another person.   It is normal for people, when they talk, to touch each other in friendly and un-self-conscious ways. Upon greeting someone, we often touch the other person's hand, arm, or shoulder. As we speak, perhaps for emphasis, we may reach out to touch another person. Do these simple gestures have meaning beyond expressing friendship or emphasizing a point? Often touching someone is an indication that one has power over the other person. It is a general social custom that more powerful people can touch people who are subordinate to them, but not vice versa (Henley, 1977).

A simple example will illustrate the power dimension of touching. Suppose a manager of a plant is walking through a production area and sees an employee he or she recognizes. The manager may quite easily walk up to that person, pat the employee on the back, and ask how things are going. On the surface this is interpreted as a friendly act on the part of the manager, nothing more; it is not usually seen as an expression of power over the worker. And yet, touching is clearly the prerogative of the more powerful person, because the opposite would rarely occur. It would be very unlikely that a worker would walk up to the plant manager and give him or her a pat on the back and ask how things are going.

One other interesting everyday case of the more powerful touching the less powerful is found in the case of adults and children. Even in public places, where an adult does not know a child, it is common for the adult to pat the child on the head or chuck it under the chin. Children can be patted, much like a friendly dog can be patted. It is a privilege that the more powerful person (in this case, the adult) has over the less powerful.

What does this general point have to do with males and females and gender roles? In everyday interaction males touch females more than females touch males (Henley, 1977). When men touch women, they are often showing that they have control over them. Men are likely to place their hands on a woman's shoulders, on the small of her back, or if the relationship is close, on her buttocks. Sometimes when men touch women it is done as a mild form of aggression. Pinching or lightly spanking are both ways in which men are allowed to touch women they know intimately. In some societies men touch and pinch the bodies of women strangers on the street, showing perhaps that they find the woman attractive, but also showing that they have the power and right to do so without reprimand.

Even forms of etiquette are often premised on the superior status of the male. Men are expected to take the arm or touch the back of women in order to guide them through crowded streets, through doors, or into automobiles. It must be noted that women actively participate in these practices. Often a woman will slip her hand around a man's arm so that she can be supported and guided by him. (This form of initiating the touching shows subordination because it "says" that the woman needs the man's assistance.) Clearly, most of these formal rituals are more symbolic than necessary, since women are quite able to get through crowded streets and in and out of doors and automobiles when not accompanied by men.

The rituals of etiquette are symbolic ways of saying that men are in control. They are stronger, and they take the action. The symbolic representation of women is that they are weaker, passive, and less competent than men.

Both the informal and ritualistic ways in which men and women touch or are touched by each other are also part of what is often called *body language.* Body language is the use of the body to convey messages, and, again, one of the messages is the relative statuses of males and females.

Standing and sitting. In addition to touching, another type of body language is the way people stand and sit (Henley, 1977). Observational studies of males and females show that women take up less space than men. When women are seated they generally hold their knees and ankles close together. If possible, they also pull their feet in at an angle under the chair. Men, on the other hand, are likely to expand the space they control by extending their legs, or crossing them by placing the calf of one over the knee of the other. The arms, similarly, may be flung over the back of a chair or clasped behind the head with elbows out. These differences in the way males and females sit indicate that males are in a position of greater freedom and in control of their personal space.

Males and females exhibit similar differences in the way they stand, with men more likely to have their feet wider apart than women. Again, by taking up more space, men are exercising more freedom and control. While touching, sitting, and standing might seem like inconsequential, even trivial, features of social life, they play their part in reinforcing the traditional gender role stereotypes of men being in control and taking action and women being subordinate and passive. These are the messages of body language, but the actual language and ways of speaking carry an even more direct message.

Language and speaking. Because language and speech are critically important features of social and psychological life, it should not be surprising that gender roles affect the use of language and the way people talk to each other (Henley and Thorne, 1977; Parlee, 1979). Research has shown that the relative power of men and women is reflected in speech and conversation patterns.

Males often expand the space they control, while females have learned to restrict their personal space.

Women are less likely in their speech to be assertive and blunt. They are more likely to qualify their statements by saying "I think," "I suppose," "I guess," and "I believe." These kinds of qualifiers make a statement weaker and less likely to influence a listener. Women also tend to speak more softly and to use "softer" language. As one writer has noted, there is a great difference between "Oh, my, such a lovely idea," and "Damn, yes, that's a tremendous idea" (Richmond-Abbott, 1983). Women are more likely to use the former phrasing, or something similar. And yet women are caught in a bind, because in many settings, if they do use stronger language they will be characterized as aggressive and unpleasant.

When women engage in conversations with men, they are also at a disadvantage because men are likely to pay less attention to what women say. This is especially revealed in studies of who interrupts whom in conversation (West, 1978; Zimmerman and West, 1975). Research in public places and in social laboratory settings shows that a man will break into a woman's line of speech (called a deep interruption) more often than a woman will interrupt a man. The following bit of dialogue recorded by Zimmerman and West, shows both how a man did not hesitate to interrupt and essentially ignore what his female friend was saying and also how the woman eventually resigned herself to being interrupted and ignored (the brackets indicate when the man and woman are speaking at the same time):

> FEMALE: How's your paper coming?
> MALE: All right, I guess (pause) I haven't done much in the past two weeks. (pause)
> FEMALE: Yeah, know how that [can . . .]
> MALE: [Hey, ya] got an extra cigarette? (pause)
> FEMALE: Oh uh sure. (hands him the pack) Like my [pa . .] .
> MALE: [How] about a match?
> FEMALE: Here you go. Uh like my [pa . . .]
> MALE: [Thanks.] (pause)
> FEMALE: Sure. (pause) I was gonna tell you [my . . .]
> MALE: [Hey, I'd] really like to talk but I gotta run. See you. (long pause)
> FEMALE: Yeah. (from Parlee, 1979, p. 52)

In one study, undergraduate male and female students who did not know each other were brought into a social laboratory for an experiment. They were introduced and told to get to know each other before the "actual" experiment. Their conversations during that get-acquainted period were recorded, and fifty-four deep interruptions were observed. Seventy-four percent of these interruptions were by males interrupting females, while only twenty-six percent were initiated by females. In same-sex couples the interruptions were nearly equal between the two conversers. (West, 1978) In another study, where the same researchers observed conversations in "natural" settings—drug stores, coffee shops, libraries—males in cross-sex conversations made ninety-six percent of the interruptions (West, 1978).

One might ask why a man would interrupt a woman's speech more than the other way around, and the answer might again be that men, by virtue of their gender role, are given more power and authority than women. But there is another level of explanation, one that is suggested by a study conducted by Esther Grief (reported in Weitzman, 1979). This study showed that when parents and young children are talking, the parents are much more likely to interrupt daughters than sons. Fathers are especially likely to interrupt their children, but both parents interrupt daughters more than sons. This study suggests that girls begin learning, even in early childhood, that what they have to say is not as important as what their brothers have to say. By comparison, boys learn that what they have to say is more significant, because their parents do not interrupt them as often. This illustrates how learning gender roles is more subtle and complex than is often supposed. When girls are treated differently from boys, even in unconscious ways, the effects may persist through life.

Research among adults does suggest that women are more hesitant about taking the initiative in conversation, and often begin with words such as "D'ya know what?" This kind of opening allows other people, especially males, to give them a go-ahead signal when they respond "What?" or "No, tell me." Apparently there are valid reasons for women needing that kind of reassurance. In an analysis of cross-sex conversation openers, men succeeded in starting their conversation topics ninety-six percent of the time, while women succeeded only thirty-six percent of the time (Pfeiffer, 1985).

These research findings about male and female speech and conversation patterns have ramifications far beyond the conversations themselves. If we think of how these patterns can make important differences in schools, in organizations, in political groups, and in the work world, we will see that they are not trivial and inconsequential. When what men say is thought to be more important than what women say (perhaps by both men and women in many instances), then men will have an advantage in obtaining positions, being promoted, and receiving career rewards and advancements. That seems to be what has happened in the world of business, occupations, and professions. Women do not fare as well as men. Obviously, this inequality between the sexes is not produced by speech interruptions alone. Interruptions are just one part of a complex of customs, norms, values, and attitudes that give males an advantage over females in the public world (education, the work world, government, religion, science, sports, and other spheres). We will now review some of the manifestations of the advantages that males have in these public realms.

Men And Women in the Public World

It is not difficult to document the dominance of men in all realms of public life. Whether it is the political world, the occupational world, or the world of the arts, there is always a recognized hierarchy of leaders, and with some notable exceptions, and some variation from field to field, males are almost always overrepresented in the leadership positions. Or, if one uses income as a measure of the positions people hold in general or the rewards they receive for their work, men once again are consistently found to have the advantage. Just a few examples of the lack of equity between men and women in the public world will document the advantaged position of men.

The political world. At the time when the Constitution and the Declaration of Independence of the United States were being written and adopted, there was much said about the inalienable rights of "men." When the leaders of this new country used the word *men,* they may or may not have been using it to refer to all people. Perhaps they were, but the fact is they set up a representative form of government in which women (along with slaves, native Americans, and others) were not given the right to vote. It was not until the 1920s, almost a century and a half later, that women finally received the right to vote.

THE WOMEN'S MOVEMENT AND THE CHANGES IT HAS BROUGHT

There was a feminist movement in the United States in the nineteenth and early twentieth centuries, but it became focused on the single issue of women being given the right to vote. When the women's suffrage amendment to the Constitution was finally ratified in 1920, the feminist movement went into a decline and remained submerged for forty years. Even World War II, which brought women into the labor force in great numbers, did not do much to change the position of women. Indeed, in the decade of the 1950s the overwhelming cultural ideal portrayed women in a stereotyped mother, wife, and homemaker role.

During this period most women and men at all levels of the society accepted and believed in the ideal of women remaining in the home, having children, and caring for them. Men, on the other hand, were to be out facing and coping with the problems of the larger world. One problem with this ideal came from the fact that great numbers of women found themselves unhappy and unsatisfied. They generally attributed their feelings of malaise to their individual and psychological shortcomings. Two events occurred in the early 1960s that brought the problems of women to a much higher level of public consciousness. One of these was political—President John F. Kennedy established a Presidential Commission on the Status of Women. The second was literary (soon to become a mass media phenomenon)—Betty Friedan published a book titled *The Feminine Mystique* (1963). The report of the Commission, coincided with the publication of Friedan's book.

The Commission report emphasized that when women worked in the labor force (as many did despite the cultural ideal to the contrary) their status, wages, and conditions of work were unfair and unacceptable. The Commission report did two things: First, it brought the issue of equity for women, especially working women, into the political arena. Second, the formation of the Presidential Commission at a national level, and the formation of fifty state commissions, gave women a communications network that provided opportunities to meet, share their ideas and experiences, and organize further to meet emergent problems (Ryan, 1983).

Betty Friedan's book struck an obviously responsive chord with many American women. It revealed to them that what they had thought was a personal psychological problem was a national social problem. It crystallized the feelings of many women who began to recognize that the traditional feminine role had placed them in a subordinate and disadvantaged position in American society.

The two catalytic events came together in 1966 when a National Conference of State Commissions on the Status of Women met in Washington, D.C. A group of women attending that conference met one evening in the hotel room of Betty Friedan and founded the National Organization for Women (NOW).

In the years since the formation of NOW, this organization has not been the only organization speaking out on women's issues. There have been splinter groups coming from rifts in the organization, and independent feminist and women's groups coming from different political and ideological perspectives. Most observers place NOW in the *liberal feminism* category of the women's movement.

Liberal Feminism

The liberal feminist approach accepts the existing economic and social institutions as they are and works for the equality of women within these institutions. Often the liberal feminist approach is characterized as having a legalistic outlook, since major efforts are directed toward changing or passing laws that affect women. Working through legislatures and the courts, the liberal feminists have made some limited gains in establishing the rights of women and achieving more equality with men in occupations, wages and salaries, credit, recreation, and other spheres of life.

The philosophical position of liberal feminism supports "individual freedom and a toleration of diverse life styles" (Anderson, 1983, p. 260). It is a philosophy that is widely accepted in American society because it gives individuals autonomy and personal choice and is thus consistent with the individualism that is so widely revered. With respect to gender roles, this philosophical tradition translates into the principle that both men and women should have the right to choose their own course in life and should not be either inhibited or treated unfairly. If a woman wishes to have a career, say as a construction engineer, she should be allowed to do so. And if she is successful she should receive the same rewards as a man in the same line of work.

To a considerable degree we now have laws that allow such freedom of choice. Even so, there are still some institutional obstructions, such as women in the military being prohibited from serving in combat positions and women in the Catholic Church not being allowed to be priests. There are also laws and court rulings that give women equal (or near equal) rights in obtaining credit, participating in sports, gaining equal access to recreational activities, and so on. Many of these legal and judicial changes have come about because of the efforts of feminist groups with the liberal feminist philosophy. But some feminists have come to believe that working within the existing institutional structure is ineffectual and misdirected. These views, which are often more ideological and intellectual than the liberal feminist approach, are divided into two types: the socialist feminists and the radical feminists.

The Socialist Feminists

Karl Marx and Friedrich Engels, when they advanced the basic socialist theory and ideology, were sensitive in some instances to the disadvantaged position of women in Western capitalist society. They were critical of the concept of private property, and considered marriage one more instance of men owning things; in this case, men owned their wives. Women, they argued, would only be liberated when the economic system of capitalism had been replaced by a classless, socialist society.

Several feminist writers in the 1970s considered this basic Marxist idea and concluded that the oppression of women could not be attributed solely to the capitalist system of private property ownership (Anderson, 1983). These writers were called socialist feminists, because they started with the Marx-Engels idea but elaborated on it. They focused on how women were oppressed in a fundamental way by a family system that made them solely responsible for reproduction and largely responsible for caring for children (Firestone, 1971; Mitchell, 1971). Just as Marx and Engels argued that the end of human oppression would come with changes in the control of economic production, the socialist feminists argued that the freedom of women would come only when they were freed from the duties of reproduction and child rearing. Only when women were so freed would they achieve equality with men in the public world of politics, economics, and the workplace.

While the socialist feminists saw the oppression of women in the reproductive system, which paralleled and supported the capitalist-productive system, there were other feminists who saw a prior and more pervasive source of oppression. These, the radical feminists, saw the source of women's oppression as patriarchy. *Patriarchy*, with respect to the family, means that a husband and father has unquestioned authority and dominance over other family members. Radical feminists have broadened the meaning of patriarchy so that it refers to any social system in which men have superior power and economic privilege (Eisenstein, 1979).

Radical Feminism

There is no single version of radical feminism, but the several distinguishable types all share one basic assumption: male dominance in social and economic relations is the preeminent fact that must be eliminated if women are to be physically, economically, and psychologically free.

Since patriarchy is seen as the dominant negative force in society, the solution of some radical feminists has been to establish "women-centered beliefs and systems" (Anderson, 1983, p. 285). In one extreme form this means establishing a separate female-centered society. One writer in this vein has argued as follows:

> *All heterosexual relationships are corrupted by the imbalance of power between men and women. . . . It follows then, that because of the inequalities between men and women in this culture, because equality is necessary to the full growth of the ability to love, and because of the essential equalness of women, the most perfect development of the ability to love, where women are concerned, can occur only in a homosexual lesbian context. (Kelly, 1972, p. 473)*

This lesbian version of radical feminism, while creating a great deal of uproar and producing some division within the women's movement, has never been accepted by more than a handful of feminists.

Another group of radical feminists has taken a very different view by emphasizing the importance of some traditional feminine characteristics, such as nurturance, affection, expressiveness, and "a commingling of feeling and thought" (Ryan, 1983, p. 339). This radical feminist view equates the male world with competitiveness, impersonality, and rational-contractual relationships—in short, an extreme ego-oriented, self-interested individualism. By contrast, these feminists see the female world as nurturing and caring, a world where enduring attachments with other people are made and maintained for their own sake and not for what can be gained from them (Thorne and Yalom, 1982). This strain of radical feminism takes note of the fact that liberal feminism urges women to enter competition in a world where the rules and the values are *man*-made. In the process of entering this male-created world, women give up the qualities of womanhood. As one writer notes, the most prominent image of the liberated woman is one who comes "complete with briefcase, career, sex partners and silk blouse, but absolutely without nurturing responsibilities" (Gordon, 1982, p. 50).

While some radical feminists are critical of the public world that males have been responsible for creating, they are usually quick to emphasize that women do have a right to seek achievement in that world, if that is their choice. They also stress that the family cannot be one that oppresses women and makes them bear the burden of injustices produced in the outside world. It cannot be the patriarchal family, in which women are called upon to provide a "haven from a heartless world" (Lasch, 1977), as many conservative commentators have wanted (Thorne, 1982; Gordon, 1982).

These radical feminists have added an interesting dimension to the picture of feminism. While recognizing the oppression of women in the traditional patriarchal system, they also emphasize how the characteristics that grow out of the "woman's experience" are worth preserving and fostering.

After this consideration of the various forms of feminism, we may ask if feminists, or perhaps other forces, have brought about changes in gender role attitudes in contemporary society? A brief look at the answer to this question will conclude this chapter.

HAVE ATTITUDES ABOUT TRADITIONAL GENDER ROLES CHANGED?

Almost everyone agrees that some things have changed with regard to traditional gender roles (both male and female). The women's movement and other social and economic forces have produced some obvious changes over the last two decades. However, to specify exactly what has changed, and how much, is difficult, because we do not generally have measurements from twenty years ago. An important exception to this lack of long-term data on gender role attitudes is found in what are called the *Detroit area studies*. In 1962 a sample of women who had borne babies in 1961 in the Detroit metropolitan area were interviewed by researchers from the Survey Research Center at the University of Michigan. These women have been reinterviewed a number of times since then, most recently in 1980. In 1980 the children who had been born to these women in 1961 were eighteen years old, and as many of the children as could be located were also interviewed (about eighty-five percent of the families from the original sample). While these samples are not necessarily representative of the entire national population, they are of great value because they cover the same area and the same people over a critical two-decade period. The fact that many of the children of these women were also interviewed is another important advantage of this sample, because it allows a comparison of generations (Thornton and Freedman, 1979; Thornton et al., 1983).

As an example of attitude changes about gender roles revealed by this study, consider how women have changed with respect to the statement "Most of the important decisions in the life of the family should be made by the man of the house." In 1962, fewer than one-third of the women disagreed with that statement. By 1980, more than seventy percent disagreed (71.3%). See Figure 2.2 for other attitude changes among these women. Interestingly, the eighteen-year-old daughters of these women in 1980 had a slightly smaller percentage disagreeing (66.2%), making the daughters somewhat more traditional than their mothers on this issue. In general, however, when comparisons were possible, daughters were less traditional about gender role issues than their mothers. That was not the case with the sons of these women, who were more traditional than their mothers. On the issue of "the man of the house making the important decisions," only forty-four percent of the eighteen-year-old sons of these women disagreed (Thornton et al., 1983). This follows a general pattern found in surveys of attitudes where men generally have higher percentages favoring traditional gender roles.

While attitude surveys have shown widespread changes in attitudes, there is still the unresolved question of whether the public expressions are backed by behavior and action—both private and public. Although many men, and women too, may follow current fashions when they make public statements, they may not follow these statements with corresponding actions in their everyday lives. We have already seen that in the world of occupations and political affairs, women have still not achieved equality with men. Certainly this leaves some doubt about how much actions regarding the two sexes are in keeping with the words. It can be said that traditional gender roles have undergone some moderating influences in recent years. But we must at least expect that traditional gender roles will still have a pervasive and persistent influence on

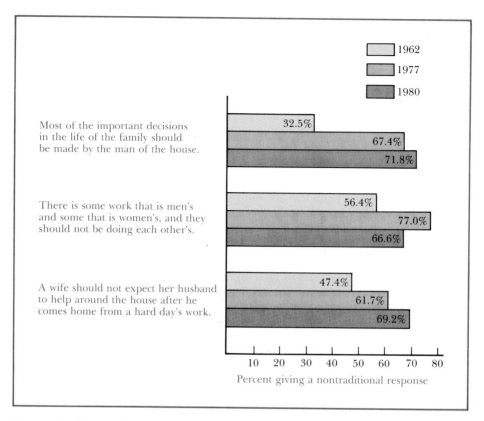

Figure 2.2 *Changes in women's attitudes about some traditional gender role statements between 1962 and 1980.* (*Source:* Thornton, et al. 1983, table 1, p. 215.)

marriage and family life. In the chapters that follow we will see that this expectation is true.

To a considerable degree the persistence of traditional gender roles will depend on how children are reared in their homes. If the socialization they receive from their parents and others stresses gender differences, the traditional gender roles will likely persist. If socialization de-emphasizes gender differences, the children will grow up with less traditional attitudes. Each family with children can consider how much or how little gender differences will be emphasized in the home. As the final issue of this chapter we will ask: Should children be raised androgynously (boys and girls the same)?

ISSUE

Should children be raised androgynously?

As we have seen in this chapter, in traditional child rearing boys and girls are raised very differently. From the most traditional perspective, parents assume that boys and girls are fundamentally different and therefore should be treated and reared differently.

Androgynous child rearing is quite the opposite. Parents of children raised androgynously begin with the assumption that boys and girls are fundamentally the same and should be treated the same. As conceptualized by Sandra Bem (Bruck, 1977), any child reared androgynously will end up possessing the personality traits associated with both maleness *and* femaleness. Such a child will not automatically accept the idea that there are some things males can do and other things females can do.

But exactly what would parents have to do if they were to raise their children androgynously? Letty Cottin Pogrebin, cofounder of *Ms.* magazine and author of the recent book *Growing Up Free: Raising Your Child in the 80's* (1980), has offered detailed guidelines for parents who wish to raise their children androgynously. First, parents would have to avoid communicating any traditional signs of gender to their children (e.g., gender-typed toys, clothing, room decor, and furniture). Second, parents' own behavior would have to be as free of gender-stereotyped patterns as possible. Both parents would be actively involved in all aspects of child care, from feeding and bathing to recreation and education. Both parents would also be involved in routine household work.

Parents raising their children androgynously would have to be constantly on guard against the reemergence of their own deep-seated beliefs and expectations about gender differences. They would have to take special care that there be no differences in discipline, praise, and encouragement for boys and girls.

Parents raising their children androgynously would also have to monitor the gender-stereotyped influences their children receive from external sources such as television, friends, teachers, magazines, books, and so on. However, these parents would have to accept the fact that they could never be totally successful in eliminating traditional gender role messages from outside sources.

With this description of what androgynous child rearing entails, we can now turn to the issue under consideration: Should children be raised androgynously?

The Arguments against Androgynous Child Rearing

Probably the major opposing argument is captured in Freud's famous dictum: "Anatomy is destiny." The core of this assertion is that there is a biological basis for gender-typed behavior. The instrumental traits associated with men and the expressive traits associated with women are accepted as natural manifestations of the biological differences between males and females. In his book *The Inevitability of Patriarchy,* anthropologist Steven Goldberg (1973) argues that male superiority in aggression, dominance, reasoning ability, and achievements in the arts and sciences all come from the male hormones. As proof for his argument Goldberg points to the fact that there is not a single woman whose genius has approached that of any number of men in philosophy, mathematics, composing, theorizing of any kind, or even painting (Goldberg, 1973).

An additional and complementary argument is built around the fact that only women can become pregnant and nurse babies. Since this is an undisputed province of women, it is believed by many that women should largely confine their energies and talents to these and related tasks.

Some have argued that there is an additional biological impediment that keeps women from taking on the instrumental roles of the society. The hormonal dynamics associated with the menstrual cycle are said to lead to periodic emotional and physical incapacities that militate against women carrying out the critical decision-making tasks of society in a steady manner.

A final biological argument is that the size and strength differences between men and women dictate that authority should reside with the males. This is especially the case in family life, where men have the responsibility of physically protecting wives and children.

To summarize these biological arguments against androgynous child rearing, they are simply that it is contrary to the natural proclivities of the sexes. Parents who try to contravene these natural tendencies will only produce frustration for themselves and their children.

A second major line of argument against raising children androgynously is the great social pressure that pushes children to conform to traditional gender roles. Once outside the supportive confines of the family, androgynous children will be severely penalized for their nonconforming and unusual personal behavior. Boys, in particular, will be condemned for feminine behavior, or at the very least for being unmanly and weak.

A last argument against raising children androgynously is that androgynous behavior might produce ineffective adults. In the world of work, business, and the professions (as well as in recreational activities such as games and sports) androgynous males would simply not compete well against more ag-gressive males. Similarly, females who show too many masculine traits would likely be viewed as aggressive and unpleasant to be around. Therefore, ironically, both males and females who have been raised androgynously could come out poorly in comparison with their counterparts who conform more closely to tra-ditional gender role expectations.

Among the arguments against raising children androgynously the foremost is a presumption that the genders are biologically different. This presumption is buttressed by a social argument that children raised androgynously will be pe-nalized in the outside traditional world. As a result they will be ineffective and disadvantaged.

The Arguments for Androgynous Child Rearing

Several major arguments have been offered in support of raising children androgynously. The first is that androgyny allows individuals more freedom to express their unique personality traits. Many individuals are simply not cut out for the roles prescribed by the society. For them, being raised androgynously al-lows a wider range of choices in personal life-styles and occupations.

Traditional gender role expectations are viewed as arbitrary and limiting for both genders, but that is especially the case with respect to women. Women are often caught in "cross-pressures" because of limitations imposed by the tra-ditional feminine role. Today, women are being told repeatedly that they can and should compete with men in the world of occupations and professions. At the same time they are likely to be told that if they want marriage, and perhaps children, they must not be too competitive.

Males are often harmed by traditional gender role expectations in quite a different way. There is ample evidence showing that the requirements for being brave, psychologically strong, aggressive, and ambitious can actually be harm-ful to the health and well-being of men. Beginning as early as the teenage years, boys are more likely to be hurt or killed in accidents, apparently because of the risk-taking that is a valued trait in males. In adulthood males often feel intensely that they must overcome all challenges, defeat all competitors, and attain great success or they are not living up to the male ideal. For those who are relatively successful in this realm, the stress can be never ending, for there is always a new challenge or a new competitor. They may become "workaholics," and liter-ally kill themselves. For the men who fare less well in the competition, or fail completely, the stresses are even greater. They must face the fact that they have failed and find some way of coping with their inadequacies as "men."

There is also evidence that women who accept the traditional feminine role often reach a period in their lives when they ask if they have made the right choice. In a society that values accomplishments in the world of work more than work done in the home, women who have given their primary service and loyalty to home and family often feel underappreciated and underrewarded. They may also feel unfulfilled, because they have sacrificed some of their own ambitions and talents in order to do the things that were expected of them as women.

Those who argue for androgynous child rearing are acutely aware of the difficulties that will be faced by adults who have been reared outside the boundaries of traditional gender roles. However, they also believe that the disadvantages of continuing to rear children along traditional gender role lines is even more harmful. It is their view that changes in the rigid gender roles of the past must begin sometime, and the sooner the better. Even if the first efforts at androgynous child rearing are not completely successful, and even if the society is not immediately transformed, it will be a beginning. Even minor and gradual changes in traditional gender roles will give more people greater freedom and opportunity in their lives, and lead the way to more changes in the future.

Summarizing the arguments for raising children androgynously, there is the greater freedom it would give to both genders. Women would be freer to enter into a wider range of activities, and men would avoid being channeled into narrowly masculine activities.

Themes

1. Gender roles are deeply ingrained and pervasive.

2. Roles are socially shared expectations about the behavior expected of people in different statuses.

3. Gender roles are made up of two compatible parts: stereotyped personality traits and expected behaviors.

4. Traditional gender roles divide along the lines of instrumental and expressive behaviors, for males and females, respectively.

5. Gender roles are learned through three complementary theoretical mechanisms: social learning, modeling, and cognitive development.

6. While traditional gender roles may be somewhat disadvantageous for men, they are much more likely to place women in subordinate, less-valued positions that call for them to make more sacrifices.

7. Traditional gender roles have a pervasive influence ranging from the seemingly trivial to the most important activities of the society.

8. The contemporary women's movement had its beginnings with a combination of events in the early 1960s.

9. There are three different philosophical strands in the contemporary women's movement: liberal feminism, socialist feminism and radical feminism.

10. There have been some clear-cut changes in attitudes about traditional gender roles in the last twenty years, but there is some uncertainty about whether these changes have been translated into behavior.

Facts

1. Experiments with animals and birds have shown that when behavior is rewarded (reinforced) it is likely to be repeated.

2. Most children have learned which gender they belong to by the age of three.

3. At somewhat older ages, children learn that their gender places them in a general category of people, e.g., females.

4. At about age six, children come to understand that the gender one belongs to is constant and will not change.

5. Children will actively seek out and adopt those things from their environment that are consistent with prevailing gender roles.

6. Touching another person is, among other things, a way of exercising power over that person, and males touch females more than the reverse.

7. When sitting or standing, men will take up more physical space than women.

8. Men interrupt women in conversation more than women interrupt men.

9. Women have made some gains in politics but are still extremely underrepresented in most high-level political positions.

10. Women are employed primarily as clerical workers, secretaries, nurses, teachers, and waitresses.

11. With equal educational qualifications, women earn only about sixty percent as much as men.

12. The liberal feminist philosophy of the women's movement emphasizes a legalistic approach, individual freedom, and a toleration of diverse life-styles.

13. Socialist feminists see the oppression of women as rooted in the reproductive and child-care systems.

14. Radical feminists see the source of women's oppression in patriarchy, both within and outside of the family.

15. Both women and men reject specifics of the traditional gender roles much more than they did twenty years ago, but men retain more traditional views than women.

Major Concepts

achieved status: A status that requires making a special effort to enter or belong to.

ascribed status: A status people are born into, such as being a male or female.

behaviorism: A theory that focuses on behavior rather than on internal states of mind (motives, intentions, attitudes). See social learning theory.

cognitive development theory: A theory emphasizing how children actively seek out and adopt those things that are consistent with prevailing gender roles.

competency traits: A label for the stereotyped personality traits associated with males.

expressive behaviors: Behaviors associated with the traditional female role, related to giving comfort, meeting emotional needs, and providing supportive service.

feminization of poverty: A term reflecting the higher proportion of households headed by women at or below the poverty level.

instrumental behaviors: Behaviors associated with the traditional male role, related to achievement and action.

liberal feminism: A part of the women's movement that accepts the existing economic and social structures but attempts to improve the opportunities of women through a legalistic approach.

modeling: Learning behavior (including gender roles) by imitating what others do.

pink-collar class: A term reflecting the high percentage of employed women in lower-level white-collar and less-prestigious professional occupations.

radical feminism: A part of the women's movement that sees the oppression of women in patriarchal systems and encourages the establishment of women- centered beliefs and systems.

role: A prescription for interpersonal behavior associated with socially recognized categories of persons.

socialist feminism: A part of the women's movement that extends the ideas of Marx and Engels by focusing on the way women are oppressed by the reproduction and child-care systems.

social learning theory: A theory emphasizing how human behavior is learned when it is rewarded by the environment, which acts as a reinforcement.

status: Any socially recognized category of persons, such as police officers, teachers, news commentators, males, and females.

stereotyped personality traits: Personality attributes that are often thought to reside in the biological makeup of males and females.

warmth-expressiveness traits: A label for the stereotyped personality traits associated with females.

3

Love
The Emotion and
The Experience

Most people would say that love is good. If there were more love in the world it would be a better place to live. We often think of love as the ultimate emotional experience. We also believe that when we give love it is the most generous of personal acts.

But some people say that love is the problem, or at least they say that love is the cause of many problems we have with marriage and family life today. As one writer archly put it, "If love is the answer, what is the problem?" (West, 1977).

If love is viewed by some people as a problem and by others as the highest emotional experience, it is clearly an issue that deserves careful consideration. In the chapter ahead we will explore the nature of love as an emotion and as an experience. After we have done so, we can return to a basic question: Do we put too much emphasis on love in this society?

Love is a complex emotion. Yet people often act as if it is the simplest and most easily understood of human feelings. One might ask, if love is so uncomplicated why is it defined in so many different ways? And why do people continue to have so many questions about it? No one ever asks, "How will I know when I am afraid?" or "How will I be able to tell when I am sad?" But how frequently people ask, "How will I know when I am *really* in love?" Even more revealing is the fact that most answers to the last question are pitifully vague and inadequate. The answer is usually something like "You'll know when it happens," or "You'll feel the chemistry." Such responses certainly raise more questions than they answer.

Rather than assume that an understanding of love is obvious, it would be better to begin with the assumption that love is not a simple emotion. The emotion of love is, in fact, very complex. Love is an emotion that has within it some very contradictory elements. A number of writers have suggested that love is, on the one hand, a self-interested or even selfish experience but, on the other hand, the ultimate caring, sharing, uniting, and generous experience (Solomon, 1981; Swidler, 1980). While it is too soon to explore this more complicated issue, it is clear that if love does have within it contradictory or opposing elements, it is more complex than it is assumed to be.

One way of seeing this complexity is to focus on love as a social and cultural ideal. The Western world has several thousand years of history, and some of our ideas about love go far back into that history. There are also widely varying ideas about the nature and importance of love in non-Western cultures around the world. These too will broaden our understanding of love.

THE HISTORICAL LANDMARKS OF ROMANTIC LOVE

An emotional, sexual attraction between members of opposite sexes is apparently a universal human capability. In most known societies the idea of love is recognized as a feeling that one human can have for another. What differs is how love is viewed and what part it plays in the normal events of life. A brief historical look at some of the cultures that were the predecessors of contemporary American culture will give some idea of how widely conceptions of love have differed.

The Classical Period of Greece

The classical period of Greek history, sometimes called the Golden Age, reached its peak some 300 to 500 years before the birth of Christ. As we all know, many of the ideas of that period have come down to our own time as important influences on our own cultural heritage. For example, the term *platonic love* is a term still used today to describe a nonsexual relationship between male and female. This usage, however, is a twelfth-century variation of an ideal of love originally described by Plato (Solomon, 1981).

Our knowledge about the ideas and lives of the Greeks comes from their mythology, their dramas, and the words of their major philosophers (most notably, Socrates, Plato, and Aristotle). Other sources of knowledge about classical Greece include histories and biographical accounts of some of the more illustrious Greek citizens. On the basis of these sources, what can be said about love among the Greeks? First, they did give the subject their attention. Indeed, one writer has called the Greeks the "inventors" of love (Hunt, 1959, p. 15). What then did the Greeks have to say about love?

Consider first the mythology of Greece, which deals with the lives of the gods. The Greek gods were very often gods with all-too-human qualities. Their tastes, their desires, and their behaviors were human, but at the same time they had superhuman experiences and abilities. The goddess Aphrodite, for example, was not born in a normal fashion but was formed in the sea from the semen that came from the genitals of her castrated father. With this beginning, having such strong sexual connections, it is not surprising that Aphrodite became the goddess of carnal love, the goddess who presided over the physical act of sexual intercourse. From the goddess Aphrodite comes the word *aphrodisiac*, which refers to something that is said to stimulate and excite sexual desires. In contrast to the very physical sexual love represented by Aphrodite, the Greeks also recognized a more spiritual love represented by the male god Eros. They called this *erotic love*, which was for them the sentimental side of love. Erotic love was a feeling of the heart and had almost nothing to do with sex. We obviously use the word erotic differently today, since it does refer to sexual feelings.

However, the spirit of Eros has been passed down to us in an indirect way. In Greek mythology Eros was a young lad who carried a quiver of arrows and a bow. When he pierced a person with an arrow, as he might do at any time it suited him, that person would be struck by feelings of love. We are familiar with this conception of love because the Romans transformed the young lad into an even

Cupid is still our symbol for romantic love.

younger, cherubic, little infant called Cupido. We call him Cupid, and he is still found on valentine cards every February. Even today, Cupid represents a kind of nonsexual, romantic love feeling, much as Eros might have represented these feelings for the ancient Greeks. We also carry on the idea that love can strike anyone at any time or place. In this view, love is something largely beyond our control (Flaceliere, 1962).

The distinction between a physical, sexual kind of love, as represented by Aphrodite, and a more spiritual love, represented by Eros, is a distinction still made today (Fromm, 1955). However, for many people sexual and spiritual love are inextricably connected (Solomon, 1981). A prevailing idea in American society is that sex without love is not acceptable, and love (romantic love) without sex is hard to imagine. While we tend to link love and sex very closely, the Greeks were much more inclined to make a separation between the two. They often characterized sexual love as an expression of one's "lower" nature. Spiritual love, by contrast, was a reflection of the higher mental qualities of humans. The Greeks tended to extol and glorify the spiritual kind of love and to treat sexual love as a necessary evil (Branden, 1981).

One of the most notable features of the way the Greeks saw love was that they applied the ideas of sexual and spiritual love to both homosexual and heterosexual relationships. When Greek writers, who were almost always male, wrote about love, they could be referring to their relations with women or with young postpubescent boys. Much has been written about the preference that the men of Greece during the classical period had for young boys. Some writers have given the impression that the homosexual liaison between middle-aged men and young boys was the only kind of love relationship in Greece. That is not the case, but it is true that for many men love affairs with young boys were the accepted, if not the preferred, love relationships. The word *pederasty* is derived from the Greek word *paiderasteia* which literally meant love of boys (Flaceliere, 1962). Today the word is used to refer to an act of sexual deviance in which an adult is sexually attracted to immature children. For the Greeks the word had a broader meaning. It could refer to a sexual relationship between an adult man and a young boy, or it could also refer simply to an affectionate relationship between them. Many times these relationships were between an older male teacher and a young man who was his student or disciple. While in many cases these may simply have been affectionate relationships, there is a good deal of evidence to suggest that these relationships were often sexual and even romantic.

One extraordinary aspect of these relationships is the youthfulness of the boys. It was said that as soon as a boy began to show signs of maturity, such as developing a beard, the relationship would end. A Greek epigram of the time expressed this view:

Desirable is the bloom of a boy of twelve. But that of thirteen is much more delightful. Even sweeter is the flower of love that blossoms at fourteen. Its charm increases more still at fifteen. Sixteen is the divine age. A boy of seventeen I would not dare to woo. (quoted in Flaceliere, 1962, pp. 68–69)

Not all Greeks of the classical period agreed, however, that affectionate, loving, and sexual relationships between men and young boys were the highest and noblest form of love. For example, the foremost playwright of classical Greece, Aristophanes, was strongly opposed to homosexual love (Flaceliere, 1962, p. 80). Among the great classical Greek philosophers, Socrates, Plato, and Aristotle, it was Aristotle who was the most hostile toward pederasty. He thought that those men who engaged in sexual love relations with young boys were depraved.

Aristotle also wrote kind words about the love between husbands and wives (conjugal love). In this he was unusual among the classical Greek writers, because, for of all the writing the Greeks did about love, very little was said about the relationships between husbands and wives. The attitude of many Greek writers toward women and marriage is expressed in the following declaration by a fourth-century B.C. lawyer:

We resort to Courtesans [prostitutes] for our pleasures, keep concubines [mistresses] to look after our daily needs and marry wives to give us legitimate children and to be faithful guardians of domestic hearths. (quoted in Flaceliere, 1962, p. 122)

Wives were thus relegated to the task of producing legitimate heirs. In general, Greek writers had a low regard for women and considered them at best a necessary evil. In the words of one Greek poet, "Marriage brings a man only two happy days: The day he takes a bride to bed and the day he lays her in her grave" (Branden, 1981, p. 16).

The Greeks, as we have seen, made distinctions about types of love (spiritual, platonic, sexual) that we continue to make today. They also contributed to the exalted status that we give to love. Plato called love "a gift of the gods, a superhuman inspiration" (Flaceliere, 1962, p. 174). Aristotle contributed an idea about love that in the long run has been even more important. He gave special significance to the love between husband and wife, a love that emphasized caring and affection more than passion. Husband-wife love, or conjugal love, is a theme that was later picked up by the Greek historian Plutarch, who wrote, "The bodily pleasure experienced is brief. But it is like a seed giving rise to the daily growth between man and wife of mutual respect, affection and confidence" (from *Erotikos*, quoted in Flaceliere, 1962, p. 185). These sentiments are reflected in many current notions about marital love. We generally expect a husband and wife to love each other passionately and sexually at the beginning of marriage, but this intense love is expected to diminish gradually into a comfortable and warm love. Passionate fires in the early stages of marriage are to turn gradually into "glowing coals."

From this classical world of Greece, we can move to a second major landmark that has shaped our views of love. This is the development of Christianity in the second and third centuries after the birth of Christ.

Early Christianity and Views of Love

Christianity, of course, grew out of ancient Judaism and thus reflects the Jewish cultural heritage. The Old Testament has no shortage of references to events and experiences that could be called romantic, passionate, and conjugal love. However, Christianity as it emerged in the second and third centuries, especially in the context of the Roman Empire, took on a character that nearly denied love, especially passionate love.

Perhaps the conditions that prevailed in Roman life had something to do with how Christianity developed. By most accounts, life in Rome, at least among the upper classes, was one where love and sex took on the character of a game or sport. Adultery, sexual affairs, and the free expression of all kinds of passions have been vividly described in the history that has come down to us from the height of the Roman Empire (Branden, 1981; Tannahill, 1980). It was in this setting that early Christianity took root. If the Romans accepted their sexual and amorous adventures without guilt, the early Christians had exactly the opposite view.

A central principle of early Christianity was asceticism, which emphasized the virtues of self-denial. In particular, Christian asceticism included human sexuality as one of the earthly pleasures to be shunned (Branden, 1981; Hunt, 1959; Tannahill, 1980). The Christian perspective on love is best understood by recalling the Greek distinction between physical, sexual love and spiritual love. The Christians raised the importance of spiritual love to a level even higher than the Greeks. However, spiritual love was not so much directed toward someone of the opposite sex as it was directed toward God. The love between marriage partners among the early Christians was closer to what has been labeled *agape*, which stresses giving to and sacrificing for the person one loves.

Sex was viewed negatively by early Christians because it was a physical pleasure and, thus, very possibly a product of the devil. However, the early Church fathers easily saw that sexual desires could not be totally repressed. At the very least, they recognized that if sex were totally denied it would lead to the extinction of their emerging religious group. The words that express this early Christian view best are those of St. Paul. He gave a begrudging approval to marriage and sex when he wrote, "let them marry, for it is better to marry than to burn [with sexual desire]" (1 Cor. 7:9).

As late as the fourth century A.D., a church leader, St. Jerome, wrote, "I should like every man to take a wife who cannot manage to sleep alone because he gets frightened at night" (quoted in Tannahill, 1980, p. 138). This clearly reflects the disdain he felt for men who were too weak to resist marriage.

This early Christian view of marriage left very little room for the experience of love, which we consider so crucial for marriage today. Passionate and romantic love were acknowledged only as negative impulses that had less than divine origins. These were considered by the early Christians to come from lust, which was probably inspired by the devil. Today, love and sex are accepted as being closely linked. At least, many believe that ideally love should be a prerequisite for sexual relations. Not so with the early Christians, who put them far apart, one representing the body, which was evil, the other representing the soul, which was pure and good.

There is one other important landmark in the development of the concept of love in Western society, but again it is not related to marriage. This is the emergence of courtly love in the twelfth century.

Courtly Love

To understand the beginnings and nature of courtly love, we might notice that, in our own lives, the ideas we have about love are likely to have been shaped by the lyrics of songs we heard as we were growing up. In a similar way, courtly love was popularized by the traveling singers and poets of France in the twelfth century. They were called *troubadours*, and they entertained aristocratic wives who remained behind while their husbands were away on the Crusades to the Holy Land. The songs of the troubadours were directed toward these ladies and often told a story of a suitor who had fallen in love with a woman he could not have. He could not have the woman of his heart's desire because she was already married.

Love in the courtly tradition, then, was not a feeling that led to marriage. Marriage in the Middle Ages, as it has been through most of history, was more closely associated with what we would think of as a business contract. Especially for the elite, marriage was a way of consolidating two families, of guarding an inheritance, or of improving the political or economic resources of the family. When the Countess of Champagne, in the twelfth century, had her chaplain Andreas Capellanus summarize the principles of courtly love, he made it his first point to proclaim: "Marriage is no good excuse against loving" (in Tannahill, 1980). This idea, perhaps perplexing at first, simply says that the fact that a person is married shall not be an impediment to falling in love.

Love, as it was characterized in the Middle Ages, was a highly emotional relationship between two people who could never have their love fulfilled, at least not by marriage and perhaps, in the ideal, not by sexual relations. Pure love according to Andreas the Chaplain, "goes as far as the kiss and the embrace and the modest contact with the nude lover, omitting the final solace, for that is not permitted to those who wish to love purely" (quoted in Tannahill, 1980, p. 265). The "final solace" was a euphemism for sexual relations and was not part of the ideal of "pure love."

Love in the Middle Ages depicted in a painting from that period called Roman de la Rose.

In the courtly love tradition, it is clear that marriage was not the expected outcome whenever two people fell in love. Put in a slightly different way, love in this early medieval period was adulterous love. It was often a love affair between a married, high-status woman and a man of lower status who yearned hopelessly to possess her (Tannahill, 1980).

By the end of the Middle Ages and the beginning of the modern era in the seventeenth century, Western culture had accumulated an extensive body of literature and thought about romantic love. We have touched only a few highlights of that history, but two points stand out. First, and most obvious, is that the *object* of love can differ greatly from one time or place to another. Among the Greeks of high status in the classical period the object of love might be a young boy; for the early Christians it was God; for a high-born woman in the Middle Ages it might be a poet-singer who had fallen in love with her despite the fact that she was already married. Clearly, the object of love feelings can vary widely.

The second major point has to do with the relationship between love and marriage. While there are historical and literary examples of deep, passionate, and abiding love between husbands and wives, through most of Western history that has not been the primary focus of love relationships. Certainly the emphasis in the major premodern Western societies has not been on the idea that two people fall in love and then marry. That idea has become prominent in the last three centuries, especially in the United States. But before we come to the modern era there is another question about love that should be addressed. Through the long history of human experience, what significance has love had for the masses of common people?

Love Among the Common People

As we have examined the classical and historical ideas about love, we have said very little about love among the masses. Indeed, it is necessary to emphasize that most of the ideas and behaviors considered were those of the elite and the upper-status members of society. The ideas and the behaviors of the common people cannot be known because their words, feelings, and experiences have not been passed down.

One possibility that many writers have suggested is that, through most of history (and even more so for prehistorical periods), the lives of the common people were so hard and so precarious that they had very little time or energy left for the luxury of experiencing love. In this view, love has been a kind of extravagance, reserved only for the rich and the high born. Only they could devote their time, energy, and thoughts to the emotion of love. The rest of the people were too busy just trying to survive.

Such a view does not, of course, deny that men and women through all of human existence have been sexually attracted to one another. Many people must surely have experienced passion, tenderness, and closeness as a part of their sexual attraction. But we might wonder whether most people lived lives in which the feelings associated with the emotion of love were negligible or nonexistent.

Even today, at the end of the twentieth century, there are millions of people on earth whose lives are so close to the edge of existence that it is hard to believe that feelings of love, as we think of them, can play a significant part in their lives. One has only to read about the lives of the Yanomamo, a society of about 10,000 people struggling for survival in the Amazon jungle along the border between Brazil and Venezuela, to see how little significance love and affection can have when life is hard and precarious (Chagnon, 1968; Harris, 1974).

The Yanomamo are by all accounts one of the fiercest, most aggressive peoples on earth. The men of neighboring villages are routinely engaged in fighting and warfare. They often raid other villages in the area and carry off women to marry. Indeed, the Yanomamo term for marriage translates to "dragging something away" (Harris, 1974, p. 77). Yanomamo wives are treated as little more than slaves and are often brutally abused by their husbands. As minor punishment the men routinely jerk the small sticks that the women wear through pierced ear lobes. As more severe punishments they jab their wives with sticks or machetes or burn them with glowing pieces of firewood (Harris, 1974). With this kind of treatment commonplace, there is apparently very little time for the expression of love, either before or in marriage. The Yanomamo women expect to be abused by their husbands and may even see this treatment as an indication of their status as wives. An anthropologist who lived among the Yanomamo for some time once overheard two women talking about the scars their husbands had given them. One said that her husband must really care for her since he had beaten her on the head so many times (Harris, 1974).

The Yanomamo are not typical of nonliterate people in the world, for they are surely extreme in their behavior. Yet they illustrate how a people living in very difficult environmental conditions can carry out their lives with almost no expression of the feelings we associate with love. Many human beings in the long and difficult development of human societies may very well have lived with a similar absence of love relationships. Many may still live so today in societies and cultures that leave very little time or energy for such a luxury.

Love Emerges as a Precondition for Marriage

We might never know how much love was a part of the lives of the great masses of people through history, but we do know that in Western Europe, beginning in the seventeenth century, an idea began to take shape that has had great influence on the millions of people who have lived since that time. Love came to be associated more and more closely with marriage. And most importantly, as in some of Shakespeare's plays, love was even viewed as the appropriate *precondition* for marriage. Nonetheless, for most Europeans in the seventeenth and eighteenth centuries, marriages were still arranged, usually on the basis of how a marriage would benefit the families of the bride and groom. To the extent that love between husbands and wives was considered, it was hoped that feelings of affection would grow after the marriage.

Not until the nineteenth century did the idea of love as the basis for marriage become widespread. In the United States in particular, the concept of romantic love as a prelude to marriage became an accepted ideal for great numbers of people. It seemed to come as part of the great political experiment that was just beginning. Along with a new democratic form of government came the "democratization of love."

The Democratization of Love

Many observers have commented on the extraordinary importance of romantic love in American society. Goode (1959) emphasized this point by describing the United States as having a *romantic love complex*. This term is used to refer to the way romantic love is valued in American culture and the significance love has for the institution of marriage. Very simply, this means that falling in love is thought to be a highly desirable part of courtship and is *the* most important issue when considering marriage. In the standard movie or television scenario when a person is agonizing about whether or not to marry, the best friend or parent has only to ask, "Do you love him (or her)?" If the answer is yes, the issue is settled. Nothing else is considered to be of equal significance in the decision. We understand this view, but many people in other societies do not, because their views about romantic love are quite different.

There are some societies in which the idea of being in love is treated as something that is laughable, or as a cause for sympathy. A person who behaves in an extreme or bizarre fashion because of love is someone to be pitied more than admired. Hunt (1959) illustrates how views about a love-driven person can differ by recounting an incident that occurred to an anthropologist who was living among the Bemba tribe in Rhodesia (now Zimbabwe). The anthropologist was telling the group an English folktale about a young prince who climbed dangerous mountains, crossed chasms, and fought dragons in order to win the hand of the woman he loved. The Bemba were bewildered by the story and remained silent until an old chief asked the question that was on the minds of all, "Why not take another girl?" This question reveals that, among the Bemba, as with many other people, the notion of "one true love" is not an important idea. It also indicates that being in love is not a necessary and sufficient reason for marrying.

Many societies and cultures fall between the extremes of those where love is considered irrelevant and those like the United States where love is given great prominence. These intermediate societies recognize the potential for a love relationship and consider it a permissible basis for many marriages. However, they also recognize that other factors, such as economic considerations, can enter into marriage decisions. These are also societies where more importance is placed on the love that can develop after marriage, even when it did not exist before marriage (Goode, 1959).

If it can be said that the United States is a society that is at the extreme end of the continuum, with a romantic love complex, the question arises as to why. One answer to this question can be found in a part of the American ideology that has existed since the founding of the nation. This is the emphasis placed on personal freedom and individual rights. The freedom of each individual to pur-

A concern with love is pervasive in American society.

sue his or her own happiness with the fewest possible constraints from governments and other authorities was so important to those people founding the United States that they wrote it into the Declaration of Independence—the rights to life, liberty, and the pursuit of happiness. Among the rights affirmed by this phrase is the right to choose whomever one wants as a spouse. And what better basis for making the choice than personal feelings of attraction? It follows easily from this idea that a person should be able to choose that individual, from all others, with whom one has fallen in love. There may have been other factors in American life that also contributed to the importance of romantic love, but the special attachment to individual freedom and choice must surely have been an important determinant.

Thus far we have been looking at love as an emergent and increasingly prominent cultural idea. The basic assumption behind this presentation is that the emotion of love is universally known to humans but that in different times and places the nature and importance of love varies greatly. This can be labeled the *sociocultural view* of love.

However, there is a very different view of love, its nature, and its significance in human life. This alternative view is that, since the early evolutionary beginnings of human life, love has played a part, and an important part, in the lives of human beings. This view, which is still very controversial and far from a proven fact, is a part of what is now popularly called sociobiology.

THE SOCIOBIOLOGICAL VIEW OF LOVE

We considered sociobiology briefly in Chapter 1, but before going on to describe this perspective on love, we must first give the general theory greater attention. The fundamental idea of sociobiology is that human behavior is significantly shaped by genetically inherited tendencies (Lumsden and Wilson, 1983; Wilson, 1975). Sociobiologists argue that the genetic tendencies inherited by contemporary humans are those that increased the chances for survival among their ancestors. If a certain human trait appeared at some time in the gene structure of prehumans or hominids that made it more likely for the carriers to survive, then that genetic trait would have a better chance of being passed on to the next generation. In the long run these traits would survive in the genetic structures of humans, while the traits that were less advantageous would disappear or become rare. Sociobiologists conclude from this that any widely observed human behavior must have been beneficial for survival and, thus, have been passed down genetically.

In the case of love, sociobiologists argue that human beings have evolved with a general predisposition for love. In the words of one advocate of this position, "the great majority of women and men are born with a genetic capacity and need for forming durable attachments of an emotional character. Some sizable majority have a propensity for sustained love" (Mellen, 1981, p. 139).

The second of these two statements is not so exceptional, nor even controversial. Indeed, as we have just noted, love is an emotion that most humans have the *capacity* to experience. This position also echoes the assertion of Goode (1959) in his famous sociological essay on love: "I suggest that love is a universal psychological potential" (1959, p. 47). To see how sociobiologists explain the *genetic emergence* of the capacity to love, we must follow the line of their reasoning. The following account is adapted from Mellen (1981).

According to anthropologists, archeologists, and biologists, some profound changes occurred as early prehumans became bipedal (started standing upright and walking on two feet). Though it is not altogether clear why, their cranial capacity increased very rapidly and allowed these protohumans to have larger and larger brains. This, too, might have been due to some kind of genetic selection. Perhaps those hominids with larger brains had a better chance of survival and thus passed on their genes more often.

However, as the heads of human infants at birth grew larger and larger, another problem was created. The larger heads became increasingly difficult to pass through the pelvic opening of the female at the time of birth. The adaptation to this dilemma was that the human infant was born with the bone of the skull still soft and malleable. The human infant at birth was not fully developed and had almost no ability to take care of itself. Born in this vulnerable and defenseless state, the human baby needed someone else to care for it or it would not survive.

Sociobiologists combine this fact of human evolution with the idea that during the time a female is pregnant, and as long as the newborn baby is nursing and dependent, she too is relatively immobile and in need of assistance. This is most clearly seen in the case of humans who depend on hunting and wide-ranging gathering for their food. These activities require mobility and speed, both of which are made very difficult for a female who is pregnant or nursing a small baby. One thing that would make the conditions of the mother easier, and increase the chances of the baby's survival, would be for someone else to do the hunting and gathering for them and bring food back to them. Ideally the woman and her baby might stay at or near a kind of home base while someone, perhaps a male, since he could not produce babies himself, would carry out this task of obtaining the food.

Sociobiologists envision that, over the course of time, some of the males might have had a tendency to feel an attachment to a particular female. This feeling might have arisen in large part out of desire to have sexual intercourse with her. Such a male might have gone out hunting some distance from a home base, perhaps in the company of other males, but when the hunt was successful he might have felt a longing to be with the female for whom he felt a special affection or attraction. If that feeling led him to return to the home base and share some of the meat, then both the female and her child would have had a better chance of surviving. Since the child, which was probably the offspring of the male, would have had a better chance of surviving, the genes of the father would have survived to the next generation. Now, if these were the genes that carried the traits of affection, caring, concern, or other such feelings, then it would follow that in the long evolutionary experience of our human ancestors, such genes would have been passed on more often in the human species.

If we imagine the negative form of this scenario, perhaps the sociobiological view will be even clearer. Suppose there was a male who did not have the tendency or ability to experience tenderness, caring, affection, or concern for females. Such a male might be without caring feelings, even for the female who had borne his child. This male might not have returned to his home base to share the food with the female and her child. He would have survived, because he would have had more food for himself. But, and this is the key, his genes would not have had as good a chance of surviving because his offspring would not have survived as often. Thus, over millions of years, through this selective process, the human species might have fostered and transmitted a genetic trait that gives people a propensity to experience an emotion we now call love.

While this sociobiological "explanation" of the evolution of love is attractively simple, it is open to criticism on several grounds. First, this particular view of the evolution of love gives special importance to the part played by males. There is a hint of sexism in the lack of attention given to females. In what way would feelings of love by a female have given *her* genes a better chance of being passed on to subsequent generations? It could, of course, be assumed that if a female developed feelings of affection for a particular male, she would have been more effective in attracting him back to herself and her child. But this is very speculative and leaves the sociobiological explanation even more problematic.

This points up a second criticism of the theory, which is that the facts and evidence necessary for proof are nearly impossible to obtain. Much of the evidence must come from the way people lived, and felt, several million years ago. We have only the dimmest of notions of what life was like for protohumans. Evidence about their lives is limited to a few scattered bones (both animal and human) and some possible primitive tools. Such evidence is far removed from any emergent feelings of love and affection in the minds of early humans.

Finally, there is also a basic question about whether emotions like love are genetically transmitted. As yet, no one has demonstrated that specific genes influence or determine temperament or specific emotions like love. It is possible that the science of genetics will someday provide evidence that supports these sociobiological ideas. With the discovery of the structure of DNA (chromosomal material that carries the genes), the science of genetics has made rapid advances, and we might some day know if love is, or is not, genetically transmitted.

For the moment, the sociobiological theory of the evolution of love must be considered an interesting speculation. The theory is plausible but greatly in need of scientifically based supporting evidence before it can be considered proven.

We have examined a variety of views about the nature of love in various times and places. It is now time to take a closer look at what love means to the individuals who experience it. For that, we turn to the love experience.

THE LOVE EXPERIENCE

This chapter began with the assertion that love is a very complex emotion. Other than that, no definition of love has yet been offered, for a good reason. There is no agreement on how love should be defined. One writer chooses to focus on a certain feature of love, while the next focuses on something quite different. Under these circumstances it is better to examine the variety of ways love is manifested and experienced. What we will see using this approach is that love can be many different things. Love can be generous; love can be selfish. Love can be a joyous pleasure; love can be an agonizing pain. Love can be healthy; love can be sick. We will examine all of these manifestations of the love experience.

Generous Love, Selfish Love

A favorite definition of love for many people is one that was offered by Harry Stack Sullivan, a noted American psychiatrist. He wrote: "When the satisfaction or security of another person becomes as significant to one as is one's own satisfaction or security, then the state of love exists" (Sullivan, 1953, pp. 42–43). This definition is appealing because its key feature is a generous spirit, which seems to many people to be what love is all about. Or at least people feel that generos-

It is appealing to think of love as primarily giving and generous, but it is a more complex emotion.

ity of spirit is what love should be about. This generous (nonselfish) view of love is also found in an often quoted biblical definition of love: "Love is patient and kind; love is not jealous or conceited, or proud; love is not ill-mannered, or selfish, or irritable; love does not keep a record of wrongs" (1 Cor. 13:4–5).

When we hear of two people who exhibit the kind of selfless generosity described in these definitions of love, it seems clear that they are truly in love. In O. Henry's famous short story "The Gift of the Magi," it is exactly this kind of generous love that makes the married couple so admirable, and their experience so poignant. In this story a penniless husband and wife each wish to give the other a Christmas gift. The husband sells his one possession of value, a family heirloom pocket watch, so that he can buy combs for the lovely long hair of his wife. However, she unknowingly cuts off and sells her hair so she can give to her husband a chain for his watch. We like this touching, but painful, story, because it reveals the generous, unselfish nature of the love between these two people.

Buscaglia (1972) has said, "The perfect love would be one that gives all and expects nothing" (p. 97). But with a standard set this high it must be nearly impossible for most people to achieve perfect love. Buscaglia himself recognizes how difficult it is to live up to this standard, when he notes, "There are few of us so strong, so totally permissive, so trusting, as to give without expectation" (Buscaglia, 1972, p. 97). And so, in most love relationships there is also a selfish dimension. Or at the very least, there is a self-interested dimension.

At least two recent analyses of love have been built around the self-interested nature of love (Branden, 1981; Solomon, 1981). Branden states his case firmly: "Of all the nonsense written about love, none is more absurd than the notion that ideal love is *selfless*" (Branden, 1981, p. 169). Branden even allows that love is an *essentially* selfish act—not in the negative sense of being indifferent to the needs and interests of the partner, but rather because people need for themselves the things they get from a love relationship.

Solomon (1981) argues similarly that many views of love, including the Christian view and the romantic view, emphasize erroneously that "true love" is selfless. He says, "this is not only not true, it is impossible" (Solomon, 1981, p. 132). It is impossible because, according to Solomon, all emotions (anger, envy, jealousy, etc.) involve the person experiencing them, which means that "we get something out of them." And so it must be with love. Solomon emphasizes that one must be able to ask the question "What am I getting out of this?" and not feel guilty about doing so (Solomon 1981, p. 132).

In order to accept the validity of these statements, we must take a closer look at the pleasures and satisfactions derived from love relationships. The first point to note is that loving and being loved are specific manifestations of the human need for *companionship*. Humans are reared from infancy in social groupings (normally a family grouping of some sort). This early experience probably plays a large part in the continuing need that most humans have for interaction with other humans. This has been called "getting hooked on people" (Campbell,

1975, p. 17). In a more practical vein, it is also a way of obtaining what is needed and wanted for survival and pleasure (food, other material goods, services, sex, etc.). But there may also be a more psychological explanation for the desire most people have for emotional closeness and intimacy with other people. In order to appreciate this idea fully it will be helpful first to examine a basic social psychological theory called *symbolic interaction theory*. The idea that people need love for "selfish" reasons flows directly from this basic theory of human behavior.

Symbolic interaction theory. Symbolic interaction is a particularly important sociological theory for understanding interpersonal relations and the social origins of personality. This theory is often helpful for understanding different aspects of marriage and family life, so a little special attention to it here will serve us well later.

Human beings have an exceptional, and perhaps unique, ability to use symbols and words. By the age of seven an average child has command of eight thousand words (Pfeiffer, 1983). People make connections with other people through these words, or symbols. Infants and children acquire many of their early symbols and words from family members, especially parents. The first words they learn are the symbols for observable, concrete things, such as mama, daddy, mouth, nose, dog, and ball. Gradually, children learn more abstract symbols—symbols that indicate not just things but evaluations as well (e.g., naughty girl, pretty kitty, or dirty garbage). Obviously, most of the evaluations that children learn are those held by family members, especially parents. Parents and other family members are referred to as *significant others* because their views have such a great influence on young children. Later in life, friends, schoolmates, marriage partners, fellow workers, religious and political leaders, and others are likely to be included among significant others.

In the process of learning language and symbols, children learn evaluations of themselves, just as they learn evaluations of other objects. In the same way that parents might convey the idea that "garbage is dirty," they might also convey the idea that "David is a good boy" when he plays nicely with his baby sister. It is through this process of learning symbols about themselves that children develop what symbolic interactionists call a *self-concept* (Rosenberg, 1979).

Self-concepts are all the thoughts and feelings people have about themselves. The most important thoughts and feelings typically come from parents; these are often carried through life. Yet, the process of acquiring and changing one's self-concept never ends. Self-concepts are constantly modified and shaped through continued interaction with other people, especially those who are significant.

One feature of the self-concept is that most people want to have, and strive to have, positive views of themselves. In Rosenberg's (1979, p. 53) words, there is the "wish to think well of one's self." The degree to which one thinks well of one's self is referred to as *self-esteem*. The notions of self-concept and self-esteem return us to the issue of why human beings have a desire to love and be loved. It will now be possible, with these two ideas in mind, to examine the "self-ish" motives for loving.

A self-interested view of love.   The idea of a self-interested motive for love rests on the principle that while people have a self-concept, they also have a continuous need for some outside validation of how they view themselves. In concrete terms, we may think of ourselves as generous or as having a good sense of humor, but we need someone else to validate or recognize these characteristics. At least occasionally someone must notice and comment on the fact that we are generous with our money (or something else) if we are to retain the self-concept of being generous. Similarly, it would be hard to maintain the self-concept of having a good sense of humor if no one ever notices how funny we can be, or how quickly we see the humor in a situation. Branden (1981, p. 73) describes the self-concept in this way: "Our 'self-concept' is not a single concept, but a cluster of images and abstract perspectives on our various [real or imagined] traits and characteristics."

This multifaceted and always somewhat unfocussed self-concept only exists in our minds, and thus it does not have the same kind of objective status as the rest of the world we experience. We can have attitudes about all the objects outside of ourselves (a new car, a pet dog, the Congress of the United States, etc.), but our selves do not have the same objective status. The very thing that is most important to us, our own selves, exists only in our minds. How, then, can we make our self-concept more objective and concrete? One way is to have someone, some special other person, tell us that the things we believe about ourselves are true. "It is in this sense that others can be a psychological mirror" (Branden, 1981, p. 76).

Solomon's ideas about the connection between the self-concept and love are very similar: "What love is about . . . is the creation of self" (Solomon, 1981, p. 142). He, too, stresses that ourselves are not firmly established but are "under-determined." "Romantic love is part of our search for selfhood. . . . it [romantic love] comes to provide what is most crucial to us . . . namely ourselves (Soloman, 1981, p. 143).

Since any number of people could probably help us see ourselves as we think we are, what is distinctive about a love relationship? The answer may be that the person we are most likely to love is one "who thinks as we do, who notices the things we notice, who values the things we value, who tends to respond to . . . situations as we do" (Branden, 1981, p. 76). That person is also more likely to view us in the same way as we see ourselves.

It is probably no accident that the person we fall in love with is likely to be someone with whom we "have so much in common." How often we hear someone who has just found a new love say, "It's amazing how many things we have in common. We spent the entire night talking and it turns out that he (she) likes the same kind of music, the same movies, the same food. . . ."

All this is familiar and plausible, but it might not be obvious why this is a self-interested explanation of love. The reason lies in our need to have a positive and objective view of ourselves. In Branden's words again, "A lover ideally reacts to us as, in effect, we would react to ourself in the person of another. Thus we perceive our self through our lover's reaction" (Branden, 1981, p. 77). And what we perceive about ourselves is very positive!

Solomon also stresses how the emotion of love and the love experience has a positive effect on our self image. It is the emotional experience that enhances our self-concept; it leads to the "maximization of self-esteem" (Solomon, 1981, p. 144). It does so, in his view, because the two lovers are often insulated from and indifferent to the outside world. In the "loveworld" they create for themselves, lovers give mutual and positive support to each other such that the self-esteem of each is increased: "I love you." "I love you, too. More than anyone or anything in the world."

To see the self-interested nature of love more clearly, Branden suggests that we consider the person who would love us. Do we want our lover to be making a sacrifice when he or she spends time with us, holds us, caresses us, makes love to us? Obviously not. We want our lover to feel pleasure and satisfaction when with us, not sacrifice. "And if it is glory that we want our partner to feel, if we want our partner to experience joy in our presence, excitement in our being, ardor, passion, fascination, delight, then let us stop talking of 'selfless love' as a noble ideal" (Branden, 1981, p. 170). Clearly, if we want our partner to feel intense satisfaction from loving us, then it follows that we, too, must feel satisfaction when we love.

Finally, it must be said that the two apparently contradictory views of love—generous love and selfish love—are not contradictory at all. There is both generosity and selfishness in love relationships. If one denies that either of these is an important aspect of love, it only leads to confusion and misunderstanding. Love is neither the ultimate consideration and generosity toward another person nor the extreme of personal selfishness. Love, perhaps at its best, is a balance or an interplay between generosity and selfishness. But, of course, love is not always at its best, as we will now see.

Love as Pleasure, Love as Pain

The good feelings and the bad feelings associated with a love experience have been described again and again by poets and storytellers. These feelings range from rapturous joy to unbearable pain. It is probably the case that the intensity of either pleasure or pain is greatest in the early stages of a love relationship. During these early stages the joy is intense when there is a mutual feeling of love and every moment together is precious. It is also during the early stages when pain can be most intense, as when one cannot, for some reason, have the person one loves. This is most extreme in the case of unrequited love, when the object of one's love does not return that love. Love can also be painful when two people in love are kept apart by outside forces. These outside forces could be families, as in the case of Romeo and Juliet, or a variety of other circumstances (e.g., one or both lovers are married already).

Let us look at some examples and some principles of love as pleasure and love as pain.

Love as pleasure.   A young woman described her ecstatic feelings of love as follows:

> After our first night together, I woke up with this strange and wonderful feeling like nothing describable or nothing I had ever felt before. . . . My delight in simply existing eclipsed everything else, and I literally could scarcely feel the ground as I walked. . . . Colors seemed more brilliant. The warmth of the sunlight on my arm as I drove to work was so acutely pleasurable that I marveled at never before appreciating it. I relived our moments of intimacy as I drove—the loving pressure of Rick's arms

'When I fell in love with you, suddenly your eyes didn't seem close together. Now they seem close together again.'

around me, the softness of his lips, and, most of all, his eyes. His look was an embrace. (quoted in Tennov, 1979, pp. 19–20)

Dorothy Tennov (1979) has interviewed hundreds of people as part of her systematic study of romantic love. The quotation above is just one of many she reports in her book *Love and Limerence*. The word *limerence* is one that Tennov coined to escape some of the problems connected with the word *love*. Limerence, basically, refers to the intense feelings that are usually associated with "falling in love." The young woman quoted above is revealing one important set of feelings connected with falling in love, or limerence, namely, the unusual euphoria that accompanies it. It is a euphoria that makes everything seem brighter and better. This feeling is often combined with an intense focus on the person one loves.

This intense focus on one's lover also includes perceiving him or her in a very special way, a way that can be called *enhancement*. Enhancement means, in part, to overlook the flaws or shortcomings of the person one loves. This part of enhancement is caught up in the old folk saying "love is blind." But there is more than this to enhancement. It is also a way of looking at the person one loves and making that person's features and characteristics special and precious. A young man described the feelings he had about the woman with whom he was in love:

I loved her clothes, her walk, her handwriting, . . . her cat, her car, her mother. . . . anything that belonged to her acquired a special magic. Her handbag, her notebook, her pencil. I abhor the sight of toothmarks on a pencil; they disgust me. But not her toothmarks. Hers were sacred; her wonderful mouth had been there. (Tennov, 1979, p. 31)

This process of glorifying another person completely is a familiar part of the experience of being in love.* Especially in the early stages of love, the mind lingers over every wonderful detail of the beloved person, "an object of shimmering beauty" (quoted in Tennov, 1979, p. 30).

Thinking about one's perfect love is not just pleasurable; it also takes up a great amount of time. Many people report how, in the early stages of love, they can hardly think of anything else. Almost every experience is immediately associated with the person one loves. A car seen on the street is the same car as he (or she) drives. A song on the radio is the theme music of the first movie seen to-

---

*The process of perceiving the loved one as perfection was labeled *crystallization* by the French writer Stendhal. The term *crystallization* is based on the following metaphor: "If one were to throw the branch of a tree into a salt mine and leave it there for some time the entire branch would be covered with crystals of salt. The branch would then be seen in a wonderful crystalline form. When a person in love beholds his or her loved one, it is similar. Crystallization occurs when the person in love is perceived as an object of shimmering beauty" (quoted in Tennov, 1979, p. 30).

gether. The chewing gum on the supermarket rack is his (or her) favorite. The list of things that can remind one of one's lover is endless. No connection is too trivial or too tenuous to be considered significant and touching. The reason why so many things remind us of the person we love is that the one we are in love with is always in our head. Thus, instead of the "other thing" reminding us of the person, it is really the other way around—the person on our mind makes the *thing* significant and important (Tennov, 1979). The car on the street, the song on the radio, and the chewing gum on the rack can in some ways be associated with the person we love because we are thinking almost constantly of that person. Even when no past connection can be made between an object and the person we love, a future connection is possible. We see an entirely new car, or hear a new piece of music, and we make a note to tell the person we love about it. Tennov interviewed a woman who saw her lover mostly on weekends. This woman recounted how great amounts of her time during the week were spent thinking and planning the next weekend:

> *A lot of it was planning conversations. If I saw a movie or read a book, I'd think about telling Stu about it, actually work out impressive sentences which I'd try to memorize. (Tennov, 1979, p. 38)*

While constantly thinking about the person one is in love with can be extremely pleasurable, there is also a darker side. If the person one is in love with does not or cannot return that love, the result is likely to be pain and despair.

Love as pain.   The experience of an unreturned love can be one of the most difficult and painful times of life. One such circumstance is when the person we are totally in love with either does not notice us or gives us only scant attention. Again, the people interviewed by Tennov provide excellent examples. One young man told an extraordinary story of how he became attracted to and then obsessed with a young French woman. This young man, named Fred, was staying in a men's residence while studying architecture in southern France. The woman, named Laura, worked there as a receptionist. Fred, after a few months, became gradually aware of a growing attraction to Laura, and while his actual contact with her was usually only for businesslike purposes, he kept a diary that recorded his hopes, feelings, and reactions. These included physical reactions that make the term *heartache* seem almost real. Fred wrote in his diary, "There is a tension slightly to the right of my middle chest, deep. Sometimes it extends down to my stomach. . . . I can see why they call it disease of the heart. . . . This passion *is* an ache" (Tennov, 1979, pp. 94–95). Fred's pain and distress continued unabated for more than a year and a half even though he never took the steps that would determine if Laura might return his feelings. In one diary entry, he wrote, "I have become distracted and unfocused. I cannot work. I am afflicted with a stupid infatuation that I refuse to idealize [sic] into something else." Later the same day, he added, "I am in great distress. . . . I want to lie down. I just want to think of her endlessly" (Tennov, 1979, pp. 98–99). Two months later, Fred described his situation by saying, "I am worse, I'm not better. It is a hideous time consuming and volcanic subterranean stirring, a whirlpool in my guts that pulls me down to my bed to daydreams and away from my work. I am hopelessly lovesick. What can I do?" (Tennov, 1979, pp. 100–101).

In other cases reported by Tennov, relationships might actually begin, and in some cases go on for long periods of time, but these too could ultimately lead to pain and distress. Usually in these cases the person one loves is either unreliable or gradually drawing away from the relationship. A person's pain and distress often comes and goes as the other person withdraws and then returns. One woman described how she met a man and after only a few dates had strong feelings of attraction toward him. However, he started to break scheduled dates, and each time he did, she felt worse. Her distress reached an extreme level when she chanced to see him walking arm in arm with another woman. After this incident she spent weeks when she thought of almost nothing else and described herself as being in intense misery (Tennov, 1979, p. 44).

Another woman, in a similar situation, said,

> If Joe forgets to call, it means I am not in his thoughts the way he is in mine. That's why it hurts so. . . . Into perfectly ordinary actions on his part I read an indication that he's losing interest and I panic. (Tennov, 1979, p. 55)

A young man exhibited a very similar reaction when he reported the following:

> It was just a little thing. Except that it wasn't a little thing. She forgot to wear the pin I had given her, even though I had asked her to be sure to wear it. I wouldn't have minded so much if she had been angry and left it at home to get even with me over something. But to forget? . . . It meant I wasn't in her thoughts as she was in mine. (Tennov, 1979, pp. 54–55)

At this point we should examine what we have seen about the experience of being in love. There is no doubt that it can be very pleasurable. This is especially true during the early stages, when one has just "fallen in love" and, most importantly, when there is a mutual feeling of love. Under these conditions the experience is extremely pleasurable. For some it is ecstasy. The pain and distress come when there is an imbalance. When the love is unreturned, or at least not in the same degree, then the person in love can be upset, distressed, or even in agony. There are no reliable statistics on the incidence of pain and distress connected with being in love, but Tennov (1979), on the basis of her hundreds of interviews, states that the most prevalent relationship she found was the one where one person did not reciprocate the same level of emotional intensity (in her terms, the same level of limerence). Indeed, she observes that since each person's feeling of emotional love changes in intensity during the course of a relationship, there will be some imbalances in every relationship. Shakespeare was

'I love this part where it's all still nice.'

probably correct when he said, "The course of true love never did run smooth" (*A Midsummer-Night's Dream*, act 1, scene 1, line 132).

To this point, we have seen that the love experience is one that combines a generosity and concern for the person one loves with a self-interested, self-satisfying component for ourselves. We have also seen that when the feelings of love between two people are balanced—reciprocal or mutual—the love experience produces a high level of pleasure. The ideal love balances generosity and self-interest, and has an emotional intensity for both partners that is equal. But the balance and equality of the ideal is difficult to achieve and even more difficult to maintain. When the balance tips, especially to one extreme or the other, the resulting love can be very unhealthy.

Unhealthy Love

The following quote illustrates how love can take an unhealthy form.

Chuck Brewer took his girlfriend horseback riding on a Lovettsville, Virginia, farm and stopped at an open grave he had dug the day before. Standing over the hole, he told Joy Keo the grave would be hers unless she agreed to revive their withering romance. (Moore, 1983)

Two months after this bizarre incident, Charles Brewer crashed into a house where Joy Keo, age seventeen, was visiting and broke into a bedroom where she was crouched in a corner. Shouting "You're gonna die bitch!", he shot her four times, leaving her with a severed spinal column. Joy Keo will be paralyzed from the waist down for the rest of her life. Charles Brewer was sentenced to fifty years in prison (Moore, 1983).

A much more widely-known case of unhealthy love is that of President Ronald Reagan's would-be assassin, John Warnock Hinckley, Jr. The object of Hinckley's love was actress Jodie Foster who had played the role of a teenage prostitute in the movie, *Taxi Driver*. Hinckley became obsessed with the young actress, seeing the film at least fifteen times (McMillan, 1982).

Foster, who did not know Hinckley, became aware of his devotion to her through the more than one-hundred poems and letters he sent to her during her first year as a student at Yale University (1980–1981). On two occasions Hinckley also made contact with Foster by telephone calls.

Finally, on March 30, 1981, Hinckley set off to prove his love for Jodie Foster, and win her love in return, by making an attempt on the President's life. Among Hinckley's possessions, found after the shooting, there was a note addressed to Jodie Foster, which closed by saying, "Jodie I'm asking you to please look into your heart and at least give me the chance with this historic deed to gain your respect and love. I love you forever." (Shaffer and Henry, 1981: p. A1).

Hinckley's belief in his love apparently remained undiminished after the assassination attempt. In written answers to questions posed by *Newsweek* magazine he ended by saying, "In closing, I would like to say hello to Ms. Foster and ask her one small question: Will you marry me? Jodie?" (*Newsweek*, Oct. 12, 1981: p. 51).

These are but two cases—one obscure, the other well-known—of the hundreds, perhaps thousands, each year where violence is committed in the name of love. In each case the young man in question believed that the need to regain the young woman he loved justified physical violence. These are examples of what has been called *addictive love* (Peele and Brodsky, 1976). The term addictive love is used to indicate that some people become addicted to the person they love in the same way as another person might be addicted to heroin. Peele and Brodsky say, "An addictive relationship, like drug addiction, is a single overwhelming involvement that cuts off a person from life. . . . the addicted lovers gradually let go of all other interests and activities" (Peele and Brodsky, 1976, p. 25). In the Brewer-Keo case cited above, Keo described how, after they started living together, Brewer became more and more possessive. She reported, "He got carried away with wanting me to himself and not wanting anybody else around" (Moore, 1983).

Peele and Brodsky (1976) observe that the number of people who can be characterized as "addicts" is relatively small but that many relationships, either on the part of one or both partners, tend toward the addicted type. In short, when a person becomes too obsessed with another person, and thus too possessive in a love relationship, that love is an addiction and can only be described as unhealthy.

Addictive love is a case of being too dependent on one's love partner. The opposite extreme is for one of the lovers to be much less interested than the other in continuing the relationship. This leads to what has been called the "principle of least interest" (Waller, 1938, p. 275). It is possible for the person with the least interest in a relationship to dominate and even exploit the other person. This, too, can be considered one of the unhealthy outcomes of a love relationship.

Once again it should be obvious that the more balance and equality there is in a love relationship, the healthier and more vital the relationship will be. We know that balance will not be found in every love relationship, or even in a given relationship at all times, but good balance is a goal worth striving for.

Throughout this chapter we have considered love from several different points of view. We reviewed the historical development of the concept of love, first as it emerged in classical Western societies and then as it came to have a special prominence in the United States. We also examined the nature of love as a personal, human experience, where it was found to have both positive and negative features. With this background, we are ready to turn to a question that is much debated today: Do we, in this society, put too much emphasis on love?

ISSUE

Do we put too much emphasis on love in this society?

Love has been the most important factor in choosing marriage mates in this society from its earliest years. Love is still nearly the only basis we use for choosing our mates. Our society is by no means unique in this matter, especially in the contemporary world. But there are many people around the world who consider "love marriages" unwise, if not foolish. A number of critics of love, even in our own society, have asked if we do not put too much emphasis on love. We will consider some of these criticisms first and then turn to the defenders of our romantic love complex.

Some Criticisms of the American Emphasis on Love

One criticism of love, especially romantic love, is that it is a fiction we have raised to a ridiculously high level in American society. This view has been most forcefully expressed in a classic statement by cultural anthropologist Ralph Linton:

> *All societies recognize that there are occasional violent, emotional attachments between persons of the opposite sex, but our present American culture is practically the only one which has attempted to capitalize on these and make them the basis for marriage. Most groups regard them as unfortunate and point out the victims of such attachments as horrible examples. Their rarity in most societies suggests that they are psychological abnormalities to which our culture has attached an extraordinary value. (Linton, 1936, p. 175)*

This view emphasizes that we have taken a particular psychological abnormality and built it up to a position where it is used for one of the most important decisions in life. Yet we have been conditioned to think that love is both normal and the best possible way to pick a marriage partner.

Falling in love, in this view, is a kind of myth. But most people, because they believe in the myth, can experience falling in love, or at least convince themselves that they have. Those who see love as an exaggerated cultural myth, however, also see it as weakening, not strengthening, marriage. In the words of one family sociologist, "to build a marriage on a romantic foundation is to build on quicksilver" (Fullerton, 1977, p. 202).

There are a number of reasons why building marriages on love can weaken marriages more than strengthen them. First, the intensity of romantic love almost never remains at the same high level. No matter how intense the feelings of love are in the beginning, the day-in and day-out routines of life are likely to diminish what Stendahl called the "shimmering beauty" of the person with whom one has fallen in love. The flaws and weaknesses that at one time seemed uniquely precious eventually become just flaws and weaknesses. The imperfections that went unnoticed in the early stages of love, perhaps because they were successfully hidden, eventually become noticed as love grows weaker.

Just because the intensity of love decreases does not necessarily mean that a relationship or marriage must also weaken. But relationships and marriages can be weakened, and even ended, by the romantic love complex when a married person becomes acquainted and falls in love with someone new. If the new love is intense enough, it can justify leaving one's marriage and perhaps entering a new one. More than a few divorce cases in American society are generated by this process. It is ironic, but true, that since love is the basic justification for marriage, it can also be the reason for ending marriage (Becker, 1981; Younger, 1981).

In recent years a number of feminist writers have expressed negative views of the romantic love complex, but for different reasons than we have so far considered. In their view, love is largely a male invention that is used to keep women in subordinate positions relative to men. Shulamuth Firestone says on this point, "love . . . is the pivot of women's oppression today" (Firestone, 1970, p. 142). There have been many statements expressing the view that women take love more seriously than do men—"Love is to man a thing apart; 'tis woman's whole existence" (quoted in Samuel, 1976: 56).

Following from this view, many feminists also believe that women are more likely to accept the "unselfish or selfless" view of love. When a woman loves a man, she will often do anything for him; make any sacrifice or satisfy any wish he has. This often means that women will sacrifice their own careers, interests and needs, all the while taking care of, supporting and assisting their men. Women thereby let the men they love make the achievements, while they themselves stay in the background, getting only reflected glory, or none at all. If the unselfish dimension of love is more accepted by women than men, then love is a mechanism for keeping women in subordinate and supportive roles.

Summing up the criticisms of the American emphasis on love, there is first the argument that we have created a vast cultural myth, which does more harm than good. Since love is the essential reason for marriage, the end result is that marriage itself will be weakened when love fades, or a married person falls in love with someone else. Some feminists have argued that love is often a kind of trap for women who have been taught to be selfless and sacrificing for the men they love.

Some Defenses of the American Emphasis on Love

Love is in some ways its own defense. Philosopher and theologian Søren Kierkegaard stated the case grandly when he wrote, "To cheat oneself out of love is the most terrible deception; it is an eternal loss for which there is no reparation, either in time or eternity" (Quoted in Pope, et al., 1980:335).

Bertrand Russell, one of the more famous philosophers and mathematicians of the twentieth century, and one who apparently had his share of loves, also believed that romantic love could be a source of the most intense delights life has to offer. But, in addition, he also saw romantic love as an escape from loneliness, which he considered a fundamental human condition. With his characteristic cynicism he described how love, even when it is temporary, can ease the burdens of life: "[Love] is the principal means of escape from the loneliness which afflicts most men and women throughout the greater part of their lives. There is a deep-seated fear, in most people, of the cold world and the possible cruelty of the herd. . . . Passionate mutual love, while it lasts, puts an end to this feeling" (Russell, 1929:122).

When critics of love say that love has an overblown importance in our society, they are missing the point that romantic love is a special and cherished part of our culture. To miss this experience would be as great as missing the great art and music of our cultural heritage. Even if love is a cultural product, as some critics claim, it can be a pleasurable part, just like the plays of Shakespeare, the music of Mozart or the poetry of Robert Frost are enjoyable parts of our culture. The emphasis on love, as we have seen, came out of the very roots of Western culture, and while there have been many different interpretations of love over the centuries, our lives have been enriched because we have inherited the idea of romantic love.

But the experience of falling in love is only part of the love experience. The more important part for many people is *being* in love. Being in love is the feeling of closeness and comfortableness that one has when the person one loves is by one's side. Being in love is the element in a relationship that gives meaning and significance to shared experiences. Being in love is also the dimension of a relationship that gets two people through the difficult times. The advocates of love believe that when two people love each other there will be greater understanding and more willingness to compromise, and if necessary, forgive. In this view, love is not a de-stabilizing element in marriage, it is the cement that holds marriages together.

To sum up the defenses of love, the advocates first point out that falling in love is one of life's great experiences. But falling in love is often only the first step in a process that leads to being in love. Being in love is a deeper more lasting feeling that gives relationships, especially between husbands and wives, strength and endurance.

Themes

1. Love is a complex emotion.

2. While love is apparently a universal human emotion, the part that love plays in the lives of people varies greatly from one society to another.

3. The Greeks gave us many words and ideas related to love, and some of the distinctions they made about types of love are still important to us today.

4. Christianity, as it emerged during the Roman Empire, elevated the importance of spiritual love but tended to minimize the importance of physical, sexual love.

5. Courtly love brought out the importance of a highly emotional or romantic love, though not as a part of marriage.

6. Only in the last three hundred years has love become associated with marriage for the common people.

7. It is quite possible that for most people, through most of human history, life was too hard and precarious for them to experience the luxury of love.

8. Two major points come from a review of the history of love in Western civilization: (a) the object of love may differ greatly from one place and time to another; and (b) in premodern times, love was not closely connected with marriage.

9. In the United States, a special significance has been placed on the importance of love as a basis for marriage.

10. The sociobiological view of love advances the position that human beings have evolved with a general predisposition for love.

11. Love is simultaneously generous and selfish.

12. Love is both a pleasurable and a painful experience.

13. Love can be unhealthy and addictive.

Facts

1. Love as an emotional and sexual attraction between human beings is apparently a universal human capability.

2. The Greeks characterized sexual love as an expression of one's "lower nature."

3. The Greeks applied the ideas of sexual and spiritual love to both homosexual and heterosexual relationships.

4. Some Greek writers accepted and even extolled affectionate, loving, and sexual relationships between men and young boys, but others did not concur, notably Aristophanes, the playwright, and Aristotle.

5. Early Christians considered passionate and romantic love to be negative impulses.

6. Among the Yanomamo, a fierce people living in the Amazon jungle, the term *marriage* translates to "dragging something away."

7. For most Europeans in the seventeenth and eighteenth centuries, marriages were still arranged. Love did not precede marriage, though it was hoped that feelings of love and affection would grow after marriage.

8. The ability of human beings to manipulate symbols and words is exceptional; by the age of seven an average child has command of eight thousand words.

9. In the process of learning language and symbols, children learn evaluations of themselves, just as they learn evaluations of other objects.

10. Through the eyes of the person we love, we perceive ourselves in a very positive way.

11. The most prevalent condition in the love relationships between two people is that the feelings of emotional intensity are not at the same level.

12. In thousands of cases each year, violence is committed in the name of love.

Major Concepts

addictive love: An overwhelming involvement with another person that cuts off a person from the rest of life and other people.

aphrodisiac: Something that is believed to stimulate and excite sexual desire.

Aphrodite: The Greek goddess of carnal love who presided over the physical act of sexual intercourse.

conjugal love: Husband-wife love.

courtly love: The principles and ideals of love as expressed by the twelfth-century troubadours in France.

crystallization: Perceiving one's love as perfection; derives from the idea that even the plain and simple features and characteristics of one's love are covered with crystals.

Cupid (*in Latin,* **Cupido**)**:** The Roman transformation of the Greek god of spiritual love, Eros.

enhancement: A way of looking at the person one loves and overlooking their flaws and shortcomings.

The Greek god of spiritual love (*see* **Cupid**).

limerence: A word coined to escape some of the problems connected with the word *love;* refers to the intense feelings that are usually associated with "falling in love."

paiderasteia: Greek word referring to a sexual, or simply an affectionate, relationship between an adult man and young boy.

pederasty: Refers today to acts of sexual deviance in which an adult is sexually attracted to immature children; derived from the Greek *paiderasteia.*

platonic love: Used today to describe a nonsexual relationship between a male and female; a twelfth-century interpretation of Plato's ideal of spiritual love.

romantic love complex: A societal pattern of placing a special value on romantic love, especially as a basis for entering marriage.

self-concept: The thoughts and feelings people have about themselves.

self-esteem: The degree to which one thinks well of oneself.

significant others: Parents, family members, and others whose views are important to individuals.

sociobiological view of love: The view that human beings have evolved with a general predisposition for love, through a process of evolutionary selection.

sociocultural view of love: The view that the emotion of love is universally known to humans, though in different times and places its nature and importance can vary greatly.

symbolic interaction theory: A theory of human behavior that emphasizes the use of symbols and language and the way people use symbols to define themselves and other objects.

4

Meeting and Dating
Getting Together, Physical Attraction, and Computer Dating

A folk saying has it that "There is someone for everyone." But a lot of restless Friday and Saturday nights are spent alone by young people waiting for their "someone" to come along. Eventually, almost everyone manages to find someone with whom there is a mutual attraction. For many people, their youth can be a carefree and fun-filled time of life, but for many others the time is filled with anxiety and stress. This chapter is about that time of life.

We will look at the ways young people in our society and others have for meeting and getting acquainted with each other. Special attention will be given to physical attractiveness as an important element in our society. And we will be considering some of the more contemporary, urban ways of meeting the opposite sex, such as computer dating and advertising.

At the end of this chapter we will consider the issue of whether we have reached a time in contemporary society when the traditional pattern of men taking the initiative and responsibilities for dating can be largely ignored. From the point of view of women, is it now possible for them to initiate dating relationships with men who interest them?

GETTING TOGETHER: ENCOUNTERS WITH THE OPPOSITE SEX

It is an obvious point, but if men and women are to enter into marriage they must have some way of getting together. Since it would be nearly impossible for any society to go on without marriages (or something like marriages), it is socially important that there be some ways of bringing marriageable people together. From society to society these ways differ greatly in their details. Even in American society the patterns of meeting, dating, and mating change from one time to another. This chapter will describe and analyze the various ways people get together and what that experience is like for the participants. The emphasis will be on contemporary American meeting and dating patterns, but we will also look at some cross-cultural and historical examples. We will begin by looking at three examples of how young people in three different parts of the world meet and choose each other. These examples will uncover both differences and similarities, which will be considered after the three descriptions.

The Saxons of Transylvania: "Going in the Gate"

Transylvania is an area of Eastern Europe that is now encompassed by the contemporary country of Romania. It is populated today by a solid and stable Germanic people called Saxons. They are farming people who live in small villages. Mating and courtship among the Saxons is an important and serious matter, because the resulting marriages determine both family fortunes and social standing in the community. For this reason, parents are very concerned that their children select appropriate marriage partners. The social and economic statuses of potential brides and grooms are carefully considered. And yet, the Saxons allow their young people to get together, get acquainted, fall in love, and have a courtship period (Barth, 1978).

Young Saxon women are generally thought to be ready for marriage when they are seventeen, and at about that age they form small social groups. During the winter season members of a group will take turns opening the "spinning rooms" of their houses for evening gatherings. The girls bring their spinning equipment and the hemp that has been raised during the summer. While spinning, they sing, talk, and joke. The young men of the village also drop in at these gatherings, where they join in the activities. About ten o'clock the group will break up, and if a boy has found a girl he fancies he will walk with her as she returns home.

When the boy and girl arrive at her gate they often stand and talk for a period of time. The more time they spend with each other in front of the girl's house, around her gate, the clearer it is that they are attracted to each other. The Saxon phrase, which would be the equivalent of our *going steady*, is literally translated as "going in the gate." If a young man continues going in the gate for an extended period of time, the girl knows he is seriously interested in her. (So also does the rest of the village.) If she feels the same, she can show her feelings by sending the boy a bouquet of flowers, which he will carry to church (Barth, 1978).

To show the strength of his feelings, the Saxon boy constructs a special tree (a May tree) in front of the girl's house. This is traditionally done on the Saturday night before Pentecost Sunday (the seventh Sunday after Easter). On the morning of the second Easter the boy will visit the home of the girl and spray her with a sweet-smelling rose water. Often he will put so much water on her that not a dry spot remains on her dress.

While the girl continues to send her suitor a weekly bouquet of flowers, the boy in return will be carving a hay rake for her. As the girl rides through the village on a cart, going to the hay and wheat fields, the rake will be seen by all the villagers. Then they know that engagement is likely. It is the custom for the engagement to be marked on "Catherin's Day"—November 24. The marriage follows in January.

The Saxon courtship system is especially interesting because even though it is in a very traditional society, the young people are given considerable freedom in the choice of a marriage mate. Yet the entire system is very orderly and ritualized, and one can be sure that everything is done under the watchful eyes of the parents (and the rest of the villagers as well).

If we turn our attention now to a society halfway around the world, we will see one where young people have even more freedom in selecting their mates. While kin and family members of the men are involved in the final decision, much of the preliminary process is left in the hands of the young people themselves.

Nepal: Selecting a Mate at the "Rice Dance"

In eastern Nepal there is a people called the Limbu (Jones, 1977). Unlike many other people in that part of the world, marriage among the Limbu is based to a considerable degree on attraction and love rather than arrangement by parents or kin. Equally novel is the mechanism the Limbu have evolved for bringing young people together. They have a dance called the *dhan nach*. This term is translated literally as the "rice dance" and comes from the fact that the dancers move around on rice straw, threshing out the grain as they dance.

The form of the rice dance is a line of people holding hands, moving in a slow rhythm, first five steps to the right, then five steps to the left, and finishing with three steps on the same spot. The dancers are arranged in a male-female, male-female manner. There may be as few as two dancers, but sometimes there are as many as twenty or thirty. The dancers sing traditional love songs as they move their feet in time with the song. Often the dancing will continue all night. As a male and female become attracted to each other, they may become "dancing friends." Being dancing friends means that they have a kind of "love" relationship. However, being dancing friends is not equivalent to being engaged. Dancing can lead to marriage, but in many instances the relationship will end after a while. Often the young man simply stops coming to the young woman's village for the dances, and thus the relationship ends. Since these dancing relationships are often quite impermanent, they serve to let young people get acquainted with a large number of potential marriage mates (Jones, 1977). This is an especially important freedom for Limbuan women. Through the rice dance they have much greater freedom than the neighboring Hindu women in the final selection of a marriage mate. The Limbuan women can, when they are interested, take some initiatives in the dance. At the very least, they have a greater knowledge of available males.

There is one other feature of the Limbu pattern that deserves some notice. While the rice dance is primarily for the benefit of the unmarried young people, it also provides an opportunity for some married people to reenter courtship. Frequently, a man or woman whose spouse is not around will participate in the dance. Sometimes this leads to nothing of any consequence, but occasionally, as one might expect, it does result in a love affair with someone new. When that occurs it can lead to divorce and a new marriage. If a married woman does get a divorce and remarry it is thought of among the Limbu as "wife theft," but the consequences are not severe. The Limbu people will speak of these instances with an air of acceptance, " 'They danced together and fell in love, so the woman left her husband' or, 'After dancing, they fell in love and had a child, so what can you do?' " (Jones, 1977, p. 295). We see from this, once again, that when love is used as the basis for marriage, it can also be used to justify leaving a marriage.

The Limbu rice dance, which brings potential marriage mates together in eastern Nepal, might seem far removed from the way American young people get together. But we can see some similarities if we take a look at one way for getting young people together in this society—the college mixer.

The College Mixer

From the two cases we have already examined we can see that in order to bring young people together there is usually an activity or function. Among the Saxons of Transylvania the young women assemble to do their spinning; among the Limbu of Nepal the dancers are threshing out the rice as they dance; at the college mixer in the United States the ostensible objective is to dance. In all cases the underlying purpose is to bring young people together so they have the opportunity to meet each other and begin what may be a more intense relationship. If two people meet at a mixer and have some initial mutual attraction toward each other, a more serious relationship might develop. If not, nothing much is lost—except, as we will see, that for some there may be a loss of pride and self-esteem.

The college mixer varies somewhat from one region of the country to another, and from one type of school to another, but it is usually found in some form as a part of college life. As the name suggests, a mixer is for the purpose of mixing people together, getting them acquainted (Schwartz and Lever, 1976). Two sociological researchers have analyzed what goes on at college mixers, focusing especially on the process of "attraction and rejection, coupling and uncoupling, in a public setting" (Schwartz and Lever, 1976, p. 416).

The particular type of mixer studied by these researchers was a dance sponsored by an all-male school to which the women of neighboring colleges were invited. This particular kind of mixer is one that accentuates the interaction that goes on at mixers of all kinds—freshman orientation week dances, sorority-fraternity exchanges, and dorm dances.

The mixer usually started about 8:30, when the women from neighboring colleges arrived by bus. Since the buses left again at 12:00 there was a particular kind of time pressure at these events. The men and women had only about

'Mother, am I pretty?'

two hours to meet each other and find out if they wished to have a longer, more involved relationship. In this respect a mixer on a coeducational campus is much less pressure laden. Nonetheless, there are many settings today where evaluations and decisions about another person must be made quickly on the basis of very limited information (e.g., in singles bars). The characteristic that is used most commonly for evaluation in these settings is physical appearance. As we will see later, in settings of all kinds physical appearance is the criterion used first and most persistently in making decisions about someone of the opposite sex.

At college mixers it is obvious to everyone, often painfully so, that physical appearance is about the only criterion being used to evaluate people. This produces a situation filled with tension. When one is repeatedly rejected, through the course of an evening, the experience can be shattering to one's self-image. "Students reported feelings of 'ugliness,' 'fatness,' 'clumsiness,' and so forth during and after the mixer situation" (Schwartz and Lever, 1976, p. 419).

Students who were interviewed about mixers nearly universally said they disliked them. They referred to mixers negatively as "body exchanges" and "meat markets." One female student expressed her feelings vehemently.

I generally think mixers are grotesque. There you are, a piece of meat lined up against the wall in this herd of ugly females. You try to stand casually as guys walk back and forth and you know you're on display. You just want to crawl up the wall. Then you're asked to dance by these really gross creatures. I'm so revolted by the whole thing. (Schwartz and Lever, 1976, p. 421)

Even a young man who claimed he liked mixers saw the "being on display" characteristics:

> *My first impression of a mixer in my freshman year reminded me a great deal of cattle auctions I'd seen. Where huge crowds of inspectors and buyers and such would climb the entryways . . . and this group of very frightened creatures would charge through the middle. (Schwartz and Lever, 1976, p. 422)*

At mixers three techniques are used to make successful contacts and deal with uncomfortable situations. These are "eye messages," the "ritualistic brush-off," and "offensive-defensive tactics." *Eye messages* are the effective use, or nonuse, of eye contact. If someone who is approaching is undesirable, the trick is to look through, past, or away from the person. If one denies another person eye contact, it is a way of rejecting that person's attentions. On the other hand, if one wishes to receive the attentions of another person (or wishes to approach another person), the eyes are allowed to meet, even if just for a moment. As one male describes it "You try to meet eyes with a girl who doesn't look happy with the person she's with, in the hope that she'll say she has to go to the bathroom. Then you pick her up on the return trip" (Schwartz and Lever, 1976, p. 423).

The *ritualistic brush-off* is an excuse or a line used to get away from someone. "Pardon me, I think I'll go for a beer" and "Excuse me, I'm going to the ladies room" are two frequently used lines. They are so ritualistic that the person being left behind is usually fully aware of having been rejected.

The *offensive-defensive tactic* is a way of avoiding being hurt or rejected in an uncertain and tension-filled situation. The tactic is one of taking the offensive as a way of being defensive. When a man and a woman finish a dance there is a moment of uncertainty about whether they will remain together. The woman may not want to take the chance of being rejected, so she can take the offensive and say "thank you" in a way that says "the interaction is now over." Men can similarly end the interaction if they are not sure the woman wants to continue with them. In some instances taking the offense as a defense against rejection can end an interaction even though both parties would rather continue it.

Mixers, as well as other social occasions where males and females have only a brief opportunity to evaluate each other, reveal important dimensions of the process of meeting and dating in our society. The experience is supposed to be one of fun, entertainment, and pleasure. Sometimes it is all of those things, but it would be misleading and unrealistic to pretend that everything about meeting and dating is pleasurable.

Some Observations of Types of Meeting and Mating Experiences

We have just examined the ways used in three societies to bring young people together. The different, and yet in some ways similar, methods and conditions in these three societies do suggest some general observations.

First, in all cases there is some ritualistic behavior. Among the Saxons of Transylvania the courtship pattern is filled with ritual. Every step of the way is part of a well-known and closely observed pattern. One might guess that once the early steps have been taken—the exchange of flower bouquets and the May tree—they lead almost inexorably to the November engagement and the January wedding. Among the Limbu there is more trial and error and more temporary and tentative relationships. There seems to be more uncertainty and more unpredictability in the process.

While the college mixer has some rituals (like the ritualistic brush-off), it seems in general to be a very uncertain situation for most participants. The uncertainty of whether or not one will be accepted or rejected, and how one is supposed to respond in either case, leads to a considerable amount of anxiety and tension. We might note that the more ritualistic and stylized the patterns of meeting are, the less anxiety pervades the situation.

A second notable difference among the three societies and their customs is the role played by parents, on the one hand, and romantic attraction, on the other. The Saxons allow for romantic attraction among their young people, but the entire courtship is closely controlled and monitored by parents. Among the Limbu, the young people are given autonomy as they choose to dance with various partners, but eventually kin members do participate in any marriage decision. In the American college mixer the entire selection process is in the hands of the young people. Family members are of little significance, except as they place their children in a particular college setting to begin with. American courtship patterns, of which the college mixer is only a small illustrative part, are almost wholly in the hands of the participants. American young people have a great deal of autonomy and freedom when they select someone with whom to become intensely involved. But that same freedom carries the price of greater anxiety and uncertainty. With this in mind, we will now take a more detailed look at the characteristics and experiences of meeting and dating in contemporary society.

OPPORTUNITY SITUATIONS AND ATTRACTION

Societies, as we have just seen, will typically provide ways in which their young people can meet. These can be called *opportunity situations*. In American society, school settings in general, both high school and college, provide nearly continuous opportunities to meet members of the opposite sex (if the setting is coeducational). Recreational settings, including dances, athletic events, beaches, arcades, bars, and even shopping malls, are all places where young people can meet and become acquainted. There are also institutional settings, such as churches, workplaces, country clubs, athletic teams and clubs, and interest organizations that serve as meeting places. Even this short list of places suggests that there is a very wide range of settings where young people have an opportunity to meet and develop relationships with members of the opposite sex.

But opportunity situations are only the beginning, since they only put young people in contact. The important next step in the process is *attraction*—if the term is used broadly, we can say *sexual attraction*. Sexual attraction can be defined as interest in another person, which includes a desire to have some sort of contact with that person (cf. Rosenblatt and Anderson, 1981). The particular contact that a person wishes to have is sexual, but sexual can mean anything from holding hands and touching to having sexual intercourse. The interesting initial question is, what causes someone to be sexually attracted to another person? That question has received the attention of a number of researchers over the last two decades. Their research provides some answers to the initial question posed above, as well as some additional ones.

Attraction to a Person of the Opposite Sex

As we saw in the case of the college mixer, physical attractiveness was the criterion most universally and regularly used to make judgments of other people. Intelligence, personality, social skills, and mutual interests were apparently of almost no importance when the men and women evaluated each other. As Schwartz and Lever noted, "All night long people are being approved or discarded on the basis of one characteristic. . . their appearance" (Schwartz and Lever, 1976, p. 418). The students readily acknowledged that appearance was the key criterion for evaluation, but they attributed this largely to the deafening noise level of the music. As one woman put it, "How can you really expect to meet someone at 400 decibels." (p. 418) But was it the noise level of the dance that made appearance so critically important? The research evidence suggests it was not.

Physical attractiveness—what we say. To assess how important physical appearance and good looks are when we evaluate members of the opposite sex it is easiest simply to ask people if good looks are important to them as a characteristic of a date. More commonly, researchers have asked "What qualities or characteristics are important to you in a person you date (or would marry)?" Sometimes a list of characteristics is provided, and other times the question is asked and respondents answer with whatever words come to mind. There have been many such studies over the years. The research findings have rather consistently shown that physical appearance and good looks are not highly rated characteristics. As we will see, however, there is at least one major exception to this generalization.

A few examples of this research will illustrate the general tendency of people to give low ratings to physical appearance as a valued characteristic in members of the opposite sex. Summaries of studies carried out between 1939 and 1975 show a remarkable consistency in the rank ordering of personal characteristics that college students look for in the opposite sex (Hudson and Henze, 1969; Kephart, 1977). Both males and females ranked dependable character and emotional stability as the two most desired characteristics. These two were followed by pleasing disposition, mutual attraction, and good health, in that order. Physical appearance and good looks are notably absent among these most desired characteristics, although they could be partially reflected in mutual attraction and good health.

In one study high school students were asked what qualities they valued most in a date (Hansen, 1977). The first five qualities, in rank order, were (1) pleasant and cheerful, (2) dependable, (3) considerate, (4) sense of humor, and (5) neat in appearance. Among these students "neatness counted," but not as much as some basic personality characteristics. Even the value placed on a neat appearance does not place an exceptional emphasis on sheer good looks or physical attractiveness. It seems likely that a neat appearance is quite possible for both boys and girls in high school without exceptional good looks. These studies of high school and college students, like a number of other studies (see Cook and McHenry, 1978, pp. 34–35), seem to show consistently that physical appearance and good looks are not what young people look for in the opposite sex. At least that is what they usually say. However, there is some contrary evidence.

Saxton (1977) reports that he conducted surveys at the College of San Mateo in California in the years 1970 and 1976. In the 1976 study, 713 randomly selected men and women students were asked to write down the three qualities they most valued in a date. Both the men and the women rated looks first and personality second. The men also valued sex appeal as the next most valued quality, while the women made thoughtfulness and consideration their third choice.

In this same study these same students were asked about the qualities they would value most highly in a spouse. The men valued looks, love, and compatibility, in that order. The women, however, abandoned looks as one of the things they would value most in a husband. Their first three choices were love, honesty, and compatibility. Indeed, for these women looks did not even make the list among the eight most valued qualities of a husband. The women also did not have sex appeal on their list. The men did value sex appeal in a wife, ranking it fourth on their list.

Two things are interesting about these last research findings. First, unlike the young men and women in most studies, these California college students acknowledged that good looks were important in their dating partners. That, as we will see, may reflect the way people actually behave more accurately than the previously described studies. The second interesting feature of these findings is that while the women valued good looks in their dates, they did not consider good looks to be important in a husband. The men, however, did want good looks and sex appeal in their wives, as well as their dates. This difference between men and women has been found in other studies and has been noted by many casual observers. It appears that when women consider marriage they are looking for more than just good looks; they want qualities that are more closely related to good interpersonal relationships. While men want these qualities to some degree, they also want their wives to be attractive and sexually appealing.

Physical attractiveness—what we do. "Your face is your fortune," is the old folk saying. In the case of attraction between the sexes it can be said that one's face is likely to determine one's fortunes. There is a substantial amount of evidence that we select and evaluate people on the basis of their looks. To be good looking refers primarily to the attractiveness of a person's facial features. But good looks are also related to body shape and weight and, for men, height.* Furthermore, the more attractive people are, the more likely we are to attribute positive qualities and characteristics to them (Dion, 1981; Berscheid et al., 1971; Dion et al., 1972; Kleck and Rubenstein, 1975).

The research supporting these statements has demonstrated that the favorable treatment we give to attractive people begins in childhood. Apparently, we learn at a very early age who is and who is not attractive, according to our particular cultural standards. One researcher presented preschool children with photographs of children they did not know. The photographs had been preselected on the basis of attractiveness. These preschool children expressed a preference for the more attractive children as ones they wished to have as friends. They also expressed the belief that the children who were more attractive would be "friendly, to not like fighting and shouting and to refrain from hitting someone, even if hit first" (Dion, 1981, p. 9). Kindergarten children in another study, again using photographs, were easily able to identify men who had the body build that is preferred in American society. These five-year-olds attributed more positive qualities to medium-built, muscular men. Men who were excessively fat or thin were described in less positive terms (Lerner and Schroeder 1971a, 1971b).

These studies show that even five- and six-year-old children know the preferred physical attributes of their culture, and, more important, they attribute positive characteristics to people who have those physical attributes. We should

---

*It should be clear throughout the following discussion that good looks and physical attractiveness are to a considerable degree cultural definitions and can vary greatly from one society to another, and from one time to another. There is very little that is absolute about physical attractiveness, except that, in general, the features near the average of the entire population are likely to be considered most attractive. In any case, we are referring in the discussion that follows to attractiveness as defined by our society in our time.

a) Sarah Bernhardt (1880s)

b) Theda Bara (1920s)

c) Marilyn Monroe (1950s)

d) Brooke Shields (1980s)

Changing standards of beauty.

not, then, be surprised if physical attractiveness plays a very important part in dating and marriage preferences of young adults. Just as the children believe that more attractive children will make better friends, so as adults we will probably believe that a more attractive person will make a better date or spouse. Despite what we say is important to us (good character, emotional stability, etc.), the fact is that physical attractiveness does play an important part in our choices.

One early study, which has now become a near classic, demonstrates clearly the importance of physical attractiveness in dating (Walster et al., 1966). In this study on a university campus, a "computer dance" was announced. The event was advertised as a dance where students would be computer matched with a person of the opposite sex. The person with whom an individual was matched was supposed to have similar interests (at least, that is what the students were told). As the students interested in the dance picked up their tickets they completed questionnaires, which were designed to measure social skills, intelligence, and personality characteristics. While the students were completing the questionnaires, four independent raters scored each student on his or her physical attractiveness. At the time of the dance the students were matched not on the basis of their similarities but randomly. The only stipulation was that the man had to be taller than the woman (conforming to our cultural preference on this point). During the intermission of the dance the partners, in private, rated their dates, indicating how much they liked them. About five months later the students were contacted again and asked whether they had continued to date their partners after the dance. After all the data had been analyzed, only one factor proved to be related to liking one's partner and continuing to date him or her. That factor was the partner's physical attractiveness as rated by the original raters. Social skills, intelligence, and personality characteristics did not predict whether the couple would like each other and continue dating. This study, and a repeat study that used nearly the same procedures, gives considerable support to the idea that physical attractiveness is the major factor in dating and mate selection (see Brislin and Lewis, 1968).

If physical attraction is especially significant in our heterosexual choices, the obvious question is why. The answer to this question might seem obvious too. One might think at first that it is clearly more pleasant to have a close, intimate relationship with an attractive person. But a second thought reveals equally clearly that it is quite possible for an attractive person to be quite unpleasant in a variety of ways. There is no assurance that attractiveness will be equal to pleasantness. The original question of why we prefer to date and marry attractive people has a more complex answer than we first suppose. Part of the answer lies in what has come to be called the *physical attractiveness stereotype* (Dion et al., 1972; Saxe, 1979).

The physical attractiveness stereotype can be summed up simply with the words: "What is beautiful is good." We have already seen how the stereotype is applied in the case of preschoolers attributing pleasant qualities to children who are attractive in photographs. It is quite appropriate in this case to use the term *stereotype*, because stereotyping means that certain characteristics are automatically attributed to a person in a particular category or with a particular appearance (e.g., gender stereotyping and racial stereotyping). There is a preponderance of evidence that persons who are physically attractive are automatically perceived as having many desirable characteristics.

In a study among college students, the people in photographs who were more attractive were also judged by both males and females to be people who were more sociable, poised, sophisticated, and sexually warm. In addition to these social skills, the attractive people were also thought to be more altruistic, kind, genuine, and modest (Dion et al., 1972). In this study there was no difference in applying the stereotype, regardless of whether the attractive person was male or female. In another study, however, when the focus was on unattractive people, there was evidence that unattractive men were not stereotyped as harshly as unattractive women (Miller, 1970).

Some research has considered whether or not there is any truth behind the physical attractiveness stereotype. It is possible that attractive people do have an edge when it comes to social skills and pleasing personalities. In one study of this issue, subjects were asked to carry on a five-minute telephone conversation with three opposite-sex peers. After each conversation they were asked to rate each person on several dimensions, including social skills. The people at the other end of the conversations were independently rated on their physical attractiveness. Since the subjects could not see how attractive the other person was, their judgments were not based on the person's appearance. In this study the more attractive people were judged by those who had not seen them, simply on the basis of the telephone conversations, to have more social skills (Goldman and Lewis, 1977). So there might be some validity to the stereotype, but since the relationship between attractiveness and social skills is not perfect, there must be some other factors that enter into the creation and maintenance of the physical attractiveness stereotype.

There are three such factors. The first is what might be called *social laziness* (Saxe, 1979). In evaluating other people it seems we only use those things that are most obvious. Physical attractiveness is a very obvious or *salient* characteristic, so we use it first. The second factor that contributes to the physical attractiveness stereotype is closely related to salience. This factor is *speed*. Ellen Berscheid, one of the leading researchers on physical attraction, has described vividly the importance of speed. She was asked in an interview, "Are people fooling themselves when they say they value social skills, intelligence, personality and good character in others more than physical appearance?" Her answer was as follows:

> *There is seemingly a paradox in what people say they regard as important in their feelings toward others and what actually influences them. I don't think people deliberately and consistently lie on this subject. We know that*

Attractive people are automatically judged as more sociable, poised, sophisticated, and sexually warm than unattractive people.

people often can't identify the forces that influence their behavior, including their feelings toward others.

Much of the unawareness of this case probably lies in the incredible speed with which the human mind processes a bit of information. For example, a person's physical-attractiveness level can be discerned from a photo . . . [which is] flashed on a screen for a bare fraction of a second. Almost instantaneously, we conjure up a mental image of that person's character.

With lightning speed, the human mind processes that information about the person's physical appearance against all the information in memory about what physically attractive and unattractive people are like. So when we see a beautiful woman or a handsome man, in the time it takes us to blink an eye we see before us a good and kind and sincere person. The fact that the individual is also physically attractive may seem incidental or just an irrelevant added bonus.

The mind works so fast that we're often not aware of where that inference of goodness and kindness came from or what information our mind used to reach that conclusion. And so we say we're responding to their character not their appearance. We're not consciously lying. For those of us who have absorbed the stereotype about attractiveness, the *effect may be virtually automatic and very compelling. (U.S. News and World Report, 1982)*

It is clear that salience and speed are most important for first impressions. Why is it that, even after two people have had an opportunity to interact and have obtained additional information about each other, physical appearance continues to be so important? One possible explanation, and the third factor on our list, is the *self-fulfilling prophecy* (Merton, 1957; Saxe, 1979). A self-fulfilling prophecy, as the label suggests, is a prophecy that comes true in part because the prophecy was made in the first place. Thus, we meet an attractive person and decide on the basis of appearance that the person will be friendly and personable. We therefore approach that person in a friendly and warm manner. Normally a person approached in that way will respond in a similar friendly way. And so by our own actions we make our initial prophecy come true.

We can briefly sum up what we know about the way in which the physical attractiveness stereotype works by noting that there are four S's operating. The physically attractive may have somewhat greater *social skills*. However, the *salience* of physical appearance allows us to make judgments with great *speed*. These produce a *self-fulfilling prophecy*, which we ourselves may help to make true.

We have now seen how very important physical attractiveness is in our reactions to other people, and how it is likely to influence our choice of dating partners. Obviously, however, not everybody can be in the "most attractive" category. In physical characteristics alone some people must be less attractive, average, or even below average in appearance. Despite this indisputable fact, most people do find someone to whom they are attracted, and the feeling is often mutual. Since this is a matter that has more than a little practical significance, we should try to understand how the process works. How is it that most of us do get matched with another person?

The *matching hypothesis* states that both men and women will choose partners whose level of physical attractiveness is similar to their own. Somehow in the process of interacting with members of the opposite sex, we learn or become aware of our own physical attractiveness. Then as the opportunities present themselves we select (or accept the selection of) someone who is roughly equal to us in attractiveness. This hypothesis is often supported by observations in our everyday lives, but experimental studies also show support. In one such study men and women who had been previously assessed in terms of physical attractiveness were asked to choose a date from a set of individuals who displayed a range of attractiveness. Those choosers who were most attractive, as expected, chose the most attractive partners. Those choosers who were less attractive were content to choose less attractive people as their dates (Berscheid et al., 1971). Field studies among couples who are engaged or have exclusive relationships show similar results (Dion, 1981; Murstein, 1972; Silverman, 1971).

People generally know their own level of attractiveness and make selections of others that approximately match their level, but that raises two additional questions: (1) How do we get a reasonably accurate perception of our own looks? (2) Why do we generally make choices within our range? Answers to both questions derive from the fact that through a number of years, as we move from childhood to young adulthood, we are immersed in a system of rating and evaluating ourselves and others. We seek to know "where we rate" compared to our peers. Many times we learn only too harshly that we do not fall into the the top levels of attractiveness. A related point is that our system of meeting and mating is, as we noted earlier, filled with uncertainty, which leads to considerable anxiety and tension. Under these conditions many people will lower the level of uncertainty by "playing it safe," not aiming too high. This, too, helps to match people more closely.

Matching between two people of the opposite sex occurs when both have assessed their personal attributes and concluded that they are roughly equal. Sociologist Erving Goffman (1952) sees the marriage proposal as a final step in the matching process. His somewhat cynical assessment is that "A proposal of marriage in our society tends to be a way in which a man sums up his social attributes and suggests to a woman that hers are not so much better" (Goffman, 1952, p. 456).

In the remainder of this chapter we will examine the nature of contemporary dating. Several lines of research have contributed to our understanding of dating and intimate relationships. First we will examine some of the popular and emergent ways people use to get acquainted.

MAKING CONTACT WITH THE OPPOSITE SEX

There are usually about equal numbers of men and women in a population, especially in the young adult years. Yet, both men and women are likely to be heard complaining about the difficulty of meeting members of the opposite sex. They do, of course, get together eventually, so how does it happen? One answer is through a friend (Knox and Wilson, 1981). When researchers asked a sample of college students at East Carolina University about how they meet people they date, the answer in one-third of the cases (both men and women) was through a friend. While the students at one university cannot necessarily be taken as representative of young people all over the country, there are at least some reasons to believe that using a friend as a go-between is a tried and true method of getting acquainted.

In traditional societies marriages are often arranged for young people, and that clearly suggests a go-between. An official matchmaker often serves as a go-

We use "love magic" in our society too. We hope that using the right perfume, after-shave lotion, deodorant, or lip gloss will attract or keep the attention of one's lover.

between who matches up the children of different families. (We will examine how this works in Chapter 5.) But in societies like our own, where families are less involved, there is a freer choice by the participants. This greater freedom, however, does require techniques that reduce the potential for ego-shattering experiences. The college mixer, considered earlier, revealed how one must tentatively show interest in another person, but not so much that one is exposed to being directly rejected. Sometimes the interest can be shown with the eyes or a few well-chosen words, but even these methods are risky. By telling a mutual friend that one is interested in a person of the opposite sex, at least the possibility of direct rejection is reduced.

Using a friend to reduce the chances of embarassment is not the only technique. In some societies "love magic" is used (Rosenblatt and Anderson, 1981). *Love magic* is like a superstition or charm that is supposed to bring a person good luck. In this case, it is to bring them the love of some special person. Like other kinds of magic and superstition, it is most commonly used in situations of uncertainty. Magic seems to relieve the tension whenever an outcome is uncertain. If a person uses love magic, and it fails to attract the other person, then the magic can be blamed for not being strong enough. It is easier to place the blame on the shortcomings of the magic than on one's own inadequacies.

The following are just a few of many known examples of love magic. Among the Chewa, a society in Africa, young men wear a bracelet with two pieces of wood on their left arm. While talking with a young woman of their choice, they rub the two pieces of wood. On Bali it is believed that a young woman will fall in love with a young man who succeeds in getting her to eat a particular leaf on which he has inscribed the image of a god who possesses a very large penis. Among the Menomini, a native American tribe, young men would wear a pouch hanging from the neck in which they could have rocks and minerals ground to a fine powder. They would also place some hair or the nail clippings of the young woman they desired into this bag, as this was supposed to win her favor. These and many more forms of love magic are found around the world (Rosenblatt and Anderson, 1981).

While love potions may seem exotic and even primitive, it is very similar to using astrological signs to anticipate whether someone will be a good match. However, we much more commonly reduce our tensions and anxieties in other ways. Alcohol, and sometimes drugs, are often used for that purpose. At singles bars, campus hangouts, parties, and dances, alcohol serves in several ways to reduce tensions. First, it is a prop, or a support, throughout an evening. Getting a drink or standing around drinking gives people something to do when they need to look "busy." Second, the physical effect of the alcohol can serve to reduce both anxiety and inhibitions. Third, as noted earlier, it gives people a way to escape when necessary—"Pardon me, I think I'll get a beer" (Schwartz and Lever, 1976, p. 413).

There are two other emerging mechanisms in contemporary society that serve the purpose of getting people together, and do so in ways that may help reduce the tensions and anxieties produced by uncertainty. One of these is the use of *personal classified advertisements* in magazines and some specialized newspapers. The second is what is loosely called *computer dating*. Both of these methods are outgrowths of our personal choice system, but personal choice in the context of an impersonal, urban society.

The personal classified advertisement. Near the back of many magazines, especially those published in urban areas, one often finds pages of short but detailed advertisements, written and paid for by people who wish to make contact with other readers. These ads usually provide self-descriptions and descriptions of the kind of person the writer is seeking. An example, made up of the words of actual ads, might read:

DWM [meaning divorced, white male] 35, handsome, creative, very affectionate, with a sexy voice. Likes travel, country music and sailing, but

*also talking, sharing, laughing, cuddling and quiet times together. I am in
search of S/DWF [single or divorced white female], non-smoker,
intelligent, attractive, slim, 28 or younger who wishes to share life.*

These ads serve the needs of many people in urban places who find it difficult in the normal course of their lives to meet the kinds of people they are looking for as mates. Marriage may or may not be the objective, but at the very least
these ads are used to meet new people. Usually the objective is to establish some
kind of companionship or intimate relationship, either short- or long-term.

The personal classified advertisement has become so popular that a book titled *Classified Love* (Foxman, 1982) has been written on the subject. The author
of this book identifies some of the advantages of this method of meeting new
people by comparing it with singles bars and other "meat markets." The first advantage of ads is that they are anonymous. "They can save you time and money
because you can list your requirements and only go out with the people you
choose" (Krucoff, 1982, p. C5). One might also add that "you go out only with
those who choose you" after seeing your self-description. The classified personal
advertisement provides not only an initial degree of anonymity but also a limited
commitment when someone responds to your advertisement. Indeed, Foxman,
who is something of an expert on these matters having written more than 300
ads (for herself and friends), suggests that the first date should be short—for
lunch or a drink—in a public place (Krucoff, 1982).

What we see reflected in these practical considerations of this contemporary mechanism of meeting is an emphasis on efficiency, anonymity, and, at
least in the beginning, impersonality. Those characteristics are even more in
evidence in a second, still growing, method of meeting potential mates: computer dating.

Computer dating.   A dating or matchmaking service that makes use of a
computer system is usually provided by a commercial, profit-making organization. A person wishing to meet someone of the opposite sex will pay a fee, complete a questionnaire, and perhaps have a personal interview with a member of
the staff. The data from the questionnaire are transferred to computer cards or
tape so they can be conveniently matched with others of similar interests and
needs. In recent years it has also become common for an agency to make videotapes of its clients. This feature allows other clients to preview the tapes of
those with compatible interests. The videotape system is especially effective in
reducing the anxiety and tensions associated with meeting others. Only those
people who themselves are subscribing to the services of the computer dating
company will see the videotape. And only those who find something interesting
and appealing on the videotape are likely to be put in direct contact with a person. This may be a critical factor in view of what we have already seen about
the importance of personal appearance when people meet for the first time.

The key to this system is that two people do not have to accept or reject each other in a face-to-face situation. Some observers would view this as the ultimate extension of an already overcomputerized and impersonal society; others see it as one of the advantages of our ever-increasing use of computers (Jedlicka, 1981). The very impersonality of a computer, they believe, makes any rejection less embarrassing and less ego damaging.

With the advent of personal home computer terminals there is even a vision of people having their first interaction through keyboards and display screens instead of in person (Jedlicka, 1981). This will be achieved through interacting computer networks and might work in the following way. One would subscribe to a computer service and provide characteristics about oneself and the kind of person being sought. This would be about the same as the classified ads we have already considered. Subscribers to the service would have a directory of all other subscribers and could communicate with anyone who seemed to possess their preferred characteristics (via computer and without actual names). Thus, a woman might receive a message from a man who was attracted by the description she had provided. But with the computer, it should be added, a woman might just as easily take the initiative. In this way the computer might be the mechanism that would help break the deeply ingrained idea that men must always take the initiative.

If a woman were to send a message to a man who was not at his terminal when it arrived, he would be informed of the message the next time he activated his computer terminal. He could then check the self-description of his correspondent. If he found it interesting, he could send a return message to her, and so the communication could go, back and forth, while each learned more and more about the other. This would be like relationships of the past that were built on correspondence through letters. The big difference would be in the speed and efficiency of the communication. Many messages could be transmitted in even a day or two, compared to weeks that might be required for letters to go back and forth.

Another advantage would be that the exchange of messages could be broken off at any time, by either party, and the unpleasantness would be less than if their interaction had been face-to-face. There would also be an advantage for people who have unusual life-style preferences, including unusual sexual preferences. It would be easier for these people to get in touch with others who had similar preferences. Again, the possible embarrassments would be minimized, and communications could be discontinued whenever it became apparent that two people had incompatible beliefs, plans, or life-styles (Jedlicka, 1981).

After two people have met, by whatever means, the relationship often grows in intensity. This could mean love, and eventually marriage. But, of course, we all know that many relationships do not last, even those that are, for a time, love relationships. Perhaps it would be useful to conclude this chapter with a brief look at breaking up.

BREAKING UP—LEAVING A RELATIONSHIP

In the movies when two lovers break up, they usually come back together at the end. That is what makes movies. In real life, however, break ups are often forever. But the topic of ending relationships has been left largely in the hands of movie writers and directors, songwriters, and other representatives of popular culture. Only a little research has been done, although a recent study of how couples leave each other has been especially informative (Rubin et al., 1981). This same study also has something to say about how men and women fall in love, so this aspect of the research findings will also be examined.

We can begin with a stereotype, the popular wisdom about men and women and their relationships. The general belief holds that men and women are different when it comes to falling in love. Women are thought to be more starry-eyed and sentimental, while men are more hard-hearted and rational. Women are believed to be more likely to fall in love at first sight and experience all the symptoms of love: a palpitating heart, an inability to eat, and an aching longing for their love. Men, on the other hand, are supposed to be more impassive, unemotional, reserved, and cool (adapted from Rubin et al., 1981, p. 822).

A related stereotype is that men are ruthless exploiters who fall out of love more easily. If they ever really were in love, they can move away from it more quickly, casually, and unemotionally. Women, on the other hand, will cling to their men, tearfully and emotionally, not wanting to see the relationship end until all hope is lost (adapted from Rubin et al., 1981, p. 822). These stereotypes of men and women and their responses to relationships are widely accepted, but what did the researchers find when they examined these matters in a carefully conducted study?

The study by Rubin and his associates (1981) was based on 231 couples from four colleges in the Boston area. These couples were recruited through newspaper ads and were almost all undergraduate college students (males were typically juniors, females typically sophomores). They were almost all dating each other exclusively at the beginning of the study, with a few having concrete plans for marriage. The researchers remained in touch with these dating couples for two years to see how their relationships developed (or ended).

The researchers wanted to know whether men or women fall in love more readily. The evidence, supported by other studies, was that men were more romantic and fell in love more readily than women. Men, for example, scored higher than women on a *romanticism scale*. This meant that they were more likely to believe in "love at first sight" and that love could overcome barriers such as differences in race, religion, or economic status. The women, by their responses, were more skeptical of these aspects of love. Men were also more likely than women to say that they entered relationships with a "desire to fall in love" (Rubin et al., 1981, p. 824). Contrary to the stereotypes, it appears that men approach relationships from a more romantic point of view. But what about leaving relationships? How do the stereotypes of men and women hold up in that context?

Two years after the beginning of this study of dating couples, twenty percent of them had married, and thirty-three percent were still dating. The remaining forty-seven percent had broken up during the two-year period.

About one-third of the original 231 couples had already broken up at the end of the first year of the study. The researchers had a measure of each partner's love at the beginning of the study and a year later after they had broken up. This measure, called the *love scale*, reflected feelings of attachment, caring, and intimacy toward the partner. It should come as no surprise that the love scores dropped far down on the scale for the couples who had broken up. By comparison, the couples who were still together at the end of one year had a slight increase in their love scores. Again, there should be no special surprise in these findings. What is interesting, and perhaps surprising, is that it was the woman's love score that proved to be the better predictor of breaking up. Among the couples who stayed together, the women's love scores at the beginning of the study were higher than those of their mates. (This is a comparison of averages, of course, and would not be true in all individual cases.) Among the couples who broke up during the year, the women's love scores were lower at the beginning of the study than the scores of their partners. Furthermore, the love scores of these women at the end of one year had dropped even more sharply than the scores of the men who had broken up. There are two ways to state the implication of this last difference: (1) women tend to fall out of love more readily than men do; and (2) men tend to cling to their love more than women do.

The latter interpretation is borne out by the fact that in this study breaking up was a more traumatic emotional experience for men than for women. Men were more likely to report that they felt depressed, lonely, unhappy, and less free than were the women who had broken up. One reason why women were less emotionally upset was that they were likely to take it better when they were the "most involved" partner (most in love). One woman said, "I don't think I ever felt romantic [about David]—I felt practical. I had the feeling that I'd better make the most of it because it won't last that long" (Rubin et al., 1981, p. 829).

This *practical approach* to relationships is one of the keys to understanding the differences between men and women. In the courtship system that has developed in Western society, and probably continues to a considerable degree, women have been much more affected by their marriage choices than have men. Often the husband's occupation, income, and life-style have shaped the marriage and determined the position of the family in the community and society. With this prevailing condition, women have had to be more cautious, practical, and realistic than men. A woman "cannot allow herself to fall in love too quickly; nor can she afford to stay in love too long with the 'wrong person.' The woman must carefully evaluate her partner's strengths and weaknesses, and must compare him to potential alternative partners, in order to make sure that she is getting the best possible 'bargain' in the marriage market" (Rubin et al., 1981, p. 831).

Men, by contrast, have had the dominant position in society and thus have more often shaped the nature of the marriage and the position of the couple in the community. Under these conditions they do not need to be as practical and realistic. Men "can better afford the luxury of being 'romantic' " (Rubin et al., 1982, p. 831).

It has often been said that women are trained (socialized) from early childhood to express their emotions or to be more emotional. That is probably true, but we see in the case of ending romantic relationships that women are apparently less emotional. This paradox is resolved if we recognize that their socialization experience puts them more in touch with their emotions. This might also mean that they can manage their emotions more effectively. There is a fairly large amount of evidence that women do have an edge on men in their ability to assess and handle their feelings and emotions (Hochschild, 1983; Hoffman, 1977; Rubin, 1970).

Having considered how men and women differ in the way they end relationships, we can now complete the circle by considering how they differ in initiating relationships. We are ready to direct our attention to the question raised at the beginning of this chapter: In today's world, should women take equal responsibility for initiating and paying for dates?

ISSUE

In today's world, should women take equal responsibility for initiating and paying for dates?

In the modern, "with-it" world of television commercials, the self-confident young woman tells us that it is quite respectable for her to ask a man over to her apartment for a glass of sherry. Or a similar young woman, as she receives her American Express card in the mail, asks her male neighbor if he would like to help her "break in" the newly arrived credit card. In the minidrama life of television commercials, these breaks with convention seem not only reasonable but, to many people, desirable. However, life portrayed on television commercials and life as we find it in reality are often very different.

While many young people feel that it *should* be possible for women to take the initiative in dating, they may also feel that there are reasons why it would not be acceptable or appropriate. We would like to present the arguments on both sides of this question, beginning with the case that women today should be able to take equal responsibility for initiating and paying for dates.

Arguments for Women Taking Equal Responsibility

Over the years, many women have chafed under restrictions imposed on them by the unwritten rules of dating, which required them to wait until a man asked them for a date. In recent years, some women have decided to do something other than just accept their "fate." They point out that there is nothing sacred about the traditional arrangements, and they argue that women have just as much right as men to initiate dates. Going one step further, they might also say that when women *do* initiate dates they should also take the financial responsibility for them.

Under the traditional dating system in the United States, a woman is in a passive, dependent state, which automatically limits her options as to who and when she dates. If the men she prefers to date don't ask her, she either has to "settle" for someone she's not attracted to or just not date anyone. Men, on the other hand, don't have to sit and wait for someone to call. They can ask any woman who interests them. This is inherently unfair to women. Thus, on the grounds of fairness alone women should have the right to initiate dating relationships.

Interestingly, it can also be argued that if women were freer to take the initiative in dating, men would feel less pressure and anxiety. Many men, of course, do not exercise their option to ask out all the women they find interesting and attractive. They often restrict the range of women they try to get to know because of shyness or fear of rejection. And, when they do ask a woman out they may worry that she is only going out with them because she doesn't have any better alternatives or because she just can't say no! If a man were to be asked out by a woman, however, he could be more confident that she really did want to spend time with him. So, if women had the same freedom as men to initiate dates, the average man and woman might actually be able to date a wider range of people. And further, the risk of rejection would be shared more equally by men and women.

The economic aspects of dating also raise interesting gender-based issues. Under the traditional system of dating, the man, by virtue of his right to initiate dates has the corresponding obligation to take the financial responsibility for the dates. Sometimes the tradition is so strong that the man pays even when the woman suggests going out. It can certainly be argued that in an age when many women have economic resources that approach and sometimes exceed those of the men they date, it no longer makes sense for men invariably to pay all dating expenses. Many women are willing and able to assume some of the financial responsibility for dating; many do so frequently.

The actual mechanics of women paying for dates also need to be examined briefly. Has anything really changed if a woman secretly slips twenty dollars to her male companion to make it appear to others that *he* is actually paying? It is quite a different matter for a woman to pick up a restaurant check openly and pay it. The women and men who break with tradition by sharing dating expenses believe that the latter method is the only "honest" course to follow.

One major argument in favor of women taking equal financial responsibility for dates is that if they do not they are incurring a kind of debt to the man they are with. There has been a hidden assumption in much dating behavior that when men pay for dates they can legitimately demand something from their companions in return. This is an example of the *fair exchange rule*, which puts pressure on women to return something of value in exchange for the money their date has spent. That "something" has traditionally been the woman's sexual favors. Many women today realize that one way to avoid being trapped by the fair exchange rule is to avoid incurring the debt in the first place.

In summary, then, there are several major arguments in favor of women's taking more initiative in asking for dates. First, it is argued that for women to do so would remove the restrictions of traditional dating and would give both men and women more options. Second, it would also equalize the psychological burden of having to ask for dates, and, thus, more equally distribute the risk of being rejected. There are also several arguments in favor of women sharing financial responsibility for dates, not the least of which is the obvious point that the costs for men would be reduced. More important, though, if women were to take on some of the costs of dating they would minimize the pressure put on them to reciprocate with sexual favors.

Arguments against Women Taking Equal Responsibility

The major argument against women taking more responsibility for initiating and paying for dates is that it would produce a great deal of confusion and misunderstanding. There would be uncounted numbers of embarrassing and awkward telephone conversations and dating experiences. The changes in long-established and well-understood social customs would simply be too radical and would therefore be unrealistic at this time. Men have been thoroughly trained to take the responsibility for dating, and their views of themselves would have to be radically altered if women were to take over. Women who would take such actions would be viewed as a threat to male independence and autonomy. The average man is not used to being placed in a passive role and would be uncomfortable with a woman who tried to put him in that position.

Another negative reaction that women risk when they initiate dates is that their invitation will be perceived as an indication of sexual availability. Women who suspect that men will react in this way might be reluctant to put themselves in such a disadvantageous position. They might recognize that a possibility for exploitation exists in their asking men for dates.

In short, the major objection to women taking the initiative for dating is that this violation of traditional social norms produces severe sanctions. The potential problems of changing traditional patterns probably are not worth the potential benefits.

There is a similar set of apprehensions when it comes to women paying for dates. Men become so accustomed to paying that allowing women to pay for them openly may be threatening to their masculinity. Having money and using it to demonstrate one's authority and manliness is deeply embedded in the average male psyche. Even when a man is able to accept the notion of a woman paying for drinks or dinner intellectually, he may still feel threatened subconsciously.

It should also be recognized that men may simply not want to give up the feeling of being in command that they derive from initiating and paying for dates. Similarly, women might feel most comfortable when they are with a man who is "in charge and responsible." The basic argument for continuing the traditional patterns of dating can be summarized as follows: "If it makes men feel better to retain control, and if women feel comfortable with this arrangement, why change things?"

Themes

1. If men and women are to enter into marriage, they must first have some way of getting together.

2. Societies differ greatly in the ways they provide for young people to get together, some having very ritualized ways, others having very unstructured conditions.

3. The more ritualistic and stylized the patterns of meeting are, the less anxiety there is for the participants, while unstructured meeting situations produce much more tension and anxiety.

4. When asked, young people usually say that personal characteristics, rather than physical appearance, are most important when they select a person they would prefer to date.

5. In actual behavior, physical attractiveness is an important factor when people are evaluating each other.

6. There is a physical attractiveness stereotype by which good personal qualities are generally attributed to people who are physically attractive.

7. Generally, both men and women will choose partners whose level of physical attractiveness is similar to their own.

8. Friends, love magic, alcohol, and drugs are all used as techniques for reducing the tensions of becoming acquainted with members of the opposite sex.

9. Two newer methods for meeting members of the opposite sex, especially in urban areas, are classified advertisements and computer dating services.

10. The stereotype, or commonly held folk wisdom, is that women are more romantic and sentimental than men when entering and leaving relationships, but the opposite appears to be true.

Facts

1. The Saxons of Transylvania have a very ritualized dating and courtship system, with most events occurring on particular religious days.

2. The Limbu of Nepal get acquainted with the opposite sex while dancing on the rice straw, which incidentally threshes out the grain.

3. At college mixers in the United States, the following techniques are found:
   a. Eye messages are used to make contact with another person, or to avoid it.
   b. Ritualistic brush-offs are recognized as ways of getting rid of another person.

   c. To defend against being rejected, individuals often take the offensive and break off contact first.

4. Several studies, over a number of years, found that "dependable character" and "emotional stability" are the most desired characteristics in members of the opposite sex.

5. In a study of California students, both men and women valued "good looks" most in a date; when asked about a spouse, men still preferred looks, but women shifted to love as their preferred characteristic.

6. Preschool and kindergarten children know the standards of physical attractiveness of their society and attribute positive characteristics to attractive people.

7. When college-age couples were randomly matched at a "computer dance," the physical attractiveness of one's partner was the only characteristic that was related to liking the partner and continuing to date him or her.

8. Physically attractive people are judged by both males and females to be more sociable, poised, sophisticated, and sexually warm.

9. Experimental studies have shown that physically attractive people do possess more social skills and pleasing personalities.

10. Physical attractiveness is a salient characteristic of a person that can be assessed with very great speed.

11. Research has shown that men are more romantic than women and fall in love more easily.

12. When romantic relationships break up, women fall out of love more easily than men, who tend to cling to their love.

13. When a romantic relationship breaks up, men are likely to feel more depressed, more lonely, less happy, and less free than women.

14. Women have been shown to be more in touch with and in control of their emotions than men.

Major Concepts

attraction: (See **sexual attraction.**)

love scale: A research measurement instrument that reflects feelings of attachment, caring, and intimacy toward one's partner.

matching hypothesis: Both men and women will tend to choose partners whose level of physical attractiveness is similar to their own.

opportunity situations The special places or events where young people can get together and have the chance to evaluate each other.

physical attractiveness stereotype: Physically attractive people are also perceived as having many desirable personal traits.

romanticism scale: A research measurement instrument that measures such things as belief in love at first sight and belief that love can overcome barriers such as differences in race, religion, or economic status.

self-fulfilling prophecy: A prophecy that comes true in part because it was made in the first place.

sexual attraction (*often just* **attraction**)**:** Interest in another person, which includes a desire to have some sort of contact with that person.

5

Sex before Marriage
Sexual Scripts of Yesterday and Today

Critics of American society used to say that Americans were sexually repressed. Sex, they said, was not discussed, and when it was it was something "dirty." But in the last couple of decades a new sexual ethic and some different sexual behavior changed that image. Beginning in the 1960s, sex was suddenly "in." Sex was acceptable, it was fun, and it was for everyone. The changes in sexual attitudes and behaviors were quickly labeled *a sexual revolution*. One of the most significant changes that came as a part of this sexual revolution was an increase in the sexual activities of young people. More and more of them had sexual relations at younger ages, often long before they married.

Because of the earlier image of Americans as sexually repressed, many people applauded, or at least looked favorably upon, the new sexual ethic. They saw it as positive and beneficial, even for the young and the unmarried. Of course, there was an opposing point of view among people who, for moral or religious reasons, decried what seemed to be a fast-moving descent to a promiscuous society.

For the most part, the popular press and other mass media either tacitly approved of the liberalization of sexual behavior or supported it openly. But in the last few years, even these sources have raised questions about the sexual behavior of Americans, especially among the young and the unmarried. Now in the media one is more likely to hear some form of the question "Is there too much sex, too soon?" It seems as though an old question has reemerged in American society. More people are once again questioning the advisability of young people having sex before marriage.

In this chapter we will see what American premarital sexual behavior has been in the past and what it is now. Along the way we will also consider the ways premarital sexual behavior is treated in other societies. At the end of the chapter we will return to the question that is being asked increasingly today: Should young people wait until marriage to have sex?

It would be a rare person who forgot the first time he or she had sexual intercourse, and not necessarily because it was such a pleasurable experience, for often the experience may have been unpleasant. We remember the first time we had sexual intercourse because of the extraordinary symbolic importance it has in our lives. *Loss of virginity* is a phrase that is loaded with meaning and significance—especially for women, but also for men. However, exactly what that meaning is and how much significance it has depends on who you are, where you are, and the time in which you are living.

If you are unmarried when you first have sexual intercourse, it can mean something quite different than if you are married. If you are a female and unmarried, the first sexual experience will mean something quite different than if you are a male and unmarried. In all cases the symbolic significance of first sexual intercourse is likely to be very different today than it was twenty years ago.

Since people do remember their first sexual intercourse experience, it is possible in questionnaire surveys or interviews to ask them about it. This has been done in a number of different studies, producing some interesting facts, and some even more interesting interpretations of the facts.

First, let us consider some of the facts. Several years ago, one study revealed that young men differed from young women in the number of times they had sex with their first partners (Gagnon and Simon, 1973). Young men reported that on the average they had sexual intercourse from one to three times with their first partners. Young women, on the other hand, usually reported that they had sexual intercourse ten or more times with their first partners. Even from these facts we can see that the initial sexual experience is very different for males and females. Somewhat less obvious is how these differences between males and females could be possible. It seems that this difference between males and females could be accounted for if a small proportion of all females were having sexual relations with many different males, often on a short-term basis. While that helps us to understand *how* the differences between men and women could occur, it still does not explain *why* it occurs. Before discussing why, there are some additional, more recently obtained, facts about the first sexual intercourse experience that should be noted.

In a study of a random sample of American young people living in metropolitan areas, researchers asked those who had had sexual intercourse a series of questions about their first sexual experience (Zelnik and Shah, 1983). The results of this study are summarized in Table 5.1. Young women who had had sexual intercourse were, on the average, 16.2 years old at the time of their first experience. The average age of their partners was 19.0. This is what one might expect, since it is very close to the normal two- to three-year age difference that separates men and women at the time of their first marriage. However, when young men reported on their ages and their partners' ages at the time of first sexual intercourse, a very different picture emerged. The young men reported that they were, on average, 15.7 years old when they had sex the first time. Their partners, however, were not younger, but older. The women partners of the young men were 16.4 years old, on the average. This age difference, with the women being nearly three-fourths of a year older than their "first-time"

Table 5.1 *Characteristics of the first sexual intercourse experience of unmarried females and males*

	Age	Partner's age	Relationship with partner	
			Engaged or going steady	Just a friend or just met
Females	16.2 yrs	19.0 yrs	65%	11%
Males	15.7 yrs	16.4 yrs	37%	43%

Source: Zelnick and Shah, 1983.

male partners, does not seem to reflect the typical male-female dating or romantic pair. Indeed, the additional information shown in Table 5.1 bears this out.

When the women were asked what their relationship was with the men they first had sexual intercourse with, sixty-five percent said they were "going steady with" or "engaged to" the man who was their first sexual partner. By comparison, thirty-seven percent of the young men said they were either going steady with or engaged to their first partner. The picture is further clarified by looking at how many women and men had sexual intercourse for the first time with someone who was "just a friend" or whom they had "just met." Eleven percent of the women had sex for the first time in this kind of casual relationship. By contrast, the males were much more likely to have had sex for the first time with someone they knew only casually—forty-three percent of the males said their first sexual experience was with a woman who was just a friend or whom they had just met.

Very similar results were reported with a sample of unmarried male and female students at the University of Wisconsin and nonstudents of comparable age coming from the same community (DeLamater and MacCorquodale, 1979). This study asked about the relationship with the partner in such a way that it was possible to determine if love was involved. Sixty-five percent of the males said their first partner was someone they were *not* in love with. Thirty-five percent of the females said they were *not* in love with their first partner.

All of these data produce a consistent picture. When young women have sexual intercourse for the first time, their partner is most likely a man with whom they are seriously involved. The number of times they have sex (more than ten times), the three-year age difference, the high likelihood of going steady or being engaged to the man, and the greater likelihood of being in love, all suggest that women are most likely to have sex for the first time when they are in a committed and serious relationship.

Young men show many fewer signs of this level of commitment. They often have sex only a few times with their first partner, and the young women they have sex with are generally older. The relationship is more likely to be casual,

The first sexual intercourse experience for a young woman is very likely to be associated with a strong feeling of love.

and they are less likely to say they are in love. So how do we interpret these differences in the early sexual behavior of males and females? Actually there are several aspects of sex that are revealed by this difference—most importantly, the gender role influences on males and females and the double standard of sexual behavior. Also, associated with both of these is the connection between love and sex.

GENDER ROLES AND THE FIRST
SEXUAL EXPERIENCE

In the discussion of gender roles in Chapter 2, we saw that the traditional feminine and masculine role expectations can be labeled expressive and instrumental, respectively. Expressive behaviors expected of females are those associated with emotion, supportiveness, comfort, and love. The instrumental behaviors expected of males are achievement and action oriented. Males are expected to do things, accomplish things, and achieve things.

With these gender role expectations in mind, let us examine the differences we have seen between males and females in regard to their first sexual intercourse experience. First, the views of sexuality and sexual attitudes of young women and men differ in ways that closely parallel the traditional male and female gender roles. When young women think about, talk about, and read about sex, they focus primarily on the personal relationship that leads to sex. If they are sexually aroused it is primarily produced by thoughts of feeling love and affection. In heterosexual relationships it is not the erotic but the emotional that constitutes the important dimension for young women (Gagnon, 1977). If we consider this in regard to the first sexual experience, it seems that for most females sexual intercourse is more likely to be both acceptable and desirable if they are involved in a love relationship. When they feel that a strong bond, an emotional commitment, exists with a man, then sexual intercourse is appropriate.

For young men, the focus is much more on the physical aspects of sex, especially in the early teenage years, when in many cases they may be almost oblivious to the romantic, expressive side of heterosexual relationships. For boys, sex is an objective, a goal, and a specific set of physical acts that they strive to experience. Sex for young men is an accomplishment, an achievement. From this perspective, having sex, especially for the first time, is a way of showing the behavior characteristically associated with the instrumental masculine role. Since sex for young men is primarily a matter of achievement, the important objective or goal is to have sex. It matters relatively little with whom one has it. Many young men do not need an emotional commitment or bond with their partner. Indeed, they may prefer that there be very little emotional commitment with their first partner. The fact that in nearly half the cases they have sex with a friend or someone they have just met would fit that preference well.

Sex has a symbolic meaning and significance that differs greatly for young men and young women. For young women the first sexual intercourse experience is likely to mean that they have given the *ultimate expression of their love.* For young men, the first sexual intercourse experience is likely to mean they have reached the *ultimate sexual achievement.*

The gender roles of our society, which help us understand the differences in male and female sexual behavior, are supported by a closely related idea. This idea is the much discussed double standard of sexual behavior.

THE DOUBLE STANDARD AND SEXUAL BEHAVIOR

All societies have rules, or norms, that require people to do some things and prohibit them from doing others. Certainly, sexual behavior is important enough for there to be rules and norms controlling what people do. These norms do not control everyone completely, of course, but they do give people some standards by which they guide their behavior. When they do not follow the standards, there is usually some punishment or penalty.

In Western societies the rules, or standards, relating to sex are not the same for men and women—thus the term *double standard.* In its simplest form the double standard allows men more freedom in their sexual behavior than it does women. This is especially the case when it is applied to young unmarried men and women. The following are some of the most familiar specifics of the *traditional* double standard:

- Young men may have sexual intercourse before marriage; young women should not.
- Young men may have sexual intercourse with women even when there is no emotional feeling or commitment; young women may have sexual intercourse when they are in love, or when there is a mutual commitment.
- Young men may have multiple sexual partners; young women should not have multiple partners.
- Young men may have sexual intercourse with women who are much lower in social status, or are "immoral" women; if a young woman were to have sexual intercourse with a man of lower status it would be viewed even more negatively than with a man of her own status.
- Young men may have sexual intercourse for recreation or to gain sexual experience and expertise; young women are not allowed to have these motives or objectives.

These interconnected features of the double standard help us to understand why the sexual behavior of young men and women is so different. Young men, since they are allowed and even expected to have sexual intercourse when they are unmarried, can and do enter into casual sexual relationships. Young women, according to the traditional standards, are not encouraged to have sexual relations before marriage. The major exception that has been allowed is that a young unmarried woman may have sexual relations with a man she is likely to marry. As the double standard has loosened its grip in recent years, a woman may, in the view of some, have sexual relations with a man that she loves, and who loves her in return. This, of course, is the same justification for premarital intercourse that is found in the traditional feminine role: love makes it right.

We can see from this consideration of the first sexual intercourse experience that gender roles, the double standard, and the close connection between love and sex are all important elements in our understanding of premarital sexual behavior. Throughout this chapter these three elements will persistently emerge as the important factors affecting premarital sex.

PREMARITAL SEX IN AMERICAN HISTORY

We often think of the Puritan period in American history as a time when sexual standards were very strict. The early colonists of the seventeenth century were noted for their intense and highly moral religious views. Moreover, their religious morality was rigidly enforced by close observation of the lives of everyone in the community. Since young people in particular were watched closely, one might think that everyone among the Puritans entered marriage in a virginal state. However, that conclusion is not consistent with the historical facts. Indeed, in the New England colonies of the Puritans, nonvirginity at marriage was rather common. A study by Calhoun (1945) found that approximately one-third of Puritan brides confessed to their ministers that they had had sex before marriage. Most of them confessed because they were already pregnant and wished to have their babies baptized. Other brides, who might have had sexual intercourse but were not pregnant, might have been under less pressure to confess (Reiss, 1981). From these facts alone we can conclude that premarital sex is not a recent invention in the United States.

Other historical sources reveal that premarital sex in the past had some of the same causes and effects as premarital sex does today. This can be vividly seen in the letters and diaries of nineteenth-century lovers (Rothman, 1983; 1984). One such couple, with the delightful names of Champion Chase and Mary Butterfield, recorded their respective feelings in letters written to each other in January 1848. They each wrote a letter to the other on the morning after the night when their passions had carried them away. Apparently, on that night they had sexual intercourse for the first time even though they had been courting for some time. Champion expressed his feelings in glowing terms, saying that he "never had such a living joyous time before" (Rothman, 1983, p. 402). Mary had more initial uncertainty about what they had done:

> *Although I love you dearly & trust you perfectly that I am perfectly willing & glad to make you happy by those favors which no one else in the wide world could obtain, yet even towards you I can not at once resign all the feelings which nature and education have fixed in my mind—I was glad afterwards when you seemed so sincerely pleased & happy—so satisfied with me. (Rothman, 1983, p. 402)*

While Mary had these early misgivings about what she and Champion had done, her later letters revealed that as they had more intimate encounters she experienced both pleasure and satisfaction with herself and her sexuality. She wrote, "I am *proud* that I can give myself to you as I am. . . . I *am* a woman now. . . . You have lifted a veil which concealed from me many beautiful paths of happiness & which taught me joys & blessings I had never dreamed of" (Rothman, 1983, p. 403).

This one short exchange between two young people of the nineteenth century proves very little about the frequency of premarital sex in that time, but it does show how the feelings and concerns of some lovers then were not much different from the feelings and concerns of many young people today. It is obvious from their words that these two young people were deeply and passionately in love. From their letters it appears that the first time they had sexual intercourse it was in the heat and passion of the moment. It was, nonetheless, an event that was taken seriously and had great meaning for them. This was especially true for Mary, whose self-definition as a woman seemed to grow out of the experience. It is also clear that her justification for having sexual intercourse was built around the idea that she was pleasing and satisfying the man she loved. While not apparent in the quotations above, it was also the case that future marriage was fully expected by both Champion and Mary. Indeed, after the night they first made love, Champion started all his subsequent letters with the words "Dear Wife." While Mary only started one of her letters "My Dear Husband," she did frequently raise questions about when they would be married (Rothman, 1983, p. 402).

Historical evidence of sexual activity by unmarried men and women, coming from letters and diaries like those of Champion Chase and Mary Butterfield, are very rich in detail, but to learn more about how widespread premarital sexual intercourse was, we have to turn to a different kind of data: premarital pregnancies. Whether or not a pregnancy (or conception) has occurred before a marriage can often be deduced from the time that elapses between the date of a marriage and the date of birth of a first child. If the time between marriage and the birth of a first child is less than nine months, there is a strong possibility that it was a premarital conception (some studies have narrowed the time period to seven months, which makes the possibility of premarital intercourse even greater).

Historical researchers often use church records of marriages and baptisms to discover how many first-born children were conceived premaritally. One such study, with data coming from various New England communities, gives an interesting glimpse at how much premarital sex there has been at different times in the history of the United States (Smith, 1978). The data coming from this study, covering the period from 1700 to 1880, are especially interesting, and are shown in Figure 5.1.

During all of the eighteenth century and nearly half of the nineteenth century (until 1840), a substantial minority of American married couples conceived their first child before they were married. The figures range between twenty-three and thirty-four percent (after 1840 the percentage drops to about fifteen percent). These figures only reflect premarital pregnancies, not all premarital sexual intercourse. Since we are primarily interested in premarital sexual intercourse, we should note why these figures might be underestimations.

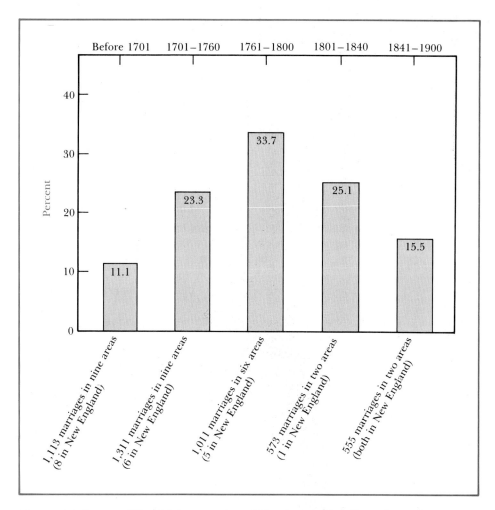

Figure 5.1 *Percent of first births occurring within nine months of marriage* (selected 17th, 18th & 19th century communities)

First, it is unlikely that all women who became pregnant while unmarried went on to marry. Some might have intentionally aborted the pregnancies, had spontaneous miscarriages, or had the children without marrying. These cases would not be reflected in Figure 5.1 because no marriages would have occurred. Second, some couples might have had sexual intercourse while unmarried and yet not have conceived a child. This could have been the result of sterility on the part of either the man or the woman, the use of some elementary form of birth control (e.g., withdrawal), or having intercourse at a time when conception was not possible. If all these considerations are taken into account, it might be possible from these data alone to guess that through long periods in American history at least one-fourth and perhaps as many as forty percent of American young people had sexual intercourse before they were married. Since the double standard of sexual behavior was probably much stronger then than it is today, we can speculate that the percentage of males having premarital sex was even greater than that for females.

In more recent historical times there is a different way of estimating the amount of premarital sexual intercourse among Americans: self-reports. While there were a number of studies of sexual behavior among college students before World War II, the breakthrough in the scholarly and scientific study of sexual behavior came in the 1950s with the publication of the work of Alfred Kinsey (Kinsey et al., 1948, 1953). The Kinsey reports of male sexual behavior, published in 1948, and female sexual behavior, published in 1953, attracted nationwide attention and gave the study of sexual behavior some legitimacy in the public mind. Kinsey and his associates conducted interviews with 5,300 males and nearly 6,000 females. However, despite these large numbers the sample was not representative of the American people because it had not been randomly drawn from the population. The Kinsey samples were strongly biased toward people who had higher educational levels. With regard to women it appears that this bias would exaggerate the amount of premarital intercourse reported, because sixty percent of the college-educated women had sexual intercourse before marriage, while for the sample as a whole the percentage was only fifty percent.

The Kinsey data did reveal some interesting twentieth-century trends. Among women born before 1900, about one-fourth revealed to the interviewer that they had had premarital sexual intercourse. Among the women born between 1900 and 1929 (who would have reached age twenty between 1920 and 1949), more than fifty percent (53%) told the Kinsey interviewers that they had had premarital sex (adapted from Reiss, 1980, p. 170). Even allowing for the greater premarital sexual activity of women at higher educational levels, it is still apparent that a great many American women in the early part of the twentieth century had sex before marriage. There are no precisely comparable data for American men, but the Kinsey sample showed, as have almost all other self-report studies, that males have rates of premarital sexual experience that are higher than females.

This brief historical review of evidence about premarital sexual intercourse reveals that it is by no means a new societal phenomenon. However, that having been said, it must quickly be added that there have been some dramatic changes in premarital sexual behavior in the last two decades. These changes have been quantitative and qualitative, which means that the numbers of unmarried people who have sexual intercourse have changed, the age at which they have intercourse has changed, and the symbolic meanings attached to premarital sex have changed.

PREMARITAL SEX TODAY

We will begin with facts. A randomly drawn sample of American teenagers living in metropolitan areas was interviewed in 1979 (Zelnik and Kantner, 1980). The following results came from these interviews:

- Of the nineteen-year-old, never-married women, 69 percent had had sexual intercourse.
- The breakdown by race was 65 percent for white women and 88.5 percent for black women.
- Of the nineteen-year-old, never-married men, 78 percent had had sexual intercourse.
- The breakdown by race was 77 percent for white men and 80 percent for black men.

From these figures alone we see that between seventy and ninety percent of unmarried American young people who live in metropolitan areas have sexual intercourse while they are teenagers. We must note also that these data do not provide the complete picture of all *premarital* sexual intercourse. Since Americans on the average do not marry until they are in their twenties, it is very likely that some of the never-married nineteen-year-olds who have not had sexual intercourse will have before they marry in their twenties. In addition, the Zelnik and Kantner study shows that among teenagers who were already married at the time of the study more than eighty percent reported having had sexual relations before marriage.

These statistics show that premarital sexual relations have increased in American society, and increased dramatically. There is also a strong indication that the age level at which young men and women are having sexual intercourse has been creeping down to even younger ages.

As an example of this age difference, we might note that the young people of the nineteenth century whose sexual experiences we considered earlier were far from teenagers. They were young adults, typically in their early twenties, who were involved in serious courtship relationships that often led to marriage. Perhaps in many cases the marriage was hastened because having sexual intercourse was a kind of implicit marriage commitment. Furthermore, as we have seen, marriage became imperative for one-quarter to one-third of the marriages in our early history when pregnancy resulted from having sexual relations. In short, we can say that until recently if people had sex before mar-

"'Adult' means 'dirty.'"

riage it was closely followed by marriage. For many people, it was literally *premarital sex*, a term we still use but which may no longer be as appropriate as it was in the past.[1]

Because of the double standard, the term *premarital sex* may not have been altogether appropriate for men in the past either. In the nineteenth and early

[1]A recently written textbook on sexuality takes issue with the term *premarital sex* because the authors feel that it ties sex too closely with a progression toward marriage. They prefer the terms *sexmaking among young singles* or *singles sex* (Nass et al., 1981, p. 141).

twentieth centuries it was considered appropriate for young men to visit prostitutes or to have relations with "loose women" in order to have sexual release and to gain sexual experience (Gagnon, 1977). So when we consider premarital sex and the changes that have occurred in the last twenty years, in a real sense the socially significant change has been in the way young women approach sex. We can consider this change and the others more effectively if we first acquaint ourselves with the concept of the *sexual script*.

SEXUAL SCRIPTS

In the opening discussion of this chapter we considered the symbolic meaning and significance of one's first sexual intercourse experience. From this case alone it can be seen that, while the act of sexual intercourse is an objective physical act, its meaning and significance vary from place to place, time to time, and person to person. A label that is becoming widely used to signify this idea is *sexual script* (Gagnon and Simon, 1973; Gagnon, 1977). The word script, of course, is taken from the language of the theater, where it refers to the instructions and words the actors are given so they will know how to act. In a similar but less specific way, we learn as a part of the society and culture we live in how to act with regard to sex: when sex is appropriate, with whom, and what it means. But this is quite abstract. We can see more clearly how sexual scripts are learned by looking at some scripts from outside our own culture. Then we can return to American society and consider the sexual scripts that are available for us, especially the scripts that can be used in the premarital years.

Premarital Sexual Scripts in Two Contrasting Societies: Ireland and Iceland

Two island societies, both located in the North Atlantic, have strikingly different views and behaviors regarding premarital sexual relations. Indeed, it would be hard to imagine two societies in which views and ideas differ more.

In Iceland in the early 1970s, seventy-five percent of all first births were to unmarried women (Tomasson, 1980, p. 94). From this fact it is obvious that sexual relations before marriage, or outside of marriage, are commonplace. A usual pattern is for an Icelandic couple to begin cohabiting and then later to become betrothed or formally engaged. Betrothal often leads to a pregnancy or the birth of a child. Marriage is likely to come when a child is on the way or has already been born. It is a very popular custom in Iceland to combine the marriage ceremony with the baptism of any child that has been born to the couple.

The Icelandic people clearly do not attach a great negative stigma to parenthood before marriage. "Unwed mothers are not looked down upon, only considered unfortunate; nor is a man stigmatized for fathering illegitimate children" (Tomasson, 1980, p. 98). While there is somewhat less illegitimacy among those Icelanders who have more education, the rates are quite high through all strata of the society. For example, over sixty percent of the first-born children of doctors and lawyers are born either illegitimately or within eight months of marriage (Tomasson, 1980, p. 96).

But the statistics and norms with regard to premarital pregnancy and birth only provide part of the picture of premarital sex. Icelandic young people report that they generally start having sexual relations at about fifteen or sixteen years of age (Tomasson, 1980). When asked about their reasons for having sexual intercourse the first time, the answers of both the boys and girls are very revealing. Almost all the young men and two-thirds of the young women report that they had sexual relations for the first time because of "curiosity" or a "sense of adventure" (Tomasson, 1980). If curiosity and a sense of adventure are the most prominent reasons for having sex, we can deduce that sex is recreational, an interesting experience that comes with growing up. There is little evidence that sex is associated with guilt, shame, or secretiveness in Iceland.

The case of Ireland is very different. Less than five percent of all reported births are illegitimate, and approximately this same percentage has persisted for nearly a hundred years (Kennedy, 1973, p. 174). Of course, the Irish may also have some premarital pregnancies that lead to hurried marriages, but even these are likely to be minimal because many marriages in the rural areas are arranged and there is almost no courtship period (see Chapter 7). Furthermore, the Irish are very moralistic about sex and rigidly control the contact and interaction between young men and women.

An example of the rigid and puritanical sexual morality of Ireland has been carefully documented in studies by Messenger (1969, 1971). Messenger and his wife, both professional anthropologists, lived on the Island of Inis Beag (a fictitious name) off the Irish coast where they studied and observed the lives of the people. These especially isolated Irish peasants probably represent an extreme in Irish traditionalism, but their behavior is at least approximated in many other parts of Ireland.

As a beginning point, sex among the Irish people of Inis Beag is rarely spoken of, *by anyone.* The result is an exceptional lack of knowledge and much misinformation about sexual matters. Young people, especially girls, are told almost nothing about sex by anyone. The boys usually hear something about sex from their peers. If young women are told anything, it is about menstruation. What little information they receive is often flawed or inadequate because their mothers have many misunderstandings and prejudices about the subject. Most young women get no information at all, so their first menstruation period is usually a very traumatic experience. In general, all things connected with sex are viewed as shameful and are mentioned as little as possible, especially by women.

Sexual intercourse is viewed as a "duty" for women, something they are obligated to "endure" as wives. There is much evidence to indicate that many of these people do not know that females can have orgasms. If they have heard of the idea they consider it deviant behavior. Men are recognized as needing and

wanting sex more than their wives, but even men believe that sexual intercourse and ejaculation can weaken them.

Boys and girls are separated in most activities at an early age, a pattern that
continues through life. During adolescence, the two sexes are kept apart almost
completely. Courtship and dating are not part of the lives of young people. The
people of Inis Beag and the anthropological observers are in agreement that on
the island of Inis Beag premarital sexual intercourse does not occur. Some
young men did boast that they had engaged in petting with women tourists and
also a few local girls. The extent of this sexual activity was limited to kissing and
some fondling outside the young women's clothing. The young men believe that
the few girls who do participate in this sexual activity get no pleasure from it.

In summary, sex and sexual intercourse among the Irish of Inis Beag is a
limited, secretive, and guilt-ridden activity. Sexual intercourse is something that
comes after marriage where its only legitimate purpose is procreation. Women
are not expected to feel pleasure from sex, and even for men it is viewed as primarily a physiological need that is periodically satisfied.

The Icelandic and Irish sexual scripts could hardly be more contrasting. If
we see a sexual script as specifying the who, what, when, where, and why of
sexual behavior (Gagnon, 1977, p. 6), then it is easy to identify these contrasts.
To Icelanders sex is for anyone who reaches physical maturity (who?). It is an
openly discussed, pleasurable activity (what?). It is appropriate when two people are in mutual agreement and have the opportunity (when and where?). And
it needs no justification other than its own pleasures and the satisfaction it
brings (why?). This does not mean that sex for Icelanders is not an expression of
love, for it often is.

For the Irish, at least those in the most traditional rural settings, the sexual
script is very different. Sex is exclusively limited to one's marriage partner
(who?). Sex is a duty for women and a physical need for men (what?). It is restricted to the marital bed, and then on a limited basis—the Irish scrupulously
avoid sex when a woman is menstruating and for months after childbirth, since
women are considered "dangerous" at those times (where and when?). Sex is
primarily for procreation and for men to satisfy a physical need (why?).

The sexual scripts of the Icelandic and Irish people are admittedly extreme.
Further, it is necessary to add that within each of these societies there are people who vary from the predominant script. For example, there is a small under-
class of urban Irish people who live in a way that is greatly at odds with the
people of Inis Beag (Peillon, 1982). These urban slum dwellers are described as
follows: "The parents exercise little control over their children, who, even at a
young age, are allowed to roam the streets . . . until late at night. Juvenile delinquency is endemic in such social conditions, and young people, left to themselves, become sexually active early on" (Peillon, 1982, p. 39). This small, deviant
segment of the Irish population does not invalidate the predominant sexual
script that guides most of the Irish people in their sexual behavior. But it does
clearly signal that within a single society there can be very different sexual
scripts. It is not unusual to find almost totally opposite sexual scripts existing

side by side within a single society. We will find this to be the case as we turn now to sexual scripts found among contemporary dating couples in the United States.

Three Sexual Scripts among Dating Couples in the United States

In Chapter 4 we introduced a study of dating couples coming primarily from four colleges in the Boston area (Rubin et al., 1981). This same sample of dating couples has provided some interesting information on sexual activities (Peplau et al., 1977). These couples, when they entered the study, thought of themselves as "going with" each other. We can assume from this that they had some type of emotional involvement and at least a partial commitment to each other. Since these were also generally college sophomores (women) and juniors (men), it is perhaps not surprising that eighty-two percent of the couples had had sexual intercourse in their current relationship. Further, seventy-four percent of the men and sixty-two percent of the women had had sexual intercourse with one or more *other* partners. Even though these figures suggest a generally liberal attitude toward sex, not all of the couples in the sample had the same sexual scripts. Three different orientations toward sex (sexual scripts) emerged.

Sexually traditional couples. One set of forty-two couples (eighteen percent of the total) had not had sexual relations in the current relationship. In some cases the males in these couples might have had some previous sexual experience, but the women were almost always virgins. Such couples were likely to reflect the double standard in their sexual attitudes, since much greater significance was placed on the virginity of the woman than the man.

While these traditional couples often expressed love for each other, this did not justify having sex. Indeed their love was partially responsible for keeping them from having sex. These couples often indicated that abstaining was a way of showing their respect and love for each other. It also showed that their feelings for each other were not simply based on physical attraction. For these couples with a traditional sexual script, sex would have to wait until marriage. As the following illustrative example shows, however, they might engage in petting that stopped just short of coitus.

> *Paul and Peggy. . . . Peggy is firmly opposed to premarital sex for herself. Raised a devout Catholic, Peggy believes that intercourse before marriage is wrong. She explained that she "can't imagine anything that would cause me to change my mind. Even if I were engaged, I wouldn't feel right about having sex." Many of Peggy's girlfriends are having sexual affairs, which Peggy accepts "for them." It's not right for Peggy, however, and she believes that Paul respects her views. For his part, Paul indicated that he would like to have intercourse with Peggy. They have engaged in extensive petting, and sometimes enjoy lying together nude. Paul commented that he sometimes finds these sexual activities more frustrating than*

satisfying, but added that intercourse "just isn't all that important for me."
He says of Peggy, "She's more conservative than I am. I'm trying to
gradually win her over to my way of thinking. (Peplau et al., 1977, p. 97)

Love justifies sex.   The most prominent sexual script in this sample of
dating couples was one that viewed sexual intercourse as permissible if the two
people loved each other. This script is the equivalent of what Reiss (1967) has labeled *permissiveness with affection*. This script does not necessarily require that
the dating couple have a long-term commitment to each other. They might be
engaged or planning marriage (perhaps vaguely), or they might not be. The key
elements of this sexual script are that mutual love is the prerequisite for sex and
that sex is an appropriate expression of the emotions and feelings of love.

For couples who held the love-justifies-sex script, sex usually came through
a gradual increase in sexual intimacy. These couples did not accept "instant sex,"
because it did not fit with their romantic view of sex as an expression of love
and caring. The following case example illustrates this sexual script:

Tom and Sandy. . . . Before they met, Sandy was a virgin, while Tom had
had coitus with three different women. Three weeks after their first date,
Tom told Sandy that he loved her. She was in love, too, and their
relationship grew quickly. In a few months they were spending weekends
together at one of their dorms. They slept in the same bed, but did not
have intercourse. Although Tom was very attracted to Sandy, he was slow
to initiate intercourse. "I didn't want to push it on her," he said. "I felt that
we shouldn't have sex until our relationship reached a certain point. Sex is
something I just can't imagine on a first date." Just before becoming
engaged, Tom and Sandy first had intercourse with each other. For Tom,
"Sex added another dimension to our relationship; it's a landmark of
sorts." (Peplau et al., 1977, p. 98).

Sex as pleasure (or sex for intimacy).   Some of the dating couples*
held a liberal view of sexual behavior, that sex did not have to be tied directly to
love or commitment. Having love was a desirable condition, but it was not a precondition for sex. Reiss (1967) labeled this sexual standard *permissiveness without affection*. Others have called it *casual sex* or *recreational sex*. Individuals or
couples with this sexual script are likely to view sexual intercourse as a pleasurable activity, one that is both expected and desired in any significant dating relationship. From this point of view, sex stands on its own merits and need not be
justified by either love or commitment. The following couple exemplifies this
sexual script:

---

*Peplau et al. (1977) do not indicate how many couples fall into this category. It is probably a
small proportion of the total number.

Diane and Alan. . . . Before they met, both Diane and Alan had had intercourse with several partners. About two weeks after they started dating, Alan asked if Diane would like to make love. She declined, saying she wasn't ready yet, but implying that she would be soon. Since they were alone in Alan's apartment, she jokingly suggested that he go "exhibit himself" across the room so she could get used to his body. They spent the weekend together, and by Sunday Diane felt ready for coitus. Diane told us that she and Alan were not in love when they first had intercourse. Nonetheless, she enjoyed the sex and felt is was "part of our getting to know each other. It led to an obvious closeness." Diane and Alan view sex as fun, and the events surrounding first intercourse suggest this playful orientation. For them, sex served as a way of developing a closer relationship. Within several months, both were in love, and their relationship continued for several years. (Peplau et al., 1977, pp. 98–99)

These three sexual scripts do catch what seems to be the essence of much contemporary thinking. The love-justifies-sex script is predominant in this particular sample of dating couples, and there is reason to believe that it is a prevailing sexual script for many unmarried couples today.

While the love-justifies-sex script is predominant, two other points must also be made. First, in different social environments (e.g., students enrolled in religious colleges, noncollege youth), the prevailing scripts might be quite different. In some settings the traditional script might prevail, in others it might be the sex-as-pleasure script that is most widely held. The second point is that there is nothing static about these scripts. At different times one might gain in importance, while another might decline. Or an entirely new sexual script for dating young people might emerge. At the moment all three scripts exist with sufficient prominence to make them viable alternatives for young people making their own decisions about sex.

ATTITUDE DIFFERENCES BETWEEN MEN AND WOMEN

The traditional couple described above (Paul and Peggy) did reveal one important aspect of sexual attitudes. Paul, as we saw, respected Peggy's conviction that sexual intercourse was wrong before marriage. She was the "gatekeeper" because her views were more traditional than his. In his words, "She's more conservative than I am." This greater conservatism among women is consistently found in research studies. For example, students at a North Carolina college were asked how many dates they should have with a person before it would be appropriate to have sexual intercourse. "Almost half the men felt it would be appropriate by the fifth date, in contrast to about 25 percent of the women" (Knox and Wilson, 1981, p. 256).

Among the couples in the Boston area sample who were not having sex, it was the men who expressed a stronger interest in having it. Even among the couples who were having sex, there was a difference between males and females. When there was an unequal interest in sex among these couples, it was the men who were more interested forty percent of the time. The women were more interested in sex only thirteen percent of the time. These few research findings show what is usually found, namely, that men are more liberal about sex and more interested in having sex.

THE CONSEQUENCES OF PREMARITAL SEX

Since so many young people have premarital sex today, it is important to ask about its consequences. One obvious and widely discussed consequence is premarital pregnancy and childbearing. The increase in sexual activity among unmarried young people has led to substantial increases in births to single women. About one in every five births in the United States today is to an unmarried woman. These births occur to women at all ages, but most are to young unmarried women. Many studies of unmarried childbearing, especially during the teenage years, have shown negative consequences for young women (Chilman, 1980; Furstenberg, 1981; Furstenberg et al., 1981; Presser, 1980). Premarital childbearing for adolescent women is associated with disrupted education, early marriage with high separation and divorce rates, and low-paying jobs and receipt of public welfare. Perhaps the most important consequences of premarital childbearing for adolescent women is that, compared to their classmates who do not become mothers, they "consistently experience greater difficulty in realizing life plans" (Furstenberg, 1981, p. 205).

But premarital sexual intercourse does not inevitably lead to pregnancy and childbearing, and there are other consequences to be considered, especially those affecting relationships and feelings about one's self.

Premarital Sex and Relationships

The study of Boston area couples discussed earlier provides some interesting information about the effects of premarital sex on the relationships. We have already seen that some of the couples had sexual intercourse early in their relationships, some only after they had been together for a time, and some never. The study also revealed that when the couples had sex, or *if* they had sex, it had no effect on the quality of the relationship, or whether it lasted. When asked "All in all, how satisfied would you say you are with your relationship?", the couples who differed on when or if they had intercourse expressed very similar levels of satisfaction. When the couples were reinterviewed two years after the beginning of the study, the researchers found that the timing of sexual inter-

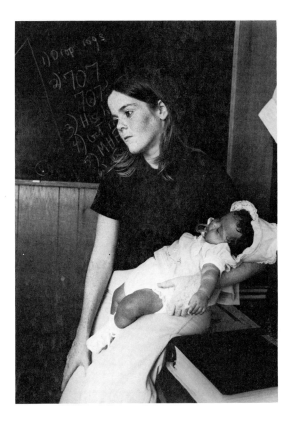

Premarital pregnancy and child-bearing in the teenage years are likely to lead to unrealized life plans.

course was not related to what had happened to the couples. In each of the three types about forty-six percent had broken up, thirty-four percent continued to date, and twenty percent had married (Peplau et al., 1977).

Another way to consider the consequences of premarital sex is to ask if it has some effect on subsequent relationships. This issue was addressed in a clever way in an experimental study that posed the following question: How are people who have differing degrees of sexual experience evaluated as potential dating partners and marriage mates? (Istvan and Griffitt, 1980). More specifically, these researchers asked if men preferred *to date* a woman who had no sexual experience, moderate sexual experience, or a high level of sexual experience, and then if men preferred *to marry* sexually inexperienced women, moderately experienced women, or highly experienced women. Women were also asked if they preferred sexually inexperienced, moderately experienced or highly experienced men as *dating partners* and as *husbands.*

In this experiment, college students at a midwestern university were first asked to complete a questionnaire that revealed their own heterosexual experience. This was done using a scale of twenty-one different sexual activities ranging from (1) one-minute continuous lip kissing to (21) (for women) mutual oral-genital manipulation with a male to mutual orgasm (Istvan and Griffitt, 1980, p.

379). The students were then told that they would make judgments about the personality characteristics of an opposite-sex individual on the basis of his (or her) responses to the sexual-activities scale. The experimenters then prepared fake questionnaires that showed individuals who had low, medium, and high levels of sexual experience.* While these questionnaires were actually created by the reseachers, the student subjects thought they were looking at real questionnaires filled out by members of the opposite sex participating in the study. The subjects were then asked to rate as potential dates and marriage mates individuals of the opposite sex who had (or so they thought) different levels of sexual experience. As it turned out, what a person preferred as a date or a marriage mate was influenced not only by the other's presumed sexual behavior but also by the person's *own* sexual experience.

Consider first what the men preferred. Men who themselves had moderate or high sexual experience preferred to date women who also had a moderate or high level of experience. With regard to marriage these men had about the same level of preference for women at all levels of experience. The big difference came from the men who were themselves sexually inexperienced. They clearly preferred sexually inexperienced women as dates and as marriage partners. They least preferred the women with high levels of sexual experience.

Women, in general, indicated that men who had a high level of sexual experience were least preferred as dates. However, the women who were themselves highly experienced did not evaluate such men as negatively as did the inexperienced and moderately experienced women. For marriage, the incxperienced and the moderately experienced women again considered the highly experienced men the least desirable. But the highly experienced women gave the highly experienced men their highest preference. For them, the least desirable marriage partners were those men who had the least sexual experience.

This experimental study does not, of course, indicate how any two people with different sexual experiences will relate to each other, but it does give us some insight into how people generally feel. There is also a reassuring complementarity in these research findings. Inexperienced men were not favorably disposed toward highly experienced women, and these women, in turn, considered inexperienced men the least preferred marriage mates. The highly experienced men were generally least preferred as dates and husbands, but the highly experienced women were fairly positive toward them, especially as potential husbands. Highly experienced men, for their part, were positive about

*Low sexual experience was defined in this study as kissing and manual touching of the clothed and nude breasts of a woman. For women, of course, this level would mean that a male had manually touched her clothed and nude breasts. Moderate sexual experience extended sexual behavior to mutual genital manipulation leading to genital secretions by the woman and ejaculation by the man. High sexual experience, in this study, included all the previous activities plus face-to-face sexual intercourse and mutual manual manipulation to mutual orgasm (Istvan and Griffitt, 1980, p. 379).

These major contraceptive methods are available to most young people today, but many who are sexually active do not use them.

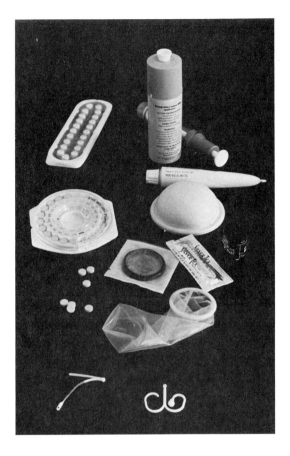

highly experienced women, especially as dates, and they also considered them acceptable as marriage partners.

These experimental research findings suggest that young people who have very different levels of sexual experience, both high and low, will be able to match up with members of the opposite sex who will find them acceptable, or even preferable. The results of this experimental study partially reflect what we saw earlier when we examined the three most common sexual scripts for dating couples. These different sexual scripts, or orientations toward sex, lead to different sexual experiences and careers. Young people, as they move through this part of their lives, adopt the scripts that suit them best. Often, though not always, they will match up in their relationships with others who have compatible scripts or will accept the script of the other.

Premarital Sexual Experience and the Self-Concept

The notion of self-concept has already been introduced. This term, which comes out of symbolic interaction theory, refers to the thoughts and feelings people have about themselves. One part of the self-concept is the degree to which people think well of themselves or have positive views about themselves. This part of the self-concept is referred to as self-esteem.

Since self-concept and self-esteem come from interaction with others, one could hypothesize that a person's self-concept would be related to sexual behavior, especially premarital sexual behavior. Researchers at the University of Wisconsin tested this hypothesis with samples of unmarried males and females who were university students and nonstudents of a comparable age (MacCorquodale and DeLamater, 1979; DeLamater and MacCorquodale, 1979). The major findings of this carefully conducted study are that premarital sexual activity is positively related to a variety of measures of self-image and self-esteem. While some of the correlations are low and could have occurred by chance, the general pattern is clear, and some specific relationships are interesting:

- The student males who had the most extensive sexual experience (number of partners, number of sexual experiences, and greatest variety of sexual experiences) were generally likely to feel that they were socially desirable, and to have self-esteem and positive feelings about their body builds and faces.
- The nonstudent males did not generally show the same correlations between extensive sexual activity and positive images about themselves. For example, having more sexual experience did not give these men positive attitudes about their body builds.
- Females, both students and nonstudents, when compared to males, had fewer significant correlations between self-image/self-esteem and their sexual behavior. However, the females who had the greatest variety of sexual experiences in their lifetimes were more likely to think of themselves as socially desirable and to feel that they had attractive faces.

There is one intriguing question that cannot be answered from this research because it is based on correlations. This question is whether the positive self-images come before or after the premarital sexual experiences. Young people who are, in fact, more socially desirable and attractive (thus their self-image may be partially based on fact) might move into heterosexual relationships more easily and when they are younger. This would lead them toward a history of more sexual intimacy by the time they reach college age. There is ample evidence that the earlier one begins, the sooner one will have more "advanced" sexual experiences (DeLamater and MacCorquodale, 1979). In concrete terms, kissing comes before French kissing, while breast and genital fondling comes before sexual intercourse, which, in turn, comes before oral-genital contact. The process is sequential, and the earlier a person begins the process, the more extensive that person's experiences will be at any given age. This could account for the correlations between positive self-images and sexual experiences. Those young people with positive self-images may have had more opportunity to start the process earlier and to arrive at sexual intercourse sooner (as well as to experience more sex and more varieties of sex).

Teenagers learn about sex and sexuality from a variety of media sources, including the music that is a prominent part of their lives.

The other possible reason for the relationship between sexual experience and positive self-image is that self-image may develop positively from the sexual experience. For males especially, since we have seen that for them sex may be viewed as an accomplishment, having success in the area of sex could enhance their self-images. For females the same reasoning would not hold, but the greater satisfaction with facial attractiveness by the sexually active women might reflect the positive evaluations they have received from their male partners.

While the causal direction of the relationship between self-image and sexual experience cannot be conclusively determined by this research, there is one statement that can be made with assurance: for this sample of students and nonstudents there is no evidence to support the notion that premarital sex produces a decline of self-image of self-esteem. Apparently, among most young people today there is not a strong feeling that they are being deviant or breaking an important societal norm when they engage in sexual relations before marriage. At least if such feelings do exist they are not strong enough to produce a negative self-concept or lowered self-esteem.

This lack of evidence for negative psychological effects of premarital sexual relations has not allayed the concerns of many people. There is, as we noted at the beginning of the chapter, more and more concern being expressed about the recent increase in sexual activity among young people. Of course, others feel that there is no special need to be concerned about the level of sex among the young. In the closing discussion of this chapter we will consider the two sides of this issue.

ISSUE

Should young people wait until marriage to have sex?

The issue here is not one of "losing one's virginity." It is possible that a person, either a man or a woman, who already had sex with someone in an earlier relationship might want to reconsider the arguments for and against having sex in a current or future relationship. One's views about sex and one's sexual behavior can change, and previous sexual experience is largely irrelevant to the discussion. If anything, previous sexual experience might give one a better basis for evaluating the arguments.

The issue of whether or not to have sex before marriage is often a difficult question in real life. Very often the question comes up in situations and circumstances that do not lend themselves to thoughtful analysis and a careful weighing of alternatives. The advantage of considering the alternative arguments here is that the context is one where there is clearly less passion. In this much less complicated situation, we will begin by considering the arguments in favor of waiting until marriage to have sex.

The Arguments in Favor of Waiting until Marriage for Sex

The most frequent and foremost argument in favor of waiting until marriage to have sex can be summarized very concisely: waiting makes both marriage and sex better. Sex is an extremely important part of marriage, especially in the early years, and if two people have been having sex long before they marry, its importance will surely be diminished. Even the excitement of sex will be lessened if sex has been a regular and routine part of the premarriage relationship.

The marriage itself is also diminished when the couple has been having sex in advance. Marriage is a significant event in a person's life; it is a transition from one status to another. Traditionally, moving into a married status has carried with it various perquisites; these are the advantages and benefits that cannot be enjoyed until the transition has been made. Sex has certainly been one of

152

these benefits, but if one has already been enjoying sex on a regular basis there will be a lessened feeling that marriage is bringing something new. The significance of marriage is thereby reduced.

A second set of arguments in favor of waiting until marriage to have sex is built around the negative consequences of having sex too early. Sex can actually confuse and confound a relationship. The pleasures of sex are often sufficiently great to convince many young people that their feelings for each other are genuine and deep. They may confuse sexual ardor and physical pleasure with something more fundamental. They may also substitute sexual interaction for other kinds of expression. Because the sexual relationship seems to convey important feelings most intensely, two people could fail to get to know each other except in a sexual sense. Even though sex might seem the best possible expression of the depth of one's feelings, that could be an illusion. A relationship built primarily on sex might be in greater danger of foundering after the sexual excitement wears off. The complementary side of this argument is that a couple should first become completely acquainted, making sure that in addition to their love they truly like and enjoy each other. If they follow this ideal until they marry, their sexual life will probably be satisfactory, and the marriage will have a good chance of lasting.

Sexual exploitation is also a factor that is not to be ignored in premarital sexual relationships. The double standard of sexual behavior, which we considered earlier in this chapter, is still present in enough cases to be important. Young women must consider whether the double standard will be used against them if they engage in sexual relations before marriage. There continue to be men who make a distinction between women they would have sex with and the woman they would marry.

As a final set of arguments in favor of waiting until marriage, there are still the remnants of some old values and practical concerns. Guilt can still intrude into premarital sexual activity. Again, this may be largely a concern of women, since they are more likely to reflect the socialization of their parents, which admonished them to keep their virginity. If guilt is not a problem, anxiety might be. Anxiety about getting caught and anxiety about becoming pregnant are both experienced often enough to be arguments against having premarital sex. Of course, the anxiety about becoming premaritally pregnant has a basis in reality. An unanticipated and unwanted pregnancy can lead to any number of undesirable decisions and outcomes. Quick and precipitous marriages are not generally advisable, if for no other reason than their high probability of ending in divorce. Abortion and adoption as ways of resolving unwanted pregnancies are frequently disrupting and disturbing for all people involved, especially the pregnant woman.

To sum up the arguments for waiting until marriage before having sex, there is first the special quality that waiting gives to both sex and marriage. Second, sex before marriage may distract a couple from developing a truly solid relationship. Third, women might be in jeopardy of sexual exploitation when they engage in premarital sexual relations. Finally, guilt, anxiety, and the negative aspects of a premarital pregnancy may be the unwanted concomitants of premarital sex.

The Arguments against Waiting until Marriage for Sex

For many young people the arguments against having sex before marriage sound as outdated as the chastity belt. They see sex as a natural human desire and experience. More important, they live in an age when contraception is easily available and there is no need to wait for marriage, which comes much later than it did a generation ago.

There was a time, not so long ago, when effective contraception was simply not available, especially to unmarried young people. The oral contraceptive, for example, did not become widely available until the 1960s, and even then single women faced some obstacles in obtaining the required prescriptions. Today, a young woman can go to a private doctor, a public health facility, or any one of a number of family-planning agencies and obtain contraceptive advice or materials with little or no difficulty. Perhaps equally important, there is little or no stigma attached to an unmarried woman asking for contraception. With contraception both physically and socially accessible, several of the problems associated with premarital sex have been minimized or eliminated.

The fact that one-half of young adults are not marrying for the first time until their mid-twenties is also an element in the acceptance of sex before marriage. Sexual maturity is demonstrably occurring at earlier and earlier ages. But sexual maturity is not simply a biological process. Young people, through music, movies, books, and their peers, are achieving earlier sexual maturity in a social as well as a biological sense. There is every reason to believe that by age fifteen young people have a high degree of awareness about sex. At that age their level of knowledge and information may not be as high as their awareness, but certainly by age eighteen most young people are fairly sophisticated about most aspects of sex. These biologically and socially mature young people are often not willing to wait as long as eight or ten years before they begin their sexual lives.

We have seen earlier in this chapter that many young people reflect another line of thinking that causes them to favor sex before marriage. They believe that sexual intimacy is a natural expression of love and commitment. Two people who love each other, and are committed to each other, can show the intensity of their bond, and at the same time strengthen it, through their sexual relationship. When sex is an expression of mutual love and commitment, the fears about sexual exploitation are substantially reduced. Of course, this suggests that sex is something that happens not at the beginning of a relationship but only after the trust and commitment have been demonstrated in many concrete ways. In other words, most of those who are positive about sex before marriage are not advocating "jumping into bed with everyone who comes along." Sex before marriage can be a responsible act and need not be a matter of living immorally or giving in to the passion of the moment.

Finally, it is sometimes argued that premarital sex, if it is with the person one is going to marry, is a kind of test of sexual compatibility. This notion is largely based on the premise that each person's sexuality is an inherent and unchanging personality characteristic. This premise may or may not be true, but it is possible that two people might be hopelessly mismatched sexually. If that were the case, they would be better off not trying to make a success of marriage.

If we assemble the arguments against waiting until marriage to have sex, the most prominent is that the waiting period is too long in view of the later age at marriage and the reduced possibilities of negative outcomes. Among the positive claims for sex before marriage there is the notion that the love and commitment two people feel for each other can be best expressed through sex. Lastly, it is sometimes argued that sex with one's prospective mate will help to avoid profound sexual incompatibility.

Themes

1. The first sexual intercourse experience is closely related to the gender role expectations for both males and females, but very differently.

2. The double standard of sexual behavior, which persists to some degree today, basically allows men more freedom in their sexual behavior then it does women.

3. Premarital sex has been in evidence throughout American history.

4. Most of our knowledge about premarital sexual behavior in the twentieth century comes from interview and questionnaire surveys and thus is based on self-reports.

5. Premarital sexual behavior has increased dramatically in recent decades and, in contrast to earlier periods, is not as closely related to marriage.

6. Sexual scripts for the appropriateness or inappropriateness of premarital sex varies from society to society, from time to time, and from person to person.

7. Premarital sex that results in pregnancies often has negative consequences, especially for young women.

8. Premarital sexual activity per se does not appear to have many negative social and psychological consequences for individuals.

Facts

1. Young women have sexual intercourse many more times with their first partners than do young men with theirs.

2. In a national study of metropolitan youth, young women who had had sexual relations were on the average 16.2 years old when they first had sexual intercourse; their partners were 19.0.

3. In the same study, young men who had had sexual relations were on the average 15.7 years old when they first had sexual intercourse; their partners were 16.4.

4. Two-thirds of the young women in the same study were "going steady with" or "engaged to" the man who was their first sexual partner. Thirty-seven percent of young men were "going steady with" or "engaged to" their first partner.

5. One historical study of colonial Puritan women showed that approximately one-third confessed to their ministers that they had had sexual intercourse before marriage.

6. During all of the eighteenth century and nearly half of the nineteenth, a substantial minority (twenty-three to thirty-four percent) of American married couples conceived their first child before marriage.

7. Kinsey's studies of sexual behavior in the twentieth century revealed that from one-fourth to one-half of American women had premarital sex.

8. In a national sample of teenagers in metropolitan areas, sixty-nine percent of nineteen-year-old, never-married women had had sexual intercourse.

9. Seventy-eight percent of nineteen-year-old, never-married men from the same sample had had sexual intercourse.

10. Black young women in American society have higher percentages of premarital sex than white young women. Black and white young men have no substantial difference in the percentage having had sexual intercourse.

11. Seventy-five percent of all first births in Iceland are to unmarried women.

12. Two-thirds of Icelandic young men and women say they had sexual relations for the first time because of curiosity and a sense of adventure.

13. Less than five percent of all reported births in Ireland are illegitimate, and this level has persisted for approximately one hundred years.

14. The preferred sexual script among a majority of college-age dating couples is that "love justifies sex."

15. Premarital childbearing for adolescent women is associated with disrupted education, early marriage with high separation and divorce rates, and low-paying jobs and receipt of public welfare.

16. Among dating couples, having sex is not related to whether couples will remain together.

17. Experimental research suggests that young men and women generally prefer members of the opposite sex who have roughly the same level of sexual experience as they have for dating and marriage partners.

18. There is no indication that having premarital sexual intercourse lowers self-esteem, and for some college-age young people sexual experience is associated with higher self-esteem.

Major Concepts

double standard of sexual behavior: Different rules relating to sexual behavior for men and women, giving more freedom to men than to women.

expressive behaviors: Behaviors associated with emotion, supportiveness, comfort, and love (see Chapter 2: Gender Roles).

instrumental behaviors: Behaviors associated with achievement and action (see Chapter 2: Gender Roles).

"love justifies sex" sexual script: Mutual love is a prerequisite for sex, and sex is an expression of love (similar to "permissiveness with affection").

"sex as pleasure" (or "sex for intimacy") sexual script: Sexual intercourse is viewed as a pleasurable activity that is expected and desired in any significant dating relationship (similar to "permissiveness without affection," "casual sex," or "recreational sex").

sexual scripts: What we learn about when and with whom sex is appropriate, and what sex means.

"sexually traditional" sexual script: A script that requires waiting until marriage before having sexual intercourse.

6

Cohabitation and Remaining Single
Living Together and Living Alone

"Do I want to get married?" That familiar old question has taken on some new meanings in recent years. In the past it usually meant, "Do I want to marry Martin?" (or ". . . Betty?", or whomever). For young people who were asking this question it was a very serious question, because they were trying to decide if "Martin" or "Betty" was *the right person*, the person with whom they wished to spend the rest of their lives. The same question, with much the same meaning, is still being asked today, but some people who ask "Do I want to get married?" are thinking of something quite different. Today, the question can mean, "Do I want to get married now, or would it be better for us to just live together for a while?" It can also mean, "Do I want to get married, or will I have a happier, more interesting, and more satisfying life if I remain single?" And for some people it might mean, "Do I want to get married *again*?"

Living together (or cohabiting),* remaining single, or remaining unmarried after a divorce are all increasingly widespread choices in contemporary life. All have become realistic options to marriage. Cohabitation has become a very popular option, especially for young people. But cohabitation is not without its critics and opponents. In this chapter we will take an extensive look at cohabitation. At the end of the chapter we will examine the arguments for and against living together before marriage.

LIVING TOGETHER, OR COHABITATION

The college campus provides an interesting place to see what has happened in the United States with regard to cohabitation. In the 1950s, at most public and private universities, males and females lived in separate dormitories (often widely separated on the campus). Males could visit female dorms, and vice versa, but they were restricted to the lobbies and common social rooms. Women

---

*Throughout this chapter the terms *cohabitating* and *living together* will be used interchangeably.

students had to be in their dormitories at a given hour (perhaps 10:00 P.M. on weeknights, 1:00 A.M. on weekends), and usually the "lockout" time was precisely observed. Being even a minute or two late could result in being restricted for a weekend. In short, male and female college students lived separately. For an unmarried college-going couple to have set up a household in the 1950s would have been regarded as scandalous behavior, a cause for expulsion from most colleges and universities.

In the 1960s college life started to change in a great many ways. The changes started with visitation rights to the rooms of members of the opposite sex, and quickly moved to coeducational dormitories and unregulated off-campus housing. But, attitudes and rules did not change overnight. In 1968 at Barnard College, in the sophisticated environment of New York City, a female college sophomore was brought before the college's judicial panel when it was learned that she was living with a man off campus. But this case and others like it soon began to sound as quaint and old-fashioned as the earlier 10:00 P.M. dormitory lockout for college women. By the mid-1970s living together or cohabiting had become a commonplace occurrence among undergraduate and, of course, graduate students. In the 1980s it is unusual for anyone to be either penalized or stigmatized for cohabiting.

There are exceptions to this general statement, since there are colleges where cohabiting is very uncommon and is considered improper when it occurs. Schools with strong religious connections often strictly prohibit cohabitation. Schools limited to either males or females are also likely to have a lower incidence of living together, at least during the normal academic year.

Since living together has emerged on college campuses, quite a number of studies have been carried out at schools around the country. On the basis of many different studies, the best estimate is that about one-fourth of all undergraduates cohabit at some time during their college careers (Macklin, 1978).

The focus to this point has been on cohabitation on the college campus, because as was noted at the outset this is where a dramatic short-term change in attitudes and behavior can be observed very easily. There is another reason that cohabitation among college students is an appropriate starting point. College students, in general, represent the middle and upper-middle classes of this society, and it is in the middle and upper-middle classes where attitudes and behaviors related to cohabiting have changed most. In the span of a decade cohabiting became respectable (or nearly so) in the middle classes. Before the 1960s there were unmarried couples who lived together, but such behavior was clearly concentrated in the lower strata of the society, and the views of the rest of the society were predictably negative about it.

When an unmarried couple lived together long enough it was held to be a common-law marriage, but the very term *common-law marriage* was a stigma, and in the minds of many people it was associated with members of the society who were breaking societal norms, religious principles, and even, in some sense, state or local laws. One rarely hears anyone today saying they live in a common-law relationship or marriage. The term *living together* suggests something different. It does not carry the same negative connotations even though the objective facts—living together in a marriagelike state—are almost exactly identical. The act of living together while unmarried has clearly moved up in the social class structure in the last fifteen years.

That upward movement of cohabitation in the social class structure has sometimes given the impression that cohabitation occurs most frequently among college students and college graduates. This impression is further encouraged because so many research studies have been done among college students. Also, the mass media have perpetuated the idea that cohabitation is found primarily among college students and the better educated. Despite the shifts that have occurred, however, it is still true that cohabitation is found most frequently among the less well educated members of the society—particularly those who have less than a high school education.

The educational and other characteristics of cohabiting couples can be seen most clearly in studies of the national population, and fortunately we do have such studies. The United States Bureau of the Census periodically draws a random sample of Americans who are fourteen years of age or older. This sample survey, called the Current Population Survey, is conducted primarily to obtain information about national employment and unemployment patterns and a number of other economic and demographic characteristics of the population. Beginning in 1967, and every four years since, a marital history supplement has been added to the Current Population Survey. This supplement provides a wealth of statistical information on American households and living arrangements. As the cohabitation trend started to grow, this Census Bureau survey has provided our most authoritative information on the trend (Glick and Norton, 1979; Glick and Spanier, 1980; Spanier, 1983).

Before examining a few statistical facts about cohabitation, there is an issue of definition that must be addressed. A formal definition of cohabitation has not yet been offered here because it is assumed that nearly everyone reading this book already has a basic idea of what the term has come to mean in American society. Later we will consider some of the distinctions that can be made about various types of cohabiting couples, but that can wait. The Census Bureau takes a very straightforward approach to the issue of definition when its interviews are conducted. For purposes of classification an unmarried cohabiting couple is one where only two adults, a man and a woman, unrelated and not married to each other, share a household (house, apartment, group of rooms, or a single room). There may or may not be children present. The Census Bureau interviewers do not ask if these two adults have a commitment to each other, or an emotional involvement, or if they have a sexual relationship. While any or all of these factors might seem to us to be important elements in a cohabiting relationship, the Census Bureau does not consider it prudent or appropriate for a government agency to probe into these matters. The result is that some households will be labeled as cohabiting couples when there is no romantic or sexual relationship. A female landlady and a male tenant, even when one might be old and the other young, would be classified as cohabiting. An older man with a live-in female housekeeper would also be so classified. Out of the nearly two million couples classified by the Census Bureau as living together, only a small minority are thought to be of these latter types (Glick and Spanier, 1980; Spanier, 1983), so the number of such cases is not likely to be great enough to distort the statistics. What, then, do we know about cohabiting couples?

COHABITING COUPLES—STATISTICS FROM NATIONAL SAMPLES

The first and unsurprising statistic is that the *number* of unmarried cohabiting couples in the United States has gone up greatly. The extent of this increase is shown in Figure 6.1. In 1970 cohabiting couples in the United States numbered 523,000 (or 1,046,000 men and women). By 1984 the number had increased to approximately two million couples, or four million men and women (U.S. Bureau of the Census, 1984). That is a 280 percent increase in the number of cohabiting couples, but to view this figure realistically we must note that the number of people between the ages of eighteen and thirty-five (the prime ages for cohabiting) also increased. The 18–35 age group grew by about forty percent between 1970 and 1984. Considering that the cohabiting population increased by 280 percent, there can be no doubt about the increasing importance of cohabitation in American society. Even if one takes into account that people surveyed in the 1980s are more willing than people might have been in 1970 to reveal that they are cohabiting, the increase is still dramatic.

There is another way that the statistics can be examined, however. Rather than focus on the absolute number of cohabiting couples, it is also revealing to compare cohabiting couples with the number of married couples in the United States. For example, in 1980 only about four percent of all couples living in households in the United States were unmarried (Spanier, 1983). The other ninety-six percent of couples in households were married. While this statistical "snapshot" of one particular time does not reveal what percentage of people have cohabited or will cohabit at some time in their lives, it does serve as a reminder that not "everyone is doing it."

The data coming from the national survey of the population also provide information on the characteristics of cohabitants in the United States.

Age

As suggested above, cohabiting couples are likely to be young adults. Approximately two-thirds of the men and three-fourths of the women who are co-

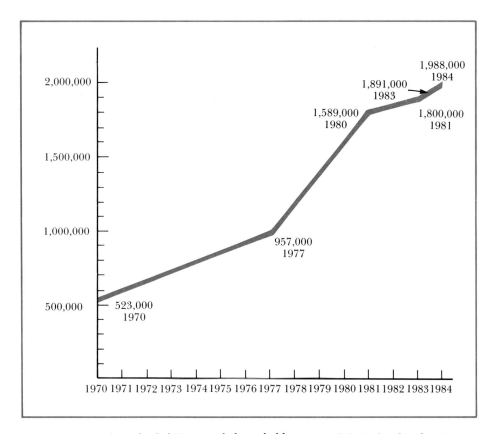

Figure 6.1 *Number of cohabiting-couple households* (*Source:* Glick, Paul and Arthur J.
Norton. Marrying & Divorcing and Living Together in the U.S. Today. *Population
Bulletin*, Population Reference Bureau, Inc. 1977. U.S. Census Bureau. *Statistical Abstract
of the United States: 1985* (105th edition) Washington, D.C., 1984.)

habiting are under thirty-five. Twenty-six percent of the men and eighteen
percent of the women are between thirty-five and sixty-four. Slightly more than
five percent of cohabiting adults are sixty-five and over.

The cohabiting adults 65 and over are of special interest because between
1970 and 1980 their numbers did not increase. The lack of change in this group
is interesting because we might have expected the opposite. One reason for expecting an increase is that the number of older people in the population increased during the 1970s. Also, one might expect that older people would have
been less reluctant to reveal their cohabitation in 1980 than they were in 1970.
Despite these factors, those sixty-five and over did not appreciably increase
their cohabiting numbers. One explanation might be a change that was made in

Social Security regulations. Before the change, two older single people, each receiving Social Security benefits, would have suffered a net reduction in benefits if they married. The regulations were changed in the 1970s, removing this "marriage penalty" and probably allowing some older people to marry instead of cohabit (Spanier, 1983).

Marital Status

Initially one might suppose that cohabiting couples would, by definition, be single. But that is not the case. About eight percent of all cohabiting adults in 1981 were married—not to the person they were living with, but to someone else (Spanier, 1983). Apparently, many such people were in the process of obtaining divorces, or were simply separated from their legal spouses.

Of course, there were substantial numbers of previously married adults in the cohabiting population. In fact, nearly half the cohabiting adults (forty-seven percent of the men and forty-five percent of the women) had been previously married. It is more likely that a previously married man will be cohabiting with a never-married woman than vice versa. While the never-married cohabiting adults tend to be under thirty-five years of age, those who have been previously married are spread fairly evenly over the age spectrum.

Children

As might be expected, if nearly half of cohabiting adults have been married, there are often children present in cohabiting homes. In 1981 slightly over a quarter (27.8 percent) of cohabiting homes had children in them. This percentage has actually gone down since 1970, when 37.5 percent of cohabiting homes had children. The reduction in this percentage might simply be due to the fact that young, never-married cohabitants increased in numbers and made up a larger proportion of all cohabitors.

It is interesting to consider some implications of children living with cohabiting parents. Children of divorced parents might have one or even both parents cohabiting. For these children, the implicit message coming from their parents is that marriage is not necessary for a sexual, emotional relationship. Children who have a cohabiting parent (or parents) are still a very small proportion of all children (probably less than one percent of all children at any one time), but for them it is a socialization experience that is surely going to influence their adult attitudes and behaviors.

Education

Cohabiting adults are found at all educational levels. For cohabiting males under the age of thirty-five, 19 percent have not finished high school, 37 percent are high school graduates, 26 percent have some college, and 18 percent are college graduates or more. These percentages are a close reflection of the overall educational attainment levels of the population under thirty-five. Among cohabiting women under thirty-five, those who have never married have nearly the same educational levels as the men. Cohabiting women under thirty-five who have been previously married, however, have distinctly lower educational levels. Only about 30 percent of them have been to college.

Race

Black Americans of all ages have cohabitation rates that are higher than the rates for white Americans. The differences are especially great in the population at ages thirty-five and over. Below thirty-five the rates of cohabitation for blacks and whites are closer, and the gap closed somewhat in the period between 1975 and 1980 (Spanier, 1983).

In summary, there have been three major trends in cohabitation since 1970. First, the number of cohabitants and the rate of cohabitation have increased greatly. Second, there has been a movement away from cohabitation occurring primarily among the less educated, lower strata of the society. Third, cohabitation has increased especially rapidly among the population under twenty-five. It has become such a familiar pattern among young adults that it is now often considered an additional step in the American courtship process.

Before taking a closer look at what cohabiting is like in contemporary life, we might note that cohabitation has also been increasing in many Western countries. As we will see, the United States has not been the pacesetter in cohabitation.

EUROPEAN TRENDS IN COHABITATION

The brief look at Iceland in the last chapter revealed that most Icelandic couples live together before they marry. Very often a child is on the way, or already born, when the actual marriage occurs. This pattern is also found in some other European countries, though not always to the same degree. Sweden seems to lead the way, with ninety-nine percent of married couples saying they lived together before marriage (Cherlin, 1979; see also, Lewin, 1982). A survey of married couples in Denmark reveals a similar but not so pronounced pattern, with eighty percent of married couples saying that they had previously lived together ("Cohabiting in Europe," 1981). In both Sweden and Denmark, many cohabiting couples have children, but even that does not necessarily prompt them to marry. In Denmark a quarter of the young cohabiting couples have children, while in Sweden the rate is somewhat higher ("Cohabiting in Europe," 1981).

These are clear indications that in both Sweden and Denmark, for a substantial number of couples, cohabitation is an acceptable substitute for marriage.

That does not seem to be the case with some other European countries. In France there has been a rapid increase in the amount of cohabitation, but it is not viewed in the same way as in the Scandinavian countries. Among French couples who married in 1976 and 1977, forty-four percent had lived together before their marriages. But cohabitation in France is for a shorter period of time (an average of just under 18 months), and by age thirty most people have married (eighty percent of the men and eighty-four percent of the women). The French almost invariably marry in the event of a pregnancy, or if a couple wishes to have children (Festy, 1980).

In assessing the European cohabitation experience, it is clear that, historically, Sweden and Denmark (along with Iceland) started the trend. In these countries the pattern was well established before it came to the United States or other European countries. It will be very interesting to see if the acceptance of cohabitation as a substitute for marriage will spread to other European countries and to the United States. Viewed from this perspective, cohabitation becomes a question of norms and social custom rather than just behavior. Most Swedish observers claim that cohabiting is seen as normal, nonstigmatized, and socially acceptable behavior. As one Swedish writer puts it, "Twenty years ago the parents of a son or daughter cohabiting with someone of the opposite sex without being married would never have admitted that to friends. . . . But now we would not even talk of 'admitting' it, for that implies that the action admitted is deviant. Indeed, we can now say that, far from being deviant, cohabitation has become a social institution [in Sweden]" (Trost, 1980, p. 19).

As we turn our attention to cohabitation norms and customs in the United States, we must return to a consideration of the meaning of cohabitation in the 1980s.

THE MEANING OF COHABITATION
IN THE UNITED STATES

One of the most prominent experts on cohabitation wrote in 1978, "Nonmarital cohabitation is fast becoming a part of the dominant culture in this country and it seems likely that in time to come a majority of persons will experience this lifestyle at some point in their life cycle" (Macklin, 1978, p. 1).

As we have already seen, cohabitation has become increasingly prevalent, but for a phenomenon to become a part of "the dominant culture," it must be accepted by the majority of people. One could also argue that such a behavior would have to be *expected of* the majority of a population. So we must ask, how do Americans feel about cohabitation today? One answer to this question can be found in public opinion polls with national population samples. Since 1980 a number of polls and surveys have included questions about living together. For example, in 1982 in a survey done for the Merit Report, the following question was asked: "In general do you approve or disapprove of unmarried adults of the opposite sex living together?" Just about one-half of the population (forty-nine percent) disapproved. Women disapproved more than men (fifty-four and forty-three percent, respectively), and people with low incomes disapproved more than people with high incomes. Perhaps there is a higher disapproval rate among people with lower incomes because there are more older people in the low-income group. Older people are generally more conservative on social issues, and thus are more likely to disapprove of cohabitation. Among adults between eighteen and thirty-four, twenty-nine percent disapproved; among adults thirty-five to forty-nine, fifty-one percent disapproved; and among adults fifty and over, seventy-one percent disapproved (Merit Report, 1982).

These general public opinion questions give us some insight into how Americans currently feel about cohabitation, but the generality of the questions obscures some important differences among types of cohabitation. To see these differences with greater clarity, a simple typology will be useful.

A Typology of Living Together

In order to measure the amount of nonmarital cohabitation among college students, one researcher used the following definition: "sharing a bedroom and/or a bed for four or more nights a week for three or more consecutive months with someone of the opposite sex to whom one is not married" (Macklin, 1978, p. 3). This definition seems to many people to be a very minimal standard. Sharing a bedroom and/or a bed for as little as four nights a week might simply mean that two people have a relatively steady sexual relationship. They also probably have an emotional commitment, but with these minimal terms this kind of living together is not like a marriage. We will call this kind of cohabitation, which falls at the minimum end of the scale, *part-time/limited cohabitation*.*

Part-time/limited cohabitation. There is a general pattern that occurs among many unmarried heterosexual couples, a pattern that can be called "drifting into cohabitation" (Macklin, 1974). The pattern often goes something like this: Two people meet and start seeing each other. After a while, if their individual living circumstances allow it, one person of the couple will start spending time at the residence of the other. At first it might be to share meals, study together, watch television, listen to music, or some other activity. The visits may

---

*This has also been referred to as the *temporary casual convenience* type and the *affectionate dating–going together* type (Macklin, 1978, p. 4).

extend over longer periods of time as the relationship grows and deepens. This might include staying overnight when the occasion allows (Friday and Saturday nights, for example). As the staying over becomes more frequent, the "visitor" brings more and more of his or her personal belongings. Toothbrushes, hair dryers, clothes, shoes, books, records, and so on are often the first things to be left in the other person's place. This can go on for some time, with the two people nominally keeping their own separate residences but spending two, three, four, or more nights a week together. Often there is no specific decision to live together. The decision, if it can be called that, is made after the fact. One day, after most of the clothes, books, and belongings have been moved in, one of the partners might say, "Well, I guess we're living together, aren't we" (Jackson, 1983, p. 43).

Since there is often no actual decision to move in together, there is also often a failure to decide other issues that are important for a cohabiting couple. They might not have established the degree to which their relationship is an exclusive relationship. They might not have worked out the details of the economic arrangements (rent, groceries, utilities, phone). And they might very well have failed to establish how their relationship is related to marriage.

Cohabiting couples who start with a part-time/limited relationship eventually reach a circumstance or situation that either changes or ends their cohabitation. Often the relationship will end because of some precipitating event. Sometimes the event is external, such as the end of a school year or the end of the summer. Other times the event is internal to the relationship of the couple. They may have a breakup or simply reach a mutual agreement to go their separate ways. Studies of American cohabiting couples, especially those who are college students, have found the average length of cohabitation to be very short. In a study carried out at Pennsylvania State University, eighty-two percent of the males and seventy-five percent of the females said their longest period of cohabitation was less than six months (Peterman et al., 1974).

On the other hand, some relationships that begin as part-time/limited cohabitation move to a more intense level, which is to say that they become more marriagelike. This leads to the second type of cohabitation: premarital cohabitation.

Premarital cohabitation. When two people plan to marry, but live together in the meantime, it can be called *premarital cohabitation*. One variant of premarital cohabitation is called *trial marriage*. The distinguishing feature of trial marriage is that the emphasis of the couple is on testing the relationship before making a final commitment (Macklin, 1978).

While premarital or trial marriage cohabitation are different in some ways, they do have some common characteristics. The cohabiting couple will typically have a single domicile, which they maintain and manage jointly. This means, in addition to carrying out the day-to-day operations of a household, that the couple is also likely to make joint purchases and share economic resources. This is often done with an awareness and expectation that at some later time they will be married.

This belief that a marriage, in all likelihood, will be in the offing is what separates premarital and trial marriage cohabitation from the final type of cohabitation: substitute marriage.

Substitute marriage. The substitute marriage form of cohabitation is a long-term commitment between two people without a legal marriage. There may be different motivations among the people who choose cohabitation over marriage, but one obvious possibility is that one or both partners is still legally married to someone else. Or perhaps a divorced person, having been affected by a previous marriage, is reluctant or resistant to enter another marriage. It could simply be that one or both members of the couple feel that "a piece of paper" is not important when two people are committed to each other.

Our previous discussion of cohabitation in Sweden, Denmark, and Iceland suggests that substitute marriage is now widely accepted in those countries. That conclusion might be tempered a little by some research on cohabiting couples by Swedish investigators. In one such study the author concluded that in Sweden "unmarried cohabitation is not an alternative to marriage but rather a variety of it" (Lewin, 1982, p. 763). This statement means that most cohabiting Swedish couples do not have objections to marriage. Cohabiting couples accept the same marital norms as married couples, especially including shared economic responsibility and sexual exclusiveness. Finally, and perhaps significantly, the majority of the cohabiting Swedes (sixty-five percent of the men and fifty-three percent of the women) "believed that they would marry their present partner" (Lewin, 1982, p. 766). The only category of cohabitors who did not seem inclined to marry were those few who had three children and had been cohabiting for at least ten years. Thus, even in Sweden, where there is seemingly very little social pressure to marry, most cohabitants still plan to marry. Even in a country where substitute-marriage cohabitation is well established, the arrangement may not be a permanent substitution.

There are probably other types of cohabitation that could be identified among the nearly two million cohabiting couples in the United States today. However, the three types we have considered (part-time/limited, premarital or trial marriage, and substitute marriage) probably cover most cohabitants. Yet even with only these three types we can see that it is misleading to treat all cohabiting couples as if they were the same.

Responses to types of cohabitation. It is also important to recognize that people respond differently to these three types of cohabitation. Parents of young people, for example, are likely to have negative attitudes about their sons and daughters cohabiting on a part-time/limited basis. This type of cohabitation may, in their view, be nothing more than "shacking up," or having a sexual relationship without making a serious commitment. This response is well illustrated by the letter of a father to his college-age daughter after she had announced that she and her boyfriend were planning to live together for the summer:

> *Why then do I object to your living with John?*
>
> *One reason by which you sought to justify your decision is that you and John plan to be married eventually; and so, you agreed, since you are both sincere and deeply committed to one another, why should you have to wait to enjoy one another's total companionship?*
>
> *I countered by suggesting that you get married now. You replied that it would be impractical because you will have to live apart next winter when you go back to school and he stays here on his job. Marriage under those conditions would, you said, impede the freedom of each of you.*
>
> *This, I believe, cuts right to the heart of the matter. You and John appear to have made a "commitment," but you don't want to be all that committed to it. (Leonard, 1981, p. 125)*

In the United States today there is likely to be an equally negative reaction to cohabitation as a substitute for marriage. The disapproval is likely to be more intense if children are born to a cohabiting couple.

At the present time, the greatest level of acceptance is likely to be given to premarital, trial marriage cohabitation. Some parents have been known to counsel their children to try living together before "jumping into marriage." This reaction is often the case when elder siblings have entered marriages precipitously and divorced a few years later. Parents, under these conditions, can often take a much more benign view of their children cohabiting, because they believe this experience may have some positive consequences.

The *experience* of cohabitation and its consequences have been topics of considerable discussion, speculation, and research, and we will now turn to this issue.

The Cohabitation Experience and Its Consequences

On one point there is strong and persistent evidence: both men and women who cohabit view their experience positively (Macklin, 1978). From the cohabitants' viewpoint, the rewards exceed the costs. They especially feel that cohabiting develops "personal growth and maturity" (Macklin, 1978, p. 7). Studies have shown that cohabitants are more likely to see themselves positively as persons. In an early study by Arafat and Yorburg (1973), for example, cohabiting college students were more likely to characterize themselves as independent, outgoing, and aggressive. Studies also show that cohabitants are more satisfied with their social and sexual relationships than are noncohabitants (Risman et al., 1981; Peterman et al., 1974). This is not too surprising since a major motivation for going into a cohabiting relationship is the desire for a closer, more affectionate and exclusive sexual relationship. Judging from the evaluations of cohabitants, they attain these goals, at least in the short run.

While most cohabitants are in agreement that the experience is positive (at least on balance), that should not hide the fact that there are also some negative features of cohabitation.

Differences in motivations and intentions.   Very often, it appears, there is a difference between partners in the motivations and intentions they have regarding living together. In many cases when females enter cohabiting relationships, they do so with the notion (or the hope) that this is the first step toward marriage, or at least a greater level of commitment from their partners. Males, on the other hand, are less likely to be thinking of marriage and more likely to be seeing the relationship in practical or convenience terms (Jackson, 1983; see also Lyness et al., 1972; Arafat and Yorburg, 1973). In the study by Arafat and Yorburg the disparity was stated even more bluntly. As a principal motive for living together, the most frequent first choice for males was sex, while for females it was marriage. One woman student in this study said, "It's a first step toward marriage, and if I don't grab him somebody else will." (Arafat and Yorburg, 1973, p. 102).

The lower level of significance and importance attached to cohabiting by males is further revealed by the following statement from a man describing what happened when he suggested living together:

> *When I first asked her she looked at me like I was asking her a momentous thing. And I scratched my head, because it wasn't momentous to me. . . . I think we discussed that once, and she said, "You don't attach much importance to this," "No" (he said), "it's just that you can come and stay with me, that's all." (Jackson, 1983, p. 41)*

Certainly, not all females who cohabit wish to marry, and not all males are uninterested or opposed to marriage. But there is some tendency for this disparity of intentions or motivations to exist, especially among the young and not previously married.

Men and women who have been divorced are especially interesting in this regard. For them, living together can be an alternative to marrying again. They may be apprehensive about marriage, or, at the least, living together may be a test or trial to make sure that a marriage has a chance of working. One woman, a divorcee, describes this view by recounting a conversation she had with the mother of the man with whom she was living:

> *One day over lunch . . . [his mother] said that she didn't approve but that she couldn't interfere with that kind of thing. At that point I laid it on her, "Look, I've been married before." That was kind of hard for me to do. . . . I didn't want her telling everybody that I had been married before and that her son was dating a divorcee, living with a divorcee. So I just said, "Look,*

there is no way I would consider marrying him unless I lived with him." I was not going to go through another relationship and get divorced again because I didn't know what I was getting into. (Jackson, 1983, p. 50)

While differences in motivations and intentions between cohabiting partners may be one problem area, it probably is not the most serious. By all accounts, the most serious problem of cohabiting couples is dealing with the negative reactions and responses of other people, especially parents.

Negative responses of others. We noted at the beginning of this chapter that as recently as the 1960s some colleges and universities still penalized students for cohabiting. By the 1970s colleges and universities, with the exception of some conservative and religious schools, had given up trying to govern this part of student life. Some other organizations did not adapt so quickly, however. In the late 1970s an FBI agent in Washington, D.C. was threatened with dismissal unless he ceased living with a woman to whom he was not married. At about the same time a woman in Virginia who was a law school graduate was not allowed to take the bar examination in that state because she was cohabiting with a man. While this latter case was overturned by the courts, it does show that a person can be penalized or stigmatized for cohabiting. There are very likely many occupations, professions (clergy, politics), and communities (small towns), that still create problems for cohabiting couples. But, these negative reactions are becoming more and more isolated and unusual.

Most often negative reactions to cohabitation come from the parents of cohabitants. From the very earliest studies of college student cohabitants to some of the most recently reported research, parents are still cited as a major source of problems (Macklin, 1972; Jackson, 1983).

Concealment and pretense are still used by many cohabiting couples because they fear that if their parents learn about their living together there will be reprimands and penalties. Often cohabiting couples are located some distance away from parents, usually going to school or working. In either case, this very distance from parents provides the initial opportunity for cohabitation. But parents do keep in touch with their children by telephone calls and occasional visits. Both of these are potential sources of stress for cohabiting couples who are trying to conceal their behavior.

Very often the telephone is the most immediate source of danger, since one partner might answer when the other partner's parents call. This dilemma is often solved by having a rule about answering. Only the ostensible resident of the apartment or house is to answer the phone. One male cohabitant described how he handled this situation:

So I could never answer the phone. They [her parents] call a lot.

Interviewer: What about when you were home alone?

Respondent: I just didn't answer the phone for six months. (Jackson, 1983, p. 45)

While the telephone problem can be handled by rigid adherence to the rules, the visit of a parent (or parents) is even more difficult. When the visit is announced in advance, the apartment or rooms have to be reordered to remove any traces of the partner living there. This is inconvenient at the least, and in many cases it is stressful and difficult. While the announced visit can be handled, the unannounced visit is nearly impossible to manage. And although such experiences might make good scenes for television situation comedies, in real life couples often find the task of concealing their relationship very stressful (Jackson, 1983).

In order to avoid the problems and the dishonesty that grow out of concealing a cohabiting relationship, some couples either tell or indirectly reveal to their parents what they are doing. This can create a new set of problems when parents cannot accept the behavior, or accept it with open disapproval or reluctance. Often couples will tell only a selected family member that they are cohabiting. This would be the member most likely to be understanding, who would then act in collusion to help keep the secret from the person who would be most upset. Obviously, family relationships of all kinds can be harmed by secretiveness, collusion, dishonesty, and guilt. While more and more parents are accepting the cohabitation of their children, though perhaps without enthusiasm, many others are still upset by it and opposed to it. The response of parents remains as one of the most common problems of living together.

DIVISION OF LABOR, TRADITIONAL GENDER ROLES, AND COHABITATION

Since cohabitation came into prominence about the same time as the women's movement, there was some early expectation that living together would introduce a new equality in relations between males and females. That hope was considerably diminished when early studies found cohabitants to be little different from married couples in breaking away from the traditional male and female roles. One researcher summarized this point by saying, "one cannot make the assumption that because people violate conventional norms and engage in cohabitation that they are therefore 'liberated' and striving for sex role equality" (Whitehurst, as quoted in Jackson, 1983, p. 44).

The persistence of traditional male and female roles is illustrated in interviews conducted by the author of this book with two cohabiting couples. In one couple the woman was a student, while her partner worked full-time. When asked who cooked the meals and washed the dishes, the couple agreed that it was the woman, since the man was tired after working all day. In the other couple the woman worked while the man was a student. This couple agreed that the woman handled the cooking and cleaning because the man had to study in the evenings.

When cohabiting couples were compared with couples who were just "going together," the cohabiting males were more liberal in their *attitudes* about

Cohabitating couples have to make a variety of daily decisions in which it becomes apparent that males often dominate in decision making.

gender roles. The females in this study did not differ in their attitudes about gender roles (Risman et al., 1981). However, despite the more liberal attitudes of cohabiting males, it appears that in their actual relationships they may still often dominate their female partners. When cohabiting women are asked about the power relationship they have with their male partners, they are much more likely to report male domination than are women who are not cohabiting, but who are "going with" someone (Risman et al., 1981). One interpretation of this difference is that cohabiting couples have had to make numerous decisions related to household tasks, the use of money, and other day-to-day things. Under these conditions of everyday living, perhaps the male dominance that is built into traditional gender roles reveals itself more often and more clearly. Thus, it may be easier for couples who are just going with each other to maintain the illusion of an egalitarian relationship (Risman et al., 1981).

In a study comparing college students who were cohabiting with college students who were married, there were some signs that married couples were more traditional about gender roles than were cohabiting couples (Stafford et al., 1977). This research focused on the division of labor in household tasks (cooking, dishwashing, vacuuming, laundering, cutting the lawn, washing the car, emptying the garbage, and others). The question the research addressed was whether the married or the cohabiting couples would have the most equality in the list of tasks. Another way to put the question is, will married or cohabiting couples have the greatest segregation in household tasks along traditional male-female lines?

The key differences showed up in the actual performance of the various tasks. Cohabiting males and females were consistently more likely to say that they shared equally in tasks that have traditionally been assigned to females in the home. For example, 36 percent of cohabiting males said that they shared the cooking equally with their partners. Only 18.5 percent of the married males said they shared equally in the cooking. Note, however, that in the majority of cases among both cohabiting and married couples, the woman did more of the cooking (77.7 percent of the married couples, 52 percent of the cohabitants). When females were reporting, the picture was generally the same; married women did more of the tasks traditionally assigned to women than did cohabiting women. This latter pattern appeared across the board in this study, as it has in others, leading the researchers to assert, "Among both married and cohabiting couples, the women are taking most of the responsibility for, and performing most of, the household tasks" (Stafford et al., 1977, p. 50).

As a summary statement about the division of labor and traditional gender role orientations, the research suggests that cohabiting couples do differ from both couples who are going together and married couples. Compared to the going-together couples, the cohabiting males dominate their relationships more often by exercising more power in decision making. This is the case even though their gender role attitudes are less traditional than those of males in going together couples (Risman et al., 1981). Compared to married couples, cohabitants share traditional household tasks somewhat more equitably (though women still do more of them). There is at least the suggestion in these research findings that traditional gender role behavior becomes stronger or more salient as couples move toward and into marriage.

COHABITATION AND MARITAL SUCCESS

The question asked more than any other about cohabitation is, "Does living together before marriage improve the chances of marital success?" There are several logical reasons for hypothesizing that cohabitation will lead to better, happier, and more successful marriages. First, if cohabitation allows two people to live together in a marriagelike situation, and they learn from this experience that they are not suited to each other, then they will have avoided entering into a marriage that would probably have been unhappy and unsatisfactory. From this point of view, in the society as a whole, many potentially unhappy and unsatisfactory marriages may have been avoided in the last decade and a half. Since the marriages that were averted never took place, it can never be proved that they would have been unhappy and unsatisfactory. All that is known is that some substantial number of couples tried living together, found it unsatisfactory, and went their separate ways.

The second logical reason for expecting cohabitation to lead to more successful marriages lies in the presumed learning experience of cohabiting. This learning includes specific knowledge about one's partner, which goes beyond what one learns in the usual romantic and courtship behavior. By living with someone it is inevitable that one will learn some of the negative features that might go undetected otherwise. If one then marries that person, there will be fewer illusions to be shattered, and the marriage should be more satisfactory.

There is also a more general sense in which a person should learn from cohabitation. One learns what it is like to go through the everyday ups and downs with a partner. The romantic notion that living with someone will be one long honeymoon is usually dispelled by the experience of living together. Thus, even if one does not marry the person with whom one has cohabited, a more realistic approach to marriage may be the result. Again, it is usually assumed that a more realistic and experienced entry into marriage will increase the chances of marital success.

While these arguments seem plausible, researchers have not had much success in showing that cohabitation has the expected effects on marriage. First, as suggested above, when two people cohabit and then break up there is no way to know what would have happened had they actually married. The most common research strategy to learn whether cohabitation makes marriages more successful is to focus on married couples, dividing them into those who did and those did not cohabit before marriage. The following summaries attempt to capture the main points of three studies of this type.

The subjects of one study were black and white married college students from two southern universities. Sixty-five percent had cohabited before marriage (not necessarily with the person they married), and thirty-five percent had not. The aspects of the marital relationship studied included sexual satisfaction, open communication, perceived attractiveness of spouse, and satisfaction of needs. In general previous cohabitants did not differ significantly from noncohabitants. However, previous cohabitants did consider their spouses slightly more attractive sexually (Jacques and Chason, 1979).

The subjects of a second study were Canadian married couples coming from all economic strata and diverse educational levels of the community. On a standard marital adjustment measure the married couples who had not previously cohabited had higher scores (greater adjustment). The difference came mostly from females, and primarily on two dimensions of marital adjustment. Specifically, women who had not cohabited prior to marriage were more likely to say there was "high agreement or consensus between themselves and their spouses on most issues" and were also more likely to be "happy or satisfied" with their marriages. In these aspects of marital adjustment the couples who had not previously cohabited came out with better marriages (Watson, 1983).

The big test of the success of a marriage is whether or not it lasts, and a third study addressed this issue. From California marriages that took place in 1972, researchers set out to learn which ones were still intact in 1976. Thirty-one percent had ended in divorce after four years, but there was no difference between the marriages that were preceded by cohabitation and those that were not (Newcomb and Bentler, 1980).

There are a number of other studies of varying quality that have also dealt with the issue of whether premarital cohabitation improves the quality or successfulness of marriage (see Macklin, 1978). Generally these studies found no differences that could be attributed to living together before marriage.

What, then, does this mean? The research evidence does not show that cohabitation before marriage makes marriages more successful, satisfactory, or durable. The expectation of benefits that some have had for cohabitation have not been demonstrated by the kind of research that has been done to date.

But we should note that there is a complicating factor that makes research on this issue difficult. The people who choose to cohabit are different in a number of respects from those who do not. Cohabitants are likely to be less religious and less traditional. Cohabiting females are more likely to describe themselves as competitive, aggressive, and independent than are noncohabiting females (Macklin, 1978). This could be why one study found couples who had cohabited to be more likely to disagree about finances, household duties, and recreation. Also, couples who had cohabited were less dependent on their spouses, considered marriage a less intrinsic part of their lives, had broken up more often, and had sought marriage counseling more frequently (Chatsworthy and Schied, cited in Macklin, 1978). The same personal characteristics that cause people to choose cohabitation in the first place may also produce some of the characteristics that are taken as signs of marital dissatisfaction and instability.

Cohabitation before marriage is a phenomenon that remains too new as a social behavior for us to understand everything about it and its effects. As a society we are still in the process of changing attitudes about cohabitation, as well as the very behavior. Nonetheless, even without all the answers many of us will have both the opportunity and the option to enter into cohabiting relationships at various points in our lives. The more we can learn about it, the more able we will be to make the decision that will suit us best.

POSTPONING MARRIAGE

In Chapter 1 it was noted that at the beginning of the twentieth century American men and women, on the average, did not marry until they were in their middle and late twenties. But, by the 1940s Americans had started to marry at younger ages. The lowest average marriage ages were reached in the mid-1950s (women at 20.1 years and men at 22.5 years). In the 1970s the age at marriage started to increase, especially near the end of the decade. By 1982 the average, or median, age at first marriage had risen to 25.4 for males and 23.0 for females (U.S. Census, 1984). An even better way to examine how young adults are more often postponing marriage is to see what percentage have not yet married at a given age. We have done this in Figure 6.2 for males and females between the ages of twenty-five and twenty-nine. For example, in 1970 only 19.1 percent of males in this age category had not yet married. By 1982, 36.1 percent of males in this age category remained unmarried. For females in this age group the percentage who had never married went from 10.5 in 1970 to 23.4 in 1982.

These higher percentages of young adults who have not yet married raise the question of whether there is simply a delay in marriage or if more people will remain single throughout their lives. Some of these young adults would surely

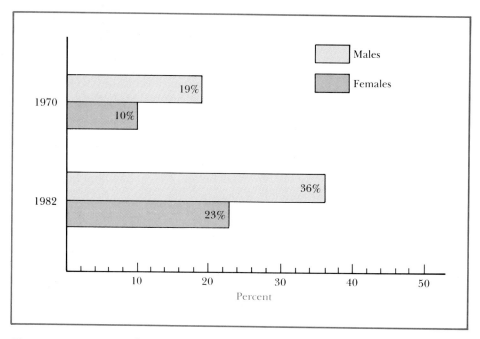

Figure 6.2 *Percentage of young adults aged twenty-five to twenty-nine who had never married (1970 and 1982)* (*Source:* United States Census, 1983. *Full Citation* United States Census, Current Population Reports, Series p-20, No. 380, "Marital Status and Living Arrangements: March, 1982," U.S. Government Printing Office, Washington, D.C. 1983.)

say they are only postponing marriage until they find the right person, but, of course, that might never occur. Others might say that they do not wish to marry, and yet at some later date they might marry anyway. As a general rule, whenever marriage is postponed it is likely that greater numbers of people will remain unmarried.

Whether being unmarried is a temporary or a permanent status, there is no question about one thing: the number of unmarried people in the population has been increasing. Since 1970, 23 million unmarried people have been added to the population over age fourteen (U.S. Bureau of the Census, 1984). Not only has the *number* of unmarried people been going up, but so has the *proportion* of unmarrieds in the population over age 14. In 1970, 28.3 percent of the population fourteen years of age and older was unmarried; by 1983 this had risen to 36.1 percent (U.S. Bureau of the Census, 1984).

The increase in the number of unmarried people comes from three sources: those who are not marrying, those who are divorcing, and those whose spouses died. The majority of the increase (14.5 million) has come from people who have never married. Divorces have added another 7 million to the unmarried population since 1970 (note that this number does not include those divorced persons who have remarried). Only 1 million of the new unmarried people are widows and widowers. Actually, because of the overall growth of the adult population, widows and widowers had a one percent decrease in their *proportion* of the total (U.S. Bureau of the Census, 1984).

Acceptance of the Single Lifestyle

In recent years much has been written about single people and the "singles life-style" in the United States. Both social researchers and the popular press have given considerable attention to this obviously fascinating social phenomenon. Along with innumerable magazine and newspaper articles, there have been quite a number of books on singles and singlehood. Some of these books are based on research (Cargan and Melko, 1982), but most are of the self-help or advice type.

Much of this attention to singles has apparently given singlehood a new acceptance in American life. It is now being claimed that people who remain single are no longer treated as inadequate or as failures. Choosing to be single is said to be a respectable alternative life-style today.

The validity of such assertions is difficult to evaluate. In one national survey, subjects were asked how they felt about the social trend of people placing less emphasis on getting married. Only fifteen percent of those responding said they welcomed this trend, fifty-seven percent rejected it, and twenty-eight percent were indifferent or unsure (*Time*/Yankelovich et al., 1982). It would appear from these data that few Americans welcome the decline in marriage.

Another way of assessing the acceptance of singlehood is to ask if young people expect to get married. In 1980, ten percent of high school senior males said they did not intend to marry. Five percent of senior females did not expect to marry. Twenty years earlier (1960), only two percent fewer males and females expected to remain single (Thornton and Freedman, 1982). Two points are obvious from these figures: (1) only a small minority of people expect not to marry; and (2) little change has occurred in twenty years.

Another kind of evidence about the acceptance of singlehood or nonmarriage can be found among the unmarried themselves. In one large (but nonrandom) sample of American singles, about thirty percent of the men and slightly over twenty percent of the women responded to an interview question with "pro-single" or "anti-marriage" answers. Among the men in this study, 10 percent said they preferred the life-style, while 20 percent disliked marriage or found it unnecessary since it is possible to cohabit. Eight percent of the single women said they preferred the life-style, while thirteen percent disliked marriage or found it unnecessary (Simenauer and Carroll, 1982).

With these kinds of statistics it is hard to say that there is a groundswell of enthusiasm for the single life-style. Yet there are a number of positive statements being made today about the advantages and justifications for not marrying. There are also, of course, negative aspects of not marrying, including the major one—loneliness.

We will look at both the advantages and disadvantages of remaining unmarried, but before doing so it is necessary to make a distinction that is important, though often overlooked. This is the distinction between *being unmarried* and *living alone*. There are a great many unmarried adults who do not live alone. This includes, of course, most of the 4 million people who are cohabiting. Also, many divorced people, especially women, live with their children, so strictly speaking they do not live alone. Many other unmarried adults (over the age of eighteen) live in apartments, houses, and dormitories with roommates or family members. Unmarried does not necessarily mean living alone, so the two terms are not synonymous. Those people who do live alone are, however, growing in number and importance in American society.

The Single-Person Household—Living Alone

Nineteen million people in the United States now live alone, nearly double the number who lived alone in 1970. It is this group that has especially fascinated many observers, since there is a widely held belief that almost everyone needs someone to "come home to." The evidence seems to bear out that belief, since the major complaint of people who live alone is "loneliness." In one sample, about eighty-five percent of the people who live alone complained about loneliness (Simenauer and Carroll, 1982). One man in this sample expressed his feelings in the following way:

> The hardest part of being alone is coming home each night and finding no one waiting for me. The house is empty. Everything is exactly in the same place where I left it in the morning. That's spooky—nothing has changed— there's no life. (Simenauer and Carroll, 1982, p. 246)

The second most common problem mentioned, especially by women living alone, is fear. Women, especially in urban places, are concerned for their physical safety, even in their own homes. One respondent described how her fears caused her to go to great lengths for protection:

> I carry mace and have a shotgun (loaded). I have eight phones in my house so I can cover myself and call the police. (Simenauer and Carroll, 1982, p. 246)

People who live alone also express concerns about their lack of sexual activity and the lack of steady, "meaningful" social relationships. There are also problems of going out for entertainment or dining without someone else along. These are, of course, the sexual and social sides of the loneliness issue. Some

Loneliness is the major complaint of people who live alone.

people who live alone express the fear that they will become too self-centered and selfish. Others feel that they are subject to social pressures and social prejudices. Men complain that friends and family assume that they must be unhappy and lonely and try to cheer them up or "fix them up." Men who live alone and who have never married are often suspected of being homosexual, even though they may not be (Davis and Strong, 1977). Women are likely to feel that they are seen by men as readily available sexual partners. A single woman who lives alone says,

> *People try to take advantage or expect things from you because you are alone. Guys will come over and think because you invite them up and [live] alone that they can stay all night. (Simenauer and Carroll, 1982, p. 251)*

While there are some obvious disadvantages connected with living alone, there are also some advantages. The most commonly mentioned advantage is "not having responsibility for anyone but myself." Those who live alone frequently mention freedom, independence, and autonomy as major advantages they enjoy. This freedom and independence means more than just having a varied social life. It also means a freedom to follow career and occupational lines without the "impediments" of spouse and family (Sanoff, 1983). Increasingly, this goes for women as well as men.

Living alone also gives some people privacy and time alone, which they enjoy as much as other people enjoy companionship. To many people who live alone this privacy means they can do what they want to do when they want to do it, especially in their day-to-day home life. It also means that they can go out alone for entertainment, recreation, and pleasure. A divorced woman living alone compares her married life with single life:

> I really enjoy going out a lot and attending different amusements. When you're living with someone you have to worry about whether you're making them mad. . . . My husband was the type that wanted to stay at home. . . . Now I don't have to worry about that. (Simenauer and Carroll, 1982, p. 254)

While these advantages of living alone are sincerely appreciated by some people, apparently the preference of many who live alone would be to have someone else with whom to live.

There have been some changes in the attitudes of Americans generally about what it means to remain unmarried or to live alone. There is at least a recognition that it is possible to have a full and enjoyable life without being married or living with others. This general shift in public attitudes has made it easier for those individuals who genuinely prefer not to marry, or to live alone. The number of such individuals, however, is by all estimates a tiny minority of all adults. Most Americans at present prefer to live with someone else, and, in fact, most prefer to be married. This is especially true for those who have never married, and it can be expected that in the foreseeable future about ninety percent of Americans will enter marriage, at least once. Entering marriage will be the subject of the next chapter.

ISSUE

Should couples live together before marriage?

In view of the earlier discussion of the three different types of cohabitation, it seems advisable to limit this discussion to what was earlier called *premarital cohabitation*. Some of the arguments may apply equally well to part-time/limited cohabitation or to substitute marriage, but others may not. In any case, to simplify the discussion the focus here will be on the cohabitation of two people who are committed to each other and are setting up a marriagelike household. This does not mean that such couples will necessarily decide to marry, for many will break up and some may continue their living-together arrangement into the indefinite future.

Arguments in Favor of Living Together

It is not unheard of today for the parents of some young adults to approve of cohabitation for their children. Some parents may specifically recommend it to their children. Sometimes these parents are reflecting their own experiences with marriage, feeling that they could have averted many problems in their own lives if they had known more about the person they married or about marriage itself. Parents may also have seen some of their older children enter marriages precipitously, only to have the marriages end in early divorces. Such parents may feel that by recommending to their children that they live together before marriage some of the same mistakes could be avoided.

This view, that cohabitation helps to avert bad marriages, is one of the major reasons given by many people, including some parents, for advocating living together. Cohabitation involves sharing responsibility for running a household (budgeting, maintenance, cleaning, cooking). Cohabitation also necessitates that two people learn what it is like to live with someone else, day in and day out. When two people begin living together, they soon find that there are differences in styles of doing things and differences in ideas, opinions, and even values that they had not previously discovered. Living together is a way of learning if these differences are insurmountable or if compromises and accommodations are possible.

Living together also provides some notion of how marriage differs from the dating relationship. For example, while living together is not exactly the same as marriage, it usually entails some restrictions on the freedom and independence one has as a single person. These restrictions are not simply a matter of not being able to go out with members of the opposite sex (a restriction entered into by most cohabiting couples). The restrictions and loss of autonomy also frequently limit what one can do with one's time, money, living style, and many other things. It is an argument in favor of cohabitation to say that two people who are thinking of marriage should find out in advance if they can handle all of these matters.

There is also the argument that two people can learn much more about the strength and depth of their love for each other if they have the experience of living together. Living in the same household with another person exposes one to the "intimate vulgarities of life." These can be successfully hidden even in the very closest and most intimate dating relationships; but they will not be hidden long when two people live together, and when they are brought into the open romantic illusions may be shattered very quickly. A relationship between two people must be strong enough to withstand these revelations. If it is not, there is less basis for a lasting relationship than a couple might have supposed. It is best that they learn this before marriage, not after.

All these arguments in favor of premarital cohabitation essentially revolve around the same basic point. It is the next best thing to marriage itself for learning if a couple is likely to have a satisfactory and lasting marriage. It is no assurance, of course, but the evidence shows that many people who think they want to spend their lives together often change their minds after trying it. Those who marry, and then become disenchanted, must go through the pains and trauma of divorce. Those who simply live together can go their separate ways with somewhat less difficulty and certainly with fewer legal procedures.

Arguments against Living Together

The most frequently voiced objection to couples living together before marriage is usually phrased in terms of a question: Why not get married? Couples who are living together may appear to be fully committed to each other but really are not if they do not "make it legal." People who oppose cohabitation for this reason argue that the lack of legal bonds, which are often seen by young people as an unnecessary sign of the commitment they feel for each other, is a fundamental difference between cohabitation and marriage.

Legal ties perform two essential functions for close relationships: they provide an external motivation for attempting to maintain the relationship, and they force others to recognize the relationship. In times of intense marital conflict the legal obligation between the spouses may be the only motive they have for attempting to negotiate their differences. Cohabitants, on the other hand, may operate under the belief that when the going gets tough, the "legally free" get going. Thus, a common criticism of living together is that because the couples are aware of how easy it is to leave the relationship they never really feel the need to "work" at it.

One obvious implication of this quasi-commitment is the uncertainty and ambiguity about sexual exclusiveness. Most cohabiting couples probably assume that their partners will be faithful, but since there has been no marriage ceremony or legal document to make this explicit there is always some room for misunderstanding.

Another difficulty that often emerges from cohabitation concerns the potential opposition of family members—particularly parents and grandparents. Very often the cohabiting arrangement has to be kept secret or treated as if it does not exist. This, of course, creates any number of charades and pretenses which can be inconvenient and guilt producing. Many parents, even when they are quite aware of their children's cohabiting, will not acknowledge it. They certainly will offer no support or encouragement to the couple to maintain the relationship. In fact, they might even try to undermine it by introducing the individual cohabitants to potential marriage partners.

There is another, more practical, objection to couples living together before marriage—potential financial problems. It is difficult, if not impossible, for two people who live together to keep their finances separate. Yet this is what many lawyers advise. At first, the only joint expenditures may involve small sums of money for utility bills or kitchen appliances. However, as the cohabiting partners acquire more and more common property (e.g., stereo systems, automobiles, furniture, and so on) their financial lives become more intertwined and more difficult to untangle. If the relationship terminates, the ownership of these items is extremely problematic because the legal rights and responsibilities of cohabitants are not as clearly defined as those of married couples.

Finally, even those who might support cohabitation in the abstract argue that as long as there are gender differences in cohabitants' motives and intents, it is better for women not to cohabit before marriage. The present structure of cohabitation represents a serious exploitation of women, who appear to have all of the constraints of marriage but none of the benefits. Not only do cohabiting women perform the bulk of household tasks and contribute more financial assets to their relationships than their male partners, on the average, but they do so in the hope that their efforts will pay off in a future marriage. They are often disappointed because their partners view cohabitation not as a deeper commitment but as a practical living situation.

In summary, then, many of the arguments against living together before marriage stem from the absence of legal bonds and the corresponding lack of total commitment. Because of the legal difference, cohabitation is not an effective preparation for marriage. It does not result in greater marital success; and it perpetuates the inequality of traditional gender roles.

Themes

1. Great numerical increases in cohabitation, especially among middle-class people, have occurred in the last two decades.

2. Attitudes about cohabitation have become more favorable as it has become more common.

3. European trends toward cohabitation, especially in Scandinavian countries, preceded the pattern in the United States.

4. There are three types of cohabitation: part-time/limited; premarital; and substitute marriage.

5. Generally, the greatest objections (particularly among parents of young people) are to part-time/limited and substitute marriage types of cohabitation.

6. While most cohabitants find cohabiting a positive experience, there are some identifiable negative features as well.

7. Cohabiting couples often have a division of labor along traditional gender role lines.

8. The impact of cohabitation on marital success has not been clearly established, in part because of differences in characteristics between cohabitants and noncohabitants.

9. There have been increases in the population of single people in the last decade, though the acceptance of singleness as a life-style is less certain.

10. There are advantages as well as disadvantages to living alone.

Facts

1. In the 1950s and 1960s college students who were caught cohabiting were often expelled from school.

2. An estimated one-fourth of all undergraduates cohabit at some time during their college careers.

3. There was a fourfold increase in the number of cohabiting couples between 1970 and 1984.

4. In 1980 only four percent of all couples living in United States households were unmarried.

5. Two-thirds of cohabiting men and three-fourths of cohabiting women are under thirty-five.

6. Nearly half of cohabiting adults have been previously married.

7. There are children residing in about one-quarter of cohabiting households.

8. Cohabitants are found at all educational levels, but in some circumstances the less educated are still overrepresented.

9. Black Americans have higher rates of cohabitation than white Americans, especially at ages thirty-five and over.

10. Among European countries, Sweden leads the way in cohabitation, with ninety-nine percent of married couples having lived together before marriage.

11. As recently as 1982, about half of all Americans disapproved of cohabitation.

12. Cohabiting males are less likely to be thinking of marriage than cohabiting females.

13. Cohabiting males dominate their relationships more than dating males, but less than married males.

14. Married couples who had previously cohabited had lower marital adjustment scores than married couples who had not previously cohabited.

15. Increases in the unmarried population come more from people who have never married than from divorced or widowed people.

16. In 1980, ten percent of high school senior males and five percent of high school senior females did not expect to marry; these figures are only small increases over the percentages of twenty years ago.

17. Loneliness appears to be the major negative aspect of living alone.

18. The most commonly cited advantages of living alone are not having responsibility for others, and having freedom, independence, and autonomy.

Major Concepts

cohabitation (census definition): Two adults, a man and a woman, unrelated and not married to each other, who share a household. There may be children present in the household.

cohabitating (or living together): A general term used to describe a man and woman who are sharing a household and are likely to have a commitment to and an emotional involvement with each other. (*See* part-time/limited cohabitation, premarital cohabitation, and substitute marriage.)

"common-law" marriage: A term used before the 1960s to describe unmarried couples who were living together—usually used in a negative way.

living together (*See* **cohabitating**)

part-time/limited cohabitation: A stage of cohabitation in which couples drift into staying together several nights a week; often, many aspects of their relationship are impermanent and unsettled.

premarital cohabitation: A type of cohabitation in which two people plan to marry, but live together in the meantime. (*See also* trial marriage)

substitute marriage: A long-term cohabiting commitment between two people without a legal marriage, but similar to marriage in many ways.

trial marriage: Premarital cohabitation in which a couple is testing the relationship before making a marriage commitment. (*See also* premarital cohabitation)

7

Entering Marriage
Marriage Forms and Marriage Contracts

When two people enter marriage there is an interest in the event that goes far beyond the two principals in the drama. Family members, religious functionaries, community members, and even the state are all likely to be involved when two people enter marriage. The state, for example, plays a subtle but important part, because anyone entering a legal marriage is also entering into a marriage contract, a marriage contract that has been developed by the state. The implications of this contract are usually only vaguely recognized since it is made up of all the laws, court rulings, and administrative regulations that affect the duties, obligations, and rights of married persons. Whether people agree with the underlying assumptions or not, they are bound by the state's marriage contract when they enter marriage.

But there is another kind of marriage contract, one that has been written about and discussed frequently in recent years. This is the *personal marriage contract*, which can be entered into voluntarily. A personal marriage contract is one that two people can prepare prior to or during their marriage (or cohabitation). A personal marriage contract can cover any issues a couple wishes to include, from economic arrangements to who does the cooking and cleaning. At the end of this chapter we will take a closer look at the nature of personal marriage contracts and then consider the arguments for and against them.

The topics we have considered up to this point (attraction, dating, love, pre-marital sex, and cohabitation) are all preliminaries to the main event—marriage. While it is true that many Americans today are delaying marriage by a few years, eventually most people do marry. By the time most Americans reach age forty they have married at least once. Figure 7.1 reveals that as far as we can tell up to this time there has been only a very slight decrease since 1960 in the percentage of American men and women who have married at least once by the time they reach age forty. Approximately ninety percent of both sexes (slightly higher for women) have married by that time.

When we consider the popularity of marriage in the United States, it must also be noted that many people enter marriage more than once. Cherlin (1981)

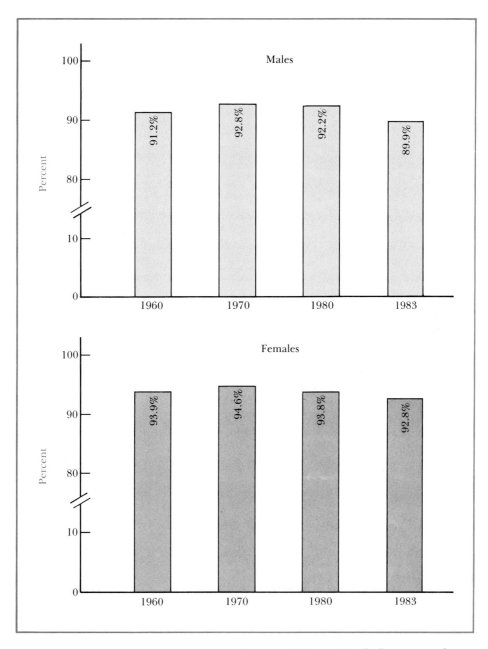

Figure 7.1 *Percentage of American men and women (1960–1983) who have married at least once by age 35–39.* (*Source:* U.S. Bureau of the Census, *Statistical Abstract of the U.S. 1985*, table 51, page 39; Washington, D.C.: 1984.)

estimates that among all American women born after World War II, more than thirty percent will remarry after a divorce. The percentage for divorced men who marry more than once is probably slightly higher (Cherlin, 1981). Add to these the men and women who remarry two or three times, and those who marry after widowhood, and it is easy to see that as a society we are very positive about marriage.

Americans are not unique in their proclivity to enter marriage, though the high percentages do stand out among the industrialized nations of the world. In the nonindustrialized countries the tendency is for nearly everyone to marry. The statistics on marriage in some countries are truly impressive. In India among the Hindu population, marriage has been nearly universal, with more than ninety-nine percent of all females marrying (Petersen, 1975). For the Indian people, marriage has been a virtual necessity for physical and social survival. Among the small preliterate tribes of the world, marriage is similarly viewed as a necessity for survival. The famed anthropologist Levi-Strauss (1956) has described an experience from his youthful fieldwork among the Bororo of central Brazil that illustrates how critical marriage is to survival. He saw a man about thirty years old who was dirty, thin, and appeared to be sad and lonely. He asked if the man were seriously ill. The answer was that he was not ill, that he was a bachelor. Among the Bororo, as in many other groups, a man who is married will have a helpmate, a wife who will provide him with the benefits of "woman's work." Among the Bororo a person who is not married is considered "only half a human being" (Levi-Strauss, 1956, p. 269).

As these facts indicate, marriage in every society is a preferred status. In every known society, in the past as well as the present, the majority of people enter marriage. However, the ways in which people marry, and the forms marriages take, are often very different from ours, so much so that at first we may have a hard time seeing that it is a marriage. And yet, a closer look reveals that even in strange and exotic marriage customs there are parallels and similarities to our ways.

As just one of many possible examples of unusual ways of entering marriage, we will take the case of the Pakhtun people who live in the mountains of northwestern Pakistan. Their way of entering marriage centers around the process of physically removing the young bride (sometimes no more than twelve years of age) from the home of her family and depositing her in the groom's family home (Lindholm and Lindholm, 1979). On the day of the marriage, the males of the groom's family march through the streets of their village to the girl's home, beating their war drums as they go. Of course, the arrangements for the marriage have been made in advance by the families of the young people. When the procession arrives at the girl's house, a male member of her family (perhaps her brother) will lift her onto a platform that will be carried on the shoulders of her new husband's male relatives. They will then proceed to carry the bride to the groom's home. The girl cannot actually be seen, because she is hidden by an embroidered cover. As the men carry the platform through the streets, bouncing it triumphantly, the small boys of the village line the route and throw stones, hoping to cause the carriers to drop the bride into the street. When the marchers reach the husband's home, the noise of their drums and the firing of their guns reaches a peak level. The bride, still covered by the cloth, is removed from the platform and placed on a cot in one room of the house. The women of the groom's family will surround the girl, talking incessantly, urging her to show her face. Later they will retire to the courtyard where they begin dancing and celebrating the bride's arrival in the household.

The groom, in the meantime, will retire to the "men's house" of a relative, while the other men in the wedding party go to a different "men's house" for a wedding feast. The groom may not join the feasting because he is expected to be in shame for losing his bachelorhood. Among the Pakhtun the marriage is joyously received by the family members, but the groom is not expected to share in the joy.

The Pakhtun bride must remain for three days in the room where she has been placed, leaving only when it is necessary to relieve herself. On the third

The bachelor party is one of the premarriage customs in American society.

night, her new husband will visit her, and they will have sexual intercourse. This experience consummates the marriage.

The Pakhtun marriage may seem unusual to us, and yet there are some features that parallel our own wedding customs. We too have public processions (usually with automobiles and blaring horns), music, dancing, and feasting. Even throwing things at the bride is a common wedding tradition, and has been in many places throughout history. We throw rice or confetti at the bride and groom, but the Hebrews threw pieces of cake, while the Greeks threw grain, fruit, and sweetmeats. In Great Britain, as recently as the last century, cake or biscuits were still scattered over the head of the bride (Monsarrat, 1974). In most of these customs from Western cultures, the things thrown are thought to symbolize fertility or fruitfulness.

But the similarities of the customs are not as important as their underlying meanings. The activities and festivities surrounding the marriage are engaged in by families, religious groups, and the community in general. It is the social side of marriage that is so important. We often think of marriage as a very personal matter, as a time when two individuals make their most lasting and sacred commitment to each other. That, of course, is true, but it is also a time when there is an intense social interest in what is happening. We will see throughout this chapter that social groups from the family to the state take a keen interest in the process of entering marriage.

In the pages that follow, we will examine the ways in which people enter marriage. We will begin by looking at three different models that describe the ways marital partners are selected.

THREE MODELS FOR ENTERING MARRIAGE

Because there are so many different forms and variations of marriage, we need some tool or mechanism to help cope with the diversity. That tool will be a trusted sociological method called *ideal-type analysis*. An ideal type is an exaggerated and extreme characterization of some social phenomenon. In the case at hand we will identify three ideal-type forms of entering marriage. Each type will be described in its most extreme, one might say "perfect," form. This will be followed by illustrative examples from our own and other societies. The most important feature of ideal-type analysis is that there might be no single society that exactly fulfills all the conditions of the extreme characterization. That does not invalidate the ideal type, since it is not being used to describe a given case precisely. It is, instead, being used as a standard, or as a model, against which any particular case can be compared and evaluated. Perhaps the use of ideal-type analysis will be clearer simply by discussing the first model or ideal type, which will be labeled the traditional-agrarian model of entering marriage.*

The Traditional-Agrarian Model

In its ideal-type form, the *traditional-agrarian model* for entering marriage has the following features:

1. Parents or other kin members select marriage mates for children when they reach marriage age.
2. The marriage partners have had little or no personal contact with each other prior to their marriage.
3. The bases for choosing a potential marriage mate will include economic considerations, the social status or prestige of the families, and often the potential for political alliances.
4. Love between the prospective marriage partners is not expected before marriage and often is of small consequence after marriage.

There are many historical examples of societies that have had the traditional-agrarian type of entry into marriage. Even today many societies retain major elements of this type. However, for a vivid illustration we will look at the historical case of Ireland in the last half of the nineteenth century. It was in this period, following a devastating famine, that the Irish modified their marriage system. As the system emerged, it came to be a nearly perfect representation of the traditional-agrarian model for entering marriage. Naturally, it had a few distinctly Irish features.

The key to understanding how the Irish approached marriage is to recognize that marriage was closely tied to taking over and inheriting a farm. It is only a slight exaggeration to say that only *if* and *when* parents were willing to turn over a farm to one of their sons was he able to marry. If there were no sons, one of the daughters could take over the farm. In this case she would bring a husband to the farm, or as the Irish country folk put it, a "son-in-law [is] going in" (Arensberg and Kimball, 1940, p. 114).

Since Irish fathers and mothers were not usually eager to turn over the control of their farm to the chosen son, they usually postponed the son's marriage as long as possible. Often the "boy" would be in his thirties, or even forties, be-

---

*The following discussion of the traditional-agrarian model and the two other models are largely drawn from the perceptive analysis of courtship by McCall (1966). McCall's work is built on Waller's (1938) early assessment of courtship as a bargaining process, and Farber's (1964) insightful and farsighted comprehension of contemporary courtship and marriage.

fore his parents were ready to turn over the farm. Only when death or the disability of one of the parents made it necessary did they see their way clear to stepping down and turning over the farm. When it did become necessary, they would set out to find "a new woman for the place."

Often a matchmaker or go-between would be used to bring the families of the potential bride and groom together. Sometimes the matchmaker would be someone who would have a nearly official status in the community, helping many different families get together on marriages. Other times it might simply be a friend of the family or even a family member who would make the first contact to arrange a meeting. One Irish countryman described how the procedure might go:

> If I wanted to give my farm over to my son and I would be worth, say, two hundred pounds, I would know a fellow up the hill, for instance, that would be worth three hundred pounds. I would send up a neighbor fellow to him and ask him if he would like to join my family in marriage. If the fellow would send back word he would and the girl would say she was willing (and the usual courtesies were exchanged), then on a day they agreed on I and the fellow would meet in Ennistymon (the local market town) and talk over the whole thing as to terms, maybe sitting on it the whole day. (Arensberg and Kimball, 1940, p. 109)

The "sitting on it the whole day" refers to hammering out a tentative financial arrangement between the two families. In the Irish case the customary procedure was for the prospective bridegroom to provide the farm, while the bride would have a dowry. The dowry might be furniture and other household goods of value, or jewelry, or livestock. By the end of the nineteenth century, however, it was usually money that had been saved by the family to ensure the marriage of their daughter. The lengthy negotiations between the fathers of the potential bride and the groom were required to make the value of the dowry equal to the value of the farm. The bargaining process was a hard-headed economic negotiation. Listen again to the words of an Irish countryman as he describes the economic bargaining:

> The speaker [matchmaker] goes with the young man and his father . . . and they meet the father of the girl and his friends. . . . The first drink is called by the young man, the second by the young lady's father. The young lady's father asks the speaker what fortune [dowry] do he want. He asks him of the place how many cows, sheep, and horses it is. He asks what makings of a garden are in it; is there plenty of water or spring wells? Is it far from the road or on it? What kind of house is in it, slate or thatch? If it is too far in from the road, he won't take it. Backward places don't grow big fortunes. And he asks too is it near a chapel and the school or near town? If it is a nice place, near the road and the place of eight cows, they are sure to ask three hundred and fifty pounds fortune. Then the young lady's father offers two hundred and fifty pounds. Then maybe the boy's

— DOWRY-WAGGON BEFORE THE BRIDEGROOM'S HOUSE —

In the nineteenth century in the Bavarian Highlands, the bride's dowry was brought to the home of the groom in an oxcart.

father throws off fifty pounds. If the young lady's father still has two hundred and fifty pounds on it, the speaker [matchmaker] divides the fifty pounds between them, so now it's two hundred and seventy-five. Then the young male says he is not willing to marry without three hundred pounds—but if she's a nice girl and a good housekeeper, he'll think of it. (Arensberg and Kimball, 1940, p. 111)

Often it was only after the bargaining had produced a tentative arrangement that the prospective bride and groom would have an opportunity to get together. A meeting place would be designated at the bargaining session. The woman would bring her friends, her brothers, and perhaps even her mother and father. The man would also bring his friends, and in this group setting the two potential marriage mates would evaluate each other. If one or the other decided at that point that they could not go through with the marriage, the arrangement could be called off. No particular public reason needed to be given; it could just be said that he, or she, "didn't suit." In one reported case the woman rejected the man who had been matched with her because he was too fat (Arensberg and Kimball, 1940, p. 114).

If the two people found each other acceptable, the marriage contract would be made final. Usually this required the assistance of a lawyer who drew up a written contract spelling out all the details of the arrangement. With the signing of the "writings," as the Irish called the contract, the marriage would usually follow very quickly (Kammeyer, 1976).

This description is the general way the Irish marriage system worked, especially in the last part of the nineteenth and early part of the twentieth centuries. This example reveals how entering marriage was largely controlled by the parents. The decision to marry was based on the success of the negotiation and bargaining about the economic aspects of the union. The Irish way of entering marriage almost totally lacked any elements of courtship or love. All of these features make the Irish case an almost perfect illustration of the traditional-agrarian model of entering marriage.

One cautionary note about the Irish case is required. Not every marriage followed the model exactly. The Irish had elopements or "runaway marriages," as they called them. Young people did sometimes become attracted to one another, perhaps fall in love, and then on their own, without parental blessing, dowry, or farm, run off to get married. Sometimes these runaway marriages would eventually gain the acceptance of parents, other times not. The Irish, like other people around the world, took a keen interest in the marriage of their children, and preferred to have them marry in the customary way. When custom is followed, there is a kind of order and steadiness in societal life, an order that is upset when young people deviate from the normal patterns.

We turn next to the second marriage pattern, the courtship model of entering marriage. This model is more common in the United States historically than is the traditional-agrarian model.

The Courtship Model

Even though the United States started its economic existence as a rural and agricultural society, the traditional-agrarian model for entering marriage never predominated (Furstenberg, 1966; Demos, 1970). The *courtship model* did, since Americans from the beginning have given young people much freedom and autonomy. They were given a much greater part in the selection of their mates than had been the case in Europe (and most of the rest of the world). Also, in the United States young people of the opposite sex were given a great deal of freedom to be together and enjoy each other's company in recreational settings. Many European visitors in the eighteenth and nineteenth centuries believed that American youngsters, especially young women, were given too much freedom (Furstenberg, 1966). Finally, from our very earliest history as a country, marriage has typically been based on romantic attachments and love, a point already noted in Chapter 2. All of these are elements of the courtship model.

But to see this model more clearly, we will begin by describing the ideal-type characteristics and then look at some examples and details. The courtship model includes the following characteristics:

1. The young people themselves have substantial control over mate selection, although at some crucial points the parents have considerable impact on the choice.

2. There are steps in the process that serve to narrow the field of eligible marriage mates.

3. Among the field of eligibles a number of potential marriage mates (sometimes many, sometimes only a few) remain in contention simultaneously as possible marriage partners.

4. Over a period of time the possible marriage partners who prove to be the "poorer bargains" are dropped from consideration.

5. The narrowing of the field of eligibles continues until at last only the two people are left. This relationship has now developed to a state of mutual love, and as opposed to previous infatuations this is "true love."

6. The two people in the couple become, at this point, committed to each other. They are likely to reach a "private understanding" between themselves, which soon will be followed by a public announcement of plans to marry (engagement).

7. A period of engagement is followed by marriage, which is a permanent contract, meant to last a lifetime.

These are the fundamental features of the courtship model of entering marriage. Examples from the American experience will illustrate some of the actual workings of this model. The classical "coming-out" party or the debutante ball, which is thought of as presenting a young woman to society, is a convenient starting point for seeing how the courtship model works. The coming-out party is the official recognition by some social group that a young woman is now ready to be seriously courted, that is, she is now ready to begin the process of narrowing the field of eligible men, until at last there is one left, whom she will marry.

The debutante ball also shows how the young woman's family enters into the choice of suitors. First, it is only a select group of families who have a sufficiently high social standing to have their daughters participate in a debutante ball. The young men who will be invited will also have to meet comparable social status standards. Certainly the families who are not quite as elite will have a little less direct control over the suitors of their daughters, but they too will find ways of narrowing the field of eligibles. The communities and neighborhoods they live in, and the schools to which they send their children, are both narrowing mechanisms. When structural impediments do not work, parents at all levels are likely simply to prohibit their children from seeing others who are of the "wrong" social class, religion, and race.

But even though the parents play a part in the selection of mates, the courtship model still puts the major burden on the young people themselves. They must meet and date a wide range of opposite-sex possibilities. In the ideal form of the courtship model, several of these possible mates are seen simultaneously. The upper-middle-class dance of the 1920s illustrates how this might occur. A young woman would attend a dance with a date, but at the beginning of the evening, if she was popular, many other young men would sign her dance card. This would give them the opportunity to dance with her and make an impression during the evening.

In this style of courtship a young woman might have a number of "suitors" simultaneously. The men, too, might be "courting" more than one young woman. Eventually, through this process, both the young men and young women would become aware of how desirable they were as potential mates. Both the women and men would gradually drop the least desirable "bargains" among those they were dating.

In the courtship model of entering marriage, bargaining is clearly going on, just as it was in the traditional-agrarian model. However, the emphasis has shifted away from economic considerations and toward personal qualities. The economic positions and economic potentials of possible marriage mates are not irrelevant, but economic considerations compete with looks, style, manners, and, most of all, love. In the courtship model, one of the key elements is to find the person "one was meant for," and ideally that will be the person who also loves one the most (McCall, 1966). The courtship process leads to one's "true love," and once that person has been found, it is expected to lead to an exclusive and permanent commitment. This is formalized through an engagement, which leads to marriage.

Shortly before the engagement, however, the parents of the two young people again take a more active part in the decision-making process. The young people are likely to visit in the homes of each other's parents. This is serious business, for now the parents will know that this relationship may lead to marriage. If the parents are going to oppose or stop the marriage for some reason, it will have to be at this juncture. In the courtship model, it is customary for the man to go to the father of the woman he wishes to marry and ask his permission.

After the blessings of both families have been obtained, there will be an engagement period. This period will last long enough for the two people to be assured that they were "meant for each other," and then they will marry. If the ideal is achieved, this will be a marriage that will last for a lifetime. Only death can end the marriage.

This model of courtship has been widely accepted and reasonably approximated for many years in American society. Some elements of this ideal still exist, though not as extensively as forty or fifty years ago. There is still the notion of "playing the field," meeting and dating a wide range of potential mates, and waiting until one falls "truly in love." Parents certainly still place their children in neighborhoods, communities, churches, and colleges that greatly influence the selection of marriage partners. But young people today are more likely to announce to their parents their plans to become engaged or to marry, rather than to ask permission to do so. And, as we saw in Chapter 6, if children enter a cohabiting relationship, they often do not inform their parents. Some remnants of the courtship model can still be found in specific practices, and in courtship ideals, but to have a clearer picture of entering marriage today we need to introduce a new model, the contemporary model of entering marriage.

The Contemporary Model

The ideal-type features of the *contemporary model* of entering marriage are as follows:

1. The selection of a mate is almost totally in the hands of the young people themselves.
2. The field of eligible mates may include every person with whom an individual comes in contact.
3. One may enter into an exclusive, intimate relationship with a new person at any time, but the commitment is not assumed to be forever.
4. A person may leave one relationship (including marriage) for another relationship whenever the costs of a relationship exceed the rewards.

At first the features of this contemporary model, especially points 3 and 4, may seem extreme and unacceptable, but a closer examination of our actual practices reveals that we often come very close to this model. Let us consider each feature of this model in turn, beginning with the assertion that choosing a mate is left almost entirely in the hands of young people.

We noted above that even when the country was young, Americans gave their children much more autonomy in the choice of their mates than did most Europeans. That practice has been extended to a point where parents are often excluded from much of the decision process. Children will usually want their parents to approve of their mate choice, but they rarely ask for their parents' permission in advance. Two cases are instructive in this regard: cohabitation and parental disapproval of a marriage choice. While cohabitation undoubtedly reflects a relationship of considerable importance, it is a rare young person who asks for permission in advance before beginning a living-together arrangement. On the contrary, as we have seen, parents are often specifically kept from knowing about the arrangement.

If parents disapprove of the person a son or daughter wishes to marry, will it deter the child? Perhaps in some cases, but if two people feel they are in love, they are very likely to consider their relationship more important than any allegiance they may have to their parents.

One counterpoint must be made with regard to contemporary parental influences on children's choice of mates. Even within the contemporary model of entering marriage, parents still give their children a starting position in the social class system of the community and society. And social class does influence who one is likely to meet and thus to fall in love with. Also, parents can manipulate their children's lives to some degree. It is usually within the power of the parents to change residence or to place their children in different school systems (e.g., a private rather than a public school) when they feel their children are going to meet and associate with the "wrong people."

However, according to the contemporary model, everyone is potentially in the field of eligibles. At least everyone with whom one comes in contact is potentially eligible. But can that statement be true? It can be true if exactly what it means is specified. It means that no one is excluded as a possible mate simply by virtue of some status that person holds—race, religion, economic position, and so on. The only exception would be immediate family members, since the incest taboo precludes them. Even this restriction is sometimes broached as when a sister and brother, or mother and son meet after a period of separation, fall in love, and choose to marry. When this violation of law comes to light, the state steps in to separate the couple, but even this does not usually change the feelings of the principals.

These exceptional cases reveal vividly how much importance is placed on being in love. And love is the key to understanding why almost everyone can be in the field of eligibles. If one is in love with a person, regardless of his or her characteristics, that person is acceptable as a marriage mate.

A complementary perspective on this matter is provided by the *principle of permanent, universal availability* (Farber, 1964). This principle emphasizes that no one is ever totally and irrevocably removed from the marriage market. Even if one is already married, there is always the possibility of meeting and falling in love with someone new. If that new person satisfies one's needs better than one's present partner, that may be a justification for moving on to a new partner.

The concept of permanent, universal availability may seem to be an affront to the sanctity of marriage and to make a mockery of the concepts of personal responsibility and commitment. While any reader can certainly take personal exception to the principle of permanent, universal availability, the real question is whether or not it reflects social reality. If this principle does reflect the kind of society in which we live, then it can help us to understand contemporary marriage and other intimate relationships.

One interesting clue to the beginnings of this pattern of moving from one relationship to another can be found in early dating behavior. Beginning at a very early age, American youngsters are likely to enter into exclusive relationships. While some casual dating does occur, there is a strong tendency for exclusive (going steady) pairs to emerge. In one study of students in Connecticut high schools, the average age for going steady was under fifteen (Gordon and Miller, 1984). By the time these students were seniors in high school, they had gone steady an average of two and one-half times. These going-steady relationships did not usually last very long: the average shortest going-steady experience was two months, and the average longest going-steady experience was only ten months. These figures show that students move into and out of most of these personal involvements with ease and speed. Indeed, two or three dates in a row by two young people is likely to be taken as evidence that they are "going together." This is vividly illustrated by an excerpt from an account by a young woman named Cheryl, whose personal description of her high school and young adult years reveals much about love, commitment, and marriage in contemporary American society (Schwartz and Merten, 1980).

Cheryl admired from afar a boy in her high school named Al. Finally she did meet him, and he asked her to go to the homecoming dance. Her description follows:

> We had a lot of fun. The next night we went to a party given by Al's fraternity, the Thetas. I don't know why, but we made out: I knew he liked me and I liked him. But I didn't like him that much! Anyhow, after that we just ate lunch together. Everyone knew we were going steady. (Schwartz and Merten, 1980, p. 81)

The authors who wrote about this young woman's account of her dating and courtship relations comment on how going steady was something that was more or less automatic in her high school:

> Al and Cheryl's relationship fits into the typical pattern at Westwood High. It begins with the awkward silence that is broken when their friends contrive to get them together. The first few dates are fine, and then, without giving it much thought, Cheryl and Al start going steady. (Schwartz and Merten, 1980, p. 82)

Before long, however, the relationship "went flat," and Cheryl found, or created, an excuse for ending it. This was the first of a number of involvements described by this young woman as she went through high school and beyond. Each relationship was more or less an exclusive commitment for the time it lasted, but it would end when one person of the pair found the costs of the relationship greater than the rewards. This pattern again exemplifies one of the themes of the contemporary model. It is part of the early and continuous training of young people as they learn how to enter and leave interpersonal relationships. One learns in this way how to form commitments, but one also learns to leave these same commitments as gracefully as possible.

Another feature of these commitments is that they are likely to become more intense and more involved as a person moves from one to the next. In general, the average length of the relationship and the level of emotional and sexual involvement increase with each succeeding relationship. Nonetheless, it is possible to leave each one in turn and move on to the next. Even marriage itself, which is the most intense involvement, may be abandoned.

Two features of social life in the last decade fit this model and its underlying principles very well. One is cohabitation, which we have already examined, and the other is divorce. Both social phenomena emerged with full-blown intensity in the decade after Farber (1964) first postulated the principle of permanent, universal availability.

Cohabitation, if viewed from this perspective, is just one more step in a series of personal involvements. It is a greater commitment than previous relationships, but certainly one that it is legitimate to leave if it becomes less than satisfactory. Indeed, in many cases of cohabitation the cohabitants declare openly that they will leave the relationship if it does not work out. Peterman et al. (1974) found that eighty-two percent of cohabitants stayed together less than three months.

By pointing out that the contemporary model allows people to leave marriage almost as easily as other earlier commitments, we do not mean to suggest that everyone in the society agrees to this in principle. Most people would not agree, but the high divorce rates of the last two decades are evidence that in practice many people do leave their marriages, despite their earlier vows to the contrary. Even when married couples have minor children, a factor that is usually thought to keep couples together, many people end their marriages. It is estimated that one out of three children in the United States will experience the end of their parents' marriage before they reach age 16 (Thornton and Freedman, 1983). While some of these marriages end because of death, most end by divorce.

In early exclusive involvements, in the increasing intensity of exclusive commitments, in the emergent patterns of cohabitation, and in the increases in the divorce rate, we see clear indications that the contemporary model of entering marriage does coincide to a considerable degree with current social reality.

Perhaps the most balanced way of using these ideal-type characterizations of entering marriage is to say that we retain some features of the courtship model but that at the same time we have adopted many aspects of the contemporary model. We still often believe in the ideal of finding the one special person who is meant for us and making the relationship work for a lifetime. Yet at the same time we recognize that two people who were once committed to each other can "grow apart" and no longer meet each other's needs. Under these conditions many people accept the idea that individuals do have a right to be happy and, if necessary, to end a relationship. Even ending a marriage where there are children can be justified under many circumstances. These two competing views are present for many people today as they consider entering marriage.

We can also see in these opposing views a reflection of the fundamental paradox of marriage in contemporary life. Marriage is probably the most important personal decision we make in our lives, and yet marriage by its very nature is an extremely social act. When a marriage ends, it means breaking a personal commitment, but it also means breaking a social commitment. Marriage is deeply embedded in social obligations and rules. In the next section we will examine the ways in which entering marriage is a process of making a social commitment even while we are making a personal commitment to another person.

THE SOCIAL CONTROL OF MARRIAGE

From our discussion above it is clear that social groups and societies have an intense interest in marriage. The interest is in who marries whom, where and when they marry, and what the conditions of the marital relationship shall be. While parents in contemporary life are in many ways excluded from their children's choices, an interesting example of the way in which parents can influence their children's marriage choices is found in Scott's (1966) analysis of the function of sorority systems on large college campuses.

Parents in contemporary American life are quite aware that where their children go to college (or *if* they go) will probably determine the type of person they marry. If parents have the economic resources to help their children go to a private school, either an elite school or perhaps a religious-affiliated school, there is a great probability they will marry someone of a similar social class or religious background. However, when by necessity children must attend municipal or community colleges or state colleges and universities, the potential marriage mates are much more problematic. State and community supported schools are likely to have lower tuition and residence costs and therefore to have a much more heterogeneous student population.

Since love is the basis of mating and everyone is "eligible" as a marriage partner—following the contemporary model—there is no assurance that children will fall in love with someone the parents would consider appropriate. Children may meet and fall in love with someone of a different race, religion, nationality, or social class level. Parents, while they may not admit it, are likely to be aware of, and in many cases apprehensive about, the possibility of a less than preferred mate for their child. While this concern may exist for both sons and daughters, there is good reason to believe that concern about daughters is somewhat greater. Women have traditionally been more likely to marry males who are higher status than they are. This tendency is called *hypergamy*. If a woman marries a man of lower status it is called *hypogamy*.

Given all these conditions, sororities can play an important part in the mate selection process, according to the analysis of Scott (1966). When a young woman on a large, heterogeneously populated college campus joins a sorority, the type of men she is likely to meet and interact with will be greatly restricted. Interaction will be governed by sorority functions, which are often reciprocal relationships with fraternities. Since the fraternity men are likely to be of similar status as the sorority women, the sorority may actually serve as a filter that simultaneously keeps out lower-status males and provides at least parallel-status males. On a large college campus where students have much personal freedom and where falling in love is the accepted basis for choosing a mate, the sorority can take the place of parents who are in no position to influence the selection of mates by their daughters.

But parents are not the only people interested in who their children marry. There are also larger social groups and organizations that exert an influence on the choice of marriage partners. Religious organizations are the most notable in this regard.

Religions and the Controls on Entering Marriage

Religions are organized and controlled by people who are almost always interested in perpetuating a particular set of beliefs. There is often the additional goal of expanding or spreading these beliefs to even larger numbers of people. One important mechanism for achieving these objectives is the control of marriage. Young members of most religions are encouraged by religious leaders to marry within their faith. Religious organizations also often have rules against marrying someone out of the faith, or procedures that must be observed if such a marriage is proposed.

The Catholic religion, for example, often requires that a non-Catholic take some religious instruction before marrying in the Church. If a Catholic is married outside the Church, such a marriage may not be recognized as legitimate.

Newly established religions are especially likely to have strict prohibitions against marrying outside the religion. The mechanisms for controlling marriage are likely to be very direct. An example of this can be found in the practices of the Unification Church, established and led by Reverend Sun Myung Moon.

Members of the Unification Church, most of whom are young people, are married after Reverend Moon selects an appropriate mate for them. Naturally the mate is a fellow member of the church. In 1982 Reverend Moon married 2,074 couples at a ceremony held in Madison Square Garden in New York City. In many cases the two people marrying were unknown to each other a week before their marriage. They came to New York from all parts of the nation and the

Reverend Sen Myung Moon married 2,074 couples in one ceremony. Many of the brides and grooms were matched by Reverend Moon personally.

world to be married. In many cases their marriage partners were chosen after their arrival. According to newspaper reports as many as 1,500 men and women were brought into a large room where Reverend Moon personally selected the mate for each (Wadler, 1982). After having an opportunity to talk, the couple could decide against the match and ask to be matched again. Most, however, did not, considering it an act of faith to marry the person chosen for them by their religious leader.

The procedure of the Unification Church is clearly an extreme example, but it does illustrate the lengths to which religious groups will go to assure that marriages are within the faith. While most religions are less intrusive in the selection process, there is no doubt that the preference is for marriages to be intrafaith marriages.

Not only do social groups take an interest in whom one marries, they also take an interest in how one marries. This can be seen in the way the church as well as the state have long required people to marry by their rules.

The Church and the State and Marriage

The Catholic Church in Europe, as it grew in strength during the middle ages, only gradually gained control over marriage. By the twelfth century, however, the Church rules governing marriage had taken shape. It was at that time that the opinions and decisions of a long string of popes, bishops, and councils were brought together and codified (Gottlieb, 1980). The most important principle to come out of this codification was that a marriage entered into secretly (called a clandestine marriage) was a valid marriage if both parties consented to it. However, if two people secretly entered into a marriage it was clear that such an action could lead to great uncertainty and problems for the Church. Church authorities noted that if one of the parties to a secret marriage later had a change of heart and denied the marriage, there would be no way of establishing if that person was telling the truth. For this and other reasons, Church authorities concluded that marriages should not be clandestine or secret. There are numerous records of court cases in the fifteenth century where couples were tried and punished by Church authorities for not being married publicly at the church door (as it was done in those days).

Church authorities sought to ensure public marriages by requiring a "reading of the banns." Reading of the banns was a public announcement generally also read at the church door on several successive Sundays before the marriage (Gottlieb, 1980). In Puritan England of the seventeenth century, Church marriages were prohibited because they were thought to be too frivolous. Only marriages performed by justices of the peace were allowed. Even so, when couples were intending to marry they were given the option of having the banns read at the church on three consecutive Sundays or in the marketplace the following three market days (Monsarrat, 1974).

Even secret engagements were considered by the Church to be punishable offenses. Gottlieb (1980) has examined cases brought before religious courts in France in the fifteenth century and uncovered many instances where couples were fined for becoming engaged secretly. As an example, there was the case of Colin Tanneur and Perrette Doulsot, who one night in the woman's family home talked about getting married. The man promised to marry her and gave her a silver ring. The woman promised to be his wife and gave him a ring with a stone of amber. One month later they were summoned into court for their actions. They admitted becoming engaged clandestinely and were fined one pound of wax each. They were also ordered to be married within a week (Gottlieb, 1980). Religious authorities did not look kindly on secret engagements or marriages in the fifteenth century. Vestiges of that view continue today as the Catholic Church still requires a reading or publication of the banns on three consecutive Sundays before a wedding.

While religious rules governing how one marries only apply to the followers of that particular religion, the rules set by the governments apply to all citizens. In the United States, individual states are able to pass unique laws governing the entry into marriage. Some states require blood tests or other medical examinations, while others do not. After obtaining a blood test, states often require a waiting period while the tests are being analyzed. Nebraska is an example of one extreme where a blood test is required five days before a marriage license can be purchased. After obtaining the license an additional three days of waiting are required. At the opposite extreme, Nevada requires no blood test and no waiting period after obtaining the license. It is not surprising that Nevada, with a very small resident population, has more marriages each year than all except the four most populous states (California, Illinois, New York, and Texas).

States also place limits on how old one must be before marriage, but again the age varies from one state to the next. In New Hampshire a female can marry with parental consent at age thirteen, provided she is pregnant and a court order has been obtained. Males in New Hampshire can marry at fourteen with parental consent, a court order, and a pregnant bride. Most states have set eighteen years as the age at which both males and females can marry without parental consent. However, at least one state (Mississippi) requires parental consent for both males and females until age twenty-one. Yet other states have different minimum marriage ages for males and females, with males having to be older than females. Alabama, Idaho, Minnesota, and New York all require a higher age at marriage for males than for females, without parental consent. In an age when gender is usually thought to be an inappropriate basis for granting rights and privileges, the marriage laws of some states still make gender distinctions.

While state governments control the ages at which people can marry, there is a much more important way the government is involved in marriage. The government has a marriage contract that one enters into at the time of marriage. Whenever two people enter a marriage, they are agreeing to all the terms and conditions that the state (this means government at any level) has attached to marriage. That, as we shall see, is a formidable array of terms and conditions.

The Marriage Contract

Imagine yourself going into a government office and signing a legally binding contract but not being allowed to see the terms of the contract. You sign the contract, but only later will you perhaps learn what your obligations, restrictions, and rights are under the terms of the contract. Any competent lawyer would have to advise you not to sign such an agreement. Yet, when people marry they do just that. Almost no one knows family law well enough at the time of marriage to be able to claim knowledge of all the conditions imposed by a legal marriage.

The hidden contract we enter at the time of marriage is very likely to be based on very traditional assumptions about the marriage relationship and the roles of husbands and wives. And when we marry, regardless of our personal beliefs or values, we will be bound by the laws based on these assumptions.

Weitzman (1981) has identified the major assumptions found in the laws of the United States regarding marriage. These assumptions grew out of English common law and have been perpetuated in the American legislative and judicial system. They include the following:

1. The husband is head of the household.
2. The husband is responsible for the economic support of his wife and children.
3. The wife is responsible for domestic services and child care.

It is true that in recent years all of these assumptions have been challenged in the courts and continue to be challenged daily. These challenges are modifying the force and range of the traditional assumptions about marriage and families, but recent court rulings have not eliminated their influence. We can see their influence in contemporary legal cases, as well as in the public norms relating to marriage and family relations.

Assumption 1. The husband is head of the family.   This assumption is revealed most clearly in the way a woman is expected to assume her husband's legal and social identity. There have been some recent important breaks in the tradition that a woman is required by law to take her husband's name (e.g., Mrs. Ebenezer Draconian), but a wife is typically expected to adopt her husband's domicile, and his social and economic status.

On the matter of names, the surname of the husband is often assumed to be the only appropriate last name for any children of the marriage. Weitzman (1981) describes a 1980 court case in which a woman named Patricia Herdman was separated from a Jason Schiffman after a six-month marriage. Patricia was pregnant when they separated and later gave birth to a girl, whom she named Aita Marrie Herdman. At the time of the divorce, Jason petitioned to have the girl's last name changed to Schiffman. The court agreed, as did the appeals court, ruling that the father had a "protectible interest" and a "primary right" in having his child bear his surname. Only when this California case was pressed at the state's supreme court level was the decision reversed (Weitzman, 1981).

The matter of domiciles is also instructive, especially regarding the way men are assumed to be heads of households. Under common-law tradition, a husband had the right to select the place of residence, and his wife had to accept and reside in the home. Many states continue to follow this basic rule. A woman who marries a man who resides in a state other than her home state may lose the residence rights she has previously enjoyed. There are cases of women losing in-state college tuition rates and the right to vote simply by virtue of their marriages to men residing in other states.

Assumption 2. The husband is responsible for economic and child-care support.   While a husband gains certain privileges upon entering marriage, the law also imposes certain obligations. Among the most important is the obligation to provide economic support for his wife and children. This deeply rooted male responsibility is built on the assumption of a strict division of labor, with husbands being responsible for the economic needs of the family and wives being responsible for the care and nurturance of husband and children.

Many couples today prefer a greater sharing of these responsibilities, which is to say that they prefer a less strict division of labor. This is best exemplified by the more than fifty percent of married women engaged in paid employment. Notwithstanding these contemporary preferences and behaviors, court rulings often seem to presume that a strict separation of employment and home responsibilities are still sharply observed by all husbands and wives. Even when laws and the courts acknowledge that women are found in great numbers in the labor force, husbands are still generally viewed as the primary breadwinners, while wives are secondary.

When the husband is considered the major economic provider, it reinforces the assumption that he is head of the household and controls the resources. Historically, under English common law, a husband acquired ownership and control over his wife's property and possessions at the time of marriage. When a woman was employed under these conditions, her husband was also entitled to her wages. As recently as 1978 in Louisiana there was a court case involving a married woman who lost a home that she had purchased with the earnings from her work alone. Her husband, without her permission and over her objection, was able to borrow money on the home she had purchased. He was able to do so because under Louisiana law he was "head and master" of the couple's property. When he failed to repay the borrowed money the credit company sought to foreclose on the mortgage. The wife filed a suit that challenged the "head and master" rule, saying that her husband had no right, without her consent, to borrow against the home she had purchased. However, the courts of Louisiana ruled against her and the U.S. Supreme Court refused to hear the case, thus letting the "head and master" rule stand. Somewhat later, Louisiana did give wives the right to control community property equally with their husbands (Weitzman, 1981).

The economic responsibilities of husbands extend also to their children. The traditional assumption of the marriage contract gives a husband the responsibility of providing economically for the couple's children. In English common law of the nineteenth century this responsibility was so firmly established that fathers were typically given custody of children in the event of a divorce. That has now changed in England and in the United States, where it is assumed that the child-care and nurturing responsibilities of mothers make her the "natural" person to have custody of the children. When the mother is awarded custody of minor children after a divorce, the father is usually required by the court to pay child support.

Regarding child support, however, a number of studies has shown that there is a great deal of noncompliance to these court-ordered payments. In 1981 there were four million mothers who were supposed to receive child support payments. Only forty-seven percent received the full amount they were due (U.S. Bureau of the Census, 1984). While the laws and court orders are flouted there are increasing efforts to make compliance more effective. On the basis of a 1978 law there is a major federal effort to locate parents (usually males) who are not paying their required child support. Agencies in each state charged with the responsibility of locating noncomplying parents are given access to Social Security records and assistance from the Internal Revenue Service. With these and other mechanisms, fathers are increasingly being held to their legal obligation to support the natural or adopted children of any marriage they enter.

Assumption 3. The wife is responsible for domestic duties and child-care services.

When a man marries, the traditional assumption is that he has obtained the services of a woman who will take care of his house, care for his children, and, in addition, provide love, affection, companionship, and sexual services. The legal term for all of these services is *consortium*. It has been the tradition under common law that the husband could sue for the "loss of consortium" if his wife's services were denied to him as a result of the negligent injury of his wife by a third party. Until recently, only husbands could sue for loss of consortium; wives could not. That too has now changed as a result of court decisions. As of 1977, in thirty-eight states and the District of Columbia, wives could also file suit for loss of consortium, if they lost the services of their husbands as a result of the action of a third party. Six states do not allow wives to file such suits, and six other states do not allow the suits to be filed by either sex.

While cases involving the loss of consortium are relatively infrequent, there has nonetheless been a consistent upholding of the principle through the cases that have arisen. In general, the courts have most often upheld the idea that a husband has the right to his wife's services, especially sexual services, and that if some third party should, for example, attract her away, he can turn to the courts to redress this loss.

If, as traditional law has assumed, a wife is obligated to perform domestic services for her husband, such an assumption has three major legal consequences. First, a woman is deprived of the legal right to her own labor. If it is "owed" to her husband under the marriage contract, then it cannot be claimed by the wife. Second, the part a wife plays in building the family's wealth and property is not considered as a contribution to the enterprise. There have been a number of tax cases and divorce cases that have reflected the view that the work of the wife accrues to the benefit of the husband only, not to the couple.

Typically, a married couple with a business or a farm will work together for the success of the enterprise. Often the wife will carry out as many of the business tasks as the husband, and yet in the case of a divorce the courts have often ruled that the wife's work has not given her joint ownership of the enterprise. All the accumulated wealth and property is presumed to be owned by the husband (Weitzman, 1981).

The third and last consequence of the assumption that a woman owes her services to her husband is that a woman may not receive wages for her work. Again, court cases have repeatedly denied requests of wives, especially in divorce cases, to be compensated for the years of "wifely service" they have rendered. In a 1973 Canadian divorce case, a woman who had worked side-by-side with her husband for twenty-five years was denied any claim to the extensive ranch land they had accumulated. She sued for divorce after her husband had beaten her so severely she had to be hospitalized. The court granted her only a two-hundred-dollar monthly maintenance payment, while her husband was left with property that made him a wealthy man (Weitzman, 1981).

Gradually states are changing their laws with regard to property accumulated during a marriage, and there is a greater recognition that the contributions of wives, both those who do and do not work for pay, must be taken into account in settlements. There are still some knotty problems remaining in this area, however, especially in divorce cases. Wives who work to put their husbands through college and professional schools often ask to share in the benefits that result from that education. In the case of a divorce this includes benefits that will be realized in the future. Sometimes the courts have ruled that wives do have a right to these benefits, but they have usually been denied any part of pensions or retirement payments due to their husbands.

We have considered only some of the major elements of the marriage contract provided by the state when we marry, but even this brief examination reveals several things. First, the laws that affect us when we marry may be very different from what we would have them be if they were based on our own values and preferences. Often the laws and court rulings are based on older traditions and assumptions relating to married life. Second, we can see that the laws and court rulings can be quite different from place to place and that they are likely to change as time goes on. With this in mind, it might be noted that even if we understand all the rights, duties, and obligations of marriage at the time we marry, they may change as time goes on. If changes in the laws, or their interpretation, do occur, we are nonetheless bound by the new forms. In the United States, even as we move from one state to another, our rights, obligations, and duties may change because of variations in state laws.

In addition to the marriage contract of the state, it is possible, as noted at the beginning of this chapter, for couples to prepare their own personal marriage contracts. At the end of this chapter we will consider the arguments for and against such contracts, but before we get to these we must examine them to see exactly what such contracts are and what they are not.

Personal Marriage Contracts

Personal marriage contracts are not new. They may seem to be very contemporary, perhaps growing out of the women's movement, but their history goes back thousands of years. Marriage contracts* dating back to 900 B.C. have been found in Egypt (Hopkins, 1980). These contracts were entered into not just by the upper strata of Egyptian society, but by people of moderate means as well. In European history there are also many instances of marriage contracts, although generally the contracts were made by royal families and families where considerable wealth was involved. (The Irish marriage contracts of the nineteenth century, discussed earlier in this chapter, are an exception to this generalization, since they were entered into by almost all people.) Marriage contracts are usually drawn up and signed before the day of the marriage; or, as in the case of the Egyptians, they may be signed on the day of the marriage. However, as a practical matter there is no reason why a contract cannot be prepared and signed at any time before or during a marriage. Also, if a marriage contract is *antenuptial* (before the marriage) it can be modified or rewritten at any later date.

What can be included in a marriage contract? One answer is that it can cover anything a couple wishes it to cover. However, under our legal system the terms may not be enforceable if they run counter to the existing laws of the state (Weitzman, 1981). For example, the courts have not generally allowed couples to write personal marriage contracts that seek to change the "essential elements" of marriage. The two provisions of marriage discussed above, the husband's duty to support his wife and the wife's duty to serve her husband, have been considered by the courts to be two such essential elements. If personal marriage contracts come before the courts and have provisions that seem to subvert these essential elements of the state's marriage contract, such contracts have often been held to be invalid (Weitzman, 1981). Also, a personal marriage contract may not include provisions that anticipate or encourage divorce. At least the courts will not usually uphold such provisions. Thus, a husband and wife cannot agree in advance to waive alimony payments in the event of a divorce. To do so would imply that the couple was anticipating divorce.

While the courts of the United States have not generally upheld provisions of personal marriage contracts that undermined the essential elements of marriage, there has been increasing acceptance in recent years of the provisions that couples include in their marriage contracts. In other words, the courts are recognizing that contemporary couples do not always accept traditional assumptions about marriage and are respecting more and more the particular

---

*In many instances we will use the term *marriage contract* in the pages that follow, even though the more precise term would be *personal marriage contract*. This follows popular usage and is less cumbersome. Also, the term *marriage contract* will generally be used to cover agreements drawn up by cohabiting couples. Again, by using only the term *marriage contract* we can avoid the new creations such as *intimate contracts, living- together contracts,* and *love pacts* (Clair and Daniele, 1980).

needs and wishes of couples who have made the effort to prepare a personal contract.*

There is one additional point that needs to be made about contract provisions that might not be upheld by the courts. Such provisions can be included in personal marriage contracts if the couple wishes. It would be of no consequence if the case did not come before a court in an adversarial proceeding (as in a contested divorce). A couple could respect and abide by the conditions of their own marriage contract even if these would not be upheld by the formal legal system.

Since anything can be included in a marriage contract, the list of possible provisions is limitless. But there are some things that are very likely to be included in most contracts. The following have been found by researchers to be the most likely issues covered (Weitzman, 1981).

Aims and expectations. Most contracts include some statement about what the two people expect to receive and achieve from the relationship. This can range from very concrete aims (the wife will be able to complete her education) to less clear-cut goals ("personal growth" or "continued emotional support"). Most commonly, aims and expectations include statements about the career objectives of one or both members of the couple. Having children (or not having them) is also an objective often mentioned in marriage contracts.

Economic and financial arrangements. Almost all marriage contracts have some provisions discussing economic matters. Historically, economic and financial arrangements were at the heart of personal marriage contracts. Today, couples are most likely to spell out who should have rights to property that the individuals had prior to marriage (or cohabitation). Couples are also likely to spell out who should own the property accumulated after the marriage. (The overwhelming majority of couples favor mutual or joint ownership of such property.)

Support and work arrangements. The majority of contemporary marriage contracts deal with the issues of work, careers, and economic support. Couples often spell out who will work, when they will work, and whose work has priority standing.

Household location and domestic tasks. Almost all marriage contracts today will give attention to where the couple will live and the circum-

---

*In early 1984 the Maryland Court of Appeals ruled that an antenuptial agreement specifying that there would be no alimony in case of a divorce was a valid agreement, and could stand.

stances under which a change of residence will be made. The following is an example of such a provision:

> *Steven and Judy both wish to reside in San Rafael. Should Steven's law practice be relocated, Judy agrees to transfer her career to the new location. Steven's career will be of major concern to the partnership since it will be the main source of support for the family. (Weitzman, 1981, p. 432)*

Other couples, of course, may deal with the same issue in quite a different way, perhaps by giving the wife's career priority.

Taking care of the household tasks is also a very frequently addressed issue in marriage contracts. Again, the particular arrangement may vary from a traditional division of labor to very nontraditional arrangements (the member of the couple doing the most housework being paid an additional income; the husband taking primary responsibility for household work).

Interpersonal relations. There are many issues affecting the relationship of a couple, and often these too are addressed in personal marriage contracts. These issues can, for example, include the surname to be used by the wife (and in some cases the husband) and the surnames to be given to any children. Other common interpersonal issues include the nature of the couple's

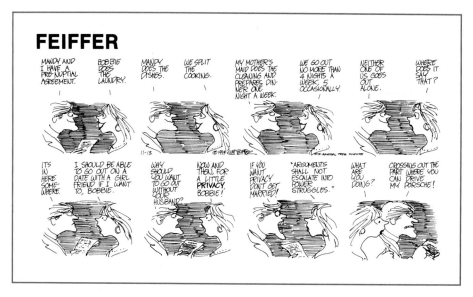

FEIFFER. Copyright © 1983, Jules Feiffer. Reprinted with permission of Universal Press Syndicate. All rights reserved.

sexual relationship, the religious affiliations and preferences of the two individuals, and the conduct of the partners in the event of disagreements. Some marriage contracts are very specific about the behavior that will be allowed and expected during disagreements: "Neither party will raise his/her voice above a reasonable level during an argument. Each party will allow the other to complete his/her statement before replying" (Weitzman, 1981, p. 438).

Children. If having and caring for children is not addressed as part of the "aims and expectations" section of a contract, the issue is often given a special section by itself. The contract might stipulate that the couple plans to have no children, or the exact number expected. Responsibility for birth control is also frequently included in contracts. And many contracts provide for who will care for the children, both physically and financially.

Wills and inheritances. Many couples anticipate in their contracts the drafting of their own wills and the disposition of any inheritances either might receive in the future.

Contract review and dissolution. Couples often recognize that the contract they are entering into may not always be appropriate or applicable under changing circumstances. Therefore, with an eye toward flexibility, they may call for periodic review of the contract and specify procedures for changing it. Some contracts provide for the kinds of "damages" that a person shall be awarded if the partner breaks the terms of the contract.

Almost all marriage contracts have some discussion of dissolution of the relationship or marriage. There is likely to be a statement about the conditions under which dissolution can occur ("if desired by either party," or "only after professional marriage counseling," for example). Many contracts deal with the issue of dividing property and providing financial support in the event of a dissolution. Child custody and support is also frequently provided for if the marriage ends when there are minor children.

This list of frequently found provisions of personal marriage contracts shows how they can range over many different topics and express the special or unique needs of particular couples. From the examples above it is clear that couples may reflect any values or views, from the most traditional and conservative to the most radical and unorthodox. Therefore, the question is not what should be in a marriage contract, but whether it is a good idea to have one at all. In the following section we will consider the arguments for and against marriage contracts.

ISSUE

Should couples have marriage contracts?

We have examined the nature of personal marriage contracts and have reviewed many of the topics they frequently cover. We are now ready to consider the basic question, what are the arguments for and against having a marriage contract? We will begin the discussion by considering the arguments against such contracts.

The Arguments against Marriage Contracts

The single most frequently heard opposition to marriage contracts is that a contract is completely unnecessary when two people love, trust, and respect each other. A marriage, it is argued, is not a business arrangement in which two people must each be careful lest the other person have the advantage. Marriage is not a question of who is getting the better "deal." When a person enters marriage it should be with the idea of *giving*, not getting. The ideal marriage is one in which the two partners are striving to give support, assistance, and comfort, as well as financial and economic benefits.

A closely related argument is voiced in very practical terms by critics of marriage contracts. They often ask, "What am I supposed to do if my husband (or wife) isn't living up to the terms of the contract? Do I bring out the contract and wave it in front of his (or her) nose? What good would that do?" This question reflects a concern that the terms of a marriage contract are not really enforceable but depend on voluntary compliance. As a concrete example, if a husband and wife have agreed in a contract to share the cooking, what is a wife to do if one evening her husband refuses to cook? Does she take him to court? Since there is very little that can force a spouse to abide by many conditions found in contracts, critics ask what good they are.

Another criticism of marriage contracts is that when two people begin a marriage this way, they are starting off on the wrong note. As one critic has argued, writing a marriage contract reflects a pessimistic outlook about the future of the relationship (Wells, 1976). It is pessimistic because it anticipates disagreements and the possibility that a partner will not perform his or her responsibilities. Contracts that make provisions for the eventuality of separation and divorce are especially pessimistic. It seems particularly inconsistent that two people who are making plans to commit their lives to each other can at the same time spell out the terms of their possible breakup.

Another criticism of marriage contracts is based more on the legal status they have, or do not have. Certainly in the past, and to a considerable degree today, marriage contracts that run counter to prevailing laws or common-law traditions have limited legal standing in the courts. Thus, it is argued, if a personal contract cannot be enforced or supported by the courts, it is nothing more than a meaningless piece of paper.

A final argument against marriage contracts is that they are inflexible and are likely to fail when they try to anticipate the areas of conflict in a marriage (Wells, 1976). Furthermore, at the time contracts are written couples are not likely to anticipate how they will change during marriage. Yet a contract can lock couples into points of view they held before marriage. For example, a man at the time of marriage may feel that the woman he is marrying is ideally suited to rear their children. At the time of marriage he might sign a contract waiving his custody rights in the event of a divorce. However, should a divorce someday eventuate, this man might have very different views about giving up custody of the children.

The arguments against marriage contracts tend to focus on their inappropriateness and ineffectiveness. Contracts are also said to set a pessimistic tone for the marriage and are frequently unenforceable in courts of law. Last, they may bind people to points of view that they would not hold later in the marriage.

Arguments for Marriage Contracts

Many advocates of marriage contracts feel that a major problem connected with marriage is that too many people marry with only starry-eyed, romantic notions about marriage in general and their partners in particular. Marriage contracts provide a way of moving to a more realistic perspective. In the course of discussions about the terms of a marriage contract, two people might reveal for the first time their views about specific issues.

A prospective wife, for example, might learn that her husband-to-be expects to have all his meals prepared for him and served at a specific time. Or he might expect her to quit working if they have a child, and not return to work until the youngest child is in high school. These and many other deeply held views may come into the open when two people sit down to discuss the provisions of a marriage contract. It is surely better, argue the advocates of contracts, if potential areas of disagreement come out before marriage. This allows the disagreements to be ironed out in advance. In some extreme cases, disagreements may be of such a fundamental nature, and the two parties so unyielding, that the marriage itself should be reconsidered.

In general, the advocates of marriage contracts see great advantages in the way contract negotiations help to clarify and bring into the open the aims, objectives, and expectations of couples before they marry. But there are several other positive features of contracts that have been identified (Weitzman et al., 1978). These include the following:

1. *Opening communication.* By requiring couples to enter into discussions of their aims, objectives, and expectations, they are more likely to establish communication and discussion as a way of relating to each other.

2. *Living up to intentions.* Couples will be more likely to live up to their intentions if they have been discussed, written down, and agreed to by both parties. The contract stands as a written guide, which can be referred to again and again as issues arise.

3. *Resolving conflicts.* When couples set down their ideals for how disputes and disagreements are to be handled, their contracts may provide a ready guide for getting through the difficult times that are likely to arise in any relationship.

4. *Providing predictability and security.* Contracts spell out some of the details of what might otherwise be unknown steps in the course of a marriage. By spelling out the details of what is anticipated, a contract can provide a sense of predictability, and thus lead to a feeling of security in a relationship.

Two of the arguments against marriage contracts have also been answered by the advocates. These are their uncertain legal status and their inflexibility. It is true that the courts have often not upheld the provisions of personal marriage contracts, especially when these provisions subvert the "essential elements" of marriage or are written in contemplation of divorce. However, there is accumulating evidence that both state legislatures and the courts are taking a new look at marriage contracts. Some states have already made major breaks from traditional family law, and some experts have said, "we predict that other states will soon join them in upholding reasonable contracts between husbands and wives" (Weitzman et al., 1978, p. 316). As couples continue to push for the validity of their personal marriage contracts, there will probably be increasing movement in this direction.

There is a similar trend with regard to upholding contracts written by cohabiting couples. Advocates of marriage contracts have welcomed this trend, because they have often argued that it is more important for cohabiting couples to have contracts than it is for husbands and wives to have them. Since cohabiting couples do not have any of the provisions of a legal marriage, they must enter into contracts if they are to have similar conditions. As an example, married couples usually have some form of "widow's rights," which ensure the widow (or widower) at least part of the spouse's property in the event of death. Cohabitants could agree to similar provisions in a personal contract and back up their agreement with appropriate wills.

It should also be noted that even if provisions of a marriage contract are not legally enforceable, a couple can still include such provisions in a contract. The contract can be as binding as they want to make it for themselves, as long as they do not ask the courts to carry out the enforcement.

The critics say that marriage contracts are inflexible and cannot deal effectively with changes occurring during marriage. This criticism is countered by advocates who point out that contracts can be changed or renegotiated. A contract may even have a built-in time period during which it will be in effect. At the end of that period the contract may be modified or amended as the couple wishes.

The principal set of arguments in favor of marriage contracts is built around their ability to open communication and discussion between marrying individuals. By working through differences before marriage, couples may avoid more serious problems later. Also, some of the alleged negative features of contracts—unenforceability and inflexibility—are not as serious as some critics suggest.

Themes

1. Marriage is the preferred way of life in most societies, including the contemporary United States.

2. Though marriage customs differ greatly from society to society, there are often underlying similarities in the meanings customs have.

3. The many different forms and variations of entering marriage can be divided into three *ideal types:* the traditional-agrarian, the courtship, and the contemporary.

4. The traditional-agrarian ideal type involves the selection of marriage mates by parents, negotiations about economic and other matters, and almost no elements of courtship and love.

5. The courtship ideal type emphasizes narrowing down the field of eligible marriage mates and settling on the best bargain.

6. The contemporary ideal type shows how people enter into relationships that they may later leave when the costs of the relationship exceed the rewards.

7. The nature of early dating behavior, cohabitation, and the high divorce rate are all consistent with the contemporary model of entering marriage.

8. While marriage is an important personal commitment, it is simultaneously a social commitment.

9. Parents are particularly interested in and concerned about the marital partner choices of their children.

10. Religious organizations are almost always concerned about the marital choices of members of their faith.

11. The state controls many aspects of marriage and creates a marriage contract that most people enter into with little or no awareness.

12. The marriage contract as defined by laws and the courts often reflects values of an earlier time. However, the law is constantly changing and adapting.

13. A personal marriage contract is an agreement between two people that can cover any topics and issues they wish it to cover.

Facts

1. By the time Americans reach age forty almost everyone (ninety-three percent of women and ninety percent of men) has married at least once.

2. In India, among the Hindu population, more the ninety-nine percent of all females marry.

3. Irish men in the late nineteenth and early twentieth centuries were often in their thirties or forties before they married.

4. Based on a study of Connecticut high school students, "going steady" begins at about fifteen, but the duration of such relationships is usually between two and ten months.

5. According to the results of one study, eighty-two percent of cohabitants stayed together less than three months.

6. It is estimated that one-third of all children in the United States will experience the end of their parents' marriage before they reach age sixteen.

7. In the fifteenth century the Catholic Church punished people who were engaged or married secretly (clandestine marriages).

8. The state of Nevada has no blood test and no waiting period for marriage, with the result that it has the fifth largest number of marriages in the country.

9. In New Hampshire a female can marry with parental consent at age thirteen, if she is pregnant and has a court order.

10. Some states have permissible marriage ages for males that are higher than those set for females.

11. There are three major assumptions that have traditionally governed family law: the husband is head of the household; the husband is responsible for the economic support of his wife; and the wife is responsible for domestic services and child care.

12. In 1981 only forty-seven percent of mothers who were supposed to receive child support were actually receiving it.

13. Personal marriage contracts go back to 900 B.C. in Egypt.

14. In European history marriage contracts were used primarily by royal and wealthy families.

15. The courts in the United States are increasingly respecting the particular needs and wishes of couples who enter into personal marriage contracts.

Major Concepts

clandestine marriage: A marriage entered into secretly, especially with regard to the Catholic Church.

consortium: All services that women traditionally owed to their husbands, according to the law.

contemporary model (for entering marriage): Young people select their marriage mates from a pool of eligibles that includes everyone; commitments are not necessarily binding for the long term.

courtship model (for entering marriage): Young people select marriage mates by narrowing down a field of eligibles; marriage is expected to last a lifetime.

dowry: Things of value that a bride brings to her husband and his family at the time of marriage.

field of eligibles: All persons who by virtue of social and personal characteristics are appropriate as marriage partners.

hypergamy: The pattern of women marrying men who are higher in status.

hypogamy: The pattern of women marrying men who are lower in status.

ideal type: A sociological method of analysis that rests on an exaggerated and extreme characterization of some social phenomenon.

matchmaker or go-between: A particular person in a community who helps families find marriage mates for their children.

permanent, universal availability: The idea that no one is ever totally and irrevocably removed from the marriage market.

personal marriage contract: An agreement drawn up by two people either prior to or after their marriage that covers any issues important to the couple.

traditional-agrarian model (for entering marriage): Parents or other kin choose mates for their children, based on economic, social, or other considerations.

8

Husband and Wife Relations
Communication, Marital Quality, and Power

An observant sociologist has noted that most people are "firmly of *two* minds" about the nature of married life (Udry, 1974). On the one hand, they believe in the ideal of two people falling in love and living happily ever after. On the other hand, the same people, but especially those who have been married for a while, are likely to say that marriage inevitably becomes a "domestic grind." They often give voice to the idea that husbands and wives will gradually move toward routine and boring relationships, with little or no romantic feeling. For generations cartoonists have amused us with scenes of long-suffering marriage partners.

Neither the idealistic nor the cynical view of married life reflects the whole truth. But there is a message in the fact that for many people the two views exist simultaneously. That message is that in a husband-wife relationship there is a continuing tension between the forces that make the relationship happy and satisfying and those that make it routine and boring, or sometimes worse. This chapter will explore these opposing tendencies and a variety of other features of husband and wife relationships.

It is obvious that when two people marry they want and expect a happy and satisfying relationship. But as we examine husband and wife relationships in more detail, we will see that what brings happiness and satisfaction to one person may not bring them to another. Indeed, two people who are married to each other may have different notions of what constitutes or produces a happy and satisfying marriage. When that occurs, there is often trouble. Again, this chapter will explore the differences people have regarding the kind of marriage they want and what they want from marriage.

Many couples have the goal of an egalitarian or "fifty-fifty" marriage. But this familiar goal is more complicated than it first seems, in large part because there are very different notions of what constitutes an egalitarian marriage. At the end of this chapter we will describe two major types of husband-wife equality, and then consider the advantages and disadvantages of each.

There are those who argue that people expect too much of marriage today. When marriages do not live up to all their expectations, they become disillusioned and disappointed. One writer has put the case strongly:

> Marriage was not designed as a mechanism for providing friendship, erotic experience, romantic love, personal fulfillment, continuous lay psychotherapy and recreation. The Western European family was not designed to carry a lifelong load of highly emotional freight. Given its present structure it simply had to fail when asked to do so. The very idea of an irrevocable contract obligating the parties concerned to a life-time of romantic effort is utterly absurd. (Cadwalleder, 1966, p. 62)

This statement emphasizes that in contemporary life we expect our spouses to satisfy our every need, forever. Critics like the one just quoted believe we have come to expect so much from a marriage relationship that it is bound to fail for most people. This is an interesting point of view, if only because it sensitizes us to some of the specifics of what we expect of a marriage. Furthermore, even the extensive list presented above does not include the equality issue mentioned earlier. If that is added to the list of things expected of a marriage, it may give some insight into why so many people leave marriages through divorce. When they fail to have all their needs satisfied, they leave it in search of another relationship that they hope will give them all they are looking for.

VARIETIES OF HUSBAND-WIFE RELATIONS

We can gain another perspective on what is expected from a marriage relationship by examining some of the different ways husbands and wives relate to each other. We will do that in part by looking at marriage systems as they exist in other societies. We will also identify some types of husband-wife relations that researchers have found in our own society. We will begin with a very unusual marriage system—one in which husbands and wives are virtually enemies.

Marriage as Warfare

In Chapter 7 we saw how the Pakhtun people of northwestern Pakistan entered marriage by carrying the bride through the streets from her parents' home to the groom's family home. We noted at the time that the groom did not join the feasting of the men in his family because of the shame he was expected to feel for losing his bachelorhood. This might have given us a clue that married life among the Pakhtun is quite different from our ideals. Such is certainly the case, for the husband and wife relationship among the Pakhtun has been described by anthropologists as a continuing state of psychological and physical warfare (Lindholm and Lindholm, 1979).

One prominent feature of Pakhtun marriage is that wives (and all women) are kept in the seclusion of the household most of the time. This practice is called *purdah.* It means that a woman must never leave the compound walls surrounding her home without her husband's permission. (The Pakhtun say, "A woman's place is in the house or in the grave"—Lindholm and Lindholm, 1979, p. 19.) It brings great shame to her husband if a wife is seen in public by other men. The punishment for a woman who violates this restriction is severe. In the past a woman who was seen by a man who was not her relative would have her nose cut off by her husband. Today, that custom has been given up, but the woman will still usually be severely beaten. If a woman is found alone with a man who is not a relative, she will be killed by her husband, because she has dishonored him in the eyes of the community (Lindholm and Lindholm, 1979).

Since women can bring dishonor to their husbands, wives are feared by their husbands. Wives, on the other hand, fear their husbands because they are always in danger of receiving physical punishment. The Pakhtun marriage is one where the wife is a prisoner in her husband's home, where she must do his bidding and still expect to be punished frequently. From the husband's point of view his wife is a threatening and treacherous enemy in his own home. With

In many contemporary Muslim societies, women are still required to cover their faces in public—a part of the practice called purdah.

this as the basis for marriage, it is small wonder that the relationship between husbands and wives is one of constant hostility and fighting. While this seems to go on through the entire marriage, it is an accepted way of life, and amazing as it may be by our standards, husbands and wives often develop a kind of respect and even fondness for each other. "Each admires the other's resolute pride and fighting ability. But the man cannot show his affection, for to do so would give the wife courage to dishonor him" (Lindholm and Lindholm, 1979, p. 19).

Some Pakhtun couples may fight less than others, but there will always be some rivalry and competition, because it is built into the social and cultural ways of these people. By the time couples reach old age the fighting seems to abate somewhat, often, it seems, because the husband is "a tired old man, without the energy for fighting" (Lindholm and Lindholm, 1979, p. 19). However, through most of married life the relationship between husbands and wives is full of strife, fighting, and violence.

In our society there are husbands and wives who have relationships that are in many ways similar to those of Pakhtun married couples, but they certainly do not represent the norm or the standard. Also, it is very unlikely that their relationships were hostile and contentious from the very beginning. Nonetheless, in a study of American middle-class couples by Cuber and Harroff (1968), there were ongoing marriages that were classified as *conflict-habituated*. Conflict-habituated couples are those who have fallen into a pattern of nearly constant fighting and arguing. These couples seem to look forward to conflict. They seem to operate under a rule that says, "No fight or argument is ever really over." The intensity may vary, but there is recurrent nagging, attacking, bickering, and arguing. The constant hostility and fighting becomes a way of life, and yet such couples may stay married for a lifetime (Cuber and Harroff, 1968).

Conflict-habituated couples are so remote from our ideal of a happy and satisfying marriage that it is difficult to understand why or how they stay together. One can conjecture that some people receive a perverse pleasure from such a high-tension relationship, but it is more likely that the explanation lies in the tendency of most people to persist in a familiar pattern of interaction. When two people gradually slip into a pattern of conflict, it becomes a habit, and like all habits, difficult to break.

Though it is difficult to understand why conflict-habituated couples remain in marriage, we do know that they exist as a reality in our society. How many such couples there are, or in what proportion to all married couples, no one can say. We only know that for some number of couples marriage can be aptly described as "holy deadlock" (LeMasters, 1959).

Role-Segregated Marriages

There are a number of societies where husbands and wives, instead of being in hostile opposition, are simply separated from each other most of the time. Their activities keep them apart or segregated. The segregated activities are largely dictated by the gender roles of males and females. The segregated roles of husbands and wives are also likely to reduce communication between them. These are called *role-segregated* couples. (This is a shortened form of the more cumbersome *segregated conjugal role-relationship* used by Bott, 1957; Rainwater, 1965).

In many Muslim societies the gender roles prescribed by the Islamic religion keep the sexes highly segregated (the Pakhtun people described above are strict Sunni Muslims). Women are often prohibited from being seen in public places. They are thus primarily confined to the home where they interact with other women and children. Husbands are away from home much of the time, engaged in work, business, or leisure activities with their male friends.

For example, in the state of Oman on the Saudi Arabian peninsula, the segregation between males and females is nearly complete. According to anthropologist Unni Wikan (1982), if one drives along the streets of the cities it is extremely rare to see a woman. Only the men will be in the marketplaces, the mosques, and on the main roads. Women will be inside their homes, for the home is their domain. Among the Omani the segregation of the sexes is such a fundamental part of life that even within the home the sexes are separated most of the time. When husbands have male guests they will sit in segregated areas of the home where they cannot be seen by members of the opposite sex. The same will be true for the female guests of wives. It is rare for any tasks in the home to be entered into jointly by both husband and wife. When husbands are away from home, which they are for most hours of the day, the wives know almost nothing about where they are or what they are doing. However, it should be noted that even though the Omani have a pattern of gender segregation it does not mean that husbands and wives are hostile toward each other (as was the case among the Pakhtun). Indeed, the case is quite the contrary, for Omani husbands and wives are usually very considerate and respectful toward each other (Wikan, 1982).

The Omani represent an extreme example of role segregation, and as such they reveal clearly the major features of role-segregated marriages. First, husbands and wives are physically apart most of the time. Second, there is a strict division of labor, with husbands and wives each having their respective activities. Very seldom do they have joint tasks or activities. Third, the level of communication between husbands and wives is limited. This means, of course, that their knowledge of each other is also limited.

Role segregation is also found in contemporary Western societies. In a classic study of London families, it was found that many working class married couples had very segregated role relationships (Bott, 1957). These English wives spent a great deal of time with their mothers, sisters, and other kin, rather than with their husbands. At the same time, their husbands were with their male friends and relatives. This high degree of role segregation extended into leisure pursuits as well as work activities. Bott observed in this study that husbands and wives were more likely to have segregated marriage roles if they had remained in the neighborhoods where they had grown up. In their old neighbor-

Among these Amish men and women, the role segregation that separates males from females in social activities is clearly in evidence.

hoods wives and husbands were likely to have social networks made up of same-sex friends and relatives.

When married couples have role-segregated relationships, their demands upon each other are lessened. There seems to be a very simple mechanism working to produce this effect. Everyone has some need for social support and interaction with other people. When husbands and wives have supportive social networks close around them, such as extended-family members and same-sex peers, they need less support from and interaction with their spouses (Lee, 1979).

The opposite side of this proposition is that when married couples are isolated from their family and kin groups (and perhaps also from the same-sex peers of their youth) they depend more on each other for support and interaction. When this occurs couples are more likely to have joint marriage roles.

Joint Marriage Roles

Marriage roles are labeled *joint* when spouses direct most of their time and energy toward each other. Specifically, this means that many marital and household tasks will be carried out together. There is also the possibility that tasks will be less rigidly assigned to either husband or wife. A couple with joint marriage roles will select entertainment, recreation, and even hobbies that can be done together. Since the couple will spend more time together, there will also be more communication between them and greater knowledge about the other person.

There is a substantial body of evidence that, with increasing modernization and urbanization, married couples have moved toward joint marriage roles (Kerckhoff, 1972). As couples form households away from their families, and away from their same-sex peers, they are more likely to turn to each other for the gratification of their needs. (The technical term for establishing a new household after marriage is *neolocal residence*, that is, a new location.) Equally important, when couples live away from their family and kin groups, they are more likely to adopt new values and orientations. They may become less traditional about gender roles; they may place more value on emotional intimacy between spouses, mutual support, companionship, and communication (Lee, 1979).

When Cuber and Harroff (1968) studied middle-class American couples, they found two forms of the joint marriage role relationship. The first of these they called the *vital marriage relationship*. The key to the vital marriage is that "the mates are intensely bound together psychologically in important life matters. Their sharing and togetherness is genuine. It provides the life essence for both" (Cuber and Harroff, 1968, p. 55). The words of one husband express how he feels about sharing his life with his wife:

> *The things we do together aren't fun intrinsically—the ecstasy comes from being together in the doing. Take her out of the picture and I wouldn't give a damn for the boat, the lake, or any of the fun that goes on out there. (Cuber and Harroff, 1968, p. 55)*

Another man, also in a vital marriage relationship, said that he had passed up a promotion because it would have meant more evenings and weekends away from his wife. He and his wife had been married twenty-two years, and he told the interviewers, "The hours with her are what I live for. You should meet her" (Cuber and Harroff, 1968, p. 55).

An even more intense form of jointness is found among those couples that Cuber and Harroff identified as having *total relationships*. The total relationship is one in which husband and wife share virtually every facet of life. They are together wherever and whenever possible.

> *There is practically no pretense between persons in the total relationship or between them and the world outside. There are few areas of tension, because the items of difference which have arisen over the years have been settled as they arose. . . . all aspects of life are mutually shared in and enthusiastically participated in. It is as if neither spouse has, or has had,*

a truly private existence. *(Cuber and Harroff, 1968, pp. 59–60; emphasis added)*

In terms of joint marriage role relations, the vital and total relationships described by Cuber and Harroff contrast vividly with relationships based on hostility or segregation. However, the contrast is based primarily on the time spouses spend together and the way they feel about each other. On the matter of division of labor between husbands and wives and the sharing or interchangeability of tasks, much less is said. It is quite possible that couples in both vital and total relationships follow traditional gender role patterns with regard to work and caring for the home. This issue will be addressed later in the chapter.

Before concluding this discussion of different types of husband and wife relationships, we must note that the research of Cuber and Harroff (1968) identified two other types among middle-class American couples. These types come much closer to one of the beliefs we discussed earlier, namely, that marriage can become a boring, unromantic, domestic grind.

Devitalized And Passive-Congenial Marriages

Many middle-aged couples acknowledge that their marriages have changed greatly since the time when they were first married. They often characterize their early years as ones when they were "deeply in love." They often say they had a period when they spent much time together, had a good sex life, and identified closely with each other, but that has all now changed. Now they spend little time together, have an unsatisfying sex life, and share few interests and activities. The things they now do together are more a matter of duty than preference.

The keynote expressed by both husbands and wives in these *devitalized marriages* is that the relationship now is dull, boring, and routine. While children, community activities, and work may keep the couple busy, the relationship between them lacks excitement and interest. One wife of such a couple expressed her frustration with the relationship when she said, "when I think of us and the numb way we sort of stagger through the weekly routine, I could scream" (Cuber and Harroff, 1968, p. 49).

Usually, devitalized relationships are not particularly marked by tension or conflict. Instead, there is a resigned acceptance that "marriage is like this." In the Cuber and Harroff sample, this view may have had some basis in reality, since these researchers report, "this kind of relationship is exceedingly common" (Cuber and Harroff, 1968, p. 50).

The last type of relationship found in this study of middle-class American couples is called the *passive-congenial relationship.* This type is very similar to the devitalized relationship, except for the fact that passivity has been characteristic of the relationship from the very start. These are likely to be people who entered marriage cautiously, often with a very calculating eye. They are definitely not people who entered marriage at the height of a torrid love affair. The cautiousness of such people reflects a measured, rational approach to life in general. One man in such a marriage expressed his views this way:

> *I don't know why everyone seems to make so much about men and women and marriage. . . . I think it's the proper way to live. It's convenient, orderly, and solves a lot of problems. But there are other things in life. (Cuber and Harroff, 1968, p. 53)*

The couples in passive-congenial marriages never did expect their marriages to be exciting and romantic. They were more likely to expect them to be convenient and comfortable. They have held these expectations from the very beginning and, thus, are different from most people, who expect more when they enter marriage.

The majority of people entering marriage have the expectation, or at least the hope, that the relationship will be vital and deeply fulfilling. Perhaps they have other expectations too, which they have not articulated completely but which are nonetheless important as they enter marriage. We will turn to some of these expectations next.

MARITAL SCRIPTS

Anyone who enters marriage is going to have some expectations about what is proper and appropriate behavior for husbands and wives. These expectations, which are likely to be unconscious and unspoken, are called *marital scripts* (Broderick, 1979, 1984). During the early stages of marriage, it is important for newly married couples to recognize and identify their own and their spouse's marital scripts, because they can often be the cause of hurt feelings and arguments over what seem to be trivial matters. The problems arise when the scripts of the two partners are mismatched. Carlfred Broderick, a sociologist who developed the concept of marital scripts, illustrates with a personal example just how important mismatched scripts can be (Broderick, 1979). Even though Broderick had known his wife since they were both in kindergarten and they had dated from the time they were in the tenth grade, he learned early in marriage that he and his wife had mismatched scripts regarding what happens when someone gets sick:

> *Every right-thinking person knows what you should do when you get sick—you go to bed. That is your part. Then your mother, or whoever loves you, pumps you full of fruit juice.*

Well, I married this woman I had known all my life, and in the natural course of events I caught the flu. I knew what to do, of course. I went to bed and waited. But nothing happened. Nothing, I couldn't believe it!

I was so hurt, I would have left if I hadn't been so ill. Finally, I asked about juice and she brought me some—in a little four-ounce glass. Period. Because, as I learned later, the only time they drank juice at her house was on alternate Tuesdays, when they graced breakfast with a drop in a thimble-size glass. My family's 'juice glasses' held 12 ounces and there was always someone standing by to refill them.

It does not matter that an issue may seem foolish to an outsider, or that it may be solved simply. The point is that mismatched scripts can so easily derail a young couple. (Broderick, 1979, p. 154)

Marital scripts, as can be seen from the illustration above, often come from unique family background experiences. Before we marry, the marriage relationship we have observed most closely is usually that of our parents. Whether that marriage was harmonious and idyllic or quarrelsome and stormy, we are likely to have picked up some deep-seated notions about the nature of the husband-wife relationship and of family life in general.

The illustration above also reveals how people do not reveal all the details of their marital scripts before marriage. This is not because they are being secretive or deceptive. It is probably because many issues have simply never arisen. Even couples who have been together for a very long time before marriage will not have encountered or discussed all their notions or views about marital life. This is likely to be true in part because many issues are so seemingly inconsequential—who, before marriage, discusses how they feel about fruit juice when sick?

One couple, whose case Broderick also recounts, nearly had a breakup in their first weeks of marriage because the bride did not clean the tub after her bath. Her husband was shocked and disgusted by the hair and bathtub ring she left behind, because in his view any civilized and considerate person would carefully clean the tub after bathing. The problem grew in intensity because he was too embarrassed to tell her what was upsetting him. He went on for weeks cleaning the tub after her, while building up increasing resentment. When she finally forced him to tell her what was wrong, the depth of his feeling, over what seemed to her to be a trivial issue, was revealed by the following exchange:

Why didn't you say something right at first if it was bugging you? Nobody's perfect, but if I knew it was bothering you I would have done something about it. Why have you let it go on so long?

Ella, frankly I find this whole conversation disgusting. I shouldn't have to tell you to flush your own toilet or to brush your teeth and I don't think I should have to tell you to clean out your own tub. I'm sorry, but you asked me and that's how I feel. (Broderick, 1984, p. 193)

"I wish you'd get another T-shirt."

It is clear that marital scripts can cover a multitude of issues, many of which are trivial until mismatching scripts are uncovered. Only then does it become clear that one of the partners had completely taken it for granted that everyone felt the same as he or she did. That, of course, is another reason that not all details of marital scripts are discussed before marriage. Why discuss things that "every right-thinking person" knows and accepts?

Since there are an infinite number of issues about which marital scripts can be mismatched, there is no way to anticipate what the specific problem areas will be for a given couple. Some major issues do commonly appear as mismatched marital scripts. These include the handling of money, relating to in-laws, and raising children. But rather than try to anticipate all issues, large and small, couples can be best prepared to deal with mismatched scripts simply by recognizing that they will emerge in the normal course of early married life. If both spouses are "armed" with the concept of marital scripts, and especially the notion of mismatched scripts, it may be possible to avert the hurt feelings and conflicts that so often result. It may be enough simply to say, "I think we've discovered a(nother) mismatched script." That will at least open up communication on an objective, nonemotional level.

COMMUNICATION IN MARRIAGE

Whether for mismatched scripts, or for almost any other problem in marriage, there is widespread agreement that communication between husbands and wives is important if solutions are to be reached. There is also agreement, supported by a great deal of research evidence, that good communication between husbands and wives is an important element in the quality of a marriage. The special importance of communication is revealed by the fact that it both produces and is an indication of marital quality. A number of researchers have shown that effective communication *leads to* better quality in marriages (Lewis and Spanier, 1979). Other researchers see "good communication" as a *measure of* the quality of a marriage relationship (Spanier, 1976). This dual position of communication is not unreasonable, for there is an interaction between quality communication and marital quality. This simply means that couples who have good communication skills will improve their relationship. As the relationship improves, the couples will be motivated to improve their communication even more (Montgomery, 1981).

There have been various attempts to specify what it means for couples to have good communication. (The preferred terms by communications specialists are *quality communication* and *effective communication*.) We would identify the following dimensions of communication as the most important: openness and honesty, supportiveness, and self-disclosure.

Open and Honest Communication

Since no one would argue that a good relationship can be built on deception and dishonesty, it may seem obvious that *openness* and *honesty* are going to contribute to the quality of a marriage relationship. Nonetheless, there are subtleties about these terms that require some exploration. One dimension of honesty in communication has been identified by Satir (1972) as *leveling*. Leveling is essentially a way of communicating that expresses a person's feelings accurately, and with no mixed messages. To communicate accurately means that if one is upset by something one's spouse has done, that feeling is expressed directly. When a wife asks her husband, "What's wrong?", and he replies, "Oh, nothing," even though he is upset by something she has done, he is not leveling. Another way of not leveling is to say the words but to express in some other way (voice tone, facial gestures, body language) that the words are not one's true feelings.

A second feature of openness and honesty has to do with whether the speaker has hidden motivations. As an example, a husband may inquire casually about one of his wife's relatives, knowing quite well that the ensuing conversation will give him the opportunity to criticize that relative's behavior. Or a wife may inquire about how much money the new employee in her husband's office is receiving, with the aim of reminding her husband about his own failure to receive a raise. This kind of deception in communication is quite subtle. Even the speakers will not always fully realize their motivations. Marriage partners should occasionally check the motivations they may have "just below the surface." If the hidden objective is to gain control or power over the other person, or to force the other person into an awkward or difficult situation, or to manipulate the other person, the communication is dishonest.

While openness and honesty are to be valued in communication, it does not follow that a husband and wife should always be completely and utterly candid and honest. It is an idealistic fantasy to think that one can be totally honest at all times. Sensitive communication sometimes requires that a person leave some things unsaid. Knowing when to and when not to say something to one's spouse requires both skill and sensitivity. Many married people know intuitively that there are limits to openness and honesty in marriage. One wife states it this way:

> I don't think anything is more difficult for us than this business of trying to be open. [She stops for a moment, wanting to clarify her position.] Look, I want you to understand that I'm not one of these people who thinks openness or honesty in a relationship means spilling my guts or telling your partner every angry thought that comes into your head. There's plenty I don't talk about—like when I wonder do I really love him sometimes, or do I want to be married. Those things don't have to be said; they're damaging. (Rubin, 1983, p. 80)

This wife understands both the limits of openness and honesty and the destructive effects of the negative feelings almost everyone has from time to time.

Supportiveness

In the most basic sense being supportive in communication means to treat the person who is speaking with attentiveness and respect. The supportive role in communication is a listening and responding activity more than it is a speaking or initiating activity. When people talk to us, it is possible to respond in a variety of ways. We can ignore them, we can reject them, or we can respond positively to them. Responding positively to what another person is saying has been labeled *confirmation* (Watzlawick et al., 1967).

It is especially important when married partners are talking to each other that they give each other confirmation. This means, first of all, that one is paying attention to what the other is saying. Through gestures and verbal cues it is possible to communicate to a speaker that one is interested and involved. Even when a listener is in disagreement with *what* is being said, it is still possible to convey the message that one is interested in the message, in the person speaking, and in the relationship that exists between them. A good relationship depends on this kind of support and confirmation, and studies have shown that when married couples possess this quality in their communication, their marital satisfaction and quality is greater (Montgomery, 1981).

Self-Disclosure

Some part of every person's life is secret. There are thoughts and feelings that one does not reveal to anyone else, because doing so would be too embarrassing or threatening. If we revealed some of our most secret thoughts and feelings, it would make us too vulnerable. And yet, if we are going to have a close relationship, we must reveal ourselves to the other person. It is the very essence of a close relationship that we can feel safe enough with the other person to reveal things that could be "used against us."

Self-disclosure has some similarities to openness and honesty, but there is a much stronger element of feelings and emotions. Telling another person about one's fears, hopes, and desires is the essence of self-disclosure. (Jourard, 1971) But, it is also more than just telling; it is an intimate interchange between two people. Lillian Rubin (1983) simply calls it *intimacy,* but her description captures the most positive elements of self-disclosure:

> *Intimacy is some kind of reciprocal expression of feeling and thought, not out of fear or dependent need, but out of a wish to know another's inner life and to be able to share one's own. (Rubin, 1983, p. 90)*

It is generally believed that husbands and wives, if they are to have a successful relationship, must not be afraid of self-disclosure. Researchers have found a generally positive association between self-disclosure and marital satisfaction (Hendrick, 1981). However, this generalization must be qualified, because just as with openness and honesty, it is possible to have self-disclosure that can be detrimental to a relationship.

When husbands and wives are in a conflict-ridden marriage, it is likely that there will be much self-disclosure, but it will be of a negative sort. If a wife reveals that she harbors hostile or angry feelings toward her husband, or a husband tells his wife that he is jealous and suspicious of her, the result is most likely to be negative for the relationship. Clearly, self-disclosure, per se, is not inevitably good for a relationship. It depends on what kind of feelings are being revealed.

There is also a view that an excessive amount of self-disclosure, even if it is not negative, can be detrimental to a relationship. Some research has revealed that when a spouse is too revealing, especially in the area of self-doubt, the effect may be negative for marital satisfaction (Cozby, 1973).

However, while too much self-disclosure might sometimes have a dampening effect on a relationship, there is a growing consensus that too little self-disclosure is the more serious problem for many married couples. Too little self-disclosure is especially harmful to a marital relationship if one spouse is disclosing more intimate feelings than the other. Even if one of the spouses perceives an imbalance in the amount of self-disclosure, the effect on the relationship is negative (Davidson et al., 1983). Following these lines, there is a good deal of research and clinical evidence that husbands in particular do not express their feelings to their wives as much as wives would wish (Hawkins et al., 1980). The resulting lack of intimate communication between many husbands and wives has led one researcher to describe marital partners as "intimate strangers" (Rubin, 1983). On the basis of interviews with 150 couples and an active clinical practice, Rubin has concluded that the search for intimacy in marital relationships is the most pervasive and critical problem among married couples.

The problem is often identified by women when they say plaintively, "He won't talk to me!" One wife describes her marriage by saying that the characteristics of her husband that are now leading to divorce are the same ones that attracted her to him in the first place: "his quiet power and his cool way of staying in control of his feelings. I remember thinking, 'this must be what a real man is like.' Then for twelve years I begged him to talk to me" (Pogrebin, 1983, p. 90). This woman longed for her husband either to ask her how she felt or to just sit around and "muse" about their lives. It was only when she reached a state where she would "get crazy" that he would say, " 'Okay, you want to talk, *talk*!' By then I felt like a jerk saying, 'I just want you to say you care' " (Pogrebin, 1983, p. 90).

And how are these silent, noncommunicative men feeling? One perplexed and exasperated man vehemently expressed his feelings to the interviewer:

The whole goddamn business of what you're calling intimacy bugs the hell out of me. I never know what you women mean when you talk about it. Karen complains that I don't talk to her, but it's not talk she wants, it some other damn thing, only I don't know what the hell it is. Feelings, she keeps asking for. So what am I supposed to do if I don't have any to give her or talk about, just because she decides it's time to talk about feelings? Tell me, will you; maybe we can get some peace around here. (Rubin, 1983, p. 66)

Males often find it difficult to express their feelings and emotions, and prefer to remain silent.

Analyzing the nature of this problem, both married couples and many social scientists have come to very similar conclusions. Women experience and have a need for a more emotional world. Men are less in touch with their emotions and thus have less apparent need for the expression of their feelings. Some suspect that men suppress or hide their emotions in order to present a strong, calm, and "manly" exterior. In other words, men are acting out what they accept as appropriate masculine gender role behavior. This view rests comfortably in the gender role learning processes we considered in Chapter 2. But there is a different, more complicated view that also bids to explain why men and women differ in the emotional component of their lives.

The alternative view finds the source of male and female differences in emotional expression in the observed fact that mothers are the primary caregivers for infant children (Chodorow, 1978; Rubin, 1983). Because mothers are the primary caregivers, especially in the first months and years of life, infants make their first attachments to women. In the continuation of this process, children make an *identification* with their mothers. They bring another person (typically mother) into their "inner psychic life" (Rubin, 1983, p. 50). This occurs for boys and girls alike. "What this says, then, is that whether in a girl or a boy, the earliest, most primitive experiences of both attachment and identification are with a woman" (Rubin, 1983, p. 50).

This identification with a woman, their mother, leads to a special problem for boys, one not experienced by girls. Because they have identified with their mothers, it is not uncommon for little boys at age three or four to say, "When I grow up I want to be a mommy." But mommy, and other people as well, are likely to set him straight about this matter, telling him firmly that he is not going to be a mommy because he is a boy. Now the boy must begin to develop a gender identity that separates him from his mother. This requires him to make a more severe break with his mother, the first intimate attachment he formed in life. For little girls the formation of a gender identity requires no such abrupt change. She can continue to identify with her mother and yet at the same time develop an independent sense of self. The essence of this theory is that girls do not have to make such a wrenching break with their mothers, the first intimate attachment in their lives, while boys must do so if they are to develop the expected gender identity and an independent sense of self.

Now let us see how this difference in the early experiences of boys and girls helps us to understand the differences in the way men and women respond to emotional attachments in adulthood. Through this process women come to adulthood having had less difficulty achieving their gender identity, which means that they have had to work less hard at establishing their sense of an independent self. To use the language of psychologists, their *ego boundaries* are less well defined because they have never had to separate themselves as completely and irrevocably as boys have done (Rubin, 1983, p. 58). This lack of sharpness in ego boundaries is thought to shape the responses of women throughout life. They are more open to their own emotions and more receptive to the emotional lives of others.

By contrast, males form their gender identities by making a more radical break in their attachments to their mothers. In so doing, their ego boundaries become much more fixed and firm. Indeed, their sense of ego boundaries (an autonomous self) may become exaggerated. It is thought by some psychologists to be a kind of defense against the pain suffered when they had to break away from their mothers. And thus, men in general, with this common early experience in emotional attachments, may have an internal psychological life that is very different from that of women. This explanation, if it is valid, may account for the commonly observed pattern of women wanting more intimacy in their relationships, and men wanting less.

As a note of caution, this interpretation is based on a psychoanalytic perspective that has found its validation primarily in clinical settings. The more straightforward interpretation, as we noted earlier, may simply be that men have internalized the traditional masculine gender role, which calls for them to be less emotional. There is nothing inherently contradictory about the two interpretations, so they may be thought of as comfortably supportive. As such, they give us some theoretical understanding of the often observed tendency among married couples for wives to want and ask for more intimate self-disclosure and for husbands to avoid it.

We have already seen in a variety of ways how satisfaction can differ greatly from one marriage to another and some of the factors that influence marital quality. It is now time to take a closer look at what is known about the nature and sources of marital quality.

MARITAL QUALITY

It is an everyday occurrence for people to describe friends and acquaintances as "happily married." It seems a very simple and obvious concept. And yet, scholars and researchers continue to analyze and debate what it means to say that a marriage is happy. The problem of unraveling this familiar idea was foreseen by one of the earliest researchers of marital happiness, who wrote more than a half century ago:

> Who is wise enough to say what constitutes a happy marriage? There are so many kinds of happiness and unhappiness incident to marriage that no weighing in the balance one kind against another can do justice to the complex emotional facts in question. (Terman, 1935, p. 167)

Since Terman wrote those words there has been a voluminous amount of research and writing on the subject of marital happiness, and yet the complexity that he spoke of is still in evidence. There is, to begin with, the matter of what term to use when we discuss this issue. Marital happiness, marital satisfaction, marital compatibility, marital adjustment, and marital quality have all been prominent at one time or another. Although the choice is arbitrary, we will generally use *marital quality*, primarily because it seems to be the most popular contemporary term. However, other terms will occasionally be used, especially when they more faithfully reflect the issue or research being described.

One distinction about terms that can be made clearly is the difference between marital quality and marital *stability*. The stability of a marriage refers to whether or not it stays intact. Instability is typically reflected by separation and divorce, but marriages can also be willfully terminated by other means, such as legal annulment, desertion, and murder (Lewis and Spanier, 1979). Marital stability is clearly distinguishable from marital quality, because many marriages with very low levels of marital quality remain intact (recall the conflict-habituated couples discussed earlier). It is also possible that a marriage in which the marital quality is reasonably good may be terminated. This can occur when one of the spouses finds a more attractive alternative (e.g., a career opportunity or a new love).

Since researchers have been most interested in what produces or influences marital quality, they have focused much of their attention on how to identify or measure whether or not a couple is happily married. One obvious way, and a method still used, is to ask married people a straightforward question: "Would you say your marriage is very happy, pretty happy, or not too happy?" When this kind of question is asked, about two-thirds of all people will answer very happy, while another twenty-five to thirty percent will answer happy (Orden and Bradburn, 1968; Glenn and Weaver, 1977). In most studies only a tiny percentage of people will say that their marriages are less than happy. Such a glowing picture of nearly universal marital happiness makes many researchers skeptical and prompts them to look for some better measure.

A similar but somewhat more elaborate way to measure marital happiness is to assemble a series of evaluative questions or statements to which individuals can respond. These are statements like the following: "We have a good marriage," "My relationship with my partner is very stable," or "Our marriage is strong" (Norton, 1983). Respondents can then agree or disagree with the statements. The responses are assigned numerical values, which are summed to give individuals a marital quality score.

The most elaborate measures of marital quality are those that break the marital relationship into various areas. For example, the degree of consensus about important matters such as philosophy of life, work and careers, and recreation can be determined with a series of questions. Statements or questions about the degree of affection that is expressed, as well as how much negative interaction occurs (arguing, fighting) are also used as parts of marital quality measures (Spanier, 1976).

There have been hundreds of studies, using these and other measures of marital quality. The principal objective of the majority of these studies has been to identify those things that are related to marital quality. Researchers, like everyone else, are most interested in what makes a happy marriage. What follows are a few of the most interesting and frequently discussed research conclusions.*

Social and Personal Characteristics

Studies have shown that when the premarital backgrounds of the married couples are similar there is a greater likelihood that their marital quality will be

---

*The following research conclusions are drawn from a careful survey of the literature by Lewis and Spanier, 1979. Original references can be found in their chapter.

higher. When marrying couples have similar religious, racial and socioeconomic background characteristics, they are said to be *homogamous*. (Homogamy literally means persons with the same characteristics marrying.) Also, when marrying couples are homogamous with respect to age and intelligence their marital quality is likely to be higher (Lewis and Spanier, 1979).

Marital quality is also positively related to personal resources and abilities. Higher levels of education and being somewhat older at the time of marriage both are related to higher marital quality. Both good physical and good mental health are also related to higher marital quality. The higher the economic and occupational status of the couple, the higher their marital quality. Religiosity is also related to marital quality; the greater a couple's religious beliefs, the higher their marital quality (Filsinger and Wilson, 1984; Glenn and Weaver, 1978).

If one has a good relationship with one's parents, and if they were happily married, the chances of marital quality are better. If one's parents like one's mate, and if the mate likes the in-laws, marital quality is likely to be higher. Approval and support from friends and community members are also related to higher marital quality. Being pressured into marriage, especially by premarital pregnancy, is likely to reduce marital quality.

Interpersonal Characteristics

As we have already seen in the case of communication between spouses, the nature of their relationship is critically important for their satisfaction with the marriage. Much research has shown that the positive regard that spouses show for each other will enhance marital quality. Positive regard is shown through favorable evaluations from one's spouse, agreement about values, mutual sexual and physical attraction, and a validation of the other spouse's self-image. Closely related are expressions of affection and love, an equalitarian relationship, companionship, and effective problem solving.

Marital quality is also enhanced by what has been called *role fit*. Basically, this means that the marital partners are in agreement about marital roles. For example, in one study husbands and wives were asked how much they disagreed about such things as housekeeping, earning a living, keeping in touch with relatives, recreation, and teaching and disciplining children. The greater the perceived consensus on these and other marital tasks, the greater was the marital satisfaction (Bahr et al., 1983).

These characteristics of marital relationships are correlated with marital quality, which can mean two different things. It can mean that they produce marital happiness, but it can also mean that they are simply reflections of marital quality. People who have these things in their relationship are likely to be satisfied with the relationship, and however their marital quality is measured, this satisfaction will be revealed. But at the same time, the couples who exhibit these characteristics in their relationships are apt to produce greater marital quality. A relationship between two people is a *process*, which means that it is an ongoing interaction. When the interaction is good it produces higher marital quality, and this in turn leads to continued good interaction.

Children and Marital Quality

Research conducted in the last two decades has shown repeatedly that when couples have children the quality of their marriage decreases. While these research results run counter to the general cultural belief that children bring fulfillment to a marriage, the two ideas are not necessarily inconsistent. When marital quality is studied the focus is on the couple (the dyad) and their relationship. Children may indeed bring some kind of fulfillment, but at the same time they put a " 'crunch' on time, energy, and economic resources" (Rollins and Galligan, 1978, p. 83).

As we will see in chapter 10, a newborn child requires a tremendous amount of energy and time from the parents, especially the mother, since she is usually the primary caretaker. This means that attention and time that might otherwise have gone to the spouse, go to the child. But marital quality is also affected as the children grow older. If anything, the research results show that satisfaction with the marriage reaches its lowest ebb when children reach school age. Many things might contribute to this relationship, but very likely the children produce tensions between parents who might be concerned about school performance and other childhood problems.

Some additional evidence that children affect marital quality and adjustment comes from a study that compared women who were voluntarily childless and women who had children (Houseknecht, 1979). The two groups of fifty women were carefully matched on the basis of education, religion, and being in the labor force. Women who were voluntarily childless had overall marital adjustment scores higher than women who had children, but they especially had higher scores on a dimension of the marital relationship called *cohesion*. In the measure of marital adjustment used in this study, this reflected the fact that childless women were more likely to engage in outside interests and work on projects with their husbands, to have more frequent exchanges of stimulating ideas, and to have more quiet discussions with their husbands (Houseknecht, 1979).

Marital Quality through the Career of a Marriage

In a number of studies, couples who have been married for different lengths of time, and who have reached different life cycle stages, have been asked about their satisfaction with various aspects of their marital relationships. These studies show that the general level of satisfaction is likely to be greatest in the early years of marriage (Rollins and Feldman, 1970; Burr, 1970; Orthner, 1975; Anderson et al., 1983). Especially before the arrival of children, both husbands and wives express a higher level of satisfaction than couples at any other later stage in the marriage. One major point about the nature of the research that produced these results must be noted. There have been no recent studies that have followed the same couples throughout their marriage careers, observing this decline in marital quality directly as it was occurring. To demonstrate with more conclusiveness that the marriage career itself produces a decline in marital quality, such "longitudinal" studies would be preferred (Spanier and Lewis, 1980). There are two studies started in the 1930s in which couples were reinterviewed as much as eighteen to twenty years afterward. These couples did show declines in marital adjustment and satisfaction over the years of the marriage (Burgess and Wallin, 1953; Pineo, 1961).

There have been some studies that have found marital quality to be somewhat higher again among couples in the later stages of marriage—especially after children have grown up and left home (Anderson et al., 1983). There has been much less consistency on this point, since other studies have not found the same improvement (Spanier et al., 1975). It must also be noted that those couples who had sufficiently poor marital quality to cause them to terminate their marriages will be automatically out of the pool of older married couples. With their downward pull eliminated from the long-time-married group, we could expect some modest increase in the overall level of marital quality.

We noted above that equalitarian marriages are related to higher quality in marriage. While equalitarian marriage is a widely shared ideal, there is some question about whether or not it can be achieved. It is to this issue that we turn next, as we consider the matters of power and decision making in marriage.

POWER AND DECISION MAKING IN MARRIAGE

Power is a word we use easily when we talk of military actions and international relations. It is also a commonplace word when we speak of governmental leaders and people who control great wealth. But when it comes to the family, we are less comfortable with the idea of power. We may sometimes refer to power when we speak of how parents have power over their children, but in relationships between husbands and wives it seems to be nearly inappropriate. There are at least two reasons why power seems to be an inappropriate word for describing how most contemporary husbands and wives are supposed to think and act toward each other. First, the very ideal of an equal-partner marriage largely precludes the idea that one partner or the other has control and authority. Since these are closely tied to power, it is inconsistent with the equalitarian ideal. Second, we have a notion that the relationship between a husband and wife is supposed to be based on cooperation and compromise, not on the exercise of power. Indeed, we sometimes subscribe to the even more idealistic notion that a marriage relationship should be one where each partner desires to give what will make the other most happy.

With all these ideals prevailing to some degree in the culture, and in our own thinking, it is not surprising that power is often neglected in discussions of husband-wife relations. And yet, if power can be found in all kinds of relationships between people, we can assume that there is a power dimension in husband-wife relations. Once we make that assumption, we can turn to two more interesting questions: (1) What is the nature of power? (2) What are the sources of power in marriage?

The Nature of Power

We have been using the word *power* in the paragraphs above assuming that its meaning is clearly understood. That assumption is not unreasonable because we all use the word in our everyday conversation. And yet, as one writer has remarked, "we all know perfectly well what it is—until someone asks us" (Bierstedt, 1950, p. 730). In other words, if we start to analyze and define power, it becomes a more complicated idea than we first supposed. Many writers and scholars have put their minds to how power should be defined, and they have not always agreed. The following definition is one that many do agree with: *power* is the ability of an individual to produce intended effects on the behavior of another individual (Scanzoni, 1979; Winter, 1973). This definition is at the individual level, but, of course, it is also possible for groups of individuals to exercise power over both individuals and other groups. One implicit feature of this definition is that power can only exist in some kind of relationship (Olson and Cromwell, 1975a). This relationship can be between an employer and employees, between members of a youthful gang, or between two nations. In marriage, power is a property of the relationship between a husband and a wife.

If in any person-to-person relationship one person has a power advantage, it can be asked where the power comes from. What gives one person power over another? There are a number of identifiable sources of power. There is, for example, *authority,* which is often described as legitimate power. Legitimate power comes from some higher source (as when the Constitution gives the president power). A society's norms or customs can also give this legitimate authority to a person (parents' authority over their children, for example). Another source of power is *expertise* and *knowledge,* and the *ability to communicate* them persuasively. Two elected representatives in Congress may have equal authority, and thus equal legitimate power, but the one who has greater knowledge or persuasive ability will often have power over the other. Being able to give *rewards* also gives a person power. A rich uncle or grandparent often has many family members doing his or her bidding. More than a few movies and television dramas have been written around this theme. But rewards can be things other than money. Anything of value, even the pleasure of being in the company of a very attractive or popular person can be a reward.

This gives the attractive and popular person power over those who want to be close to and identified with him or her. Entertainers and other celebrities are frequently reported to have hangers-on and lackeys who will do anything their idol requests. Finally, power is also given to those who have the ability to punish or in other ways do harm to those who fail to comply with their wishes. This has been labeled *coercive* power. This is what gives even the unpopular bully on the playground his power over other children.

All these sources of power may seem quite remote from the relationships of husbands and wives in marriage, but as we will see next, some of the same factors may be operating. We will begin with a consideration of *patriarchy*, a traditional source of authority in the family.

Patriarchy as a Source of Power

Western society has an extremely long history of giving ultimate authority in the family to the husband and father. The sacred writings of the Judaic and Christian religious traditions make this patriarchal authority very clear. The Hebrew tradition, as reflected in the Old Testament, makes it clear that men have the authority to dominate their wives and children. The Christian tradition, as represented by the New Testament, similarly gives such rights to males. "Wives, submit to your own husbands, as unto the Lord. For the husband is the head of the wife, as Christ is the head of the church" (Ephesians 5:23–24).

This patriarchal tradition was passed down through the Roman and European cultures and came to be faithfully reflected in American society. In the nineteenth century the marriage manuals of the time, which were largely written by clergymen and physicians, were fully committed to the patriarchal view of marriage and family life (Gordon, 1978, p. 208). In this view, a wife was to be obedient, reverent and submissive to her husband. The husband, for his part, was asked to temper his "authority with love, prudence and wisdom" (quoted from Brandt, 1892, in Gordon, 1978, p. 208).

While Biblical authority legitimizing men's power may have diminished somewhat, it has by no means disappeared in contemporary society. One current spokesperson for this view is Phyllis Schlafly, who says women recognize that "there is a valid and enduring purpose behind this recognition of different roles for men and women which is as relevant in the twentieth century as it was in the time of Saint Paul" (Schlafly, 1977, p. 50). Another writer in this tradition observes that most egalitarian marriages evolve into marriages in which wives exercise a veto power and husbands gradually give in on more and more decisions. This, he believes, leads to marriages without proper direction and guidance. He concludes by saying, "I believe that . . . egalitarian marriage is a mistake" (Alexander, 1981, p. 26). Schlafly echoes the same idea, drawing an analogy between running a ship or flying a plane and a marriage. "When I fly on a plane or sail on a ship, I'm glad there is one captain who has the final responsibility and can act decisively in a crisis situation" (Schlafly, 1977, p. 50). Regarding marriage, she says, "If marriage is to be a successful institution, it must likewise have an ultimate decision maker, and that is the husband" (Schlafly, 1977, p. 50).

While a belief in the absolute power of males, as reflected by the traditional patriarchal view, is not widely held in contemporary society, there are still enough vestiges of it to give males some power in marriage. Sometimes it has a religious base, but more commonly the greater authority of males is found in gender roles. Males are still believed by many to have the "final word" if a husband and wife cannot agree.

Resources as a Source of Power in the Family

We have seen that an individual who has rewards to give another person will gain power over that person. In marital relationships, these rewards have been labeled *resources,* and a theory of marital power built on this dimension is called *resource theory* (Blood and Wolfe, 1960). Resources are anything that one spouse has that can be given to a partner to satisfy their needs, wishes, desires, or interests.

Resource theory posits that husbands and wives in any marriage will each bring resources to the relationship. But which resources they bring, and how many (or how much) they bring, will determine who has the most power. The things that can be valued resources are as varied as human beings are varied, but those who support resource theory have focused primarily on economic resources. Specifically, income earned is the primary economic resource of a household. Closely associated is educational attainment level and occupational status and prestige.

Some critics of this conception of resources have called it too narrow, because it is almost automatically more favorable to males (Safilios-Rothschild, 1970). According to this view there are noneconomic resources that are also important for a household, and these are often more closely associated with women. Companionship, emotional support, entertaining skills, sexual favors, and a positive home atmosphere, are just a few of the resources that wives have traditionally held (or withheld) as resources that might give them power.

The debate here is not over what should be more valued, but rather over what is more valued in our society. It is easy to argue from an ethical standpoint that companionship, emotional support, and so forth are as valuable as or more valuable than income and occupational prestige. But in American society there is no denying the great value placed on money, status, and prestige in the occupational world. The person in a home who can say, "I'm bringing in the money that keeps this place going," is almost always going to prevail over the person who says, "I'm keeping this place clean, pleasant, and comfortable." It may not be fair, but it seems to be the reality of a materialistic and money-oriented society.

This state of affairs does give men in most marriages a resource advantage over their wives, because men typically have higher educational levels, higher incomes, and higher occupational prestige. Even though women are continuing their educations and joining the work force in increasing numbers, only a relative few are achieving higher status jobs and higher incomes than their husbands. But the issue here is not why these differences exist between husbands and wives, it is rather what the implications are for power within marriages.

There has been a substantial amount of research on this question, and the results have stimulated a variety of discussions and criticisms (Allen, 1984; Blood and Wolfe, 1960; Burr, 1973; Olson and Cromwell, 1975b; Scanzoni, 1979; Turk and Bell, 1972). The most important among these criticisms is that power has not been adequately measured or that decision making has not been adequately conceptualized and measured. We cannot go into all the issues that have been raised, but some of them are important enough to consider here, beginning with how researchers measure power in marital relationships.

Measuring Power

A commonsense approach to measuring power between marital partners is to ask, "If a husband and wife disagree on a course of action, whose position is likely to prevail?" One method of getting an answer to that question is to *observe* couples as they make decisions, to see who dominates in the decision-making process and who "wins" if there is a difference of opinion. Couples are sometimes observed in interview situations to see who exercises the most influence and who seems to have "the last word" (Hill, 1965). Sometimes couples are put in a laboratory-like situation and given a hypothetical decision to make (e.g., "If you were given $300 to spend, what would you buy?"). Observers can then observe which person most influences the final decision and, if there is a disagreement, whose view prevails (Kenkel, 1957).

While observation of this sort has been used in a number of studies, it is time-consuming and sometimes difficult to arrange and conduct a significant number of such sessions. There are also difficulties connected with being objective in the observations. To be certain that observers are being objective in their conclusions, it is preferable to have multiple observers. To avoid some of the problems and costs of this method, many researchers have turned to the *self-report* method to determine which marital partner has the most decision-making power.

The self-report method of measuring power usually relies on questionnaires or interviews. Wives and husbands are asked a series of questions about who makes the "final decisions" about a variety of family matters. For example, in one early study, interviewees were told, "In every family somebody has to decide such things as where the family will live and so on. Many couples talk such things over first, but the *final* decision often has to be made by the husband or the wife. For instance, who usually makes the final decision about what car to get?" (Blood and Wolfe, 1960, p. 282). Other questions asked about buying life insurance, taking a house or apartment, taking jobs (both husband and wife), spending on food, selecting a doctor, and deciding on a vacation. The person being interviewed could choose any of the following answers for each of these questions: husband always; husband more than wife; husband and wife exactly the same; wife more than husband; and wife always. By summing up the numerical values assigned to these responses, a score reflecting husband or wife decision-making power could then be assigned to each interviewee.

While this method of studying husband-wife power relationships has been criticized on both technical and substantive grounds, it continues to be used in many studies. These technical criticisms may have some validity, but many researchers find this method adequate for establishing the general pattern of power, and it still has its defenders (Allen, 1984). A more fundamental criticism is that this method only concentrates on the *outcome* of couple decision making and does not tell us anything about the *process* that actually allows couples to reach decisions (Scanzoni, 1979). This is a reasonable criticism, since we know that the interaction between any two people, especially husbands and wives, is likely to be complicated and filled with subtleties. Nonetheless, without denying this fact, it is still possible to conclude that self-reports of decision making in marital couples have validated resource theory. Researchers using this measure of power have demonstrated again and again that the resources two individuals bring to the decision-making process will influence the distribution of power.

Insofar as there have been exceptions in the research literature, they too have proved to be interesting and revealing. In a few studies of marital power, especially those conducted among lower socioeconomic classes and in other countries, the relative resources of husbands and wives have not been so clearly related to their power (Komarovsky, 1962; Safilios-Rothschild, 1967). However, these results do not negate resource theory. In these negative cases, the study was typically being done among people where the *ideology of patriarchy* prevailed and men had power regardless of what their resources were. These cases simply underline the fact that the resources a wife may have cannot override the power that men hold if patriarchy prevails. Resource theory can only operate in settings where the ideology is at least tending toward equalitarianism (Rodman, 1972; Burr, 1973).

Other Sources of Power in the Family

Closely related to resources are expertise, knowledge, and the ability to communicate persuasively. These, as we have seen, are related to power, and again in husband-wife relations, husbands very often have the advantage. The same higher levels of education and more prestigious occupations that give husbands generally higher income than their wives also give them greater skills in decision making and manipulating other people. The anecdotal case that illustrates this well is the woman who remains in the home to care for the children while her husband has a job where he is called on to face the competition in the outside world. Such women have often complained about spending their days "having no one to talk to who is more than three feet tall." While caring for children may be a challenge, it does not develop or polish the interpersonal skills that are equal to those of someone who is out in the occupational world.

Of course, the woman who remains in the home full-time to care for children is not as commonplace today as she was a generation ago. Women are entering the labor force in ever-increasing numbers, and when they do they are both bringing home resources and enhancing their expertise, knowledge, and skills. These resources do seem to increase the power of women relative to their husbands. However, the fact that husbands often have still higher educational levels and correspondingly more prestigious occupations continues to give them a resource advantage over their wives.

In terms of the ability to persuade another person, husbands may have another advantage that we should note in passing. Men are typically older than their wives. This slight age difference, which only averages about two or three years in first marriages, may not make a great deal of difference, but if any advantage accrues it would tend to be to the husband.

One final point of marital power is that from a theoretical viewpoint the threat of physical punishment or harm can give a person power (called *coercive power* above). It is a fact that the physical stature and strength of males generally exceeds that of females, and one must then wonder if this feature gives husbands greater power in decision making. Perhaps even the threat of physical violence gives some power advantage to men. Perhaps also, physical power comes into play only in extreme cases of disagreement, but then it is usually used by men more than women. Some years ago we would hardly have given this idea any credibility, but research has made us aware that physical violence in the home is much more widespread than was previously assumed (Gelles, 1980; Straus and Steinmetz, 1980). While the phenomenon of *wife abuse* has received the most attention, it is clear that this represents only the extreme of the range of physical violence between marital partners. This issue will be addressed more fully in Chapter 13.

It is apparent from the preceding discussion of power that under existing conditions it is generally the case that power in family decision making will gravitate toward husbands rather than wives. While an unquestioned and absolute patriarchal ideology is not widely supported today, continuation of male gender-role advantages does still give husbands some "legitimate" power. If we add to that the advantages that come from the generally greater resources of males, as well as several other of the advantages discussed above, the power advantage of husbands is even more assured. As the final issue of this chapter, we will consider two alternative ideals of husband and wife equality. These are labeled the equalitarian and equal-partner models.

ISSUE

Is an egalitarian marriage better than an equal-partnership marriage?

There are several different interpretations of what it means to have equality in marriage. For this discussion we will distinguish between the *complementary equal-partnership* marriage and the *egalitarian* marriage. The complementary equal-partnership marriage is one in which husbands and wives each have their separate responsibilities and tasks, but these are thought to be equally important. Each partner contributes things of equal value, and the decision making about important family matters is done jointly.

The egalitarian marriage has a number of dimensions that make it different from the equal-partner marriage. First, an egalitarian marriage is distinguished by the nearly identical activities of husbands and wives. Both have employment or careers, and the work of each is equally valued. Spouses share the breadwinner and domestic roles equally and interchangeably. Parenthood is optional, but if there are children the task of caring for them is equally divided between husband and wife (Scanzoni, 1980).

There is another interpretation of the egalitarian marriage that concentrates solely on equal rights between husbands and wives, without regard to their activities. In this interpretation, husbands and wives have equal power and equal rights, regardless of what each does. This means that even if there are differences in earning power, occupation, educational attainment, or even intelligence, the differences are to have no influence on the equality of the spouses. In this view of egalitarian marriage there is a "pure" equality between the spouses that transcends all their personal characteristics. This conception of an egalitarian marriage has been articulated by Daryl Bem and Sandra Bem (1979).

The Bems use an extreme example to illustrate the essence of this interpretation of an egalitarian relationship. A wife who is not employed may wish to leave a community where her husband has a good job. Even though she has no plans or prospects for employment in another community, she has a right to have her wishes considered equally with those of her husband. The fact that he has superior earning power and a job is extraneous and irrelevant. The equality between them is unaffected by any other considerations. Of course, the same principle would apply if the situations of husband and wife were reversed.

For purposes of the following discussion, we will make the assumption that those who favor the egalitarian marriage are speaking primarily of marriages in which the activities of the spouses are basically the same. Each has roughly equal domestic responsibilities, and each has outside work or a career that carries the same importance.

We are now ready to compare the *complementary, equal-partnership* relationship with the *egalitarian* relationship. We will begin by considering the case for complementary, equal-partnership relationships.

The Case for Complementary, Equal-Partnership Marriages

Arguments for the complementary, equal-partnership marriage are built around the idea that a husband and wife can have equality without having to be doing the same thing. There is often an assumption that certain things are best done by men, while other things should remain as the special province of women. There is no implication that women are less able or intelligent than men. On the contrary, women are assumed to be much more competent and talented when it comes to providing a warm, loving, and comfortable atmosphere in the home.

There are several practical considerations behind the advocacy of the complementary, equal-partnership type of relationship. The first of these is that if there are children born to the couple, it will necessarily have to be the wife who will carry much of the initial burden. The wife will usually take some time off from her employment or career while she is having the baby. Also, she will probably choose to be responsible for much of the early child care, which may include breast-feeding—a task only she can do. Some social scientists claim that women, because of their hormonal endowments, are uniquely suited for the task of parenting children when they are infants (Rossi, 1984).

Thus, if couples are to have children, the work careers of the wives are going to be interrupted for greater or lesser periods of time. Accepting this fact, many couples believe it makes sense to acknowledge that the wife's work or career cannot be given the same importance or prominence as that of the husband. A division of labor, which gives the husband primary responsibility for earning a living and the wife primary responsibility for running the home and caring for children is a compromise with reality. However, couples who accept this view do not concede that there is a substantial loss of equality thereby.

There is another kind of reality that some husbands and wives take into account when they opt for the complementary, equal-partner arrangement. That is the reality of the workplace, which gives men an advantage over women. To begin with, husbands often have higher educational levels than their wives. But, even if they do not, it is a reality that men have an easier time moving up occupational ladders than do women. Again, that militates for couples to make a rational decision that favors the husband's work over the wife's work.

Along with all these more or less rational arguments for the complementary, equal-partner relationship, there is the old-fashioned preference, expressed by many men and women, for marriages in which the partners are equal and yet the husband is the head of the household. Many women specifically state that they prefer to play a supportive role, while letting their husbands face the rigors of the outside world. If that means that their husbands have somewhat more power in the marriage, they are willing to accept that, too. Similarly, men often express a preference for being the "head of the family." They feel the role is natural, that it is their birthright as men.

Advocates of the complementary, equal-partner relationship argue that in the division of labor there is generally equality, but not in every sphere of life. Men have greater authority in matters that relate to their work and economic matters, and, of course, many times that authority carries over into the home. Women have greater authority with regard to domestic and child-care issues. The result is a kind of balance between husbands and wives that reflects both the realities of life and some deeply embedded preferences of many men and women.

The Case for Egalitarian Marriages

Advocates of egalitarian marriage consider the complementary, equal-partner relationship to be inherently unequal. The division of labor it promotes does not give the same advantages to women as it does to men. No matter how much good will there is on the part of husbands, there will always be inequality as long as their economic position is given priority. Their breadwinning responsibilities will be overvalued, and the child-care and household management responsibilities of women will be undervalued.

But there are other arguments that reflect the benefits that flow to both husbands and wives when they have true equality. One of these is a reduction in the pressure on many men when they have final authority (and responsibility) in their marriage relationships. This pressure is often not remarked upon, perhaps because it is unrecognized by many men and women. But when husbands and wives have relationships that give them equal rights as well as equal responsibilities, the effect is positive for both. Wives develop greater respect for themselves and their opinions, while husbands can relax because they are not under constant pressure to be "in charge."

Greater equality in the realms of child care and other work in the home can also be satisfying for both sexes. Men who are able to take more time from their work and devote more time to their children have an opportunity for experiences that are unparalleled in the outside world. Women who have help with these responsibilities are usually very happy to have some of the burdens of child care taken from them.

But most important, the greatest positive benefit found in truly egalitarian marriages is the quality it adds to the relationship between the two married people. When they can treat each other as two equal adults, the ramifications extend through all aspects of marriage. Women in unequal relationships often have to be indirect, subtle, and perhaps servile to get what they want from their husbands. In an egalitarian relationship they can be open and direct. On the other hand, men in unequal relationships can never be totally sure they are not being manipulated and maneuvered by their wives. When a husband and wife are completely equal their entire relationship is likely to be marked by greater openness and honesty. This is viewed as the outstanding benefit of the egalitarian marriage.

To summarize, the advocates of egalitarian marriage start by seeking equal and interchangeable work and domestic roles for husbands and wives, because they generally believe a strict division of labor is inherently unequal. But they also believe that greater equality reduces the tensions and pressures of traditional gender-related tasks. This same equality provides pleasures that cannot be obtained when there is a strict division of labor. But the most important argument for complete equality is that the relationship is more honest and open, and therefore more satisfying for both husband and wife.

Themes

1. In contemporary life we expect our marriages to provide a great many things.

2. Marriage relationships can take a number of different forms. The types of marriage relationships vary from one society to another and from couple to couple in our own society.

3. Individuals bring marital scripts to their marriages, which can cause problems for newly married couples when their scripts are mismatched.

4. Quality of communication between husbands and wives is an important element in satisfactory marital relationships.

5. The dimensions of communication that are most important are openness and honesty, supportiveness, and self-disclosure.

6. Married partners should give confirmation to their spouses by responding positively to what the other person is saying through gestures and verbal cues.

7. Self-disclosure is important for any close relationship, but there may be limits to how much is good for a marriage.

8. There is widespread agreement that one of the serious problems in many marriages is the inability or reluctance of many men to reveal their most intimate feelings.

9. This tendency among males may be a product of gender role socialization, or it may result from the specific problems of establishing gender identity when children are primarily reared by mothers.

10. Marital quality has been the most widely studied aspect of married life.

11. Marital quality is related to both the social and personal characteristics of the partners, and to the nature of their interpersonal interaction.

12. Children appear to have a negative effect on marital quality.

13. Marital quality varies over the life cycle of a couple, with the highest quality in the early stage of marriage.

14. Power is a significant and normal aspect of the relationships between husbands and wives.

15. Power has a variety of sources, including tradition and individual attributes.

16. Patriarchy has a long history in Western societies, and vestiges of it remain in the traditional gender roles.

17. Patriarchy, gender roles, and resources give husbands a power advantage over wives.

Facts

1. Marriage among the Pakhtun follows a societal pattern of continuing warfare between husbands and wives.

2. Traditional Muslim societies often follow a custom of role segregation between husbands and wives.

3. Role segregation is also found among many working-class families in both the United States and Great Britain.

4. Role segregation between the spouses is more likely to prevail among couples who have remained in the neighborhoods in which they have grown up.

5. Joint marriage roles are associated with modernization and industrialization.

6. Joint marriage roles are typified by vital and total marriages.

7. Devitalized marriages are those in which the relationship has become dull, boring, and routine.

8. Passive-congenial marriages are those that typically started on a passive note and have remained at that level.

9. The earliest identification with another person, for both boys and girls, is typically with a woman—their mother.

10. Boys reared primarily by their mothers must develop a gender identity and an independent sense of self (ego boundaries) by separating themselves from their mothers.

11. Marital stability refers to whether or not a marriage stays intact; it is distinct from marital quality.

12. Generally, more than ninety percent of married couples will say that their marriages are "very happy" or "happy."

13. Marital quality is likely to be greatest if the partners have similar social and personal characteristics, high education, intelligence, and income, strong religiosity, and good relationships with parents.

14. Marital quality is reflected in a high positive regard for one's spouse, and satisfaction with all parts of the relationship.

15. Voluntarily childless wives have higher marital quality than wives with children, which is consistent with the general tendency for children to reduce marital satisfaction.

16. Research has shown that couples early in marriage are most satisfied with their relationship; some studies also show an increase in marital satisfaction in the later stages of marriage.

17. Husbands often have "resources" such as education, income, and prestigious occupations that give them power in relation to their wives.

18. In research on marital power, observation and self-reporting are the two principal methods used to measure power.

19. Resource theory as an explanation of marital power can only operate in settings that tend toward equalitarianism.

Major Concepts

authority: Legitimate power, power that comes from some higher source, such as the Constitution, norms, or customs.

coercive power: Power based on the ability to punish or do harm to another person.

complementary, equal-partnership marriages: Marriages in which husbands and wives have separate tasks, thought to be equal in importance, and decision making is done jointly.

confirmation: In conversation, responding positively, through word or gesture, to what another person has said.

conflict-habituated couples: Married couples who have fallen into a pattern of nearly constant fighting and arguing.

devitalized marriages: Marriages that have become dull, boring, and routine. Husbands and wives spend little time together, have an unsatisfying sex life, and share few interests and activites.

egalitarian marriages (used interchangeably with *equalitarian marriages*): Husbands and wives have nearly identical activities, both in employment or careers and in the home. Parenthood is optional, but taking care of any children is equally divided between husband and wife.

equalitarian marriages (*See* **egalitarian marriages**)

homogamy: Marriages between persons with the same or similar characteristics, such as religion, race, and socioeconomic status.

joint marriage roles: Marriage roles which have husbands and wives directing most of their time and energy toward each other and carrying out marital and household tasks together.

leveling: A way of communicating that expresses a person's feelings accurately and with no mixed messages.

marital scripts: Unconscious and unspoken expectations about what is proper and appropriate behavior by one's spouse.

passive-congenial marriages: Marriages that lacked excitement and romance from the beginning and are characterized by passive husband and wife relations.

purdah: A custom practiced in many cultures (especially Muslim cultures) that keeps women generally secluded in their homes and limits their visibility in public places.

role-segregated marriages: Marriages in which husbands and wives carry out their activities separately.

9

Marital Sexual Life
Variations in Sexuality and Sexual Behavior

Two people who are married for twenty-five or thirty years will probably have sexual intercourse more than 3000 times if their weekly average is close to the overall average reported for American couples. In light of this statistic alone, it is safe to say that sex is a most important part of married life. Some people would say that sex is *the* most important part. For particular couples that might be true, because sex for some people can be the cornerstone of marriage. At the opposite extreme, there are also couples for whom sex is inconsequential. Most couples fall somewhere in between.

In this chapter we will be giving our attention to various aspects of sexual behavior among married couples. We will examine the sexual ways of the past and then see how, in recent years, both sexual attitudes and sexual behavior have changed. We will find that recent changes have brought about a greater amount of sexual activity and diversity. Included among these changes are recent increases in extramarital sexual activity, with an estimated half, or more, of all married men and women having had extramarital sex. With this statistic in mind, it is obvious that extramarital sex is a significant marital issue. Since extramarital sex is widespread, it can reasonably be asked what should be the course of action if the sexual infidelity of one's spouse is uncovered? At the end of this chapter, we will consider alternative answers to this question.

To understand our own sexuality and our sexual relationships, we must go beyond the view that sex is purely biological. This is not to deny that sex has a biological foundation. But a purely biological approach leads to the questionable idea that sex is basically a "natural" behavior. This leads to the closely related fallacy that there is "normal" sex. A keynote of this chapter is that what we learn about sex is much more important than "what comes naturally."

One way to begin to see how much sexuality is learned is to take a cross-cultural perspective. By looking at how people of other cultures view sex and experience sex, we can find clear signs that much of what we may think of as natural is, instead, learned. To see the validity of this point, we will begin with the simple issue of what is considered sexually exciting or "sexy" from one culture to another.

CROSS-CULTURAL VIEWS OF SEXINESS

American popular magazines often publish polls and surveys that claim to establish which parts of the male and female anatomy are most sexy. Females are often said to favor the buttocks (coquettishly called the "tush") as the sexiest part of a male. Males are similarly attracted to the *derriere* as one of the sexiest parts of a woman, but both breasts and legs come in for some favor. Apparently, almost no American males select the armpits as one of the features of a woman that arouses them sexually. Fewer still choose the neck as sexually exciting. Yet there are males in different parts of the world who would select these as the sexiest parts of a woman's body. Indeed, they would think it strange that men in other societies would not consider them sexy. For instance, among the Abkhasians, a group of people living in the southern part of the Soviet Union, it is the female's armpit that is especially sexually exciting (Benet, 1974). It would be unthinkable among the Abkhasians for a woman to allow a man other than her husband to see her armpits. Japanese males, on the other hand, are said to think of a woman's neck as a particularly sexual part of her body. They are especially attracted to a long, swanlike neck. For a number of years the Hollywood film actress Audrey Hepburn was very popular among Japanese men, precisely because one of her most striking features was a long slim neck. While this feature might have appealed to some American males, it is doubtful that very many would have seen it as sexually arousing.

Even in our own society, around the turn of the century, the standards of sexual attraction were quite different from today. With the dress styles for women being floor length, a glimpse of a woman's ankle or calf might have given a man quite a thrill. In addition, photographs of that period, especially those showing women posing nude or seminude, reveal that the preference then was for a woman's body to be relatively heavy and very well padded.

While the sexual attractions of females are those most often noted by contemporary Western people, it is sometimes the case that the males of a society are the objects of sexual attention. Among the Wodaabe, a nomadic tribe in Central Africa, young males are the center of attraction, especially during ceremonies held several times a year. These are times when dances are performed by the young males, who compete with each other to be chosen the most beautiful and charming (Beckwith, 1983). Their costuming and makeup, along with the parading and performing before tribe members, are comparable to a Miss America contest in the United States. The most handsome young men of the tribe stand in a kind of chorus line where their attractiveness is judged largely

In the Wodaabe tribe of Central Africa the males are the objects of sexual attention.

on the basis of their exaggerated facial expressions. An observer describes the scene as follows: "Eyes roll; teeth flash; lips purse, part and tremble; cheeks, inflated like toy balloons, collapse in short puffs of breath" (Beckwith, 1983, p. 508).

These facial features, especially the large rolling eyes, are particularly alluring for the women of the tribe, who may cry out in ecstasy when a man performs well. The charm and magnetism of these facial gestures may bring multiple wives to the most handsome young men of the tribe. American women would not likely find these facial gyrations sexually attractive, but the Wodaabe women clearly do.

These few examples show that even at the fundamental level of physical body features, human beings learn to find very different sexual attractions. When we turn to the broader realm of sexual customs and beliefs, the range of preferred behaviors is unbelievably varied and diverse. We have only to look at our own history to see this demonstrated.

CHANGING VIEWS OF SEXUALITY

Married Sexual Life in the Past

Social historians generally believe that married life in general, and married sexual life in particular, is very different today from what it was even a hundred years ago. Both in Europe and the United States in the nineteenth century the authority and supremacy of the husband and father in the home (called patriarchy) dominated all parts of life (Shorter, 1982). In regard to sex, patriarchy meant that husbands could dictate when they would have sexual intercourse with their wives. In this powerful position, men often showed little regard for either the feelings of their wives or the physical repercussions of their actions.

A very grim picture of sex between husbands and wives in the nineteenth century and earlier has been drawn by a number of social historians, but some cautionary notes should be issued before we proceed. An obvious point is that not every pre-twentieth-century man behaved in the same way. There were certainly loving and considerate husbands who were sensitive to the emotional and physical feelings of their wives. The social historians are describing the more general condition that prevailed among the majority of people.

The second point regarding the work of social historians on the matter of sexual relations is that the evidence is undeniably sketchy and anecdotal (Shorter, 1982). There are no systematic surveys or interview studies of sexual behavior going back to the nineteenth century and earlier. For evidence of what sexual life was like it is necessary to use diaries, journals, reports of doctors and midwives, folk songs, sayings, stories, and poems as sources.

This type of evidence suggests that the attitude of most men toward their wives was one of indifference to their physical health and emotional well-being. In the words of one historian of the family, "intercourse in the traditional family was brief and brutal, and there is little evidence that women derived much pleasure from it" (Shorter, 1982, p. 9). There is evidence that many husbands did not abstain from having sex with their wives either during pregnancy or immediately after the birth of a child. Despite the warnings of doctors and midwives that the health of the wife would be endangered, especially by infections, many women embarrassedly reported that their husbands paid no heed (Shorter, 1982).

And how did pre-twentieth-century women view sex? Many viewed it with fear, because sexual intercourse might very well mean another pregnancy. The typical wife living on a farm, or in a village or town, had no knowledge of contraception or even of a "safe" period during her menstrual cycle (Shorter, 1982, p. 3). Every time her husband approached her to have sex, except if she were already pregnant, it might mean another pregnancy. A married woman who lived through her entire reproductive period might, as a general average, have seven or eight pregnancies, and perhaps six live births. In addition to the problems

*Rigid views of female sexuality
prior to twentieth century even
found expression in the manner
of dress.*

and difficulties of pregnancy itself, there was always a very real danger of death
at the time of giving birth. Even when a woman survived the rigors of childbirth, the cost to her health of bearing and rearing numerous children could
easily lead to an early death. With all this a painful reality for women, it would
not be surprising if sexual intercourse were viewed at least with apprehension
and probably with dread. And so it was for many women.

Why, then, did they not avoid sex by using one subterfuge or another? Perhaps many did, or tried to do so, but there is another dimension to sex in the
pre-twentieth-century period that explains why many did not. Sex, even among
the educated classes, was viewed as a "right" of husbands and a "responsibility
or duty" of wives. This view of sexuality has been revealed in an interesting
study of American marriage manuals (today often called sex manuals) by Gordon (1978).

By studying nineteenth-century marriage manuals, Gordon has been able
to show how Americans, especially those who were middle class and well educated, viewed sex. While marriage manuals certainly do not show us how all
married couples behaved in their bedrooms, they do reveal the prevailing beliefs and ideals about marital sex.

One major theme found in marriage manuals of the 1800s is that sexual desire is generally very limited among women. A classic statement of this view appeared in an 1869 marriage manual in which the author asserted the following:

> *As a general rule, a modest woman seldom desires any sexual gratification for herself. She submits to her husband, but only to please him and but for the desire of maternity, would far rather be relieved from his attentions. The married woman has no wish to be treated on a footing with a mistress. (Hayes, 1869; quoted in Gordon and Shankweiler, 1971, p. 460)*

This statement, while it most prominently claims that women have a low level of sexual desire, also makes some other implicit assertions. One is that a woman "submits" to her husband in order "to please him." This implies, first, that the man does have a strong(er) sex drive and, second, that a wife must satisfy that drive. Sex is a duty of marriage, and under the best of conditions a wife submits in order to please her husband.

A second idea revealed by this quotation is that women should be sexually motivated only by a "desire for maternity." This is often called the *procreative* view of sex. In the nineteenth century this view, at least as an ideal, was expressed by many writers. They advocated sex only for procreation because sex was seen as an "exhausting," "draining," and "debilitating activity." For males in particular the loss of "vital body fluids" was seen as leading to all sorts of negative effects on health and vitality. One marriage manual stated

> *The ordinary results of an abuse of the conjugal privilege [excessive sexual intercourse with one's wife] are, in the man, very much the same as those brought on by self-abuse [masturbation]. Locally there is overexcitation, irritability and possibly inflammation. The digestion becomes impaired, dyspepsia sets in, the strength is diminished, the heart has spells of palpitation. . . . (Napheys, 1869; quoted in Gordon, 1978, p. 62)*

With the dangers of excessive sexual intercourse in mind, many writers of marriage manuals addressed the question of how often a married couple should have sex:

> *Few should exceed the limit of once a week; while many cannot safely indulge oftener than once a month. But temperance is always the safe rule of conduct. (Trall, 1866; quoted in Gordon 1978, p. 63)*

By the end of the nineteenth and beginning of the twentieth centuries, some different views about marital sex were coming on the scene. Some marriage manuals, especially those published after 1900, were starting to consider the pleasurable aspects of sex, along with the procreative function. One twentieth century writer wrote on this issue, saying

> *We must reiterate our opinion that the sex instinct has other high*
> *purposes besides that of perpetuating the race [procreation], and sex*
> *relations may and should be indulged in as often as they are conducive to*
> *man's and woman's physical, mental and spiritual health. (Robinson, 1917;*
> *quoted in Gordon 1978, p. 67)*

An equally important development in the twentieth century was the view
that women as well as men could experience sexual desire. In the nineteenth
century, this was only begrudgingly admitted, and women who too openly admitted or revealed their sexual desires were often labeled mentally ill or deviant
(Barker-Benfield, 1976). While in the beginning of the twentieth century women
were thought to have some sexual desires, their sexuality was still seen as distinctly different from that of men. The sexuality of women was seen as passive
or dormant, waiting to be aroused by a man. As one 1914 sex manual put it,

> *Men's sexual appetites are, on the average, far keener and more insistent*
> *that those of normal women. Women's desire for sexual gratification*
> *often needs . . . awakening. (Geddes and Thompson, 1914; quoted in*
> *Gordon 1978, p. 67)*

This brief historical look at the different views of sexuality that have prevailed in American society underlines how social beliefs and ideas change and
vary over time. It would be only too easy to see these ideas as amusing misper-
ceptions and myths. They may be that, but the most important point to be
drawn from this discussion is that our current views about sex and sexuality
are just as much social constructions as those of the past. Current social views
about sexuality influence our sexual behavior in the same way that social views
of the nineteenth century shaped the behavior of the people who lived then.
Sexuality is related in some fundamental way to a biological impulse, but it
clearly can be affected by changing social views. And just as views about sex
and sexuality changed from the nineteenth to the twentieth centuries, so too
they have continued to change right up to the present day.

Changing Views of Sexuality: The Mutual Orgasm and "Sex as Work"

By the middle of the twentieth century sex was no longer seen as being simply for procreative purposes. While women were usually thought to be somewhat less sexual than men, most sex manuals of the 1950s stressed the mutual
enjoyment that sex could give to both husband and wife. Indeed, this idea of
mutual enjoyment came to be centered on the mutual orgasm. In the 1950s
there was a great emphasis on married couples controlling and orchestrating
their sexual encounters so that both husband and wife would reach their orgasms at almost exactly the same time. In order to achieve the mutual orgasm, it
was usually assumed that the husband would have to control his own emotions,

while simultaneously and skillfully bringing his wife to her peak of sexual excitement.

If it appears that the ideal of the mutual orgasm made sexual experiences methodical, carefully controlled, and almost worklike, that view is not without validity. In fact two researchers studied the most popular sex and marriage manuals of the 1940s and 1950s and concluded that in many ways sex was seen as work (Lewis and Brissett, 1967). Sexual intercourse was often described in terms that were almost exactly like those used for successfully completing a job or task.

The sex manuals of the 1950s emphasized that proper preparation is an important ingredient for doing any task well. So it was for sex, also. Careful study, of course, would be the first task. The advice of marriage manuals in this regard was not unlike the instructions for a new piece of equipment—"Study this manual carefully before you begin to use it."

Studying the manual revealed to the reader that certain tasks had be learned and performed in order to achieve successful sex. A husband would have to learn about the various "erogenous zones" that could be manipulated in some prescribed manner so that his wife would be properly aroused.

The sex and marriage manuals treated sex as an orderly and systematic process, which couples would have to follow in an unvarying manner if they were to perform the task successfully. One important step in the process was labeled *foreplay*, which one manual asserted "should never last less than fifteen minutes even though a woman may be sufficiently aroused in five" (quoted in Lewis and Brissett, 1967, p. 15).

An emphasis on time and planning was one of the keynotes of the "sex as work" view. There were specific warnings against spontaneous or impetuous sex. One marriage manual warned that "spur-of-the-moment" sex sounds very romantic, but that it leaves one's clothes in a shambles, plans for the evening shot and birth control program incomplete. The preference was for a planned time period so that sex could be properly entered into and completed. "Husbands and wives should rarely presume to begin loveplay that may lead to coitus unless they can have an hour free from interruptions" (quoted in Lewis and Brissett, 1967, p. 15).

Of course, the "sex as work" theme is shown clearly by the emphasis placed on the mutual orgasm. Sex is like work when there is a clear-cut objective, an objective that one strives to achieve. If the objective is not achieved (no orgasm, or only one orgasm) then the entire experience, when viewed from this perspective, is judged a failure (or semifailure). It is likely that a generation of married couples (at least in the middle classes) guided and evaluated their sexual behavior in terms of the mutual-orgasm view.

The "New Sexual Ethic"

Beginning in the mid-1960s, some far-reaching changes occurred in the sexual ideals, beliefs, and behaviors of Americans. We have already seen in Chapters 5 and 6 how premarital sex changed in the late 1960s and the 1970s. These changes were fostered by the publication of books and magazines that provided Americans—both married and unmarried—with a "new sexual ethic" (Gordon and Shankweiler, 1971, p. 461).

With the "new sexual ethic," there was a very different emphasis. One of the themes of the new ethic was that rigid and limiting rules and procedures for sex could be ignored. No phrase of the 1970s captured the new sexual ethic better than the overworked "whatever turns you on." This cliche was used for any kind of behavior, but it had a special meaning with reference to sex. It meant that one could be sexually aroused by almost anything or any experience and each individual was free to go in any direction that was pleasurable or satisfying. The writers of sex manuals for the new sexual ethic not only condoned an "anything goes" style, they consciously and explicitly encouraged it.

The same two researchers who looked at the sex and marriage manuals of the 1950s took a new look at the sex manuals of the 1970s (Brissett and Lewis, 1979). What they found was a nearly opposite picture from the marriage manuals of only a decade or two earlier. Instead of a restrictive, limiting, and rigid set of prescriptions for sex, they found a new sexual philosophy that emphasized individual freedom and choice. Their overall assessment is the following:

> Upon encountering the newer sex manuals, one quickly realizes that he/she is embarking on a large-scale reinterpretation and redefinition of human sexuality. (Brissett and Lewis, 1979, p. 64)

The "new sexual ethic" was announced by an outpouring of books that described vividly how sex could be interesting, varied, and exciting for everyone.

This reinterpretation and redefinition of sexuality has numerous components, not the least of which is an attempt to break from the interpretations and definitions of the past. *Liberated sex* is a dominant theme. The old ways, the traditional ways, are attacked as no longer appropriate for contemporary life. Liberated sex can mean (depending on the particular writer) sex that is at odds with "the official attitude and code of morals." The suggested breaks with restricted sexuality include sexual alternatives to sexual intercourse, extramarital sex, and even displays of sexuality in the presence of one's children. Liberated sex also carries the idea that satisfying sex can be enjoyed by everyone—"young, elderly, impotent, frigid, and the physically or emotionally handicapped" (Brissett and Lewis, 1979, p. 66). The new sex manuals stress that everyone can and should learn how to enjoy sex.

Liberated sex also means a wide range and variety of sexual expression. Sex manuals both picture and describe the variations for having sexual intercourse, but sex is by no means limited to intercourse. In the sex manuals that exemplify the new sexual ethics, oral sex has not only come into the open, it is often urged as a way of adding variety to one's sexual life. Similarly, masturbation, which a century ago was routinely called "self-abuse," is now heralded as an acceptable part of people's sexual lives, including the lives of married couples, in which masturbation can occur when they are together or alone.

Contemporary sex manuals also recommend and give instruction on the use of sexual equipment (vibrators, dildos, clothing, and so forth). They encourage couples to have sexual experiences in unusual places and to act out their most personal sexual fantasies. In short, they encourage almost everything and anything that is sexually stimulating and pleasurable.

The new sexual ethic is simply one more human construction and interpretation of sexuality. As such, it does not absolutely determine everyone's sexual behavior, anymore than did previously held ideas about sexuality. However, it does have consequences for our personal sexual lives. We live in a socially constructed world, and to some degree our personal experiences, including our sexual experiences, are shaped and modified by the social context in which we live. This principle is clearly illustrated by the experiences of people who grew up in one sexual world and then lived through changing times into the new sexual ethic. Lillian Rubin (1976) has studied the lives of working-class married couples and found that many of the wives in these couples have been caught between the old and new ways.

Often their husbands have become aware of various features of the new sexual ethic and have found it relatively easy to integrate these new ideas into their thinking. As an example, husbands have learned about the greater expression of sexuality among women. These working-class husbands studied by Rubin are no longer the stereotypical insensitive brutes who think only of their own satisfaction. They want their wives to enjoy sex too. They want them to be freer and to be active participants in a mutually satisfying sexual life. But the wives often find these new attitudes of their husbands a mixed blessing. Most of these wives grew up learning a very narrow definition of what was sexually appropriate, especially for women. Indeed, for many of these women sexuality was something they had to learn to control and repress. When it came to sex, the guiding principle was "Men *use* bad girls, but *marry* good girls" (Rubin, 1976, p. 136). Bad girls in this context were those who were sexually free and uninhibited. They were the girls who had a reputation for being sexually loose. By repressing their sexual desires, working-class women tried to avoid the label.

Now these wives are being urged by their husbands to take a new attitude toward sex. Often the same message is coming from the mass media, even in the usually staid and conservative "women's" magazines. Now they are hearing from all sides that they should "loosen up" about sex.

There are several areas of sexual life that give these women special problems. On the matter of mutual enjoyment, and especially the female orgasm, many of these women cannot achieve the ideal. Often they are not as concerned about this as their husbands. One woman told Rubin plaintively,

> *I rarely have climaxes. But if it wouldn't bother my husband it wouldn't bother me. . . . I keep telling him it's something the matter with me, not with him. (Rubin, 1976, p. 152)*

One woman read in a magazine the fact that some women have multiple orgasms, and she worries that her husband might learn of this higher standard:

> *It's really important for him that I reach a climax, and I try to every time. He says it just doesn't make him feel good if I don't. But it's hard enough to do it once! What'll happen if he finds out about those women who have lots of climaxes? (Rubin, 1976, p. 153)*

Working-class men are also urging their wives to take the initiative in sex, to be less passive. But here, too, this is a new standard, a new demand, that is contradictory to the sexually passive role that women of the past were supposed to take. One woman says on this issue,

> *I just can't. I guess I'm inhibited. All I know is it's very hard for me to start things up or tell him something I want. Maybe that comes from back when women weren't supposed to enjoy sex. (Rubin, 1976, p. 143)*

The stresses produced by the new sexual ethic, especially for working-class women, are seen most clearly in the area of unconventional sex. As a case in point, oral-genital sex has increased greatly in recent years among working-class couples. Rubin found that seventy percent of the working-class couples in her study reported that they had had some form of oral-genital sex. This compares to seventy-six percent of middle-class couples. On the surface this seems to be a great change from the time when standard sexual intercourse (with the man on top, the woman on her back) was nearly the only form of sex. However, as Rubin points out, many couples who said they had tried oral-genital sex had done so only once, or it occurred only a few times a year. Even more important, while many working-class couples have some oral-genital sex, the women in these couples often have negative feelings about the experience. Many women share the sentiments of one wife who says,

> *I sure wish I could make him stop pushing me into that (ugh, I even hate to talk about it), into that oral stuff. I let him do it, but I hate it. He says I'm old-fashioned about sex and maybe I am. But I was brought up that there's just one way you're supposed to do it. I still believe that way. . . . How can I change, when I wasn't brought up that way? (Rubin, 1976, p. 138)*

We can learn a lot from the women and men interviewed by Rubin. We can learn things that go far beyond the particular sexual problems of working-class couples. Their experience with the new liberal ideas of sex can help us to see that the sexual lives of all of us are played out in the context of some larger social definitions of sex. We learn about sexuality, what it is, how we are expected to behave, what we are to enjoy and not enjoy, from the social world in which we live. Perhaps in the normal course of most people's lives the definitions, meanings and ethics of sex remain relatively constant. But in contemporary society there is continuing and often rapid change. When this is true, we must learn, unlearn, and relearn about sex and sexuality. As we have seen in the case of working-class couples, such learning and relearning can be the source of problems.

The most basic lesson of the cross-cultural and historical examples of variability and change, and Rubin's contemporary study, is that sex is more than the natural expression of a biological urge. It is a complex and varied human behavior that is often intensely loaded with social significance and psychological meaning. As we continue, in the remainder of this chapter, to consider various aspects of marital sex, it will be important to keep in mind that sex always has social and psychological significance beyond the physical act itself.

MARITAL SEX

When speaking of marital sex, it is clear there is no one standard of quantity, quality, or variety that would be right for everyone. Also obvious is that there is no ideal or even optimum level of sex between two people. Individual variations in sexual interest are simply too great. And, of course, the sexual behavior of any couple will be determined by the particular combination of the two people involved. With these cautionary notes sounded, it is still of some interest to know something about what the marital sexual experience is, generally. We can begin by looking at the statistics for frequency of sexual intercourse, or coitus.

Frequency of Coitus

There are parts of Polynesia where, it is said, a husband and wife are expected to have sexual intercourse at least once each night. If a Polynesian wife is disappointed in this regard, she may complain to her women friends, and soon her husband will become the butt of teasing and joking in the community (Reiss, 1980). While this may be the standard of sexual activity among Polynesians, there is no evidence that more than a few American couples maintain this level of sexual activity. Those who do are most likely to do so in the first years of marriage and then to experience a reduction.

The evidence on the frequency of coitus among American couples is far from perfect, but a basic pattern emerges from the available studies, and this pattern is in accord with casual reports and informal observations. (Figure 9.1 shows the overall pattern visually.) Serving as a kind of baseline data source, we have the ground-breaking studies of Alfred Kinsey and his associates (1948, 1953) conducted in the 1940s and early 1950s.

As noted in Chapter 5, Kinsey and his associates collected sexual life histories from many thousands of American men and women, but because people with higher levels of education were overrepresented in these samples, there may be some overestimating of sexual activity. With this in mind, we may first consider what the married women in Kinsey's sample reported about their sexual behavior during the first several decades of the twentieth century. Married women between twenty-one and twenty-five years of age reported they had an average of about two and a half coital experiences a week. From twenty-six to thirty years of age, the average dropped to slightly over two times per week. For women in their thirties the number went down from slightly less than twice a week to about one and a half times. And women aged forty-one to forty-five reported having sexual intercourse slightly less than once a week.

One interesting feature of the Kinsey data is that women who were born before 1900 reported that they had sexual intercourse more often than women born after 1900. We can interpret this relationship in light of our earlier discussion, where we saw that sex in the nineteenth century was often no more than a wifely duty and that husbands had the prerogative to demand sex whenever they wanted it. Under these conditions, sex may have been more frequent because husbands simply demanded their sexual rights and disregarded the wishes of their wives.

Since the time of the Kinsey studies, there have been a number of studies of American sexual behavior, including two based on random samples of the population of married women under the age of forty-five (Westoff, 1974). A 1965 sample included over 4,600 women, and a 1970 sample had over 5,400 women. By having these two sample surveys that were conducted five years apart, we can get a picture of any change that might have occurred during that period. Also, it is possible to make a rough comparison with the earlier Kinsey data.

In 1965 American married women under age forty-five had sexual intercourse an average of about one and a half times per week (the median was 1.48,

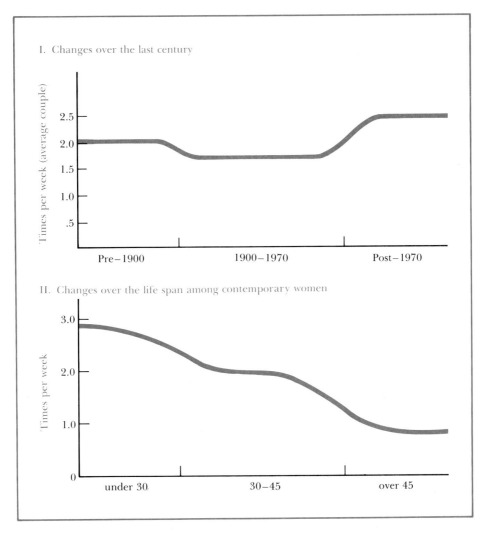

I. Changes over the last century

Times per week (average couple)

2.5
2.0
1.5
1.0
.5

Pre−1900 · · · · · · 1900−1970 · · · · · · Post−1970

II. Changes over the life span among contemporary women

Times per week

3.0
2.0
1.0
0

under 30 · · · · · · 30−45 · · · · · · over 45

Figure 9.1 *Two major trends in coital frequency* (*Sources:* Kinsey, et al, 1948,
1953; Westoff, 1974; Tavris and Sadd, 1977; Hunt, 1974; Blumstein and Schwartz,
1983.

while the mean was 1.70). The 1970 survey revealed a statistical increase in sexual intercourse, with the average going up to nearly two times per week (median, 1.88; mean, 2.05). These comparisons of averages may seem like small increases, but they are increases of at least twenty percent (Westoff, 1974).

Comparisons with earlier generations of women, as represented in Kinsey's study of females, are difficult because we do not have the 1965 and 1970 women divided by age. A very rough averaging out of the Kinsey data for women under forty-five would put the median at about 1.75 times per week. Since this figure for American women born in the early decades of this century falls between the 1965 and 1970 figures, it is perhaps safest to say that these major studies do not reveal a great amount of change. Over the first seventy years of this century, American women have generally reported having sexual intercourse about one and a half to two times per week.

When *Redbook* magazine invited its female readers in 1974 to respond to a questionnaire on their sexual behavior, 100,000 did so (Tavris and Sadd, 1977). This is a very large number of respondents, but it is also a nonrandom and volunteer sample and thus may not have the scientific credibility of Westoff's earlier study. This mid-1970s study uncovered a higher level of sexual intercourse than had previously been found. The weekly average, as measured by the median, was 2.3 times. Another major 1970s study was conducted by Morton Hunt (1974), and even though the scientific quality of the sample left much to be desired, he also found that couples were having sex more than twice a week. Broken down by age, Hunt's sample of women between sixteen and twenty-five reported they had sexual intercourse about three times a week. Women between twenty-six and forty-five said they had sexual intercourse about two times a week, and those between forty-five and sixty reported that they had sexual intercourse on an average of once a week.

A recent study of American couples has been conducted by Blumstein and Schwartz (1983). This study is distinguished by the fact that in addition to married couples the research also gave attention to gay, lesbian, and cohabiting couples. Regrettably, it must be noted again that the 12,000 couples in the study (both partners had to agree to participate) were not drawn randomly from the population, and the representativeness of the sample is therefore in doubt. Since all but about 15% of the couples had at least some college, it is likely that this sample is again skewed in favor of higher status Americans. Despite this note of caution, it must be said that both the quantitative and qualitative reports from this study provide important information and insights into the sexual lives of contemporary couples in the United States.

Regarding the frequency of sexual intercourse, Blumstein and Schwartz divide the married couples according to how long they have been married. Three categories are used: less than two years, two to ten years, and more than ten years. Forty-five percent of the couples married less than two years have sex three times a week or more. Between two and ten years, the number having sex three or more times drops to twenty-seven percent, and over ten years the number is eighteen percent. Turning to the couples who have been married longest, sixty-three percent of couples married ten years or more have sexual intercourse at least once a week, and one in five of these couples has sex at least three times a week. It is very interesting to note that when these married couples of ten years or more are compared to either gay men or lesbian couples of the same duration, the married couples, on average, have more sex.

The data on frequency of marital sexual intercourse among the couples in the Blumstein and Schwartz study are not easily compared with those of the earlier studies of married couples. However, even a casual examination of the data indicates that the average married couple today has sex at least twice a week. These estimates continue to provide evidence that sex among married couples today is probably more frequent than it was before 1970.

This study also considers the relationship between the frequency of sex and satisfaction both with the sexual relationship and with the marital relationship generally. Among couples who have sex three times a week or more, both husbands and wives say in eighty-nine percent of the cases that they are satisfied with their sex lives. Among couples who have sex once a month or less, only about one-third say their sex lives are satisfactory. When couples have sex infrequently, they also have a tendency to be dissatisfied with their marriage relationship generally. It is not easy to say if the decrease in sex leads to dissatisfaction with the relationship or vice versa, but the researchers in this case feel that having problems in other parts of the relationship will be likely to influence the sexual part of life. In their words, "Other problems come into the bedroom and make it less likely that the couple will want to have sex together" (Blumstein and Schwartz, 1983, p. 201).

Thus far the focus has been almost exclusively on sexual intercourse, but as we saw in the case of working-class couples sex can include oral-genital sex, as well as other sexual variants. The sample of married couples studied by Blumstein and Schwartz provides further indication of how often oral sex is a part of marital sexual activity. For heterosexual couples there are two forms of oral sex: *fellatio,* the women taking the man's penis in her mouth; and *cunnilingus,* the man using his tongue and mouth to stimulate the woman's genital area. Forty-three percent of the couples reported engaging in fellatio sometimes, twenty-four percent reported usually, and five percent said it was every time they had sex. Among the remaining couples eighteen percent said rarely, and ten percent said never. The percentages of couples reporting on how much they engaged in cunnilingus are nearly identical (sometimes, 42%; usually, 26%; every time, 6%; rarely, 19%; and never, 7%). The similarity of these percentages strongly suggests, though it does not prove, that when couples have oral sex it is often mutual or reciprocal.

These percentages indicate that for about three-fourths of American couples oral sex is a part of their sexual repertoire. This estimate may be slightly high in view of our earlier noted point that the Blumstein and Schwartz sample has an overrepresentation of higher status, more educated couples. As we saw above, when Lillian Rubin asked her sample of working-class couples about oral sex a decade earlier, the number reporting affirmatively was seventy percent. But as we have said, many of these couples had tried oral sex only once, or reported that it was something they did only occasionally (three to ten times a year).

The 1980s sample of American couples studied by Blumstein and Schwartz tends to support Rubin's earlier finding that men are more interested in and

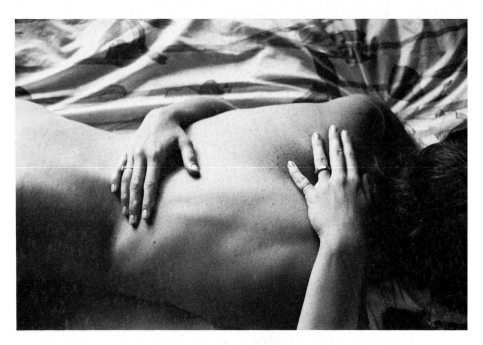

The sexual lives of married couples can often be greatly improved if husbands and wives take the time to learn the personal sexual scripts of their partners.

pleased by oral sex than women. Men who perform and receive oral sex are both happier with their sex lives and happier with their relationships generally. By comparison, women who perform and receive oral sex are no happier with their sex lives, or their relationships, than women who do not. While many women do enjoy oral sex, there is evidence once again in this study that some married women agree to have oral sex because it is something their husbands want. Women often confide to interviewers that they agree to oral sex because "it means so much to him." One woman described to the interviewer how she feels about oral sex with her husband:

> *It makes him feel good, truly good. I don't find it unpleasant. I don't say I wish I could do it all the time. I don't equate it with a sale at Bloomingdales. I could do that all the time. But it's not like going to the dentist either. It's between two extremes. Closer to Bloomingdales than the dentist.*
> *(Blumstein and Schwartz, 1983, p. 234)*

For some married women there are indications that oral sex is something they equate with submissiveness or degradation. And for a few, the old negative taboos about their genitals make them uncomfortable when their husbands perform cunnilingus.

These varied reactions, where oral sex for some women is very pleasurable and desirable, while for others it is uncomfortable and undesirable, reveal again how different individuals can be when it comes to sex. There is no right or wrong about these differences. They simply mean that individuals attach different meanings and values to the same objective behavior. These different meanings and values attached to various sexual behaviors are further illustrations of sexual scripts. This concept was introduced in Chapter 5 when we discussed the various sexual scripts of unmarried couples. Now, as we consider marital sex, we wish to develop and expand the concept of sexual script, especially to emphasize how each individual can have his or her own personal, idiosyncratic sexual script.

Personal Sexual Scripts

A *personal sexual script* is the meaning and significance an individual attaches to any and all sexual behavior. An individual sexual script comes from all that one has learned about sex from all sources. Sometimes elements of a sexual script may be relatively trivial and superficial ("I get turned off by wet kisses" or "I find heavier women sexually exciting"). Other elements of a sexual script may be more deeply embedded in basic ideas about sex and procreation. For example, the research of Kristin Luker (1984) has revealed that some women experience some of the pleasure of sexual intercourse from the possibility, and even the mildly exciting danger, that sex might result in a pregnancy.

The idea of sexual scripts can be a useful tool for married couples, both to enhance their sexual lives and perhaps to resolve sexual problems. To be useful as a tool, the two persons in a couple must first accept the idea that each has a sexual script. To do so will give them a basis for discussing their individual sexuality and their personal sexual responses. One immediate advantage of such a discussion is that it may allow a couple to acknowledge that even though they are sexually attracted to each other, each is a unique sexual person. This may help to avoid the problems that come from saying to one's spouse, "Other women (or men) I have known, like to do this. Why don't you?" The answer, from a sexual script perspective, can be, "It doesn't seem to be consistent with my personal sexual script." One may or may not know why it is not consistent, but that is not the point. What is the point, and what can be extremely important for a couple's sexual life, is a recognition and acceptance of the uniqueness of the other person's sexuality, that is, of their sexual script.

In the most positive case a couple may learn that they have perfectly matched or complementary scripts. He likes doing what she most enjoys and she likes doing what he most enjoys. More often there will be areas where the matching of scripts is less perfect, but each partner, understanding what the other person likes and wants, will try whenever possible to satisfy those desires. Even when certain actions do not have the same sexual meaning or significance for the acting partner, it may still be important and satisfying to give pleasure to the other partner.

There are, of course, many instances when the sexual scripts of two people are mismatched. What one person finds sexually stimulating and exciting, the other may experience as distasteful or even repulsive. The case of oral sex, as we have seen, is for many husbands and wives a vivid example of mismatched sexual scripts. But, there are many, many other possibilities for mismatched sexual scripts. When the sexual scripts of a couple are seriously mismatched, it may not be possible to resolve the problem simply by discussing it. Yet, if two people do discuss their sexual problems from the point of view of their personal sexual scripts being mismatched, it may sometimes be possible for them to work out a satisfactory accommodation. It may also be possible for one or both to change their sexual scripts. Sex therapy and counseling are more and more widely used by couples today. It may be possible through therapy or counseling to understand the origins of personal sexual scripts, but at present this is more an art than a science. Even more problematic is the potential for making changes in one's sexual script through therapy, counseling, or other means. The major hope for doing so lies in the primary assumption that sexual scripts are learned. At least this assumption holds out the hope that what has been learned can be modified or replaced by new learning.

Sex as Power

The preceding discussion of sexual scripts has dealt with sexuality in purely sexual terms. But this is a limited view that ignores the other meanings that sexual behavior can have. Sexual behavior, especially between husbands and wives, does have other meanings, especially including what has been called "the balance of power in the bedroom" (Blumstein and Schwartz, 1983, p. 206). Sex can be used, and is used, as an instrument for wielding power over one's partner.

Connecting sex with the term *wielding power* may conjure up images of couples locked in a struggle or battle, where there is no love and caring but only a concern for controlling the other person. There are couples who fit this image, but that is not what we are talking about. We are talking about many average, "happy" couples who nonetheless use sex as an instrument of power. This is often done through the necessary acts of *initiating* sex and *refusing* it. Someone has to take the first step, and when either the husband or wife does so, the other person has to respond. That response can be positive or negative. Both of these actions have implications about power. How individuals use these actions can tell us about how much power each partner has and how sex can be used to control the other person (Blumstein and Schwartz, 1983, p. 206).

When husbands and wives are asked who initiates sex, most of the time they are in fairly close agreement (Blumstein and Schwartz, 1983). As Figure 9.2 shows, about half of all husbands and wives acknowledge that in their marriages it is the husband who is likely to initiate sex. On the other side, in twelve percent of the marriages it is said by the wives that they are more likely to initiate sex; in fairly close agreement, sixteen percent of husbands say their wives

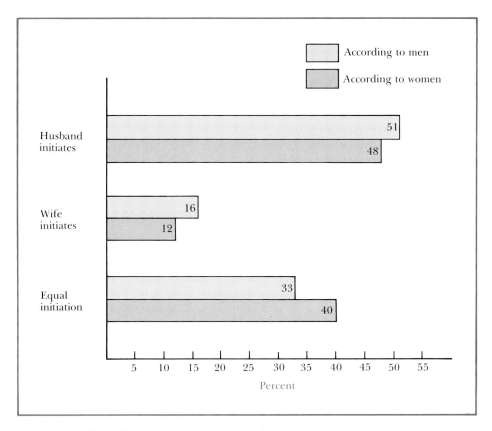

Figure 9.2 *Who initiates sex?* (*Source:* Blumstein & Schwartz, 1983, p. 207)

are more likely to initiate sex. This leaves a substantial minority who say that initiating sex is about equally divided (thirty-three percent of husbands and forty percent of the wives feel it is equal).

One important reason women give for not initiating sex more often is that doing so is a potential threat to their husbands. Traditionally the male role calls for them to be the initiators. While there have been modifications in this regard, there is ample evidence that for many men this idea is still deeply embedded in their attitudes. When their wives become the initiators, they become threatened. Sensing that their initiatives are threatening to their husbands, many wives who want to have sex more will pull back. Often they do so because they believe, or know, that their actions only worsen the situation. One wife described why she had become less assertive sexually:

> In the beginning I would put pressure, sexually too. I would say, "When are we going to make love?" and I realized that it was just no good for him.

Because he would get very anxious; he would pace the house and I'd wait. (Blumstein and Schwartz, 1983, p. 213)

Thus, many women come to recognize, or know intuitively, that they will be creating tension if they take too much initiative sexually. This violation of the traditional gender role of men will produce tension, and in many cases men may feel that their very manhood is called into question if they are not the ones initiating sexual activities.

The same traditional idea of men being the initiators of sex is the basis of another common pattern and a potential sexual problem. This is the case of the husband taking the initiative and the wife refusing. When wives refuse to have sex, husbands are often disappointed and upset, but, we should note, the traditional male gender role is left intact. The husband who is frustrated can still retain a positive view of his own sexuality and "sexual drive."

While initiating (and refusing) sex can be a problem for many couples, there are some positive signs that many couples today are achieving relative equality, in regard to both initiating and refusing sex. When they do have equality in either initiating or refusing sex, they are also more likely to be happy with their sex lives in particular and their relationships generally. Both husbands and wives are more positive about their sex lives and their overall relationship when they are about equal in initiating and refusing sexual overtures (Blumstein and Schwartz, 1983). There are a number of possible reasons for these characteristics of couples to be correlated. One of these is that when husbands and wives are equally committed to a relationship there is a greater freedom to share equally in initiating sex and being able to refuse without seriously hurting the other.

Some indirect evidence for this interpretation is found in the observation that the partner who is more committed to the relationship (more in love) is more likely to be refused after taking the initiative. When husbands are more in love than their wives, their requests for sex are refused much more often than when the wife is more in love. This suggests that refusing sex (or not refusing it) is not simply a reflection of sexual desire, but is used as an instrument of power. In the words of Blumstein and Schwartz, "When a person refuses sex, he/she can be a force to be reckoned with" (1983, p. 219). Inequality in sex, especially in sexual refusal, may then be a sign of unequal commitment or love, whereas equality in sex may reflect a more equal commitment and therefore a more satisfying sexual and overall relationship between two people.

SEX OUTSIDE OF MARRIAGE

If there is any doubt about the symbolic meaning and significance of sex, it is only necessary to recall the reactions we have to extramarital sex. We use terms

"So this is adultery!"

like *having an affair, cheating, playing around,* and *adultery* to refer to sex outside of marriage. The actual sexual acts are neither more nor less than marital sexual acts, but we can easily see that negative emotions are very often evoked by such acts.

As is seen so often from the historical record, this form of sex is not a new phenomenon. Recent historical studies of life in colonial America reveal numerous cases of adultery. Even though colonial America was intensely religious and morally restrictive, some people found the opportunity and the desire to engage in sex outside of marriage. When discovered, such persons were summarily tried and punished. Often, as the law provided, the punishment was death (Morgan, 1983).

In contemporary American life we penalize much less severely those who are discovered having an extramarital sexual relationship. Of course, there are many distinctions that can be made to make the offense much less or much more serious. A married woman with small children who has an extramarital affair and abandons her husband and family is likely to be very heavily criticized. By contrast, a middle-aged married man who discreetly, or secretly, keeps a mistress while continuing with family obligations is likely to get off very lightly, even if discovered. On these comparisons, people are likely to apply a double standard by giving men more leeway. We are likely to apply a kind of social calculation in which a woman with young children would be thought of as violating more of her social obligations if she has sex outside of her marriage. The same would be true of a clergyman, who might be held to a higher standard than men in other occupations.

While these and many other distinctions are made to judge the seriousness of having an extramarital affair, there is in American society a general disapproval of sex outside of marriage. Despite the more liberalized attitudes coming from the sexual revolution of the last twenty years, seventy-five to eighty-five percent of Americans say they disapprove of extramarital sex (Glenn and Weaver, 1979; Nass et al., 1981; Blumstein and Schwartz, 1983). While numerous public opinion surveys consistently show people disapproving of extramarital sex in principle, statistical studies of actual practices reveal a different picture.

Many Americans apparently are caught in a moral dilemma that one writer has labeled the "I-know-it's-wrong,-but-I-feel-so-good" syndrome (Mathias, 1981, p. 5). While the statistics on extramarital sex are not absolutely established, enough evidence exists to make some educated estimates. The most established, and certainly expected, fact is that married men are more likely than married women to acknowledge that they have had sex with someone other than their marital partner. Kinsey's studies found that about fifty percent of married men had experienced extramarital sex by age forty, compared to twenty-six percent of married women. This two to one ratio may not hold today, because while the percentages have increased for both sexes, it appears that women have increased their extramarital sexual activity more. On the basis of different surveys of varying quality, some experts believe that "60 to 65 percent of married men and 45 to 55 percent of married women experience extramarital sex by age forty" (Nass et al., 1981, p. 297). Among high income men, those earning $60,000 or more a year, an estimated 70 percent have extramarital affairs (Richardson, 1985).

These percentages are especially high for women in a society where public opinion reflects a negative feeling about extramarital sex. The same may be said for males, except that the previously mentioned double standard probably makes their violation of the norms seem somewhat less inconsistent. Cross-cultural comparisons probably also influence our attitudes about the extramarital behavior of American men, since even sixty-five percent may be far below the incidence for men in many other societies. In Japanese society, for example, almost all married men have some extramarital relations, though Japanese married women seldom do (Maykovich, 1976).

The significant increase in extramarital sexual activity among married women has been the subject of much conjecture and discussion. The most widely accepted explanation for the increase is that women are employed outside the home much more than previously. Working provides the opportunity and the freedom to meet and become involved with members of the opposite sex. It is a fundamental axiom that opportunity must exist if someone is to have an extramarital sexual relationship. The workplace provides that opportunity.

In addition to opportunity, there must also be some motivation. Both men and women who are having extramarital sex often report that relationships with their spouses are not satisfying or fulfilling (Atwater, 1979, 1982). Especially women who are having extramarital affairs, while they will acknowledge the problems, will often emphasize that their outside relationships are very fulfilling and pleasurable. Most important, they find in their lovers closeness, expressiveness, and communication. Unlike their husbands, who are often described as unexpressive, the men with whom they are having affairs are described as men they "can talk to" and "communicate with" (Atwater, 1982). Many women who are having affairs also find that their sexual behavior is more varied and their sexuality heightened. Some women feel a sexual constraint with their husbands that they do not feel with their lovers (Atwater, 1982).

But along with the positive reactions there are negative ones as well. Guilt is one of the common reactions, and fear of being found out is second. One young wife told an interviewer how she felt about her only affair, including her explanation for why it happened:

> I was resisting the thought of being married. . . . I was restless. . . . There really is no excuse. . . . I consider it an unhealthy thing to have done and I selfishly put a lot on the line for very little. He doesn't know, and he's not going to know about it. It won't happen again, I'm sure. (Blumstein and Schwartz, 1983, p. 277)

Both guilt and the fear of discovery show through in this statement. Many people like this young woman have these reactions, and a single, often brief, affair reveals the negative side of a romantic or sexual experience. Indeed, there is evidence that many married people have only one extramarital experience and then return to being consistently monogamous. One break from a monogamous commitment does not necessarily mean a continuing pattern of extramarital sex. Often an extramarital affair is simply to satisfy curiosity. One woman expressed her feelings in the following way: "I have not told [my husband] this, but I would hate to think that I would die knowing only one man" (Blumstein and Schwartz, 1983; p. 278).

Open Relationships

There has been much discussion in recent years about couples who have an "agreement" about outside sexual activities. Such an agreement may allow a degree of freedom to have sexual relationships with others. The label for such an agreement is *open marriage* or *open relationship.*

The amount of discussion about open relationships may be much greater than is merited by the number of couples actually in open relationships. In the sample of couples questioned by Blumstein and Schwartz (1983), about fifteen percent of married couples claim they have some form of an open relationship. Specifically, they reported to the researchers that they had discussed sex outside of the relationship and had decided that "under some circumstances it is all right." Some interesting comparisons can be made between married and non-married couples. Among opposite-sex cohabitants, twenty-eight percent claimed an open relationship. Lesbian couples had a very similar response, with twenty-eight percent having open relationships. Gay male couples had a much higher percentage, with sixty-five percent reporting open relationships (Blumstein and Schwartz, 1983).

The widespread discussions of open marriage have brought to light many of the problems connected with this arrangement. While some couples claim to have successfully negotiated these problems, almost everyone agrees that an open marriage in the sexual sense is not something to be entered into without careful consideration. The earliest advocates of open marriage, Nena and George O'Neill, make this point very clearly in their widely discussed book (O'Neill and O'Neill, 1972). Their basic notion is that a married couple can enhance the marital relationship if the partners do not have to focus all their attention on each other. Each partner, they argue, should engage in different activities with other people (of both sexes). These activities should be entered into openly, with the awareness and concurrence of the spouse. Reports and descriptions of these outside activities can then be brought back to the marriage and can serve as a source of renewed energy for the marital relationship.

The O'Neills counsel that a married couple must move into an open relationship slowly, and with continuous open discussion. If both partners find the openness comfortable, then ultimately it might be possible to move to the level of having sexual relationships outside the marriage. Again, this would have to be with the awareness and concurrence of both spouses. There is no expectation that all couples will be able to accept an open marriage that includes extramarital sexual relations.

The criticisms of open marriage include those of Nena O'Neill (1977), one of the coauthors of the original book putting forth the premise. O'Neill points out that sexual fidelity is usually promised at the time of marriage and is associated with feelings of trust and security. Even when the partners agree that their sexual lives need not be exclusive, there is often a feeling that the trust has been broken and that security is imperiled when an outside relationship is announced. Often the partner feels the same anger, rejection, and insecurity as when a secret affair is uncovered (O'Neill, 1977). One serious problem stems from the feeling that if one's partner is choosing to have a sexual relationship with another person, it must somehow reflect negatively on oneself (Mintz, 1981).

Taking these problems into account, it appears that for an open marriage to include a sexual dimension a married couple must meet some important preconditions. The marital partners must have nearly perfect communication and complete trust. Each person must be psychologically secure. And most important, the relationship must be cooperative, not competitive. Some couples might meet these criteria, but most do not. For the majority, a sexually open marriage is probably not possible.

Yet as we have seen, husbands and wives do have extramarital relations in a very high percentage of contemporary marriages. This is done secretly, and often the spouse never learns of it. But when an act of infidelity does come to light, it is a critical period for the relationship and the future of the marriage. In the section that follows, we will consider this issue and the alternative responses.

ISSUE

What is the best way to respond to the infidelity of one's spouse?

Almost no one in our society enters marriage with a premeditated plan to be sexually unfaithful. For most people who are marrying the vow of sexual exclusiveness is a cornerstone of the marriage. Obviously, with all the evidence about the amount of extramarital sex, many people change their views sometime after they are married. And there is only a small minority of couples who have an "agreement" that allows some outside sexual activity. For the rest, having sex with someone outside the marriage is done with the intention of keeping it secret from the husband or wife. Very often, however, the secret is uncovered, and when it is, the couple faces the question of how to handle what is usually a serious problem for the relationship. There are no simple answers as to how marriage partners should respond, if the problem does come up in their marriage. However, it is possible to identify a number of alternative responses, especially by the "injured" spouse. As a basis for your consideration and discussion, we will offer three alternative responses. They represent basic points along a continuum, which ranges from ending the marriage to ignoring the issue. These are clearly starting points for more extended and deeper discussions. It is suggested that readers ask themselves the question, "What would I do if I learned that my husband or wife had been having a sexual relationship with someone else?"

End the Marriage

Many people feel that infidelity deals a fatal blow to marriage. There are a number of reasons for this view. First, sexual exclusivity is considered a sacred vow of marriage, and it cannot be violated without making marriage meaningless. In the eyes of both the law and many major religions an adulterer is guilty of a major offense. But a second reason goes beyond mere legal or even theological considerations. Infidelity is such a breech of the relationship that there is little hope of repairing the damage. When a spouse is unfaithful, it means that the love and respect necessary for a marriage relationship are gone. And once gone, these qualities are not likely to be restored.

A related point is that once a marriage relationship has been damaged by unfaithfulness it will never again be a healthy relationship. There will be, at the very least, suspicions and doubts that will plague the marriage throughout its existence. But even more damaging is the strong possibility that there will be anger, bitterness, and perhaps hatred. As long as these feelings prevail, the marriage will be a "hell" for everyone concerned. Under these circumstances, it is better simply to end the marriage and start anew.

Discussion and Negotiation

There is a broad middle ground of responses to the infidelity of one's spouse that we will label *discussion and negotiation*. One initial point of discussion could be about the nature of the sexual relationship and the conditions under which it occurred. Many people would agree that there is a great difference between an ongoing love affair and one isolated, unplanned incident. By openly discussing these matters it may be possible for some people to handle the infidelity of a spouse. However, learning the details of an infidelity, such as when and with whom it occurred, is an extremely delicate matter. On the one hand, there is a natural reaction to want to know "everything," but it is quite possible to learn too much and thus intensify pain and hurt.

In any case, couples who go in the direction of discussion and negotiation will have to spend a considerable amount of time and psychic energy in this process. They will often have to examine what is lacking in their own relationship, for these shortcomings may have contributed to the infidelity. Perhaps also it is something in the personality of one of the spouses, especially the unfaithful spouse, that will have to be analyzed more deeply. These kinds of discussions, perhaps with the aid of outside counseling or therapy, can be difficult and are often painful, because they can open issues that are more sensitive than the original problem of sexual infidelity.

Another key element in discussion and negotiation is for the couple to work out how they are going to handle the future. This could range from the threat that any future extramarital sex will automatically mean divorce to an agreement between the marriage partners that they will have a sexually open marriage. The particular agreement about the future of the relationship depends on the needs and wishes of the individual couple.

Ignore or Downplay the Matter

In an age of greater sexual freedom and more relaxed attitudes about sex generally, some individuals can accept with calm and equanimity the sexual infidelity of a spouse. Sex is recognized as an enjoyable and pleasurable activity. Furthermore, the pleasure is often heightened by the novelty of a new partner.

Since extramarital sex is tempting, it is therefore accepted that some spouses are going to succumb to the temptation occasionally.

Not only is there temptation, there is also opportunity. Both men and women today are often in work situations with members of the opposite sex. They often travel, perhaps with someone from their place of work, to cities where they are not known and are thus freed from normal restraints. With such opportunities and freedoms, extramarital sex becomes easier and more tempting. By recognizing these facts of contemporary life, some people are able to accept the sexual infidelity of their spouses more easily.

For those who accept these views, it may not even be appropriate to think in terms of "infidelity." They may not see having a sexual fling, or even a love affair, as a breech of faith or a violation of the marriage relationship. It is simply something that happens occasionally in a marriage. From this viewpoint, if one does learn about the extramarital sex of a spouse, it may be the most prudent course of action to treat it casually, or even ignore it. Unless it is producing a break in the marriage itself, it may simply be treated as one of those things that will happen periodically but will probably pass and be forgotten.

There are also some practical reasons why some people choose to ignore the extramarital sexual activities of their spouses. If one is getting everything else one wants from a marriage (such as companionship, children, a home, money), it may be of little importance that one's spouse is sexually involved with someone else. While this situation may not be considered ideal by many people, it is a reason that some married people give for "looking the other way." However, the more likely reason for someone either to ignore or to downplay the extramarital sexual activity of the spouse is that such behavior is at least tacitly accepted as a part of contemporary life.

Themes

1. Sexuality is, to a considerable degree, learned behavior and varies from one culture to another.
2. Sexuality is more than just a natural expression of a biological urge.
3. Social historians have painted a grim picture of sexuality in the nineteenth-century and earlier, in Europe and United States.
4. Within a patriarchal family system, husbands controlled marital sex, and wives viewed sex as a duty and responsibility.
5. In the early twentieth century there was an increasing recognition that women too had sexual desires.
6. Before the emergence of the new sexual ethic, marital sex was often viewed as work.
7. The new sexual ethic fosters and encourages a very wide range and variety of sexual expression.
8. The new sexual ethic has often led to problems for people who received their socialization about sex in a different era.
9. In the last two decades there has been an increase in the frequency and variety of sexual behavior among American married couples.
10. The individual sexual scripts of a husband and wife can be matched or mismatched and thus can affect their sexual life.
11. Sex can be used as a power factor in a marital relationship.
12. Sex outside of marriage is imbued with symbolic meaning and significance.
13. The "open marriage" relationship, which some couples claim to have, is difficult to control and maintain.

Facts

1. In different societies, a variety of physical features may be considered sexually attractive, including, for example, the neck and armpits, and large rolling eyes.
2. Before the twentieth century an average married woman would be likely to have as many as eight pregnancies and six live births.
3. In the 1950s there was great emphasis in marriage manuals on the mutual orgasm.
4. The frequency of sexual intercourse, according to Kinsey's study of women, was greater for women born before 1900 than after.
5. Several studies confirm that the frequency of sexual intercourse increased among American married couples after 1970.

6. The frequency of sexual intercourse for married couples under age forty-five is more than two times a week; after forty-five it is about once a week.

7. Married couples who have sexual intercourse infrequently are less satisfied with their marriages.

8. Oral-genital sex is in the sexual repertoire of about three-fourths of American couples.

9. Men are more interested in oral-genital sex than women.

10. In one-half of marriages, husbands and wives agree, the husband is most likely to initiate sex. Wives initiate sex much less often (between twelve and sixteen percent), because to do so might be threatening to their husbands.

11. The majority of Americans (seventy-five to eighty-five percent) disapprove of extramarital sex, but some experts estimate that more than sixty percent of married men and between forty-five and fifty percent of married women have an extramarital sexual experience by age forty.

12. In Japanese society nearly all men, but very few women, have extramarital sex.

13. "Open marriage" relationships are claimed by fifteen percent of married couples, twenty-eight percent of cohabiting and lesbian couples, and sixty-five percent of gay male couples.

Major Concepts

cunnilingus: A form of oral sex in which a man uses his tongue and mouth to stimulate a woman's genital area.

fellatio: A form of oral sex in which a woman takes a man's penis in her mouth.

liberated sex: A dominant theme of the "new sexual ethic," which attacked traditional morality, opposed restricted sexuality, and advocated a wide range and great variety of sexual expression.

mutual orgasm: An objective of sexual intercourse greatly emphasized in marriage manuals of the 1940s and 1950s.

new sexual ethic: A view of sexuality emerging in the 1960s encouraging individual freedom and personal choice and a general liberation of sexual behavior.

open marriage (or, open relationship): An agreement between husband and wife (or a cohabiting couple) that allows some degree of freedom to have sexual relationships with others.

personal sexual scripts: The unique psychological meanings individuals may attach to various sexual behaviors.

procreative view of sex: The view that women should be sexually motivated only by a desire for motherhood, especially prominent in the nineteenth century.

sex as work: Prescriptions for sexual behavior in marriage manuals of the 1940s and 1950s that described sexual intercourse in terms almost exactly like those used for successfully completing a job or task.

sexual scripts: The different meanings and values individuals attach to various sexual behaviors. These meanings can be at a social or psychological level. (*See* personal-sexual scripts)

10

Having Children
The Choices of Parenthood

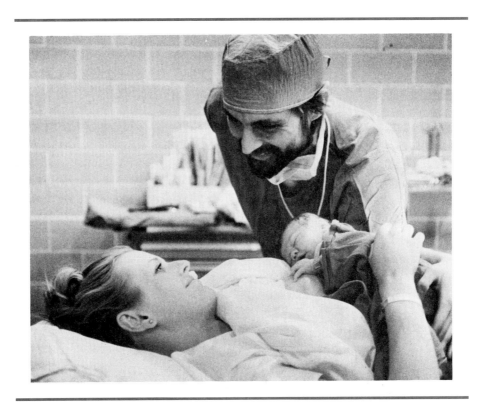

Lillian Rubin found in her study of working-class couples that the average time between the date of the marriage and the birth of the first child was nine months (Rubin, 1976). With this as the average time interval, it is obvious that many of the women must have been pregnant at the time of marriage, and, indeed, forty-four percent were. But whether premaritally pregnant or not, the nine-month average reveals that there probably was not a great amount of deliberation among these couples about becoming parents.

Rubin (1976) also interviewed middle-class, professional couples, and they, by comparison, had their first child an average of three years after their marriage. But even this time period means that the average middle-class wife became pregnant after slightly more than two years of marriage—this despite the fact that most of these wives held jobs after they were married.

The wives in the Rubin sample, most of whom had married in the late 1960s, are close to being characteristic of the total population. Studies of American couples have shown for years that most newly married couples had their first child during their first two or three years of marriage. Until recently, marriage for most people has meant that parenthood would soon follow. Becoming parents was not so much a result of a conscious decision as it was a more or less automatic next step after marriage. This pattern reflects the old refrain, "Love, marriage, baby carriage" (Daniels and Weingarten, 1982, p. 33).

But today there is widespread acceptance of the idea that having children is a matter of choice. It certainly is true that couples marrying today can decide *if* they want children, and if they do, how many they will have and when they will have them. This chapter will examine all these choices, and at the end of the chapter we will focus on a very specific choice: Should women wait until after age thirty to have their first child?

While it is accurate to say that couples (or individuals) can make many different decisions about parenthood, it is another thing to say that they do. This is one of the important topics to be explored in this chapter. We will be especially interested in why and how people make decisions to have children

To answer these questions we will examine the social, psychological, and technological contexts in which people make decisions. In order to have a clearer perspective on childbearing choices, we will begin by taking a brief look at some cultures where people have little or no choice about whether or not they will have children.

CULTURES WITH LIMITED CHILDBEARING CHOICES

In the plains states of the northern Midwest and in southern Canada there is a fundamentalist religious group called the Hutterites. The children of these vigorous and prosperous farm people usually marry in their late teens or early twenties. Hutterite married couples use no methods to control their childbearing, and the result is as one would expect. As recently as the 1950s Hutterite women had an average of eleven children (Stockwell and Groat, 1984). Population scientists believe that the Hutterites come closer than any other group to reaching the maximum natural fertility. Individual women can, of course, bear much larger numbers of children—it is reported in the *Guiness Book of World Records* that a Chilean mother has had more than 45 children (Boehm, 1985).

The Hutterites are important because they illustrate a group where there are either no choices or very limited choices with respect to having children. Of course, it could be argued that the Hutterite couples do make a choice. Their choice is to have as many children as they are biologically capable of having. But since their religious principles both preclude the use of contraceptives and encourage couples to have as many children as possible, individual couples have little choice but to follow the group ways.

It is safe to say that, historically, many people have lived under conditions where childbearing has been similarly uncontrolled and decision making quite limited. It is estimated that in the United States in 1800 the number of children born to each married woman was 6.9 (Stockwell and Groat, 1984). This is far short of the Hutterite number, but it is large enough to suggest that for most married couples there was very little decision making with regard to the number of children they would have or when they would have them.

In many places in the world today it is the norm, and indeed the preference, to have nearly as many children as one can have. In a number of African countries (Kenya, Senegal, Sudan) the average preferred family size among women between forty-five and forty-nine years old is from seven to nine children. In some Latin American countries the preferred family size among women forty-five to forty-nine is from five to seven children (Lightbourne and Singh, 1982). For these women who have largely completed their childbearing, there must have been very little decision making about how many children to have. However, it is important to note that younger women in these countries, those who are between fifteen and nineteen and still have their childbearing years ahead of them, are expressing a preference for slightly fewer children. On the average they want one less child. While these family sizes are still very large by American and European standards, there are indications that some decision making about family size is emerging, even in these traditional societies (Tierney, 1986).

One might ask why people in many parts of the developing world want to have large numbers of children. There are, of course, many reasons, and they vary from society to society, but one of the most important is that children are necessary. They are often literally necessary for survival (Mamdani, 1972). Many rural people, because they live at the margins of existence, put their children to work at a very early age. But more important, children also provide a means of support when parents reach old age. In some societies, couples who have no children are destined to be paupers when they grow too old to work. Without children to provide for them, they will have to depend on the mercy of other community members. It is also the case that children, especially sons, provide physical security for their parents in old age. Without them, the old people might be robbed or cheated by criminal or enemy groups (Mamdani, 1972). Under these and many similar conditions, children are not a matter of choice, they are a matter of necessity.

In many societies where children are so critically important, women who do not bear children are held in low regard and are often treated badly. In some societies of Africa, the Middle East, and Asia women can be summarily divorced by their husbands if they do not bear children. In societies as separate as the Aowin people in Africa and the Punjabi in India, childless women are thought to be witches or to possess evil spirits (Ebin, 1982; Homans, 1982). Among the Aowin, at the funeral of either a man or woman who has had no children, the corpse is called derisive names, it is physically abused, and the mourners command the spirit of the dead person never to return again (Ebin, 1982). Interestingly, in societies around the world the cause of infertility is more often attributed to the female, even though it is caused by the male thirty to forty percent of the time (McFalls, 1979). While these reactions to infertility may seem extreme, perhaps they also indicate how seriously social groups take childbearing. It is as if the entire society is offended by the failure of a person to have children. But why should the larger social group care if an individual is childless? To best understand the answer to this question, we must take a sociological view. This will allow us to see why people react negatively to the person who remains childless and also give us some insights into our own reasons for having children.

A SOCIOLOGICAL VIEW OF CHILDBEARING

It is a fundamental sociological assumption that the institutions and the culture of any society are humanly created. This simply means that the ways people do things and the things they value are shaped over time as the people interact with each other. The ways of doing things are the *institutions* of a society, and the values are key elements of the *culture* of the society. As a case in point, we have frequently seen in earlier chapters that from one society to another different aspects of marriage and family life can take very different forms. Similarly, the things people value and think desirable can vary greatly. But while the institutions and cultural values vary tremendously, they must ultimately allow the society to continue. If not, the society will disappear, and so will the particular institutions and values.

Applying this basic idea to the issue of childbearing will show concretely how it might work. Every group of people, every society, must have a set of institutions and cultural values that will enable and encourage people to have and rear children. If not, the group will not survive. One could imagine, for example, a group of people adopting a system that required all adult members to abstain from sexual relations. This is a nearly unthinkable possibility, perhaps, but many societies require celibacy of some people at least some of the time. Very often religions and religious groups require celibacy on the part of at least some of their adherents. And there are some extraordinary historical cases in American society of religious groups prohibiting sex for all members. The best known of these groups are the Shakers and the Rappites (Kephart, 1976; Muncy, 1973).

The Shakers were a part of the society of Quakers and were given their name because of the violent and unusual movements they made in moments of religious ecstacy. One group of Shakers came to the United States from England in 1774. The leader of that group, Ann Lee, insisted that sexual lust was sinful and developed a theology requiring members to be celibate. However, not all Shakers were absolutely required to abstain from sexual intercourse, because they divided themselves into the Inner Order and the Outer Order. Members of the Inner Order were those believers who had reached a higher state of perfection by giving up sex completely. The Outer Order members could have sexual intercourse, but it was to be accomplished without lust and solely for the purpose of procreation. This did give the Shakers a method of obtaining new members, which along with some recruitment of outsiders kept the group in existence through the nineteenth century. By the early years of the twentieth century, however, only six hundred members remained (Muncy, 1973). Today only a handful of elderly Shaker women survives.

The Rappites also came to the United States from Europe, but somewhat later than the Shakers (in 1803). They established several different towns in the United States but the last permanent settlement was in Economy, Pennsylvania. In 1807, the leader of the group, George Rapp, abruptly declared that henceforth all members would refrain from sexual relations. Families continued to live together in the same households, but husbands and wives could no longer sleep in the same bed. When new members joined the group, they had to give up having sexual relations. This group, too, survived for nearly a century. There were apparently some lapses in the practice of celibacy, and some new members were brought into the group, so it was not until 1905 that Rappites became extinct (Kephart, 1977; Muncy, 1973).

The Shakers and the Rappites demonstrate the obvious; when a society adopts institutions and values that prohibit childbearing, its days are numbered. Usually societies and religious groups have stressed the opposite approach, often following some version of the biblical dictum: "Be fruitful, and multiply" (Genesis 1 : 28).

This admonition illustrates how successful societies coped with the high death rates of infants and children—and mothers dying in childbirth—which made the survival of the group precarious. The societies that were able to maintain and even add to their populations were those that developed institutions and values that supported and rewarded childbearing. Societies that provided less support and fewer rewards for having children might simply have disappeared. If we take these factors into account, it is not surprising that we find societies existing around the world with strong reward systems for people who have children and, as we saw in the case of the Aowin, negative penalties and punishments for those who do not.

This sociological interpretation of the motivation for childbearing would lead us to believe that in contemporary societies, including American society, there are still likely to be rewards for people who have babies, and perhaps even punishments for those who do not. Since we have emphasized that childbearing in contemporary society is a matter of personal choices, perhaps it would be well to examine how much individual decisions are likely to be shaped and influenced by external social influences.

The Social Pressures to Have Children

If we were to identify all the pressures, large and small, that encourage or induce people to have children, the list would be long. But there are a few very important and obvious pressures that should be recognized.

The family. When a young couple marries today, there is usually no immediate pressure from parents or grandparents that they have a child. In the past, especially in societies with extended families, that may have been the case. But today parents are likely to encourage the young couple to wait until the marriage relationship has been firmly established. However, if a married couple does not have a child after four or five years of marriage, there are likely to be questions and hints from parents (or grandparents). They will inquire if

While almost all married couples have children, the large family is very rare today.

"something is wrong," or ask jokingly about when they are going to be presented with a grandchild. Not all parents and grandparents, of course, will follow this pattern, but it is commonplace enough to be clearly recognizable as a pressure to have children.

Religion. Almost all religions, and certainly Western religions, make the bearing of a child a positive and significant event. The Catholic Church, for example, through its doctrinal pronouncements, makes it clear that the purpose of marriage, and sex within marriage, is procreation. While other Christian religions are usually less explicit on this matter, the general themes are certainly supportive of childbearing.

In the United States the Jewish leadership has noted with some concern that Jews tend to have very small families. This is threatening because of what it portends for the size of the Jewish population in the future. A number of conferences have been held to determine both the causes of the low childbearing pattern and what might be done about it.

As a general rule the newer, smaller, and more sectlike a religious group, the more emphasis is placed on having children. The Hutterites, the Amish, the similar religious groups have very large numbers of children (the Shakers and Rappites are, of course, an exception to the rule). The Nation of Islam religion, as it became established among blacks in American society, put a great deal of emphasis on members having large families. It is understandable that new and small religious groups would want to encourage having children, since the growth of the religious body would be ensured by this means.

Other social pressures.   In addition to family and religious pressures to have children, ethnic groups frequently support and encourage more children among their numbers. Government policies, from income tax deductions for children to child support payments of various kinds, are all basically supportive of childbearing. In the economic realm it would be difficult to ignore the vast amount of advertising devoted to portraying babies and children in a positive way. While these images presented in the mass media may not cause people to have children, they are certainly consistent with the other positive supports for parenthood.

If one takes the entire complex of institutional and cultural pressures to have children, it is small wonder that most people do genuinely feel that they want to have children. This pervasive pressure for having children has been called a "cultural press" for childbearing (Kammeyer and Ginn, 1986). Of course, ultimately this cultural press must operate through the individual who grows up and lives in this environment. It is, in the end, the individual person who absorbs all of society's messages and concludes that she or he "wants to be a parent." It is this point of view that we will consider next.

Personal motivations for parenthood.   A popular "women's magazine" a few years ago published a piece titled "Baby Hunger" (Davitz, 1981). The author, a female psychologist, recounted how she had, at the age of twenty-nine, suddenly experienced a deeply emotional urge to have a baby. While up to that time in her life she had never apparently given the matter much more than a passing thought, now she was consumed by an interest in babies. She attributes this newly-found urge to a kind of biological "hunger" to have a baby. The author claims to have found other women who have had similar experiences and concludes that this desire for a child should be recognized and accepted as a "natural, biological" urge (Davitz, 1981).

There is no reason to doubt the author of this magazine piece probably did experience a sudden interest in and desire for a baby. Nor can one doubt that other women have had similar feelings. What can be doubted is whether this is a biological urge, or whether the desire to have a baby is a product of the accumulated societal and familial messages that most females (and males) receive from childhood on. (Surely every little girl has had some adult say, "When you grow up to be a mommy. . . .") There is no certain answer to the question of where the "urge" to have babies comes from. But some part of it must come from the social and psychological supports and rewards for having children. Thus, for childless women to experience an interest in babies as they near the age when many women have finished having children is quite understandable.

Some women and men do remain childless, despite the social and psychological pressures (and possible biological urges), and they do so voluntarily. Remaining childless by choice is a very interesting contemporary phenomenon, and it has in recent years received the attention of social researchers. By taking a look at this research we can both learn something about the people who make this choice and also, incidentally, learn more about the general social and psychological pressures to have children.

THE CHOICE TO BE CHILDLESS

In 1960 it was possible for American researchers to declare with some confidence that among married women those who were able to have children but chose not to were so few as to be a "nearly extinct" group (reported in Mosher and Bachrach, 1982). Then as now, of course, some percentage of married couples were childless because of infertility. Overall, about four percent of American women end their childbearing years being *involuntarily* childless (Mosher and Bachrach, 1982).

We will return to the issue of infertility later, when we review some of the new methods and techniques that allow infertile couples to have children. At the moment our primary interest is in those couples who choose to be childless, or as some prefer to say, "childfree." The very term we customarily use to refer to those people who do not have children (childless) implies that they are missing or lacking something.

Concentrating on the voluntarily childless, a number of important questions come quickly to mind. The first and most obvious is how prevalent is this phenomenon in our society? As every researcher who has studied this question has noted, finding the answer is much more difficult than might be supposed (Mosher and Bachrach, 1982). There are two basic obstacles: arriving at an acceptable definition and gathering data from a representative sample of the population.

On the matter of definition, Veevers (1979) has offered the strictest standards. To be voluntarily childless, one must "forego parenthood, either biologically or socially through adoption, and . . . successfully maintain a lifelong commitment to that decision" (Veevers, 1979, p. 4). This definition would exclude a childless woman who marries a man who already has children from a previous marriage. Veevers estimates that in Canada and the United States about five percent of all couples might meet the terms of this definition. However, analyses of data from the United States suggests that an even smaller percentage of couples are voluntarily childless.

One of the most careful and reliable estimates of voluntarily childless couples has been made by Mosher and Bachrach (1982), using two random samples of women in the United States who were between the ages of fifteen and forty-four. Among the women who were currently married, 1.8 percent said they were voluntarily childless. If formerly married women were included, the percentage rose to 2.2 percent.

But there is an additional problem in estimating the amount of voluntary childlessness. This problem stems from the fact that there are some women who have not yet had any children but who say they will in the future (the "temporarily childless"). Some of these women will probably end their childbearing years not having had children, apparently by choice, and thus they too should be included in the voluntarily childless category. But how many of these are there? Mosher and Bachrach are unwilling to guess, although they do report that if every "temporarily childless" woman remained childless, the percentage would go up to just over ten percent. They do not expect this to happen, however, so Veevers's (1979) estimate of five percent of couples remaining voluntarily childless is probably an acceptable figure.

Given the large amount of attention and publicity that has been given to the voluntarily childless issue in the last fifteen years, it may be surprising to learn that only five percent of couples (or women) choose to be childless. Further-

Childless couples find a wide variety of interests and activities, including pets, to add interest and fulfillment to their lives.

more, current estimates are that since 1975 the percentage is either going down or leveling off (Houseknecht, 1982a). This trend is especially surprising since the two characteristics that are most clearly associated with voluntary child-lessness are still on the increase. Every study has shown that women who are voluntarily childless are more likely to have higher levels of education and to be participating in the labor force with a career commitment. Since both of these factors have increased since 1975, it is perplexing that there have been no corresponding increases in voluntary childlessness (Houseknecht, 1982b).

Perhaps part of the explanation lies in the process of decision making that surrounds voluntary childlessness. It is not, as we will see, a single, uncomplicated decision.

Making the decision to be childless. When we think of making decisions, it is easiest to use examples where there is a thoughtful deliberation, a careful weighing of alternatives, and finally a decision is made. If we set out to buy a new automobile, we weigh the merits of the various models and their basic costs, we may shop around among different dealers to see where we can get the best buy, and then we make our purchase. By comparison, our decisions to have children (or not to have children) are often made very differently. Indeed, it can be said with some justification that most people deliberate more carefully about purchasing a car than they do about having children.

Studies of voluntarily childless couples have shown that there are basically two ways the decision is made. Some people make the decision not to have children at an early point in their lives. Veevers (1980) found that about a third of her sample of childless couples fell into this category. On the basis of the national United States sample of women, Mosher and Bachrach (1982) found forty-three percent of the childless couples had entered marriage agreeing that they would not have any children.

The reasons why some people make the decision not to have children are not very clear, sometimes even to the people themselves. One woman gives the following account of her experience:

> *My first decision never to have children was formed when I was fifteen and all us girls sat around talking about sex and marriage and husbands. Everyone else would always talk about the kids they were going to have, like it was just taken for granted. I couldn't sit and talk about it with the same enthusiasm as the others did. It finally came to me that I just didn't want to have children. It was a shock because all my life, you know, you're sort of groomed for it. (Veevers, 1980, p. 18).*

When a woman or a man makes the decision to be childless before marrying, they must then find a mate who will agree with their decision. Apparently, in about a third or more of the cases they are able to do so, though it is impossible to know how many minds are changed when individuals meet and marry a person with different views.

Since these early decision makers constitute only a minority of the voluntarily childless couples, what about the others? How do they come to be childless? In many ways they are the more interesting and revealing decision makers, because they mirror some of the characteristics of the couples who go on to have children. They certainly begin at the same place, because they enter marriage with the conventional expectation that they will eventually have one or two children. Typically, they have not given the matter very much serious thought, and in this regard also they are like most marrying couples (Veevers, 1980).

For these couples who eventually end up being childless, the process of decision making is one that goes through a series of stages. In a sense, these stages do not represent a decision as much as a series of postponements, with corresponding reassessments about parenthood. We can see this more clearly if we examine the stages that typify the experience.

Postponement for a definite time.   In this first stage these voluntarily childless couples are again like most other contemporary marrying couples. They avoid conception through the use of some kind of contraception so that they can achieve certain goals before starting a family. The typical goals may be "graduating from school, travelling, buying a house, saving a nest egg, or simply getting adjusted to one another" (Veevers, 1980, p. 21). If there is one way that these couples differ from other married couples, it is that they use contraception conscientiously and carefully. They do not become haphazard about contraception, as is so often the case among couples who become parents not long after marriage.

Postponement for an indefinite time.   The second stage is marked by increasing vagueness about the length of the postponement and the reasons for it. While the couple still believes that they will have children someday, they no longer have a notion of when the time will come. Their reasons for postponement are more vague and general, such as when they can "afford it" or when they "feel more ready."

Deliberating the pros and cons of parenthood.   Stage three is the first time that the couple openly considers the possibility that they might remain childless. It is a time of considerable uncertainty and ambivalence. One woman interviewee expressed the indecision she and her husband were feeling when she said, "We haven't decided to have children right away, and we haven't decided never to have them either. We just keep postponing the whole thing. We might or we might not. We can worry about that later" (Veevers, 1980, p. 23). In the case of the couples who remain childless, the "later" comes with the fourth and final stage of the process.

Accepting permanent childlessness.   If there is a decision for this type of childless couple, it comes in the fourth stage, and it is more a recognition that

"*We've decided not to have children.*"

a decision has been made. It might more aptly be described as a retrospective acknowledgment that all the postponements of the past have added up to a decision to be permanently childless.

Nancy Friday, the author of a best-selling autobiography, *My Mother/My Self* (1977), describes some of the uncertainty and indecisiveness she and her husband went through on their way to becoming childless. After recounting how they had once nearly drifted into parenthood without even discussing it between themselves, Friday writes, "about two years ago Bill [her husband] and I decided not to have children. No, to put it correctly, the decision went like this: One day he said, 'Isn't it a good thing that we didn't have children' " (Friday, 1977, p. 428). This was a retrospective recognition, not a decision.

Social pressures on the childless.   Regardless of how the decision to remain childless is made, after a few years of marriage childless couples report frequent social pressures and negative or even hostile responses to any indication that they may remain childless. While the severity of these reactions varies, they often reach a peak in the fourth and fifth years of marriage.

One feature of the social pressure childless couples are subjected to is the way relatives, friends, and even strangers freely ask for explanations and give unsolicited advice. It seems that parenthood is so positively valued that many people feel justified in asking a childless couple why they are not having children. When couples admit that this is their preference, the advice is usually that they should think carefully about such a position and not wait until it is too late.

Childless couples often become sensitive to the intrusions into their personal lives and develop strategies to deflect or disarm their well-meaning advisors. One tactic is to say or imply that they cannot have children because of infertility. Another is to say that they are contemplating adoption. Most childless couples agree, however, that while such techniques usually work with friends, co-workers, and strangers, it is parents that present the most persistent problem. The most common strategy for dealing with parents is not to tell them about any final decisions, often holding out the possibility of parenthood at some later date. In practice, this often means that long after a couple knows with certainty that they will have no children, they have not told their parents. "Parents are literally the last to know" (Veevers, 1980, p. 145).

If voluntary and involuntary childlessness are the case for only about ten percent of the total population, then the overwhelming majority of people do experience parenthood. Since entering parenthood is nonetheless a decision, it is important that we understand as clearly as possible both the positive and negative features of this process. It is to the process of becoming parents that we turn next.

BECOMING PARENTS

The experience of becoming parents is naturally divided into two parts. The first part, the pregnancy, or more technically the gestation period, is approximately nine months long and is literally shaped by nature. The second part, which has been called the "second nine months," is the initial experience of being parents. This second part, in the sociological and psychological literature is referred to as "the transition to parenthood." We will begin by considering the pregnancy experience.

The Pregnancy Experience

In television situation comedies, and perhaps in a few PG movies, pregnancy is handled through a series of stereotypes. The first stereotype is the "pregnancy announcement," which is usually a scene in which a wife informs her husband, who then reacts with a combination of excitement, joy, and bewilderment. The second stereotyped scene is at the beginning of labor, when the nervous and rattled father-to-be falls apart, leaving his calm and slightly bemused wife to handle the situation. The third stereotype is after the birth of the baby and shows the proud and beaming father with the glowing new mother, who is usually holding the baby. In real life there may be some occasions that are similar to the fictional stereotypes, but reality usually has a way of being a bit less sugarcoated.

In order to develop a more realistic picture of the pregnancy experience we will draw primarily on the research findings of two major studies of first pregnancies. The first is a carefully done interview/questionnaire study of 120 wives and 60 husbands (all Caucasian) from Baltimore, Annapolis, and the suburban Maryland communities around Washington, D.C. (Entwisle and Doering, 1981). The second is an observational and interview study conducted in a London, England, hospital. The main data for this second study came from sixty-six women who were having their first babies (Oakley, 1980).

The first awareness of pregnancy is often a physical change experienced by the woman. Aside from missing a menstrual period, the most common early signal of pregnancy is morning sickness, which typically involves nausea and vomiting. In the American sample, about half of the women experienced this kind of sickness *often* in the first three months of pregnancy. While morning sickness declined after that, several other symptoms increased (backache, heartburn, insomnia, painful sexual intercourse, shortness of breath, and swollen ankles). While the list of physical symptoms experienced by these pregnant women is quite extensive, they nonetheless described themselves as "having fairly easy pregnancies" and "looked upon themselves as being healthy" (Entwisle and Doering, 1981, pp. 51, 53).

Sexual activity during pregnancy changes in three ways. First, there is a reduction in the frequency with which couples have sexual intercourse. Studies by Masters and Johnson (1966) revealed a pattern of reduced sexual activity in the first three months of the pregnancy, some increase again in the second

A number of physical changes and symptoms, not all of them pleasant, accompany pregnancy.

three months, and a decrease again in the last trimester. Some researchers, but not all, have confirmed this pattern. Entwisle and Doering interviewed couples in the sixth and seventh months of the wife's pregnancy and found that twelve percent of them had not had intercourse at all in the previous two weeks. The remaining, sexually active couples were still having sexual intercourse an average of two and a half times per week. When asked about their frequency of having sexual intercourse before the pregnancy, the wives reported an average of every other day, or three and a half times per week.

The second change is a decline in interest in sex reported by many women. During the course of the pregnancy, from fifteen to twenty-six percent of the sample of women studied by Entwisle and Doering reported that they "often" had less interest in sex than before their pregnancy. An additional thirty-four to forty percent reported "occasionally" having less interest than before. While lack of interest in sex was slightly more common in the last trimester, it was certainly not limited to that part of the pregnancy.

The last change in sexual behavior is stopping intercourse completely. Most couples in the Entwisle and Doering sample did not stop having sexual intercourse until they were at least into the eighth month of the pregnancy. And a third of the wives said they were not going to stop at all during the pregnancy. If couples do stop having intercourse, the timing is closely related to the feelings of the wife about sex. When wives feel very negative or even mildly negative about sex near the end of the pregnancy, the couple has almost always stopped by the eighth month. Husbands' feelings about sex are also of some importance, however. In forty percent of the cases husbands indicated they had a reduction in their "sex drive" during the pregnancy (Entwisle and Doering, 1981).

The birth experience.   The experience of labor and the delivery of the baby is, understandably, an unforgettable event, especially for women. Reactions to the birth process and to the newborn infant are extremely varied. When a sample of wives was asked how they felt, thirty percent gave negative answers about their emotional states, and almost half (forty-seven percent) were negative about their physical states (Entwisle and Doering, 1981). Similar results were found in the study of English women having their first child, with approximately half saying that the birth experience and the pain connected with it was worse than they had expected (Oakley, 1980).

For many women the birth experience can be appropriately labeled "the agony and the ecstasy" (Oakley, 1980, p. 85). The fear that surrounds an unknown experience and the pain that comes from labor and the delivery are agony for most, but not all, women. On the other hand, Entwisle and Doering (1981) found that for fourteen percent of their sample of women it was a "peak experience." One woman described her elation and excitement just moments after the baby was born:

I kept yelling to my husband: "Get the camera! Get the camera!" [How did you feel?] Really ecstatic. I felt really great. I was just so happy. I was ready

*to get up and call everybody. It was really great. I was just sitting there all
smiles. (Entwisle and Doering, 1981, p. 96)*

However, seeing the baby for the first time in the delivery room is not a
positive experience for all women. One-third of the women were either negative or very negative about the appearance of their babies. When asked about
their feelings toward the baby at first, eight percent were negative, and twenty-
two percent were neutral (Entwisle and Doering, 1981). In the British sample,
the new mothers were asked how they felt about their babies the first time they
held them. While ten percent were euphoric, and twenty percent were amazed
and proud, fully seventy percent said they were not much interested in their
babies (Oakley, 1980).

The research findings on the pregnancy and birthing experiences may
seem unduly negative, accentuating the disagreeable aspects more than the
agreeable. There may certainly be many positive aspects to the experience, but
many women, especially those who have found the childbearing experience
more difficult than they had been led to believe, feel that a realistic portrait is
better than a totally rosy one. Oakley has stated the case for this view:

*Some readers may feel that the portrait of motherhood given here is too
bleak, too depressing, an inaccurate rendering of the satisfaction many
women derive from having . . . a baby. . . . [But] many of the women who
were interviewed said . . . that they were misled into thinking childbirth is
a piece of cake. (Oakley, 1980, p. 6).*

If some women feel misled about just how easy, or difficult, child*bearing* is,
there is a different kind of reaction to the warnings and advice that are given
about the first weeks and months of parenthood. Indeed, there seems to be a
continuing drama, played out year after year, generation after generation, with
the parents of children telling prospective parents how much having a child will
change their lives. The parents-to-be say, "Yes, we know." And they do believe
they know, or understand. Or they may think that they will be different, that
they will be able to handle parenthood and make the necessary adjustments
better than others. Then, after having a baby, they say, "We knew it would be
difficult, but not *this* difficult." It seems to be difficult to communicate with
words, what it is really like to make the transition to parenthood.

The Transition to Parenthood

Becoming a parent for the first time has been called a crisis. There is debate
about whether this word is too strong. Some feel that a milder word, such as *adjustment,* should be used. Perhaps the exact word is not so important, but in a
study of more than one hundred events in life that are potentially stressful, a
sample of 2,500 American adults ranked the birth of the first child as sixth most
stressful. It ranked immediately after a marital separation, which is nearly uni-

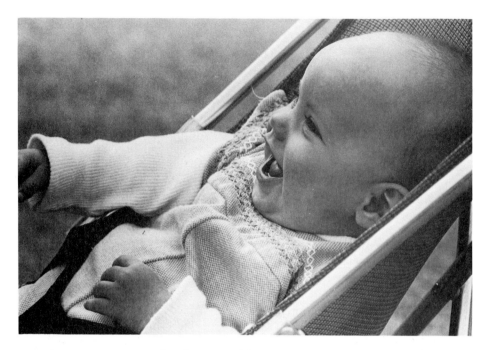

The transition to parenthood is a stressful period in the lives of most married couples, but the first smile of a baby can make up for many of the difficulties.

versally experienced as stressful (Dohwrenwend et al., 1978). There are three characteristics of having a first child that contribute to making this a stressful event in life. The first is that having a new baby in one's home is not just a change in living conditions, it is an abrupt change. The second characteristic is that a new baby requires taking critically important actions. Sometimes caring for a baby literally involves life-or-death decisions. The third characteristic is that the changes that come from having a new baby are pervasive.

On the issue of abruptness, becoming a parent involves a change in one's daily routine and life-style that is nearly unequalled, not even by marriage itself. One day a couple is living the life of two adults, albeit one that has been complicated somewhat by the pregnancy. The next day, or after a brief hospital stay, the lives of these two people are almost totally wrapped up in the care of the newborn child. Caring for the child is not simply the routine feeding, diapering, and bathing, although these things all take time and require learning. The fundamental issue of care is making sure that this nearly helpless organism is kept alive and healthy. Even though a healthy human infant is probably quite resilient and viable, the new parent is acutely aware of its vulnerability. There is a constant awareness that something could happen to the child—smothering, choking, or something else—and the responsibility is awesome.

The pervasiveness of parenthood is both short-term and long-term. Taking care of a child is a twenty-four-hour-a-day job, not just in the first year or two of life, but for many years. Parents must either be with the child, or know where it is, what it is doing, or who is caring for it. In the long-term sense, once one becomes a parent, it is a lifelong commitment. One may end a marriage, or almost any other relationship, but except when a child is given up for adoption, it is not possible to end parenthood.

At a more concrete level, couples with a new baby experience a number of problems, although the intensity varies from couple to couple and often from the first baby to the second. The sheer level of the physical demands is the thing that most new parents comment on first. One mother who kept a diary during her first pregnancy wrote after her daughter was a month old, "A month is only four weeks . . . but it has been an eternity for me. I'm a zombie. Four weeks of night feedings and little sleep. I haven't read a paper. I barely have time to shower and wash my hair" (Lowenstein and Lowenstein, 1983, p. 18).

Naturally, if one is too busy to take a shower and is not getting much sleep, a great many other aspects of married life are also being sacrificed. Perhaps most important, the time that the husband and wife spend with each other, especially without the baby present, is greatly diminished. Closely connected is the reduction in sexual activity, either because of reduced opportunities or fatigue (Sollie and Miller, 1980; LaRossa, 1983).

In summary, the stresses of parenthood (especially first-time parenthood) are likely to lead to physical and emotional fatigue, and to strains in the husband-wife relationship. There are also feelings that opportunities are being lost or that one is being restricted from social and economic activities (Sollie and Miller, 1980).

These outcomes of childbearing have been documented with great consistency and are supported by personal accounts and innumerable popular magazine articles ("How Motherhood Can Threaten Marriage," "Is There Marriage after Children?", "How a New Baby Changes a Marriage"). Parenthood thereby becomes a rather threatening and discouraging prospect, and one can reasonably ask if there is any hope. Can one avoid, or at least minimize, some or most of the problems and tensions? Fortunately, recent research does seem to provide some cause for optimism about minimizing the problems and stresses of parenthood.

Reducing the Stresses of Parenthood

One important key to reducing the stresses and problems of parenthood is *preparedness.* As one researcher puts it, "Preparing for the worst helps" (Glass, 1983, p. 377). This principle can be carried back even to the stresses of childbirth that we discussed earlier. Entwisle and Doering (1981) found that women who went to childbearing preparation classes and were taught what to expect during pregnancy and delivery had more positive experiences. In these classes women were forewarned about some of the unpleasant events that could occur. The women in these classes could then express their concerns, and it seems that by doing so they could weather the actual experiences better. Also important for the childbirth experience is that the women who were best prepared encouraged their husbands to participate in the birth experience. The participation of the husbands had a positive effect for them as well as their wives (Doering and Entwisle, 1975).

The principle of being prepared for the worst (some would say being realistically prepared) seems to apply equally well to the early parenting experience (Glass, 1983; Kach and McGhee, 1982). Those parents who underestimate how much energy and effort the baby will require are more likely to report problems after the baby is born (Kach and McGhee, 1982). Ann Oakley, who conducted the English study of women as they went through their childbearing experiences, describes her own unrealistic notions at the time she had her children:

> *I thought babies made people happy and failed to realize that you had to make the baby happy first, even if this meant three months of sleepless nights and days with no time to oneself. (Oakley, 1980, pp. 2–3).*

Oakley's unrealistic views were followed by an unexplainable depression and unhappiness. Though she thought her two children, born sixteen months apart, were "absolutely lovely," what followed was a nightmare:

> *The time that followed was an unhappy haze of nappy [diaper]-washing and pill-taking, as I found I could not make my dream of domestic contentment come true. I felt depressed and oppressed. I felt constantly tired, I felt isolated, I felt resentful of my husband's freedom, I felt my life was at an end. (Oakley, 1980, p. 2).*

In this individual case, and perhaps in an extreme form, we have a vivid picture of what can happen when one is unrealistically prepared for parenthood. On the positive side, it seems that the more carefully and realistically one is prepared for being a parent, the easier and more positive the experience is likely to be.

While preparedness for parenthood comes primarily during the pregnancy period, there are some things that can occur after the child is born that can also make the experience more positive. It is a commonplace occurrence for grandparents (especially grandmothers) to give assistance at the time a child is born. Even in contemporary society, where young couples frequently live great distances from their parents, the new grandparents are likely to give emotional and financial support (Belsky and Rovine, 1984). Parents and other kin, as well as friends, constitute the social networks of couples, and these usually provide valuable social supports during the difficult period of early parenthood (Belsky, 1984; Tinsley and Parke, 1983; Young and Willmott, 1964).

When family social supports for new parents are not readily available, as they sometimes are not in contemporary urban life, new organizations spring up to fill the gap. One such group, Parents After Childbirth Education, was formed by two mothers who had what they called "bad bouts with the new baby blues" (Breathnach, 1984, p. C5). These women reasoned that many other new mothers experience similar stresses and thus formed their organization. Workshops for new mothers are held for eight-week periods. During these sessions the mothers, with their babies in tow, share their experiences and discuss their problems and fears. Through these group sessions they learn that they are not alone in their uncertainties and anxieties about mothering, and this helps them through the difficult transition to parenthood.

Pregnancy, childbearing, and the transition to parenthood are all demonstrably difficult for a great many people. So why do people continue to want and to have children? It would strain credibility to suggest that the social and cultural pressures for childbearing are so great that more than ninety percent of the people are duped or pressured into parenthood. It seems more reasonable to say that, while social and cultural pressures exist, they operate through individuals who must experience children as a positive part of their lives. If this were not true, especially in contemporary urban society, people would not have children.

As a result of some recent surveys, we now have a better understanding of why people value children (Hoffman et al., 1978; Hoffman and Manis, 1979). In a seven-nation survey of both parents and nonparents, the following question was asked: What would you say are some of the advantages or good things about having children compared with not having children at all? The subjects were married women under age forty and their husbands. Many had already had children, while others were nonparents. The people gave a great variety of answers to this open-ended question, but most were similar enough so they could be reduced to a few basic reasons for having children. The seven basic reasons given by American adults are shown graphically in Figure 10.1. Although we will be concentrating on the American responses in the following discussion, there will be some comparisons with the responses of people from other countries.

Among American adults, the number one reason for having children is because they provide "primary group ties and affection." In more everyday terms,

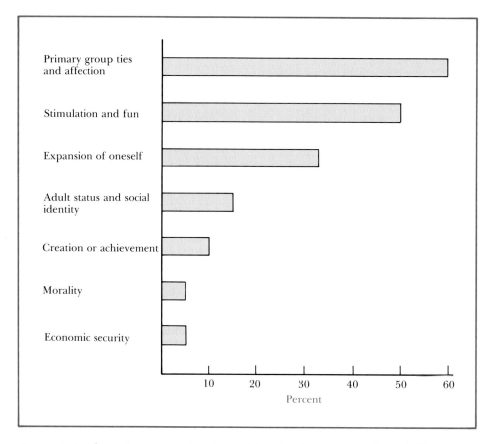

Figure 10.1 *The major reasons American adults give for wanting to have children.*
(Based on Hoffman et al., 1978)

people say that children "bring love and companionship." Children also are said
to "complete the family" and make for a "closer family life." Children are also
seen as "benefitting and expressing the husband-wife relationship." In short,
children are seen as something to love, to be loved by, and to express love. They
are thought to bring individual family members closer together. In the United
States, about sixty percent of husbands and wives, parents and nonparents,
mention these advantages. In Turkey, this is also the primary advantage, being
mentioned by eighty-six percent of the respondents. In Indonesia, it is the second most mentioned advantage, and among the urban population of Sudan it is
again the most mentioned advantage (Hoffman et al., 1978).

Among Americans the second most popular answer, mentioned by nearly
half of the respondents, is that children provide "stimulation and fun." People
say, "With children around, there is always something going on." "They keep

you young." Children are said to bring "joy, happiness, and fun" (Hoffman and Manis, 1979).

The third most common answer, given by about one-third of American respondents, is that children give one an "expansion of self." Children give a "purpose to life;" they provide a "learning experience;" and they give a parent a kind of "immortality, by leaving a part of oneself behind."

The fourth advantage of children, mentioned by about fifteen percent of the Americans, is that children give "adult status and a social identity." In many societies, including the United States, becoming a parent is a way of gaining adult status almost instantly. This can be seen most clearly in the case of young teenagers who become parents. Their parents and other relatives generally bring them into the adult segment of the family, even while their unmarried peers continue to be treated as adolescents.

The fifth advantage is that children are seen as a "creation or an achievement." Somewhat more than ten percent of Americans mention this reason for having children. Apparently there is a feeling that producing and, even more, rearing children is a reflection of the parents' efforts and abilities. However, it is interesting that this reason is given more often by nonparents than by people who have already had children. The fact than nonparents mention this advantage of parenthood more than parents may mean that it "exists more in the anticipation than in the actual day-to-day experience of parenting" (Hoffman et al., 1978, p. 100).

The sixth advantage for having children is associated with "morality." While not mentioned by many American adults—only about five percent of the respondents—becoming a parent is sometimes viewed as a virtuous act, an act that demonstrates one's goodness. Having a child is seen as giving up selfish and self-indulgent ways. And, according to some parents, having had the experience of rearing children has made them better people.

The seventh advantage of children, again mentioned very infrequently by American adults, is "economic utility, and security in old age." As we said earlier, in many countries of the world it is necessary to have children if one is to survive economically and be provided for in old age. The survey results from both Indonesia and the Philippines bear out this contention, since the economic motive was the number one reason mentioned in both countries. It is not surprising that only slightly more than five percent of Americans mention this advantage. Even though children do provide an income tax deduction (mentioned by about two percent of American respondents), the costs of raising a child are much greater than the economic benefit they provide.

The exact dollar cost of raising a child in contemporary American society has been variously estimated by researchers. One estimate is that it will cost $85,000, in 1980 dollars, to provide for a "moderate-cost" child; this estimate covers the costs of childbirth and the costs of providing for the child until age eighteen, plus four years at a public university (*Intercom*, 1982). But this estimate is low compared to the projections of Olson (1983), who assumes that

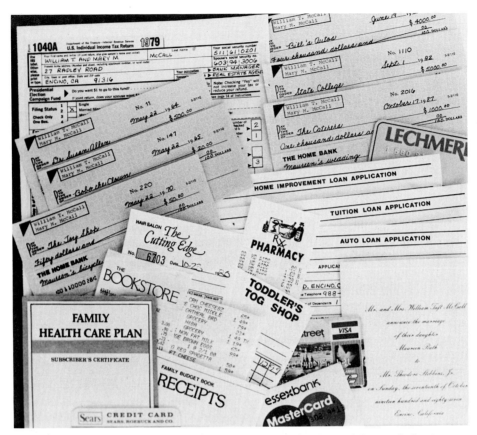

The costs associated with rearing a child today are far short of the tax deduction for a dependent child allowed by the Internal Revenue Service.

American families in the future will spend the same proportion of their incomes on their children as they have in the recent past. If this assumption were to hold true, a child born in 1980 would cost an average United States family $226,000 for a firstborn son and $247,000 for a firstborn daughter. The higher cost of rearing a daughter is attributable to the moderately higher costs for transportation, along with sharply higher costs for "entertainment and weddings, cosmetics, travel, jewelry and toys" (Olson, 1983, p. 56). Sons require greater expenditures for food, housing and medical care, but these costs do not offset the higher costs of the items provided for females.

Even though the cost of raising children is high, there is almost no evidence that potential parents in the United States are deterred from having children because of the money it will require to raise them. This applies at least to the first, and probably to the second, child. It may be that some parents are deterred from having larger numbers of children because of the costs involved. Surely, however, any of these child-rearing cost figures make it abundantly clear that most families in the United States are not likely to have children because they are going to be an economic asset.

To sum up, we can say that Americans have children for the love, affection, fun, and stimulation they provide, or are expected to provide. Children are seen as an opportunity to expand a parent's personality, or to attain adult status or a social identity. Children are also thought to give an opportunity to shape and create a new person. Other advantages, such as enhancing one's morality, realizing economic gains, and increasing personal power, while likely to be important in some other societies, seem to be much less important in the United States.

Deborah Churchman, who describes herself as a free-lance writer who "gave birth to two children deliberately," expresses very well the American ideals about having children. "The reason people have children is to love someone completely and unselfishly" (Churchman, 1979, p. C5).

She goes on to say that, unlike any other relationship a person might form, the relationship of parent to child is one that is not based on give and take. For parents,

> *Having a child is a lifetime lesson in giving, in reaching into your innermost recesses for all your talents, abilities, knowledge, patience, calmness, justice, humor and joy, and sharing these, using them to mold and buffer and bolster and protect and project your little human into society. (Churchman, 1979, p. C.5).*

These ideal motives for having children are a few of the positives that must be balanced against the realities we considered earlier.

Since 1960, and especially in the last decade, there have been a number of revolutionary developments that affect the way we have children today. These developments and their ramifications are the topics of the next section.

TODAY'S TECHNOLOGY OF CHILDBEARING

Contraceptive Technology

While there have been many highly publicized breakthroughs in the technology of childbearing, we will begin by discussing contraception. Developments in the techniques of contraception, and in their availability and use, have revolutionized control over childbearing in the last twenty-five years. Two-thirds of all married women in the United States between fifteen and forty-four use some kind of contraception (Bachrach 1984). Many of the remaining one-third either want to get pregnant or are infertile.

The single most popular method of contraception is the birth control pill, used by over one-fourth (28.6 percent) of all women between the ages of fifteen and forty-four who are using contraception (Pratt et al., 1984). However, this overall percentage is somewhat misleading, because the birth control pill is much more likely to be used by women under thirty than women over thirty. Among women over age thirty, sterilization becomes increasingly important as the method of contraception. Sterilization is most likely to be for the female, but in a substantial number of cases it is for the male who is her mate. Figure 10.2 shows the usages of the four most popular methods of contraception in the United States today. This graph shows that the pill, and to a lesser extent the condom, give way to the two sterilization procedures as couples reach age thirty.

Two other methods of contraception, the intrauterine device and the diaphragm, reach their peaks of popularity between the ages of twenty-five and thirty-five, when each accounts for about ten percent of the users. The rhythm method, which is an effort to confine sexual intercourse to those times of the ovulation cycle when conception is least likely, is never used by more than five percent of contraceptors.

While most methods of contraception are widely accepted today, it has not always been that way. Well into the twentieth century it was illegal to send information on birth control through the mail because it was considered pornography. Until the 1930s all major religions in the United States prohibited the use of contraception. Today, although the Catholic Church officially prohibits the mechanical, chemical, and surgical methods of contraception, Catholics differ only slightly from Protestants in the methods used (Pratt et al., 1984).

But if contraception is not used, or if it fails, it is still possible to avoid having children through the means of abortion. The legal availability of abortion in the United States has only recently been *reestablished.* It might be surprising to learn that abortion has not always been illegal in the United States. In the first part of the nineteenth century, American women were able to use various substances and techniques, often under a doctor's supervision, to "restore their menstrual flow" after they had missed a period or two. As long as the fetus had not yet been felt to move in the uterus, these methods were accepted and apparently widely used. In effect, this allowed abortion until sometime in the fourth month of pregnancy (Mohr, 1978). But as the nineteenth century progressed, more and more restrictions were passed that made abortions illegal (Mohr, 1978). As a result, for the first two-thirds of the twentieth century there were very few legal abortions in the United States—though there were countless illegal and self-performed abortions.

But abortion policies started changing in the 1960s as a number of state legislatures passed legislation that liberalized conditions under which abortions could be performed. In 1973 there was a dramatic change in policy when the

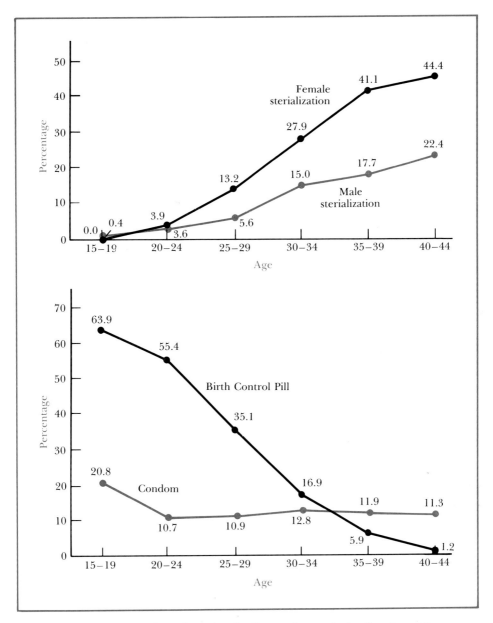

Figure 10.2 *Percentage of couples using the four major methods of contraception arranged by the age of the wife. (Source: Pratt et al., 1984)*

Supreme Court ruled that women had the right to choose abortion. Specifically, the Court ruled that states cannot pass any special laws or regulations governing abortion during the first trimester (approximately thirteen weeks) of pregnancy (Jaffe et al., 1981). In the second trimester the state can regulate abortion, if the regulation is related to the woman's health. In effect, the United States has had abortion on demand since 1973.

While this policy has been vigorously and heatedly attacked by some individuals and groups, it is nonetheless a very important element in our childbearing patterns today. The statistics tell just how important it is. In recent years about 3.6 million babies have been born yearly in the United States. Abortions have numbered more than 1.5 million yearly (U.S. Bureau of the Census, 1984). These figures indicate that roughly thirty percent of all births that could occur do not. At this level of magnitude, abortion cannot be dismissed. It is a technological capability that large numbers of people use to control and influence the number of children they have.

Even while legal abortion is widely used, however, there is a heated public debate about whether or not it should be allowed. Without attempting to give a full airing of the issues, a few observations can be made. First, the two sides in the debate focus on entirely different issues, and almost never do they address the arguments of the other side. On the antiabortion side, the critical argument is that human life begins at the moment of conception and that the preservation of that life is paramount. This view may be grounded in a humanistic philosophy that puts great emphasis on the sanctity of each individual life, or it may grow out of a theological position that imbues each human life, from conception onward, with a spirit or soul. From this viewpoint, aborting a fetus is immoral, criminal, or sinful, because it kills the fetus-as-human.

On the proabortion side of the debate, the emphasis is placed almost entirely on the rights of the pregnant woman. The proabortionists believe that a woman has the right to make a choice about whether or not she should carry the fetus and bear the child. From this view, any law that abridges this right is a law that makes pregnancy, once it occurs, compulsory (Hardin, 1968). There are some subsidiary arguments, such as the claim that an unwanted child will be disadvantaged and possibly mistreated. But the principal argument is that a woman who has to carry, bear, and often shoulder the primary responsibility for rearing the child is not accorded her rights if the state prohibits her from ending an unwanted pregnancy.

The issues surrounding abortion and abortion rights have been taken to the courts, where the legalities have been established on the basis of constitutional law. The current prevailing policy is based on the constitutional guarantee of the right to privacy (Jaffe et al., 1981). The right to privacy is interpreted as covering the right of a woman to choose abortion during the first two trimesters (26 weeks) of a pregnancy. The abortion issue has thus been legally resolved for the time being, though certainly not to the satisfaction of all people. While public opinion polls have shown that the majority of Americans favor the availability of abortion, especially under some conditions (e.g., mother's health in danger), there is a minority vigorously opposing abortion for any reason (Jaffe et al., 1981).

Most of the legal issues surrounding abortion have been resolved, though some, like the rights of the father to stop an abortion, are still being contested in the courts. This issue is similar to a variety of legal issues that are emerging with respect to some of the newer reproductive techniques that are now just beginning to influence childbearing. In the next section we will consider some of the legal and personal issues raised by the newest reproductive technology.

The New Reproductive Technology

The terms and labels of the new reproductive technology can be found almost daily in newspapers, magazines, and book covers. Among the most popular are artificial insemination, sperm banks, surrogate mothers, test-tube babies, genetic engineering, and gender selection.

In 1984, a French court had to rule on whether the wife of a deceased man had the rights to the semen he had placed in a sperm bank before his death. The woman, who had been married only two days before her husband died, wished to have herself impregnated with the sperm. The French court ruled that she did have the rights to her dead husband's sperm (Maubouche, 1984). This is but one example of many issues, both legal and moral, that are coming out of the new techniques of reproduction. While the legal issues are fascinating, there is the equally important point that we, as individual decision makers, must consider how we feel about these techniques. To get a glimpse of the possibilities and the problems, we will examine some of the current options.

Artificial insemination and test-tube babies   Most dairy farmers have been artificially inseminating their cattle for at least three decades, some much longer. In some respects it is surprising that artificial insemination with humans is still in its infancy. The technology has obviously been available, so there must have been some other kind of impediment to its adoption. In all likelihood, the reluctance of couples to use artificial insemination comes from the fact that the sperm implanted in a woman's uterus often does not come from her husband. Usually, the woman's husband is sterile, and another man serves as a donor. There may be other cases when a donor's semen is used, such as when a couple determines that there is a high likelihood of a genetically transmitted disease. And in recent years it has become more common for women who are not married to choose to be artificially inseminated so that they can have children.

While these are all possible reasons for artificial insemination, there are still relatively few couples who avail themselves of this option. The exact numbers are unknown, but estimates range from 6,000 to 25,000 pregnancies a year in the United States are produced by artificial insemination (Hartley, 1981; Nass et al., 1981).

The so-called test-tube babies are produced in part by the techniques of artificial insemination, but the key difference is that ova are removed from a woman's body and fertilized *in vitro* in a laboratory. The sperm used for fertilization may be from a woman's husband, or from any other donor. This technique is still very rare, but it has been successfully performed, and it is probably just a matter of time until it has been perfected. It is clearly in demand from couples who are kept from having children because the fallopian tubes of the woman are blocked and there is no hope of surgical repair (Nass et al., 1981).

Surrogate mothers. Another emerging technique that employs artificial insemination is called surrogate mothering. When couples cannot have a baby because the woman is infertile, the husband's sperm may be used to impregnate another woman. This woman has agreed, through a legal contract signed in advance, that she will turn over the baby to the couple at the time of birth. While there have been hundreds of these arrangements, and organizations are springing up around the country to provide surrogate mothers, there are many unsolved problems and unanswered questions. Some of these problems and questions are legal, but others are personal and emotional. There has been at least one case where the surrogate mother, after carrying and delivering the baby, decided that she wished to keep the child. It was, after all, at least half hers since she provided the ovum and carried the fetus. Under existing legal customs it is extremely difficult for a father to obtain custody of a child if a mother wishes to keep it. This is true even when a mother has signed a contract earlier agreeing to give up her rights to the child.

Another problem may arise when a child is born with birth defects and neither the father nor the surrogate mother wishes to keep the child. Such a problem has already arisen in the case of a baby born in Michigan. The contractual father argued that the child was not his, and in this case the blood-type evidence supported him, but that did not resolve the problem of an unwanted child. This case also illustrates another problem, which is that the surrogate mother must not have sexual intercourse with other men, even her own husband if she is married, for the period of time it takes to become pregnant (Krucoff, 1983).

There have been attempts to establish laws and regulations governing the surrogate mother business, but it has been difficult to enact the laws because regulation has often been opposed by those who favor and those who disapprove of the practice. One critic complained that passing regulatory legislation would give approval to "premeditated abandonment [by the surrogate mother]" (Mathews, 1983 p. A2).

Sperm banks. One mechanism for facilitating artificial insemination is to store the sperm of males. Since frozen male sperm can be stored for an indefinite period, the possibilities are quite numerous. For infertile couples, where the semen of the husband has a low sperm count, his sperm can be collected and stored until there is a sufficient supply to impregnate the wife. If husbands are known to carry a hereditary disease, the couple may prefer to go to a sperm bank to use the sperm of some other male (Chico and Hartley, 1981).

Other potential users of sperm banks are unmarried women and lesbians who wish to be mothers. In these cases, the women can be quite selective, choosing the sperm of just the kind of man they prefer, in terms of physical characteristics and mental and intellectual levels and achievements. (Couples have these same options, of course, if they wish to use the sperm of a man other than the husband.) For those people who wish to be selective about the sperm they are using, there are now sperm banks that specialize in the sperm of eminent men. Among the most notable of this type is one in California that is popularly called the "Nobel sperm bank." This enterprise specializes in storing the sperm of famous and successful scientists, and counts among its donors three Nobel prize winners (Mathews, 1982).

The premise behind the "elite" sperm bank is that the characteristics of the donors will be passed on genetically to the offspring. This is a forerunner of what has been called genetic engineering. Using genetic engineering techniques, scientists may soon be able to select out preferred characteristics from the genetic structures of humans and carry out breeding programs that will reproduce these characteristics in the offspring. Or, in other cases, genetic engineers could eliminate genes carrying undesirable traits such as diabetes, hemophilia, sickle-cell anemia, or Tay-Sachs disease.

To many people, these methods of selecting "elite" donors and gene manipulation are frightening examples of scientific and rational control over an area that should be left "natural." And yet, a number of the techniques just discussed are eagerly sought and used by infertile couples and others who could not otherwise have children. The era of controlling these aspects of childbearing is just beginning, but with scientific and medical advances coming each year, the issues raised here are only going to grow in significance.

Gender selection. Many of the new technologies of childbearing are applicable only to selected segments of the population (infertile couples, lesbians, unmarried women who want to have babies). But there is one area that is potentially relevant to all couples; the gender selection of their children. The technology has now reached a point where parents (or a parent) can, if they wish, select the gender of a child (Hilts, 1983), though it must be said that the only sure method is probably unacceptable to most couples. By using amniocentesis, a process of drawing a small amount of amniotic fluid from the uterus of a pregnant woman, it is possible to determine if the fetus is male or female. Thus, it would be possible to abort the pregnancy if the fetus were not of the desired gender. However, since the determination of gender by amniocentesis is typically done in the fourth month of pregnancy, the abortion would have to be performed well into the second trimester (Williamson, 1978). The use of abortion, especially a relatively late abortion, for the purpose of determining the gender of a child, has generally been viewed as unacceptable to most people.

There are some other techniques that have been used with uncertain levels of success, but they do have the advantage of not requiring abortion. Sperm separation combined with artificial insemination appears to have considerable promise, though techniques have not been perfected. The sperm bearing the male (XY) and the female (XX) chromosomes do have different physical properties, with the male sperm being faster swimmers but shorter lived (Williamson, 1978). If these characteristics could be used to sort out the two types, then it would be only a matter of inseminating with the sperm of the desired gender. While claims have been made for some sorting techniques, they have not yet been tested adequately enough to say that they are effective (Intercom, 1976; Williamson, 1978).

Timing of sexual intercourse, relative to the time of ovulation, has also been offered as a technique for changing the probabilities of having one gender or the other. While claims of success have been made by using this method, the scientific evidence is limited and not especially compelling (Williamson, 1978).

Except for the amniocentesis-abortion method, there is not yet a sure way of determining the gender of one's child. However, it is probably just a matter of time before the techniques will be developed that will allow couples to make this decision. With this possibility in mind, two questions become immediately apparent: Do couples want to have the power to make this decision? And if they do, what would be the outcome? On the first question, national surveys have shown that a little over one-third of adult women approved of the idea of being able to predetermine the sex of their children. However, a substantial majority (59.1 percent) disapproved (Pebley and Westoff, 1982). The question was general, and abstract, in that no method was identified and no conditions were specified. Many more people, for example, might approve of gender determination in the case of a gender-linked hereditary defect (Chico and Hartley, 1981). Some greater approval might also be given if a couple already had two or more children of the same sex and wanted their last child to be of the opposite sex.

One outcome of gender determination that has frequently been predicted is an excess of males, especially firstborn males (Etzioni, 1973; Williamson, 1978). If American women who have not yet had children were to satisfy their gender preferences, among their firstborn they would have 189 boys born for every 100 girls (Williamson, 1976a). The preference for boys is worldwide, found in country after country. Only five societies have been found that preferred girls over boys. All were very small, and only two still exist as they were described in the anthropological literature (Williamson, 1976b). With these minor exceptions, it can be said that the vast populations of the world, India, China, the Middle East, Latin America, and Africa, all have a strong preference for males. If there were a method by which people in these countries could select the gender of their children, they would surely display this preference. However, at this time the techniques are not feasible in these developing areas. In the developed areas of the world, including the United States, the prospect of choosing the gender of one's children is a realistic possibility in the near future, but it remains to be seen how much and under what circumstances it will be used.

We have seen in the preceding pages a wide array of choices that can be made with respect to parenthood. Many of these are closely tied to new technological developments and the latest scientific discoveries. Often these developments are relevant to only a small proportion of the childbearing population (for example, couples unable to conceive children naturally). But there is one choice of childbearing that applies to everyone, and it generally does not depend on the newest technological developments. This choice is *when* to have children. This is the issue that we will consider as the closing discussion of this chapter.

ISSUE

Should women wait to have children until after age thirty?

Since childbearing is a choice today, many young women, especially those with college educations and career plans, are considering not only *if* they should have children but also *when* they should have children (Wilkie, 1981). Often with their husbands, they are considering whether it would be better to have their children relatively soon after marriage, or better to wait. Age thirty is frequently the point that women see as a watershed in their lives. That particular age is somewhat arbitrary, but it does give focus to the discussion and allows the arguments to be stated with more precision. We will take up this issue by considering first the arguments against having children after age thirty, and then turning to the arguments for having children after thirty.

Arguments against Having Children after Age Thirty

The major arguments against waiting until after thirty to have a first baby are centered around the physical condition and health of the mother and the baby. The two major physical and health problems are the declining ability of women over thirty to conceive a child and the increasing chance that the child will have a birth defect. The ability to conceive after age thirty, and especially after age thirty-five, is still a subject of some scientific controversy. In 1982 *The New England Journal of Medicine* reported a French study of two thousand women who, because their husbands were sterile, were trying to become pregnant by artificial insemination (Schwartz and Mayaux, 1982). This study showed that only sixty-one percent of women aged thirty-one to thirty-five, and fifty-four percent of women over thirty-five, were able to get pregnant. This led the journal editors to warn women who wanted careers and children to have children in their twenties and concentrate on careers later (Russell, 1982). Other researchers (Bongaarts, 1982) have argued that the French study is misleading and that it overstates the amount of infertility after age thirty. While that may be true, the fact remains that some women who wait until after thirty to have children may find that they are no longer able to do so (Hendershot et al., 1982).

The increased chance of having a baby with Down's syndrome after a woman reaches age thirty has received wide publicity. The statistical studies show that the increases are as follows: at ages twenty-five and thirty, approximately one per thousand live births; at age thirty-five, somewhat over two per thousand; and at age forty approximately ten per thousand (Rinehart et al., 1984; Daniels and Weingarten, 1982). Clearly, the probabilities for a child with Down's syndrome do increase and couples planning children after age thirty, and especially after age thirty-five, do have to take this risk into account. Even though it is possible to have the fetus checked by amniocentesis, couples must face the possibility of aborting a fetus that is as much as four months old if the tests are positive. For many couples this would be a difficult decision, and for some it would be impossible (Daniels and Weingarten, 1982).

There are other pregnancy risks that also increase with the increased age of the mother. These include early miscarriage, toxemia of pregnancy, breech presentation of child at birth, hemorrhage from placental abnormalities, and chromosomal abnormalities (Daniels and Weingarten, 1982).

These medical and physical arguments against having a child after thirty are often augmented by the claim that older parents will not enjoy their children as much as if they had had them when they were younger. Couples who are older when they have children may not have the stamina and energy to do all the things necessary for good childrearing. Older parents may thus enjoy their children less because they will be too fatigued and exhausted much of the time.

Even if older parents have the energy and strength to do what is important for rearing children, they may be unwilling to make the necessary sacrifices, or if they do they may be resentful. Married couples who have had a number of years of the carefree (childfree) life may have become so accustomed to their freedom that they will be unwilling to give it up. If they do make the required sacrifices, the result could easily be resentment, depression, and even hostility toward the child. If older parents do not give the child the attention it requires, the child may suffer.

The foremost arguments against waiting until after thirty to have children are centered around the lessened ability of a woman to conceive after that age and the negative health implications for both the child and the mother. The second major argument against having children after thirty is that parents by that time will have developed a style of life that makes children an imposition or a resented burden.

Arguments for Having Children after Age Thirty

The arguments for waiting to have a baby center around work and career goals, economic security, marriage quality, and personal freedom. Women today, especially those who have higher levels of education, are not only likely to be in the labor force but are very likely to have career objectives. When these women have children they leave the work force either for several years or for a brief period around the time the baby is born. If this occurs in their twenties when their careers are just starting, the effects on careers are likely to be negative. By waiting until age thirty a woman will have had a better chance to establish herself in an occupation or profession before having to take time off for a child, or children. The argument is that the interruption and distraction of having a child will not be as great at this later point in a woman's career. A related advantage is that the economic position of a couple in their thirties is likely to be better than it was in their twenties.

Since most couples will probably have been married in their twenties, they will have been married for five or more years when their first baby is born. Since marriages ending in divorce are most likely to break up in the first three to five years, there is a greater chance that the couples who have babies when they have been married longer are going to stay married. A related point is that the strains of pregnancy and parenting, which often have a negative effect on the quality of a marriage, may have a greater effect on marriage relationships that are less well established. By giving themselves a few extra years of marriage without the burdens connected with having a child, a couple may have a more stable and sound relationship at the time they have a first baby.

Many married couples are clear in wanting to have the first years of their marriage free of the responsibilities of children. These years can be spent traveling, engaging in hobbies or sports, or doing other recreational activities. Having a child will usually limit these activities severely.

Finally, if one is to argue for having a first child after age thirty, it is necessary to deal with some of the health and physical factors that are said to be a problem in later childbearing. Some would say that the physical stamina and energy levels of women in their thirties will be too low to have and care for children. The counterargument is that in contemporary society, with women having an average life expectancy of nearly eighty years, there is no reason to believe that health or physical stamina are greatly reduced by the mid-thirties.

Of course, the medical problems connected with having a baby after the age of thirty are not to be denied. However, an examination of the facts reveals that their seriousness is not as great as some people believe. For example, even when mothers are thirty-five years old, the chances of having a baby with Down's syndrome are only about two-tenths of one percent. Furthermore, for those couples willing to use amniocentesis and abortion, this defect can be detected and the problem averted. In general, with the health levels of contemporary women and the quality of medical care available, most of the physical and health problems can be dealt with if women prefer to wait until after thirty to have children.

To sum up the arguments for waiting until after thirty, the main advantages are that careers and marriages are going to be more established and stable by that time. Couples will have had a period in which to enjoy each other, and thus by age thirty will be eager and able to have children. While some health considerations are not negligible, they are far from overwhelming or insurmountable.

Themes

1. In the United States in the recent past, having children was a nearly automatic step after marriage.

2. Today, couples and individuals can make decisions about having children, how many they will have and when they will have them.

3. Historically, many people have lived under conditions where childbearing has been uncontrolled and decision making was limited.

4. For societies to survive under conditions of high infant and maternal mortality, it was essential that institutions and cultural values enabled and encouraged people to have and rear children.

5. There are social and psychological pressures that still encourage and induce people in contemporary society to have children.

6. The pregnancy and childbirth experiences, as well as the transition to parenthood, are often much more difficult than people are led to believe or expect.

7. Both parents and nonparents feel that having children has many positive features.

8. The ready availability of contraception and abortion in contemporary society are important contexts for childbearing.

9. New reproductive technologies have produced complicated legal and moral problems and have added new dimensions to personal decision making about parenthood.

Facts

1. Through the 1960s most wives had babies during the first three years of marriage.

2. Maximum natural fertility is illustrated by the Hutterites, who had an average of eleven children per woman.

3. Preferred family size in many African and Latin American countries is still between five and eight children, even among young women.

4. In many developing societies, having many children is necessary for economic survival and assistance in old age.

5. The Shakers and the Rappites were religious sects that prohibited sexual intercourse, illustrating what happens when a society does not produce children.

6. An estimated four percent of married couples are involuntarily childless, and five percent are voluntarily childless.

7. There are two types of decision-making processes for voluntarily childless couples, Thirty to forty percent decide to be childless before marriage, while the remainder postpone having children until a time when they recognize a decision to be childless has been made.

8. When wives are pregnant, most couples do not stop having sexual intercourse until they are in the ninth month of pregnancy.

9. Studies of new mothers reveal that substantial numbers are either negative or neutral about their babies at the time of childbirth.

10. Being adequately and realistically prepared for childbirth and the transition to parenthood is the most effective way of reducing the problems and stresses of those times.

11. American adults are most likely to value children because they bring love and affection and strengthen family ties, provide fun and stimulation, lead to an expansion of the self, and provide adult status and social identity.

12. It is estimated that raising a child in the United States in the years ahead may cost as much as $226,000 for a firstborn son and $247,000 for a first-born daughter.

13. The birth control pill has been used by about one-half of all married women under thirty since 1970.

14. Abortion during the first four months of pregnancy was not generally illegal in the United States in 1800.

15. Approximately thirty percent of all pregnancies today end in abortion.

16. Artificial insemination may now account for as many as 25,000 pregnancies each year in the United States.

17. Gender selection of children is now possible by a combination of amniocentesis and abortion, but this method is unacceptable to most couples.

Major Concepts

amniocentesis: A process of drawing a small amount of amniotic fluid from the uterus of a pregnant woman. This fluid can then be used for a variety of tests.

artificial insemination: Impregnating a female by implanting male sperm in her uterus at the time of ovulation.

"baby hunger": An alleged, biologically-grounded emotional urge to have a baby that is experienced by some women.

involuntary childlessness: Remaining without children because of biological infertility.

maximum natural fertility: The average number of children that women can have during a reproductive lifetime if they are exposed to sexual intercourse and use no contraception.

sperm banks: Repositories of male sperm that can be used by those who wish to be artificially inseminated.

surrogate mothering: An agreement by a woman to be impregnated and to bear a baby for another woman or a couple.

"test-tube babies": Artificially inseminating ova that have been removed from a woman's body.

transition to parenthood: The series of pervasive changes that parents of firstborn children experience in the first weeks and months of a baby's life.

voluntary childlessness: Remaining without children because of personal choice.

11

Child Rearing
Socialization, Parenting, and Child Care

It has been estimated that over two hundred popularly written books on parenting and child rearing are available in the United States. During a recent five-year period, over twenty-three million of these books were sold (Cagan, 1980). These facts alone reveal that in this country child rearing is taken very seriously. But it is not just book sales that show how much people care about child rearing, for there are also innumerable magazine and newspaper articles published each year on this topic. These too are read and discussed avidly. If there were some way to know the hundreds of thousands of hours spent discussing the rearing of children, one could see even more clearly that there are very few issues that get more attention.

But this outpouring of words about child rearing also carries another message: there is no one "correct" or "perfect" way to raise children. If there were, far fewer words would be needed. And yet, many writers, and some fortunate parents whose children have "turned out well," are confident that they have the answers. Perhaps some do, but one can be justified in being just a bit skeptical of such claims.

As we approach this complex issue of rearing children, we will take a much more modest view. Rather than claiming to have the answers, it will be the objective here to identify and discuss the most important and pressing questions. At the end of the chapter we will raise the question that ultimately all parents face: Do children have the same rights as adults?

W e will begin our consideration of child rearing with a brief examination of what we know about the lives of children in the past. The history of childhood is still under debate among scholars, but some surprising, and even shocking, details have emerged.

THE HISTORY OF CHILDHOOD

One important key to understanding child rearing is to understand the way we see childhood as a distinct stage of life. Most of us, if asked, could confidently identify the early stages of life as beginning with infancy, and then continuing to childhood and adolescence. We would also have fairly good agreement about the ages at which one moves from one stage to another. It might, then, be surprising to learn that over great periods of Western history, childhood was not recognized as a distinct stage of life. This, at least, is the view of social historian Philippe Ariès (1962) who assembled evidence to support the thesis that in the Middle Ages a child went through infancy directly into a kind of adulthood. The most common image of the medieval child, as Ariès found in the paintings of that period, was that of a kind a miniature adult. Obviously, if parents did not recognize a stage of life that we recognize as childhood, they were likely to treat their children very differently than we do. We can only imagine what some of these differences were, but one guess is that children of that era were expected to carry a heavier load than most children today.

Evidence for the argument that childhood was not recognized as a distinct stage of life during the Middle Ages is limited, and is still being debated. But there is a substantial amount of evidence that children were treated more carelessly and harshly in the past than they are today. By contemporary standards, parents generally did not care for their children as well, either physically or emotionally. Some historians associate the careless and even brutal treatment of children with the fragility of life and the resulting high rates of infant mortality.

Infant and childhood death rates were so high that in many places half of the children born did not reach adulthood. Infectious diseases and various unidentifiable fevers were frequent killers of children. There were almost no effective defenses against these many causes of death. (Even as recently as 1918 in the United States an influenza epidemic swept through the country with such virulence that almost every family lost some children.) Under such conditions of very high infant and childhood mortality, perhaps parents of medieval times and later could not allow themselves to become too attached to their infant children. Thus, their apparent callousness was a defense against repeated heartbreak (Ariès, 1962).

Others who have studied the history of childhood claim that the insensitive and harsh treatment of children continued beyond the Middle Ages. One of the strongest exponents of this position says, "the history of childhood is a nightmare from which we have only recently begun to awaken. The further back in history one goes, the lower the level of childcare, and the more likely children are to be killed, abandoned, beaten, terrorized and sexually abused" (deMause, 1974, p. 1).

Infanticide and Abandonment

Infanticide and abandonment have been documented as part of the history of Western society, though the incidence of such acts is nearly impossible to establish (Langer, 1973). However, after surveying the evidence coming from as recently as the eighteenth century, one observer has concluded, "there is no question that there was a high incidence of infanticide in every country in Europe" (deMause, 1974, p. 29).

The difficulty of estimating the amount of infanticide stems in part from the fact that the intentional killing of an infant can easily be disguised. Just as child abuse today is often covered up by claiming a child has suffered an accident, so it was also possible to cover up a killing. Furthermore, it appears that many infant deaths were, in fact, semiaccidental. Under crowded living conditions, many infants slept with their parents, other relatives, or a nurse. It was often reported that infants were suffocated during the night. While suffocating an infant may have been accidental, it may also have been wanton carelessness.

While accidents and carelessness account for some infant deaths, there are many recorded instances when infants were intentionally killed. As late as the end of the nineteenth century, there is a description of an eastern European village where mothers sent their babies to "killing nurses." The methods of doing away with the infants included "exposing them to cold air after a hot bath; feeding them something that caused convulsions in their stomachs and intestines; mixing gypsum in their milk, which literally plastered up their insides; suddenly stuffing them with food after not giving them anything to eat for two days" (deMause, 1974, p. 29).

One indirect form of infanticide is abandonment of a baby, although in this case if someone finds the baby before it expires it is given a chance to live as a foundling. Abandoning babies was so widely practiced in Europe that it led to the establishment of foundling homes. Thomas Coram of London opened a Foundling Hospital in 1741 "because he couldn't bear to see the dying babies lying in the gutters and rotting on the dung-heaps" (deMause, 1974, p. 29). As late as the 1890s it was still common to see dead babies on the streets of London. (Rolph, 1969).

Wet-Nursing and Swaddling

While the killing and abandoning of infants was clearly deviant and even criminal behavior, there were a number of "normal" child rearing practices that were of dubious merit and very likely harmful to children. One of these was the practice of *wet-nursing*, which was widely practiced in Europe in medieval times and well into the eighteenth century. Wet-nursing is the practice of hiring another woman to nurse one's baby. Generally this involved turning over the baby full-time to the wet nurse in her own home. Typically the families with money would hire as a wet nurse a woman from the lower classes. Naturally, for a woman to have breast milk it was necessary for her to have had a recent

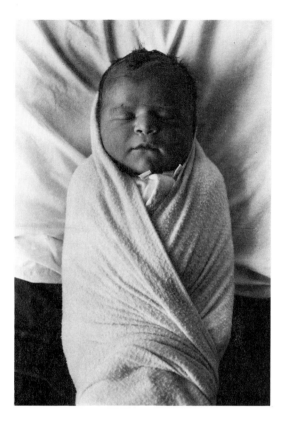

Swaddling babies, by wrapping them very tightly with cloths, was very common in Europe before the nineteenth century. It is still practiced in Mongolia today.

baby. Since women who served as wet nurses were often poor, it was not uncommon to send babies to live in homes that offered less healthy conditions than the parental home. Nonetheless, on the European continent, especially in urban France, the use of wet nurses was very common into the eighteenth century (Robertson, 1974).

Another very common practice with infants was swaddling. Essentially, *swaddling* means to wrap a baby very tightly with cloths, making it impossible for the baby to move either its arms or legs. The arms are pinned to the sides and the legs are straightened and bound tightly. In many cases, swaddling involved a rigid board to which the baby was wrapped. A baby was typically swaddled for one to four months of its early life.

The ostensible purpose for swaddling was to protect the newborn infant from thrashing around and hurting itself. There was the additional concern that if the legs were not held in a straightened position the child might walk on "all fours" like an animal. Swaddling a baby was a time-consuming process and obviously a task that would not have been carried out if it had not been thought necessary. In other words, it was done for the baby's own good. And yet, perhaps parents and nurses found some advantages in it for themselves, for babies that are swaddled are very passive and docile. Swaddled babies cry less and sleep more. It is said that when babies were swaddled they were often cared for simply by placing them in some convenient out-of-the-way place, or even by hanging them on a hook.

There are also some incredible reports that swaddled babies were tossed about between adults as a kind of game or sport. Even a royal child, the brother of Henri IV of France (sixteenth century), was being passed from one window to another for amusement when he was dropped and killed (deMause, 1974). This practice was common enough for doctors to complain about parents who broke the bones of their children in the "customary" tossing of their babies. Ironically, one of the justifications for swaddling was that infants would not so easily have their bones broken if they were protected by the swaddling cloths and boards (deMause, 1974).

While swaddling babies goes far into antiquity and has been found in many societies, the practice was discontinued in England and America by the end of the eighteenth century. In France and Germany, however, it persisted until the nineteenth century (deMause, 1974).

Discipline and Punishment

Parents through the ages have used various means to control or discipline their children. Oftentimes physical punishment was administered routinely and severely. According to one judgment, "The evidence which I have collected on methods of disciplining children leads me to believe that a very large percentage of children born prior to the eighteenth century were what would today be termed 'battered children' " (de Mause, 1974, p. 40). This may be an overstatement, and is very likely limited to the European and American experiences, but there is ample evidence that physical punishment for children was the norm. One evidence of this is a thirteenth century law that said, "If one beats a child until it bleeds, then it will remember, but if one beats it to death, the law applies" (deMause, 1974, p. 42).

Well into the nineteenth century, in the United States amd Europe, children were routinely whipped by parents and teachers. A typical whipping involved the use of some instrument like a brush, strap, belt, or switch. In schools where children were often spanked and whipped, special paddles and yardsticks were retained for the purpose. One German schoolmaster estimated that he had, through his career, administered "911,527 strokes with the stick, 124,000 lashes with the whip, 136,715 slaps with the hand, and 1,115,800 boxes on the ear" (deMause, 1974, p. 41).

There was one pervasive justification that parents used for hitting their children: to break their will or spirit. There was repeated testimony, coming from parents and other authorities, claiming that it was necessary to break, subdue, and bridle children. Children were viewed as wild and willful little animals, who might never be brought under control if they were not broken early. Early often meant in infancy, as soon as the child showed signs of independence or willfulness. Esther Burr, the wife of the Princeton College president, described in her 1755 journal how she had already "whipped" her ten-month old daughter. She believed her daughter understood when she had done something wrong, and concluded, " 'tis time she should be taught" (Walzer, 1974, p. 366). Another mother of that period said about her children, "When turned a year old (and some before), they were taught to fear the rod, and to cry softly" (deMause, 1974, p. 41).

By the 1840s in the United States, the whipping of children, at least as an automatic and routine part of child rearing, had fallen out of favor. Of course, corporal punishment of all types continued to be used, just as it continues to be used today.

In summing up childhood through history, it is necessary to conclude that the lives of children must have been hard and harsh and that many did not survive to adulthood. In fairness, it must be acknowledged that life for everyone was more difficult and dangerous before the modern era. Conditions of contemporary life, at least in developed societies, make the childhood experience very different, because life for everyone is easier. It is time now to direct our attention to contemporary child rearing.

CONTEMPORARY CHILD REARING

There is a small and relatively isolated parish in the west of Ireland called Ballybran, in which an anthropologist named Nancy Scheper-Hughes lived for a year. She has described the way in which people of this village view the rearing of their children (Scheper-Hughes, 1979). Her account is especially interesting because some of the views of these Irish families contrast so much with the prevailing views in the United States today. Let us look at how the Irish parents view the matter of their children's behavior and personalities.

The Irish parents do feel, as parents generally do, that they should instill in their children a respect for proper and right behavior. They are likely to say, "Beware of the habit you give them" (Scheper-Hughes, 1979, p. 212). But despite this admonition, these Irish parents are strong believers in the idea that a child's basic personality, talents, abilities, and nature are largely determined by birth and inheritance. Parents and other villagers use the term *dutcas* when they refer to the characteristics of a particular child. *Dutcas* is translated as blood, stock, or breeding, that is, the things one inherits from one's ancestors. Thus, "the mother of two particularly unruly little boys, throws her hands up in despair and says, ' 'tis no use, the more I kill them, the worse they be. They're too full of their father's *dutcas*' " (Scheper-Hughes, 1979, p. 213).

But the *dutcas* of a child does not have to come from an immediate parent, for the Irish parents believe that the characteristics of any particular ancestor can pop up in a child. Thus, one son may be said to inherit his thriftiness from a particular grandfather, while another son may get his laziness from a ne'er-do-well uncle.

Essentially, the Irish parents believe that what a child inherits from parents or other ancestors will determine his or her personality. By comparison, the Indian (Hindu) belief about the personality of a child comes from a very different source (Kakar, 1979). Indian religious, medical, and folk beliefs hold that life begins at conception when the spirit from the carnation in a previous life joins with the fertilized ovum. Thus, a major portion of the personality comes not from ancestors but from an already existing spirit that has lived in another body at a previous time. However, there is an opportunity to modify the spirit while the fetus is in the mother's uterus. The critical period for influencing psychological development of the baby comes in the third month of the pregnancy. According to Indian tradition, it is in the third month of pregnancy that the feelings and wishes of the fetus, which come from its previous life, are transmitted to the mother. These are revealed to the mother in the form of cravings for particular foods. These cravings of the mother, which are really the wishes of the fetus, are not to be denied, for their fulfillment will ensure the proper psychological development of the child.

The personality of the Indian child is thought to be largely determined by the spirit coming from a previous life, though this might have been modified while it was in the uterus. With this view in mind, it is not surprising that Indian parents are highly indulgent with their children. Mothers do not try to mold their children into a particular desired image. They are inclined to follow rather than lead the child in its development (Kakar, 1979).

These two views of childhood personality formation, coming from Ireland and India, are very different from many of the views held by most parents in American society. Of course, some Americans do subscribe at least partially to the view that personality traits can be inherited from parents or ancestors. There is also a long-standing folk belief that what the mother does during her pregnancy will affect the character of her baby. This view has recently been popularized in a book called, *The Secret Life of the Unborn Child* (Verny and Kelly, 1984). Verny, a psychiatrist, has collected cases that lead him to conclude that from the sixth month of pregnancy, a fetus can begin learning and responding emotionally to its mother. He reports a case in his book of a young conductor of a symphony orchestra knowing an entire score of music, even though he had never seen it before. This is alleged to have occurred because his mother had played this piece of music while she was pregnant (Breathnach, 1983).

While some people might believe that the personalities of children are inherited from ancestors, and a few might believe that they can begin to shape a child's personality while it is still in the womb, these are not prevailing and overriding beliefs. There is a much stronger likelihood that American parents will put more emphasis on the influences of their parenting. Many Americans, especially those who are middle class and college educated, do believe that they can shape the personalities of their children. This notion needs to be examined.

Can Parents Shape the Personalities of Their Children?

It is a testimony to the success of the social sciences, especially sociology and psychology, that so many people now believe that they can shape the personalities of their children. Through most of the twentieth century these fields of study have carried the message that children are largely a product of their environment. Even more pointedly, there has been an emphasis on the crucial role played by parents in the process of shaping children's personalities. The views coming from sociology and psychology are essentially correct, and yet it might not follow that parents can consciously set out to produce a certain kind of child and succeed in producing what they want.

Many young, modern, and well-educated parents seem to conceive of child rearing as a process of direct, straightforward transmission. Their view might be expressed in the following way: "If I want my child to be independent, I will teach independence, and my child will be independent. If I want my child to be frugal or neat, I will teach those things." This view of child rearing often leads parents to wonder, "Where did I go wrong?", when their children do not turn out exactly to their expectations. To understand why this approach might not work, we will take a look at the basic process called *socialization*.

Socialization is the process by which a person learns and generally accepts the ways of a particular social group or society. The objective of socialization is to make sure that the new members of a society will do things in about the same ways as they have been done. It is almost always the responsibility of the older, more experienced members to guide and instruct new members in the ways of the group. Socialization begins very early in life, with parents taking the responsibility of socializing their children.

There is no doubt that this process does work. Hard-working and industrious parents often have children who grow up to be hard working and industrious. Catholic parents are likely to have children who follow the teachings of Catholicism, while Jewish parents are likely to have children who identify with Judaism. But the system is certainly not foolproof. There are hard-working and industrious parents who have lazy children. And there are children of Catholic and Jewish parents who do not accept or follow those religions. If socializing children were a direct transmission process, it would always work. Obviously, it does work much of the time, but it certainly does not work always. Why some children seem to absorb socialization directly and others do not is still not fully understood.

One reason why socialization does not seem to work in all cases is that it can be both more subtle and more complex than we suppose. Socialization occurs constantly, especially in the family. Socialization is as likely to occur by example as by verbal means. A father who tells his children to try to get along with other people and be friendly might often engage in disputes with his neighbors when his children are present. This father is socializing his children as much in the latter instance as in the former. Example is as much a part of socialization as verbal training.

The complexity of socialization is increased by the fact that, in the home, there are typically two parents, who may be sending "mixed signals" to the child. Furthermore, there may be other family members, especially siblings, who also play a part in socializing a child.

There are also nonfamily socializing agents. At a fairly early age children begin to be socialized by the media of communication, especially television. Somewhat later, playmates and friends, the schools, and the print media (magazines, newspapers, and books) play some part in the socialization of children.

Because socialization is such a pervasive, subtle, and complex matter, and because outside socializing agents compete with familial ones, parents are unrealistic when they assume that they can consciously shape the personalities of their children. This does not invalidate the sociological and psychological prin-

Children who watch television from a very early age will receive some of their socialization from the programming and advertising. In many cases, the message will be different from the socialization of their parents.

ciple that socialization influences human behavior and individual personalities. It simply means that the process is too complex and pervasive for any parent (or parents) to understand completely and to manipulate successfully. We will now take a more in-depth look at what typically happens in the early interaction between parents and the infant child.

Early Parent-Child Interaction

The human baby is born with needs that are largely biological and with limited capabilities for filling those needs. A baby can make sounds, primarily crying, and has senses that allow it to experience comfort and discomfort. In the first weeks of life, babies cry when they are uncomfortable and are relatively quiet when they are comfortable. Their usual discomforts are hunger, wetness, coldness, and pain. Babies cry reflexively when these discomforts occur. Since human infants are helpless, they must have some other human present to give them food and keep them warm, or they will not survive. When babies cry because they are uncomfortable, adults usually come to attend to them. The connection between comfort and another person is one of the first things babies learn. It is the first step toward humanness, or what is loosely called human nature.

Human nature is a popular term that many people use to imply that there is something inborn or inherent that makes people behave in certain ways. But the idea that human nature is natural, always there and waiting to blossom, is quite inaccurate. It is more accurate to think of human nature as developing when a human organism interacts with other humans. Absolute evidence for this assertion is limited, since it is impossible for any human to stay alive in the first three or four years of life without human contact and support. There are only a few reported cases of human infants who have survived with little human contact (Curtiss, 1977; Davis, 1940, 1947). There are some verified cases of parents who have locked their babies away, giving them only enough food and water to keep them alive. When these children finally were discovered in early childhood, they did not possess the characteristics we think of as human. They did not talk (in one widely known case, the mother was a deaf mute), and they did not show the emotions that we usually believe to be a part of human nature (crying, smiling and laughing, responding to human gestures of friendship, and the like). The few documented cases of extreme isolation demonstrate that human beings do not become "human" if they do not have at least some human contact.

To see how a baby does become human and develop a personality, we need to look again at the infant who cries when it is uncomfortable or in need of food. As already mentioned, the baby absolutely needs adults for comfort and survival. Parents will generally respond to these needs by giving the infant those things that make it more content. The parents give these comforts freely, expecting little in return from the baby. However, after a while, parents will begin to ask for something in return. Mothers and fathers will feed and change the diapers of the baby, but eventually they want something in return, even if it is only a smile. If they get the smile, they may give something else—a hug, or a cuddle, or a tickle. If the baby responds again, more comforting rewards are given.

This is the beginning of a process by which children learn what has been called the *norm of reciprocity* (Gouldner, 1960). Reciprocity occurs when two interacting people give one another something of equal or almost equal value. People want to continue to interact with one another if they are receiving something that is roughly equal in value to what they are giving. This is a basic element in a theory of human behavior called *exchange theory*, which emphasizes the importance of give and take, costs and rewards, in all human interaction.

Reciprocity is probably the earliest social lesson. Describing reciprocity from the point of view of what is happening to the infant, one writer has said, "We have probably stumbled here upon a most important truth about socialization. . . . The human infant is both highly dependent and pleasure seeking. Put these two things together, and it follows clearly that he [or she] must have the help of others in securing his [or her] own gratification. This simple fact is the root-source of a process that we shall call, quite unscientifically, 'getting hooked on people'" (Campbell, 1975, p. 17). "Getting hooked on people" means that after a while the baby needs more than the food and the diapers the adult provides. The baby also needs the smiles, the attention, the hugs, and the comforting words of the adult who delivers the other necessities.

As the babies grow older, parents start demanding more and more from them in return for what they are giving. Thus, babies must slowly give up their selfish ways. They have to start doing some things that they do not want to do and stop doing other things. Eating solid foods instead of warm milk, especially milk coming from the mother's warm body, comes just one step before sitting on the cold potty. And so the process of making a responsible member of society begins. Later, the smiles, the praise, and the affection of parents are bestowed in response to brushing teeth, keeping the room clean, sitting quietly in church, bringing home A's on report cards, and otherwise behaving as the parents desire.

Parents also use negative sanctions or punishments, which they have at their disposal by virtue of their powerful position relative to children. They may supplement their reward system by scolding, spanking, withholding desserts, restricting telephone privileges, or "grounding" in order to make a child or adolescent to do what is "right."

But the reward and punishment system is not required all the time or forever to make children behave in a reasonably "proper" way. Something else happens in the socialization process that cannot be explained by the simple ideas of rewarding good behavior and punishing bad behavior. Children do what their parents and others expect of them even when their parents are not around to see what they are doing. Children will generally do the "right" things without constant reward and punishment. We saw some features of this process in our earlier introduction of symbolic interaction theory (Chapter 3). A brief review of that theory will point up how children internalize their socialization experiences and come to govern their own behavior.

Symbolic interaction theory is built around the central idea that human behavior is deeply influenced by the human ability to understand and use words and language. It is through words and language that we are able to comprehend and respond to the world around us. We also learn to respond to our own selves with the same words and language. The meaning and the value of things, including ourselves, is conveyed by significant others (parents, other family members, friends). Thus, a little girl who is told often enough that she is cute and adorable may eventually come to take that attitude toward herself. That is, she may evaluate herself with the same words or symbols as do her significant others.

But there is one more step in the socialization process. People ultimately evaluate themselves not only according to how specific individuals respond to them, but also according to how others *in general* will respond to them. People are likely to behave according to the general rules, norms, and values that prevail in their societies, and not just in response to specific other people. For example, most of us will not cheat on an examination, or cheat on a spouse, even though we might not be caught. The reason is likely to be that we would have a difficult time "living with ourselves" if we did. Such a statement probably means that we have internalized the rules, norms, and values of our society and that we evaluate ourselves accordingly.

These, then, are the basics of parent-child relations and the early socialization process. Now we will turn to some of the specifics of child care and child rearing. We will begin with some major questions that are being asked today about parenting.

MAJOR QUESTIONS ABOUT PARENTING

Everyone agrees that a child needs to be cared for and nurtured. There is some agreement that natural parents should do a substantial part of the required child rearing. But there is much less agreement about exactly who should do what. There is both discussion and debate about the different effects on the children if the child rearing is done by mothers or by fathers, or some kind of day-care service. To deal with some of these issues, we will consider the following questions:

1. Do women have a natural or inherent inclination toward mothering?

2. What will be the effects on children (and on men) if fathers take over more of the child-rearing responsibilities?

3. What are the effects on children if more child-rearing is done outside the family (especially in day-care facilities)?

Mothering: Is It Natural for Women?

It is not too uncommon to hear people speak of a "maternal instinct," though social scientists have all but abandoned the term. In the 1960s and 1970s, the spokespersons of the women's movement rejected even the suggestion that women had a natural proclivity for mothering. The feminist critique of the "mystique of mothering" argued that women learned mothering as part of learning the feminine role. Some feminist critics argued that when women were socialized to believe that it was "natural" to want to be mothers it was an "instrument of oppression" (Mitchell, 1966).

Feminists were also highly critical of motherhood because they wanted to expose what one has called "the darker, often unspoken experiences of motherhood" (Thorne, 1982, p. 12). This darker side of mothering included the isolation that mothers often feel when they devote themselves completely to caring for their children. It also included the guilt that mothers feel when they resent the way their devotion to their children robs them of their individuality and their opportunities. Feminists also called attention to the ways in which a strict gender segregation with regard to child care separated fathers from their children (Thorne, 1982).

But feminism has moved beyond this stage, and there is a different view of mothering. Of course, the women's movement, as we saw in Chapter 2, does not speak with a single voice, but several examples of this new view are worth noting. Betty Friedan, who is often given credit for giving a start to the women's movement in the 1960s, is now arguing that women must not ignore and deny the importance of home, children and family life (Friedan, 1981).

Even among some of the more radical feminists, there is an expression of the view that women are intrinsically different from men. Women, in this view, are more nurturant and mutually caring than men (Rich, 1979; Thorne, 1982). The argument is now being made that women should not suppress these tendencies; they should be fostered as an alternative to the competitive and egocentric tendencies of males (and the male-created world).

Another prominent feminist of the 1960s and 1970s, sociologist Alice Rossi, argues that there are some biological differences between the sexes that affect the way they relate to their infant children (Rossi, 1984). Rossi draws part of her conclusion from the research that has been done on fathers who take a primary role in parenting. When fathers in egalitarian families take primary responsibility for the care of their children, they put much more emphasis on teaching, training, and developing the skills of their children. By contrast, mothers are much more likely, especially with infants, to give comfort and nurturance.

As an example of how fathers often deal with their infant children, consider the words of a father who cares for his infant son four mornings a week while his wife is teaching.

I give him a bottle; he's just learning to hold it up for himself now. I continually will teach him things or try to: how to hold his bottle, how to get it if it's fallen over to one side. . . . Right now I am trying to teach him how to roll over . . . he should know by now, but he's got this funny way. He tries to roll over with his arms stuck straight out. . . . also I will interact with him by trying out new toys. (LaRossa and LaRossa, 1981, p. 195).

This father, apparently like many fathers, is primarily interested in his son because of the new skills he can be taught. This accounts for a second difference that Rossi feels is very important, namely, that fathers become much more interested in their children after they are no longer infants. At about eighteen months of age, when both verbal and physical skills begin to develop rapidly, fathers often show much more interest in their children. Of course, this difference in parenting styles between fathers and mothers could simply be the result of the different socialization that men and women have received. Many writers believe this to be the case, with females being socialized to emphasize human relationships and males being socialized to accomplish tasks. However, Rossi believes that the differences in parenting styles rest in something more fundamental. She believes that the evolutionary process has produced essential differences between the sexes and that these lead to the observed differences in parenting (Rossi, 1984).

Specifically, Rossi attributes parenting differences between the sexes to male and female hormones. The hormonal levels of males and females are very different when the fetus is in the uterus, and again at the time of adolescence and young adulthood. To conclude that the hormonal differences do account for the differences, Rossi employs two criteria. First, caring for the young is done by females in almost all species. Second, women are the primary caregivers for the young in almost all cultures. Indeed, in many societies fathers are so little involved in caring for the very young that their contribution is exceeded by that of other children in the family (Rossi, 1984; Weisner, 1982; Whiting and Whiting, 1975). These criteria, while consistent with the hormonal hypothesis, are far from conclusive evidence for its validity.

The debate about whether mothering is an inherent trait of women is far from over, and much more research will have to be done before a final conclusion can be reached. In the meantime, this debate completely misses the point that males can play a much greater role in parenting than has traditionally been the case. Whatever biological tendencies there may be that influence parenting, they can be exaggerated or reduced in any particular culture. In contemporary American society, there is a tendency for fathers to be more actively involved in the rearing of their children. This is the issue we will turn to next.

Father as Parent

In the past, the word *parenting* usually meant mothering. The phrases *caring for children* and *rearing children* only brought mothers to mind. Fathers have been the missing parents. They have not played a large part in caring for children, especially young children. Until recently, there was very little feeling that they should, but that seems to be changing. More and more people are saying that fathers should take more responsibility for child care. It is said that doing so would be good for the fathers and good for their children (not to mention that it would provide benefits for mothers, whose child-care load would be lightened). Before going on to consider some of the possible benefits of fathers caring for children, we must first examine what fathers are doing today in this regard. How much do fathers interact with and take care of their children, especially their infant children? A number of researchers have addressed these and related questions, and their studies do give us some reasonably clear answers (Baruch and Barnett, 1981; Belsky et al., 1984; Katsh, 1981; Lamb, 1981).

One very carefully conducted study involved researchers visiting in the homes of couples who had infants that were one, three, and nine months old (Belsky et al., 1984). By going directly into the home, this study improved on studies where the interaction between parents and infants was observed in a laboratory setting. Laboratory observations of parent-child interaction had shown that fathers are as capable of being highly involved and caring for their infant children as are mothers (Parke and Tinsley, 1981). However, what happens in the controlled conditions of a laboratory and what happens in the natural and normal home conditions are very different. Observations in the home, in which couples were told to "go about their everyday household routine and ignore the observer to as great an extent as possible," revealed that fathers were much less involved with their infants than mothers (Belsky et al., 1984, p. 695).

The couples in this observational study were distinctly middle class, with fathers on the average having educational levels beyond college. Even so, on all measures of relations with the infants, mothers were significantly more involved than fathers. The only household activities that fathers had significantly more of than mothers were "reading and TV watching." It can be said that by the age of nine months the difference in the amount of infant care and attention given by mothers and fathers did become less pronounced. However, this occurred because mothers reduced their level of involvement, not because fathers increased theirs.

In a study by Beverly Katsh (1981), fathers and mothers of three-week- and three-month-old infants were asked to report how many times they had performed five routine child-care tasks during the preceding week. According to these self-reports, fathers "put the baby to sleep" about fifteen to twenty percent of the time. The fathers "diapered"and "bathed the baby" about ten percent of the time (though when the baby was only three weeks old it was only five percent of the time). Naturally, feeding the baby varied greatly according to whether the baby was being breast-fed or not. When the baby was not being breast-fed, fathers of three-week-old babies fed the baby about twenty percent of the time, and "got up during the night to attend the baby" about one-fourth of the time. At three months the fathers had increased getting up at night to about

There are often important influences on the father as well as the child when fathers care for their children. Presently, however, fathers generally contribute only a small portion of their time to child care, especially where infants are concerned.

forty percent of the time (feeding the baby remained at slightly over twenty percent).

In this study, for obvious reasons, if the mother was breast-feeding the father was substantially less likely to feed the baby or to get up at night to attend to it. But, more interestingly, the husbands of women who were not breast-feeding were more involved in all aspects of infant care than were the husbands of women who were breast-feeding (Katsh, 1981). The exact reason for this difference is not known, but perhaps the couples who were breast-feeding were somewhat more traditional than those who were not.

Summarizing the results of these and other studies, we may say that the degree of participation of fathers in the care of their infant children is only a small fraction of the degree provided by mothers. Even by their own reporting, which could be inflated, fathers seldom carry more than twenty percent of the load in the routine tasks of infant care. While there has been much talk and speculation about fathers taking a more active part in the care of their children, the research evidence does not show fathers doing anywhere near half the work.

Being "The Father You Wish You'd Had"

"Don't be the man you think you should be, be the father you wish you'd had" (Pogrebin, 1982, p. 43). This line is a theme of Pogrebin's (1981) book *Growing Up Free*, and has struck a responsive chord with many men who feel they never really knew their fathers. They did not know their fathers, in part, because their fathers were not around the home very much. But, equally important, even when their fathers were around they were distant and reserved and, thus, unknowable. Fathers have often retained this kind of distance from their children, perhaps because they have thought it unmanly to show emotion and affection, especially toward their sons.

There are now testimonies coming from men who have taken on the primary responsibility for rearing their children, testimonies emphasizing how their feelings and priorities have changed as a result of caring for their children full-time. Such men have reported that caring for a child, especially a small child who is almost totally dependent on them, has made them less self-centered and more sensitive to the needs of others. Just having a small, helpless child brings out qualities that are usually associated with "maternal" feelings. There is the interesting possibility coming from these isolated reports that what has so often been attributed to a maternal "instinct" is in actuality a result of the unique responsibility of caring for and responding to the needs of a trusting and helpless infant (Fein, 1983).

At a more concrete level, fathers who have taken over the primary care of their small children frequently report that their life priorities change. One such father, whose former wife had moved some distance away while he was given custody of two children aged three and four, reports how his attitudes about career changed:

> The transition from full-time career person to father/career person has gone surprisingly well. . . . I was wholly involved in my work—actually almost consumed by it. . . . What I have discovered, to my considerable astonishment . . . is that I don't miss my careerism at all. . . . The children, in effect, "forced" me to put my personal and professional lives in proper perspective. (Weigand, 1973, p. 30)

Of course, a few case examples of fathers taking primary responsibility for the rearing of their infant children do not prove that this experience will profoundly affect the feelings and career attitudes of all men. These reports are provocative, however, and do suggest some interesting possibilities for more systematic research. Even though the numbers are small, if a sample of men with full-time responsibility for taking care of their children could be studied systematically over time, the results would be informative.

Another dimension of the "fathering" question is what effect it would have on children if fathers took a more active part in child rearing. Some tentative answers to this question are apparent. First, children would know their fathers better. If fathers increased their contribution to child care even to half the total time required, it would provide a much greater opportunity for children to know their fathers as complete persons. This means that they would learn their fathers' weaknesses as well as their strengths. As a full-time father puts it, "I am never afraid of saying that I am sorry to the children, or confessing when I have made some goof, like burning the dinner beyond repair" (Weigand, 1973, p. 31).

But seeing their fathers as whole persons is more than just seeing that they, too, make mistakes and errors (children always learn eventually that their fathers—and mothers—are not perfect). Much more important is seeing fathers as humans who experience the entire range of feelings and emotions, not just those of the strong and calm "daddy." Again, the words of a full-time father show what this can mean:

> And there are moments when, if I hear one more fairy tale or see one more episode of "Sesame Street," I know—and the children sense—I will go crazy. They give me privacy then, with neither hurt nor resentment. They know when Daddy asks to be alone, he really means it. (Weigand, 1973, p. 31)

At present, only a tiny minority of fathers take care of their children on a full-time basis. A much more significant feature of child care today is the care that children receive from people other than their parents. Baby-sitters, child-care services, and day-care centers are now important sources of care for many American children. We turn next to the issues related to these forms of child care.

Baby-Sitters and Other Child-Care Services

Is it bad for children, especially infants, if they are separated from their mothers (or parents) and left with baby-sitters or in day-care centers? This question has been debated for years and still evokes strong feelings from many people. Some argue that taking the child away from contact with the mother in the early years of life may be permanently damaging to the psyche. Psychoanalyst Selma Fraiberg has written a book called *Every Child's Birthright: In Defense of Mothering* (1977), in which she specifically argues that a child away from its mother during the early formative years will have lifelong problems in forming attachments with other people. Others, like psychologist Jerome Kagan (Kagan et al., 1977) and child-development specialist Sandra Scarr (1984), have concluded from their research that children in day-care centers do not suffer any special adverse effects. We will review these arguments more closely later, but first we will consider some facts about child care in the United States.

About thirty percent of American families with young children use some form of child care for ten hours a week or more ("Family Day Care Study," 1981). The most common kind of child care is called *family day care*. Family day care refers to those cases where children are cared for in the homes of relatives, friends, or neighbors. About forty percent of all children who receive care from others are under these relatively informal arrangements. Only about six percent of such homes are licensed or registered ("Family Day Care Study," 1981). Slightly less than a third of children receiving care remain in their own homes. Fifteen percent of children receiving care are in day-care centers or nursery schools (U.S. Bureau of the Census, 1984). These are usually licensed or registered facilities with trained staffs ("Family Day Care Study," 1981). Figure 11.1 shows the breakdown of child-care arrangements for employed women who have at least one child under five years old.

It scarcely needs to be said that the type and quality of care received by children in these different kinds of arrangements can vary greatly. Certainly when questions about the effects of outside child care are being debated, one must assume that appropriate standards of child care prevail. Indeed, there is some evidence that most parents find satisfactory child care. Despite recent highly publicized accounts of child sexual abuse in a few child-care centers, most parents express satisfaction with their present child-care arrangements ("Family Day Care Study," 1981). While parental satisfaction is not a certain guarantee

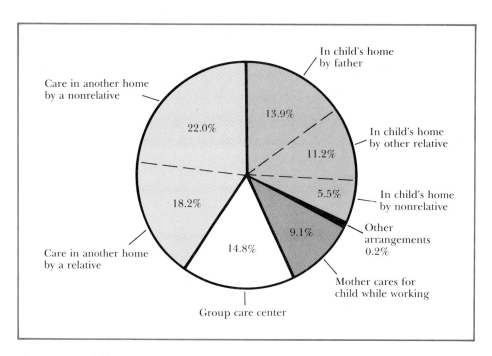

Figure 11.1 *Child-care arrangements for employed women who have at least one child under five years of age. (Source: U.S. Bureau of the Census, 1984)*

that the care is of high quality, it does indicate that reasonable standards are being maintained.

Research on the effects of child care.   The argument that a child separated from its mother in the early months and years of life will be a child (and adult) incapable of forming lasting relationships is based on the notion of mother-child bonding (Fraiberg, 1977). During the first eighteen months of life, the child is said to develop a healthy ego when its mother gives it constant, dependable, and unlimited love and devotion. Fraiberg's claim is that a child so reared will have a sure sense of self and will develop the ability to love and trust. The opposite side of the coin is that a child who has not had its mother more or less constantly will be lacking in these qualities. The fundamental research evidence for this position comes from studies of children who were extremely separated from any close and warm relationship with another person. Critics have been very skeptical about whether studies done on children in "such extreme sterile and affectionless surroundings" can have any meaning for children in child-care situations (Whitbread, 1978).

More important, several researchers have approached the issue more directly. They have set up research situations in which very young children who were in day-care centers were compared with matched samples of children who were cared for in their homes by their parents. One such researcher, Jerome Kagan, had been an early critic of day care for young children. Then during the 1970s he and his colleagues set up a day-care center and conducted a five-year study (Kagan et al., 1977). Children entered the center when they were between three and a half and five and a half months of age. About fifteen months into the study, the researchers set up an experiment to see if the day-care experience had affected attachments of the children to their mothers. The child-care infants had been separated from their mothers for five days a week from 8:30 A.M. to 4:00 P.M. They were compared to infants who had remained at home. In the experiment, each day-care and home-reared toddler was brought into a room with his or her mother, a stranger, and a familiar woman. In the case of the day-care youngsters the familiar woman was their day-care teacher. The children were allowed to play freely with the toys provided until they became bored or distressed. Then the observers noted the woman to whom the child went. There were no differences between the day-care and home-reared infants, and the overwhelming preference of all children was for the mother. Furthermore, when the mothers left the room there was no difference in "separation anxiety" between the day-care and the home-reared children (Kagan et al., 1977). The alleged "attachment problem" of children who were separated from their mothers while in day care, did not seem to be in evidence in this experimental study.

Summarizing the results of his research, Kagan has said, "We showed that you can take a very young child and keep him away from his mother most of the day, five days a week, all year long, and not hurt him or his relation to his mother" (quoted in Whitbread, 1978, p. 36). It must be said, however, that the day-care center set up for this experiment was a high-quality, well-staffed facility. There were only three children enrolled for each adult caretaker (Norman, 1978). Therefore, the most judicious conclusion from this study is that a well-run day-care facility, like a stable and attentive family, will produce children who are likely to be normal in their psychological development.

There have been some studies in which children from day-care centers surpassed children who were cared for full-time in their homes. In a study by Caldwell the babies reared in day-care centers had an average increase in IQ of seventeen points between the ages of two and three; a comparison group of home-reared infants had a drop of six points (cited in Whitbread, 1978). Similar results were found by Lally (cited in Norman, 1978), who studied children from low-income families. Again, at three years of age the children reared in day-care centers had an average IQ level fourteen points above the home-reared children. While the differences between the two groups diminished as the children reached school age, the day-care experience obviously did not harm the children in their intellectual development.

In addition to psychological and intellectual development, there is also evidence that children who have day-care and nursery school experiences develop more rapidly in their social skills. One writer describes how she has observed "babies who . . . inch their way across a playpen pad, at four months, gurgling enthusiastically, to welcome a special pal in the morning. Toddlers too young to talk, will run to alert a friend to a parent's arrival at pickup time" (Whitbread, 1978, p. 36).

It must be emphasized again that in any experimental study of the influence of day care on young children, the quality of the day care is likely to be at a higher than average level. Not all day-care centers, and certainly not all unregulated family day care and baby-sitting is going to be up to the same standard. But when the attention to the children is both intensive and of high quality, there is no evidence that day care is detrimental to the child. Even a very young child can be separated from its mother (or father) for long parts of each day without creating psychological problems. Such children even appear to gain advantages in both intellectual and social development.

BEYOND INFANCY: PARENTING IN THE CHILDHOOD AND ADOLESCENT YEARS

By the time children reach school age, and especially as they approach the teenage years, the tasks of parenting shift. The child becomes increasingly self-sufficient and independent, which makes the job of parenting easier in some ways but harder in others. Parents usually feel that they must continue to guide and control the lives of their children, while children are striving for autonomy and independence. Under these conditions, the relationships between parents and their children revolve around two interconnected spheres: (1) the things parents want from their children; and (2) the methods they use to achieve their objectives.

What Parents Want from Their Children

Almost universally, parents want the same thing for their children. They want their children to have good lives. But enclosed in that very broad statement there are many, many different notions of what children must and should do to ensure that they have the best possible lives. We can not deal with all the many variations, but research on the values that parents have when they socialize their children is very revealing.

In a series of studies, Melvin Kohn and his associates have identified two critical sets of values and have shown how they differ among parents (Kohn and Schooler, 1969; 1973; Kohn, 1977). The major finding of these studies can be summarized as follows. Some parents put the greatest emphasis on "self-direction" in their children. They want their children to show autonomy, creativity, and per-

"While we're at supper, Billy, you'd make Daddy and Mommy very happy if you'd remove your hat, your sunglasses, and your earring."

sonal responsibility for their behavior. Other parents place much greater emphasis on conformity and obedience to rules. They want their children to show respect for authority, which includes both the people in authority and the rules or laws they have established.

These two opposing values—autonomy and obedience—are found among parents in different parts of the society. Parents who have higher than average educations and white-collar, managerial or professional jobs tend to value autonomy in their children. In general, these might be called middle- and upper-middle-class parents. Parents who have lower levels of education and blue-collar or manual occupations are more likely to value obedience in their children. These parents are generally referred to as working class.

There are probably good reasons why middle-class parents value autonomy, while working-class parents value obedience. The reasons may be seen most clearly in the occupations of these parents, especially the fathers. Middle-class parents are likely to be employed in occupations in which they are rewarded for individual initiatives and responsibility, that is, for autonomy. They are expected in their work to take initiatives, be responsible, and act independently. Generally speaking, the more they do so, the more they are rewarded. By comparison, working-class parents are much more likely to be employed in work settings where they must do exactly what they are told, and where individual initiative is not especially valued or rewarded. People who work on assembly lines know that they must do the work in the way they have been instructed if they want to keep their jobs.

Middle-class parents expect, at least implicitly, that their children will enter the occupational world at levels where they will be expected to show individual responsibility and self-direction. They socialize their children with this in mind, so that they will get along best and most successfully when they enter the white-collar, managerial, and professional occupations. Working-class parents have experienced a different kind of work world, one where they do what they are told, when they are told to do it. They assume that their children will enter the same kind of world, so they teach their children obedience and conformity, in order for them to survive in that world. One might say that if working-class parents are sometimes arbitrary and unfair in their demands for obedience from their children, it is their way of forewarning their children about adult life.

The differences in the values of middle-class and working-class parents can be seen in the ways they discipline their children. In Kohn's research, he explored the reasons that parents (especially mothers) gave for punishing their children. He found that working-class mothers punished their children directly or immediately after the child misbehaved, without asking questions. Middle-class mothers were more likely to punish or not punish their children according to how they interpreted the child's intentions when committing the act. Middle-class parents judged the child's misbehavior by considering whether or not it seemed to violate the long-range goal that their child be able to demonstrate autonomy and individual responsibility. Working-class parents punished misbehavior if it violated some rule. They wanted obedience to the rules they had set down for their children, and they did not want discussion or argument about them. They were also much more likely to use physical punishments such as hitting, slapping, or spanking.

Changing Parental Values about Child Rearing

The values of autonomy and obedience have been picked up in surveys of American parents; in addition to showing the social-class differences just discussed, the surveys have found indications of some recent overall shifts in emphasis (Alwin, 1984). Sample surveys of parents in the Detroit metropolitan area have been taken for many years, and since these surveys asked parents the same questions at different times, changes can be identified in their socialization values. In surveys taken in 1958, 1971, and 1983 parents were asked, if they had to choose, which item from the following list they would pick as the most important for a child to learn to prepare for life:

a. To obey
b. To be well liked or popular
c. To think for himself
d. To work hard
e. To help others when they need help

The parents were then asked which items came second, third, and fourth in importance. The answer "to think for himself" is an indication of autonomy or self-direction. The answer "to obey" is clearly an indication of the value placed on obedience.

Over the years the most highly ranked answer has been for the child to "think for himself." For the total sample of parents at each time period, autonomy has been the most preferred quality as preparation for life. "To obey" and "to help others" have generally been the next most popular choices. However, by the time of the 1983 survey "to work hard" had also moved up to be a popular choice. In every survey, "to be well liked" was thought by parents to be the least important quality (Alwin, 1984).

Perhaps the most significant feature of this comparison of parental values over time is that while the autonomy measure has been increasing in popularity, the obedience measure has been decreasing. In all the surveys, including the one taken in 1983, the blue-collar parents have been likely to favor obedience more than the white-collar parents, but there has been a clear shift by both classes toward autonomy and away from obedience. The only exception to this pattern is found among black parents in the Detroit sample, who in the 1983 survey had a slight tendency to prefer obedience more than they had in earlier surveys. Their preferences for autonomy, while high, did not appear to change much over time (Alwin, 1984).

A close analysis of the data coming from these surveys shows that it was the Catholics in the sample who made the greatest changes since 1958. Through the decades of the 1960s and 1970s, Catholics have become much more assimilated into the mainstream of American society, and the religious policy of the Church has placed a greater emphasis on individual autonomy (Alba, 1976, 1981; Greeley, 1977).

Since these surveys come from only one metropolitan area in the United States, it is not certain that the results can be generalized to the whole society. However, the trend they reflect is consistent with the increasing levels of education in the society, the reduction in blue-collar occupations, and probably the influences of the mass media. The general message coming from the latter— magazines, books, television, and movies—is that the individuality of children should be respected. The additional message is that children should be taught to make responsible judgments as soon as they are able to do so. Children, it is said, who learn to think for themselves and to be responsible for their actions will be better equipped to handle their problems. This is especially important as they move through the adolescent years and into young adulthood.

In principle, there is widespread agreement on the last point: children should be given as much freedom and autonomy as possible, so that they can learn how to make good decisions and develop sound judgment. However, the principle does not come to grips with the reality of the relationship that exists between parents and children. Parents and their children often have very different ideas about when the children are old enough to make good decisions. They also may differ about the specific areas of life in which children at any given age can make decisions. These questions raise a basic issue: Do children have the same rights as adults? It is this practical issue of child rearing that we will consider as the concluding question of this chapter.

ISSUE

Do children have the same rights as adults?

The term *children's rights* has been widely used in recent years. However, an element of confusion has crept into the discussions of this issue because the term has been used in two distinct ways. The two different meanings of children's rights can be distinguished by noting that one refers primarily to the *welfare* of children and the other to the *freedom* of children.

Children's rights from the welfare perspective is illustrated by the United Nations Declaration on the Rights of the Child (1959), which specifies a number of things that should be guaranteed to every child. For example, every child has the right to receive the things necessary for health, well-being, and security. These include such things as an adequate diet, shelter, clothing, education, and so on.

Children's rights from the freedom perspective refers to the right of children to choose for themselves the way they wish to live. The advocates of children's rights from the freedom perspective argue that children have the same rights as adults to make decisions that affect only themselves.

It is the freedom perspective of children's rights that we are addressing in the presentation of the issue that follows. In a way, the issue is not a yes or no question, but is really a matter of when and on which issues children do have rights. From the parental side, the question is, when do they give up control and on which issues. From the children's side, the question is when are they able to make the decisions about their own lives. The answers to these questions are not easy or obvious, but since the questions must be faced by every parent and child, they deserve a full airing.

The Arguments for Children's Rights

The advocates of children's rights see children as the last major group in this society still systematically denied the rights to self-determination. Children's rights advocates point out that over the course of our history we have gradually given several groups the right of self-determination and autonomy, even though earlier generations considered these same groups incapable of handling these rights. Black Americans were not thought to be capable of coping with freedom or the full rights of citizenship. Workers were not allowed to join together into labor unions and engage in collective bargaining. Women were not allowed to vote. At the time these rights were denied to blacks, workers, and women, it seemed reasonable to many people, just as it now seems reasonable, to restrict the freedom of children.

But exactly which rights and freedoms do the advocates of children's rights want for children? The answer is, the same rights and freedoms as adults. One spokesperson for this view puts it this way: "Children, like adults, should have the right to decide the matters which affect them most directly" (Farson, 1974, p. 27). Freedom for children, just as for adults, does not mean license. A. S. Neill, the founder of a school noted for the freedom it gave to children, defined license as an act that interferes with someone else's freedom. He said, "in my school a child is free to go to lessons or to stay away from lessons because that is his own affair, but he is not free to play a trumpet when others want to study or sleep" (Neill, 1966, p. 7).

A major argument against children's rights is that children may do things that are not good for them, and may even be psychologically or physically damaging. Anticipating such arguments, the advocates admit that there is some risk, but they counter by saying that there are always risks in life, and children will be better off learning that the decisions they make for themselves may have bad consequences. A child who decides to stay up until midnight will learn that not having enough sleep will make the next day unpleasant.

Some advocates of children's rights focus their attention on the rights of children in the late teenage years rather than early and pre-teenage years. Indeed, it is during the adolescent years that the demands of children to govern their own lives come most often into conflict with the wishes of parents. The advocates say that if children have been taught to take responsibility for their actions when they are young (perhaps under parental guidance and even control) they will be able to make better decisions for themselves when they reach the late teenage stage of life. Children of this age should be able to pick their own friends, their styles and tastes in clothing and appearance, and their general life-style. (As a small but often significant example, in recent years the earring for males has been a point of contention in many families.)

Summing up the case for adolescent children's rights, it is the right of children to decide what they will do with their lives, even before they reach the age of legal majority (generally assumed to be eighteen). Certainly after that age there should be no question about complete autonomy. While parents may give advice and counsel, they can no longer expect to control their children.

The Arguments for Parental Control

The arguments for parental control have already been touched on in the preceding discussion, but they deserve a fuller presentation. At the preteenage level, parents often feel that a very strong controlling hand is necessary. There are really two fears that are most often expressed by those who would maintain strong control over children. First, there is the fear that children free to make their own decisions will make harmful or detrimental choices. Second, there is the fear that if a child is not controlled at younger ages an uncontrollable "monster" will be created.

Regarding harmful or detrimental effects of too much freedom for children, there is a concern that children simply cannot see the long-range consequences of their actions. Parents, by contrast, have much greater experience and a clearer perspective on the repercussions of particular actions. A child who is not interested in putting effort into schoolwork, for example, is not looking ahead to the impact this will have on admittance to college, or to the limitations a poor school record will place on occupational choices. The underlying concern about giving children freedom to make their own choices is that they simply do not have enough knowledge, experience, or good judgment to make the best decisions for themselves.

The second concern with giving children too much freedom is that an uncontrolled child will be ill equipped to go out into the real adult world. A child who has always had the freedom to do whatever he or she wishes may feel as an adult that this is an absolute right in any and all circumstances.

There is an extension of this idea that is often invoked for children in their teenage and adolescent years. The assumption is that teenage children will often test the boundaries of their freedom and independence. This route may take them into realms that are far beyond the behavior they know is expected of them by their parents, but there is an impulse to test how far they can go. Many parents and child-behavior specialists believe that adolescents want to have limits and controls set by their parents. Thus, parents who fail to set controls and limits are going to allow their children to get into unreasonable and even dangerous situations. Ironically, according to this view, the children themselves want to be told by their parents that their behavior is unacceptable.

The crux of the parental-control position is that parents have the right to control their children, and they have the responsibility to do so. In the long run the children themselves will be grateful for the controls placed on them by their parents.

Themes

1. In American society a great emphasis is put on parenting and child rearing, but the diversity of philosophies indicates that there is no "correct" or "perfect" way to raise children.

2. Children and childhood were viewed very differently in the past than they are today.

3. By today's standards, much of the treatment of children historically can be characterized as abusive and negligent.

4. Routine and severe physical punishment was the norm in American and European societies well into the nineteenth century.

5. People in many societies believe that the personality of a child is formed before the child is born.

6. In contemporary American society, there is a widely held belief among parents that they can directly shape and determine the personalities of their children, but the complexity of socialization makes that unlikely.

7. While feminists in the 1960s and 1970s argued against the "mystique of mothering," some contemporary feminists are inclined to believe that women should acknowledge and develop their nurturing tendencies.

8. However, there is a continuing debate about whether nurturing is a learned or genetically inherited characteristic of women.

9. Fathering is receiving more and more attention, with fathers taking a more active, but still a minority, role in caring for their children.

10. When fathers take a more active role in caring for their children, there are likely to be influences on both the fathers and the children.

11. There is continuing debate and discussion about the effects on children of child care outside the home.

12. Research has not revealed any psychological, intellectual, or social negative effects resulting from being in child-care facilities.

13. Parents socialize their children in ways that they hope will give them the best chance in life, but the views of people in different parts of the social structure vary greatly.

Facts

1. During the Middle Ages in Europe childhood was not recognized as a distinct stage of life; children passed directly from infancy into adulthood.

2. Prior to the twentieth century, and especially in earlier historical periods, infant and childhood mortality were so high that half of all children did not reach adulthood.

3. Infanticide and abandonment have been documented as a part of the history of Western society.

4. Swaddling infants and sending them out to wet nurses were common practices in Europe until the eighteenth century.

5. Human infants who have been deprived of contact and interaction with other humans do not possess the characteristics we think of as human.

6. Through the socialization process, people learn to evaluate themselves as well as other social objects.

7. Fathers put more emphasis on teaching and training their small children, while mothers are more likely to give comfort and nurturance.

8. When they are observed in their homes, fathers are much less involved with their infant children than are mothers. Fathers seldom carry more than twenty percent of the infant child-care load.

9. About thirty percent of American families with young children use some form of child care for ten hours a week or more.

10. Only about six percent of child-care facilities are licensed or registered.

11. Children who are cared for full-time in quality day-care centers identify with their mothers in the same way as children who remain in their homes.

12. White-collar parents favor "autonomy" in their children, while blue-collar parents regard "adherence to the rules" as more important.

13. The national trend in recent years has been for parents to move toward favoring autonomy and self-direction in their children. Catholic parents in particular have moved toward wanting their children to show greater autonomy.

Major Concepts

autonomy: A socialization value emphasizing self-direction, creativity, and personal responsibility.

children's rights (freedom): The right of children to choose for themselves the way they wish to live.

children's rights (welfare): A concern that every child will be guaranteed those things in life that provide health, well-being, and security (adequate diet, shelter, clothing, education, and so on).

dutcas: An Irish term meaning blood, stock, or breeding; that is, the characteristics one inherits from one's ancestors.

exchange theory: A basic theory of human behavior that emphasizes the importance of give and take, costs and rewards, in all human interaction. (*See* reciprocity)

infanticide: The practice of killing infants, or allowing them to die by abandonment or neglect.

obedience: A socialization value emphasizing conformity and respect for authority and rules.

reciprocity: The practice of two people, as they interact with each other, giving each other things of equal or almost equal value.

socialization: The process by which a person learns and generally accepts the ways of a particular social group or society.

swaddling: Wrapping a baby very tightly in cloths, making it impossible for the baby to move its arms or legs.

symbolic interaction theory: A social psychological theory built around the idea that human behavior is deeply influenced by the human ability to understand and use words and symbols.

wet-nursing: The practice of hiring another woman to nurse one's baby.

12

The Family and Work
Breadwinners/Homemakers, Dual-Earners, and Commuter Marriages

We are accustomed to making a sharp separation between the family and work. They are so very different in place and purpose. But a moment's thought quickly shows that these two very important areas of life are closely intertwined. What happens in the family is going to influence what happens at work, and what happens at work is equally likely to influence family life. Losing a job, being transferred to another office, or falling in love with a co-worker are just a few of the ways that one's work life can have an impact on marriage and family life. Similarly, worrying about a sick child, having a fight with one's spouse, or planning for a daughter's wedding can all influence one's work performance.

This chapter will consider a wide range of areas in which work life and family life are intertwined. While there are some areas in which the family and work are complementary or mutually supportive, it is more often the case that they are in conflict or opposition. This is often true because the needs of the family call for one course of action while the demands of work call for another. This conflict is, if anything, becoming more intense as women enter the labor force in greater numbers and with more serious career intentions. At the end of this chapter, we will consider one of the more intense decisions faced by many married couples today: When the career of one spouse calls for moving to a new place of residence, but the career of the other requires staying, how is the decision made?

Not many years ago the relationship between work and family was divided mostly along gender lines. Men went out into the work force and earned the money (or at least most of it) that provided for the economic needs of the family. This was called the *breadwinner* or *good-provider* role (Bernard, 1981; Davis, 1984). In this system, women remained in the home, where they provided for their husbands and cared for their children. Their contribution was called the *homemaker* role. (The term *housewife* was widely used until it started to take on negative connotations. Being a housewife came to be associated with staying in the home and performing a repetitive cycle of unimportant and mindless activities.) In combination, these gender-related roles were called the *breadwinner/ homemaker* system.

Everyone agrees that today in the United States the breadwinner/homemaker system is no longer the prevailing family form. In statistical terms, only thirty percent of married couples have the breadwinner/homemaker arrangement today. For more than half of all couples (fifty-two percent), both husband and wife are employed. In the remaining eighteen percent either the wife alone is employed, or neither is (Presser and Cain, 1983).

Yet, even though the breadwinner/homemaker arrangement is now a minority type, it is still an ideal for some Americans. For many others it may be preferred in some modified form, perhaps with the wife working only part-time, or working only after children reach a certain age. There is also possible indication that even among couples who are committed to the dual-earner system, the older more traditional way is romantically idealized.

The breadwinner/homemaker system has existed long enough to be traditional, but its history is not quite as long as might be supposed. Indeed, the history of males becoming the breadwinners and women moving into homemaking on a full-time basis seems to have emerged sometime in the nineteenth century. The exact date is not easy to pin down, in part because the emergence is tied to the Industrial Revolution, which occurred at different times in different places. The Industrial Revolution came as a result of the transition from human power to power generated from water, coal, and steam. These energy sources powered machines that increased the productivity of workers hundreds of times over what it had been with hand labor alone (Davis, 1984).

It was as a part of this change that the place of labor went from the home to the factory. This was a dramatic change, since throughout most of history the primary workplace had been the home or on the land surrounding it. Farmers and peasants, for example, almost always worked where they lived. Before the Industrial Revolution, even the production of nonagricultural goods, such as shoes and clothing, usually occurred in a home or attached workshop, with all family members contributing. Under these conditions the idea of a breadwinner was meaningless, since virtually every member of the family contributed to the family enterprise.

But when workers started working outside the home for wages, the nature of economic life changed greatly. At first, in some cases, such as the English cotton industry around 1800, entire family units (fathers, mothers, and children) went to work in factories (Smelser, 1959). Eventually, however, children were prohibited from working in factories because of child labor laws, and women were increasingly relegated to the home.

This movement, keeping women in the home while men went *out* into the work world, started in the first half of the nineteenth century in the United States and was most effective in the years between 1860 and 1920 (Davis, 1984). At the beginning of the twentieth century, only about five percent of married women were employed outside the home. After that, the percentage started

The paintings of Grandma Moses depict farm families where all members of the family contributed to the family enterprise. Under these circumstances, the idea of husband as sole breadwinner was meaningless.

(Grandma Moses. Apple Butter Making. Copyright © 1982, Grandma Moses Properties Co., New York. 'Grandma Moses, born in 1860, devoted many of her 101 years to raising a large family. Mother of five, grandmother of eleven, she was eventually recognized as 'Grandma' to the whole world on account of her heartwarming paintings of traditional American values.')

climbing, and it has not stopped. Now, over fifty percent of all married women are in the labor force (U.S. Bureau of the Census, 1984) (see Figure 12.1).

This nineteenth-century movement, which separated women from the economic workplace and kept them in the home as full-time homemakers, has a dimension that goes beyond simple labor force statistics. A new cultural role for women emerged during the nineteenth century, which transformed how women and motherhood were viewed. This new cultural role has been called by historians a "new image of womanhood" (Lerner, 1969; Welter, 1966). This new

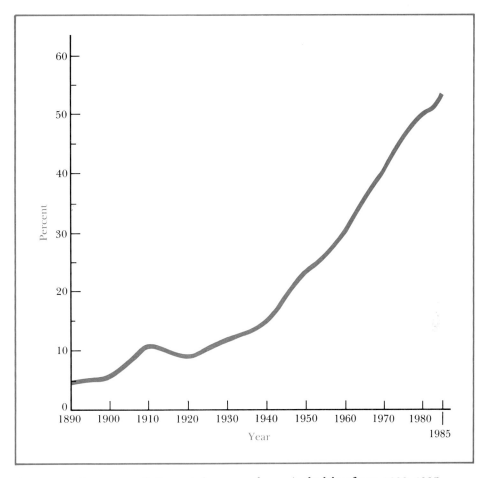

Figure 12.1 *Percentage of all married women who are in the labor force, 1890–1985.*
(*Source: U.S. Bureau of the Census, 1984*)

image especially stressed that women had a moral duty and responsibility to remain in the home and care for their families. The "cult of true womanhood" raised women to a lofty, even saintly, level as they were praised and rewarded for taking care of their children and husbands. In return for their efforts, they were to be provided for by their husbands who would bring home the rewards of their work in the industrial and business worlds.

This cultural ideal of women in the home was strongly reflected in the emergence of women's and homemaker's magazines in the nineteenth century (Gordon, 1978). As this ideal developed in the United States, it embodied several related dimensions. One key idea was that women were said to be responsible for maintaining the virtues of home and family life. The outside world was seen as corrupting and harsh, while the home was pure, warm, and comforting. Women were also charged with the responsibility of rearing their children in such a way that the next generation would carry on the best qualities of the culture. A slogan that was repeated again and again was, "The hand that rocks the cradle, shapes the nation."

An implicit but less frequently articulated feature of the cultural ideal of women in the home was that the quality of the home and the children served as a kind of community display for the economic success of the husband. "The wife became a billboard for her husband's achievement, and the manner in which she dressed, the activities she engaged in, and the kind of home she managed all served to tell the world of her husband's success" (Gordon, 1978, p. 204).

Many would view the last of these as a negative element of the wife-as-homemaker ideal, since it reveals how married women could only have a community status through their husbands. The breadwinner/homemaker system put wives in a dependent and subordinate role. While the earlier system of patriarchy gave males the dominant position in their households, just by virtue of their gender, this newer system added to their dominant position because they were the sole economic providers for the family. Women could not command economic resources on their own and thus were totally dependent on their husbands' earning ability and the willingness of husbands to share what they earned with their families. When husbands did share their earnings, they gained power from doing so.

"Very pleased to meet you. What does your husband do?"

The breadwinner/homemaker system has been breaking down for many years as women have been returning to the labor force. And yet, the cultural ideology supporting the system has persisted. We need only look back to the decade of the 1950s to see this ideology in full force in American society. In that decade, Americans in all strata of society believed fervently in the ideal of women in the home and men earning the living—this despite the fact that twenty-five to thirty percent of all married women were working in the 1950s. Many of those working women, however, did so out of economic necessity. And when these women had young children they were often plagued by feelings of guilt, for the prevailing ideology held that they should be in the home.

In the 1980s, there are still vestiges of the breadwinner/homemaker system and the ideology that supports it. The breadwinner/homemaker system can still be widely found among the upper socioeconomic strata of the society. We will begin by examining how this system works for them.

THE BREADWINNER/HOMEMAKER SYSTEM

The Wife as Helpmate—A Vestige of the Past?

Wives who are homemakers are found in all strata of society, but there is a prominent representation among the wives of men who have high-status professions or are in the upper echelons of business (Kanter, 1977). The wives, while they are not employed, do have the "job" of being helpmates of their husbands. They take care of home and children, and they do the things necessary for the success of their husbands' careers. They are the epitome of the often-heard assertion, "behind every successful man there is a woman" (Fowlkes, 1980, p. x).

A revealing study of the wives who are in the wealthiest class has been conducted by Susan Ostrander (1984). These women, whose husbands controlled the largest businesses and corporations in the country, were interviewed and asked to describe their lives and the meaning they attached to what they did. Their "work" is of two types. First, they must manage the households of the men who run the major businesses of the country. This means entertaining and keeping social ties with the right people among the social elite. It also means rearing the children properly so that when these children grow up they will be prepared to take their positions in the business and social worlds. Second, these wives work at fund-raising and managing the major charitable, educational, and cultural institutions of the communities in which they live.

The women of this upper class take very seriously both the running of their households and the activities in their communities. They have obligations to their families and to their communities, and by fulfilling these obligations they maintain the position and power of their social class (Ostrander, 1984).

The women homemakers of the upper class are an elite minority, but some of the same patterns exist, though to a lesser degree, among professional and business families in which women are more likely to remain out of the work force. One study at this socioeconomic level compared the wives of medical doctors with the wives of college professors (Fowlkes, 1980).

This study showed that the wives of medical doctors were distinctly more likely to be in the traditional homemaker role than were academic wives. A majority of the doctors' wives were neither in paid employment nor in credit-earning educational studies. Three-fourths of the wives of academics, by contrast, were either in a paid job or in school. The doctors' wives, especially the older ones, were likely to subscribe to the sentiments of "A Physician's Wife's Prayer," which states: "Dear God, please grant me a full awareness of my responsibilities as a helpmate to my physician husband. Help me to cultivate, practice and love the virtue of unselfishness that he may see in me the perfect wife and helpmate" (The Women's Auxiliary of the American Medical Association, as quoted in Fowlkes, 1980, p. 44).

In order to be the "perfect helpmate," doctors' wives were more or less obligated to be active in the auxiliaries of the district medical society and the local hospitals. This was especially the case when their husbands were first starting to practice in the community. Many of the wives joined auxiliaries and other voluntary associations willingly, both to become socially active and to contribute to their husbands' careers. As one doctor's wife put it, "You have the sense of 'you should.' . . . To my way of thinking it would be wrong not to do your part. It's possibly helpful to your husband's work" (Fowlkes, 1980, p. 49). While some doctors' wives resented this kind of obligation, they nonetheless usually acquiesced and "did their time."

In addition to community and volunteer work, doctors' wives were also expected to participate in and host a variety of social functions. These included cocktail parties, dinners, coffees for the wives of new doctors, and other similar social affairs. Again, most doctors' wives entered into these activities and social responsibilities with a willing attitude, though a few resented them or resisted openly.

While the average age of the doctors' wives in this study was less than forty, it is significant that the older women often spoke disdainfully of a "new breed of wives." These younger wives were often viewed as being less willing to take on the traditional role of doctor's wife. And, in fact, a few of the younger women did express the feeling that they wanted to be "just wives," not "doctors' wives." This seems to indicate that some changes are occurring even in this generally traditional professional group.

This study of medical and academic wives reveals that even when women do not fully accept the role of adjuncts to their husbands' careers, they still often play "supportive" roles. The nature of the supportive role is most clearly revealed in the following statement: "The ideal wife, then, is one who provides her husband with a support system that enables him both to maximize his professional opportunities and goals, and meet the day-to-day demands of professional work in a trouble-free state of mind" (Fowlkes, 1980, p. 79). Thus, the supportive role means that a wife provides an atmosphere that allows her husband to devote the maximum amount of his time and energy to his professional career. In specifics, this can mean anything from providing an encouraging word to keeping the children from being noisy when he is trying to work.

The following statements of wives show further details of what it means to play a supportive role (Fowlkes, 1980). The first two have to do with subordination to the husband's career and the remaining three have to do with providing a supportive home environment.

> *I knew I would mostly be the second-best thing in his life; medicine would always come first. (p. 82)*

> *I helped him to get established in those early years by understanding about his hours and why he had to spend them. If I hadn't it would have detracted from what he had to do. (wife of an academic, p. 89)*

> *I feel somewhat restricted as to what I can do in the house when he works here. I can't listen to music in the morning. (p. 104)*

> *He really requires a lot of attention. . . . My husband is very dependent. He doesn't like to be left alone and have to do things in the house for himself. (p. 105)*

> *The position he's in now has many problems and I'm a good buffer. . . . He finds it helpful to have someone he can talk to about those problems. (p. 109)*

Comparing the wives of doctors and the wives of academics, it is generally the case that academic wives are less likely to give automatic priority to their husbands' careers. This may be due in part to the generally higher prestige that doctors receive in this society, but it may also be attributable to the higher incidence of working or studying among academic wives. When women are not full-time homemakers, there is a greater likelihood that they will be more autonomous and will reduce, at least to some degree, the support they provide for their husbands' careers.

Some Dangers of the Helpmate Role

When wives do remain out of the work force, and devote themselves more or less completely to maintaining the home and supporting their husbands' careers, they face some dangers connected with the end of marriage through death or divorce. Without the economic support of their husbands, these women often face an abrupt loss of income and a decline in their level of living. If a marriage ends because of the death of a husband, there may be substantial insurance and other death benefits. In the case of divorce, there may be alimony and child support, though the former is becoming less and less common. In either case, the economic condition of a woman who has no independent income is very likely to decline with the end of a marriage.

Even among women who have college educations or professional degrees, it may be difficult to find satisfactory employment because they have not been active in the labor force. More than likely, the level of the job and the pay they receive will be far below that of their former husbands.

The plight of women who have followed the homemaker course, only to have their marriages end unexpectedly, has been vividly demonstrated in recent years by the lawsuits such women have filed. As a case in point, the wives of military personnel have often had to forego their own careers during the years their husbands were on active duty. In part this was because they were expected to carry out the homemaker role as adjuncts to their husbands' careers. But, also, because the military careers of their husbands called for frequent relocations, it was difficult to establish and maintain their own careers. The expectation was that after twenty or thirty years of active military service their husbands could retire from active duty and receive military retirement pay. Until Congress passed new legislation in 1982, it was not possible for the courts in a divorce case to award to a spouse part of a military person's retirment pay. Now the courts, in divorce decrees, can give former spouses of military people a part of military retirement pay. However, how much a woman receives from the pension of her former husband will depend on the ruling of the court hearing the divorce case.

The fundamental problem of women helpmates whose marriages end in divorce is that the original assumptions of the marriage are negated by the divorce itself. Husbands and wives in such marriages begin with the idea that theirs is a joint effort, to which both will contribute and from which both will eventually benefit. But if the couple divorces, these earlier commitments often carry little moral weight. Divorcing husbands continue with the careers they have established, while wives are left with little to show for their contributions.

With the increases in divorce rates in American society in the 1970s, the breadwinner/homemaker marriage partnership became a more dangerous alternative for women. This may be one of the reasons why married women entered the labor force in increasing numbers during that same decade. There are certainly other reasons as well, but there can be no doubt that concerns about financial security have played some part in the movement of married women into the labor force. In the next section we will focus on couples in which both husbands and wives work, giving special consideration to those instances where the work of the wife is not just a job, but a career.

DUAL-EARNER COUPLES

As we begin this discussion of dual-earner couples, there are a few terms that should be clarified. While the term *working wives* is understood by most people to mean wives who are gainfully employed in the labor force, it does have the disadvantage of implying that wives who remain in the home do not work. Some people have appropriately objected to that implication, so we will generally use the term *employed wives* when we refer to women in the labor force.

When discussing couples in which both husband and wife are employed, they are often referred to as a *dual-career couple.* However, a career implies an occupation that requires special training and where there is the potential for moving up a hierarchical ladder of related, but increasingly higher status, jobs (Aldous, 1982). Many people simply have jobs, not careers. To cover both types, there is an increasing preference for the term *dual-earner couples.* We will use this as a general term to cover all couples where the husband and wife are both employed, and use the term *dual-career couples* only when we wish to discuss couples where both have careers.

Types of Occupations

Men and women in the labor force have very different jobs, even though in some instances these differences are masked by the official statistics. As an example, eighteen percent of women who are employed have professional-technical occupations, while men have a slightly smaller percentage in that category (Hayghe, 1982). However, the specific professional-technical occupations of men and women are very different. While men are overrepresented in the professions of medicine, law, and engineering, women are overrepresented as nurses, elementary school teachers, and librarians. The differences in the prestige and pay of these professions clearly favor men.

Employed women are also very highly concentrated in clerical and service occupations (Hayghe, 1982). Thirty-five percent of all employed women are in clerical jobs, where they serve as typists, word processor operators, and so forth. Another fifteen percent of all employed women are in "service" occupations, which include, most prominently, waitressing. These two categories, when combined, put half of all employed women in relatively low-paying or low-prestige jobs.

These statistical facts about the differences in occupational statuses of employed men and women make it likely that most married men will have more prestigious jobs and earn more money than their wives. These differences are very likely to influence husband-wife relations and an array of other family matters. We should also note that when the situation is reversed—when wives earn more than their husbands, or have more prestigious occupations—that,

Women who are employed are highly concentrated in the clerical and service occupations, for which they receive relatively low incomes.

too, will have implications for marital relationships and family functioning. We will examine the research on this topic later. But first we will consider some basic issues and problems among dual-earner couples.

Time and Family Work

In the last decade, there have been many studies on the amount of time husbands and wives spend on family work in the home. *Family work*, of course, is primarily cooking, cleaning, and caring for children. These studies have often compared households where the wife is and is not employed. Several general statements can be made that summarize this large body of research (Berheide, 1984; Berk and Berk, 1979; Geerken and Gove, 1983; Szinovacz, 1984).

Wives who are employed do approximately sixty-five to eighty percent of the family work (the percentage varies from study to study).

Wives who are not employed do approximately eighty to ninety percent of the
family work.

In terms of hours spent, employed wives are involved in family work significantly less than nonemployed wives. (A common pattern is for employed
wives to spend about four hours per day, while nonemployed wives spend
seven or eight hours per day on family work.)

Husbands who have employed wives spend only slightly more time on family
work than husbands whose wives are not employed. (Often the difference
is a small fraction of an hour.)

The picture that these statistical results reveal is remarkably consistent in
showing that husbands do only a small fraction of the family work, whether or
not their wives are employed. Indeed, when their wives are employed, husbands have not generally shown any substantial increase in the amount of family work they do.

The evidence showing that women who are employed have only slightly
more help with the work of home and family is a situation that has been commented on widely. Scholars are likely to express their views in an understated
fashion: "Pervasive changes are taking place in women's lives, largely as a result
of increased labor force participation, but comparable changes in the division
of labor and in the roles of men have lagged considerably (Hess, 1984, p. 249).
Journalistic writers are more blunt: "We 'Liberated' Mothers Aren't. We're doing it all, not having it all, with too little help from men or society" (Crittenden,
1984, p. D1).

Some researchers believe that since the 1960s there has been a modest increase in the percentage of family work done by the husbands of employed
women (Maret and Finlay, 1984; Pleck and Rustad, 1981; Szinovacz, 1984).
There are at least two major reasons why one might suppose that husbands
would contribute more to family work today than they did two decades ago: (1)
a loosening up of rigid gender role distinctions between "men's work" and
"women's work"; and (2) improvements in the occupational status of women,
which might give them more leverage with respect to their husbands. Research
has been done on both of these possibilities.

In a recent study of men and women who were college and university ad-
ministrators, the major finding was that husbands who had less traditional gender role orientations were much more likely to share in family tasks (Bird et al.,
1984). Husbands in this sample were also more likely to share in family work if
their wives were employed, and especially so if their wives had careers as opposed to noncareer jobs (Bird et al., 1984). Among the women in this sample of
professionals, the higher their individual incomes, the more likely it was that
their husbands would share in family tasks (Bird et al., 1984). Two major studies
using national random samples of adults have supported the same conclusion.
As a woman's income increases relative to her husband's income, his share of

the household work increases (Ross et al., 1983; Maret and Finlay, 1984). The researchers in one case make an interesting observation on this pattern: "Employers who persist in discriminating against women because of their supposed domestic responsibilities may be perpetuating a self-fulfilling prophecy that promotes women's secondary status in the work place, thus ensuring their primary responsibility for domestic tasks" (Maret and Finlay, 1984, p. 363).

One recently reported study, however, did not find the relative (or absolute) income of husbands and wives to be the most important determinant of how much household work married men do (Coverman, 1985). Among the subjects of this study of dual-earner couples, the husbands contributed most to family work when they were younger, when there were children in the home, and when the occupation of the husband required fewer hours on the job. According to this research, the contributions that husbands make to family work are largely a function of the *demand*, such as the presence of children, and of their *capability of responding*, as reflected by shorter work hours (Coverman, 1985).

The fact that younger men, in this study, were more likely to contribute to family and household work does suggest that changes are occurring among American working couples. One must be cautious in making this interpretation, however, since this relationship might only reflect greater contributions of husbands in the early stages of marriage, and not a societal trend.

Balancing Family and Work Obligations

Since 1950 there has been a steady increase in the percentage of wives employed, but the increases in recent years have been greatest among those wives with children (see Figure 12.2). When both parents work, a fundamental problem is finding time to meet both family and work obligations. The word most often used to characterize this problem is *balancing* (Bohen and Viveros-Long, 1981; Nock and Kingston, 1984). The word *balancing* conjures up a number of relevant images. There is first the idea that both work and family need their fair share of attention, and neither can be neglected. The words of one husband, an attorney, express this idea:

> *From a male perspective it is not either/or family or work. It's both. As a practical matter it is not open to sacrifice the career or the family . . . at least you're damn crazy if you do. . . . In that direction lies suicide, divorce or drug addiction. (Bohen and Viveros-Long, 1981, p. 159)*

A second image evoked by the balancing of career and family is one of near-frantic running from one to the other trying to keep everything going. Many wives and husbands have this feeling as they leave their children with baby-sitters or in day-care centers, rush off to work, meet deadlines and assignments, pick up their children at the end of the day, shop for groceries, prepare dinner, bathe the children and put them to bed, do the laundry, and get ready for a new day. All these daily routines are frequently intensified as couples prepare for holidays, buy gifts, entertain guests and visitors, and cope with occasional crises (large and small, both at home and at work). The result is a frenetic daily and weekly round that seems to keep life at a continuously stressful level.

The sociological term that has been applied to this tension between the demands of work and the demands of home is *role strain*. The expectations of work and the expectations of family are conflicting, in two different ways (Voydanoff and Kelly, 1984). First, there is *overload*, which means that the demands of the two roles are more than a person can adequately handle. There are just not enough hours in the day to do everything. At the end of every day there is the feeling that the person is just a little further behind schedule.

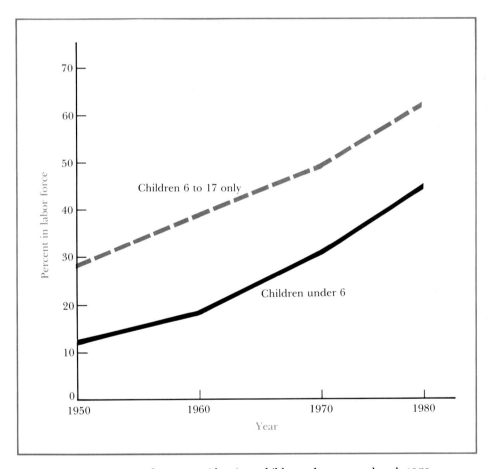

Figure 12.2 *Percentage of women with minor children who are employed, 1950–1980. (Source: U.S. Department of Labor, Bureau of Labor Statistics, 1980, table 26, Johnson and Walkman, 1981, table 3)*

The second kind of role strain is *interference*: the job calls for one thing to be done, while family obligations call for another. This type of role strain is illustrated by the case of a parent who has to decide whether to work on a report due the next day or on Halloween costumes for the children. All parents, fathers as well as mothers, have felt the pressures that come when children need one thing and work requires something else. Of course, family obligations can be things one should do for a spouse as well as for children. When an important client needs to be entertained on the same night as one's wedding anniversary, the role strain can be equally severe.

Empirical studies of the role strains produced by time shortages yield results that are to be expected from what we have already seen. Among dual-earner couples it is women, especially in families with preschool or school-age children, who experience the greatest pressures from time shortages (Voydanoff and Kelly, 1984). It is also not surprising that idividuals who report three or more important changes in their lives in the last year experience greater time shortages. These changes, such as divorce, death, new relationships, and increases in expenses, all reflect conditions that require more time.

One interesting research finding is that among couples in which the wife's occupation has greater prestige than her husband's occupation, both husband

Working women usually have the responsibility of caring for their children, but it is unusual to bring the child along to the workplace.

and wife report higher time shortages (Voydanoff and Kelly, 1984). One can speculate, as did the researchers who uncovered this fact, that the husbands in such couples are being asked to do more family work than other husbands. Since the wives in these couples also experience greater time pressures, we would guess that the demands of their jobs are greater than average, and that their husbands, despite their somewhat greater contribution to family work, are still not reducing their wives' family work loads by very much (Voydanoff and Kelly, 1984).

Work Schedules of Dual-Earner Couples

When both husband and wife are employed, they might have work schedules such that they go to work at the same time and return at the same time. At an opposite extreme, their work schedules might require that they work at completely different hours. The range of possibilities for matched or mismatched work schedules has become increasingly interesting as more and more husbands and wives are employed (Pleck and Staines, 1982). Several questions arise regarding these possibilities. First, when both husband and wife are employed, what is the extent of their having matching or mismatching schedules? Second, if husbands and wives have different work schedules, do these differences come from attempts to accommodate to the presence of children in the home? Third, if husbands and wives have different work schedules, what are the positive and negative effects of working at different times? We will address these questions in order.

Matched and mismatched work schedules. The evidence from national samples of employed couples reveals that it is rare for couples to have perfectly matched schedules—the same number of hours worked at exactly the same times (Nock and Kingston, 1984). Only eight and a half percent of all working couples have perfectly matched work schedules, leaving over ninety percent with mismatched schedules. It is true that many working couples have working schedules that are fairly closely matched, with about half having less than a three-hour difference in the particular hours they work. However, there is a substantial minority of couples who do work at very different times. Most often this is because one or the other is working at some time other than the "normal" working day. This is called *shift work*, and typically includes many service occupations. Frequently, these are occupations filled primarily by women, such as nurses (both professional and practical), waitresses, salesworkers, and telephone operators.

It has recently been observed that more than one-third of all employed couples with children under fourteen have at least one spouse working shift-work hours (Presser and Cain, 1983). The fact that shift work is so common among couples who have young children suggests that couples might adjust their work hours so that they can care for their children. As evidence supporting this idea, when wives are on shift work, especially as waitresses and practical nurses, in thirty percent of the cases their husbands take care of the children while the wives are at work (Presser and Cain, 1983). It is likely that many women who are on shift work choose it so husbands can care for the children rather than having to use other child-care services.

There is some qualitative research evidence that supports the conclusion that many married couples with children do meet some of their child-care needs by electing to work at different hours (Ferree, 1984; Robboy, 1983). Men working the night shift said that their major reason for choosing this shift was to give them an opportunity to assume routine child care while their wives worked. Some men said that shift work allowed them "to become more involved with their children" (Ferree, 1984, p. 71).

Positive and negative effects of mismatched work schedules. Since so many husbands and wives do have mismatched work schedules, we can reasonably ask about the positive and negative effects of this arrangement. While research has provided only limited answers to the question, some observations can nonetheless be made.

From the point of view of child care, we can guess that many couples see it as an advantage if a parent is caring for the children rather than someone else. The children are able to remain in the familiar surroundings of their own homes and with one of their parents. It is also an arrangement that does not require any cash payment to an outside party, so it carries an economic benefit as well. Finally, from a somewhat different perspective, it can be viewed as good that fathers as well as mothers have the experience of caring for their children. This is an issue we discussed in Chapter 11, where we saw that fathers who care for their children often feel that they gain insights about both their children and themselves that they would not otherwise have.

While there are some benefits with regard to child care when employed parents work different hours, the effects on marital relationships do not appear so positive. In the extreme case, there are couples who work completely different hours of the day. Eleven percent of working couples were found to have this degree of dissimilarity in their work schedules (Nock and Kingston, 1984). These husbands and wives must often be like "ships passing in the night," since the study shows that many have less than an hour between the time one spouse returns home and the other leaves for work. One can add to these another substantial group in which one spouse must leave for work before the other returns home.

One would suspect that mismatched work schedules would put strains on a marital relationship. However, there has not been enough research on couples with mismatched schedules to know whether these suspicions are correct. There is research on how dual-career couples fare generally, and, of course, couples with mismatched schedules are encompassed in this larger category.

Working parents often work at hours other than the 'normal' working day (shift work), so the other parent can care for the children.

We should keep this in mind as we see how dual-earner couples adjust to this arrangement.

There are two types of studies that tell us something about the effects of both husband and wife being employed. First, there are studies of the psychological effects on wives and husbands. Second, there are studies of the effects on the marital relationship.

The Psychological Effects of Employment on Women

Research on the psychological and mental health of married women who are employed has usually focused on the deleterious effects of not working (that is, being a full-time housewife) or on the potential positive or negative effects of having a job as well as family and household responsibilities. On the first point, there is research support for the idea that when women are full-time housewives, and especially when they have small children, their mental health is poorer than that of married women and mothers who are employed (Gove and

Geerken, 1977; Radloff, 1975). There are, however, some studies that have not confirmed this relationship, since they did not find greater psychological distress among full-time housewives (Pearlin, 1975; Wright, 1978).

With regard to the housewives, there is research evidence that their attitudes about employment are important determinants of their mental health. If full-time housewives do not want to have a job, they have much better mental health than housewives who want to be working (Gove and Peterson, 1980).

When we consider the potential positive or negative psychological effects on women who do have both job and family responsibilities, it raises the issue of role strains we considered earlier. While there is no doubt that dual obligations produce feelings of time shortages, it remains to be seen if they actually produce harmful psychological outcomes for women. On the one hand, it might seem that competing role obligations would naturally lead to psychological distress. But there is another perspective, one that emphasizes that when women have multiple roles they are exposed to more sources for gratification. In its simplest form this view depicts the housewife (and mother) as "housebound," carrying out a nonchallenging and low-prestige job. This view of the housewife role, insofar as it is held by women, could lead to more depression among housewives than among women who have outside jobs, since the latter would have other sources of self-esteem and gratification. Evidence for such a view can be found in the fact that women with jobs do tend to have higher self-esteem (Ferree, 1976; Gove and Peterson, 1980). Of course, even with this supporting evidence there is still some uncertainty about the direction of the causal relationship. It is possible that women with higher self-esteem are the women who will seek out jobs and enter the labor force, while those with lower self-esteem will remain at home.

At this point, the evidence on this issue can be summarized by saying that married women who have jobs generally seem to have better psychological health and higher self-esteem than married women who do not. But, as we will see below, this general statement may be modified in the light of how husbands feel about their wives being employed. We will return briefly to this point after we consider the psychological effects on husbands when their wives are employed.

Effects of Wives Working on Husbands

In recent years there has been considerable interest in whether husbands experience psychological distress when their wives are employed. Most researchers have hypothesized that husbands will have more depression, anxiety, loss of self-esteem and other symptoms of poor mental health when their wives are employed. This hypothesis comes from several related views, including the idea that when their wives work husbands will have doubts about their own abilities as breadwinners for their families. There is also the view that husbands will become psychologically distressed when, as a result of their wives working, they lose some of their power in the home and have to shoulder more responsibility for the work of the household.

While these ideas seem plausible, the research testing the hypothesis that husbands of employed women will suffer poorer mental health has not been strongly supportive. There are scattered pieces of positive evidence, but one researcher who examined the results of five other studies, plus his own data, concluded by saying, "There is no evidence to support the hypothesis that husbands whose wives work report more distress than husbands whose wives do not" (Fendrich, 1984). This statement can be accepted if it is qualified by adding "except under some conditions." For, as we will see, there are some circumstances under which some husbands do suffer negative psychological consequences when their wives are employed.

One of the most interesting interpretations of the circumstances under which husbands will suffer psychologically from their wives' employment has been offered by Ross et al. (1983). These researchers posit that there are four types of couples and that some types (both husbands and wives) will experience much greater psychological depression than others when the wife is employed. The four types of couples are the following:

Type I. This type of couple is one in which the wife cares for the home and children and the husband is the breadwinner, and both approve of this arrangement. (This is, of course, what we earlier called the breadwinner/ homemaker system, but it is important to note that in this conceptualization there is an attitudinal dimension: both husband and wife favor this division of labor.)

Type II. This type of couple is one in which the wife enters the labor force, usually for economic reasons. The wife takes a job because either the couple needs more money or they wish to achieve a particular standard of living. However, neither the wife nor the husband has a positive attitude about the wife working. The husband feels he is failing in his responsibility as breadwinner, and the wife feels she would not have to work if her husband were a better provider.

Type III. In this type of couple, the wife is working, and she and her husband are not negative about her doing so largely because the employment of women is more widespread. The husband may have fewer economic pressures because his wife is working. However, the Type III husband is not likely to give his wife much help with family and housework.

Type IV. This type of couple is one in which the wife is working because she wants to, and her doing so is enthusiastically accepted and supported by her husband. Furthermore, the husband is willingly providing support and assistance with housework and other family work.

In a cross-sectional national sample of United States married adults, all of these marriage types were still found (Ross et al., 1983). However, it is probably the case that a few decades ago the Type I couples predominated, only to be gradually replaced in many cases by Type II couples as women entered the labor force in greater numbers. In the last decade Type III couples have become more common, and even more recently, some couples have adopted the Type IV characteristics.

Most important for the question at hand, the effects of wives working are shown to be very dissimilar for the men in the different types of couples. The most important difference is the high level of depression among husbands in Type II couples. These men had wives who were working, but neither they nor their wives approved of having them do so. At the opposite extreme, among husbands who approved of women working and who backed their feelings by doing a greater share of the housework, the depression level was lowest (Ross et al., 1983).

The latter research finding is important because it is consistent with other studies showing that when men do contribute more to family and housework they do not have lower mental health (Kessler and McRae, 1982). Their wives do, however, have better mental health (Kessler and McRae, 1982; Ross et al., 1983). This raises again our earlier discussion of how working affects the mental health of married women. It is among the Type IV wives that the mental depression level is lowest, just as it is among the husbands of Type IV (Ross et al., 1983). The very important implication of this research is that the employment of married women does not have negative psychological effects for either husbands or wives if employment for women is viewed positively.

The further significance of the relationship comes from the way in which it reveals past and possibly future trends. If, as one might suppose, it becomes more and more common for wives to be employed, and if attitudes about their employment become more favorable among both men and women, then one can expect any negative effects of female employment on the mental health of men to be less and less in evidence. The same should be true for the mental health of women, especially if husbands take a more equal role in the care of children and other work of the household.

Dual-Earners and Marital Relationships

Our earlier discussion of the mismatched working schedules of many working couples, and time pressures in general, led to the question of how much marital relationships suffer when both husband and wife work. The research evidence is again mixed, but as one could easily anticipate from the preceding discussion, when a husband and wife disagree about the wife's working, they are likely to have a less happy relationship (Blumstein and Schwartz, 1983). This pattern might help to explain why one study has found that in the early stages of marriage, before children, the marriage relationship is better when the wife works than when she does not, but later, after there are children, the couples where the wife is not working are more satisfied with their relationship (Geerken and Gove, 1983). It may be that the stresses connected with having young children are exacerbated when both husband and wife are employed. At least one study has shown that among couples where wives are working there is more arguing about how the children are being raised (Blumstein and Schwartz, 1983).

Other recent studies have produced mixed results on the issue of marital quality. Two major studies found no differences in marital quality between dual-earner couples and couples in which the husband is the sole earner (Fendrich, 1984; Locksley, 1980). A study using a national sample of both husbands and wives found that the wife's employment enhanced marital quality for both husbands and wives (Simpson and England, 1982). Without denying that there are some contrary research results, it is reasonable to say that both husband and wife can have full-time jobs without its being detrimental to their marriage relationship. Whether it is detrimental or not depends on attitudes of both husband and wife (and especially whether they are in agreement or disagreement) about gender roles, housework, and child rearing.

When men feel that their own self-esteem is wrapped up in being the sole providers for their families, it is not surprising that it would be harmful to their marriages if their wives work. Consider the words of one husband on this point:

> Do you know what I think when I hear these guys who have wives that work while they have kids? That these guys have no respect for the family, and those women have no respect for themselves or their husband. I don't think my wife should respect me if I can't make enough money for her to stay home and raise the kids and have some time for herself. (Blumstein and Schwartz, 1983, p. 119)

While this is a very strongly stated point of view, it is not an isolated example. Among the thousands of married couples interviewed in this study, one-fourth of the wives and one-third of the husbands did not believe that both should work (Blumstein and Schwarz, 1983). It hardly needs to be said that the people who hold this opinion are assuming that it will be the husband who does work.

As a final point on the matter of dual-earners and marriage relationships, it is interesting to consider the couples in which traditional patterns are reversed—namely, the circumstance in which the woman is employed while her husband is not (or has a less prestigious job). One such case, of course, is when husbands are unemployed because they are unable to find work. The evidence on this situation is clear-cut. When men are unemployed and are unable to find work, it can be devastating for their marital (and family) relationships (Furstenberg, 1974; Komarovsky, 1940; Larson, 1984). In light of conventional expectations that all men will have jobs, and the traditional view of many that the man should be the major breadwinner of the family, it is not surprising that marital discord follows a period of unemployment. It is especially likely in blue-collar families that breakdowns in communication will occur among family members when the husband and father is unemployed (Komarovsky, 1940; Larson, 1984). It is often difficult for other members of the family to feel positive toward an unemployed husband and father. However, if men have had loving relationships with family members before they lose their jobs, it is much easier for them to retain their position in the family when they are out of work (Aldous et al., 1979).

A very different circumstance arises in those cases in which wives have occupations that are more important or more prestigious than their husbands' (Rubenstein, 1982). Most theoretical predictions suggest that there will be more marital disharmony in this situation. Husbands are expected to be more dissatisfied with their marital relationships when their wives have higher-status occupations. The research of Hornung and McCollough (1981) found that when wives had higher status occupations than their husbands there was more marital dissatisfaction. In a further study a more ominous product of wives having higher occupational status than their husbands was uncovered (Hornung et al., 1981). Among such couples there were higher rates of psychological abuse—insults, threats, swearing, kicking, and smashing of objects—and higher rates of life-threatening physical abuse—violence with a knife or gun. Both husbands and wives might be the perpetrators of these acts. This psychological and physical violence between husbands and wives was especially likely to be found among couples where the occupational status of the husband was lower than might be expected on the basis of his educational level (an "underachiever").

These signs of conflict among couples where the wife has an occupational status higher than her husband would lead one to expect higher marriage dissolution rates among such couples. A study of married couples over a seven-year period between 1967 and 1974 confirms that expectation (Philliber and Hiller, 1983). During this period, fifteen percent of the wives who had higher status jobs than their husbands obtained divorces. Among wives with lower status jobs than their husbands, nine percent were divorced during the same period (Rubenstein, 1982). One interpretation of this difference is that women with higher status jobs might have been more economically able to leave unsatisfactory marriages. An alternative interpretation is that husbands found it uncomfortable to be in marriages where their wives had higher status jobs. Both interpretations could, of course, contribute to the greater likelihood of divorce among couples where the wife has a higher status occupation.

While many couples in which the wife's job is of a higher status than that of her husband are in that position unintentionally, there are some couples who are there by choice. In one interesting study, two researchers located and interviewed a number of such couples. Atkinson and Boles (1984) identified forty-six married individuals (twenty-six wives and twenty husbands) who agreed that the wife's occupation would be more important than the occupation of her husband. Specifically, the husband and wife agreed that the couple would relocate for the wife's career, that moving for the wife's job would take precedence over the husband's work, and that "marriage and family life were organized around the wife's rather than the husband's career" (Atkinson and Boles, 1984, p. 862).

Among these couples with this special agreement, most of the wives' occupations were in traditional male fields and were higher than average in status (college professors, physicians, ministers, politicians, and business owners or executives). Husbands in these marriages had somewhat lower status occupations, when they were employed. They also typically had occupations that gave them a certain amount of flexibility in their working hours. Often, the husbands had been in careers but had either left them or retired.

Most of the respondents in this study acknowledged that there were some social costs connected with this occupational arrangement. They were often perceived by their relatives, friends, and co-workers as deviant. One father said of his son, who was relocating to accommodate a career move by his wife: "If he were any kind of a man, he wouldn't be following her like that" (Atkinson and Boles, 1984, p. 864). Women, as well as men, were often critical of the arrangements of these couples. Often the couples would reduce the social costs by hiding or concealing what they were doing.

Among many of these couples, the wives appeared to compensate for the possible costs incurred by their husbands who gave up part of the traditional masculine role. Female respondents spoke of doing some things with and for their husbands that overemphasized certain aspects of the traditional feminine role (appearing sexy, preparing romantic dinners, and catering to every whim of their husbands). Interestingly, in light of our previous discussion about home and family work, the wives in these households still claimed to spend more time on household tasks than their husbands. The husbands did not always agree, often seeing the housework as more evenly divided. However, this is not unusual, since a number of studies have shown that husbands think they do more household work than their wives think they do (Stein, 1984). The researchers concluded in this case that the wives' perceptions were more accurate and that they did do more of the household work than their husbands (Atkinson and Boles, 1984).

Even among these couples who had opted for the wife's job to be more important than her husband's, the influence of traditional gender roles can be seen in the behavior of both husbands and wives. While gender role orientations are changing, they are still strong enough to create special problems for couples who organize their working lives in alternative ways.

Throughout this chapter we have been dealing with the issues of work and family while making at least the implicit assumption that a family is made up of husband, wife, and usually children. While that assumption does have validity, it also neglects a large and growing category of family households: the single-parent household. In the next section we will give attention to the special circumstances of the single parent who works outside the home.

WORK AND THE SINGLE PARENT

The term *single-parent household* refers to a household in which there is one adult living with his or her minor child or children. However, while both fathers and mothers can be single parents, in about ninety percent of the cases it is the mother who heads the household when only one parent is present (Fuchs, 1983). Most single-parent families (about eighty-five percent) today are produced by divorce or separation rather than the death of a spouse. In addition, some single-parent households are produced when women have children but remain unmarried. Both divorce and unmarried parenthood increased greatly during the 1970s, resulting in a fifty percent increase in the proportion of children living with only one parent.

These are the demographic facts about single-parent families, but the most important fact is that female-headed households are the most impoverished segment of the American population. (See Figure 12.3) During the 1970s the number of families living in poverty changed very little, but the composition of these families changed dramatically. The number of poor families headed by males (a category that includes families with both parents as well as father-only families) dropped by about twenty percent, while the number of poor families headed by women increased by one-third (Pearce and McAdoo, 1981). This trend has led to the phrase "the feminization of poverty."

The poverty of women, and especially women alone who have minor children, stems from two basic sources. First, these women carry the major burden of child rearing. This means that the burden of physically caring for children falls to them, but it also means that the economic burden is largely theirs as well. Substantial evidence shows that divorced and separated men provide only a small part of the child support they are legally obligated to pay. One study in the 1970s revealed that only twenty-five percent of those women eligible actually received child support. Among those who did receive child support, sixty percent received less than $1,500 in a year (Pearce and McAdoo, 1981). It is stating the obvious to say that this amount is inadequate to meet the needs of a child.

For single parents who have never been married (almost always mothers), only eight percent were ever judged eligible by the courts to receive support from the fathers of their children. Only five percent actually received any payments (Pearce and McAdoo, 1981). These single parents are found in study after study to have the highest percentages living below the official poverty level.

A second major reason for poverty in female-headed families is that, in general, opportunities for women in the labor force are limited by occupational segregation and gender discrimination (Pearce and McAdoo, 1981). Women with college educations earn about the same amount as men with eighth-grade educations; thus, "the opportunity for a woman with an eighth-grade education to earn a 'living wage' is considerably limited" (Pearce and McAdoo, 1981, p. 18). A further exacerbating factor is that among the one-parent families in the United States there is an overrepresentation of black families. Thirty-seven percent of

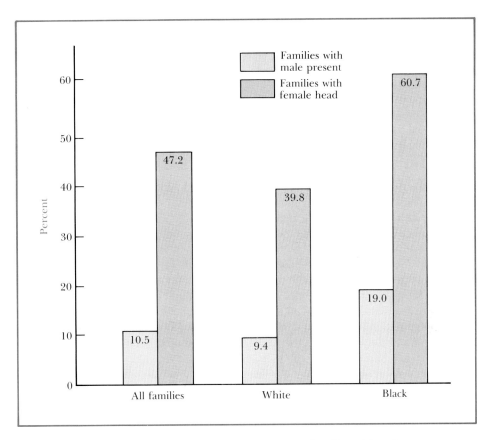

Figure 12.3 *Percent at or below the poverty level among families with male present and headed by a female. (Source: U.S. Census, Current Population Reports, Series P-66, No. 147. "Characteristics of the Population Below the Poverty Level: 1983." Table 19, pp. 72–75)*

all children living in one-parent households are black, while only fifteen percent of all children under eighteen are black (Gongla, 1982). Since blacks are still subject to racial discrimination in the occupational world, the plight of black female heads of families is made even more difficult.

Before proceeding with a further consideration of the problems of the one-parent family, it is necessary to issue a cautionary note. There is a tendency among many observers to classify all one-parent families as social problems and the source of social pathologies. This reaction comes, in part, from the association with poverty just identified. However, as Gongla (1982) has pointed out, the one-parent family is also perceived as a problem because it deviates from the "normal" two-parent family. This bias might mask some of the strengths of the one-parent family. In such families, the relationship between the children and the parent might be closer and more supportive than exists in many two-parent families. One should also avoid assuming that one-parent families will automatically produce pathologies in children. Most children who grow up in one-parent homes are as "normal" as children who live in two-parent homes (Gongla, 1982; Herzog and Sudia, 1968).

With this point made, it is nonetheless the case that the contradictory demands of job and family that we have seen in dual-earner couples are intensified in single-parent families. An empirical study of employed, divorced mothers with children under the age of thirteen addressed the issue of how mothers handle the conflicts between job demands and the needs of their children (Johnson, 1983). In general, the findings of this study showed that, when there was conflict, it was the interests of the children that took precedence over the demands of the job. In most cases the mother herself handled the problem rather than turning it over to someone else. The most common needs of children are illness or injury while the mother is working, or is supposed to be working. Another recurrent problem is that children have appointments with doctors or dentists during the mother's working hours.

A number of anticipated conflicts between job and children had never arisen for the divorced mothers in this sample. For example, only a minority of them had been required to travel out of town for their jobs or had been required to work on a holiday. However, the fact that their jobs had not created these conflicts is largely a function of the level of jobs they held. Most of these divorced mothers were in clerical or service occupations, which had relatively low-level demands on their time. If a family matter (the illness of a child) demanded attention, it was apparently fairly easy for these mothers to miss or leave work. However, this may imply two things regarding income. First, the general salary level for such jobs is low (in 1977 the women in this sample earned an average of $8,400). Second, many of these women, especially those in service occupations (i.e., waitressing), are likely to lose hourly wages or tips when they take time off from work. Thus, while the demands of work do not seem to create insurmountable obstacles to meeting family needs, the level of income derived from these jobs is low. As other studies have shown, this leads to greater amounts of social and psychological stress in life (McLanahan, 1983). Female heads of families, compared to male heads, have lower self-esteem, less feeling of control over their lives, and less hopefulness about the future. All these negative psychological effects probably reflect, at least in part, the considerably lower incomes of female-headed families (McLanahan, 1983).

THE FAMILY AND WORK IN THE YEARS AHEAD

In the twentieth century, and especially in the last twenty years, the most significant change with regard to work and its relationship to the family has been the return of large numbers of women to the work force. Some women work because they have to, while others work because they want to, but for a great many women the reason for working is both need and the satisfaction that comes from having a job. Women, no less than men, work because it gives them a "sense of participation and purpose in society which having a job can provide" (Ferree, 1984, p. 73). In terms more closely connected to the family, many women work for the same reasons that men work: by doing so they are making a contribution to the well-being of their families (Ferree, 1984).

As we try to look ahead to the relationship of working and the family in the future, we must remember that being employed, for many people, is not the same thing as having a career. The idea of a career is more relevant for the highly educated and the middle and upper-middle classes. A career is an occupation that one enters with the idea of making advances, and if possible climbing to the top of a profession or field. The working classes, especially, but perhaps many in the middle class as well, do not see their occupations in this way (Ferree, 1984). From the working-class view, "a good job is a means to a good living, but achievement in a specialized vocation is not the measure of a person's worth, not even for a man" (Komarovsky, 1962, p. 57). Clearly, if a job is not thought of as a career for a man in the working class, it will probably not be so considered for most women in the working class (Ferree, 1984).

Thus, as we look toward the future of working and its relation to the family, we can expect that a great many Americans will continue with a very "traditional" view. Men will have jobs, if possible, and their jobs will be seen as the primary economic support of the family. Wives will have jobs when family finances call for them to supplement the husbands' income (or, in the event of unemployment, to keep the family economically afloat). For these Americans there may not be much movement toward more equalitarian notions of gender roles in the family, although some research among blue-collar families has found that as a wife's work becomes more an economic necessity for the family she is able to negotiate a more equitable sharing of household labor (Ferree, 1984).

Moving to the level of Americans who have higher educational and professional training, where careers are possible for both husbands and wives, a different picture emerges. First, some couples at this level will continue some version of what we called the breadwinner/homemaker system. In all likelihood this arrangement, with the husband the full-time earner and the wife playing a complementary and supportive role, will be found most prominently in cases where men have very high-status professions or executive positions.

A modified version of this arrangement is what has been called the "senior partner/junior partner" arrangement (Scanzoni, 1980). In this type of arrangement, the husband has a career, which is viewed as the primary and most important source of income and status for the family. The wife may also have a career, but it will be one that is secondary, in terms of both income and status. The wife in this arrangement may simply have a job that provides either extra discretionary income or simply the opportunity to get out into the work world.

It is, however, the dual-career couple that is most often discussed as the "emerging" arrangement among the middle and upper-middle classes. This arrangement is one where "the rights and responsibilities of each spouse relative to the occupational system, and also to the household, [are] relatively interchangeable" (Scanzoni, 1980, p. 127). In a regional sample of young wives, Scanzoni found twenty-three percent saying in 1975 that they and their husbands shared equally in the financial support of the family. The wives among these couples also report more often than do the wives of the other couples in the sample that their husbands participate in household tasks. However, there is no evidence that the husbands in these marriages are sharing this work equally.

The researcher who carried out this analysis estimates that in the years to come this type of marriage arrangement will "edge upward" (Scanzoni, 1980, p. 128). But that view is not shared by all. To begin with, there is scant evidence, as we have already seen, that husbands and wives are moving toward sharing the family work equitably. Even among couples where the wife's occupation is viewed as primary, women are still doing slightly more of the household work. Among most couples the wife continues to carry a substantially disproportionate part of the load.

But there is yet another view of the future of work and family. This view is that among husbands and wives who both wish to have careers, with both pushing toward full achievement, it will be necessary to give up a substantial part of family life (Hunt and Hunt, 1982). Specifically, the argument is that in order to be fully competitive in two high-level careers it will be necessary for a married couple to give up having children and the accompanying features of family life. As an alternative, one or the other of the couple might push for a successful career, while the other plays a supportive, or junior-partner, role. In that case, it would be possible to have children, but that would put couples back into one of the two more conventional marriage arrangements.

What these observers expect for the future, at least among the higher status groups, is that many couples will consciously decide to have children and a full family life. But at the same time, believing in an equalitarian relationship between husbands and wives, they will recognize that *both* will have to give up some achievement in their careers. Neither will play the necessary supportive role that would have allowed the other full concentration on career achievement (Hunt and Hunt, 1982). Exactly how accurate this assessment is, and if it is accurate how many couples will opt for it, is difficult to say. It does, however, represent an option that is often overlooked when considering the future of work and family relationships.

There is one additional view about the family and work that is a by-product of computers becoming an ever more influential part of our society. As home computers become more versatile and effective, it is possible that more and more working people can remain in their homes while doing their work (Toffler, 1980). Linked by telephone to a computer in some central place, it will be possible to receive work assignments and send in completed work without ever leaving one's home. If both husband and wife have such jobs (or careers), family life could be transformed in ways that are nearly unimaginable. Child care, just to take one example, could be handled *while* parents are at work. Or parents could "work around" the times when their children need them. Fathers could easily have more time available to care for their children, and thus reduce the weight of child care that currently falls to mothers. And, to be very speculative, all of these factors could possibly lead to an increase in the number of children couples might be able to have, even though both husband and wife were employed.

In the more immediate future, we can be sure that for the majority of married couples both husband and wife will be working, at least during some periods of the marriage. Exactly how their respective jobs (or careers) will influence and shape marital relationships and family life will depend on how they define the relative importance of "her work," "his work," and family work.

For those husbands and wives who define their respective jobs as equally important, there is one issue we have not yet addressed. What should married couples do when the job of one requires moving? We live in a mobile society, and often career or professional advancement comes in the form of an opportunity in another state, or even in another country. But often the opportunity of one spouse may work to the disadvantage of the other. When a couple faces this situation, a decision must be made. Perhaps the decision can be made on the basis of whose job or career should take precedence. But when both jobs or careers are of equal importance, couples may have to consider a different solution. They may have to weigh the merits of setting up two households and living separately much of the time. Such an arrangement has been variously called the *two-household*, the *long-distance*, or the *commuter marriage* (Gerstel and Gross, 1984). As the closing issue of this chapter, we will consider the arguments for and against commuter marriage.

ISSUE

Weighing the costs and benefits of a commuter marriage

Commuter marriage is not so much a philosophical or moral issue as it is a practical issue. Generally, couples consider entering into a commuter marriage because of necessity, not because it is a preferred style of life. There may be exceptions to this rule, but we will begin with the assumption that couples who consider the possibility of a commuter marriage are attempting to evaluate whether the costs will exceed the benefits. Usually they are asking if the advantages related to career or occupational objectives can outweigh the disadvantages of living apart. They can do this only by marshaling the advantages and disadvantages on both sides of the issue and making a decision on the basis of the greatest relative benefit. We will follow the same procedure in the discussion that follows.

For the purposes of this discussion, some major dimensions of a hypothetical couple who might be considering a commuter marriage will be arbitrarily defined. First, it will be assumed that the couple has no children, since children would be an additional complicating factor. One of the spouses has a career or occupational opportunity that requires moving to another state, too far away for daily commuting. The other spouse must remain in the present community because of his or her career or occupation. These circumstances require that separate residences be established in both communities and that the couple will not be able to be together except for intermittent weekends and holiday periods. While this arrangement will not be permanent, it will last for at least a year and probably more. With these conditions specified, we are now ready to consider the arguments on both sides of the issue, beginning with those against commuter marriage.

Arguments against Commuter Marriage

The fundamental disadvantage of a commuter marriage is that it runs counter to the very essence of what marriage is supposed to provide. Most people marry because they want the regular companionship of another person. They want to spend their lives with someone they love, are friends with, and feel comfortable with. For many people the world of work is filled with problems, competitors, deadlines, and tensions, while home and marriage provide a "safe haven" where they can find relaxation, companionship, and rejuvenation for the next working day. In a commuter marriage many of these comforts are lost. Certainly it is possible for a couple in a commuter marriage to use the telephone as a substitute for face-to-face conversation and companionship, but that is both limited and expensive.

The economic costs associated with commuter marriage are not to be ignored, for the expenses of maintaining two residences, traveling, and calling long-distance are substantial. Only couples who expect to make a considerable financial gain from their respective jobs are apt to be able to afford such a costly arrangement.

But even if economic considerations are not prohibitive, there are other noneconomic costs that must be considered. Couples who live apart often report that their leisure time is not fully satisfying. First, and obviously, leisure time spent with the spouse is severely limited. It should be noted that this includes time spent in sexual and other romantic activities. These are important parts of married life that often must be packed into a brief weekend. As a related problem, many couples who live separately report that when they are together there is a "re-entry time" during which they have to become comfortable with each other again.

Other leisure time activities are also affected by commuter marriage arrangements, including especially the spontaneous, spur-of-the-moment things that married couples do when the mood strikes them. When couples have only a weekend every month or so there is scarcely any time for spontaneity, and many commuter marriage couples report a tendency to plan activities in order not to waste any of their precious time (Gerstel and Gross, 1982).

The commuter marriage has another disadvantage related to leisure time, but it is of a more social nature. Apparently "married singles" face the same kinds of problems as divorced and widowed persons in a largely married world. Married couples often find it difficult to integrate the single, but married, person into their social activities. As a result, commuter marriage individuals do not receive as many social invitations, or, if they do, other people often do not know how to deal with them (Gerstel and Gross, 1982).

Finally, one of the major drawbacks of a commuter marriage is that it can raise the specter of extramarital sexual relations and the possibility that marital partners may grow apart because they are separated so much of the time. Research studies have not found extramarital sexual relationships to be especially related to commuter marriages, but certainly the potential exists, and at the very least suspicion and jealousy can easily emerge. Couples who consider a commuter marriage must examine the soundness and flexibility of their relationship very carefully, or they may encounter serious problems. If a marriage is shaky to begin with, it may crumble when it becomes a commuter marriage.

Summing up the negative arguments, the commuter marriage removes some of the major pleasures and comforts of marriage. It is costly in an economic sense, and in a social sense, because it can isolate a person from pleasant social company. Commuter marriage can also lead to serious problems in a marriage, especially if the marriage is not basically sound at the outset.

Arguments for Commuter Marriage

Since the usual purpose for a commuter marriage is career advancement, one obvious advantage of this arrangement is that couples can maximize their individual occupational opportunities. When a job or career calls for moving, the opportunity may be too great to pass up. At the same time, the other spouse may find the costs of moving too great to bear. The pluses on one side and the minuses on the other may add up to a very strong case for having separate residences.

Career advancement may be particularly enhanced by commuter marriages because spouses who live alone can give their uninterrupted and undivided attention to their work. Husbands and wives who live separately can concentrate on work without having to adapt to another person's schedule or needs. If people living alone feel like skipping dinner to continue working, or if they wish to get up at three in the morning to start working, they can do so without taking into account how it will affect their spouses.

Many commuter marriage couples find advantages for husband-wife relations as well as for careers. Day-in and day-out marriage can lead to a certain routineness and even boredom with the relationship. When two people live apart most of the time it is certainly much more difficult for them to become bogged down in daily routines with their spouses. Many commuter couples report that each new meeting is like a fresh start and a time to be cherished. Their relationship is given the highest priority; and they often report that during times together they do not take each other for granted. They are also likely to avoid arguments about "tremendous trifles" (Gerstel and Gross, 1982).

As a last advantage of commuter marriage, many couples note with pleasure how living separately has helped them break out of many traditional gender role behaviors. Both men and women learn that they can handle things they had previously treated as appropriate only for the opposite sex. Men learn that they can prepare meals and sew on buttons, and find a new pleasure in doing so. Women likewise find new confidence in doing things they had always left to their husbands.

In summary, the greatest advantages coming from commuter marriage are usually associated with individual career advancement for both members of a marriage. But there may be several latent advantages for the marriage relationship itself. The foremost is that commuter couples learn to appreciate and make the most of the time they have together. The breakdown of rigid traditionalism along gender lines is also valued by many husbands and wives.

Themes

1. The areas of family and work are closely intertwined, with events in one affecting the other.
2. In the recent past, the relationship between work and family was divided along gender lines, with men as "breadwinners" and women as "homemakers."
3. The emergence of the breadwinner/homemaker system emerged with the advent of the industrial revolution in the nineteenth century.
4. The "cult of true womanhood" idealized the role of women as caregivers for husband and children.
5. The breadwinner/homemaker ideology was still in full force in the 1950s but has been breaking down since that decade.
6. The breadwinner/homemaker system today is still found among the wealthiest families and many professional families.
7. Among dual-earner couples there has been only a modest increase in the amount of household work done by men.
8. Many dual-earner couples have mismatched work hours, which allows one parent to be in the home caring for children while the other is working.
9. The psychological health of women is better among women who work outside the home. The psychological health of husbands is more closely related to the attitudes that they and their wives have about the wives working.
10. The psychological health of men is closely tied to their own employment, and is especially influenced by unemployment.
11. Single-parent mothers have a special economic burden in American society, and often have lower self-esteem and a feeling of less control over their lives.

Facts

1. The movement of women out of the work world and into the home reached its greatest heights between 1860 and 1920.
2. At the beginning of the twentieth century, only about five percent of married women were employed outside the home.
3. Currently, over fifty percent of all married women are in the labor force.
4. In professional occupations, men are overrepresented in medicine, law, and engineering, while women are overrepresented in nursing, elementary education, and as librarians.
5. Thirty-five percent of all employed women are in clerical and service occupations.
6. Husbands whose wives are employed spend only a fraction of an hour more on family work than husbands whose wives are not employed.

7. Marital disharmony is greater when wives have more prestigious occupations than their husbands.

8. Among dual-earner couples, women experience the greatest pressure from shortages of time.

9. Over one-third of all employed couples with children under fourteen have at least one spouse working shift work.

10. Ninety percent of single-parent households are headed by women.

11. During the 1970s there was a fifty percent increase in the number of children living with only one parent.

Major Concepts

balancing: A word used to characterize the problem of finding time to meet both family and work obligations.

breadwinner/homemaker system: Label given to the arrangement under which husbands provided for the economic needs of the family while wives remained in the home caring for husbands and children.

commuter marriage: Husbands and wives living in separate places because of their jobs or occupations (*Also* **two-household and long-distance marriage**).

"cult of true womanhood": An ideology regarding women that emerged in the nineteenth century, emphasizing how women were responsible for maintaining the virtues of home and family life.

dual-career couples: A term used to refer to couples where both husband and wife have occupations that require special training, and there is potential for moving up to higher status positions.

dual-earner couples: A general term to cover married couples where both husband and wife have paid employment. *Compare with* dual-career couples.

family work: Work done in the home or for the family, such as cooking, cleaning, and caring for children.

interference: A type of role strain that comes from having to do something for one's work at the same time as something needs to be done for one's family.

long-distance marrige: **See commuter marriage.**

overload: A type of role strain that comes from having too many things to do, and too little time.

role strain: The tension created by the conflicting expectations of work and family obligations.

senior partner/junior partner arrangement: A marital arrangement in which a married couple agrees that the husband's career is primary and the major source of income, while the wife's career or occupation is secondary.

two-household marriage: **See commuter marriage.**

13

Conflict and Violence in the Family

Husband-Wife Conflict, Spouse and Child Abuse, and Sibling Conflict

In several earlier chapters we encountered instances of conflict and violence between husbands and wives, as well as among other family members. We noted in the chapter on love (Chapter 3) that among the Yanomamo people of northern Brazil wives in some instances considered the abusive treatment they received from their husbands as a sign of their love. In Chapter 8 when we considered husband-wife relations, we observed that among the Pakhtun people of Pakistan husbands and wives have relationships with such continuing conflict and fighting that their marriages have been characterized as "warfare." The Pakhtun home may be a virtual prison for the wife, where she frequently receives beatings from her husband. But when her husband is in the home he often faces a hostile adversary who returns as much as she gets in fighting and aggression (Lindholm and Lindholm, 1979).

In the chapter on child rearing (Chapter 11), we saw how children of the past, in both Europe and the United States, were severely punished, mistreated, abused, and even killed. All these examples, and there are others that could be added, tell us clearly that conflict and violence do occur within the family. Yet we may easily discount these illustrations as happening in other places and at other times and as having no particular relevance to our own society in the present.

Of course, in recent years we have heard much more about "battered wives" and "abused children" because of the amount of media attention they have received. Yet, even though we are aware of conflict and violence in contemporary American families, these may still be dismissed as being unusual, deviant, or pathological. In other words, we may define conflict and violence as things that occur to "other" people, people who are "sick" or mentally ill, or even criminal. That may be an appropriate interpretation of some issues, but we will also see that it is not possible to dismiss all conflict and violence as something that occurs to others, or as something done by "bad" people.

As we take a closer look at conflict and violence in the pages ahead, two major themes will emerge clearly:

1. There is some conflict in every marriage and in all families.
2. Violence occurs more often in marriage and family life than we suppose.

These two themes have practical implications and significance for our personal lives. By understanding the characteristics and causes of conflict and violence, we will be in a better position to cope with them, wherever and however we encounter them. It may be that we will encounter conflict and violence in our personal lives, or in the lives of our friends and co-workers, or perhaps through the kind of work we do. Very few of us will be completely spared from experiencing the conflict and violence that occurs in marriage and family life.

The primary focus in this chapter will be on husbands and wives and their relationships. However, both conflict and violence also occur between parents and children, and between siblings. Some attention will be given to these family relationships later in the chapter.

CONFLICT IN MARRIAGE

There are some married couples who become habituated to conflict. Their marriage relationships, which have been called conflict habituated, are virtually built around more or less continuous bickering, arguing, and fighting. But these couples represent only a minority of all married couples, and we need not focus exclusively on them as we examine the issue of conflict. We will see below that conflict also occurs in the lives of average, "normal," and "happily-married" couples.

To understand conflict between husbands and wives, it is necessary to take a closer look at the concept of conflict. The meaning of *conflict* may be obvious in the sense that we can all recognize it when we see it, but we must give it a little closer analysis if we are to understand it fully.

The Meaning of Conflict

Without usually recognizing it, people often use the word *conflict* to refer to several different things (Gelles and Straus, 1979). When one says, "There was a conflict about where Bill and Mary were going on vacation," it can mean something quite different from when one says, "Bill and Mary had a conflict over where they would go on vacation." The first sentence might simply mean that there was a difference of opinion, or that Bill had one preference about where to go and Mary had another. In this sense, the word *conflict* is closer to the way it is used when referring to a "schedule conflict" in an academic program. Two things are competing, and one cannot have both.

The second sentence, "Bill and Mary had a conflict . . .", implies something closer to a fight, or at least an argument. Conflict in this usage is closely related

Conflict between marital partners refers to means, methods, or behaviors used to resolve conflicting interests. These two individuals are using words, gestures, body language, and facial expressions.

to the way in which one would speak of two countries being in an "armed conflict."

One might also speak of "the conflict between Bill and Mary," meaning that the two of them dislike or are hostile toward each other. In this sense the word conflict refers to a negative emotional feeling between two people, or more simply, hostility.

We now have three ways in which the word *conflict* can be used, and if we are going to be clear about what we are discussing, we will have to keep the distinctions among them as clear as possible. To make the necessary distinctions, we will use three different terms: conflict of interest, conflict, and hostility (Gelles and Straus, 1979). These follow the order of the three usages above, but for convenience they can be summarized as follows:

Conflict of interest: the competing opinions, preferences, desires, or needs of two people (or groups).

Conflict: the means, methods, or behaviors used to resolve conflicting interests.

Hostility: the negative emotional feelings (dislike, hatred) that can prevail between two people (or groups).

With these distinctions in mind, some further observations can be made about conflict within families. The first of these is a refinement of the earlier assertion that there is conflict in every marriage and in all families. We can now be more precise by saying there is *conflict of interest* in every marriage and in all families. There is, in fact, a sociological theory, called *conflict theory*, that makes this assertion for all social groups, including the family. This general theory will be sketched out briefly here because it will sensitize us to the important point that neither the family, nor any other social group can avoid "conflicts of interest." And if any group, including the family, does so, it would probably be bad for the group.

Conflict Theory

There are a number of expressions of conflict theory in sociology, but we will limit our consideration here to those elements of the theory that are most important for our discussion of the family (Collins, 1971; Coser, 1956; Dahrendorf, 1959; Scanzoni, 1972). A basic proposition of conflict theory is that every social group will have positions (or statuses), and these positions will be arranged according to power. Often, individuals in the higher positions will have power because their positions are vested with authority. This means that the individuals who are in those positions will have *the right* to exert power over other people in the group. As we have seen a number of times, the traditional patriarchal system gives the father power over other family members.

Even if power is not vested in a position by some tradition, power will be held by someone, if for no other reason than their superior physical strength. Here, too, males usually have the advantage over females and children. Some writers hold the view that the physical advantage of men over women and children is the original source of the patriarchal system (Collins, 1971).

According to conflict theory, those persons in a group who are in the subordinate positions are rather continuously trying to have their interests and needs met, even though such interests and needs are in conflict with the interests of the person (or persons) in power. Perhaps the clearest family example of the workings of this principle is the way in which children try, in the face of the superior power of their parents, to have their interests and needs met. A sixteen- or seventeen-year-old is likely to see an automobile as an important need, but parents often feel it is best to keep teenagers from driving (an obvious conflict of interest).

Conflict theorists argue that the open expression of conflicts of interests among members of a group is also good for the health and well-being of the group. This may seem like a strange and even ridiculous idea, but perhaps their point will be clearer if we examine the extreme and opposite case. Suppose one person in a group has supreme power over all other members, so that there can be no expression of conflicts of interest by the subordinate members of the group. Supreme power means that one person has a life-and-death control over other members of the group. The all-powerful one can be as unreasonable or capricious as he (or she) wishes to be, and there is nothing the others can do. Just on an intuitive basis, this does not seem like a healthy kind of group, and there are some examples that bear out that intuition.

As one example, it has been argued that the absolute power that slave owners in American society had over their slaves in the nineteenth century produced a number of negative outcomes. The slaves who lived under the absolute control of slave owners are said to have developed impaired personalities because they had so little control over their own lives (Elkins, 1959). The slaves often developed an outside demeanor that was submissive, while on the inside they harbored deep hostility and resentment. A parallel case has been found in the circumstances of the Jews and others who were held in German concentration camps during World War II. Again, the camp inmates were completely dominated and controlled by their prison guards. In this system, too, where absolute power was in the hands of one group, it produced both personality impairment (submissiveness) and hostility among those who were so dominated (Elkins, 1959).

In the family, a comparable situation exists in those reported cases in which one member of the family (often the father) dominates and terrorizes other family members. Consider the following report of a woman named Mary McGuire describing how her husband used terror to dominate members of his family:

> I know the horrors of beating; of being shot at and pistol whipped; of being tied up to watch while my grave was being dug; of having my husband hold a gun to my child's head demanding obedience and threatening to pull the trigger; of trying to prevent my 12-year old daughter from being raped by my husband, while Father laughs, "I am king of this house and can do as I damn well please." (Meyers, 1983)

The wife in this case was driven to the extreme of trying to solicit someone to kill her husband and served a five-year prison sentence for that offense.

Such cases, where some members of a group have virtually no ability to press for their interests, do suggest that absolute control does not make a very healthy social system. This is consistent with the view of conflict theorists, who say it is better for the well-being of groups if members can press for their particular interests, desires, and needs. The conflict theorists' major argument is that groups allowing this kind of action by their members are going to be able to change, adjust, and adapt better than more rigid groups. From their view, change is not only inevitable in any social system, but it is a positive value.

Perhaps the best argument for allowing group members to press for their interests, even when they are in conflict with those of other members of the group, is that if they are not allowed to do so hostility builds up. Eventually, when suppressed hostility finally breaks out, it can be very explosive. This issue will be discussed in more detail shortly, but for the moment it can stand as a tenet of conflict theory.

To summarize the insights from conflict theory, we can say that conflicts of interest will exist among members of every social group. To allow these conflicts of interests to have expression is good for the individuals and for the group as a whole. Thus, conflict theory leads us to a very different conclusion than one we might have started with. If one were to ask the average person on the street, "Which is best for the family, conflict or no conflict?" the answer in many cases would probably have been the latter. If we agree now that we are specifically talking about the freedom of family members to press for their conflicting interests, even when they are in opposition to the interests of more powerful family members, perhaps we can see that some degree of conflict is a better choice. At the very least, it now becomes a more open question.

One final point about conflicts of interests can be made here. When the family was organized along patriarchal lines, there was probably relatively little expression of conflicting interests by the less powerful members of the family. But in the twentieth century, as the egalitarian ideal came to be accepted by most people, and this ideal was supported by the increasing resources of women (through their education and employment), the gates have been opened for more, not less, open expression of conflicting views between husbands and wives. We should keep this trend in mind as we examine conflict among married couples.

The Issues That Produce Conflict

It will help to understand marital conflict if we know more about the issues and topics about which couples commonly disagree. A number of surveys have asked couples about their areas of disagreement, and while the results of these studies are not always exactly the same, there is enough consistency to see the most likely points of conflict in marriage.

The two issues that show up prominently in every survey are *money* and *children* (Scanzoni and Scanzoni, 1981; Straus et al., 1980). Usually these are at the top of the list, with money being the most common area of conflict. One survey based on a national sample of married couples, however, found *housekeeping* to be a more prominent area of disagreement than either money or children (Straus et al., 1980). A fourth area that creates disagreement for many couples is *sex*. We will review these four major sources of conflict, beginning with problems over money.

Conflict over money. American married couples often argue about making money, particularly about not making enough. But even more frequently they argue about spending it. It hardly seems too strong to assert that if a husband and wife have the same standards and principles about making money and spending it, they will have considerably reduced their chances of marital conflict.

On the earning side, couples who are dissatisfied with their incomes are also more likely to report that they are dissatisfied with their marriages. "It is difficult to be poor but happy" is the way two researchers put it (Blumstein and Schwartz, 1983, p. 67). However, having disputes about too little money does not mean that couples are worried about their physical survival, at least not usually in American society. Money is a symbol for many other things. Earning money is a symbol for self-worth (especially for men); money is a symbol for security (especially for women); and money is often a symbol for the success of the marriage (Blumstein and Schwartz, 1983). It is understandable, therefore, that couples who are having a hard time economically would find this a conflict area in their lives.

However, even when couples are doing well economically, there are still often problems about managing money. Indeed, "couples argue more about how [their] money is managed than about how much they have—and this holds true despite their actual income level" (Blumstein and Schwartz, 1983, p. 77). It is very common in marriages for wives to have the traditional role as buyers for the family. If husbands in these marriages do not second-guess the purchasing decisions of their wives, the system can run smoothly. However, conflict frequently arises when husbands in these marriages are critical of the way their wives handle the family purchases. One wife in this type of marriage complained vehemently to an interviewer about her husband's reactions:

> We fight about money. . . . When he sees the bills and how much is on the charge, he has a f——, s——fit . . . we have a fight because I get really insulted. . . . I feel it's a personal insult when he starts yelling about how high the bills are. (Blumstein and Schwartz, 1983, p. 82)

For other couples the situation is reversed, and it is the husband's spending that upsets the wife. One woman described her former husband's style of buying as follows:

> He would go out and get a fancy job and then he would buy a hundred things because he thought he could afford it. So we'd have instant debt as soon as we had instant money, and then he'd get fired and all we had were debts. The highs weren't worth the lows. . . . It got to where we couldn't stand the sight of one another. (Blumstein and Schwartz, 1983, p.69)

Attitudes about money and the use of money are usually deeply ingrained, and often have their origins in early family life experiences. When two people marry, their independent attitudes about money and the use of it must somehow be integrated. Judging from the research on marital conflict, many couples do not have the same attitudes about money, and their marriages suffer when they fail to achieve a satisfactory level of agreement on this issue.

Conflict over children.   We know from an earlier chapter that marital quality goes down when married couples have children. There may be many reasons for this, but it appears from the research on marital conflict that couples often have disagreements that center around their children.

However, exactly what parents find to disagree about is not as clearly known. We can certainly guess that a major area of disagreement is over how children are to be raised. Again, as with attitudes about money, most adults probably formulated their attitudes about child rearing while growing up in their own families. Perhaps many people do not even recognize their deep-seated ideas about the appropriate ways to rear children until they actually have them. This is a variant case of what, in an earlier chapter, we called *marital scripts*. In this case, we can call them *parental scripts*, which can be defined as unconscious and unspoken expectations about what is proper and appropriate parenting behavior.

A husband and wife may very likely have entered parenthood without ever discussing their parental scripts, except in very superficial ways. Their areas of disagreement may surface only when they have their first child. This is borne out by one national study where nearly one-half of couples with young children reported that they had "open disagreements or fights" about how to raise the children at least once every few months (Blumstein and Schwartz, 1983, p. 561). Among couples where the wife is working full-time, the likelihood of disagreeing or fighting about how to raise the children is just slightly higher than among couples where the wife is not working. This suggests that the dual-earner couples are having some of the problems of time management we discussed in the last chapter. However, even among the couples where the wife is not working, forty-five percent report that they have disagreements or fights at least once every few months over the issue of child rearing.

As children grow older, parents are often faced with various crises or problems that are brought on by the behavior of the children. When these arise, there is often no well-defined norm for how to deal with the situation. In the absence of clear-cut principles or rules, it is not uncommon for two parents to have differing views. As the crises or problems increase in seriousness (delinquency, truancy, drug abuse, running away from home) they produce high levels of anxiety and tension in the family, which may also contribute to disagreements and fights between the parents.

Conflict over housekeeping and housework. In most studies housework is not found to be the major reason for couple conflict, but in at least one study, "things like cooking, cleaning, and repairing the house" were mentioned most frequently as causes of disagreement (Straus et al., 1980). In this study, a surprising one-third of the respondents said that they "always" disagree about these household tasks. This survey finding is consistent with studies showing that husbands who treat their wives violently often do so in the context of disputes over cooking or cleaning. Frequently these are cases where husbands expect their wives to do all the household tasks and demand near-perfection in the way things are done. One such husband, in attempting to explain why he abused his wife, described his reactions when he arrived home from work as follows:

> *I came home tired and beat. The house was a mess, the dogs were loose,
> and she was in the bedroom taking a nap. Supper wasn't even started yet.
> I fixed a drink, turned on the news. She came out, yelled at me for having
> that drink. I'd heard that a thousand times before. I couldn't take it
> anymore. I threw the drink in her face, grabbed her arm and yelled,
> "Where's my goddamned supper? You never do anything around here."
> (Denzin, 1984, p. 501)*

An abused wife described her husband as a man who could not bear anything being wrong with his food. "I did his breakfast in a hurry and he complained about the grease. . . . He threw the plate at me" (Dobash and Dobash, 1979, p. 95).

While these examples typify cases where husbands initiate conflict (and also violence), there may be other cases when wives initiate conflict about housekeeping tasks. We saw in the last chapter that even though many wives have jobs they still usually have to do most of the housework. Under these conditions, it is understandable that they might express their dissatisfaction with the amount of household work they have to do, and disagreements could follow. Whatever the reasons, it is not difficult to accept the research finding that household work is a source of husband and wife disagreement and conflict.

Conflict about sex.   The degree to which married couples have conflict over sex is quite variable from one study to another. In some studies, sex is so infrequently mentioned as a source of marital conflict that it is placed in the miscellaneous category (Scanzoni and Scanzoni, 1981). But in one study sex was the second most important area of disagreement, with more than a quarter of the respondents saying they "always" disagreed about sex (Straus et al., 1980). The differences in these study results may lie in the methods of asking the questions. In some research the respondents are simply asked to name the things that they and their spouses disagree about most often. This is an open-ended question, which puts the burden on the respondent to bring up the sometimes sensitive issue of sex. With this method of questioning, sex is rarely mentioned as an area of disagreement (Scanzoni and Scanzoni, 1981). In studies where sex is offered as one of the choices, it appears much more prominently as a source of marital conflict.

We saw in Chapter 9 on marital sexual life, that when couples have sexual intercourse less often they are also likely to be more dissatisfied with their marriages. However, as noted at that time, it is difficult to say if it is problems over sex causing problems in the marriage, or problems with the marriage causing sexual problems. We can be sure that some couples do have disagreements and conflicts over sex, but in many cases these may be symptoms or reflections of other kinds of conflict. It may also be that sex is such a sensitive area that couples themselves may avoid open conflict about it.

There is one other sex-related matter—extramarital sexual relations—that can be an intense source of conflict in marriage, although again it does not show up as one of the most frequent areas of conflict. It is usually included with the general category of "activity disapproved of by spouse," which includes drinking, gambling, flirting, and so on. These can be very serious areas of conflict among particular couples, but they do not affect as many marriages as the issues we have already discussed.

Couples without Conflicts

There are some couples who report that they have no conflicts. In several reported studies the percentages ranged between nine and seventeen percent of respondents who said that there was "nothing" or "nothing specific" about which they and their spouses disagreed (Scanzoni and Scanzoni, 1981, p. 484). There are several ways to interpret these responses. First, there may be couples who have reached such a state of harmony and integration that they do not have any notable conflicts of interest. Second, in this kind of social research there is the possibility that some people are giving what they think is the "socially appropriate" response. It may be embarrassing for them to admit that they have disagreements in their marriages. Third, and perhaps most likely, there are probably couples who have what we earlier called conflicts of interest, but when they arise they resolve them without anger, argument, or fighting. In other words, conflicts of interest are resolved so amicably that they are not seen as conflicts by the participants. In the next section we will give some attention to the ways in which it may be possible to resolve conflicts of interest without anger, argument, and hostility. This is often called conflict management.

Conflict Management

There is no shortage of ideas on how to manage conflict. There are books of all types, educational films, scholarly journal articles, and popular magazine and newspaper pieces that give advice, suggest techniques, and simply offer pious hopes ("look at it from the other person's point of view") about how to manage conflict. We will take a brief look at some of these ideas, giving special attention to those that seem to have the most validity and empirical support.

As an example, there is the extensive research by Gottman (1979) who used videotaped sessions of husbands and wives to gain a better understanding of how couples argue. One interesting feature of Gottman's research is that he taped the arguments and conflicts of couples who were identified in advance as either "distressed" or "nondistressed." Distressed couples were those who were seeking marriage counseling and had at least one partner scoring below the average on a marital happiness measure. The nondistressed couples were those who responded to a newspaper advertisement calling for couples with "good" marriages and who scored above average on the marital happiness measure (Gottman et al., 1977). For convenience, we will refer to the two types of couples as *happy* and *unhappy*.

The videotaped arguments of nearly five hundred couples led to the identification of three stages of an argument. First is *agenda building*, followed by *arguing* and finally *negotiation*. Happy and unhappy couples are likely to handle these stages differently, with unhappy couples much more likely to be stuck on one of the first two stages (or to revert back to one) and never to reach a point of successful negotiation.

Agenda building is a term that can be translated as "listing one's complaints." Some couples even have difficulty listing their complaints, because they *suppress* them. Suppression sometimes occurs when people deny, perhaps even to themselves, that there is a conflict of interest. Another form of suppression is an unwillingness to state openly that one has a complaint. A husband or wife will be upset about something, but instead of bringing it into the open he or she will stop communicating, or grow cold and distant. Then the spouse must sense that something is wrong and try to guess what it is.

There is much agreement that suppression is bad for a relationship. Suppressing a grievance or complaint is likely to result in a conflict surfacing in some indirect way (depression, psychosomatic illness) or in an explosive way (Fullerton, 1977; Straus et al., 1980). A rule of thumb for keeping this from happening is for couples to agree that each partner has the right to express a complaint (or, in the terminology just introduced, to build an agenda).

Expressing complaints or building an agenda, however, does have many pitfalls. A very common mistake is to express a complaint by making a statement that casts *blame* on the other person. "You are spending too much money. There is no way we will be able to make it unless you stop your spendthrift habits." These words express the speaker's complaint, but they do so by putting blame on the other person and putting him or her on the defensive. Being defensive is a second pitfall of agenda building. As two spouses express their complaints, they become so focused on defending their own views and themselves from the complaints of the other that they pay very little attention to what the other is saying.

How, then, does one avoid making blaming statements and putting the other person in a defensive position? One suggestion is to use the technique of making "I" statements (Gordon, 1970; Blood and Blood, 1978). The person who is concerned about his or her spouse spending too much money begins the complaint with the word *I*, as in, "I have been getting more and more worried about how we are going to handle all the bills, and I think we need to discuss our spending." With this statement the spouse is not immediately put on the defensive, and the problem is first of all that of the speaker, and then a joint problem.

One other problem connected with agenda building is that it can easily lead to *cross-complaining*. A complaint by one partner leads to a cross-complaint from the other. The following dialogue illustrates cross-complaining:

Husband: You're late again. We agreed to meet at two o'clock, and I've been waiting for forty-five minutes.

Wife: I had a hard time catching the bus. If you hadn't taken the car this morning, or if we could afford to buy a second car, I wouldn't be so tied down. Either you should get a better paying job or you should let me go to work again.

Husband: You know how I feel about your working while the children are young. And besides, you just want to get back into your old office so you can be around Joe again.

Wife: I don't see what you have to talk about, with all those young cuties around your office, hanging on your every word.

By engaging in cross-complaining, these two people have built up quite an agenda in a short period of time. Either they have been suppressing some complaints, which are now coming into the open, or they are dredging up a number of old ones.

It is not uncommon for husbands and wives, in the course of an argument, to bring up issues or complaints from the past. Of course, doing so only makes the conflict more intense and insoluble. Yet, while it is easy to point out what people do wrong when they argue, it is not easy to resist cross-complaining. Some couples never move beyond this stage of trading charges.

After the agenda-building stage comes the *arguing* stage, which is roughly what was called conflict earlier—the means, methods, or behaviors used to resolve conflicting interests. This is the stage when two adversaries use whatever means are at their disposal to make cases for their respective positions. This stage is often heated, and even happily married couples will raise their voices, stomp around, and so on (Brandt, 1982). But videotapes of couples arguing have revealed some subtle differences in the arguing styles of happy versus unhappy couples (Gottman, 1979). The couples who are basically happy with each other will listen to what their partners have to say and will acknowledge the other's words in subtle, yet significant, ways. As an example, a husband might be expressing a complaint or making a point, and while he is doing so his wife says, "uh-huh," or nods her head to show her husband that she is listening, and even perhaps showing some sympathy for his view (Brandt, 1982). Happy couples are likely to do this in arguments, unhappy couples are less likely to.

Another feature of the arguing stage occurs when the two people arguing interject comments about the communication that is taking place. One person might say, "You're shouting at me; you don't need to do that." Among the more happily married couples, the other person is likely to respond along the following lines: "You're right, I was shouting. I'm sorry" (Brandt, 1982, p. 41). This level

CHENEY   *"Would you please pass the salt, too?"*

of communication during the heat of an argument is likely to be a sign of positive feelings between two people. Couples who are hostile toward one another are more likely to let the interjected statement lead to a subargument ("I'm *not* shouting at you, but you deserve to be shouted at").

If arguments are to be resolved, there must be some effort at *negotiation*, the final stage. The two partners must try to offer a solution or compromise from which each will get some satisfaction. But that is the most difficult task of all after an intense argument. Couples who have developed much bitterness toward each other find it very difficult to reach these mutually satisfactory conclusions. Indeed, when couples reach a stage in their relationship where they are no longer friends, and they persistently see each other as enemies, it may be impossible for them to conclude an argument successfully. Psychologist John Gottman, who has observed many such couples, has concluded that when a marriage has reached the bitterness stage it cannot be easily saved, and perhaps it cannot be saved at all (Brandt, 1982).

Is Conflict Healthy?

We have already noted that conflict theorists believe social groups will be healthier and more adaptable if members can express their conflicting interests. There is a similar idea coming from psychological theory rather than sociological theory. The psychological idea is called *catharsis*, which refers to expressing "bottled-up" emotions in order to get rid of them. In this view, individuals are thought to be emotionally healthier if they can "blow off steam" occasionally. A major assumption of this theory is that people have built-in aggression, which is going to come out eventually. A proposition that follows from this assumption is "that people need to be able to discharge their aggression in ways that are minimally harmful" (Straus et al., 1980, p. 167).

The advocates of catharsis have been numerous, and their views have often been popular with the public. Apparently the basic assumption that people have built-in aggression is a widely held view of "human nature." Perhaps the most vivid symbols of the catharsis approach are the foam rubber bats that are sold commercially. The idea is that people (including married couples) can buy these bats and more or less harmlessly beat on each other, in the process getting rid of their pent-up aggression. A number of similar physical techniques for releasing aggression have been advocated by psychologists and marriage counselors. These include "punching pillows, biting a plastic baby bottle while imagining it is someone you are angry with, and smashing a board in order to 'let it out' " (Straus et al., 1980, pp. 167–168).

Some believers in catharsis put less emphasis on physical objects and more on verbal aggression. In the "encounter groups" that had considerable popularity in the 1970s, one of the themes was for participants to use the experience to express their innermost feelings and frustrations (Berkowitz, 1973). The general idea was that this kind of verbal catharsis would make their relationships better generally, and in particular would minimize the chances of physical violence.

Researchers have made several efforts to test the validity of both conflict theory and catharsis theory (Berkowitz, 1973; Straus, 1974; Straus et al., 1980). As a major example, Straus and his associates examined the data from a national sample of 2,143 couples to see if their verbal aggression lessened physical violence. They tested the catharsis theory hypothesis that "letting off a verbal blast at one's husband or wife helps avoid a physical explosion" (Straus et al., 1980, p. 169). The evidence is strongly to the contrary. Indeed, the results of the research are exactly opposite of what the theory would predict. Couples who had little or no verbal aggression (saying something to spite the other person, or threatening to hit or throw something at him or her also had little or no physical violence (pushing, grabbing, slapping, hitting, or threatening with a weapon). At the other extreme, couples with a high amount of verbal aggression also had a high amount of physical aggression. Among those subjects who were in the top five percent in verbal aggression, more than eighty percent had engaged in one or more physical fights during the previous year. Clearly, this test and others like it do not bear out the theory that letting go verbally will reduce the chances of physical violence.

A test of conflict theory was also carried out among the same sample of couples. The theory, as noted earlier, accepts the idea that there will be conflict in families and that expressing conflicting interests can be healthy. However, when the couples in this national sample were asked about the amount of conflict they had over money, children, sex, housekeeping, and social activities, the ones who had the most conflict also had the highest levels of physical violence. Just bringing the conflict out in the open, as the theory suggests, does not seem to have the effect of reducing physical violence (Straus et al., 1980).

The researchers in this study reasoned, however, that it might make a difference *how* couples handle their conflict. If they use more reasoning and negotiation when they have conflicts, as conflict theory would suggest they do, then perhaps violence would be diminished even in the face of conflicts of interest. However, in this case again the theory was not supported. The fact is that the couples who had the most areas of conflict, *and* who used reasoning and negotiation *most often* in their arguments, had by far the highest amount of physical violence. At least this aspect of conflict theory also fails to find support from empirical research.

This leaves the conclusion that might have been anticipated at the outset. Married couples who have the most conflicts of interest, and who engage most often in verbal arguments, or even negotiation, are also most likely to engage in physical violence. It is to this issue—physical violence in the family—that we turn next.

VIOLENCE IN THE FAMILY

As with conflict, if we are going to examine violence in the family we must give some attention to what is meant by the term *violence*. We can start with a definition: violence is "an act carried out with the intention of, or perceived as having the intention of, hurting another person" (Gelles and Straus, 1979, p. 554). Several features of this definition require some elaboration. The first is the *intention* of the person committing some physical act. Sometimes a person will not intend to hurt another person (e.g., squeezing another person's arm) and yet it will hurt. Therefore, the definition of violence must include the perception of the person who is the object of another person's act.

If we interpret this definition of violence broadly, family violence includes any act that inflicts physical pain on another person in the family (spouse, child, parent, sibling). Therefore, acts ranging from spanking, slapping, and hitting to beating and killing would be counted as family violence. Some people might object to having the term violence applied to spanking. Spanking is viewed by many people as a normal and acceptable when it is done by a parent as part of child rearing. As we will see at the end of the chapter, spanking or not spanking is a debatable issue, but an interesting point is made by Gelles and Straus (1979). They note that if an adult applied the same physical punishment to a co-worker as parents give to children by spanking, it would be considered a chargeable assault. We will return to the issue of spanking children at the end of this chapter.

Conjugal Violence—Spouse Abuse

Researchers who have studied violence in the family have concluded that a marriage license is widely viewed as a "hitting license" (Straus, et al, 1980, p. 31). There are two reasons for reaching this conclusion. First, there is a widely ac-

Violence in the family is widespread and affects many different areas of family life.

cepted social norm that it is legitimate to hit family members—under some circumstances. Second, there is in actuality a substantial amount of hitting in families. We will examine both of these reasons.

A norm that justifies hitting other family members is difficult to document, even though its existence can certainly be inferred. Because the family is thought to be a place where love, affection, and support are supposed to prevail, it is difficult for people to acknowledge that hitting and violence are acceptable. Especially in an interview situation, or in answer to a questionnaire, it is difficult to express such a sentiment. Even so, a substantial percentage of both men and women are willing to affirm that violence is acceptable. In a national sample survey, Americans were asked if they thought there were circumstances in which it would be all right for a husband to hit his wife and for a wife to hit her husband (Stark and McEvoy, 1970). The following summarizes their responses:

All right for a husband to hit his wife?
Women approving = one out of six
Men approving   = one out of four

All right for a wife to hit her husband
Women approving = one out of five
Men approving   = one out of four

In another national study the respondents were asked to evaluate the phrase "couples slapping each other around" (Straus et al., 1980, p. 47). Approximately one out of three husbands and one out of four wives saw this type of violence as at least "somewhat necessary," "somewhat normal," and "somewhat good" (Straus et al., 1980, p. 47).

Since this kind of behavior is directly contrary to the norm of the family being a place of love, affection, and supportiveness, these figures are interestingly high. Of course, survey results only reveal what people will say in response to an abstract question. It is just as revealing to hear what people say when they are dealing with concrete cases, either their own or those of other people. Marital partners, for example, often justify hitting a spouse, or being hit by a spouse, for one of two basic reasons: (1) the spouse is doing something wrong in the eyes of the aggressor; or (2) the spouse "won't listen to reason" (Straus, 1980, p. 693).

An example of both these justifications can be found in a case described by LaRossa (1980), which was uncovered in an interview with a young married couple named Jennifer and Joe. Jennifer described herself as a strong-willed person who had been independent for much of her life and wanted to "run things" in her marriage. Her husband concurred in this evaluation, but he had opposing ideas about who was to dominate the marriage. When the interviewer asked Jennifer if she still wanted to run things, the following interchange occurred:

> *Interviewer:* Do you think you run things now?
>
> *Jennifer:* No, I tried hard, though!
>
> *Joe:* She tries. One day we had a conflict and she more or less tried to run me and I told her no, and she got hysterical and said, "I could kill you!" And I got rather angry and slapped her in the face three or four times and I said, "Don't you ever say that to me again." And we haven't had any problems since.

Joe analyzed his use of violence in the following way:

> *You don't use it until you are forced to. At that point I felt I had to do something physical to stop the bad progression of events. I took my chances with that and it worked.*

Later in the interview, Jennifer said,

> *Joe doesn't usually use force. That was the first and last time he'll ever do that. It was my fault. I was trying to dominate him, that's for sure. (LaRossa, 1980, pp. 160–161)*

Joe, in this case, was justifying his use of violence by implying that Jennifer had gone too far in trying to dominate him. But in addition, by saying that she was getting "hysterical," he was justifying what he had done on the grounds that she was beyond reasoning. For her part, Jennifer made it clear that it would be the last time he would hit her, but then she immediately added that it was her fault.

Perhaps neither of these two people would have supported violence in the abstract if they had been asked about it by an interviewer. But, while they both expressed some ambivalence about this occurrence (especially Jennifer), both seemed to think it was justified at that time, and in that particular situation.

Both the survey results and case examples provide evidence for a social norm sanctioning violence, at least by a substantial proportion of people. However, it is the actual amount of violence among American couples that supports equally well the assertion that a marriage license is a "hitting license."

The Extent of Conjugal Violence

A national sample of 2,143 husbands and wives, the study we referred to above, gives a good indication of how widespread conjugal violence is in the United States (Straus et al., 1980). In this study, the following acts were identified as conjugal violence: threw something at spouse; pushed, grabbed, or shoved spouse; slapped spouse, kicked, bit, or hit with fist; hit or tried to hit with some object; beat up spouse; threatened spouse with knife or gun; and finally, used knife or gun. In the year prior to the survey about sixteen percent of all couples (one out of every six) had engaged in at least one of those acts. Considering the duration of the marriage, instead of the previous year, twenty-eight percent of the couples had experienced at least one of these acts since they had been married. The most common of these acts was to "push, grab, or shove" one's spouse.

The most extreme kinds of violence—beating up a spouse or actually using a knife or gun—each occurred in about two percent of the couples during the year preceding the study. In about one in twenty couples there was at least one instance in the preceding year of beating up the spouse.

Even though these statistics reveal an extensive amount of family violence, there is a fairly good chance that the amount of reported violence turned up in a survey of this kind is an underestimate of the actual amount. This is the view of the researchers, because, as already noted, many people will probably be reluctant to admit that they use violence. A separate study by a different investigator supports this view of underreporting. Simply by asking both the wives and husbands of couples about violence, the total number of couples reporting violence goes up considerably. As an example, in one survey of couples, seventeen percent of the wives and sixteen percent of the husbands reported violence by the husband. But because husband and wife reports were not always in agreement, in twenty-six percent of the *couples* either the wife or the husband, or both, reported violence by the husband (Szinovacz, 1983).

In view of the great amount of attention that has been directed in recent years to the issue of "wife battering," there is one intitialy puzzling finding from the study of the national sample of couples: husbands and wives report being the aggressors in approximately equal numbers (Straus, 1980). At first glance, this equality in aggression might mean that as much attention should be paid to "husband beating," as to wife beating. That is not justified, however, because while a wife may strike first or throw the first object, it is almost always the husband who strikes the most damaging blows (Straus, 1980). Research on cases of spouse assault that come to the attention of police and appear in court records also support the claim that husbands do more damage. Out of 1,044 cases of assaults between family members in two Scottish cities, 791 wives were victims compared to only 12 husbands (Dobash and Dobash, 1979).

The fact that women are so much more often the victims of physical assaults from their husbands accounts for the concerns about wife beating. Battered wives are justifiably receiving the attention of both researchers and the mass media today (Dobash and Dobash, 1979; Gayford, 1983; Pagelow, 1981; Straus and Hotaling, 1980).

Wife Beating

The primary question about wife beating is why it happens. What causes husbands to beat their wives? There is no simple answer, because there is no single factor that provides a perfect causal explanation. Instead, there are different answers at different levels of analysis.

Thinking in terms of the cultural level first, there are two intersecting cultural themes that make the beating of wives possible, and to some degree probable. First, there is what has been called "the culture of violence" (Gelles, 1974). The obvious point is that many cultures, including American culture, place a positive value on violence, especially violence as a way of solving disputes or problems. Warfare, Western movie shoot-outs, the execution of criminals, and vigilante attacks on urban muggers all illustrate the way violence is seen as a positive solution to problems. The culture of violence, and violence specifically directed toward wives, can be found in the following bit of folk verse:

> *A woman, a horse, and a hickory tree*
> *The more you beat 'em, the better they be*
> *(Quoted in Straus, 1977/1978, p. 455)*

But, as some critics of the culture-of-violence argument have pointed out, if it is a violent culture that causes violence in families, why is it that husbands make their wives victims of violence more than vice versa? Part of the answer is that males, given the traditional masculine gender roles, are socialized to value this part of the culture more than are females. But a further answer lies in the intersecting cultural value, patriarchy (Dobash and Dobash, 1979). We have examined patriarchy previously and know that it gives men nearly absolute control over other members of the family. This dominance of males in a patriarchal system may, in extreme cases, make men feel they have the "right" to beat their wives. The act of wife beating may also be seen as a method some men use to maintain their dominant position in the family.

To summarize the cultural explanations for wife beating, we may agree with those who claim that the culture of violence legitimizes intrafamily violence generally, but it is necessary to add that the cultural value of patriarchy can be seen as giving men the "right" to hit their wives (Pagelow, 1981). Furthermore, it can be added that husbands are most likely to invoke this right when their power is threatened (recall the words of Joe, above, when Jennifer tried to "dominate" him).

Turning from the cultural level to examine other explanations for wife beating, there is a belief—we should call it a myth—that wife beating is primarily a lower-class phenomenon (Pagelow, 1981). Researchers now agree that wife beating is certainly not limited to the lower classes but is found at all class levels. Some studies have found wife abuse to be somewhat more frequent in families with lower education, income, and occupational statuses (Gelles, 1974; Szinovacz, 1983). However, these moderate differences among status levels must be assessed very carefully. In public-data studies there may simply be more *reported* incidents of spouse abuse among lower status couples because the police are called in more readily. Even in scientific surveys lower status persons may be less likely to hide or cover incidents of abuse. There are also indications that middle-class men use somewhat less obvious and more elaborate methods of hurting and terrorizing their wives. For example, it appears that higher-status men are more likely to hit their wives in places on their bodies and in ways that are less visible. Lower class men are likely to hit their wives on the face and neck, while middle-class men more often strike the breast or abdomen (Pagelow, 1981).

There are also a variety of beliefs and myths about the personality and psychological characteristics of men who beat their wives, and about women who are beaten by their husbands. Regarding the personalities of women who are beaten, the most extreme explanation is that these women are masochistic and actually seek out men who will treat them violently. In other words, the women themselves have some kind of psychological pathology that either leads to, or allows them to tolerate, the beatings. The flaw in this explanation is that too many women who are beaten by their husbands seek to escape, do escape, and even if they do not, make it quite clear that they both fear and detest being beaten. Also, this kind of explanation is an example of making the victim the cause of the crime. *Blaming the victim* is an often used approach, but it is not an acceptable explanation for another person's actions.

There are other, similar explanations that also place blame on the women who are beaten. They are said to be "weak women" who are unwilling to leave after the first attack, or women who have a "learned helplessness" (Walker, 1979). Again, to place the blame on a wife for the beatings she receives from her husband is to find the cause in the wrong person.

An even more common explanation for wife beating is to locate the cause in a mental illness or psychological problem of the husband. The line of reasoning for this explanation is, in some ways, airtight. Any man who repeatedly beats his wife, especially on the slightest provocation, must obviously be mentally ill. Therefore, wife beaters are mentally ill. One problem with this explanation is that it simply gives wife beating a new name, but it doesn't really explain anything. Another problem is that in case after case of men who beat their wives, there is ample testimony that most of the time they are normal men who function very well socially. Even their wives often attest to their normal, and even loving, behavior much of the time (Pagelow, 1981).

On the other hand, there is a great incidence of alcoholism and drug use among men who beat their wives. If either of these two behaviors is viewed as a psychological pathology, then one could say that many men who beat their wives have at least the signs of a mental problem. Interestingly, many wives of these men have reported that their first beatings, and many others, came when their husbands were drunk, but they also note that many later beatings came when their husbands had not been drinking (Pagelow, 1981).

Another psychological characteristic that is often associated with wife beating is jealousy. Many wives who are beaten report that their husbands are obsessively concerned about infidelity. These husbands are suspicious of every move and often restrict the comings and goings of their wives greatly. One could argue that this intense jealousy and suspicion is a kind of mental illness, although there are probably other husbands who are equally jealous who do not beat their wives.

This leads back to the question of why some men (and women in some cases) use violence as a way of expressing their feelings or emotions, or as a way to solve problems. One answer to this question is that violence as a way of responding to problems is learned in the home as children grow up.

The Family as Training Ground for Violence

There is a widely held view among those who have studied family violence that the family itself provides the training ground for future violent behavior (Gelles, 1974; Steinmetz and Straus, 1973; Straus et al., 1980; Straus, 1980). According to this view, children learn about violence when they themselves are struck or beaten, or when they see their parents hitting each other. There is evidence from a national sample of American adults to support these views (Straus et al., 1980). The more men and women had been struck when they were growing up, especially during their teenage years, the more likely they were to engage in violence against their spouses. And when men and women had seen their parents strike each other, they were much more likely to strike their own spouses than were men and women whose parents had been nonviolent. Furthermore, when both were true, that men and women were struck as teenagers and that they saw violence between their parents, they were even more likely to engage in violence against their spouses (Straus et al., 1980).

Men who experienced the greatest amount of these forms of family violence as they were growing up had about a one in ten chance of being wife beaters. The researchers who conducted this study note, "This is a 600 percent greater rate of wife-beating than we found for husbands who came from nonviolent homes" (Straus et al., 1980, p. 113). This pattern also appeared for wives who came from violent homes. Indeed, it was slightly stronger, with one in eight who came from the most violent homes having "severely assaulted" their husbands in the year preceding the study (Straus et al., 1980, p. 113).

These research findings support the widespread observation that violence can be passed on from one generation to another. The mechanism is no particular mystery. It is the familiar process of socialization, which we considered in Chapter 11. Children learn when they are young that it is permissible, and even appropriate, to use violence against family members. These lessons learned in childhood influence the way they relate as adults to their spouses and other family members.

This entire line of analysis suggests that family violence is a general phenomenon that manifests itself especially in husband-wife relations but also pervades all other family relationships. We will now direct our attention to other kinds of violence in the family, beginning with the abuse of children.

Child Abuse and Maltreatment

In Chapter 11 we saw that there is a long history of treating children harshly in Western societies. In contemporary times, at least comparatively, children are generally treated with much more care and compassion. Nonetheless, there is substantial evidence that many children, in countries around the world, are both seriously harmed and shamefully neglected in their own homes (Taylor and Newberger, 1983; Kamerman, 1983). The term *child abuse* has become a distressingly familiar topic in public and professional discourse. The initial interest in the "battered child" has now expanded to cover a wide range of child maltreatment. There are a number of specific forms of child abuse, but the major categories are *physical abuse, sexual abuse*, and *physical neglect*. Other types of maltreatment can be added to the list, including medical neglect, educational neglect, emotional abuse, emotional neglect, and abandonment (Watkins and Bradbard, 1982). Our discussion will be limited primarily to physical abuse, or what has been called child battering, and sexual abuse.

It is difficult to document the scope and dimensions of child abuse. The principal obstacle is the "hidden" nature of the problem. Spouse abuse is also often hidden from the outside world, even though the person being victimized is an adult and is usually fully aware that what is happening is wrong. Children who are abused, however, are in a very different situation. Especially as infants and small children, they have no way to judge and evaluate what is happening to them. They are essentially trapped in a life that, to their knowledge, has no alternatives. In recent years various professionals (doctors, teachers, and others) have been sensitized to the signs of children being battered and often uncover cases of child abuse. However, unless the child is severely hurt, or there are repeated injuries of a suspicious nature, the abuse of a child may go undetected, perhaps forever.

An added problem of detection comes from the fact that the treatment of children by their parents ranges on a continuum from no physical harm to brutality and even murder. Exactly where on this continuum physical abuse begins is very unclear. When the 1940s Hollywood actress Joan Crawford reared her two children, she punished and restricted them in a variety of ways. She often told her children that she wanted them to learn how to work and behave properly. When her daughter published an autobiographical account of the way she and her brother had been treated as children, many readers concluded that the children had been mistreated and abused (Crawford, 1978). And yet, it seems that Miss Crawford's colleagues, friends, and visitors saw her only as a strict and demanding mother whose children always behaved perfectly. Even in this well-documented case it is still difficult to assess whether it should be called child abuse or not (we have primarily the daughter's account, published after her mother's death). Most people, on the basis of this record, would say that the children were abused, but some people might discount the daughter's account and give to the parent the right to rear her children as she saw fit.

Recognizing the hidden nature of child abuse and the lack of precision about what constitutes excessive physical punishment, it is not surprising that we have only very rough estimates of how widespread the abuse of children is. One estimate is that one child in forty suffers some type of abuse or neglect each year (Halperin, 1979). Viewed from the perspective of abusive parents, a national study found that about twelve percent of American parents had committed acts against their children that were "severe enough to put the child at risk of physical injury" kicked, bit, hit with fist, etc.] (Straus et al., 1980).

When one looks for the causes or explanations for child abuse, they are similar to the explanations that have been proposed for wife abuse. There are psychiatric and psychological explanations that look for causes in psychological illnesses or personality abnormalities of parents. Several personality characteristics have been found to be highly represented among abusive parents. For example, abusive parents have lower self-esteem, are more insecure, and are less sure of being loved. Abusive parents also appear to derive less satisfaction from parenting and have less understanding of the development of children (Watkins and Bradbard, 1982).

Other explanations of child abuse locate the causes in parental isolation, stress, and frustration. These are characteristics of the parenting and family situation, and can be the product of poor housing and impoverished living conditions (Garbarino and Sherman, 1980). Closely related to these living conditions, and perhaps a cause of them, is unemployment. There is a greater likelihood of child abuse when fathers are unemployed (Gelles, 1973; Gil, 1970).

A number of studies have shown that parents may be selective in the abuse of their children. One particular child, often one who has some particular physical, mental, or behavioral characteristic, may receive the major share of parental abuse (Frederick and Boriskin, 1980).

In child abuse, just as in spouse abuse, there are indications that it is a learned behavior. Investigators agree that parents who abuse their children were likely to have been abused, neglected, or maltreated themselves as children (Watkins and Bradbard, 1982). The research by Straus and his associates found that when mothers had been hit by their parents as teenagers, there was a one in four chance that they would treat their children in an abusive manner. This compares to one in ten mothers who had not been hit as teenagers (Straus et al., 1980, p. 107). This study also revealed that parents who had been in homes where their parents hit each other, were also likely to treat their children abusively. We can see in this, again, that the family itself can be the birthplace of violence that is passed on from one generation to another.

The Sexual Abuse of Children

In addition to child battering and beating, the sexual abuse of children has also come to the awareness of the public in recent years. While the sexual abuse of children has occurred throughout history, it has been called "the best kept secret" because it has been so little acknowledged and discussed (Rush, 1980, p. i).

The sexual abuse of children can occur either in the family or outside the family. Inside the family, the most common circumstance is for a young girl to be sexually abused by a father, stepfather, brother, or other male relative living in the home. It is also possible for young boys to be sexually molested in similar circumstances, but the incidence is considerably lower. Even if the sexual abuse occurs outside the family, the aggressor is typically either a friend or relative of the family, or someone who has been charged with responsibility for the child.

The results of a study conducted among college students at the University of New Hampshire showed that 19.2 percent of female students and 8.2 percent of male students had been "sexually victimized" sometime during childhood (Finkelhor, 1979). It may be that some of these were isolated incidents rather than long-term and repeated violations of these young people, but the incidence is still surprisingly high.

Within the nuclear family there are two types of sexual relations that are illicit and often involve the abuse of children: sex between siblings and sex between parents and children. The most common of these is sexual relations between siblings. If we focus on instances of brother-sister relations, victimization or abuse is often involved, but not always. In those cases where both brother and sister are preadolescent at the time they are involved, a more appropriate description is "sexual experimentation." But abuse does occur between siblings, and the most common abusive situation is for an older (or stronger) brother to force a sister to engage in sexual relations (Finkelhor, 1979).

While much less frequent, observers agree that the most severe form of sexual abuse occurs when fathers force their daughters to have sexual relations. The imbalance of power in this situation is so overwhelmingly in favor of the father that it must be labeled sexual abuse. Furthermore, there are many reported cases in which daughters are extremely young—often preschool age—when their fathers begin to molest them (Meiselman, 1978). Most of the information we have about the families in which fathers sexually abuse their daughters comes from psychiatric or criminal cases. These may be presenting a biased picture, but the evidence suggests some common patterns in family relationships when fathers sexually abuse their daughters (Herman and Hirschman, 1981).

The father appears to be the key actor in families at risk for father-daughter incest. They are typically the dominant parent, often bordering on being intimidating and tyrannical with other family members (Herman and Hirschman, 1981; Nass et al., 1981). Often these fathers engage in violence against their wives and children. It is not uncommon for these fathers to be heavy users of alcohol or problem drinkers (Meiselman, 1978).

Mothers in these cases are often withdrawn in some way from the family. They may be ill, either physically or psychologically, alcoholic, or simply absent for periods of time from the home. In many cases they have had large numbers of children (Herman and Hirschman, 1981).

Daughters who are sexually abused by their fathers have often taken over some of the responsibilities of the household that might normally be done by their mothers. In many cases it is the oldest daughter in the family who will take this role and whom the father will exploit for his sexual gratification. Not infrequently, when the first daughter rebels and leaves the home, the father will move on to younger sisters. Generally, the daughter will keep the sexual molestation by her father a secret because of his threats. In many cases women do not reveal what their fathers have done until many years later, often in conjunction with seeking help for psychological problems. However, it should be noted again that much of what is known about the effects of incestuous relations comes from populations of clinical patients. While there are cases where no apparent severe psychological damage is incurred by the victims (Koch, 1980), father-daughter incest must be identified as sexual abuse because fathers are in the more powerful position in the family.

Violence between Siblings

For anyone who has grown up with brothers and sisters, it may not come as a surprise to learn that the most common form of family violence has yet to be addressed. That, of course, is violence and aggression between siblings. Both national samples and special surveys reveal that physical and verbal aggression are endemic among brothers and sisters. According to the parents in a national sample, forty percent of the children in their families had hit a sibling with an object in the preceding year, and eighty-two percent had engaged in some form of violence (Straus et al., 1980). The entire list of violent acts siblings engage in is shown in Figure 13.1.

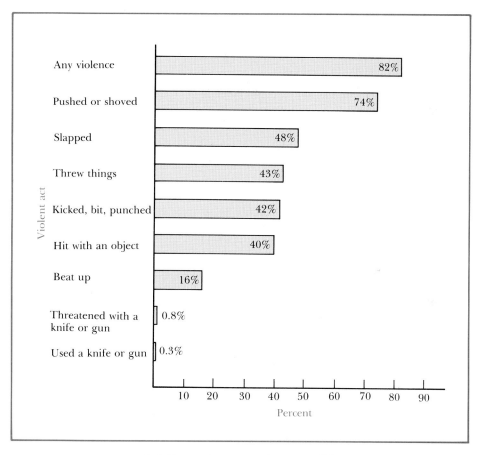

Figure 13.1 *Percentage of children who were violent to a sibling in previous year, according to parental report. (Source: Straus, Gelles, Steinmetz, Behind Closed Doors: Violence in the American Family. New York: Anchor Doubleday, 1980, p. 81)*

Perhaps the higher rates of violence between siblings do not seem either surprising or serious. Even though sixteen percent of children have beaten up a sibling in the previous year, it has a much less ominous sound than if, say, sixteen percent of parents had beaten up their children. We seem to have a much greater tolerance for children beating up on children than we do for other kinds of interpersonal violence. There appears to be a normative expectation that kids will just naturally fight "like cats and dogs." People may not approve of siblings fighting, but it is clearly more tolerated.

In research on sibling aggression, some interesting patterns have been found. It would be expected that boys would fight with siblings more than girls, and that is in fact the case. But the difference is so slight as to be almost negligible. Indeed, in a sample of college students who were asked about the amount of physical aggression they had with their siblings, the difference between males and females was so small that it could have occurred by statistical chance (Felson, 1983). Interestingly, while girls fight with their siblings just about as much as boys do, they almost never fight with other children—neighbors, schoolmates, and friends (Felson, 1983). Age is another factor that influences sibling fighting. When the sample of college students was asked how much they fought with the sibling nearest to them in age, the amount varied according to whether that sibling was older or younger than the respondent. These students were more likely to report fighting with a sibling if the nearest sibling was younger. The same pattern held for the sibling who was next nearest in age (Felson, 1983). The most promising note with respect to age is that as children grow older, especially as they move into middle adolescence, the amount of fighting between siblings decreases.

The commonplace explanation for why siblings fight is "sibling rivalry." *Sibling rivalry* is based on the notion of jealousy between brothers and sisters, particularly as they contend for the attention of their parents. The theoretical literature on sibling aggression stemming from jealousy describes it as an angry, expressive conflict that does not have a realistic basis. In the study of college students referred to above, the researcher tested whether the aggression reported was of this type or was "realistic conflict." *Realistic conflict* is conflict over different or divergent interests, values, or goals (if a brother is using his sister's sweater to clean his bicycle, for example, there is a realistic basis for conflict). The results of the research did not support the widely accepted sibling rivalry interpretation of sibling aggression. When siblings had fights, they were almost always over real and tangible goods and issues (Felson, 1983).

The things siblings fight over are not surprising. They fight most frequently over property, or the use of it (toys, television, the telephone, clothes). The second most frequent cause of fighting is over the division of work and chores. The third most frequent cause is objecting to the behavior of a sibling—teasing, insulting, spying, and so on (Felson, 1983).

One unusual finding in this study of sibling aggression is the role that parents play in one particular situation. When younger siblings are in conflict with

The most common form of family violence is between siblings. Parents, as well as adults, generally have a greater tolerance for violence between children.

older siblings, they are more likely to call for help from their parents. If parents respond to these requests, and especially if they are likely to punish the older sibling, there is apt to be more fighting between the siblings. It seems that under conditions where parents are likely to intervene, the younger sibling is more willing to fight with an older, stronger sibling. Parental intervention, in this case, leads to more aggression, not less (Felson, 1983).

A New Sensitivity to Family Violence

In the past twenty years there has been a significant increase in awareness and attention given to violence in the family. As we have seen, an awareness of child abuse came first, in the 1960s, followed by awareness of spouse abuse, and especially wife battering, in the 1970s. The trend has been for researchers to move away from the simple pathological or illness models to broader explanations of all kinds of family violence. Essentially, this leads to the view that violence in the family is a product of the workings of the family, itself, and is not simply the actions of "bad," sick, or ill individuals. A broader view also directs our attention to the cultural and societal conditions in which family life is immersed. Understanding and reducing family violence requires a recognition of some of these familial, cultural, and societal contributors, as well as individual causes.

As we conclude this chapter on conflict and violence, we are going to address an issue that we have occasionally touched on, but have not fully explored, in the preceding pages. This issue is spanking. The question is whether parents should or should not spank their children.

ISSUE

Should parents spank their children?

As we begin our consideration of spanking as an issue, we must try to separate this form of physical punishment from child abuse. There is no question that child abuse is wrong. But if the following discussion is to reflect the feelings of many people who favor spanking, we must begin with the assumption that spanking is a nonabusive form of punishment. Those opposed to spanking may argue otherwise, but those who speak in favor of spanking usually make a clear distinction between physical punishment and child abuse.

Thus, we will try to define what constitutes spanking, at least for purposes of this discussion. A spanking is physical punishment administered by a parent to his or her child when the child's behavior is deemed to be inappropriate in some way. The punishment typically consists of hand-administered slaps, usually to the buttocks or lower body, of sufficient force to inflict pain but not to injure (to hurt without harming). Sometimes instruments such as belts, sticks, paddles, or hair brushes are used to administer the punishment. The objective of the punishment is to change the behavior of the child.

Arguments in Favor of Spanking

The most reasoned arguments in favor of spanking begin with two assumptions. First, spanking is not to be done routinely or regularly, but only when the behavior of the child is of such a nature that strong measures are warranted. Second, spanking should generally be a last resort after other methods of changing the child's behavior have proved to be ineffective. Ideally, both of these conditions should be met before spanking occurs.

With regard to the matter of the seriousness of the child's behavior, advocates of spanking often single out those behaviors that might be physically harmful to the child. A small toddler who persists in darting out into the street or a child who plays with matches even after having been warned of their dangers are examples of cases where spanking seems justified. After all, it is argued, if the child who runs into the street is hit by a car, the results will be much more harmful than a spanking. The same is true for the child who plays with matches. Spankings, while painful, will be much less harmful than the alternatives.

Referring again to a child who is still a toddler, it is often argued that when children are very young, and before they have a full command of language, a spanking is the only way a parent can get his or her message across. It may not be possible to explain to small children how serious the consequences would be if they were struck by a car. The words and the illustrations would be too abstract, whereas the spanking would be concrete and clear. The assumption is that small children may not know why they should stay off the street but that they will understand if they do go into the street it may bring another spanking.

The argument that spanking should be used as a last resort carries the notion that some (perhaps most) children will soon get used to verbal admonitions and punishments, which then become ineffective. When this occurs, parents will be justified in turning to their "ultimate weapon," the spanking. This is a punishment that by its very nature the child cannot easily shrug off. The pain is real and cannot be ignored. Thus, if a child does not respond to scoldings or other nonphysical punishments, the spanking is justified.

One of the interesting arguments for spanking is advanced by many adults who were themselves spanked as youngsters. They often say, "My parents spanked me and it didn't do me any serious harm, and probably did me some good." Often there is a nostalgic recollection of particular spankings that a father or mother administered. There is the further idea that the spankings may have made them better persons. Extending this line of thinking, some advocates of spanking conclude that the society would be better generally if all parents used a "firm hand" when rearing their children. If every child learned that bad behavior would be followed by a "good spanking" the society would be both safer and better.

To summarize the arguments in favor of spanking, this punishment should be used only when the severity of the behavior calls for it and when other methods of punishment have been tried. At a more general level, the "good, old-fashioned" spanking is viewed as a way of producing a better, more law-abiding society.

Arguments against Spanking

Those who are opposed to spanking question whether children learn what they are supposed to learn when they are being spanked. Does the child who is spanked after darting into the street really learn about the danger of automobiles, or simply that when parents get angry (or frightened) they will hit and hurt? Whenever parents attempt to modify or control a child's behavior, by whatever means, the action taken by the parent will be interpreted by the child. It is always possible that the child's interpretation will be different from the lesson the parent intends to teach. For example, a parent may find an older sibling hurting a younger brother or sister. The parent may spank the older child in order to discourage such behavior. However, instead of learning that one should not hurt smaller brothers and sisters, the child may learn that a big person may hit a little person. Rather than discourage the child from hitting siblings, the spanking may teach the child that causing someone else pain is an acceptable way of dealing with other people (Skolnick, 1978).

When parents spank or hit their children, even "for their own welfare," it has been observed that children are also learning some auxiliary or "unintended" lessons, such as the following (Straus et al., 1980):

1. Those who love you the most are also those who hit you.
2. It is morally right for family members to hit other family members.
3. Hitting someone is all right when other things do not work.

Thus, even the childhood spanking is a way of learning that it is acceptable to hit family members. Rather than leading to less violence in the society, it may lead to more.

The opponents of spanking also take the view that children are never too young to understand the words, expressions, and voice tones of parents. This includes the words and behaviors of parents when they are unhappy and upset with a child's behavior. If the child will not respond to verbal scoldings and punishments, the parent can always resort to other physical acts, such as restricting play or withholding foods the child likes.

Spanking, its critics say, is more a reflection of the failure of the parent than the child. Parents are often extremely frustrated and angry when they spank their children. The spanking is largely a way of venting this frustration and anger, and often has little to do with helping or improving the child.

Finally, even though spanking is supposed to be a punishment of last resort, parents who start using it as a disciplinary method will often turn to it more easily and frequently. When this occurs, the child takes spankings less and less seriously, and they lose whatever effect they might have had.

Summing up the arguments against spanking, the lessons taught by spankings may not be as clear to the child as parents assume. The lessons can sometimes be quite the opposite of that intended by parents, and may well include the lesson that it is acceptable to resolve differences between people by hitting and using violence. Spanking is unnecessary because other methods of reprimand and punishment can always be used, even with very young children. Finally parents often spank because of their own frustrations and anger rather than for the good it will do the child.

Themes

1. There is some conflict in every marriage and in all families.

2. Violence occurs more often in marriage and family life than we suppose.

3. Conflict theorists say it is better for the well-being of groups, including the family, if members can press for their particular interests, desires, and needs.

4. The task of managing conflict requires avoiding a series of pitfalls.

5. The popular idea that "blowing off steam" in family conflicts is healthy has been called into question by researchers.

6. There is a widely accepted social norm that under some circumstances it is legitimate to use physical force and even violence against family members.

7. Physical and violent ways of dealing with family members are passed on from generation to generation.

8. Child abuse tends to be a hidden form of family violence, but in recent years various professionals and the public at large have become more sensitive to the signs of battered children.

9. Sexual abuse in families, especially adult males forcing younger females to perform sexual acts, has also been hidden, but many cases of this form of child abuse are also coming to light.

10. Violence between siblings is probably the most widespread and accepted form of family violence.

11. Studies of family violence have revealed that it is not simply a matter of pathology and mental illness, but that it grows out of family, societal, and cultural conditions.

Facts

1. The major conflicts between husbands and wives center around money (especially the use of it), children, housekeeping, and sex.

2. There are three stages to an argument: agenda building, arguing, and negotiation. However, many couples do not successfully achieve all three stages.

3. Happily married couples have different styles of arguing than unhappily married couples.

4. Verbal aggression is highly related to physical aggression.

5. A substantial minority of Americans (from one-sixth to one-fourth) agree in surveys that it is "all right" for spouses to hit each other under some circumstances.

6. Hitting a spouse is most often justified by one of two reasons: (a) the spouse is doing something wrong in the eyes of the aggressor; or (b) the spouse "won't listen to reason."

7. Survey responses reveal that twenty-eight percent of all couples have engaged in some form of violence during their marriages.

8. Wives are most often the most serious victims of marital violence.

9. Wife beating is found in all social classes, but is more commonly reported in families with lower education, income, and occupational prestige.

10. There is a strong association between alcohol abuse and men who beat their wives.

11. Men and women who experienced the greatest amount of violence in their childhood homes are most likely to use violence against their spouses and their own children.

12. It is estimated that one child in forty suffers some type of abuse or neglect each year.

13. One parent out of eight commits a physical act against his or her child to put the child at risk of physical injury.

14. Mothers who abuse their children have been found to be insecure and have lowered self-esteem. They are also likely to be isolated, frustrated, and living in poor housing and impoverished conditions.

15. Fathers who abuse their children are more likely to be unemployed than fathers who do not.

16. A study of college students revealed that 19.2 percent of females and 8.2 percent of males had been "sexually victimized" sometime during childhood.

17. In families where fathers molest their daughters sexually, the father is often dominant, intimidating, and tyrannical, while the mother is often withdrawn, passive, or absent from the home.

Major Concepts

agenda building: Listing one's complaints in a discussion with another person, especially a spouse—the first stage of conflict management.

arguing stage: A stage of conflict management where two people try to resolve their conflicting interests. *See* **conflict.**

blaming the victim: Finding an explanation for aggression in the behavior of the victim of that aggression.

catharsis: Expressing "bottled-up" emotions in order to get rid of them.

conflict: The means, methods, or behaviors used to resolve conflicting interests.

conflict of interest: The competing opinions, preferences, desires, or needs of two people (or groups).

conflict theory: A sociological theory that has as its basic tenet the idea that there will be conflicts of interest in every social group, including marriages and families.

cross-complaining: Responding to a partner's complaint by voicing a complaint of one's own.

culture of violence: Placing a positive value on acts of violence, especially as a way of solving disputes or problems.

hostility: The negative emotional feelings (dislike, hatred) that can prevail between two people (or groups).

"I" statements: Voicing one's complaints and concerns in such way as not to blame the other person, best accomplished by making statements beginning "I. . . ."

negotiation: The final stage of conflict management in which partners with conflicts of interest try to offer a solution or compromise from which each will obtain some satisfaction.

parental scripts: Unconscious and unspoken expectations about what is proper and appropriate parenting behavior.

sibling rivalry: Jealousy between brothers and sisters, particularly as they contend for the attention of their parents.

violence: An act carried out with the intention of, or perceived as having the intention of, hurting another person.

14

The Family in Middle and Later Life
Mid-life Changes and Intergenerational Relations

When, as young adults, we think of our parents and the home in which they live, we often think about them as the stable reference point in our own changing, shifting lives. There is a seeming constancy and stability about our parents and our family homes that keeps us from seeing that *change* is also the key feature of marriages and family life in the middle and later years of life. For example, when children leave home, it is an important change in the lives of parents. After having children around them for as long as twenty years or more, parents are left in a home that is picturesquely called "the empty nest." This change can lead to other changes, as for example, when women who have not been employed earlier enter the work force to occupy their newly found free time.

But there may be other, less obvious, changes occurring at about the same time for husbands and wives. There may be changes in attitudes, values, and even personalities as people cross the middle years of their lives. For some these changes will be minor and quite unnoticed. But for others the changes may be so severe as to be a *crisis of mid-life*. The new attitudes and values and personality changes can lead to other changes, such as new responses to work and career, or in extreme cases, intrusions into the marital relationship that lead to breakup and divorce.

After the middle years of life come the years when people leave the work force, or change the intensity of their work. With retirement there may be a change of residence, which can mean a completely new community and style of life.

While all these changes are occurring, there is the accompanying inevitable change called *aging*, with all that implies, both physically and psychologically.

Even this brief discussion of changes shows that while parents and home seem to be the rock of stability and constancy, change of dramatic proportions is happening. These transitions of life are no less important than the earlier movement from youth to adulthood or the change from being single to being married.

In this chapter we will look at some of the major changes in the middle and later years of marriage and family life. As we do so, two things will stand out: (1) there are great differences in the ways in which people pass through the middle and later years of life; and (2) people in the middle and later years of life are importantly affected by the family members in the generations on either side of them; and they, in turn, have important influences on the members of other generations. These, too, will be our concerns in the pages ahead.

At the end of this chapter we will look at one of the more interesting contemporary issues reflecting the relationship between generations. This is the relationship between parents and their adult children who return home to live after having been on their own for some years. The question that many parents ask today is, are parents obliged to provide a home for their adult children if they wish to return home to live?

Suppose we take fifty years of age as being the heart of the middle years of life. If we were to dip into the population of fifty-year-old men and select two at random, it is entirely possible that we would pick the following two cases:

Mr. A. is a machinist with a large company who takes great pride in the quality of his work. He often volunteers to work extra hours of overtime if the company is trying to meet a production schedule. He has always been active in sports, though now he concentrates on coaching a soccer team for eight- to twelve-year-old girls and a winter basketball team for his church. He and his wife enjoy having friends over for their casual dinners and cookouts. But as a couple, dancing is their love, and they find time every two weeks or so when they can enjoy being together. They also travel, sometimes visiting their grown children and other times visiting national parks and historical sites.

Mr. B. is a man who has a respectable job, but one that he describes as "paper shuffling." He is looking forward to the time when he is eligible for retirement and can leave the grind of daily work. He stays close to home when he is not working, mostly puttering around the house and watching television. He and his wife have drifted into a routine that has no social highs or lows. They get along congenially, but there is no intensity in their relationship. He likes his children, but feels that visiting them would take too much effort and probably cause him to miss his favorite weekly television shows.

Men (and, of course, women too) with life-styles and attitudes this different are not hard to find, and they emphasize the point that middle-aged people can be very different. They may be the same age chronologically, but chronological age is not the only determinant of how people live. Of course, what is true for fifty-year-olds is also true for sixty- and seventy-year-olds. There are people who reach advanced ages who have great vitality and enthusiasm for life, while others seem to have been beaten into submission by the lives they have led.

Both women and men in the middle and later years of life vary greatly in attitudes and behavior. Sometimes light can be shed on the reasons for these variations. Other times, while trying to generalize about these life stages, it will be important to remember the variability that does exist in the overall picture of family life in middle age and beyond.

THE DEMOGRAPHICS OF MARRIAGE IN MIDDLE AND LATER LIFE

Between the ages of fifty and sixty-four, more than four-fifths of all men and more than two-thirds of all women are married. However, even in this late middle-age stage of life, about fifteen percent of women are widows who have not remarried. Only five percent of the men in this age group are widowed. The pattern of more men being married and fewer widowed is a trend that becomes increasingly pronounced in the later stages of life. Figure 14.1 shows that between the ages of sixty-five and seventy-four the percentage of males who are married remains a relatively high eighty percent. However, for women between sixty-five and seventy-four the percentage who are married drops below fifty percent. At ages seventy-five and above, seventy percent of men are married. By contrast, women aged seventy-five and above are married less than twenty-five percent of the time (United States Census Bureau, 1983).

These demographic figures are important background factors for understanding the lives of middle-age and older Americans. Essentially, they tell us that from age fifty onward, women in the population are much less likely than men to be married. There is a high probability that a woman will spend a significant number of years as a widow. By contrast, a male, even over the age of seventy-five, still has a high likelihood of being married. There are two reasons for more men than women being married after age seventy-five. First, since women have a greater life expectancy than men, the men are less likely to have been widowed (recall that wives are also likely to be younger than the men they marry). Second, if men have been widowed, there is a greater likelihood that they will have remarried, since there are many more women than men in the population over age sixty-five.

While the life expectancy of females is greater than that of males, the fact is that life expectancy has gone up greatly for both males and females in the last half century. Life expectancy at birth for males is now over seventy-one years; for females life expectancy at birth is over seventy-eight years. In 1920 the life expectancy for men and women was fifty-four and fifty-five years, respectively. One obvious implication of this greater length of life is that married couples, if they do not divorce, have more and more years together as husband and wife.

Since there are more long-term marriages today, there is an increasing interest in the quality of married life among older couples. In Chapter 8 we took a brief look at the quality of marriage for couples who were in long-term marriages. We noted that over the entire range of marriage, some researchers

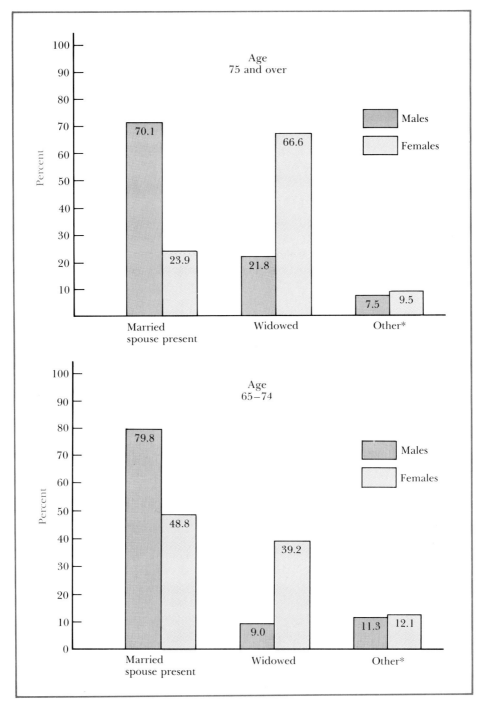

Figure 14.1 *Marital status and living arrangements of men and women aged 65 and over. (Source: U.S. Bureau of Census,' Marital Status and Living Arrangements,' March 1983, Current Population Reports, Series P-20, No. 389)*

found an upturn in marital quality in the later years of married life. Specifically, after marital quality has dropped to a low point during the years when children are in school, it rises again in later life, at least according to some studies. This issue of marital quality in long-term marriages now requires a closer look.

MARITAL QUALITY IN LONG-TERM MARRIAGES

The question of why some researchers have found a modest increase in marital quality in the later stages of marriage, while others have not, has been the subject of a substantial amount of debate and discussion among family researchers (see Ade-Ridder and Brubaker, 1983, for a summary of more than twenty-five studies). Often these debates have centered around conflicting ideas about how to conceptualize marital quality, or about measurement procedures, sampling, and other technical details of research. These are complicated matters that cannot be adequately presented or resolved here, so we will focus on some areas about which there is greater agreement.

Most observers agree that even if some samples of long-term married couples show some upturn in marital quality, it is far short of the level of marital quality found in the earliest stage of marriage. Thus, the outlook is for marriages over time to decline steadily in quality or, at best, to make a slight resurgence in quality in the later years. This picture of long-term marital happiness is rather bleak. But a closer look does reveal some bright spots about marriage.

One simple way to describe what happens in a long-term marriage is to say that some things get better, and some things get worse. As an example, in one recent study of married couples who were in various life cycle stages (from beginning marriage to postretirement), the researchers focused on the level of love and problems (Swensen et al., 1981). In this study, love was measured by asking married couples about their actual behaviors toward each other. The focus of the questions was on "the things that people in love say to each other, do to or for each other, or feel for each other" (Swensen et al., 1981, p. 846). On the negative side, the couples who were in the later stages of marriage had the lowest scores on this measurement of love. Other studies have confirmed this decline in love, especially among men (Peterson and Payne, 1975).

However, while lower expressions of love are a sign of declining marital quality, other signs indicate an increase in quality. Marital problems decline to their lowest levels in the "empty nest" and postretirement stages of marriage, even lower than in the beginning stage of marriage. This is consistent with research showing that "negative sentiments" go down steadily through marriage careers (Gilford and Bengston, 1979). Negative sentiments can be interpreted as the amount of sarcasm, anger, criticism, nonnormal talking, and disagreement.

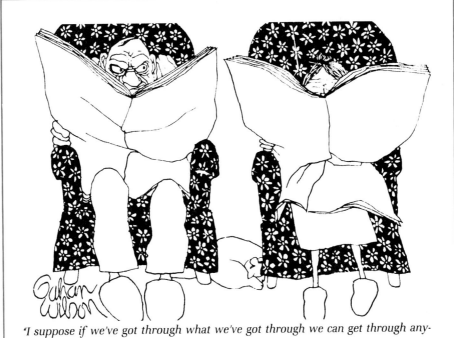

'I suppose if we've got through what we've got through we can get through anything.'

If we combine the decline in love with the decline in negative sentiments,
we begin to get a more favorable picture of long-term marriages. Indeed, the
picture seems to be one of decreasing intensity, in both negative and positive
emotions. When married couples are first married, their expressions of love
are at a high pitch, but so also are some of their tensions, which are probably expressed in negative sentiments. Both of these expressions are at a much lower
level after couples have been married for many years.

There is another positive feature of long-term marriages that can be seen
from these studies. During the stage of marriage when school-age children are
in the home, the level of "positive interaction" between husbands and wives
goes down to its lowest level. Positive interaction is reflected in the husband
and wife working together, discussing things, laughing, exchanging ideas, and
having a good time. As might be expected, couples who are just beginning marriage have the highest level of positive interaction. But, in later marriage stages,
after the low point of the child-rearing years, the level of positive interaction
goes up again, not as high as it was in the first stage of marriage, but up to an
intermediate level (Gilford and Bengston, 1979).

These several competing positive and negative features of the quality of married life in the later stages probably help explain why different researchers have reached conflicting conclusions. As researchers have directed their attention to different aspects of married life, they have sometimes identified those aspects that improve with the length of marriage, and other times those aspects that deteriorate.

These studies of marital relationships in different life cycle stages give us some insights into the nature of long-term marriage. But there are some features of middle and later life that can be especially influential for the quality of married life. Three of these features are important enough to give special attention: (1) the "mid-life crisis" and mid-life transitions; (2) the sexual lives of middle-age and older people; and (3) retirement.

THE "MID-LIFE CRISIS" AND MID-LIFE TRANSITIONS

It is difficult to say if the idea of a mid-life crisis is a scientific concept or the product of "pop psychology and sociology." It has certainly received its share of mass media attention, with any number of magazine and newspaper articles, books, television shows, and even movies on the topic. At the same time, scientific disciplines, especially psychiatry, counseling psychology, and sociology, have also given the mid-life crisis serious attention (Brim, 1976).

Even though the mid-life crisis has had so much attention, it proves to be an elusive concept. At a psychological level it is a rapid and substantial change in personality (Brim, 1976). A mid-life crisis often involves a questioning of one's personal sense of identity. Going through a mid-life crisis can mean questioning most of what one has believed and accepted without doubt up to that point in life. The previous values placed on work, reputation, material things, family, and even marriage may be less meaningful and important than had previously been assumed. With this breakdown of previously held values, a person going through a mid-life crisis may, with dramatic suddenness, make major changes in work and life-styles (Brim, 1976).

Almost all writers acknowledge that the mid-life crisis is overwhelmingly a male experience. There have been some efforts to bring females into the discussion, but both popular and scholarly writing has largely focused on males. When a more general term, *mid-life transition*, is used, females are much more often given consideration equal to that of males. Perhaps the best way to treat this topic is to concentrate on the male mid-life crisis first and then turn to the more general topic of mid-life transition.

The Male Mid-Life Crisis

The male mid-life crisis is best understood as a reaction to a number of changes that occur in mid-life. There is no exact age at which this occurs, but the general opinion is that it occurs most commonly around age forty (Levinson et al., 1978). It is about this time in life that physical, occupational, psychological, and social changes occur in the lives of most men. It appears that for some men, going through these changes is a period of considerable upheaval and distress. Concentrating on the specifics of these changes will give a clearer picture of what the mid-life crisis is.

Physical changes.   As one writer put it, "The hormone production levels are dropping, the head is balding, the sexual vigor is diminishing" (Lear, 1973). One could augment that partial list by adding fading eyesight, declining athletic ability, more aches and pains, and other signs that the body is not the same as it was in earlier years. The specifics of the hormonal declines are diminishing testosterone, cortisol, and androgen levels from age thirty on. We know little about the effects of these diminishing hormonal levels, either physiologically or psychologically, but they certainly may contribute in some way to a feeling of physical decline.

Work and career.   Many men enter the work force with a notion or "a dream" about what they will do in their lifetime. During their twenties and thirties they invest the major part of their time and energy in their work. By the time most men reach forty the major outlines of what they will accomplish in their work or careers have been drawn. More than likely when they reach that age there will be a realization that some of the dreams and objectives they had when they were young will never materialize. Even most of the men who have been reasonably successful by the usual standards of money and prestige will see that the future is not going to find them doing much better. Indeed, because of young people coming up, they may have to work harder and "run faster," just to keep their places. In the most devastating cases, these men who have been successful in their careers may lose their jobs. In short, the dreams and ambitions of youth meet head on with the reality of middle age. For many men this requires a reassessment of what they are ultimately going to accomplish in their lives.

Facing death.   The decline of physical health and the recognition that time is running out for one's ambitions and objectives both signal that time is running out for life itself. For the first time in life, men in middle age see that they are reaching a point where the road is going downhill instead of uphill. There is a change in the time orientation of men at this midpoint in their lives. They stop thinking of the time they have had since birth and begin to think of the time they have yet to live (Neugarten, 1968a).

This dramatic change in time orientation is often intensified by the death of a parent, or a last parent. This critical event often triggers the realization that it is just a matter of time before one's own death. "Death—at the conscious level—instead of being a general conception, or an event experienced in terms of the loss of someone else, becomes a personal matter, one's own real and actual mortality" (Jaques, 1965, p. 506). "Death represents to the middle-aged man the fact that he will not achieve what he thought he was going to achieve" (Brim, 1976, p. 5).

These are the critical events that often converge at mid-life: physical changes in one's body, a realistic recognition of what one is going to accomplish in life, and a recognition of one's mortality. Many men negotiate these three difficult events with apparent ease and steadiness. Many others go through some dramatic psychological changes, which in turn lead to changes in life-style and social relationships. These changes can be difficult, and even destructive, especially for marriages and marital relationships. Some marriages end during this crisis period, but often it will simply be a time of life when married couples have to work through a series of transitions.

The male mid-life crisis is common enough to be widely observed and is therefore an empirically verifiable phenomenon. However, systematic attempts to identify men who go through a genuine crisis of mid-life have shown that not every man follows the classical pattern. In one sample of three hundred men entering middle age, two researchers claim that they found only twelve percent of the men who showed the classic signs of mid-life crisis. These are men who showed strong signs of alienation, dissatisfaction with work, anxiety, and psychological symptoms such as agitation and restlessness. Perhaps most revealing, there are men who overwhelmingly reported "thinking about the kind of person I am and what I really want out of life." They were also likely to wish they "could start afresh and do things over, knowing what I do now" (Farrell and Rosenberg, 1981, p. 81).

The fact that only a small minority of middle-aged men displayed the classic symptoms of the mid-life crisis might seem to be a very positive sign. However, this study presents a more discouraging picture. While another one-third of the men seemed to be well adjusted and satisfied with their lives (both work and family), the remaining fifty-six percent of this sample of men displayed more negative responses to their mid-life circumstances. Strictly speaking, these men were not exhibiting mid-life crises, but their psychological states and life views were severe enough to merit attention.

A portion of these men appear on the surface to be making a satisfactory adjustment to mid-life changes, but the researchers see this as a cover-up and a facade. Various psychological measures show these men to be hiding "feelings of desperation, loss and confusion" (Farrell and Rosenberg, 1981, p. 213). These men claim initially to be happy with their work, but when drawn out in interviews they reveal "boredom, conflict and a sense of being passed by. They harbor fantasies of starting a new career or regrets about not pursuing vague dreams" (Farrell and Rosenberg, 1981, p. 214). They also claim to have happy

Men respond to middle and later life in a variety of ways. Today, many make an effort to remain healthy and fit through intensive running programs.

marriages, but these too are found on closer examination to be denials of the reality of their relationships with wives and children.

Finally, in this study of middle-aged men fully thirty percent had never really succeeded in life and were living lives of bitterness and disenchantment. The general description of these men conveys a dismal life picture:

> *They report deprivation, neglect, and brutality in their homes during childhood. Although they may attempt to escape this environment, catastrophic failures in young adulthood, early marriages based on the need to escape, followed by a trend of drifting from job to dead-end job, losing friends, and drinking have led to a repetition of their parents' circumstances, attitudes, and life styles. (Farrell and Rosenberg, 1981, p. 216)*

As these men reach middle age they are not experiencing an abrupt crisis that is typical of the mid-life crisis. They are continuing what has become a state of chronic discontent.

This grim image of middle age may be realistic for many men, though one must be careful about accepting the results of one study and generalizing to the entire population. Indeed, the authors of this research, themselves, caution about the generalizability of their research. Nonetheless, their work does demonstrate that middle age, with its several critical changes, can intensify discontent or produce crises for many men.

Because most of the writing about mid-life crises has focused on men, so has our discussion to this point. Obviously, the changes discussed above (physiological and body changes, reassessment of youthful aspirations, and a recognition of one's mortality) are changes that occur to women as well as men. Indeed, the physiological change of menopause among women is generally more noticeable and focused than the hormonal changes in men. Women who have invested some of their self-image in their reproductive capability may also react psychologically to menopause. And there is the further, often discussed, adjustment that many women are presumed to make to the "empty nest," when their children leave home. The general assumption is that women who have devoted their lives to rearing and nurturing their children must feel some kind of loss or purposelessness when they no longer have their children to care for (Troll et al., 1979; Spence and Lonner, 1971; Lowenthal and Chiriboga, 1972). This view is challenged by some writers who find that for many women it is something of a relief when their children leave home. If some women have anxiety during this period of life, it may be because they face the task of finding something to do with their lives that will give new meaning and significance (Rubin, 1979).

All these changes suggest that women as well as men have to make some adjustments and transitions in mid-life. We will examine these transitions next, especially those that are reflected in personality changes of men and women in middle adulthood.

Mid-Life Personality Transitions for Men and Women

The most frequently noted change occurring in mid-life is a personality shift in which men and women seem to take on more of the traits of the opposite sex. Men become more reflective and sensual, and have more interest in family relationships and love. They become less aggressive and are less interested in power and mastery (Brim, 1976; Guttman, 1979; Zube, 1982). The most common explanation for these shifts among middle-aged men is that in earlier years of their lives they suppressed the more emotional and sensitive aspects of their personalities. They did so in order to play out the masculine role expectations of succeeding in work and providing for their families. It is in mid-life, when these expectations have been met (at least, as well as they are going to be met), that men can recover the other, more "feminine" sides of their personalities. These personality changes coincide with some of the features of the mid-life crisis we discussed above.

For women, the personality changes tend to be in the opposite direction. It is in mid-life that they are able to pull away from the nurturing role somewhat, perhaps in part because, as noted above, children have left home and no longer need to be nurtured as much. Furthermore, there is also a tendency for women in mid-life to become more aggressive and assertive and less sentimental. During these middle years of life women often try to satisfy their own needs, especially for personal growth and self-expression (Neugarten, 1968b). This means that women in middle age often look for opportunities outside the home that are not family related. The irony of this countermovement of men and women in mid-life has not gone unnoticed. Just at the time when women are moving in an outward direction, away from home and family, men are turning toward this realm with increased interest (Zube, 1982).

The mid-life crisis and mid-life personality transitions are likely to have some important influences on marital quality. Certainly, if a man or woman experiences a severe crisis at mid-life it can be devastating for a marriage. But that need not be, and is not always, the case. Husbands and wives weather these transitions and work out their adjustments. As husbands and wives remain married there is one continuing aspect of married life that may either help or hinder their relationship; their sexual lives. It is time now to consider what happens in the sexual lives of middle-aged and older people, both in and out of marriage.

SEXUAL LIFE IN MIDDLE AGE AND LATER YEARS

A recurring question, especially from young people, is whether sex continues to be interesting and exciting after a couple has been married twenty or thirty years, or more. A closely related question is whether people retain ther sexuality and sexual interest when they reach old age (whether married or not). The answer to both questions is yes, but as is so often the case it must be a qualified yes.

Apparently there are many beliefs and myths about the sexual lives of older people. Among them are the following: most older persons are not sexual; those older people who do retain their sexual functioning suffer rapid declines as they grow older; an interest in sex by elders is abnormal or a perversion; sexual activity in old age is harmful (Palmore, 1981).

One kind of evidence that contradicts these myths is the information we have on how often older married couples have sexual intercourse and whether or not they are interested in sex (frequency and interest). In studies conducted by researchers from Duke University, married persons between the ages of forty-six and seventy-one were interviewed four times over a six-year period (George and Weiler, 1981; Palmore, 1981). They were asked whether they were sexually

Through middle and later life the majority of people continue to be actively inter-
ested in sexual relationships.

active and, if they were, what was their frequency of having sexual intercourse.
The youngest group of men in this study, those aged forty-six to fifty-two, were
all sexually active at the time of the first interview. Sexually active in this case
simply meant reporting that they still had sexual relations. At the end of this
study, six years later, five percent had become sexually inactive (Palmore, 1981).
All other age categories, from fifty-three to seventy-one, also had declines in the
percentage who were sexually active. For example, about seventy-five percent
of the men in the oldest group (late sixties to early seventies) were sexually active at the beginning of the study. Six years later, about sixty-four percent of
these men were still sexually active. The married women in the sample also had
declines in the percentage who were sexually active, and in general their rates
of decline were faster than the men in the sample. Nonetheless, among the
oldest group of women in this study (those in their late sixties and early seventies), fifty percent were still sexually active in the sixth year of the study.

These statistics, which are supported by a number of other studies, show
clearly that the vast majority of married people over age fifty, sixty, or seventy
still have sexual intercourse. While these statistics reveal that there is a decline
in being sexually active, especially after age sixty, the frequency of having sex-

ual intercourse remains relatively stable for those who do continue to have sex. Furthermore, in the Duke University studies, sometimes as many as twenty percent of these older married people increased their frequency of having sexual intercourse from one interview period to the next (Palmore, 1981). This is important because it reveals that sexual activity, while it generally declines with age, can also increase in later life.

Several additional observations have been made about the sexual lives of older married people on the basis of surveys of this type. One is that there is almost always a higher percentage of women than men, at any of the later ages, who indicate that they have "no interest in sex" (Garza and Dressel, 1983). A second observation is that women also report a lower frequency of sexual intercourse than do males. And yet, at the same time, several studies have shown that when married couples stop having sexual intercourse entirely, both husbands and wives agree that their stopping is more often attributable to the husband (Pfeiffer et al., 1974; Roberts, 1980). Finally, the sexual interest or drive of older couples is highly correlated with the level of sexual interest and drive they had when they were younger. The greater the interest they had as young couples, the greater it is when they are older. This is consistent with studies going back as far as the Kinsey research, in which it was observed that a strong early interest in sex was related to a strong continuing interest in later life (Kinsey et al., 1948).

Statistical studies of sexual activities of married older people clearly show that there is a substantial and continuing interest in sex into advanced ages. But the sexuality and sexual vitality of older people is conveyed much more vividly by their own words. A survey in which older people, both married and unmarried, volunteered their answers to a variety of direct questions about their sexual lives, leaves no doubt about how they feel about sex (Starr and Weiner, 1981). Consider a few of their written answers to the question "Do you like sex?" (Starr and Weiner, 1981, pp. 36–37):

(Female, widow, age 74) "I like sex tremendously with my sweetheart."

(Male, married, age 67) "Very much. I love the fondling, touching, nakedness and all the methods of achieving the end result."

(Female, divorced, age 79) "Yes. Feeling of deep response and communication with my partner. Gives me zest for life."

(Male, widowed, age 74) "Yes. It is one of the supreme pleasures of living."

These older people, and many more like them, were volunteers for a study of sexuality, and thus many of them might have been especially positive about sex. Of course, there were some older people in this volunteer survey who were negative about sex or were no longer interested. But they were clearly a minority. The majority, in answer to a question about how sex now compared to when they were young, said that sex was the same as it had been, or better. A surprising forty-one percent of the older women in this sample said that sex was better now. Twenty-seven percent of the males said it was better. As one widow of sixty-seven put it, "Better. You have no worries about getting pregnant or raising a family," and a married woman of eighty-one answered, "Better, as we have more time for bed-talk and are more relaxed" (Starr and Weiner, 1981, p. 43).

These statements, and many others on all aspects of sex, give vivid testimony to the fact that most people have a continuing interest in sex throughout life. Of course, various kinds of health problems can eventually interfere with sexual activity, but that happens to some younger people as well. Perhaps the most important inhibiting factor is that many older people (especially women) have no sexual partners. For them, sexual intercourse is not possible, but masturbation is. In the volunteer sample just mentioned, slightly less than half (forty- six percent) of the men and women said they did masturbate, and eighty percent said that masturbation is an acceptable outlet for sexual needs (Starr and Weiner, 1981). Considering that many of these people grew up in an era when masturbation was widely believed to be bad for both body and soul, this is a substantial level of acceptance.

In reflecting on the sexual lives of older people, it has been noted that both researchers and the lay public often seem to hold older people to a sexual standard that is special for them as a group (Garza and Dressel, 1983). Many people seem to make an implicit assumption that sexual intercourse within marriage is the only expected or appropriate sexual activity for older people. Most studies of the sexual lives of older people give little or no attention to extramarital sex, nonmarital sex, homosexual sex, oral sex, and masturbation (Garza and Dressel, 1983). All these nonnormative forms of sexual activity are part of the sexual lives of younger people, but the elderly seem to be held to a more rigid and limiting standard. And yet, it is in later life that these alternative forms of sexual expression can become more important, not less. (Garza and Dressel, 1983).

Focusing only on the frequency of sexual intercourse of older people has another implication, which should be noted. We learn from research that there are declines in the frequency of sexual intercourse as people become older, and we may be inclined to attribute this to a loss of sexual interest or energy. But it may simply be that sexual intercourse, especially the frequency of sexual intercourse, is an inappropriate measure of sexuality for older people. For them, sexual satisfaction might come as much from manual stimulation, oral stimulation, caressing, touching, and tenderness as it does from sexual intercourse to orgasm. Holding older people to the sexual intercourse standard, might be applying a "youth-oriented, genitally focused model" that is very inappropriate (Garza and Dressel, 1983, p. 105). The sexuality of older people may be more appropriately and satisfyingly expressed in other ways.

RETIREMENT AND MARITAL LIFE

Retirement from the work force is said to be a time that many people look forward to with great positive anticipation. But retirement is also thought to be associated with a number of negative outcomes, for both individuals and married couples. On the negative side it is often said that retirement is a time when people lose their interest in life, have lowered morale and depression, and even experience declines in physical health. Frequently, retirement is associated with much lower income levels, and in extreme cases it causes people to drop below the poverty level. Finally, with regard to marital relations, postretirement husbands and wives are sometimes believed to be together too much, getting on each other's nerves and creating marital strife. Wives, especially, are alleged to complain, "What do I do with him 24 hours a day?" (Keating and Cole, 1980).

If these generally assumed negative outcomes of retirement are valid, and if husbands and wives in retirement do get on each other's nerves, we can expect the worst for marital relationships during the retirement stage of life. It is fortunate, therefore, that the research evidence on retirement is not supportive of many of these widely held notions. Some may have partial validity, for a small percentage of couples, but most prove to have little widespread validity and importance. To see why, some general features of retirement need to be reviewed.

The Nature of Retirement Today

In 1979 the federal government passed legislation outlawing compulsory retirement at age sixty-five. Most classes of workers can now remain in the labor force until age seventy if they choose to do so (Blau et al., 1982). However, despite this legislation, more and more workers are retiring earlier than ever. The trend is especially notable among males, since historically they have been almost universally employed during their adult lives. Now, one out of eight men is no longer working between the ages of fifty and fifty-nine, and this number is increasing. Among men aged sixty to sixty-nine, more than half are not working (fifty-three percent), whereas in 1940 only thirty percent were not working. The simple explanation for this trend is that more and more men are financially able to retire.

Since women (especially married women) have not been in the labor force as much in earlier decades, the same trend toward earlier retirement is not evident in the statistics. However, between the ages of fifty and fifty-nine, approximately half of all women are not employed. Between sixty and sixty-nine, three-fourths of women are not employed. Whether because they have never been in the labor force or have retired, most women are not gainfully employed in their fifties and sixties.

Not only are men and women leaving the labor force earlier, they are also living longer. This means that the retirement years are probably more and more likely to be years of good health and vitality for both husbands and wives. These concurrent trends are just beginning to be reflected in existing research on the marital lives of retired couples. Even so, most of the negative images of retirement listed above have not found support in the studies of retirees that have been completed.

Income, not surprisingly, goes down substantially with retirement, and puts some elderly Americans into poverty. The official poverty level among the elderly is fairly high, with fourteen percent of the population over the age of sixty-five living in households below the poverty level in 1983 (U.S. Bureau of the Census, 1984). But the overall level of poverty does not reveal the great differences that exist within the elderly population. For example, thirty-six percent of the black elderly live below the poverty level. Twenty-three percent of the elderly who are of Spanish origin are below the poverty level. In general, elderly women, especially those who are members of minority groups and not married, are the hardest hit by poverty. Over age sixty-two, more than forty percent of black women are living in poverty (U.S. Bureau of the Census, 1984). See Figure 14.2 for a breakdown of poverty levels among American elderly men and women who are members of major ethnic and racial groups.

Even though poverty is a severe problem for many older Americans, there are circumstances that can reduce the severity of economic hardship in old age. Nearly everyone who reaches sixty-five years of age is eligible for social security payments, but, in addition, retirees today often have other pensions and retirement plans to supplement their social security payments. For those elderly who are fortunate enough to have purchased and paid for a home, the cost of housing is greatly reduced. The medical needs of the elderly, which can be considerable, are substantially covered by Medicare today. However, to be completely covered it is necessary to have supplemental private health insurance, which is difficult for those elderly with limited financial resources.

While there is no doubt that health problems increase in old age, there is a commonly held belief that retirement per se leads to declines in health. However, the empirical studies that have been done have not shown that health declines or illnesses increase as a result of retirement (Atchley and Miller, 1983; Palmore, 1981). There have been some studies that indicate the existence of mental illness among retirees, but the causal sequence can go in both directions. Some people leave the labor force because they have mental illness. On the other hand, among people who are retired, mental illness can be brought on by lack of social contacts, poor living conditions, and poor physical health. But then one must ask if it is retirement or some general conditions of life that produce the mental illness.

Generally, retirement does not seem to produce mental illness, since it does not lead to lower life satisfaction or morale (Atchley and Miller, 1983; Palmore,

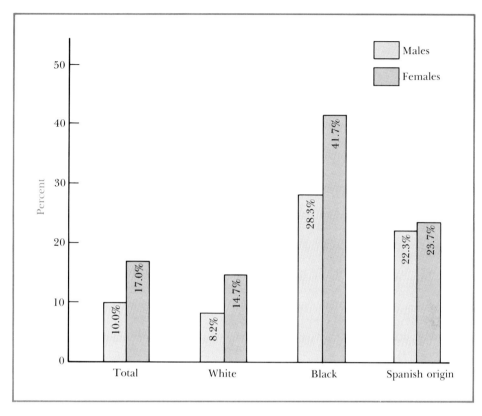

Figure 14.2 *Percentage of the population aged 65 and over living in poverty. (Source: U.S. Bureau of Census, 1984, Series P-60, No. 145, 'Money, Income, and Poverty Status of Families and Persons in the U.S.: 1983,' Table 17, p. 25)*

1981). Some research has even shown higher levels of morale among retired couples than nonretired middle-aged couples (Keating and Cole, 1980).

To sum up the research on retirement, people are retiring younger than ever before, while they are still vital and healthy. Many, but not all, are economically better off than previous generations of retirees. There is no evidence that retirement has a negative effect of health, either physical or mental, for the majority of retirees.

Retirement and Marital Relationships

There have been several studies that have examined how marital relationships are affected by retirement. In one such study the subjects were limited to couples in which the wife had not been in the labor force and the husbands had retired from school teaching. Among these couples, the general effects of retirement on the marital relationship was most positive. There was a generally high level of satisfaction with retirement, especially among the husband retirees. The major disadvantage seen by the wives was a reduction of privacy and personal freedom. However, it appears that many wives were willing to ease their husbands' adjustment to retirement by giving more of their time and attention to their husbands. The researchers note, "For these women pleasure of time with spouse and satisfaction in feeling needed seemed to offset loss of personal freedom" (Keating and Cole, 1980, p. 86). There were signs in this study that wives who had not entered the labor force were willing to resume a nurturing role that might have been important to them earlier in the marriage.

An interesting and unusual study of the effects of retirement on marital quality focuses on the retirement of wives (Szinovacz, 1980). The retirement of wives is often related to the time when their husbands retire (Atchley and Miller, 1983; Palmore, 1981). Since they are typically younger than their husbands, women often retire earlier than sixty-five (if the trend toward earlier retirement of males continues, it may be even earlier in the future). When the husbands and wives in this sample were asked how the wife's retirement had affected the quality of the marriage, only one husband out of twenty-four said that the marriage was "worse." About half of all husbands and wives said the marriage was about the same. The remaining forty-six percent of husbands and forty-eight percent of wives said that there had been at least slight improvement in the marriage. Among the wives who said there had been improvement, twenty-eight percent said that the marriage was "much better" (Szinovacz, 1980).

Those wives who saw an improvement in their marriages were most likely to attribute this change to a reduction in their levels of stress that had been caused by overloads on their time and conflicting time schedules. This would not come as a surprise in the light of what we saw about these problems in Chapter 12. A second reason offered by the women of this study for seeing improvements in their marriages was that retirement gave them more opportunity for joint activities with their husbands, if the husbands were also retired. And a third reason mentioned by the traditional husbands and wives in this study was a reduction in conflicts about the wife's housekeeping performance. When wives are expected to care for the home in addition to working, as they so often are among most traditional couples, retirement reduced this source of conflict. One traditional husband expressed it this way:

When she was working everything was messed up with clutter. . . . But since she retired things seem to be better since she is home all the time. I come home and the house is cleaned up. I think that is the difference there. (Szinovacz, 1980, p. 434)

While Szinovacz found a few retired wives who considered it a bother to have their husbands "underfoot" all the time, this attitude is rarer than mythology would have it. Most women in her sample said they enjoyed being with their husbands all day.

Some retired husbands and wives do, however, resolve whatever problems there might be in this regard by living segregated lives. Sometimes, even while they are in the same house together, they are involved in separate activities and interact only minimally. Or, in the extreme cases, husbands and wives may live separate lives, indicating a disenchantment with the marriage. As one wife described her life with her husband,

> *We don't see each other too much even now that we're retired. He works in the basement and I work upstairs, or I go into town shopping and he's doing something else, working in the yard or something. (Szinovacz, 1980, p. 48)*

There are many different ways to adjust to retirement, but segregation, while possible, is neither the most common nor the likely trend in the future. The research that has been done on past retirees indicates quite clearly that retirement usually has a fairly positive influence on marital relationships. The major exception is the case where retirement is brought on by ill health, especially that of the husband (Atchley and Miller, 1983). The trend of earlier retirements by healthier retirees who are often more economically secure would seem to bode well for many older people who are increasingly called the "youthful old."

Up to this point, our consideration of middle age and later life has focused attention primarily on the relationships between husbands and wives. But for the married couples in the later stages of life there are a number of other very important family relationships. There are the relationships between the middle aged and their adult children. There is also the relationship between middle-aged couples and their own parents. And if middle aged and older have grandchildren, there will be a relationship with them also. Generally, as people enter middle age they are likely to be part of a three- or four-generation family complex. In the remainder of this chapter we will focus on the major issues of these inter-generational family relationships.

FAMILY RELATIONSHIPS IN MIDDLE AND LATER LIFE

To deal with the complex of family relationships just referred to, it will be most convenient to direct our attention to couples in the age range between forty-five and sixty-five. Married couples of this age (as well as people who are widowed and divorced) are likely to have parents in the later stages of life, as well as adult children and grandchildren. We will begin by considering the relationships between the middle-aged and their adult children.

The Middle Aged and Their Adult Children

About eighty percent of all people who have been married and are in their late fifties and early sixties have living children (Troll et al., 1979). These children to a considerable degree are independent, and yet, as we will see, the ties between generations are strong. It is nearly universally expected in American society that when children move into adulthood they will establish a residence separate from that of their parents. This is especially the case when a child marries. The formal term for this system is *neolocal residence.*

While most young adults follow this residence pattern, a surprisingly large proportion live close to their parents. For example, a study of married young adults in the Minneapolis area found that seventy percent saw their parents at least weekly (Hill et al., 1970). After evaluating a substantial number of such studies, one specialist estimates that between eighty and ninety percent of all older people with living children see at least one child once a week or more, and speak to them on the telephone with about the same frequency (Cicirelli, 1983).

There is some likelihood that living in close proximity to parents is more characteristic of young adults in the working class than in the middle and upper-middle classes. Generally, occupations and professions that are higher paying or more prestigious require people to be more geographically mobile. This is a process that begins even as young people get college educations and advanced degrees, for the higher the educational level, the more likely a person is to migrate out of their home community (Kammeyer and Ginn, 1986).

There is evidence that living near parents is not just a matter of occupations and education but is, in fact, the preference of most people (Troll and Bengston, 1979). Furthermore, it should be noted that those adult children who do live greater distances from their parents are still interacting with them. There is a substantial amount of evidence that interaction between generational members continues to be fairly high even though face-to-face contact is limited by distance. Telephone communication is both convenient and commonplace today and is used regularly to keep the generations in touch with each other. Even face-to-face contact is possible with convenient and relatively inexpensive air travel commonplace.

The amount of interaction between generations has been extensively documented by a great amount of research in the last couple of decades. This research was stimulated by a debate among sociologists and other family scholars about the fundamental nature of the family system in contemporary society (see Troll, 1971). On one side of the debate, there was a characterization of the family as an *isolated nuclear family system.* This means that the nuclear family, composed of wife, husband, and their minor children, lives in a separate household and leads lives that are independent of the other generations. On the other side of the debate were those who said that there was too much interaction, especially in the form of aid and assistance between generations, to say that the nuclear family was isolated. The term preferred by those on this side of the debate was *modified extended family system.*

The debate about which term is the most apt description of the present-day family system has never been completely resolved (Gibson, 1972; Troll et al., 1979). On the one hand, the nuclear family lives separately from other generations and by and large operates independently of other generations of kin. How many young married couples will, for example, ask either the wife's or the husband's parents if they may, or should, buy a new car, or have a baby, or move to a different state? In an extended family system these decisions would probably not be made independently by the young married couple. And yet this same young couple may very well ask for and receive financial help from parents to do any of these things (Cheal, 1983). Also, in the case of having a baby or moving, parents or other kin members may be on hand to help out during the most difficult or important times. These ties between generations reflect more closely an extended family system, at least in a modified form.

It is the preference here to describe the family system in the United States as an *independent nuclear family system.* This term allows us to avoid the word *isolated,* which produces an image of a nuclear family that is not attached or linked to anyone but exists in a kind of solitary confinement. Using the term *independent nuclear family* identifies the basic decision-making unit as the nuclear family, and also reflects the reality of nuclear families living in separate residences (generally) and having separate financial lives (almost always). But the terminology is, in the long run, not as important as the reality it stands for, and we need now to examine a few more aspects of the relations between generations in this society.

The Middle-Aged Couple as a "Generational Bridge"

It has been noted by a number of writers and researchers that a couple in middle age, with both adult children and living parents, serves as a kind of bridge that links the generations (Hill et al., 1970). In two different senses, the middle-aged generation is advantageously placed. In the first and most obvious sense, the middle-aged generation, since it is also the middle generation, has the closest ties with each of the other two generations. The second sense of being in an advantageous position refers to the economic advantages of the middle-aged generation. When it comes to giving aid, especially economic, it is the middle generation that is most often called upon to help both their children and their parents. While they are in the best position to give this aid, it nonetheless puts added pressure on the middle generation (Hagestad, 1981).

While the economic transactions between generations are important, it has been noted that noneconomic transactions may be increasingly important (Smelser and Halpern, 1978). This often means simply giving advice or emotional support, both routinely and during difficult times. For example, many elderly people have the economic resources to be able to take care of their business affairs, but they may still need help with confusing or incomprehensible bureaucratic regulations and requirements (Shanas and Sussman, 1977). Medicare regulations, supplementary health insurance programs, the Social Security System, insurance, investments, taxes, and so on involve a complex array of ever-changing bureaucratic paperwork that the elderly are often ill-equipped to handle. While many of these might be equally confusing to their middle-aged children, it may nonetheless be comforting to be able to ask for advice and counsel from children rather than from a bureaucrat.

In a parallel way, there are also noneconomic supports middle-aged parents can give to their adult children. To take only one example, if adult children go through divorce, they often turn to their parents for help and support. Of course, a child getting a divorce might need economic help, but often, equally importantly, the child needs emotional support. Parents may be disappointed about the divorce, but they still usually try to give the emotional support their child needs. Parents also frequently take responsibility for informing grandparents about the separation and possible divorce of a grandchild. By serving as interpreter and discussant of this family crisis, the middle generation can often reduce the degree to which grandparents will be upset. This, of course, is another example of the way in which the middle generation serves as a generational bridge.

Another way of looking at the term *generational bridge* is to see it as a way of maintaining the solidarity of the family, or kin group. The middle generation is sometimes called the "kinkeeping middle generation" (Hill et al., 1970, p. 330). Kinkeeping can also be seen from the point of view of the particular individuals in the family who take the responsibility for maintaining intergenerational relations. The evidence on this point is clear: kinkeeping is done by women.

Women as Kinkeepers

In the relations between generations, the evidence clearly points to the significance of the mother and daughter relationship. Whether measured in terms of the amount of contact or the feelings of affection and intimacy, it is the relationship between women in the family that is closest (Adams, 1968; Troll et al., 1979). Males are not as close to their parents or to their children as are females. The reason for intergenerational relations being gender related is not altogether obvious. It can be said that women being kinkeepers is simply an extension of the traditional feminine gender role. If women are expected to be responsible for the expressive and emotional aspects of family life, then it follows that maintaining generational links would be part of that task. As for men, it has been suggested that when they reach adulthood they must break away from their parental families and establish their autonomy. When they marry, they are expected to give their primary loyalty to their wives and children, thus separating them even further from their parental families (Turner, 1975).

Since women are more likely to be the kinkeepers in families, and the mother-daughter relationship is the closest intergenerational link, it is not surprising that this relationship has received the most attention from researchers. The mother-daughter relationship has also been discussed in a number of popular books and articles in recent years. The book *My Mother/My Self* by Nancy Friday (1977) drew a great deal of attention when it characterized this relationship as one of lifelong ambivalent conflict. According to this view, daughters are never able to escape their early experiences with their mothers, even though they lead to negative consequences throughout life. Daughters feel attachment to their mothers but also at least a latent hostility toward them. While this book may have struck a resonant chord with some women, the general thesis does not receive support from systematic research. Studies show repeatedly that all but a few mothers and daughters express affection and liking for each other (Adam, 1968; Baruch and Barnett, 1983). Indeed, many women are aware that it is currently fashionable to view mothers negatively (and as the source of personal problems) and are nearly apologetic about liking their mothers. In one study a married woman of thirty-five was asked whom she liked to be with when she was feeling "down." She answered, "It's really embarrassing to say so, but it's my mother" (Baruch and Barnett, 1983, p. 605).

In many mother-daughter relationships there is probably an increase in friction during the daughter's adolescent period (Fischer, 1981). However, the relationship usually improves when daughters get married, and especially when they have children of their own (Fischer, 1981). One case example, described as an "ideal type," reveals what happens to many mothers and daughters as they move from the period of the daughter's adolescence to her marriage and motherhood. In this case, the daughter, as an adolescent, did everything she could to shut her mother out of her life. Her mother describes that period as "pretty bad." But then the daughter married and the relationship changed. Even on her wedding day the signs of change started to appear. As the mother recalled the day of the wedding, her daughter cried nearly the entire time. And when it came time for her to leave on her honeymoon it was nearly impossible to separate her from her family.

> It was time for them to go and friends were taking them to the airport. She could not leave. I am not kidding when I say they physically forced her in the car. "We've got to go. We're going to miss the plane." "I know . . . I know. Where's Jimmy?" (her brother). And then she had to come to me first. And then she went to her father. She went to Jimmy who she adores. She's out in the car and I hear her scream: "I didn't say goodbye to Mummy!" (Fischer, 1981, p. 616)

Her mother says, "The fact that we have this beautiful relationship [now] is the high point of my life" (Fischer, 1981, p. 616).

This same study showed that when daughters become mothers themselves, they often idealize their own mothers' mothering abilities. Generally, this takes the form of seeing their mothers' abilities with children in the light of their own experiences. One daughter with small children expressed her feelings as follows:

> *Now that I had children I realized what she had been through. Before that . . . it just didn't dawn on me what kind of responsibility she had. (In what specific ways?) Well, her patience—she really understood. I never realized how much she did understand—what we were going through when we were teenagers and when we were younger. She was really almost, I consider, almost a saint. (Fischer, 1981, p. 618)*

These positive sentiments of married daughters with children are also reflected in the numbers of visits and telephone calls to their mothers. About ninety percent of the married daughters with children who live within twenty miles of their mothers visit their mothers at least once a week. Only about fifty percent of the nearby daughters who are single or married without children visit their mothers this frequently. The same pattern prevails for daughters who live more than fifty miles away. In addition, married daughters with children also telephone their mothers more often, whether they live close or far away (Fischer, 1981).

As daughters themselves reach middle age, the relationship they have with their mothers may change again. Now their mothers are becoming elderly and are in different circumstances. They may be widowed and in need of more care and assistance, either because of financial need or declining physical or mental health. We will consider this relationship in the next section, in the context of the general relationship between adult children and their elderly parents.

Relationships between Adult Children and Their Elderly Parents

There are two major aspects of the relationship between adult children and their elderly parents: (1) interpersonal and emotional relations; and (2) aid, assistance, and economic support. These two dimensions are quite different but are often closely intertwined. There is probably a general historical trend toward a lessening importance of the latter, while the former continues to be very important in the relations of middle-aged people and their elderly parents. We will begin by considering interpersonal and emotional relations, and then move to the issue of caregiving.

Just as we have seen in the earlier considerations of intergenerational relations, most adult children feel very close to their elderly parents, while the parents return the sentiment even more strongly. In a study by Cicirelli (1981; 1983) eighty-seven percent of adult children felt "close" or "very close" to their elderly fathers, and ninety-one percent felt "close" or "very close" to their elderly

Almost all adults and their elderly parents have mutually positive feelings. While they may have areas of disagreement, they tend to avoid those issues that are potentially explosive.

mothers. This overwhelming expression of positive feelings between children and their elderly parents is encouraging, and certainly contradicts the sometimes heard assertion that older people are rejected and ignored by their children.

While there is no reason to doubt that there is genuine affection between adult children and their elderly parents, there are a few minor qualifiers that must be introduced. To begin with, there is probably a certain amount of social pressure to say that one feels close to one's parents or one's children, even though the actual feeling is a little more mixed or even negative. This pressure may be a little stronger for the adult children than for the elderly, since elderly people are noted for expressing their feelings with particular candor and honesty. Almost all elderly say they have positive feelings about their children, but as Bengston and Kuypers (1971) have noted, the older generation has a special stake in seeing the younger generation in a positive light. Since the parents have "produced" their children through upbringing and socialization, there is a desire to see them as good products.

There is another, perhaps more important, element in the relations between parents and children in the later stages of life that influences interpersonal feelings. It can be assumed that both parents and their adult children
genuinely wish to be friendly with each other. In the interests of accomplishing
that, both sides are careful, especially avoiding those topics and issues that
could produce problems for the relationship. The adult children often simply
do not reveal details of their personal and intimate lives that they believe will
upset their parents.

This process of the two generations avoiding conflict has been called *interaction management* (Hagestad, 1981). Both sides, the parents and their middle-
aged children, have learned through the years which topics are potentially
explosive, and they carefully avoid raising them. Their conversations have *de-
militarized zones* (Hagestad, 1981, p. 30). Perhaps to take the place of these explosive topics, family members learn to "pick their fights" (Troll, 1972). They
can then argue and debate issues, and perhaps let off some steam, but everyone
recognizes that these are issues of no great consequence.

Family members also may use a technique of manipulating the settings in
which they interact with each other, thus making them safe. Hagestad (1981) reports that many people she interviewed could tell her exactly the conditions under which they could get along smoothly with family members. Sometimes it
might be alone with the other person, other times it might be in a group, or perhaps by using certain other people as buffers. There are some signs that middle-
aged children and their parents often use grandchildren in this way (Hagestad,
1981).

While the vast majority of middle-aged children and their elderly parents
get along well, there are instances when there is conflict between these older
generations. Cicirelli (1983) says that five percent of his sample of adult respondents report frequent conflict with their elderly mothers, and six percent report frequent conflict with their elderly fathers. The most common reason for
conflict is that one party is critical of or intrudes into the activities or habits of
the other party. This statement is broad enough to cover most conflicts between
people, whether related or not, but some illustrations might be helpful.

Elderly parents might object to certain aspects of the way their children
live, such as their drinking behavior, marital conduct, or religious behavior (or
lack thereof). The author once purchased a used book on the patriarchs and
prophets of the Old Testament that contained the following handwritten inscription from a mother to her son:

> *To Robert* _____
>   *from Mother*
>   *for Father's sake.*

> *May you read this as you did in the days of long ago. May its lessons bring
> you back from the broad road followed by the scorner and disobedient,*

whose conscience slumbers to certain ruin. May you be given wisdom
before it is too late, is the anxious daily prayer of your loving,

Mother

While poetically composed, and with an expression of love, this motherly message is a stinging attack on what she considers her son's "scornful" and "disobedient" ways. One can imagine that more than a few family conflicts preceded this inscription.

Many parents and children acknowledge that while they get along well together they might have more conflicts if they were to live together. This is perhaps one reason that most older people want to live near their adult children, but not with them. And yet, about fifteen percent of all people over the age of sixty-five do live in households with a child (Smith, 1981). In a study of households in which elder relatives (ninety-one percent of whom were parents or parents-in-law) were being cared for, there were substantial indications that both stresses and conflicts were regular occurrences (Steinmetz and Amsden, 1983). The elders in these households were often reported by their caretaking children to be making excessive demands, being disruptive, and attempting to maintain an authority role. When caretakers and the elders were asked how these problems were resolved, the most common answer was "by talking." However, nearly half added that "screaming and yelling" were also used (Steinmetz and Amsden, 1983).

But there is an even more extreme indication of conflict in homes where elders are taken care of by their children. There is now increasing recognition that just as there is child abuse and wife abuse, there is also elder abuse. Insofar as facts have been established, and they are scanty at this time, the victims are most likely to be females over sixty-five years of age. The abusers are most likely to be their daughters (Pedrick-Cornell and Gelles, 1982; Rathbone-McCuan, 1980).

Research shows that when middle-aged children do take care of their parents, it is again the daughters or daughters-in-law who do the bulk of the caregiving. Since women of middle age are often in the labor force, the task of taking care of aging parents is a considerable additional burden. They must now meet the demands of the job, take care of their household responsibilities, and care for an aging parent. The strain on middle-aged women who must juggle these competing demands is very great (Lang and Brody, 1983; Stoller, 1983).

Research on middle-aged children and their parents, shows repeatedly that elderly parents are more satisfied with their lives and their children if they can remain independent. The reverse is also true, with middle-aged children feeling more positive toward their parents if they are not obliged to care for them. It is an irony of this relationship that the greater the amount of support and care the children provide for the elderly person, the poorer their relationship. If a parent is in need of assistance, either economically or physically, the children will nearly always meet this filial responsibility by providing the required support and care. But this very act of caregiving can lead to feelings of less independence by the parents and less satisfaction with their children. From the side of the adult children, the problems and stresses produced by caring for a parent are likely to contribute to declines in the quality of the relationship between generations.

Widowhood

One specific transition that can lead to the need for increased aid for elderly parents is widowhood (Anderson, 1984; Morgan, 1984). As we saw earlier in this chapter, women over sixty-five are likely to be living without a spouse, while men over sixty-five are very likely to be living with a spouse. A big contributor to this difference is, of course, widowhood, which is much more common for older women. Not only do wives usually outlive their husbands, but when men are widowed they are much more likely to remarry. If a woman is widowed after age fifty-five, there is only a five-percent chance that she will remarry. By contrast, most men who are widowed are likely to remarry if they are under age seventy (Troll et al., 1979). Among older people there are five widows for every one widower (Miller, 1978).

Very few widows (or widowers) move into the homes of their children after their spouses die. Since they have been running their own homes, it is difficult for them to move into a home where they would have a subordinate role. Also, if they move into the home of a child, they will suddenly be in the midst of the problems and pressures of that household. Their very presence would, as we have seen, very likely contribute to those problems and pressures, and most elderly people are reluctant either to lose their autonomy or to create problems for their children.

As would be expected, however, at the time a spouse dies the amount of interaction with children increases. There are the immediate problems of arranging for a funeral and providing necessary emotional support. While children provide this immediate help, they also provide continuing emotional support and help with personal problems (Anderson, 1984). But, in addition to children, widows and widowers increase their interaction with other kin members, especially with their siblings (Morgan, 1984). Often they turn to these kin members, instead of their children, when they are worried, ill, depressed, or short of money (Anderson, 1984).

The Grandparent-Grandchild Relationship

Thus far we have said very little about one of the most interesting family relationships: the relationship between grandparents and grandchildren. Two statements can be made immediately about the role of the grandparent. First, it is the least well defined of family relationships. There is little consensus about what the rights and duties of grandparents are. This leads to the second point, which is that there is an extremely wide range of behavior among grandparents with respect to their grandchildren (Hagestad, 1981).

One image of grandparenting is more myth than reality. This is the image of grandparents as old people sitting in their rocking chairs, living out the last years of their lives. Given the marriage ages and childbearing ages of the last forty years, a grandparent is most likely someone in mid-life who is still active and employed (Troll et al., 1979). The most common age for a woman to become a grandparent is about fifty; for men it is about fifty-two (Troll, 1983). In other words, a grandparent today is likely to be a vigorous and active person. Perhaps great-grandparents come closer to being people in the postretirement years of life. With the length of life that is commonplace today, especially for women, it is likely that most children will know at least one great-grandparent.

It is usually the grandparent, not the grandchild, that sets the style of grandparenting behavior. Several different styles of grandparenting have been identified by researchers (Neugarten and Weinstein, 1964; Wood and Robertson, 1976). The following types summarize these styles:

Remote-uninvolved: Some grandparents choose to be relatively detached, both from the role of grandparent and from interacting with the grandchild. They are unlikely to mention that they are grandparents and will make only limited efforts to do things with or for the grandchild.

Formal-symbolic: Some grandparents accept the social status of grandparent, but in a relatively formal and symbolic way. They will do the things that grandparents are supposed to do—give praise and gifts, take an interest in accomplishments and development—but they will make few additional efforts to be with and interact with the child.

Personal-pleasure: Some grandparents find great personal satisfaction in the grandparent role and pleasure in their grandchildren. This type of grandparent might display the automobile bumper sticker that reads: "Ask me about my grandchild." They truly enjoy being with their grandchildren and are often surrogate, but "fun," parents.

There is general agreement that relationships between grandparents and grandchildren are mutually beneficial. However, there is also a recognition that too much grandparenting can be disadvantageous. Parents sometimes complain that after a grandparental visit they have to cope with a different child. Grandparenting, it has been suggested, is subject to a "Goldilocks effect" (Hess and Waring, 1978). It can be "too much," and it can be "too little." But it is best if it is "just right."

While there may be an optimum level of grandparenting, there is widespread agreement that it is mutually beneficial for grandparents and grandchildren to interact with each other. It seems that grandchildren receive a special benefit from this contact because the relationship is uncomplicated and honest.

This can be detected in the words of grandchildren when they responded to the question, "What is a grandparent?":

> *Grandad grows lovely raspberries and always pretends not to notice us eating them. (Tracey, age 8)*
>
> *She's the person who tells me all the things about my parents they would rather not have me know. (Sarah, age 15)*
>
> *She leads an empty life of her own which is filled by the lives of others. Most of all she is a person who will always have time to see you when the rest of the world is busy. (Gill, age 14)*
>
> *(From* To Grandma and Grandpa, *Richard and Helen Exley, eds., cited in Tinsley and Parke, 1984, p. 161–162)*

These statements tell us that grandparents can be pleasant and supportive friends to children in a rich variety of ways.

As a final issue for this chapter, we will return to the relationship between middle-aged parents and their adult children. There is an assumption in our society that children, once they leave home, will be on their own thereafter. But in recent years many young people who have lived away from their parents have returned home. Some people have called this the "refilled nest syndrome." When adult children move back home after having had a relatively autonomous life for a while, new dimensions are added to parent-child relations. When parents have had a home without their children for a while, the return of children requires some readjustments. The issue for many parents is whether or not they are obliged to provide a home for their adult children whenever the children wish to return home.

ISSUE

Are parents obliged to provide a home for their adult children?

An often-quoted line of poetry is one by Robert Frost that describes and defines what *home* means:

"Home is the place where, when you have to go there,
They have to take you in"

(From 'The Death of the Hired Man' by Robert Frost)

While that line of poetry gives nearly everyone a feeling of instant recognition, the issue for many parents today is more problematic. They may ask themselves whether they really want to share, once more on a full-time basis, their homes and their lives with their now-grown children. Young adults may themselves question whether the disadvantages outweigh the advantages when they return home to live. In the discussion that follows, we will consider the issue primarily from the point of view of the parents, but, of course, many of the same concerns can be considered equally well from the perspectives of the children.

The Positive Aspects of Adult Children Returning Home

Parents want the best for their children, which means that children who want to return home after being on their own for a while will not usually be denied by their parents. Very frequently returning home has an underlying economic cause. The expenses of normal living, including renting an apartment, buying food and clothing, and maintaining an automobile or paying for transportation can easily run beyond the means of young people, even though they may have relatively good jobs. Of course, for children who have lost their jobs, have encountered unusual expenses, or have become ill or incapacitated, the economic stresses are even more severe. Most parents will, under any of these

severe economic conditions, be more than willing to help their children by letting them return home.

Even when economic needs are not so intensely pressing, parents will often
be happy to help their children by letting them live at home for a year or two (or
more). A young adult who has a job can get an important economic boost in life
by living with his or her parents for a few years. The money saved on housing
costs, as well as other of life's needs, can be money put aside for what is often
called "a good start in life." The parents can feel good about helping their children in this way, and the children will usually deeply appreciate what their parents are doing for them.

Indeed, appreciation for parents is one of the advantages often mentioned
as a by-product of returning home. A psychiatrist specializing in family therapy
says that after young people have lived with roommates who leave dirty dishes
in the sink, "Suddenly, parents don't seem so bad after all. They [the parents]
generally pick up after themselves" (quoted in Bumiller, 1982).

Since children who return home are in the postadolescent years of life and
have had away-from-home experiences, both parents and children can view
each other in a new light. Often parents and their children are able to relate to
each other as two adults rather than as parent and child. Many parents and children who are once again living together report that they truly enjoy each other's companionship, even for simple things such as cooking or shopping.
Parents also get some tangible rewards from their more experienced and
knowledgeable children. In the words of one mother, "there are rewards in
having the children home again: they help with engine rattles, making rum
cake, and pinning hems, and they provide company for afternoon tea and
scrabble. What's more, one learns so much . . . like putting on mascara, raising
a spinnaker, and basic yoga" (Foote, 1982, p. 362).

To sum up, the positive aspects of adult children returning home are often
primarily economic advantages for the children. Parents can get their rewards
from helping their grown children, either in times of economic need or just to
give them an economic helping hand. Often the experience of returning home
gives both the children and the parents new and more positive views of one
another.

The Negative Aspects of Adult Children Returning Home

From the point of view of parents, having adult children return home requires some adjustments and adaptations. These may not result in serious problems, but there are several potential areas where difficulties can arise. The
problem most often mentioned by both parents and children is that of modifying "parenting" behavior. After children have been on their own for a few years
and are used to having autonomy and freedom, it is often difficult for them to
live under even limited parental control again. Parents, for their part, find it
very difficult not to intrude in their children's lives when they disapprove of or

are concerned about certain behaviors. If parents do try to impose their views on their adult children, relationships can become severely strained. If no accommodation or compromise is reached on this very fundamental issue, the end result, in the extreme case, is that the child may be asked to leave home. If this occurs the break between parents and child may take years to heal.

Of course, there are other, generally less serious, issues that can produce problems between parents and their adult children. One of these is that with the initial departure of their children, parents may change or modify their lifestyles and homes. The return of the same children often requires changing back or adapting. Even physical space can become a problem as children who have accumulated their own belongings return home. One mother complained that after her son left home she had transformed his room, outfitting it with a white rug and bedspread. When he returned with his dog to reclaim his room, some obvious problems arose. The young man's mother may have been pleased to have her son at home, but she had not redecorated the room with him and his canine friend in mind (Bumiller, 1982).

The daily coming-and-going routines of households are also dramatically altered when adult children return home. Parents may have enjoyed feeling that their schedules were at last of their own making, after years of accommodating to the activity demands of their children. When children return home, parents may once again have to conform to their children's needs.

Some observers, especially those who take a broader view of the returning-home pattern, think there may be deeper significance to some children returning home because of "economic need." In the case of children who come from middle-class and relatively affluent homes, they may have been conditioned to expect always to have everything they want in the way of material goods and comforts. Out on their own they want to continue living at the same level as they did while they were growing up and their parents were paying the bills. When they learn how much it costs to pay the rent for a nice apartment, to keep a car running, and always to have enough money for recreation and entertainment, they return to their parents instead of lowering their expectation levels. In short, for some young adults, returning home to live with parents may mean that they want to live in an affluent life-style that they cannot personally pay for.

The major negative aspect of adult children returning home is likely to be the adjustment that both parents and children must make to this new situation. Children must often give up some of their autonomy, and parents must give the children more freedom. At the same time, parents will once again have to make more accommodations to their children. In the view of some observers, when children return home it often reflects a degree of self-indulgence and an addiction to material things.

Themes

1. Middle and later life is a time of change in the family.

2. Among people who are middle aged, there are great variations in life-styles and attitudes, making generalizations difficult.

3. Several demographic facts greatly influence the marital opportunities of men and women over the age of fifty.

4. The overall picture of marital quality in long-term marriages is generally positive.

5. The "mid-life crisis," which is especially likely to affect males, can have a great impact on marital life in the middle years of life.

6. Sexuality continues to be a vital factor in the lives of most people throughout life.

7. For most people, retirement appears to have a fairly positive influence on marital quality.

8. Despite the emphasis on the nuclear family in this society, there are strong relationships between the typical three- and four-generational family.

9. Middle-aged couples serve as a "generational bridge" between the older and younger generations.

10. Women are the "kinkeepers of families, and maintain the closest intergenerational ties.

11. The relationship between middle-aged adults and their elderly parents are more often interpersonal and emotional today, and less often economic.

12. Widowhood is a time when the elderly need more help and support from their children and other kin.

13. The role of grandparent is not clearly defined, leaving much room for individual variation.

Facts

1. Between the ages of fifty and sixty-four, more than four-fifths of all men and two-thirds of all women are married.

2. Men above sixty-five continue to be married about seventy-five to eighty percent of the time, while the rate of marriage for women falls to twenty-five percent by age seventy-five.

3. In long-term marriages, there are declines in expressions of love, but there are also declines in marital problems and negative sentiments.

4. Experiencing a mid-life crisis appears to be most closely related to physical changes, work and career realities, and a recognition of one's eventual death.

5. While the classic symptoms of mid-life crisis appear to affect only a small minority of men, many more experience withdrawal, disappointment, and disenchantment in the middle-age years.

6. The most frequently noted personality change in mid-life is for both men and women to take on more traits of the opposite sex.

7. The majority of married people continue to be sexually active into their sixties and seventies.

8. More people are retiring earlier, and in better health and economic circumstances, than ever before.

9. The retirement of wives is often related to the time when their husbands retire.

10. Nearly half of all husbands and wives acknowledged some improvement in their marriages after retirement.

11. Eighty to ninety percent of all elderly people see at last one of their children once a week or more.

12. Contrary to some popular assertions, adult women and their mothers almost always have positive feelings toward each other.

13. Approximately ninety percent of middle-aged adults feel close to their elderly parents.

14. There is a greater likelihood of conflict between adult children and their elderly parents if they live in the same household.

15. About fifteen percent of all persons above the age of sixty-five do live in a household with one of their children.

16. If a woman is widowed after age fifty-five, there is only a five-percent chance she will remarry. Men who are widowed are very likely to remarry if they are under seventy.

17. Today, people are likely to be grandparents at about age fifty, which makes it unlikely that they will fit the stereotypical image of "grandma and grandpa in rocking chairs."

Major Concepts

empty-nest syndrome: A characterization of the parental home after children have grown up and left.

formal-symbolic grandparent: A type of grandparent who accepts the social status of grandparent but interacts with his or her grandchild only in a formal and symbolic way.

"generational bridge": The link between adult children and elderly living parents, provided by the middle-aged generation.

independent nuclear family: The pattern of generations living separately and having independent decision making and separate financial lives, and yet having substantial interaction between generations.

interaction management: The process by which generations avoid conflict by avoiding potentially explosive topics and selecting "safer" issues about which to debate or argue.

isolated-nuclear family: The pattern of wife, husband, and their minor children living in a separate household and leading lives independent of other generations.

kinkeeping: Activities aimed at maintaining the solidarity of the family especially across generational lines.

mid-life crisis: Rapid and substantial personality changes in middle age that lead to questioning personal identity and previous values placed on work, reputation, material things, family, and marriage.

mid-life transition: Gradual changes, especially in personality, experienced by many men and women during middle age.

modified-extended family: The pattern of different generations living separately but having extensive interaction in the form of mutual aid and assistance.

neolocal residence: The pattern of children as they move into adulthood establishing a residence separate from their parents.

personal-pleasure grandparent: A type of grandparent who finds great personal satisfaction in his or her grandchildren.

remote-uninvolved grandparent: A type of grandparent who is detached from and has limited interest in his or her grandchildren.

"return-to-the-nest syndrome": The pattern of adult children returning to live in their parents' home.

15

Separation and Divorce
Causes, Correlates, and the Divorce Process

Jeremy, in his first year in high school, chose to write a term paper on divorce. He explained in his introduction, "I was interested in divorce because my mother and father had a divorce and I had a vague idea of what was going on, but I did not fully understand and now I do." He concluded the introduction to his paper by writing, "Some joker has said the major cause of divorce is marriage. However, we all know this is no joke" (from Wallerstein and Kelly, 1980, p. 302).

Divorce is no joke. There has been some talk in recent years of divorce becoming easier and easier to obtain. It is said that because divorce is so commonplace, people get divorced with hardly a second thought. There have been books and articles written about "creative divorce" and "amicable divorce." While there may be truth to some of these characterizations, they do not aptly describe the typical divorce experience. Couples who separate and begin the divorce process, even after many years of wanting to end their marriages, often find the experience painful and disorienting. Children of parents who divorce usually feel hurt and distressed by the breakup of the family and the changes in their lives. Even parents whose adult children are going through separation and divorce suffer along with their children and grandchildren. Except for some rare and fortunate people, divorce is not a happy or pleasant experience; to say that it is ignores the reality that is all around us.

This chapter will examine the social and legal nature of divorce, especially as it has evolved in Anglo-American societies. This will give us a clearer standard by which to evaluate the nature and extent of contemporary divorce. The chapter will also take a close look at the statistics of divorce, both to see how these are best interpreted and what they tell us about the patterns of divorce. Much of the research on divorce has revealed which social factors are closely associated with divorce. An examination of these factors can provide some of the reasons that divorce has reached its current levels and perhaps even indicate what might be expected in the future. In the latter part of the chapter we will examine the different aspects of the divorce experience, since divorce is not simple but is a complex array of different actions and experiences.

One of these experiences, one that affects over a million divorcing couples each year, concerns child custody. Through much of the twentieth century, mothers have routinely been awarded custody of all minor children, but more couples today are considering some form of joint custody. Under joint custody both husband and wife retain both rights and responsibilities for their children. There are many advocates of joint custody, but there are also critics. At the end of the chapter, after we have considered the nature of child custody both in the past and more recently, we will present the arguments for and against joint custody.

We have seen in previous chapters that the people of all societies value marriage, so it will not be surprising to learn that once a marriage is formed the people of most societies prefer to have the marriage remain intact. But there is generally a recognition that some marriages will not work out, and thus most societies have some mechanism for ending marriages. In some societies, couples may end their marriages by very simple procedures, as when a man may simply say to his wife, "I divorce thee," or a woman may place her husband's possessions outside the front door of their home where he will see them when he returns. Yet, in many other societies the process is difficult, complex, and expensive, making divorce virtually impossible for most people. When this occurs, it is not uncommon for people of lesser means to end marriages in some other fashion. For example, in England in the early 1800s, when divorce was so expensive and difficult that it was only available to the very rich, some English couples were divorced by having the husband auction off his wife in the village marketplace. This was not quite a legal divorce, but for many of the village people it was viewed as an appropriate and valid way of ending a marriage (Menefee, 1981). To see this method of divorcing in its proper perspective, it is necessary first to take a brief look at English divorce laws and procedures, as they developed after the medieval era.

DIVORCE IN ENGLISH HISTORY

Prior to seventeenth century, the only official way of ending a marriage in England was to have it annulled by the Church (the Roman Catholic Church before, and the Anglican Church after, the Reformation). If the original marriage was judged by the Church to be "spurious," and not a "true" marriage it could be ended. A *spurious marriage* might be one, for example, where the husband and wife were too closely related to each other. Church laws spelled out just how closely a husband and wife could be related, so if a couple could find some witnesses to testify that the rules had been violated, their marriage could be annulled. However, if the reason for the divorce was adultery, desertion, or physical cruelty, the laws of the Church did not allow a full divorce (one which allowed remarriage). In these cases, the Church would only grant what was called a *separate bed and board divorce.* With this type of divorce, the legal obligations of marriage remained, except that the husband and wife lived separately. Since remarriage was not possible, this type of divorce created a great hardship for many people. For those people who were rich and titled, this limited form of divorce could lead to a circumstance of not having legitimate heirs for their wealth and titles (Menefee, 1981).

Apparently as a result of pressures brought by the English aristocracy, a law was passed that made it possible for a full divorce to be obtained by the passage of a private act of the House of Lords (Cott, 1983). This was very expensive, costing several thousand pounds, and was thus only available to the rich. In fact, there were only ninety such private acts by the House of Lords between 1697 and 1785, even though England had a population of nearly seven million in the eighteenth century. All these divorce awards were to husbands, and all were based on grounds that the wives had committed adultery (Cott, 1983). The fact that no wives were granted divorces because of adulterous husbands surely reflects a double standard of sexual conduct and shows that this divorce law was primarily for the benefit of males.

The rules for getting a divorce, either from the Church or from the Parliament, were so limiting that most married people were effectively excluded from divorce. At least, they were excluded from getting a divorce that would allow them to remarry. It was under these circumstances that some of the English people chose the method of "selling wives" as a way of ending their marriages. Of course, the very terminology reveals that women were viewed as the property of their husbands, which reflects the patriarchal system of marriage that prevailed at that time.

The most common examples of wife-selling occurred in cases of adulterous wives. If a married woman took a lover and her husband learned of it, he might very likely choose to end the marriage. The wife, too, might want to end the marriage and marry the man with whom she was having a sexual relationship. Under these circumstances there was often an act of collusion between the husband, his wife, and her lover, in which they would agree in advance that the lover would make the purchase. The public occasion for this event must have been a bizarre sight, for according to custom the husband would bring his wife to the marketplace with a rope or halter around her neck. When the sale was made, usually to the prearranged buyer, the rope was handed over to the new owner. Often the money was paid to the husband for all to see, and many times a formal bill of sale would be drawn up (Menefee, 1981).

An analysis of these proceedings reveals, first, how women were viewed in marriage. The acts of leading a woman to the marketplace, selling her at auction, and turning over the rope around her neck to the buyer emphasize how much a woman was viewed as the property of her husband. But there is another, more subtle message in this transaction, which should also be noted. The fact that the sale was held in a public place, with members of the community observing the event, is important. For just as the marriage ceremony was a social and public event, so also was this form of divorce. It may not have been recognized by the Church or the government, but it was recognized by the people of the community who knew the married couple. It was clear to the folk of the community that when a woman was sold by her husband she was no longer obligated to him. Her marriage vows no longer had validity or force. As for the husband, everyone would now know that he no longer had responsibility for the woman who had been his wife. The members of the community understood that these two people were no longer married. The woman was now the wife of the man who had purchased her, and the husband was free to remarry.

In 1857 the English changed their divorce laws in order to make legal divorce more accessible to the majority of the people. With the Divorce Act of 1857, divorce became possible on the grounds of adultery and on several other grounds as well, including extreme cruelty by the husband or desertion for at least two years by the husband (Menefee, 1981). In the United States, many of these grounds for divorce had been accepted for many years by the time the English passed their divorce reform legislation. However, in the early colonial period, divorces were nearly as difficult to get as in England.

DIVORCE IN THE HISTORY
OF THE UNITED STATES

According to a search of the court records of early Massachusetts by historian Nancy Cott, there were 229 divorce petitions filed in that colony and state between 1692 and 1786 (Cott, 1983). However, only half of these petitions actually resulted in divorces. Among the other half of the divorce petitions, about thirteen percent were dismissed or not granted by the court, and another twenty-five percent were left unresolved. Of the remaining petitions, the court annulled eleven marriages and granted the "separate bed and board" divorce in seventeen other cases. The separate bed and board divorce in the colonies, like in England, meant a partial divorce that did not allow remarriage.

If the divorces, annulments, and separate bed and board decrees are added together, a total of 143 marriages were legally ended in Massachusetts in the ninety-four years between 1692 and 1786. Except for desertion, which some

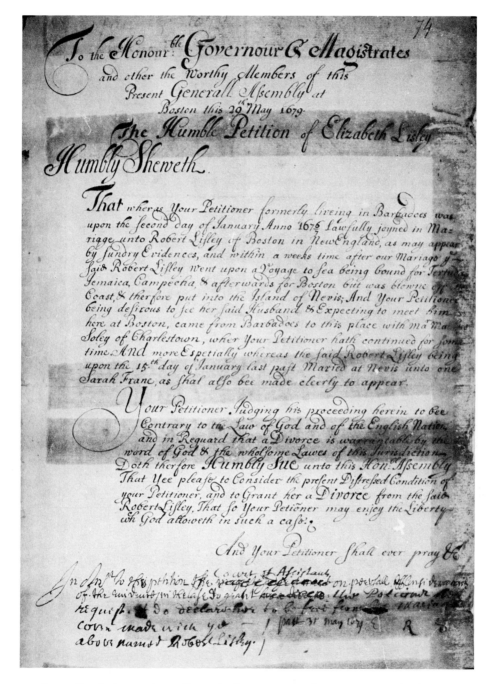

In pre-Revolutionary times, divorce in the American colonies was rare. The divorce petition above was based on the bigamous marriage of the woman's husband.

married people resorted to, there is no indication that Americans had any other mechanisms for ending marriages. Thus, during a period of nearly one hundred years, the population of Massachusetts, which probably averaged around 200,000 people, had a very low rate of divorce. To see just how low the divorce rate was by contemporary standards, suppose we were to ask, "How many divorces would there have been in Massachusetts over the same ninety-four years, if current United States divorce rates had prevailed?" The answer, based on the current divorce rate of 4.8 divorces each year for every 1000 people in the population, is over 90,000 divorces, instead of 143!

This hypothetical statistic tells us two things we would probably have guessed: divorce was rare in the colonial period of United States history, and the divorce rate is high in the present-day United States. Before we take a more complete look at current divorce statistics, there are several other features of the historical record of divorce in the United States that are worth noting.

Although divorce was rare in colonial America, the laws governing divorce, especially grounds for divorce and the divorce rights of women, were liberalized in the United States sooner than they were in England.

While there is only one recorded case of a woman in seventeenth-century Massachusetts receiving a divorce on the *sole* ground of adultery, by the eighteenth century women were beginning to be treated somewhat more fairly (Gordon, 1978). In some of the earliest recorded divorce cases in Massachusetts, the grounds in addition to adultery were cruelty, desertion, and bigamy. *Bigamy,* which is marriage by a person who is already married, was fairly common in this historical period. Often a married man would migrate from England or move from another colony with the intention of sending for his wife after becoming established. Because there might be no knowledge of his marital status, it was possible to marry another woman in the new place and simply never call for the earlier wife. When these cases were discovered, a divorce petition might be filed on the grounds of bigamy (Gordon, 1978).

The divorce laws in colonial Connecticut were noted for being especially liberal. There was much less use of the separate bed and board divorce, so that virtually all petitions that were granted in the eighteenth century were "true" divorces (Gordon, 1978).

By 1843, in addition to the grounds already mentioned, Connecticut added "habitual intemperance" (alcoholism) and "intolerable cruelty" to the list of grounds for divorce (Gordon, 1978). An interesting case of Connecticut granting a divorce on unusual grounds came as early as 1675, when a woman named Elizabeth Rogers was granted a divorce because her husband was a "free thinker." Apparently, Elizabeth Rogers's husband came before the court and declared that he renounced all types of worship being conducted in New England and declared himself "against the Christian Sabbath as a mere invention" (Gordon, 1978, p. 284). The Connecticut court found this antireligious expression sufficient grounds for divorce.

During the nineteenth century, many but not all states liberalized their divorce laws greatly. One important liberalizing law is called the *omnibus clause.*

Indiana was the first state to have such a clause in its statute of 1824, but a number of states across the country followed. The Indiana law listed a number of grounds for divorce, such as those already mentioned—adultery, cruelty, one-year abandonment—and then went on to say, "Any other cause for which the court shall deem it proper that a divorce should be granted" (Gordon, 1978, p. 286). This omnibus clause, of course, opened the gates for any kind of complaint that spouses might have as a basis for requesting a divorce.

Another important development in divorce law occurred in California, where a series of nineteenth-century court decisions expanded the concept of cruelty to include mental cruelty (Griswold, 1982). Today, mental cruelty is very broadly interpreted and can include any act or behavior that is psychologically damaging to one's spouse. In 1857 a California judge ruled that it was unacceptable cruelty when a woman's husband had accused her of adultery. The judge's decision was very much rooted in the nineteenth-century conception of women as being more moral and more sensitive than men. He stated in his opinion, "To a lady of delicacy of feeling, purity of thought and refined sensibilities, I can conceive of no greater cruelty than by falsely charging her with prostituting her person" (Griswold, 1982, p. 19). Another court decision in the same year echoed that sentiment by stating that a false accusation of adultery is "the grossest act of cruelty which can be perpetrated against an innocent female" (Griswold, 1982, p. 19). In 1863 the Supreme Court of California greatly expanded the meaning of mental cruelty when it offered the following opinion: "We think that any conduct sufficiently aggravated to produce ill-health or bodily pain, though operating primarily on the mind only, should be regarded as legal cruelty" (Griswold, 1982, p. 20). In 1870 the state legislature followed the court's lead and redefined cruelty so that it included "mental suffering" (Griswold, 1982, p. 20).

The liberalization of divorce laws in California and many other states, especially in the West and Southwest, set the stage for divorce as it has evolved in the twentieth century. Before turning to a consideration of divorce in contemporary United States, it is necessary to give some attention to a matter about which there is considerable confusion—divorce statistics.

THE STATISTICS OF DIVORCE

There is a substantial amount of misinformation and misunderstanding about divorce statistics. One important reason for the confusion and misuse is that some of the most appealing statistics, those that seem to have intrinsic meaning for many people, are either misleading or more complex than they seem. And while the best statistics for understanding trends in divorce are rates, these rates often do not convey as much information as people would like and thus are less appealing. We will first examine some divorce statistics that are not as good as they seem on the surface.

Divorces as a Percentage of Weddings

A measure of divorce that is often used and yet is considered inappropriate by most specialists on divorce is one that compares the number of divorces in a year to the number of marriages occurring in that same year (for a city, state, or county). If, for example, a state has 60,000 marriages in a given year and 30,000 divorces, it is easy to see that there were fifty percent as many divorces as marriages. That much is accurate, and it may be interesting, but it is not a good indication of the rate of divorce. There are several reasons why this is not a good divorce rate. First, and most important, a good rate would compare the number of divorces with the *population at risk.* The number of people getting married in a given year is only a small portion of the population at risk for divorce. All married couples, whenever they were married, are at risk for divorce.

Comparing divorces in a given year to marriages in the same year is also a poor measure of divorce because it can be influenced as much by the marrying behavior of people as by their divorcing behavior. If, for some reason, the state with 60,000 marriages in one year suddenly has a drop in marriages to 40,000, and the number of divorces remains at 30,000, the result would be an apparent rise in the "divorce rate."

The most serious misuse of the comparison between divorces and marriages in a given year is the assumption that somehow the comparison indicates what percentage of marriages end in divorce. Because it is easy to obtain the statistics on numbers of divorces and marriages occurring in particular states or cities in any given year, this mistake has often been made. This can lead to ridiculous statements such as one once made on a national television program claiming that in some California counties the "divorce rate" was more than one hundred percent!

Percentage of All Marriages Ending in Divorce

If the divorce rates of a society are said to be high, it is understandable that people would want to know what their chances are of having a marriage that does not end in divorce. The question is meaningful and interesting, but the answer is not always what it seems. Consider, for example, the couples getting married in American society this year. What can we say about their chances of divorce? In one sense, unless we have some way to see into the future, we can say nothing. But we can perhaps make the assumption that couples marrying this year will be divorced at about the same rate as couples who were married in previous years. That assumption should be true if we are comparing couples married this year with couples married last year, or perhaps even in the last three years. However, the further back we go in time, the less confidence we can have in our assumption that couples marrying today are going to be similar to, and have divorce records similar to, couples of the past. Now the problem begins to become apparent. Couples married in the last three years have not yet gone through enough of their married years for us to say much about their divorce histories. In fact, the only couples for whom we do have more or less complete marriage and divorce histories are those who married many years ago—say twenty or twenty-five years. But can we make the assumption that couples marrying this year are going to be like couples who married that long ago? Many things have changed in the last twenty-five years—more women are in the labor force, the women's movement has changed our thinking, the economy is different, many more couples cohabit before marriage, couples are waiting longer before they marry, and so on.

Yet, we often hear the statement that "fifty percent of all marriages end in divorce." Where do such statistics come from and what do they really mean? The answer to the first question is that a number of researchers have carefully assembled the divorce statistics for couples who were married five, ten, fifteen, and more years ago (Preston and McDonald, 1979; Weed, 1980). The most recently analyzed marriages took place in 1973, and the couples in this group had only been married four years when the study took place (Weed, 1980). These researchers are acutely aware that when they extrapolate from recently married couples and couples married many years earlier, they cannot use these data to speak of currently marrying couples. The serious researchers make their statements very carefully, usually emphasizing that *if* the couples who have recently married follow the same divorce patterns as those who married many years earlier, *then for them* the percentage who will ultimately divorce *may* reach a certain percentage. Unfortunately, their cautious scientific statements are either not heard or are ignored by most people who speak glibly about the percentage of all marriages ending in divorce.

The most meaningful way to describe and assess statistically what has happened and what is happening with regard to divorce is to examine and compare the rates of divorce for those years where data are available.

Divorce Rates

The population at risk of getting a divorce is obviously the population of married couples. Thus, the most meaningful measure of divorce would be produced by comparing the number of divorces in any given year to the total number of married couples in the society for that year. This is customarily done by dividing the number of divorces (and annulments) in any particular year by the number of married women (fifteen years of age and over) in the population. As an example of how the calculation of this divorce rate is made, we will take the figures for the year 1982, when there were 1,170,000 divorces and annulments and 53,927,000 married women fifteen years of age and older. The number of divorces is first divided by the number of marriages, as follows:

$$\frac{1,170,000}{53,927,000} = 0.0217.$$

The result is a small decimal fraction, 0.0217. To avoid the small decimal fraction, it is the custom in creating rates to multiply by some constant number. In the case of the divorce rate this constant number is 1000. When 0.0217 is multiplied by 1000 the result is 21.7. This is the divorce rate for 1982, and it can be described in a very straightforward manner: for the year 1982, there were 21.7 divorces for every 1000 marriages in the population.

The main advantage of calculating rates of divorce in this way is that it is possible to disregard the absolute sizes of the married and divorced populations when making comparisons from year to year. The population of the United States has grown greatly in the last sixty years, but it is still possible to compare the divorce rate in 1982 with the divorce rates in 1972, 1952, and, if the data are available, 1932. These data are available, and in the next section we can use divorce rates to see clearly what the trend in divorce in the United States has been since the 1920s.

UNITED STATES DIVORCE RATES

The rates of divorce in the United States between 1925 and the present are shown in Figure 15.1. In addition to the divorce rate discussed in the preceding section, a second rate (the lower trend line) is also shown. This second rate is based not on the married population, but on the total population. One might reasonably ask why the entire population is used as a basis for calculating a divorce rate when only the married population is at risk of divorce. The answer is that by using the total population in the calculation it is possible to obtain a more current measure of what is happening to the rate of divorce. The size of the total population is known at all times, but the size of the married population is only determined by periodic surveys and censuses. By comparing the number of divorces with the total population we can have more up-to-date measures of the divorce rate. An examination of Figure 15.1 shows that the two rates tend to parallel each other, although the divorce rate based on the total population tends to be less volatile in its fluctuations.

There are several features of the divorce rate trend between 1925 and the present that deserve comment. The overall trend in the last sixty years has obviously been upward, but the steepest part of the increase in the United States divorce rate started in the early 1960s and continued until the end of the 1970s. During this fifteen-year period, the divorce rate more than doubled (by either measure). This rapid increase in the divorce rate has shaped much of our thinking about divorce, and in fact about marriage itself.

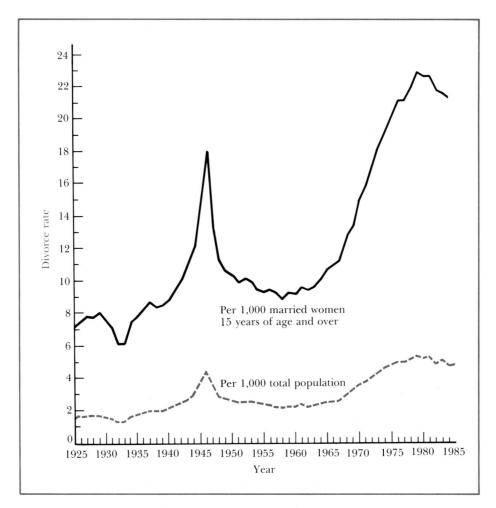

Figure 15.1 *Divorce rates for the United States, 1925–1985. (Sources: National Center for Health Statistics, 1985. 'Advance Report on Final Divorce Statistics, 1982.' Vol. 33, No. 11. And, National Center for Health Statistics, 1985. 'Births, Marriages, Divorces And Deaths for 1985.')*

Several other features of this divorce trend line are interesting. There is a substantial dip in the divorce rate in the early 1930s. This dip corresponds with some of the most difficult years of the economic depression of that decade. This suggests that divorces are less frequent during times of severe economic depression. Since research conducted in the 1920s also revealed that divorce rates generally went down during economic hard times, there has been a long-standing belief that the divorce rate goes down during economic depressions and recessions. Even though the decline in the divorce rate in the 1930s is indisputable, research conducted on the post–World War II period has failed to show the same relationship. Indeed, since 1947 the divorce rate has tended to go up during periods of economic recession (South, 1985).

A second very noticeable pattern in Figure 15.1 is the high peak of divorce in the middle 1940s. This peak corresponds with the end of World War II and reflects how the war affected marriages. Two major factors increased the divorce rate during this postwar period. First, many married couples were separated by the war, and, perhaps because of their experiences while apart, many chose not to return to their prewar married lives. Second, many marriages were entered hastily and precipitously during the war years. After the war, perhaps these marriages had lost some of their initial appeal. Interestingly, with regard to the two major wars since World War II, the divorce rate went down during the Korean War and up during the Vietnam War (South, 1985).

While the depression and war divorce patterns are interesting, there is one other pattern that is more closely connected with our own time. As Figure 15.1 shows clearly, the divorce rate has been going down since 1979. The decline in the five years between 1979 and 1984 has been about as steep as the increases of the 1970s. It may be premature to speculate very much about the causes of this decline, since it has not been going on very long, but the downward trend cannot be ignored, since there may be some plausible explanations for it (Kammeyer, 1981). In the pages that follow, as we consider some of the factors associated with divorce, we will consider if some of them can account for the recent declines in the divorce rate.

FACTORS ASSOCIATED WITH DIVORCE

We can begin to understand both the increases and the decreases in the divorce rate in the United States if we examine some of the factors that have been found to be associated with divorce. These factors are most appropriately called *correlates*, which simply means that they are characteristics of individuals or couples that are correlated with divorce. Without necessarily taking up these correlates in order of their importance, the first one we will consider—age at marriage—is universally agreed to be of great significance.

Age at Marriage

All available evidence points to the fact that if one marries at an early age, there is a greater likelihood of divorce (Booth and Edwards, 1985; Glenn and Supancic, 1984; Teachman, 1983). Couples who marry under age eighteen are particularly prone to divorce. The effect of early marriage on divorce holds for both males and females, but the "earliness" is relative to the general ages at which the two sexes marry. In other words, males who marry at eighteen or nineteen have about the same chances of divorce as females who marry at sixteen or seventeen, and the same is true up the age scale (Glenn and Supancic, 1984)

There are a number of likely explanations for the high rate of breakup of marriages among couples who marry young. One explanation is that people who marry when very young are poorly prepared for the role of marriage. Being poorly prepared, they fail to meet the needs and expectations of their spouses and experience more dissatisfaction. This explanation can be labeled *poor preparation for marital role performance* (Booth and Edwards, 1985; Lee, 1977).

A second explanation for the high divorce rates among those who marry young grows out of the idea that the chances of divorce increase if there are attractive alternatives to the marriage (Levinger, 1979). It may be that individuals who marry when they are very young will perceive that their chances for remarriage are good if they do divorce their present spouse (Booth and Edwards, 1985). This explanation can be called *attractive alternatives after divorce.*

A third explanation, again coming from the ideas of Levinger (1979), is that people who marry young have fewer barriers to divorce. Couples who marry when very young often do so without the wholehearted approval of their parents, sometimes despite actual parental disapproval. This means that they often do not have a sense that parents and other relatives will oppose their divorce (Booth and Edwards, 1985). Without this barrier to divorce, it may be easier to end the marriage if it is not going well. This explanation can be called *barriers to divorce.*

These three alternative explanations for higher divorce rates among couples who marry young have been evaluated in a study conducted by Booth and Edwards (1985). In interviews with a national sample of 1,715 married adults, marital instability was measured by a series of questions about whether the couple had considered or taken steps toward separation or divorce. In this study neither alternative attractions nor the lack of barriers to divorce was able to account for greater amounts of marital instability among those couples who married early. However, the research did provide support for the idea that the greater marital instability among early marrying couples is related to poor marital role performance. Poor role performance, which was found much more often among those who married early, was revealed by more frequent expressions of dissatisfaction and negative behaviors by both marital partners. There was more unhappiness with the way one's spouse performed with respect to understanding, love and affection, sex, breadwinning, home care, companionship, and faithfulness. Poor role performance was also indicated by one or both members of the couple getting angry easily, having feelings easily hurt, being jealous, being domineering, being critical, being moody, not talking to the other, having had a sexual relationship with someone else, spending money foolishly, drinking or using drugs, and having been in trouble with the law. According to this study, these reflections of poor role performance among the early marrying couples contributed to their marital instability (Booth and Edwards, 1985).

There is a high rate of marital breakup among couples who marry young. Research suggests that a major factor may be the poor performance of marital roles.

Another kind of explanation for the greater marital instability among couples who marry when they are in their teens is that often early marriage follows premarital pregnancy (Furstenberg, 1979). There are several possible reasons why premarital pregnancy may lead to more unstable marriages. If young couples are not prepared for the marital role, they are even less likely to be prepared for the parental role. We saw in Chapter 10 how having a baby creates stress for all married couples, and the less realistically one is prepared for parenthood the more stressful it is. Also, having a baby in the first year of marriage is an added economic strain on young couples who are already likely to be under some economic pressures (Furstenberg, 1979).

The research evidence on the effects of premarital pregnancy on marital instability is somewhat mixed. Some studies have found that pregnancy before marriage contributes to marriage breakup (Coombs and Zumeta, 1970; Furstenberg, 1976, 1979). Other studies have found that premarital pregnancy does not affect marital instability, but that having a child before marriage does (Bumpass and Sweet, 1972; Teachman, 1983).

If we accept that marriages precipitated by pregnancy or marriages that follow the birth of a child both contribute to marital instability, we may have uncovered some of the reasons for the decline of divorce since 1979. There is evi-

dence that premarital pregnancy is not as likely to lead to marriage as it was
two decades ago. Even though we saw in Chapter 5 that more young people are
engaging in sex before marriage, this has not meant an automatic increase in
pregnancy-prompted marriages. One reason for this is the increased use of contraceptives by unmarried teenagers (Zelnik and Kantner, 1980). However, even
when pregnancies do occur, they do not lead to marriage as often as they would
have in previous decades. The major reason for this is the dramatic increase in
legal abortion during the 1970s. In the latter part of this decade about one-third
of all legal abortions were for women under age twenty (U.S. Bureau of the Census, 1984). In 1979, thirty-seven percent of unmarried teenage women who became pregnant ended their pregnancies with abortions (Zelnik and Kantner,
1980). Without abortion, some of these pregnancies would have led to teenage
(pregnancy-prompted) marriages. In some cases these pregnancies would have
led to the birth of a child without marriage, and research has shown that wom-
en who marry after having had a child are particularly likely to have divorces
(Teachman, 1983). Since these high-risk marriages did not occur, the overall effect would be a decline in divorces, just as has been observed during the 1980s.

In his study of the effects of unwed childbearing on the breakup of marriages, Teachman (1983) found very high instability in the marriages of black
women who had a child before marriage. For example, a black woman marrying at age 16 or 17 *after* having had a child had only a thirty-eight percent
chance of still being married after fifteen years. For white women under the
same conditions, the chance of still being married after fifteen years was sixty
percent (Teachman, 1983). This pattern of black women having poorer chances
of their marriages surviving is a general pattern, regardless of age at marriage
or premarital pregnancy. The factor of race is the second major correlate of divorce, and we will consider it next.

Race

Every study that has considered black-white differences in separation and
divorce has found higher rates of marital breakup among blacks. In the combined data coming from seven different random samples of the United States
population, the rate of divorce and legal separation was fifty percent higher for
blacks than whites (Glenn and Supancic, 1984). Studies comparing black and
white marital dissolution rates have also revealed that blacks are more likely to
remain in the separated category longer than whites (Cherlin, 1981). According
to the results of one national sample of women, one-half of the black women
who separate from their husbands are not divorced five years after the beginning of the separation. By comparison, only one-tenth of white women have not
divorced five years after separation (McCarthy, 1978). One result of this difference is that at any given time the black population has a much larger percentage
of its population in the separated category. In 1983, about twelve percent of the
black female population between 25 and 44 was separated, while only three

percent of the white female population between those ages was separated (U.S. Bureau of the Census, 1983).

The higher rate of marital instability among black Americans has been the subject of a considerable amount of discussion and debate. Scholars, politicians, and many others have all made attempts to account for the greater marital instability of the black family in the United States. The explanations include the legacy of slavery, in which black families were often broken up, the disruptions caused by migrating from rural places, high unemployment among black males, and the presumed effect of government social welfare programs (Cherlin, 1981). It is not a simple task to decide which of these different explanations is most valid, but Cherlin points out that most of the divergence between black and white family patterns has occurred since World War II. He therefore feels the explanation probably comes from "the response of the poorest, most disadvantaged segment of the black population to the social and economic situation they have faced in our cities over the past few decades (Cherlin, 1981, p. 108). Linking the greater instability of black families generally to the conditions of those who are most disadvantaged is consistent with the general evidence we have about the effects of socioeconomic status on marital stability.

Socioeconomic Status

Marital instability is more frequent among people in the lower socioeconomic strata of society than the higher strata. Research has shown repeatedly that people with higher educational levels, higher incomes, and higher status occupations have lower rates of marital dissolution (Norton and Glick, 1979). However, the recent research on this pattern by Glenn and Supancic (1984) has led them to say that socioeconomic factors may be somewhat overrated as correlates of divorce and separation. While that may be true, their research continued to show that, generally, married couples who are in higher educational, income, and occupational categories have lower rates of separation and divorce. There are many possible reasons for higher status people having less marital instability. One possibility is that usually more years of education are needed for higher socioeconomic status levels, and more education typically requires later marriage. We have seen that later marriage leads to greater marital stability. There is also the possibility that there are fewer crises and disruptions in the lives of people in the higher socioeconomic status levels. As a last possibility, it is believed by some that higher status people have more to lose from divorce than lower status people, especially in terms of social status. This belief may be somewhat dubious today, since divorce does not generally carry the same stigma that it did even a generation ago, although in some higher status occupations, such as among the clergy and politicians, divorce may still be detrimental to status.

When educational attainment levels are used as a measure of socioeconomic status, one pattern often appears that points to something beyond simple social or economic status. Studies have shown that people who do not complete high school or college are more susceptible to marital breakup than those who do. For example, people who attend college for one to three years have a much higher marital breakup rate than those who complete four years of college, but, more important, they also have a higher marital breakup rate than those people with high school degrees. In a study of the national population based on seven sample surveys, college "dropouts" had the second highest marital disruption rate, exceeded only by the people who did not complete high school. This pattern has led some researchers to speculate that people who do not finish school (both high school and college) may be categorized as having a lack of persistence (Glick, 1957). According to this interpretation, not finishing school and not sticking with marriage reflect a common personality trait.

Religion

It is probably not surprising to learn that religious preferences and religiosity generally are related to separation and divorce (Glenn and Supancic, 1984). The more often people attend religious services, the less likely they are to have a marital breakup. Among the major religious denominations of the United States, Protestants as a group have slightly higher dissolution rates than Catholics, while Jews have lower rates than Catholics. The highest marriage disruption rates are among those people who claim no religion. Among the Protestant denominations, some that are most conservative in their theology, such as the Nazarenes, Pentecostalists, and Baptists, have relatively high marital disruption rates (Glenn and Supancic, 1984; Thornton, 1978). There might be several reasons for this unexpected relationship. It may be related to the relatively lower socioeconomic status of the membership of these denominations, or it may be that these denominations are concentrated in the South, where the divorce rate is higher than many other regions of the country (Glenn and Supancic, 1984).

This discussion of the correlates of divorce provides an overall picture of divorce and some of the factors contributing to divorce rates. Some of the foregoing discussions also gave us glimpses of how divorce might come to individual couples. But to see how individuals experience divorce, we need to examine more closely the process of divorce.

THE DIVORCE EXPERIENCE

Many descriptive and colorful words and phrases have been used to describe the experience of going through a divorce. The process has been described as traumatic, as a highly stressful experience, as the death of a marriage, and so on. All these descriptions contain some truth, but the most realistic description of divorce is that it is a very complex phenomenon. To say that divorce is complex is to recognize that divorce is not a single or unitary act. There are different aspects to divorce, and they all may be happening at once. According to one analyst, there are at least six different "stations of divorce" (Bohannan, 1971, p. 33). Calling these six aspects of divorce *stations* is not quite apt, because this term suggests that divorce is a series of six steps that must be negotiated in some order. But the stations of divorce do not always come in the same order. Indeed, quite the opposite is true, as Bohannan recognizes when he says,

> *The complexity of divorce arises because at least six things are happening at once. They may come in a different order and with varying intensities, but there are at least six different experiences of separation [and divorce]. They are the more painful and puzzling as personal experiences because society is not yet equipped to handle any of them well, and some not at all. (Bohannan, 1971, pp. 33–34)*

To provide an overview of the six stations of divorce, each will be described briefly; we will then consider the details of each.

1. *Emotional divorce*—the recognition that the emotional relationship with a spouse is deteriorating and the marriage is ending
2. *Legal divorce*—the process of meeting the requirements for divorce that have been established by the state
3. *Economic divorce*—the division of money and property and a determination of the level of continuing economic support (e.g., alimony or maintenance awards)
4. *Community divorce*—the changes necessary in dealing with friends, relatives, and associates during and after the divorce
5. *Coparental divorce*—the determination of the custody of children and visitation rights
6. *Psychic divorce*—the process of regaining an individual identity and autonomy

The Emotional Divorce

There is widespread agreement that most people experience the greatest stress at the time when they begin to recognize that their marriage may actually end. It could hardly be otherwise, since in this society people select marriage partners largely on their own and because of love. They marry because they want to spend the rest of their lives with the person they love, and then some time later, maybe only a few months but often years later, they recognize that just the opposite is likely to occur. Even couples who have had stormy and difficult marriages often have a sense of loss, disappointment, and failure as they near the actual breakup. One woman, who had left her husband after years of being extremely unhappy in the marriage, described how she felt as she and her husband started the actual process of getting a divorce. "And, midnight, I was sitting in bed, eating vegetable soup, my first meal of the day, and I wanted to call him and say, 'What a colossal mistake we've made. I only feel together when I'm with you.' " (Weiss, 1975, p. 46).

In some divorces the emotional divorce is exacerbated by the fact that one spouse wants a divorce and the other does not. There is evidence that the noninitiators or rejectees have a more difficult time of accepting the end of the marriage and adjusting to the stress of separation and divorce (Goode, 1956; Petit and Bloom, 1984). However, the time period during which noninitiators resist the divorce more than the initiators appears to be relatively short. In one study that covered a period of eighteen months after separation, the noninitiators at the end of that time did not differ from the initiators in desiring a reconciliation (Petit and Bloom, 1984).

This research finding supports a general conclusion that the beginning of separation is the most difficult emotional part of ending a marriage. The actual divorce, which comes much later in the process, is stressful too, but by that time the emotional divorce has usually been experienced and adjusted to by most divorcing people.

One particularly interesting feature of this adjustment to the emotional divorce is the way in which individuals who are divorcing develop *accounts* of what has transpired (Weiss, 1975). An account is a final history of how the marriage ended. A typical account will summarize the important events, explaining what each spouse did and why he or she did it.

The account of a divorce is something that must be developed over time because often when people are going through the emotional divorce they are confused, ambivalent, and uncertain. There is not only confusion and ambivalence about the feelings and behavior of one's spouse, but even more important, there is likely to be confusion and uncertainty about one's own feelings and behavior as well. Ultimately, however, all divorcing people will establish an account of what happened.

An account is not necessarily objective truth. It is not at all uncommon for the accounts of a husband and wife to be quite different. For example, in one divorce case where both husband and wife were interviewed, the husband accounted for his divorce by elaborating on how flirtatious his wife was. The wife, on the other hand, said the divorce was caused by her husband's resistance to her attempts to improve herself by returning to college (Weiss, 1975). Whether the accounts are in agreement or not is not the important issue. What is important is that every divorcing person, in going through the emotional divorce, must review and process the events until it is possible to come to terms with the fact that the marriage is ending.

The Legal Divorce

We have already seen in this chapter how divorce in the United States evolved through legislation and the courts. Until the 1960s, the only way divorce could be obtained in any state was through an adversary procedure, in which one member of a married couple filed a complaint against the other member. It was necessary for at least one party to be guilty of some kind of marital misconduct in order for the courts to grant a divorce. Even if both members of a married couple agreed they wanted a divorce, it was necessary for one to file a complaint of some sort against the other.

This legal requirement often caused couples to exaggerate their complaints, or even to commit perjury in order to obtain divorces (Bahr, 1983). Until 1966, adultery was the only ground for divorce in the state of New York. Before that date there were reports of New York married couples staging adulterous scenes, complete with cooperative private detectives who would testify in court that one partner had been "caught in the act of adultery." As a result of such open flaunting of the law, there was increasing pressure during the 1960s, as the divorce rate was moving upward, for divorce laws that would allow divorce without marital misconduct. California and New York were the first states to pass such laws, which are popularly known as "no-fault divorce" laws (Weitzman, 1985). The *no-fault divorce laws* typically grant divorces on the grounds of irreconcilable differences, irretrievable breakdown, or incompatibility. In 1970, California eliminated all types of marital misconduct as grounds for divorce (however, "permanent insanity" is still allowed). By 1985, all states except South Dakota had passed some form of no-fault divorce law (Weitzman, 1985).

The passage of no-fault divorce laws has clearly made divorce easier to obtain than the earlier adversary divorce laws. This has caused some people to ask if the liberalized laws might not have caused, or at least contributed to, the increase in divorce rates in the 1960s and 1970s. With respect to the nation as a whole, the increase in divorce rates had started about eight years before the no-fault laws were passed (Sell, 1979). A number of studies of individual states have been made on a before and after basis, and researchers have been unanimous in their conclusion that the changes in divorce laws do not account for the rise in divorce rates (Bahr, 1983; Dixon and Weitzman, 1980; Schoen et al., 1975).

Since many people believe that the ease of obtaining a divorce should increase the divorce rate, this issue may deserve a little more careful examination. The first point that should be made is that even with no-fault laws, divorce is not easy (in several senses of that word). No-fault divorce laws do not diminish the stresses and the trauma of the emotional divorce. And as we will see below, no-fault divorce does not eliminate the problems of the economic divorce, the problems connected with the care and custody of children (if there are children), and the problems related to the community or psychic divorce. These problems are likely to be just as severe and taken just as seriously as in an adver-

The speed and ease with which one may get a divorce varies greatly from one time to another and from one country to another.

sarial system of divorce. Furthermore, a no-fault divorce is not automatic; it takes time. Many states require a one- or two-year period of legal separation before the final divorce decree will be granted. In short, while no-fault divorce reduces some of the cumbersome mechanics of the adversarial divorce, it does not make divorce so easy that it can be obtained on a whim or capriciously. This does not mean that the mechanisms for obtaining divorce cannot sometimes be shown to influence divorce rates. The case of the Soviet Union is instructive on this point.

Divorce in the Soviet Union. Prior to the Russian Revolution in 1917, only husbands had the right to obtain divorces, and usually the grounds were adultery (Moskoff, 1983). However, according to the philosophy of communist theoretician Friedrich Engels, as interpreted by Lenin, marriage under a patriarchal system kept women in slavery. Therefore, marriage could only be based on the free choice and the mutual love of husband and wife.

Immediately after the revolution, consistent with this philosophy, all existing divorce laws were abolished, and a new simplified court registration system was adopted (Moskoff, 1983). The new procedure allowed either husband or wife to request an end to the marriage. If both made the request, it was immediately registered and took effect. If only one spouse made the request, it was registered with the court, where matters of child custody, alimony, and so on would be handled (Mace and Mace, 1963). This law made divorce in Russia infinitely easier to obtain, at least for women, who could now get a divorce as easily as men. But in 1926 the divorce law was further revised, so that divorce became even easier. Between 1926 and 1936 the citizens of the Soviet Union were able to get what was quickly labeled the *"postcard divorce."* This label was applied because married persons had only to stop in at a registry office and either orally or in writing indicate that they wished to have a divorce. According to the law, the spouse had to be informed by postcard within three days that the marriage was over (Mace and Mace, 1963; Moskoff, 1983).

While the divorce statistics of the Soviet Union during this period are not easily obtained or completely reliable, there is evidence that the divorce rate did reach high levels, especially in the cities. There were also many tales of couples marrying and divorcing capriciously. There were reports of the same couple being married and divorced as many as fifteen different times. Another report describes a man of about thirty who filed for divorce from one wife, and then married another, all in less than fifteen minutes. As he filed for divorce, the young woman sat beside him. "She watched the details of the divorce with interest and then proceeded to marry the man" (Mace and Mace, 1963, p. 208).

Apparently, Soviet officials became concerned about the uses and abuses of this convenient form of divorce, and in 1936 they began a series of retreats that made divorce increasingly difficult and expensive. By 1944, divorce was effectively taken out of the hands of the citizens and given over to a cumbersome legal process. The divorce rate of the Soviet Union was thus reduced and remained low until 1965, when there was a dramatic simplification of the law. In the next year the divorce rate made a substantial jump, as people apparently availed themselves of the easier methods. The Soviet divorce rate rose through the decade of the 1970s, though it remained below that of the United States.

Other aspects of legal divorce in the U.S. Today in the United States, even though no-fault divorce is available in almost all states, adversarial procedures have certainly not been eliminated. It is still possible in many states to file suit for divorce on one or more of the traditional grounds of marital misconduct (Weitzman, 1985). Often, when one spouse does file a suit for divorce and charges misconduct, there is a high level of rancor and hostility involved. Frequently, attorneys for the two opposing parties use all measures at their disposal to protect the rights of their clients. This often produces a divorce experience that transcends the personal feelings of the divorcing couple. One woman interviewee explained how the legal process was forcing her to say things she did not want to say: "I think it could work out. Ours could. But to help myself, I have to go there and tell things that are husband and wife business, and he has to do the same. I don't want to hurt him. I want to be fair" (Spanier and Casto, 1979, p. 214). But many times divorcing spouses get caught up in the legal battles of a contested divorce, with resulting hostility and bitterness that influences their relationship for years after the divorce.

Even with no-fault divorce laws, there is still usually an aspect of the divorce process that involves attorneys and the courts and is a part of the legal divorce. Divorcing couples must divide the economic and material things they have accumulated during their marriages, and if they have children they must reach some agreement about their economic support and custody. Usually these arrangements are worked out in a separation agreement, which both parties agree to before it is filed with the court. Once again, in this process husbands and wives, with the assistance of their attorneys, often engage in conflict over the specifics and details of the separation agreement. It is not uncommon for couples to fight intensely over things that have nothing to do with the original reasons for divorce (e.g., who will get which automobile, or who will get the children during special holidays). Even so-called amicable or friendly divorces often end up with hostile and acrimonious exchanges over disputed terms in the separation agreement.

The Economic Divorce

As we have just noted, the legal divorce often revolves around economic matters, which are a very important part of any divorce. Every marriage is an economic partnership, and if divorce comes the accumulations of that partnership must be divided. Many marriages also end with debt obligations, and these too must be allocated between the partners at the time of divorce. The third economic aspect of divorce is the continuing economic support that one spouse may be obliged to provide the other after the divorce (alimony or maintenance awards). And finally, if the couple has minor children, it will be necessary to establish the level of child support payments and the extent of other economic obligations for a noncustodial parent. These are the key elements of the economic divorce.

One way to look at the economic divorce is to recognize at the outset that divorce has economic costs for husbands and wives. The old proverb, often used to encourage marriage, says "two can live more cheaply than one." Ironically, the validity of that statement is most clearly revealed at the time of divorce. When separating couples set up individual households, the costs in housing, utilities, transportation, new household furnishings and appliances, child care, and so on, may not double, but they do increase greatly. In this period, when expenses are suddenly increasing, incomes may go down because of missed days of work and lost productivity. The economic costs of divorce must also include attorneys' fees and perhaps medical, counseling, or psychiatric services for spouses or children.

While divorce is expensive for all concerned, there is a growing body of evidence that the economic costs for women are greater than they are for men (Weitzman, 1985). In the postdivorce period, men usually bounce back to their predivorce levels rather quickly, while women often remain below their predivorce levels. A study of California divorces occurring after the no-fault law went into effect, showed that one year after a divorce the economic standard of living for divorced men went *up* 42 percent, while the economic standard for divorced women went *down* 73 percent (Weitzman, 1985). In a study of divorced individuals in eight Western states, almost half (forty-eight percent) of divorced women said their income was much lower than that of friends and relatives. Almost none of the divorced women reported much higher incomes than their friends and relatives, although a quarter of the divorced men did (Albrecht et al., 1983). The same pattern appeared in a small Pennsylvania sample of divorced men and women, in which only one man out of twenty-two reported major economic problems after divorce. The majority of the women, and especially those who had been married longer, said they were worse off (Spanier and Casto, 1979).

There are a number of ways to explain the diminished economic circumstances of women after divorce, but the simplest is a recognition that the major share of incomes coming into American families is from husbands. We have seen in previous chapters that a substantial percentage of married women do not have any paid employment, that many who are employed have only part-time jobs, and that even when women do work they usually earn less than their husbands. As long as families are intact, these arrangements can be viewed, from an economic point of view, as a strength for the family (Becker, 1973; Ross and Sawhill, 1984). But the weakness of an arrangement that has wives working for no pay (in the home) or low pay in the labor force is quickly revealed in the case of divorce. Then, wives, especially wives who have been married for many years, are suddenly left without the major part of their predivorce economic resources.

One way for women to retain some of that income is to receive alimony or maintenance from their former husbands and, if they have children, child support as well. However, the liberalized no-fault divorce laws we discussed above, combined with other laws and court rulings, have reduced the amount and extent of alimony or maintenance awards (Bahr, 1983; Weitzman, 1985). In two California studies after the no-fault divorce laws went into effect, there were fewer alimony or maintenance awards for women, and when awards were made they were smaller (Seal, 1979; Dixon and Weitzman, 1980). The same tendency has been found in Georgia and the state of Washington after the passage of no-fault divorce laws (Welch and Price-Bonham, 1983). There is now a prevailing spirit in the courts that alimony or maintenance is to be used as an aid until a divorced person is self-supporting, not as lifetime guaranteed income. The courts have also made it clear that alimony is not to be viewed as a punishment for the spouse who must pay it (Weitzman, 1985).

A minor legal aspect of alimony or maintenance awards is a recent Supreme Court ruling that makes husbands as well as wives eligible for economic support after divorce. While alimony has been awarded to men in a small number of publicized cases, the general impact of this ruling is negligible.

The no-fault divorce laws have also had a negative effect for women in property settlements accompanying divorce. As with alimony or maintenance awards, in the years after California passed its new divorce laws, women received lower property settlement awards than they had under the old law (Seal, 1979; Weitzman, 1985). Similar studies conducted in Georgia and the state of Washington found some tendency for lower property settlements for women in Washington, but not in Georgia (Welch and Price-Bonham, 1983).

With regard to the economic divorce, it can be said that in general there are economic costs whenever there is a divorce. But women have suffered more economic deprivation after divorce than men, and recent changes in divorce laws have tended to increase their disadvantage.

The Community Divorce

The community divorce is the most purely social aspect of divorce, since it involves the changes necessary in dealing with friends, relatives, and associates during and after the divorce. The community divorce is a mirror image of the social side of marriage. Just as marriage is a way of making a social commitment to another person, the community divorce is the process of letting relatives, friends, and associates know that now the marriage is ending. The community divorce begins when the separating couple informs other people that a separation is either contemplated or has actually occurred.

This initial step in the community divorce is often very difficult for several reasons. First, when two people are in the process of separating, the stresses of the emotional divorce are usually at their peak. A husband and wife may be

"Look. Let's at least stay together until the Crockers' party."

having a difficult time admitting to each other, and to themselves, that the marriage is going to end. This is often not just a matter of admitting to oneself that one was wrong about the marriage in the first place but is a reflection of true ambivalence. Almost every person who is separating has feelings of uncertainty and reluctance. On the one hand, there are reasons for wanting the marriage to end, but, on the other hand, there are reasons for wanting the marriage to continue. Under these conditions of ambivalence that so often prevail in the early stages of divorce, it is difficult to make announcements to family and friends that the marriage is, indeed, ending.

The problem of making the announcement is often more difficult because married couples have a tendency to present a false image of their marriage to the outside world. This facade of secrecy about the problems of the marriage may have been maintained through some of the early stages of separation, but ultimately it is necessary to tell family members and friends what has been happening and what is probably going to happen. When the announcement is made, family members and close friends are often shocked and surprised

(Weiss, 1975). Almost everyone at some time or another has said, on learning of a marital separation, "I always thought of them as the perfect couple."

A final reason why it is difficult to make the initial announcement of a separation and potential divorce is that there are no social customs or norms that govern how it should be done. The announcement of a separation is typically awkward for the person who makes it and for the person who hears it. The uncertainty of the situation is revealed in the experience of one man who, when he told an associate about his impending divorce, was asked, "Do I feel sorry for you or congratulate you?" (Bohannan, 1971, p. 37). Most people respond to the announcement with "Oh, I'm sorry to hear that." This is roughly what one says on hearing of a death in the family of an acquaintance and seems to be borrowed at least in part from that social situation.

There is another problem area in the community divorce, and in the long run it is a more serious problem for many divorcing people than the initial announcement. Most people who divorce have the experience of changing social worlds. Often one spouse will leave the community entirely, which certainly means establishing new friends and other social relations. But even when former spouses remain in the same community, there are inevitably changes in social relationships. Almost all divorced persons report that some of the friends they had while married are no longer friends. Apparently, it is especially difficult for married friends to remain friendly with both the husband and wife after a divorce. "Many divorcees complain bitterly about their 'ex-friends.' " 'Friends?' one woman replied [in response to an interview question], 'They drop you like a hot potato. The exceptions are those real ones you made before marriage, those who are unmarried, and your husband's friends who want to make a pass at you.' " (Bohannan, 1971, p. 59).

Many divorced couples have a period of transition when they feel isolated and alone because of the loss of former friends. Establishing new relationships can be difficult, especially for those who divorce after many years of marriage. Often people in this situation turn to organizations such as Partners Without Partners or other "single or divorced" clubs to make the social transition easier.

Another part of the divorced person's social world that often changes with divorce is relationships with in-laws. Whether or not a divorced person remains in social touch with the parents and siblings of a former spouse is another area where there are no clear social norms. Several factors will influence how much divorced persons maintain social relationships with in-laws after divorce. Having children is one such factor, especially for custodial parents. Grandparents are much more likely to remain in contact with a former daughter-in-law if she has custody of their grandchildren. Even if relationships with in-laws are maintained after divorce, there is usually a qualitative change in their nature and intensity.

The Psychic Divorce

Gradually, as people go through the emotional, legal, economic, and community divorces, they are also having to move toward the psychic divorce,

Many people going through separation and divorce need the help of support groups and counseling.

which is an internal process of regaining individual identity and autonomy. Not everyone is immersed in marriage to the same degree, but it is nearly impossible to be married for any length of time without having a part of one's identity wrapped up in one's spouse. Psychic divorce is the process of separating from the personality and influence of an ex-spouse.

For many people, the psychic divorce is a slow process that can go on long after the actual divorce. A divorced man who still will not buy striped shirts, only because his former wife did not like them, could be said to be working toward his own psychic divorce. Now it is true that some divorced couples claim to maintain a close and friendly relationship after divorce, and for them perhaps a psychic divorce is not an issue. However, most divorced people fare best if they accept the divorce as a complete discontinuation of their former husband-and-wife relationship. For divorcing couples who have children, especially when they share custody, the psychic divorce may be especially difficult, if for no other reason than that as parents they continue to come into contact with each other. We will consider some of these circumstances in the consideration of the last type of divorce: the coparental divorce.

The Coparental Divorce

In each year since 1972, more than one million children under the age of eighteen had parents who divorced (National Center for Health Statistics, 1985). Over the last thirty years, the number of children with parents who have divorced has increased steadily each year. The rate at which children under age eighteen have been involved in divorce has tripled during that same time. Figure 15.2 shows that in 1950 there were 6.3 children out of 1000 who had parents who were divorcing. During the 1980s, the rate has been between

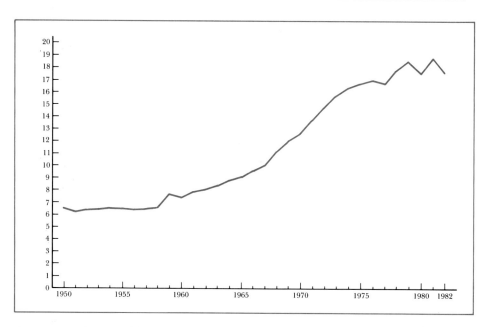

Figure 15.2 *The rate of divorce effecting children under 18 years of age, 1950–1982.*
(Note: the rate is interpreted as the number of children out of every 1000 children
whose parents divorced in any given year.) (Source: National Center for Health
Statistics. 'Advance Report on Final Divorce Statistics, 1982.' Vol. 33, No. 11.)

seventeen and eighteen. Only one measure of children affected by divorce has
decreased: the number of children per divorce. This decline probably reflects
the fact that the birth rate has decreased since the mid-1960s.

These figures tell us that many couples must make decisions about their
children at the same time they are going through all the other aspects of divorce. There are two fundamental divorce decisions that relate to the parental
role: (1) Will the divorce be harmful to the children? (2) If the decision is to have
a divorce, how shall the custody of the children be handled? These two major
issues growing out of the coparental divorce will be considered in the remainder of this chapter.

THE EFFECTS OF DIVORCE ON CHILDREN

Most parents, no matter how much they are dissatisfied with their marriages,
will give some thought to the impact that divorce will have on their children.

Many parents explicitly acknowledge that they remain married for the sake of their children, perhaps planning to wait until the children are older or grown up before they separate. Yet a great many other parents obviously do go ahead with divorce even though they have children. These parents must weigh the presumed advantages of divorce against the possible negative effects a divorce might have on their children.

There are two popular and widely held beliefs about how divorce affects children. The first and more general is that children whose parents are divorced are likely to be damaged psychologically and socially. The second is that children are not hurt as much by the divorce of their parents as they are by living in a household where there is continued strife and hostility. Clearly, these two widely held notions are at least partially contradictory. While there is perhaps a grain of truth in each, it is no longer necessary to rely just on these general assertions. There is now a considerable amount of research-based evidence on the effects of divorce on children, and while there are still many unanswered questions, there are also some general statements that can be made.

There is ample evidence that when couples are in the process of separating there is a great deal of stress on children, except for those who are still infants (Hetherington et al., 1978; Longfellow, 1979; Wallerstein and Kelly, 1975, 1976). Beyond infancy, there are different reactions at different ages, presumably reflecting the reasoning ability and understanding of the children. Those children who are in the later preschool years, between the ages of three and one-half and six, reason egocentrically about the separation of their parents. More specifically, they often blame themselves for one of their parents being gone. A child of this age might say, "Daddy left home because I was a bad boy—I didn't put away my toys that day" (Longfellow, 1979, p. 300).

Children of school age, especially between six and twelve, have a wider range of negative emotions when their parents separate and divorce (Wallerstein and Kelly, 1976). Initially, children of these ages tend to cover their fears and feelings, often by focusing on their own activities or play. Eventually, however, anger, fear, a loss of identity, and loneliness emerge. Interviews with children of this age show that they often blame one parent or the other for breaking up the marriage and creating the problems of the family. Children often have fears about the loss of the parent they are living with, since they often feel they have already lost one parent (Wallerstein and Kelly, 1976).

The reactions of adolescents to the separation of their parents include anger, sadness, a sense of loss or betrayal, and sometimes shame or embarrassment. But at this age children also exhibit a more detached and analytic attitude about their parents and their relationships with their parents. Adolescents have more insight into their parents' marriages, which allows them to develop more differentiated interpretations of what brought about the divorce (Longfellow, 1979; Wallerstein and Kelly, 1974).

Thus, with respect to the age of children when their parents go through separation and divorce, it appears that those who are not yet into adolescence

All children experience anxiety and fear when their parents separate and divorce. Often younger children especially will have to be reassured that they are not to blame for the divorce.

have the most stressful time. This is especially true of preschoolers who know what is happening but cannot fully understand why, and often blame themselves.

Among all children there are likely to be above average problems during the period of separation. Problems manifest themselves in the home and, for those who are old enough, in school as well.

One of the most encouraging results of the research on children of divorce is that the upset caused by the separation is relatively short-lived. Studies have shown that a year and one-half after the separation most children have gotten over the most severe negative reactions. In a ten-year follow-up study of children who had been preschoolers and had shown great distress at the time of their parents' separations, the children had no serious aftereffects of the experience (Wallerstein, 1984).

A number of studies of national or very large samples have supported the conclusion that in the long run there are no systematic impairments, either psychological or social, among children who come from broken homes (Kulka and Weingarten, 1979; Kurdek, *et al.*, 1981; Levitan, 1979). Of course, there are children who come from divorced families who have psychological or social problems that reflect the divorce. But researchers studying this issue are more and more agreed that it is not divorce per se that causes problems, but the quality of family relationships. For example, if parents continue to engage in conflict through the divorce and after, a child is likely to be at greater psychiatric risk (Longfellow, 1979). If parents, either one or both, engage in behaviors that are upsetting to the child (alcoholism, sexual promiscuity), the child will suffer. If one or both parents ignore or do not see the child, it is likely to be harmful to the child. In short, if a child lives in an atmosphere that produces instability, uncertainty, and stress, either during or after the divorce, there can be negative repercussions for the child (Wallerstein and Kelly, 1980).

This conclusion also sheds light on the question of whether a child is better off living in a home where parents are continually fighting and hostile or going through the agonies of a separation and divorce. The probable answer is that a divorce may, indeed, be better for the child, *if* the divorce is not accompanied and followed by continued parental conflict. If the divorce is of such a nature that it brings about some resolution to family problems, it may well be the better course of action for the welfare of the child. If not, the divorce may only add to the child's problems by adding the separation or estrangement from one parent.

Since divorce so often leads to a degree of separation from one of the parents, parents must make a decision about how the matter of custody of children is to be handled. They must often balance their personal interests against the welfare of the children. Only a decade or two ago it was expected, and nearly automatically the case, that the mother would receive custody of any minor children. Today, more and more divorcing couples are discussing and deliberating over the custody of their minor children, since it has become a more problematic aspect of divorce.

CHILD CUSTODY

Divorce, as we have seen, is the legal means by which the state ends a marriage. Even though parents who are divorcing are not divorcing their children, the courts, in the process of granting divorces, take responsibility for the disposition of any minor children a divorcing couple may have. Historically, and to a considerable degree in the present, the courts have granted custody of any minor children to only one of the divorcing parents. When custody is granted to one parent, it means that the court intends for that parent to have all the rights and responsibilities for the child that had previously been possessed by the two parents together. The courts have usually emphasized that the rights and responsibilities of the custodial parent are centered around the "physical, moral and mental well being of the minor" (Weiss, 1979, p. 332).

In different cultures and historical periods, the particular parent who is given custody has varied greatly. In the United States since the 1920s the custody of children has almost invariably been given to the mother. But that may be the exception when compared to earlier historical periods and other cultures.

Very often, if the family system is organized as a patriarchal system, the father automatically receives custody of minor children. Two cross-cultural cases concerning peoples from Nigeria and also a look at American history will illustrate how these systems work.

Among the Fulani, a society in southern Nigeria, there is never any doubt that the husband will receive custody of any children in the event of divorce (Adegboye, 1981). If there is a divorce, the husband remains in the home and the wife returns to her family home. If at the time of the divorce the wife is still nursing a child, that child will remain with her. But as soon as a young child can walk and has been weaned, it is returned to its father. The mother can visit her children if she wishes, and in her old age she can choose to return to live with her children (Adegboye, 1981).

The Kanuri people, also of Nigeria, but in the northeastern part, are noted for their extraordinarily high rate of divorce (Cohen, 1971). While the Kanuri value marital stability, they do not expect it, and they consider attempts to make divorce difficult or impossible as ridiculous. The result is that forty-five to fifty-five percent of all Kanuri marriages end before reaching the fourth anniversary. As with the Fulani, the children of any divorcing couple remain in the home of their father. "This means that almost all Kanuri children have 'lost' a mother through divorce" (Cohen, 1971, p. 232). This does not necessarily mean that they have lost touch with her, but it does mean that they were probably reared by one of their father's other wives (the Kanuri, as well as the Fulani, are polygynous). In some cases of divorce, the children are given by the father to one of his sisters, since it is believed that they will receive better treatment than from their "stepmothers" (Cohen, 1971).

In the United States and England prior to the twentieth century, custody was also routinely given to husbands in the event of divorce (Luepnitz, 1982; Roman and Haddad, 1978). In keeping with the patriarchal family structure, it was assumed by the courts that fathers had a property interest in their children. Also, since women were virtually legal nonentities and were themselves thought to be in need of protection, they were not seen to be qualified to take responsibility for their children (Luepnitz, 1982).

Gradually through the nineteenth century, however, there was a change in legal philosophy that reflected several social changes. Married women, as we saw in Chapter 12, were increasingly restricted to the home, where they had the major responsibility for rearing the children. The "cult of ideal womanhood" held that women were uniquely suited to give children the nurturance and moral guidance required in proper child rearing. This also reflected a basic change in views about child rearing, which in the early part of the nineteenth century (and before) stressed discipline and moral guidance (tasks that fathers seemed ideally suited for). With the coming of the Victorian age in the later part of the nineteenth century, the emphasis in child rearing moved toward love and nurturing, which seemed the natural, or even "instinctive," province of women (Luepnitz, 1982; Roman and Haddad, 1978).

American law in the nineteenth century started to take notice of the special problems of dealing with children who were very young when their parents divorced. In a divorce case in 1839, "a girl of twenty-one months was awarded to the mother as 'the most proper person to be entrusted with such a charge, in relation to an infant of this tender age' " (Roman and Haddad, 1978, p. 33). This daughter of "tender age" was awarded to her mother, but when she turned four years old, she was returned to her father.

Gradually, this doctrine of *tender age* was extended to later and later ages. In one sense, the change from giving fathers custody in the nineteenth century to giving mothers custody in the twentieth century was accomplished by increasing the tender age to higher and higher ages. More and more, a child was considered by the courts to be better off with his or her mother until reaching the age of majority. An additional legal concept, *the best interests of the child,* was also applied as the changes in custody patterns occurred in the twentieth century. Essentially, the courts came more and more to the conclusion that it was in the best interests of children to be in the custody of their mothers. In recent decades in the United States, more than ninety percent of children have been placed in the custody of their mothers after divorce (Watson, 1981).

Until very recently, there were only a very small number of divorce cases in which mothers voluntarily gave up partial or complete custody of their children after divorce. Usually, if a father was granted custody of children, it was because he had been able to demonstrate to the court that the mother was either imcompetent or unfit. But there are two changes in child custody currently taking place. One is the use of *mediation,* and the other is *joint custody.*

Mediation is a method of resolving contested issues between the divorcing parties by having a neutral person clarify the issues, identify alternatives, and move the disputants to a mutual agreement (Bahr, 1981). Mediation can, of course, be used for all contested issues, not just child custody. The advantage often claimed for mediation is that it takes disputes out of the hands of opposing lawyers and gives them to a mediator who is working for the good of both husband and wife. In child custody disputes, the use of mediation is seen as serving the best interests of the child by keeping hostilities to a minimum. There is the further argument that when husband and wife make an agreement through mediation, they will abide by it more closely than one imposed on them by the courts (Bahr, 1981).

The issue of joint custody is being considered by an increasing number of divorcing parents today. The essence of joint custody is that both parents retain both responsibility and authority for the rearing of their children (Clingempeel and Reppucci, 1982). Under single-parent custody, only one parent has these basic rights and responsibilities, although the noncustodial parent may exercise limited authority, especially during times of visitation. Usually, with joint custody the concept of visitation no longer applies, since both parents will alternate having physical custody of the children. Some arrangement will be worked out so that children live with one parent for a given period and then live with the other parent. The lengths of time are worked out by the couple, but it is not uncommon for children to stay with one parent during certain days of the week and the other parent on other days of the week. In each residence, the children are likely to have clothes, toys, and other possessions.

State laws providing for the possibility of joint custody have only a short history. In 1975 only North Carolina had such a law, but twenty-nine additional states have since enacted joint custody laws, and many others have them pending (Derdeyn and Scott, 1984). Even when states do not have such laws, the existing divorce laws may allow the courts to accept joint custody arrangements.

While joint custody has gained in popularity in recent years, support for this method of arranging custody is not universal. There are those who find flaws and shortcomings in joint custody arrangements. We will consider the arguments for and against joint custody as the final issue of this chapter.

ISSUE

Is joint custody of minor children better than sole custody?

When parents divorce, they divorce each other, but they do not divorce their children. Most parents want to remain in contact with their children as much as possible and make every effort to achieve that objective. It is not uncommon for parents to take their disputes over child custody to the courts (or to mediation) when they cannot agree on the custody arrangements for their children.

When parents fight for the custody of their children, they may be motivated by many different factors. In some cases, it seems that parents who battle for their children are simply extending the conflicts of their marriage and their divorce. When this is the case, the parents are not usually acting in the best interests of their children, even though they may think they are.

But divorcing parents who have the welfare of their children uppermost in their minds still have to consider carefully their decisions about custody. One possibility is to opt for sole custody, in which one parent retains the legal rights and responsibilities for rearing the child, while the other is limited to informal influences on the way the child is reared plus periodic visitation rights. The other possibility is joint custody, which gives the two parents equal power and authority over the rearing of the children. Often, joint custody means that each parent will have physical custody of children for equal or nearly equal amounts of time. Parents who divorce today will want to weigh the arguments for and against joint custody and compare them with the arguments for and against sole custody. The arguments for joint custody will be considered first.

The Arguments for Joint Custody

When both parents wish to play an active part in the upbringing, education, and general welfare of their children, then joint custody is more fair than sole custody. Many who make the case for joint custody consider the fairness argument to be one of the strongest. If each parent truly wishes to be active in the parenting of their children, and wishes to continue as a vital force in the children's lives, how can either parent be denied that wish? As an incidental point, the argument that sole custody by the mother is a more natural, and thus more beneficial, arrangement for the child is rejected out of hand by the advocates of joint custody. They consider this belief to be an outgrowth of an outdated philosophy that is both sexist and unfair to fathers.

The supporters of joint custody believe that from the point of view of the children, too, there is generally a strong desire to continue to see and be with both parents, not just one. This point of view is supported by the findings of several studies, which show that most children make a better adjustment to divorce if they have continuing contact with both parents.

Supporters of joint custody also believe that when both parents have about the same amount of time with their children, one of the often noted problems of sole custody is avoided—namely, the problem of the parent who sees the children only occasionally for short periods of time and who thus gravitates toward being an "entertainment parent." Noncustodial parents, because they see their children infrequently, seem to want to make the most of the opportunity, so they often plan an endless round of entertainment and fun during their children's visits. When one parent provides only trips to the zoo, movies, eating out, and other entertainment, it is unfair both to the children and to the parent who has custody the other ninety percent of the time. Many times, custodial parents complain about the unfair comparison between a weekend of fun and entertainment and the more mundane everyday kind of life they can provide for the children. With joint custody arrangements, children usually spend enough time in the home of each parent that they are more than just visitors or guests. Each parent's home is also a home for the children, with all that implies about chores, schoolwork, and boredom.

Joint custody is also believed by many to reduce the problems of the sole-custody parent in another way. Many times when one parent has the full responsibility of caring for children day in and day out, the role strain and role overload are great. Especially if a custodial parent is employed, the problems of doing everything that needs to be done are intense. This includes having leisure time for social and recreational activities, which could lead to new relationships and possibly remarriage. Joint custody gives both parents time off from parenting so they can have free time for recreation and meeting new people.

Joint custody also tends to be more equitable from an economic standpoint. When both parents take full responsibility for meeting the needs of the children, it is more likely that each will contribute a fairer share to the financial burden of child rearing.

To summarize the arguments for joint custody, it is a fundamentally fairer arrangement if both parents want to have custody of the children. Children seem to adjust better to divorce if they continue to have extensive contact with both parents, and since joint custody allows this more often than sole custody, the edge goes to joint custody. Joint custody avoids the excesses that so often occur when a parent has the children for only short periods of time. And, finally, joint custody also allows a fairer distribution of child-care burdens in terms of both time and money.

The Arguments against Joint Custody

The most basic argument against joint custody is that it may be too difficult for children to have two homes, between which they are repeatedly shuttled. This feature, above all others, leads many critics of joint custody to believe that it is not in the best interests of the children, even though parents may want or prefer it.

There are a number of features of alternating between parental homes that are potentially disruptive and disturbing to children. For example, while joint custody does not necessarily mean that time with parents will be divided equally, or nearly so, it usually is. Couples may have their children on alternate weeks, or even months, but a very common arrangement is to have the children spend two or three days with one parent, after which they move to the home of the other parent for a similar period. Opponents of joint custody point out that children may find it difficult to make these shifts from one home environment to a completely different one every few days, or every week. Their rooms will be different, as well as their clothes, toys, friends, eating times, and general living conditions. The two parents may also have very different philosophies of child rearing, so the children will have to learn to live under two different parental regimes. The adjustment can become even more complicated if one or both of the parents remarry and bring yet other parents into the lives of the children.

There are also some concerns that when children are moved so frequently from one household to another, the effect is to increase the number of times children have to make separations from their parents. Each of these separations can be psychologically wrenching for the child, as well as the parent, and may interfere with the adjustment to divorce.

Critics of joint custody also point out that this system requires regular and extensive contact between the divorced parents, who must plan and coordinate their own schedules and have accurate knowledge of their children's schedules. For example, each parent must know who is delivering and picking up which children, at what time, and where. If not, there are likely to be some anxious moments and unpleasant situations. This high level of communication and coordination can work if the parents are on good terms, but often there will be residual anger and hostility from the divorce, which can make each contact an uncomfortable exchange. If joint custody parents have their conflicts intensified by frequent contact, it can be harmful to the parents and the children. This view is supported by some research evidence showing that continued parental conflict after divorce can be harmful to the post divorce adjustment of the children.

Joint custody arrangements between angry or bitter parents can also lead to a continuation of some of the more harmful ways parents use children during divorce. One parent may criticize the other parent in front of, or directly to, the children; this situation can occur more often with joint custody simply because the parents are in contact more often. A parent may also use children as "spies" to report what the other parent is doing, and this, too, can occur more often if children are moving frequently from one home to the other. Both of these examples show again that joint custody may be workable if the divorced parents are on good terms, but may be harmful to the children if they are not.

Summing up the arguments against joint custody, one great concern is about the possible negative effects of moving the children back and forth between two different environments, making their lives unstable and discontinuous. The difficulties of children separating from a parent are increased simply because separations occur more often. Joint custody requires a great amount of cooperation and communication, which may be difficult for parents who remain bitter or angry after divorce. When hostility persists, the increased amount of contact may be harmful, especially for the children. Children may also be hurt by observing the continued fighting of their parents and made to feel guilty if they are involved in their parents' conflicts.

Themes

1. In the past, divorce has often been difficult to obtain, expensive, and reserved for the wealthy.
2. People of lesser economic means have often ended their marriages in less formal ways.
3. The liberalization of divorce laws in the United States started even in colonial times but accelerated greatly in the nineteenth century through a series of state laws and court decisions.
4. Many measures of the extent of divorce in the society are ill conceived and inappropriately interpreted.
5. There are a variety of correlates of divorce, including age at marriage, socioeconomic status, and religion.
6. The divorce experience is a complex phenomenon, not a unitary act.
7. Historically and cross-culturally, there have been widely varying ways of awarding custody of children after divorce.

Facts

1. In the nineteenth century, divorce in England was sometimes achieved by husbands selling their wives.
2. In colonial times in America, divorce was very rare.
3. The concept of mental cruelty came to be a basis for divorce in California in the 1850s.
4. Measuring divorce by comparing divorces in a given year to weddings in that same year is inappropriate and misleading.
5. Statements about the percentage of all marriages ending in divorce are based on data coming from previous cohorts of married couples and projections into the future.
6. The divorce rate in the United States increased dramatically in the 1970s but has been decreasing somewhat since 1979.
7. Couples who marry while they are teenagers have much higher chances of divorce than couples who marry later.
8. Black Americans have higher rates of marital breakup than white Americans.
9. Marital breakup is more frequent among people in the lower socioeconomic strata of society than in the middle and higher strata.
10. With regard to religion, people who claim no religion have the highest rates of marital breakup.

11. There is no evidence to support the claim that liberalized divorce laws have caused the divorce rate to increase.

12. California and New York were the first states to pass no-fault divorce laws in the 1960s.

13. In the Soviet Union it was very easy to obtain a divorce in the 1920s and 1930s, but it was made legally cumbersome in the post–World War II period. In 1965 the Soviet Union again made divorce more accessible to its citizens.

14. The economic costs of divorce are much greater for women than for men.

15. The rate of divorce for couples who have children under age eighteen has tripled in the last thirty years.

16. Children are likely to have their greatest problems with their parents' divorces during the separation period.

17. Preadolescent children are likely to have greater problems than older children when their parents divorce.

18. Research has not uncovered any general, long-term negative effects on the children of divorced parents.

19. In the first part of the nineteenth century in the United States, the custody of minor children was regularly given to husbands in the event of divorce.

20. Since 1920, and until recently, mothers have received custody of minor children almost automatically.

Major Concepts

account: A final history of how a marriage ended, as interpreted by a husband or wife after the divorce.

adversary divorce: Divorce granted after a complaint filed against a married partner has been upheld by the court.

annulment: Ending a marriage by church decree, when the marriage is judged a "spurious" or not a "true" marriage.

community divorce: One of the "stations" of divorce; the changes necessary in dealing with friends, relatives, and associates, during and after divorce.

coparental divorce: One of the "stations" of divorce; the determination of the custody of children and visitation rights.

economic divorce: One of the "stations" of divorce; the division of money and property, and a determination of the level of continuing economic support.

emotional divorce: One of the "stations" of divorce; the recognition that the relationship with one's spouse is deteriorating and the marriage is ending.

joint custody: A custody arrangement in which both parents retain rights and responsibilities for rearing their children after divorce.

legal divorce: One of the "stations" of divorce; the process of meeting the requirements for divorce established by the state.

mediation: A method of resolving contested issues between divorcing parties by having a neutral person clarify the issues, identify alternatives, and move disputants to a mutual agreement.

no-fault divorce: Divorce granted on the basis of irreconcilable differences, irretrievable breakdown, or incompatibility, without an adversary proceeding.

"postcard divorce": A name applied to the easy divorce process in the Soviet Union in the 1926–1936 period.

psychic divorce: One of the "stations" of divorce; the process of regaining an individual identity and autonomy after divorce.

"separate bed and board" divorce: A type of divorce granted historically, in both England and the United States, that continued the legal obligations of marriage, even though the husband and wife lived separately.

six "stations" of divorce: Six different aspects of a divorce that must be handled, often simultaneously.

"wife selling": A method of divorcing in eighteenth and nineteenth century England.

16

Life after Divorce
Adjustment, Binuclear Families, and Remarriage

The period after divorce has been described in the following vivid terms:

> . . . a period of stumbling blindly through a dark, boulder-strewn, humid valley which at times is frightening beyond endurance, until at last, through luck and the will not to give up, one staggers in the right direction—whether toward a new marriage or a fulfilling independent life—there is light again. (Westoff, 1977, p. 24)

There have been many other descriptions of life after divorce, including some that end on less optimistic and hopeful notes. But there is widespread agreement that divorce means having to make some critical and dramatic life adjustments. It is not too strong to say that after divorce it is necessary to establish a new life.

For many divorced people there are three major steps in establishing this new life. First, it is necessary to make a psychological and social adjustment to the divorce itself. Second, for divorced couples with children (and most do have children at the time of divorce), it is necessary to work out a relationship with one's former spouse and the children. And third, for the majority who remarry, it means working out a new marriage and family life.

By all accounts, remarrying leads to a marriage and family life that is more complicated than first marriages. Remarriage can also be very rewarding, but the complications are undeniable. One of the most difficult of the complications is establishing and maintaining relationships with the children of one's new spouse. More and more remarrying couples are facing the issue of how to cope with the delicate and often difficult relationship between stepparents and stepchildren. At the end of this chapter, we will focus on this issue.

ADJUSTMENTS AND CHANGES IN THE POST-DIVORCE PERIOD

The Emotional and Psychological Adjustments

Divorce and its aftermath is often a traumatic, stressful, and unsettling experience. Yet it is encouraging to note that for most people who go through the experience, there is a strong tendency to bounce back. In interviews with a sample of divorced individuals from eight western states, the subjects were asked whether the most difficult period in their lives was before, during, or after the divorce (Albrecht et al., 1983). More than half (fifty-five percent) said the most difficult time was before the decision to divorce, which supports the research findings that the separation period is most difficult. A little more than twenty percent of divorced men and women said the period just after the divorce was most difficult, and only three percent said that their current period was most difficult (Albrecht et al., 1983). In answer to another question in the same study, ninety-three percent of divorcees said that the present is better than the predivorce period, which is more evidence that most people do make a satisfactory adjustment after divorce.

While other studies have also found positive evaluations of life after divorce, the levels are somewhat lower. In a study of divorced couples from Marin County, California, two-thirds of the husbands and slightly over half of the wives, five years after their original separations, said that the divorce had been beneficial and had enhanced their lives (Wallerstein and Kelly, 1980). Even many of the individuals who had initially opposed divorce had come to see its benefits. One woman said of her divorce, "When I look back, I wish I had gotten out earlier, before things were so desperate. . . . He forced me into divorce by humiliating me. When a person does everything to make you let go, it's time to let go" (Wallerstein and Kelly, 1980, p. 187). The researchers who conducted the postdivorce study in eight western states reached a conclusion that corresponds well with this woman's statement, when they said, "Despite the personal stress associated with divorce, most respondents demonstrated a clear recovery and were quite convinced that the price they had to pay in terminating a bad marriage was worth it" (Albrecht et al., 1983, p. 137).

It is encouraging to learn that many divorced people can look back a few years after their divorces and say that they are better off than they were either before or during the divorce. However, this should not obscure the fact that many people do have a period after the divorce when it is difficult to adjust and adapt to their new life situation. Many observers see these adjustments and adaptations after divorce as a natural process, much like the adjustment one must make after the death of a family member. It is a process that most people have to go through after a divorce. Researchers have found, however, that more women than men report adjustment difficulties in the postdivorce period (Albrecht, 1980; Wallerstein and Kelly, 1980).

For some people the emotional and psychological adjustments that started during the separation stage have either not been completed or are revived at the time of the final divorce. One factor that seems to play a part in emotional and psychological adjustment is the way in which people started the divorce. One very important dimension of divorce is the degree to which a person wanted or opposed the divorce at the beginning. In a substantial number of divorces, one spouse wishes to end the marriage (sometimes labeled the *leaver*), while the other spouse is reluctant to end it (the *left*). It is not surprising that the person who is left usually has a more difficult time adjusting to the divorce. Being left by one's spouse is often devastating to self-esteem and feelings of self-worth.

Often a marriage partner who is left does not wish to end the marriage because of a continuing emotional attachment or love for the leaving spouse. Continuing to be in love with the person from whom one is divorced does, of course, make postdivorce adjustment much more difficult. In the words of one man, "I think of her every day of my life. I wonder who she is with, if she's working, how she's treating my daughter, and lots of other things. I still love her quite a lot" (Spanier and Casto, 1979a, p. 219). Divorced people with this emotional response are very likely to experience depression and loneliness. They often long for the way things were in the past and find it difficult to move ahead with a restructuring and rebuilding of their lives.

Another response of people who are forced into divorce by a spouse is anger, because they feel betrayed or misused. When the anger is intense it often extends into the postdivorce period and interferes with establishing a new life. In one study, the children of divorced couples were interviewed five years after the original separation, and more than a quarter (twenty-nine percent) reported that they still observed intense bitterness between their parents. An even larger percentage said they were aware of continuing friction and mild anger (Wallerstein and Kelly, 1980). When there is evidence of anger after the divorce it is more likely to be displayed by the spouse who has been left than by the leaver (Spanier and Casto, 1979b). The anger of a spouse who has been left is likely to persist longer if that person has a difficult time establishing new heterosexual relationships (Spanier and Casto, 1979a). With regard to the spouse who has been the leaver, the most enduring emotion is a feeling of guilt or anguish, but there is less evidence that this interferes as much with postdivorce adjustment (Weiss, 1975).

Even when divorced people have successfully negotiated the emotional and psychological aspects of divorce, the postdivorce period is still a period of considerable difficulty and complexity. It is a period when a new life-style has to be established. Although the process of reorganizing and reorienting one's life will probably have started during the separation period, it is after the symbolic watershed of the divorce itself that a new way of life has to be worked out. In the sections that follow, we will consider the aspects of postdivorce life that are most important and often present the greatest challenges.

Coping With the Role of Divorced Person

There are two social factors relating to divorce that make establishing a new life after divorce especially difficult. First, to be a divorced person is to be in a status that still carries, at least for some people, a negative stereotype or image. Second, to be divorced is also to be in a status where the accompanying role expectations are ambiguous or unclear. We will consider the negative images of the divorced person first.

Negative images of the divorced person. It is not uncommon to find divorced people who think of themselves as failures or who believe that others think of them as failures. In interviews with divorced men and women in England, many reported feeling ashamed or complained that others responded negatively to their divorced status (Hart, 1976). One particularly degrading experience remarked upon by most divorced men and women is the courtroom experience at the time of the divorce. One man of fifty-five said, "I felt dirty when I came out of the courtroom. I went to sit in a church to try and restore a sense of being clean" (Hart, 1976, p. 149). Others in the same study complained that when one was divorced other people applied negative stereotypes. A divorced female of twenty-four said, "People look down on us. . . . It's like living with a label on" (Hart, 1976, p. 153).

Some even complained that being divorced was a negative element in work settings and affected evaluations of their work (Hart, 1976).

The negative stereotypes attached to being divorced are likely to be experienced differently by people of different ages, educational levels, and religions. When divorce is more commonplace in a population, the stereotypes are likely to be less negative, although it is still possible to hear a twice-divorced person say, "I'm going to be very careful; I don't want to be a 'three-time loser.' " There is also a particular negative stereotype that still attaches to divorced women. Many women report that after divorce they are considered by many men to be sexually available (Kohen et al., 1979). In the words of one woman, "Men think we are easy game" (Hart, 1976, p. 155). Not infrequently, the husbands of female friends view the separated or divorced woman as "easy game." One woman described how the husband of a neighboring couple with whom she had been friendly offered to walk her home after a visit. She described what happened then:

> *Maybe I should have known what was going to happen. I turned around at my door to say, "Thank you for walking me home," and it was pawing and grabbing and, "You poor thing, what are you doing for sex? You really*

As they go through separation and divorce, many people find that they are dropped by their friends.

must be hurting." And I said, "You goddamn bastard. I'm friends with your wife. Don't you ever, ever, put your hands on me again." (Weiss, 1975, p. 160)

It is likely that in an age of greater sexual freedom this image of divorced women may be less widespread and less negative than formerly, but it does still have some impact on the dating and courtship experiences of divorced women.

While the negative stereotypes of the divorced status may not be as strong as in the past, there is still the problem of the lack of clarity or the greater ambiguity with regard to role expectations. The problem can be defined and illustrated here with some initial examples, but the ambiguity of postdivorce roles is pervasive, as will be apparent in several later discussions.

Role ambiguity of the divorced person.   Roles, as we have noted before, are expectations about the behavior of people who hold a particular social status. For most statuses there are some widely shared understandings as to what these expectations will be. For the status of divorced person, the expectations are much less clear, and there are several areas where there is great uncertainty. From a sociological perspective, we can say that our society has not yet worked out, at least not very clearly, what the role expectations of divorced persons are.

As an example of the problems coming from role ambiguity, it will be recalled from the last chapter that many divorced people lose friends from among those they had while they were married. Divorced people often feel that their former friends have inexplicably rejected them and are understandably hurt by this behavior. However, since this pattern occurs so frequently, one must look for answers that extend beyond individual personality characteristics and consider some social causes.

There are several reasons that divorcing and divorced people are dropped by friends, especially by married friends. First, as we saw above, a divorced (now single) person poses a sexual or romantic threat (real or imagined) to married couples. But of equal importance, divorced people no longer fit the standard married-person role. Friends feel awkward with them and do not know what to say. The standard topics of conversation—kids, family, and home—are either gone or are too sensitive to discuss. In other words, the roles of married people make it clear what they are interested in and how they will respond. The divorced-person role is perplexing, unclear, and possibly even threatening to married friends. As a married man put it in describing the uncomfortableness he and his wife felt when they talked with friends who were separated, "we were really awkward with them. We just didn't know how to talk to them. How do you talk to somebody who is so totally removed from your situation?" (Weiss, 1975, p. 148).

One of the most ambiguous and unclear areas in the postdivorce period is the relationship that one has with a former spouse. As several observers have noted, the lack of clarity is signaled even in the lack of an appropriate word or name for former husbands and wives (Ahrons, 1981; Mead, 1971). *Former husband* or *ex-wife* (or the vulgar *"my ex"*) are terms that only reflect the former connection, not the postdivorce relationship. The available terminology gives no guidance as to what is an expected or appropriate relationship with one's former spouse. Without clear social expectations, individual divorced couples must work out their unique relationship with very little guidance. In the section that follows we will consider the kinds of relations that divorced couples do establish, especially in relation to the care and custody of any children they may have had in the marriage.

Relations between the Formerly Married

Two people who divorce after only a year or two of marriage, especially if they have had no children, are likely to go their separate ways quite quickly and with relative ease. Very likely each will remarry in a fairly short period of time, which will tend to reduce even further their interaction with each other. Even for those couples who divorce after many years of marriage, when their children have reached (or will soon reach) adulthood, there may be little or no contact between the former spouses after the divorce. But other couples, those married five, ten, or up to twenty years, are likely to have minor children and as a result continue to be in contact after divorce. Statistically, half of all divorces reported in the United States* are granted to couples who have been married between five and twenty years. Of course, some couples who were married for only a short period of time and some long-time married couples may also have minor children at the time of divorce. In the discussion that follows, the focus will be on all couples with minor children.

The range of relationships between former husbands and wives extends all the way from spouses (usually husbands) who simply disappear, either physically or socially, to former married couples who remain close and even intimate. As an example of the latter type, researchers in one study found a case where a former husband and wife occupied the two halves of a duplex (Ahrons, 1979). Their children had specified times when they were to be living with each parent, but the children were encouraged to go freely between their parents' households. The divorced couple in this case maintained a friendly and continuing relationship. They had no intention of reconciling but felt their living arrangement was desirable because it gave the children "spontaneous access" to their parents. This couple recognized some potential drawbacks of living in such close proximity, the most important of which was that the personal life of each could be easily observed by the other. This type of continuing close relationship has the potential for being a problem, because formerly married couples often find it difficult to remain detached and objective about the personal behavior of a person to whom they have been married.

This issue highlights a general problem faced by divorced couples who have children and remain in contact with each other primarily for the welfare of their children. To see the general nature of the problem, it is helpful to make a distinction between the *coparental* role and the *husband-wife* role. The coparental role calls for both parents to maintain an interest in the welfare of their children. This involves the social and psychological well-being of the children, as well as their physical well-being. The husband-wife role, of course, calls for two married people to be concerned with the welfare of each other. Again, this welfare can include social, psychological, and physical dimensions. In a legal sense, when two people are divorced they no longer have a responsibility or even a right to involve themselves in the welfare of their former spouse. The major exception to this general principle is court-ordered alimony or maintenance awards, whereby one spouse must provide economic resources for the other.

---

*In the United States today, only thirty-one states provide detailed divorce data to the National Center for Health Statistics. Estimates of the percentage of divorces occurring between five and nineteen years of marriage are based on these reporting states.

The distinction between the coparental role and the husband-wife role may seem quite obvious in the abstract, but in practice many divorced couples have a difficult time recognizing when their behaviors slip from one to the other. Also troublesome is the fact that there are some legitimate gray areas where a certain behavior could fit with the coparental role and yet could also be interpreted as falling within the husband-wife role. Some concrete examples will help to demonstrate the problems faced by many divorced husbands and wives.

A divorced person is legally free to remarry, since that is the essence of a legal divorce. It follows from this that former spouses cannot object to, or interfere with, the marriages of their former mates. But consider the hypothetical case of a divorced woman who has joint custody of two school-age children with her former husband. Suppose that this woman is dating, cohabiting with, or proposing to marry a man who is objectionable to her former husband on the grounds that the man or the relationship will be a bad influence on the children. (The genders of the spouses could as easily be the other way around.) Does the former husband have any right to interfere in the personal affairs of his former wife? Since a former spouse no longer has husband-wife rights and responsibilities, the answer is no. But a former spouse does have the coparental right to look out for the welfare of his or her children, so on this basis the answer is yes. In this hypothetical case, a former husband could, of course, take legal action, perhaps attempting to gain sole custody of the children. But a legalistic response to this problem misses the point, for former spouses cannot, and do not, turn to the courts every time an issue comes up. They must try to work out these problems by themselves, and it is not always easy.

Most divorced couples probably fare best if they keep clearly in mind the distinction between their coparental rights and responsibilities and their *former* husband-wife rights and responsibilities. However, as the case above illustrates, that distinction is not always clear-cut, and in many instances former husbands and wives inadvertently slip back into the old roles they had when married. In the lives of people after divorce, there are many examples of former husbands and wives objecting to the ways their former spouses spend their money, maintain their homes, use their leisure time, and so on. And yet, if these behaviors do not adversely affect the welfare or well-being of their children, they have no right to interfere in the personal lives of someone to whom they were once married.

This does not mean that divorced couples cannot involve themselves in the personal lives of their former spouses, if that is their mutual wish. We have already seen in the earlier example that some divorced couples do choose to maintain very close relationships. In a study of divorced couples from San Diego, some divorced people described former spouses as their "best friends," but these were roughly balanced by those who said they were "bitter enemies." The vast majority of divorced people said that former spouses were "neither friend nor foe" (Ahrons, 1979, p. 505).

The fact is that many couples do remain in contact after their divorce because there are children that necessitate that contact. The children very often move back and forth between the homes of their parents, keeping in close contact with both. This continued interaction of divorced couples and their children has led to the development of the binuclear family (Ahrons, 1979, 1981).

THE BINUCLEAR FAMILY

The *binuclear family* has been defined as "two interrelated households, maternal and paternal, which form one family system" (Ahrons, 1981, p. 425). Another way to describe the binuclear family is to say that it is "two households, but one family" (Ahrons, 1979). This type of family form is frequently found among divorced couples who have joint custody arrangements, but it is also found in cases where one parent has sole custody, if the noncustodial parent is involved in the rearing of the children in some way.

Three different types of binuclear families have been found in research (Ahrons, 1979). The first type is characterized by divorced spouses who continue to be good friends and choose to spend time together, both for enjoyment and to keep the two households united. These families are likely to have occasional meals together, both for the shared family experience and for family confer-

"Well, against the odds, here we are—Fran, her ex, me, my ex, Dick, my ex's new, Phil, Fran's ex's new, Pearl, Fran's ex's ex, David, Fran's ex's ex's new—CHEERS!"

ences. These families are, by their own description, very child centered in their activities.

A second binuclear family type exists where husband and wife are "neither friend nor foe," so there are relatively few occasions when the entire family does something together. The exceptions are significant events that the children are involved in, such as school plays, sports events, and graduations. The parents in this type of binuclear family usually communicate by telephone, which they do frequently but only with regard to the activities of the children.

A third type of binuclear family is influenced by the unresolved conflicts between the parents. If both the father and mother attend an event involving the children, they remain separate from each other. When the parents in these families do interact about the children, there is usually hostility and competitiveness (Ahrons, 1979). In this type of binuclear family, the children are in considerable danger of being used by their parents as a way of hurting or gaining advantage over the former spouse. The methods and techniques are many; they include criticizing the other parent, undercutting the respect and authority of the other parent, and asking the children to spy on the other parent. When the parents are hostile toward each other, encounters are usually unpleasant and are therefore avoided, if possible. This leads to failures in coordination, which only adds to problems and strife. One divorced woman complained about her husband, who refused to make arrangements with her when he was taking the children to his home:

> I asked their father to call me and deal with me on situations around visitation. "Don't call them, because they then have to tell me, and I don't know what the story is, and they are just put in the middle." (Weiss, 1979a, p. 143)

Often, the parent who goes directly to the children is primarily interested in establishing that the other parent is not in complete control of the children. This is often an effort to wrest some power from the parent who has custody of the children (Weiss, 1979a). The opposite line of attack from the custodial parent is to create obstacles that make it difficult for children to visit the other parent (Wallerstein and Kelly, 1980).

It is to be expected that children who are in a binuclear family where the relationship between their parents is regularly hostile and competitive are not going to fare as well as when the parents are cooperative. The research evidence supports this point, with children making the best adjustment to divorce when there is continued involvement by the father (in cases of the mother having sole custody) and where there is a cooperative atmosphere between the parents (Jacobsen, 1978).

One minor counterpoint might be offered to the general proposition that children fare best when their parents are cooperative. There is much evidence that children of divorced parents fantasize that their parents will remarry.

Young children are especially inclined to harbor this idea for some time before accepting the reality of their parents' divorce (Wallerstein and Kelly, 1980). One wonders if, when divorced parents continue to have a very close relationship, children might not be encouraged in their fantasies that the family will be made whole again. There may be no harm in this, since these fantasies serve as psychological defense mechanisms for the children, but divorced parents who remain on close terms should probably make special efforts to be sure that their children understand what this does and does not mean.

While the relationship between their divorced parents influences the behavior of children, the parent-child relationship is itself interesting and important. In the section that follows, we will consider how parents relate to their children and children relate to their parents in homes where there is only one parent.

RELATIONS BETWEEN DIVORCED PARENTS AND THEIR CHILDREN

Even though the family after divorce may appropriately be called a binuclear family, the households in which children live are single-parent homes. At least until such time as a parent remarries, children of divorce typically live in a home that has only one adult figure; and the parent in such a home is without the immediate presence of another adult. This set of conditions produces what one researcher has called "a different kind of parenting" (Weiss, 1979a, p. 66).

One of the most widely noted changes in parent-child relations after divorce is the way in which children increase in significance and importance for their parents. Children take on a new meaning with the end of a marriage, because they represent all that is left of the family after the husband-wife relationship has been severed (Weiss, 1979a). It is also likely that parents of divorce place an increased emphasis on the success of their children. This may be in part because with the marriage itself a failure, the children can be a compensating success. Also, many divorcing parents continue to be uncertain about whether ending the marriage may have been too harmful for their children. Divorced parents may watch their children very closely, often to assure themselves that the children are "normal" or "doing all right" after the divorce. If the children are doing well, it seems to justify the divorce and remove some of the guilt that many parents feel (Weiss, 1979a).

Divorced parents who live with their children often grow much closer to their children. Children become primary sources of support and love. Even very young children are "pressed into being advisors, practical helpers, buffers against loneliness and despair, replacements for other adults" (Wallerstein and Kelly, 1980, p. 103). Many parents report that they are closer to their children after divorce than they were before. A father of two school-age sons who had

Divorce produces a very different relationship between parents and their children. Parents who see their children on a limited basis may put too much emphasis on fun and recreation.

his sons half of every week said, "It's weird, but we are much closer than we would have been if I had stayed married. . . . They are able to be more relaxed with me. . . . And, I'm much more open with them" (Weiss, 1979a, p. 71–72).

An interesting explanation for the increase in closeness between divorced parents and their children is found in the concept of *parental echelon* (Weiss, 1979a, p. 73). The parental echelon is the parental level of authority in the intact family. This parental echelon, or parental level of authority, is reflected in the way parents typically try to maintain a solid front when dealing with their children. One feature of echelons in authority structures is that people who are at higher levels cannot side with people who are at lower levels (Goffman, 1961). In a family with both a father and a mother, parents are expected to give their first loyalty to each other and, in particular, not to side with the child or children. Obviously, real families do not always achieve the goal, but it is nonetheless the normative standard.

Clearly, when there is only one parent in the household, the parental echelon loses its meaning. Parents in one-parent homes can make alliances with children without having to be concerned about undercutting the other parent. Of course, a lone parent will not necessarily make alliances and agreements with children, but with the parental echelon no longer in place, he or she *may* do so. When this occurs, the parent and child become more equal in rights and responsibilities. This leads the child in the single-parent home to "grow up a little faster" (Weiss, 1979a, p. 82).

Parents in one-parent homes are more likely to treat their children as equals, giving them greater rights and responsibilities.

The process of growing up a little faster by the children of divorce has several dimensions. First, when children experience the divorce of their parents, they also usually lose a great deal of innocence and naivete. As long as marriages remain intact, children usually give relatively little attention to the relationship between their parents. Generally, parents produce this situation by not telling the children what is happening "behind the scenes" in the marriage. But separation and divorce bring the relationship out into the open. Children see their parents arguing and fighting. Or parents, especially when they are upset, may tell the children what is happening to the marriage. In any case, by the time the divorce is over, children are well aware that married couples do not always live "happily ever after."

A second dimension of growing up fast is that single parents are very likely to ask their children to take on new responsibilities in the household. A mother who has custody of her children, for example, will often take a course of action similar to that of the following woman, who had custody of her four children. She describes how,

> *As soon as I was on my own, I sat down with the children . . . and I told them, "Now things are different. Instead of, more or less, it being a family*

*of mother and four children, we're all one family with all equal
responsibility, and we all have a say, and we're all very important. (Weiss,
1979b, p. 100)*

When women with custody are working, they are especially likely to ask
their children to take more responsibility, both for themselves and for the
household. Since economic resources are often diminished after divorce, children will also become much more sensitive to the use of money. Single parents
may simply have to be candid about the sacrifices necessary to make ends meet.

Children who are quite young may be called on to assume nearly adult responsibilities. Children as young as ten and eleven may be expected to have
some of the dinner prepared when their parent comes home from work, or in
many cases children simply have to fend for themselves with regard to meals. It
is often reported that sons are expected to "fill their father's shoes" when they
live with mothers. This might include both the heavy work around the yard or
house and serving as the authority figure with regard to younger children. One
woman describes how her son had taken on the responsibilities of a father as
follows:

*My oldest son has taken on that role of being a parent, telling the others
what they should do and what they shouldn't do, and how he will send so-
and-so to bed if so-and-so doesn't do this or that. And he'll take on all
kinds of responsibilities. And I don't think it's good for him, because he's
only eleven. (Weiss, 1979b, p. 102)*

There are also many instances when children actually reverse roles with
their parents, worrying about them, comforting them, and acting almost as
their parents (Weiss, 1979a; Wallerstein and Kelly, 1980). Sometimes the parents encourage that kind of behavior by their children because it makes them
feel that the entire burden of taking care of the family is not theirs alone. A
woman with a fourteen-year-old son tells about how "he'll come over and say,
'Now Mom, calm down. I'll take care of it.' And, I really love that. When he does
that I really feel good" (Weiss, 1979a, p. 87).

Other parents sometimes complain that their children become too watchful
and parentlike. One mother reported how her ten-year-old son tried to control
her behavior, much like her own mother had done when she was much younger:

*I called my house and Mark said, "When are you coming home?" And I
said, "Pretty soon." And he said, "Ma, it's quarter to eight. Now you had
better get home quick." And I said, "Okay, Mark. I'm just having drinks
with a few friends." And he said, "Well, don't drink too much, and be home
soon." . . . And I got off the phone, and I said, "I did this with my mother
. . . I'd have to call up and have to give these excuses! I'm still doing it and
I'm twenty-nine years old." (Weiss, 1979a, p. 87)*

In some instances the reversal of roles, with children taking care of their parents, reaches disturbing dimensions. In one case a twelve-year-old boy decided to live with his father in order to take care of him. The father was depressed about the divorce and threatening suicide. The boy pressed ahead with his plan to care for an apartment and his father, but he proved to be too young for such an imposing task. When researchers followed up on this case after the divorce, they reported that "Although a gifted student, he dropped out of school and spent a restless and aimless adolescence, embroiled in a variety of minor delinquencies. He appeared to have been depleted by the responsibility which he had accepted prematurely" (Wallerstein and Kelly, 1980, p. 117).

Most children of divorce do not have such strenuous demands placed on them, even if they sometimes reverse roles with their parents. And on the positive side, many parents *and* children view the divorce experience in retrospect as one that gave the children greater maturity and strength earlier than other children (Wallerstein and Kelly, 1980; Weiss, 1979a).

There is one other significant experience that children may have after their parents divorce. Unlike most children of intact families, the children of divorce often see their parents dating, entering into sexual relationships, falling in love, and, in many cases, remarrying. These, too, are often broadening and maturing experiences, though for many children it can be embarrassing or even upsetting to see their parents in a romantic context.

DATING AND COURTSHIP AFTER DIVORCE

Since the majority of divorced people do remarry after divorce, it is apparent that they must enter the world of dating and courtship. For many divorced people, reentering the world of dating has a number of special difficulties. For almost all divorced people, dating, courtship, and remarriage are approached with different points of view than their first experience. There is greater caution and a greater sense of realism about moving toward a new marriage commitment.

The Difficulties of Dating after Divorce

Many divorced men and women find it difficult simply to start dating. The degree of difficulty is somewhat related to age at the time of divorce and to length of marriage, since those who divorce while young generally have very little difficulty picking up where they left off before marriage. It is also generally less difficult for men than for women to begin dating after divorce, especially if the divorce comes after a relatively long-term marriage.

There are several reasons why divorced women are at a disadvantage in dating, including the continuing gender bias that makes it difficult for women to initiate dates. There is also a cultural bias that gives men greater latitude in the ages of the women they may date. For example, men in middle age may date women who are their age, but they may also date women who are as much as fifteen or twenty years younger than they are. It is relatively rare for women to date men who are substantially younger. Divorced women can date older men, of course, but beyond middle age there are simply fewer men in the population. Also, as we saw in Chapter 14, most men who are middle aged and older are married.

Many people who divorce after years of being married report that they find it difficult to start dating again, in part because it seems to be something slightly inappropriate for them. As a divorced woman in her early forties put it, "To me the term 'dating' should be updated or something, you know, to make it more our age" (Weiss, 1975, p. 278). Many people who divorce after a number of years of marriage feel uncertain of what is expected of them in current-day dating situations.

But the most serious impediment to dating for many divorced people is simply that they are not in social networks where they are likely to meet prospective dating partners. Again, this is a more serious problem for those who divorce after being married for many years and are older.

For younger parents who divorce and have custody of their children, the children may also be an impediment to dating. Again, women are most often at a disadvantage in this regard, because they are most likely to have custody. Children require time and attention, which makes it difficult for custodial parents to get out where they might meet potential dating partners. Simply having the children in the household may make entertaining and other social activities in the home more difficult. Romance itself may be impeded by the presence of the children. If remarriage is a prospect, a potential mate may also object to having a "ready-made" family.

There are also psychological reasons why both men and women who divorce after long-term marriages find it difficult to enter into dating. For some who have just gone through bitter divorces or tumultuous marriages, there may be an emotional resistance to becoming involved with another person again. Although most eventually overcome this resistance to involvement, their attitudes have often been changed and shaped by the experiences of their first marriage and the divorce experience. Their attitudes as they approach dating and courtship are marked by greater caution and a more realistic view of what marriage means.

Caution and Realism during Courtship

A very common sentiment expressed by many divorced people, especially if they are contemplating remarriage, is that their approach to marriage is much

The return to dating after divorce is difficult for many people, especially if the divorce comes after a marriage of many years.

more practical and pragmatic and much less romantic than it was before their first marriages (Furstenberg and Spanier, 1984). Divorced people often view their first marriages as having been forced by social pressures and characterized by a lack of good judgment. They express a strong determination not to make those same mistakes again.

The greater practicality of the dating and courtship process is reflected in the tendency of couples to discuss much more fully all the implications of a proposed marriage. One woman, now remarried, said to an interviewer, "Before marrying, we sat down and discussed different things that happen in a marriage. We brought out our views and ideas, and decided that the only way a marriage can work would be to be honest, outspoken, and ready to accept each other's criticism" (Furstenberg and Spanier, 1984, p. 56).

Couples who have previously been married also tend to give up traditional dating behaviors fairly early in their relationships. Instead of limiting their contact to formal dating situations, where there is a tendency to display only one's best side, these couples move quickly to a pattern of informal association, with more continuous and less formal interaction. In interviews, they often acknowledge that early in their courtship they deliberately tried to present themselves as they really were, not as some idealized image. They were quite willing to let their dating partners see them in hair curlers and old clothes (Furstenberg and Spanier, 1984).

With regard to love, divorced people still usually believe in the importance of strong emotional attachments, but they commonly play down the importance of romantic love. They often reject ideas such as "uncontrollable emotional feelings, indulgence in fantasies and unconditional commitment" (Furstenberg and Spanier, 1984, p. 61). Divorced people have often experienced the souring of such intense romantic feelings in their earlier marriages and realize how easily changes can occur. Indeed, they often say they expect these feelings to diminish. As one woman divorcee put it, "Well, romantic love is, I think, temporary. It comes and after awhile, it will leave" (Furstenberg and Spanier, 1984, p. 61).

The extreme expression of both practicality and a sense that love may fade or die is found in the willingness of some previously divorced couples to discuss openly before marriage the possibility of their marriage not working out. Having been in marriages that were painful, they often agree in advance that they will not endure another bad marriage. In an interview, a divorced woman described her feelings on this point in the following way: "I would try my damndest [to make the marriage work] and hope he would try the same way, but if we couldn't work it out, then we wouldn't stay together . . . it's a little different from what I thought the first time" (Furstenberg and Spanier, 1984, p. 192).

Through this more cautious and realistic dating and courtship process, many divorced people do reach the decision to remarry. A second marriage, much like the dating and courtship that precedes it, is different in many ways from a first marriage. The reasons for the differences are many, as we will see in the next section.

REMARRIAGE AFTER DIVORCE

Remarriage has a long history in American society. Even though divorce was very rare in pre–Revolutionary War times in the United States, remarriage was a relatively commonplace occurrence because of early death. According to the research of Demos (1970), about one-third of all men and one-quarter of all women who lived in the Plymouth Colony and lived full lifetimes remarried after the death of a spouse. This pattern of remarriage as the result of widowhood more often than divorce, persisted until the 1920s. Since that time, remarriage has more commonly followed divorce than death, and recent rapid increases in remarriage have reflected increases in divorce. By 1982, about ninety percent of all men and women remarrying were previously divorced (National Center for Health Statistics, 1985).

Another way of seeing how much remarriage has increased in American society is to consider what percentage of *all marriages* in a given year are by people who have been divorced. In the year 1900, only three percent of all women marrying had previously been divorced. In 1930, the percentage had increased to nine percent (Cherlin, 1981). In 1982, approximately thirty percent of all women who married had previously been divorced (National Center for Health Statistics, 1985). Among men who married in 1982, the percentage was slightly higher, at thirty-one percent.

These figures point to the general fact that most people who divorce do remarry. About five out of six men and three out of four women remarry after divorce. Those who divorce when young have a much higher percentage remarrying, and men at all ages are more likely than women to remarry (Cherlin, 1981; Thornton and Freedman, 1983). The great tendency to remarry after divorce is an indication that most people, when they divorce, may be giving up on a particular marriage but apparently are not disillusioned with marriage as an institution (Thornton and Freedman, 1983).

With all the remarriage in recent decades, the American family system includes a great many "remarried couple households." A *remarried couple household* is "a household maintained by a married couple, one or both of whom have been previously married" (Cherlin and McCarthy, 1985, p. 23). About one out of five of all married couple households today are remarried couple households (Cherlin and McCarthy, 1985). There are about 9.2 million remarried households, and in these homes live about 4.8 million children under eighteen who are stepchildren (Cherlin and McCarthy, 1985). Since mothers most often receive custody of children after divorce, it is not surprising that most often children in such homes are those of the wife, making the husband the stepparent.

When remarrying couples have children from earlier marriages, the numbers and ages of such children, and with whom they live, are factors that immensely complicate remarriage. In the most complex case, both the remarrying husband and wife will have custody (either sole or joint) of their minor children. If this couple also goes on to have children, the family form becomes even more complex.

When one or both partners of a remarriage bring children to the marriage, the resulting family is usually called a *reconstituted* or *blended family* (Duberman, 1975; Furstenberg, 1979). Both terms suggest that two separate families are being combined, but neither gives much indication of the complexity, the uncertainty, and the problems that can ensue when that occurs. These problems and other, more general, problems of remarriage have been considered by a number of writers, and while positive features of remarriage can also be found, it is difficult to escape the problematic nature of remarriage. At the societal level, it has been said that a number of problems stem from the fact that remarriage is an "incomplete" institution (Cherlin, 1978).

Remarriage as an Incomplete Institution

The conventional first-marriage family in American society is a social institution with relatively clear social norms and social roles. In everyday terms, this means that in first marriages there is a high degree of understanding about what is expected of husbands, wives, and children, with regard first to how they relate to each other and second to how they relate to other kin, such as in-laws and grandparents. But when marriages are remarriages for one or both spouses, and families are composed completely or partially of the children of divorce, the resulting family system is not completely institutionalized. The institutionalization is incomplete because there are positions without clear roles and relationships between family members or related individuals without clear norms and expectations (Cherlin, 1978).

There are many examples of the incomplete institutionalization of the families of remarriage. Consider, for example, the matter of authority over children's behavior. Generally, the norm in American society is that parents control and provide guidance for the behavior of their children. Furthermore, traditional gender roles give fathers a particularly prominent role in this regard. Yet, because of traditional custody awards, many remarried households have children of divorce who belong to the mother, making her new husband stepfather to her children. In remarried households, stepfathers outnumber stepmothers by a ratio of six to one (Cherlin and McCarthy, 1985).

The stepfather role has many ambiguities. When and how much should a stepfather be involved in the teaching, guidance, and control of his wife's children? How is his role affected if his wife's former husband has joint custody and has the children roughly half the time? There are no institutionalized answers to these questions, so each remarried family must work out its own individual arrangement. This process is filled with uncertainty and has great potential of producing misunderstandings and even conflict. Very often people must deal with these problems in contexts where relations among family members are either strained or hostile. The former husband and wife may still be bitter or angry as a result of the divorce. Sometimes the remarriage itself may have produced new resentments on the part of a former spouse. From the point of view of the children, they too often experience uncertainty and confusion about whether they owe their first allegiance to their natural father or to the husband of their mother, whom they often see much more on a day-to-day basis. Sometimes, children in these circumstances also resent the fact that a parent has remarried and harbor a certain amount of hostility toward their new stepparent.

It should be noted as we consider this one example of the ambiguity of the stepfather role, or the stepparent role generally, that remarriage after divorce presents a set of conditions that differs greatly from remarriage after widow-hood. If the former spouse has died, the stepparent's role is much less ambiguous and complicated. A stepfather in this case has a much clearer mandate with regard to his wife's children, because he is expected to take the place of their natural father, insofar as possible.

To further illustrate how remarriage is an incomplete institution, Cherlin (1978) has noted that both our language and our legal system fail to give us guidance for our behavior. Regarding language, as the example above suggests, the word *stepparent* was originally used to refer to stepping in to fill the role of a dead parent. Today with remarriage coming most often after divorce, the new parent is not so much a replacement as an additional parent (Bohannan, 1971b). Furthermore, the words *stepmother* and *stepfather* often have very negative connotations, as in the "wicked stepmothers" of fairy tales and other folktales. Yet there are very few alternative words that do not present some problems. In one remarried family, a researcher found that the children of the mother wished to call her new husband *dad,* but his children were also living in the home, and they refused to allow this usage (Cherlin, 1978). Stepchildren often use the first name of their parent's new spouse. In one reported case, a little girl of nine had a mother who had been married four times. The girl called her natural father, the mother's first husband, *daddy.* "The other three she called Daddy-Tom, Daddy-Dick, and Daddy-Harry" (Bohannan, 1971b, p. 135).

Even though it is somewhat inappropriate and has negative connotations, the word *stepparent* is still widely used because its meaning is widely understood. But there are many other relationships in remarried families where there is no usable word of any kind (Cherlin, 1978). For example, if children live with their divorced mother when their father remarries, there is no term that can be used to express their relationship with their father's new wife. Stepmother in this case is even less appropriate since the children may only live in the household of their father on a limited visiting basis. American children, at least of a certain age, usually resort to phrases such as "my dad's wife." But that label quite clearly leaves much uncertainty in those times when the children are in their father's household and "dad's wife" is serving as a surrogate mother. Again, the lack of appropriate words for these and many other relationships is only symptomatic of how remarriage is an incomplete institution.

The legal system is similarly inadequate for dealing with many aspects of remarriage after divorce. The field of family law has largely developed under the assumption that marriages are first marriages (Weitzman, 1974). This assumption leaves many of the circumstances of remarried families unattended to or unclear. One resulting legal problem is that there are competing obligations between previous and present spouses and children. For example, under common law, as we saw in Chapter 7, husbands have financial obligations for their spouses and children. When husbands divorce and remarry, the law says little about the relative financial obligations they have to their previous and current families. The current family obligations may be further complicated if the new wife brings children to the marriage, for which her former husband has some obligations. And then, too, the remarried couple may have children of their own, which further complicates the financial obligations toward children (Cherlin, 1978).

One area where these financial obligations become especially sensitive is in the writing of wills. When remarried couples are writing their wills, they must consider how they will distribute their estates to their children of different marriages, including their own..Furthermore, if either or both of the remarried couple should die without a will, the legal battles that ensue among the competing heirs are likely to be monumental.

Another area in which the legal system has little to say about the remarried family is the prohibition of sex between family members connected by the remarriage (Cherlin, 1978). While incest laws prohibit sexual relations between close family members in first marriages, the law is not always clear on what is illegal among steprelatives. Is it illegal for a stepmother to have sexual relations with a stepson who has reached the age of majority? Or is it illegal for a stepsister and stepbrother to have sexual relations in adulthood?

These examples of unresolved issues in the legal system, along with the inadequacies of the language system, are indications of just how incomplete the institutionalization of remarriage is. These sources of difficulties are seen from a societal-level perspective. Many of the same problems can be seen as stemming from the structure of the reconstituted family. The most noticeable structural feature of the reconstituted family is the expansion of its boundaries (Albrecht et al., 1983; Walker and Messinger, 1979).

Expanded Boundaries of the Reconstituted Family

The boundaries of the first marriage are usually well defined, enclosing a relatively small number of people with well-defined positions (husband, wife, and children). The boundaries of reconstituted families often include a larger number of people, and as the discussion above has already indicated, the positions often have unclear role expectations.

It can be taken as an axiom that the more people there are in a family system, the more difficult decision making can be. Consider the example of a decision that many families make each year: where and when to take a summer vacation. Even in the conventional first-marriage family this can be a complicated decision if both husband and wife are working and two or more children are engaged in their particular summer activities. Just to find a time when everyone can be free of obligations at the same time is often difficult. In the reconstituted family, the difficulty of this decision is greatly complicated because so many more people are involved. To begin with, the desires and often the legal rights of ex-spouses must be taken into account. If a noncustodial father has been granted the right to have his children for a month in the summer (a common arrangement), then his schedule must be part of the planning for a family vacation.

This is but one example of the many ways in which the workings of the family can become exceptionally complicated for the reconstituted family. Obviously, if both spouses in a remarriage have children from a previous marriage, the decisions become even more complex. It takes only a little imagination to see that when divorce and remarriage are widespread, there can be long chains of interlocking reconstituted families that must somehow accommodate each other.

The boundaries of remarried families are also expanded by the addition of extended-family members. The case of grandparents can illustrate this expansion of boundaries. A remarried couple with children from both previous marriages *and* with children from their present marriage can have four sets of grandparents for their children. All of these grandparents might want to have time with their grandchildren. Without wishing to complicate the matter unduly, it is necessary to mention that any set of grandparents could also be divorced and remarried. In the extreme case, a particular remarried couple could have eight sets of grandparents to accommodate! This is unlikely to happen in reality, but most remarried families have grandparental obligations that extend beyond the four grandparents that typify first-marriage families. Of course, in the same way that grandparent relationships can proliferate, so also can other extended kin (aunts, uncles, cousins). All these extensions of family boundaries mean greater complications, and in some cases more problems.

The problems and complications of remarried and reconstituted families that have thus far been identified may make it seem as if the obstacles for success are nearly insurmountable. Indeed, one of the most commonly asked questions is whether or not remarriages can succeed in the face of the many intrinsic difficulties in this form of marriage and family life. In the next section, we will turn to that question.

The Success of Remarriage

One obvious measure of the success of remarriage is the frequency with which remarriages end in divorce. The evidence on this point has been quite consistent in all analyses that have been done. Divorce is more likely to occur in a remarriage than in a first marriage (Glick, 1980). A major exception to this general pattern, found in one study, was that for black Americans second marriages were more likely to remain intact than first marriages (McCarthy, 1978).

While the pattern has been for remarriages to end in divorce more often than first marriages, the difference is not very large. In one set of projections of the percentage of marriages expected to end in divorce, thirty-eight percent of first marriages and forty-four percent of second marriages were expected to end in divorce (Glick, 1980). Another projection, using more recent data, estimated that 47.4 percent of first marriages and 53.5 percent of remarriages would end in divorce before the twenty-fifth anniversary (Weed, 1980). Recog-

"I do, again."

nizing that these figures are largely projections, and as we noted in the last chapter must be interpreted carefully, they do show that people who remarry have a slightly higher chance of divorcing than people in first marriages.

But there is another factor that must be considered when divorce is used to compare the intensity of marital problems or marital dissatisfaction in first and second marriages. This factor is one that could make remarriages compare quite favorably with first marriages. It has been observed that people who get divorces and thus are eligible to remarry are not representative of the total set of people who enter first marriages (Glick, 1980; Halliday, 1980). There are probably many people in the population of first-marrieds who will not get divorced, regardless of how dissatisfied they might be with their marriages. For example, there are many people who are unwilling to divorce because of their religious beliefs, since many religious denominations either prohibit divorce or view it as improper behavior (Halliday, 1980). There may also be other, nonreligious, reasons for people to reject divorce, even when their marriages are unsatisfactory (family honor and economic considerations, for example). It follows, then, that the remarrieds do not include that segment of the population who will not divorce. Looked at from the opposite perspective, remarrieds are made up of those people who will use divorce when their remarriages are unsatisfactory, because they have already done so at least once (widowed people are not being considered among the remarriers in this analysis). In view of these considerations, the marital quality of remarriages may compare very well with first marriages, despite a slightly higher divorce rate.

But there are other measures of marital quality than the comparative statistics on divorce. People who have remarried after a divorce can be asked to evaluate the quality of their marriages, and their responses can be compared with the responses of people who are in their first marriages. Comparisons can also be made with regard to the general well-being and life satisfaction of remarried people and first-married people. A number of researchers have used these kinds of questions to ascertain whether remarried people fare as well as those who remain in their first marriages.

Remarriage and Marital Quality

National surveys over a number of years have included the following question on marital quality: "Taking things all together, how would you describe your marriage? Would you say that your marriage is very happy, pretty happy, or not too happy?" (Glenn, 1981, p. 65). Data from seven national surveys conducted between 1973 and 1978 were used to make comparisons between people who had been divorced and remarried and those who were married and never divorced (Glenn, 1981). The findings from this analysis can be summarized as follows:

- Remarried white women reported moderately lower marital happiness than white women in their first marriages.
- Remarried black women reported much lower marital happiness than black women in their first marriages.
- Remarried white men reported slightly lower marital happiness than white men in their first marriages.
- Remarried black men reported *greater* marital happiness than black men in their first marriages.

The most prominent pattern in these research findings is that women who have remarried are less happy in their marriages than women who are in their first marriages. Incidentally, these differences are not produced by age or socioeconomic status differences between the people with different marriage histories. However, one influence that could not be ruled out is the fact that some divorced people who remarried and were dissatisfied might have ended their marriages again. The effect would be to remove from the remarried group those least satisfied with their marriages, so the marital happiness scores among the remarrieds may be somewhat inflated.

The fact that women who divorce and remarry are less happy than women who remain in their first marriages is interesting and calls for some explanation (Glenn, 1981; White, 1979). The explanation may lie in the possibility that women who divorce have their general psychological health more negatively affected by marriage failure. It may also be that women, more than men, who are maladjusted and chronically unhappy are more likely to be divorced and therefore in the remarried population. Neither of these two explanations is as widely accepted as a third, which is based on a recognition that women who remarry after divorce have a much poorer choice of marriage mates than do men. The "marriage market" for divorced women, as we noted earlier, is less favorable, which could lead more women then men "to settle for marriages with which they are less than pleased" (Glenn, 1981; p. 69).

In addition to marital happiness, researchers have also examined the general well-being or life satisfaction of remarried people compared to people in first marriages. In the national samples of adults mentioned above, respondents were also asked the following question: "Taken all together, how would you say things are these days—would you say that you are very happy, pretty happy, or not too happy?" (Glenn, 1981, p. 65). On this measure of overall or global happiness, there were no significant differences between the people who were remarried and those in their first marriages.

In a study of divorced persons conducted in central Pennsylvania, their general psychological and social well-being was measured at a time early in the separation and divorce process and again two and one-half years later, after many were remarried or cohabiting. In this study, there was a general improvement in well-being between the separation period and the postdivorce period. However, at the time of the second interview, there were no significant differences in well-being between those divorced people who had remarried and those who had not (Furstenberg and Spanier, 1984). This is somewhat surprising because in the national samples of adults there were great differences in well-being between divorced people who had remarried and those who remained unmarried (Glenn, 1981). The divorced people who had not remarried were found in these surveys to be the unhappiest of all the marital statuses. These national findings would coincide with national data showing that divorced (and not remarried) people have the highest death rates in the population from suicide, homicide, automobile accidents, and alcoholism (Gove, 1973). All these causes of death are indicative of some kind of psychological or social problem.

The authors of the Pennsylvania study propose that the reason for no differences in well-being between those who have and those who have not remarried comes from the fact that the remarried population is made up of two types.

There are those who have remarried and have done so successfully, who are high in their psychological and social well-being. But there are also those who have remarried and have been as disappointed with their second marriages as they were with their first. These remarrieds are likely to be very low in their psychological and social well-being. Since the two groups have opposite psychological and social profiles, they tend to cancel each other (Furstenberg and Spanier, 1984).

The research that has been done on the psychological and social well-being of people who remarry after divorce is well summarized by the following words: "The data . . . show a remarkably high level of well-being among persons remarried after divorce" (Glenn, 1981, p. 70). This positive note about remarriage is a theme that is emerging with increasing frequency in recent years. Since this chapter has devoted considerable attention to many of the problems and difficulties of remarriage, it is appropriate that the concluding section be devoted to some of the strengths of remarried families.

Strengths of Remarried Families

Families in general tend to show great strength in times of difficulty or crisis. Remarried families certainly have their special problems, but they, too, often respond strongly and positively to the situations they face (Knaub et al., 1984; Pasley and Ihinger-Tallman, 1984). Because the problems faced by remarried families are not covered by norms and social roles, the members of these families are often especially creative and inventive (Furstenberg and Spanier, 1984). If the language does not provide a ready-made term for members of the immediate or extended family, a term is often invented for the occasion. If the norms do not specify exactly what authority a stepparent has over children, families often sit down together and discuss what the stepparent's role will be. It may not always be easy for families to negotiate the uncharted areas, but it is by no means impossible if they are willing to discuss and work out the arrangements.

There are two characteristics of remarried people that make them more willing to enter into discussions and work out new arrangements: they tend to be more honest and more tolerant (Westoff, 1977). Remarried couples report again and again how in their second marriages they are able to talk about more things with greater candor than they were in their first marriages. First marriages may be linked too closely with dating and courtship, where young people often present their best characteristics and hide their flaws. When they enter marriage for the first time, they continue to "keep up a front" to some degree. In second marriages, people are more inclined to present themselves openly and directly, even, as we saw above, during the dating and courtship period. One remarried woman described her new openness in the following way: "If we fight, I'm a better fighter now, more verbal. I don't withdraw as much. I'm more direct. If you can talk about a problem, you can resolve it" (Westoff, 1977, p. 131).

The greater tolerance of remarried couples probably stems from their experience with marriages that failed; they have a more realistic perspective about how bad married life can be. Many remarried couples report that minor irritations do not bother them as much as they did in their first marriages. They understand that married life will not be perfect all the time. Remarried couples know they will not please each other at all times. A remarried doctor told an interviewer, "I may be getting older, but I'm more tolerant. I'm really happy, so little things don't bother me so much. And you certainly want to make it work. . . . It's a searing experience to break up a marriage. . . . Thank God you have a second chance" (Westoff, 1977, p. 133).

It has been suggested at several points in this chapter that the relationship between stepparents and stepchildren is one of the most crucial areas of remarried family life. As a final issue of this chapter, we will consider some alternative ways in which the sensitive relationship between stepparent and stepchild can be handled.

ISSUE

What is the best approach to stepparenting?

Unlike many of the other issues connected with marriage and family life, the issues growing out of stepparenting are not as well-defined or polarized. Everyone agrees that stepparenting is difficult, but the different points of view about how best to manage this difficult task have not emerged as clearly opposing positions. In the presentation below, two approaches to stepparenting are identified and elaborated, but they serve primarily to prompt and stimulate discussions of how best to carry out the task of stepparenting.

One approach to stepparenting is to try to establish a relationship with stepchildren that approximates as closely as possible the "normal" or biological parental relationship. An alternative approach is to define the stepparent role as different from that of the biological parent. With this latter view, many of the rights, responsibilities, and emotional ties that are generally enjoyed by biological parents are not necessarily expected by stepparents. We will consider these as alternative views toward stepparenting, and begin the discussion with the idea that stepparenting should be as much like the parenting of a biological parent as possible.

Stepparenting as a "Normal" Parent

Marrying a person who has custody of children from a previous marriage is not done without prior knowledge that parenting will be part of the new marriage. It is not possible to be part of a home as an adult married person and ignore the fact that one's spouse has children. With these facts obvious enough, one school of thought about stepparenting is that one must work from the very beginning, even before the marriage, to establish oneself as a parental figure in the home.

Establishing oneself as a parent involves a number of important dimensions, which usually come quite naturally in the biological family but which must be worked at in the reconstituted family. It means, first of all, that no matter how complex the family unit (his children, her children, full-time, part-time) the effort must be made to create a close-knit, happy family. To achieve this, there must be regular and patterned family interaction and activities. Even though children in reconstituted families may not always be eager to join into family activities, establishing patterns of close family interaction can be used as a mechanism for bringing the family together.

For a stepparent to take on the parental role fully, and for children to view a stepparent as their parent, it is also necessary to take an active part in setting limits and disciplining. If the natural parent does not have the active participation of the stepparent in the disciplinary side of parenthood, then the authority of the natural parent will suffer. This will be particularly true if the stepparent takes the role of a "friend" or "pal" with respect to the children. It is probably best, from this point of view, if stepparents are called by a parental name rather than by a first name, because the latter would undercut parental authority.

The issue of love and emotional attachment is a more difficult area for stepparents to negotiate, but to be a full-fledged parent to one's stepchildren, this, too, must be cultivated. Stepparents may not feel an instant love for the children of their new spouses, but the children should feel that they are receiving love and warmth from the beginning. Stepparents should not, of course, attempt to weaken or diminish the love of the child for its natural parent. The aim is not to take the place of the natural parent as an object of love but rather for the stepchild to be receiving love from the stepparent as well. Developing a love between stepparents and stepchildren that is deep and mutual will probably take effort and time, but it should be the goal of stepparents throughout the new marriage.

To sum up, one approach to stepparenting is to create in a reconstituted family, a family that is as close as possible to the first-marriage family. This kind of family would be organized around the family activities often characteristic of biological families. It would also be a family in which stepparents accept the parental roles of setting limits for and disciplining the children whenever necessary. Finally, stepparents would strive to develop a loving and affectionate relationship with their stepchildren.

Stepparenting on a Nonparental Model

Many people who have thought about and experienced the stepparent role have concluded that life in a reconstituted family is better if stepparents do not try to be full-fledged parents to their stepchildren. As they see it, the reconstituted family is so different from the "natural" or biological family that it is misguided to act as if they are the same, or even that one can be made into an approximation of the other.

A reconstituted family, according to its definition, is created from the elements of a broken family. The children who have gone through the breakup of their parents' marriage are often unwilling to accept the new family, with its substitute parent, as a simple replacement for the first. Under these circumstances, it is often nearly impossible to create a happy family immediately after a remarriage. Many stepparents look back after a few years and recognize that they tried too hard to create a happy family setting when the odds were against them from the beginning. The disappointment and distress produced by this effort is often harmful to the marriage relationship.

The goal of achieving instant parenthood, by stepping into limit-setting and disciplinary responsibilities, is also considered by many observers to be counterproductive and distressful. Stepparents will almost always have styles and methods of discipline that differ from those of the children's natural parents. The children will very likely notice the difference in discipline styles and will probably express dissatisfaction. This disturbance can affect the new marital relationship as well as the relationship between stepparent and children.

On the issue of discipline, it is also possible that stepparents do not have the same degree of tolerance as natural parents for the misdeeds of the children. Stepparents may more easily "see through" and discount the explanations and protestations of children when issues of wrongdoing come up. If this is true, it makes disciplining children an especially sensitive area for stepparents to enter. It could be argued on this basis alone that stepparents are well-advised to forego the disciplinary aspect of parenting whenever possible.

Love and affection between stepparents and stepchildren is often achieved only gradually over a long period of time. Many observers now feel that it is very unlikely that "instant love" can be achieved and therefore that it is harmful even to act as if it exists. There is no absolute requirement that adults and children who have been connected only through a marriage must have a relationship that is the same as parent-child love. It may be that respect and friendship will serve very adequately for many years as the primary elements in a relationship between stepparents and their stepchildren. Perhaps over time love will develop, but it is not necessary, and it is certainly not considered advisable for either the adult or the child to display a false or sham love.

This view of stepparenting can best be summarized by saying that it is not necessary for stepparents or reconstituted families to either strive for or act as if they are biological parents or first-marriage families. It may be much more realistic, and healthier for all family relationships, including the marital relationship, for reconstituted families to establish their unique ways of operating. Then the reconstituted family can be shaped to meet the special needs and circumstances of all family members.

Themes

1. While most divorced people can look back on their divorce experience and feel that they are better off than they were before or during the divorce, the postdivorce period is nonetheless a period of adjustment.

2. Establishing a new life after divorce is made difficult because of the negative images of divorced people and the ambiguities that surround the divorced role.

3. Divorced couples who have children are likely to continue some kind of relationship after the divorce.

4. Divorced couples with children often have difficulty distinguishing between the coparental role, which continues, and the husband-wife role, which does not.

5. The concept of the *binuclear family* reflects the fact that in a divorce where there are children, there is a family system made up of two households, the maternal and paternal.

6. When children of divorce live in households with only one parent, the relationship between parent and children takes on a new character.

7. As a result of the divorce of their parents, children tend to grow up a little faster.

8. Dating and courtship after divorce is difficult and complicated, especially for divorced women.

9. Remarriage is not new in American society; in the nineteenth century it was usually the result of the death of one spouse, but in the twentieth century it is more likely to result from divorce.

10. Remarriage after divorce is made complicated by the lack of clear norms and social roles; thus, remarriage has been called an *incomplete institution.*

11. The stepparent role, in particular, has many ambiguities and uncertainties.

12. The reconstituted family that results from a remarriage between people who already have children has wider, less clear boundaries than the conventional first-marriage family.

13. While the complications and difficulties of remarriage and reconstituted families are undeniable, these family systems also have their strengths.

Facts

1. Surveys of divorced couples have found that the overwhelming majority say that the divorce was beneficial and that they are better off after the divorce than they were before.

2. Divorced persons who were left by their spouses, much more than spouses who were the leavers, suffer from a loss of self-esteem, are lonely and depressed, and often harbor anger and bitterness.

3. The adjustment of children to the divorce of their parents is made more difficult by continuing hostility and conflict between their parents.

4. Parents often report that their relationships with their children have become closer after divorce; this is especially true of parents who have custody of their children.

5. Males after divorce have better chances of remarriage than females, in part because a cultural bias gives men a wider range of ages to choose from and also because after middle age there are fewer men in the population.

6. The dating of divorced people tends to move quickly toward informal interaction.

7. About one-third of all men and one-quarter of all women who lived in the Plymouth Colony and lived full lifetimes remarried after the death of a spouse.

8. About one in five of all married-couple households today are remarried households.

9. The word *stepparent* originally referred to "stepping in" to take the place of a deceased parent.

10. Divorce is slightly more likely after remarriage than after first marriages.

11. Divorces are likely to be higher among remarried than first-married couples because some number of first-married couples will not divorce regardless of how unsatisfactory their marriages are.

12. Remarried women tend to report lower marital happiness than women in their first marriages.

13. Remarried black men tend to report greater marital happiness than black men in their first marriages.

14. In national surveys, divorced people who had not remarried were found to be much less happy than divorced people who had remarried.

Major Concepts

binuclear family: The two interrelated households, the maternal and the paternal, which form one family system after a divorce in which children are involved.

blended family: (*See* **reconstituted family**)

coparental role: The continuing responsibility divorced parents have to be interested in the welfare of their children.

husband-wife role: The responsibility of married people to be concerned with the welfare of the spouse, which no longer necessarily applies to divorced couples.

incomplete institution: A description of remarriage as a family system in which the positions are without clear roles and relationships between family members or related individuals are without clear norms and expectations.

negative stereotypes: In regard to divorce, the negative characteristics that are often attributed to divorced persons—e.g., losers, failure, and (particularly for divorced women) sexually easy.

parental echelon: The parental level of authority, which in the intact family is higher than that of the children, and is the level to which parents typically give their first loyalty.

reconstituted families: Remarried-couple households where one or both of the partners have brought children from a previous marriage. (Also called a blended family)

remarried-couple households: A household maintained by a married couple, one or both of whom have been previously married.

role ambiguity: In regard to divorced persons, the lack of clear understandings about what kinds of behaviors are expected of them.

REFERENCES

Chapter 1

Blood, B. and Blood, M. *Marriage.* 3rd ed. New York: The Free Press, 1978.

Blood, Robert O. *Love Match and Arranged Marriage: A Tokyo-Detroit Comparison.* New York: The Free Press, 1967.

Chandrasekhar, S. *A Dirty Filthy Book.* Berkeley, Calif.: University of California Press, 1981.

Fullerton, G. *Survival in Marriage.* 2nd ed. Hinsdale, Ill.: The Dryden Press, 1977.

Gordon, H. and Kammeyer, K. "The Gainful Employment of Women With Small Children." *Journal of Marriage and the Family* 42 (1980):327–336.

Oboler, Regina Smith. "Is the Female Husband a Man? Woman/Woman Marriage among the Nandi of Kenya." *Ethnology* 19 (1980):69–88.

Pogrebin, Letty Cottin. *Family Politics: Love and Power on an Intimate Frontier.* New York: McGraw-Hill, 1983.

Rosenberg, Morris. *Conceiving the Self.* New York: Basic Books, 1979.

Rubin, Lillian Breslow. *Worlds of Pain.* New York: Basic Books, 1976.

Samuel, Dorothy T. *Love, Liberation, and Marriage.* New York: Funk & Wagnalls, 1976.

Skolnick, A. *The Intimate Environment.* 3rd ed. Boston: Little, Brown, 1983.

Stannard, Una. *Mrs. Man.* San Francisco: Germainbooks, 1977.

Trivers, Robert L. "Parental Investment and Sexual Selection." In *Sexual Selection and the Descent of Man*, edited by Bernard Campbell. Chicago: Aldine, 1972.

Vincent, Clark. "Familia Spongia: The Adaptive Function." *Journal of Marriage and the Family* 28 (1966):29–36.

White, Gregory. "Inequality of Emotional Involvement, Power, and Jealousy in Romantic Couples." Paper presented at the annual meeting of the American Psychological Association, San Francisco, 1977.

Chapter 2

Anderson, Margaret L. *Thinking about Women: Sociological and Feminist Perspectives.* New York: Macmillan, 1983.

Broverman, I. K., Vogel, S. R., Broverman, D. M., Clarkson, F. E., and Rosenkrantz, P. S. "Sex Role Stereotypes: A Current Appraisal." *Journal of Social Issues* 28 (1972):

Bruck, Connie. "Professing Androgyny." *Human Behavior* 6 (1977): 22–31.

David, Debbie, and Brannon, Robert (eds.). *The Forty-Nine Percent Majority: The Male Sex Role.* Reading, Mass.: Addison-Wesley, 1976.

Eisenstein, Z. (ed.). *Socialist Feminism and the Case for Capitalist Patriarchy.* New York: Monthly Review Press, 1979.

Fehrenbach, Peter A., Miller, David J., and Thelen, Mark H. "The Importance of Modeling Behavior upon Imitation: A Comparison of Singular and Multiple Models." *Journal of Personality and Social Psychology* 37 (1979):1412–1417.

Firestone, Shulamith. *The Dialectic of Sex.* New York: Bantam, 1971.

Forisha, Barbara Lusk. *Sex Roles and Personal Awareness.* Glenview, Ill.: Scott, Foresman, 1978.

Friedan, Betty. *The Feminine Mystique.* New York: W. W. Norton, 1963.

Frieze, Irene H., Parsons, Jacquelynne E., Johnson, Paula B., Ruble, Diane N., and Zellman, Gail L. *Women and Sex Roles: A Social Psychological Perspective.* New York: W. W. Norton, 1978.

Goldberg, Herbert. *The Hazards of Being Male.* New York: New American Library, 1976.

Goldberg, Steven. *The Inevitability of Patriarchy.* New York: Morrow, 1973.

Goode, William. "Why Men Resist." In *Rethinking the Family: Some Feminist Questions*, edited by Barrie Thorne and Marilyn Yalom, pp. 131–150. New York: Longman, 1982.

Gordon, Linda. "Why Nineteenth Century Feminists Did Not Support 'Birth Control' and Twentieth Century Feminists Do: Feminism, Reproduction and the Family." In *Rethinking the Family: Some Feminist Questions*, edited by Barrie Thorne and Marilyn Yalom. New York: Longman, 1982.

Heiss, Jerold (ed.). *Family Roles and Interaction: An Anthology*. 2nd ed. Chicago: Rand McNally, 1976.

Heiss, Jerold. "Role Theory." In *Social Psychology*, edited by Morris Rosenberg and Ralph Turner. New York: Basic Books, 1981.

Henley, Nancy M. *Body Politics: Power, Sex and Nonverbal Communication*. Englewood Cliffs, N.J.: Prentice-Hall, 1977.

Henley, Nancy M., and Thorne, Barrie. "Womanspeak and Manspeak: Sex Differences and Sexism in Communications, Verbal and Nonverbal." In *Beyond Sex Roles*, edited by Alice G. Sargent. St. Paul, Minn.: West Publishing, 1977.

Homans, George F. *Social Behavior: Its Elementary Forms*. New York: The Free Press, 1961.

Irvine, Lucy. *Castaway*. New York: Random House, 1983.

Kelly, Janis. "Sister Love: An Exploration of the Need for Homosexual Experience." *The Family Coordinator* 21 (1972):473–475.

Kohlberg, Lawrence. "A Cognitive Developmental Analysis of Childrens' Sex-Role Concepts and Attitudes." In *The Development of Sex Differences*, edited by Eleanor E. Maccoby. Stanford, Calif.: Stanford University Press, 1966.

Lasch, Christopher. *Haven in a Heartless World: The Family Besieged*. New York: Basic Books, 1977.

Maccoby, Eleanor E., and Jacklin, C. N. *The Psychology of Sex Differences*. Stanford, Calif.: Stanford University Press, 1974.

Mitchell, Juliet. *Women's Estate*. New York: Pantheon Books, 1971.

Parlee, Mary Brown. "Conversational Politics." *Psychology Today*, May 1979, pp. 48–49.

Perry, David G., and Bussey, Kay. "The Social Learning Theory of Sex Differences: Imitation is Live and Well." *Journal of Personality and Social Psychology* 37 (1979): 1699–1712.

Pfeiffer, John. "Girl Talk—Boy Talk." *Science 85*, January/February 1985, pp. 58–63.

Pogrebin, Letty Cottin. *Growing Up Free: Raising Your Child in the 80's*. New York: McGraw-Hill, 1980.

Richmond-Abbott, M. *Masculine and Feminine: Sex Roles Over the Life Cycle*. Reading, Mass.: Addison-Wesley, 1983.

Ryan, Mary P. *Womanhood in America*. New York: Franklin Watts, 1983.

Skinner, B. F. *The Behavior of Organisms: An Experimental Analysis*. New York: Appleton-Century-Crofts, 1938.

Stockard, Jean, and Johnson, Miriam M. *Sex Roles: Sex Inequality and Sex Role Development*. Englewood Cliffs, N.J.: Prentice-Hall, 1980.

Thorne, Barrie. "Feminist Rethinking of the Family: An Overview." In *Rethinking the Family: Some Feminist Questions*, edited by Barrie Thorne and Marilyn Yalom. New York: Longman, 1982.

Thorne, Barrie, and Yalom, Marilyn (eds.). *Rethinking the Family: Some Feminist Questions*. New York: Longman, 1982.

Thornton, Arland, and Freedman, Deborah. "Changes in the Sex- Role Attitudes of Women, 1962–1977: Evidence From a Panel Study." *American Sociological Review* 44 (1979):832–842.

Thornton, Arland, Alwin, Duane F., and Camburn, Donald. "Causes and Consequences of Sex-Role Attitudes and Attitude Changes." *American Sociological Review* 48 (1983):211–227.

Weitzman, Lenore. *Sex Role Socialization: A Focus on Women*. Palo Alto, Calif. Mayfield, 1979.

West, Candace. "Actions Speak Louder Than Words: Communicating Control in Cross-Sex Conversations." Paper presented at the annual meeting of the Southern Sociological Society, New Orleans, 1978.

Zimmerman, Don, and West, Candace. "Sex Roles, Interruptions, and Silences in Conversation." In *Language and Sex: Difference and Dominance*, edited by Barrie Thorne and Nancy M. Henley. Rowley, Mass.: Newbury House, 1975.

Chapter 3

Becker, G. *A Treatise on the Family*. Cambridge, Mass.: Harvard University Press, 1981.

Branden, N. *The Psychology of Romantic Love*. New York: Bantam, 1981.

Buscaglia, Leo. *Love*. New York: Fawcett Crest, 1972.

Campbell, E. Q. *Socialization: Culture and Personality*. Dubuque, Iowa: William C. Brown, 1975.

Capellanus, Andreas. *The Art of Courtly Love*. Translated by John Jay Parry. New York: W. W. Norton, 1969.

Chagnon, N. *Yanomamo: The Fierce People*. New York: Holt, Rinehart & Winston, 1968.

Firestone, S. *The Dialectic of Sex: The Case for the Feminist Revolution*. New York: William Morrow, 1970.

Flaceliere, R. *Love in Ancient Greece*. Translated by James Cleugh. New York: Crown, 1962.

Fromm, E. *The Art of Loving*. New York: Harper and Brothers, 1955.

Fullerton, G. P. *Survival in Marriage*. Hinsdale, Ill.: The Dryden Press, 1977.

Goode, W. J. "The Theoretical Importance of Love." *American Sociological Review* 24 (1959):38–47.

Harris, M. *Cows, Pigs, Wars and Witches: The Riddles of Culture*. New York: Vintage Books, 1974.

Hunt, Morton. *The Natural History of Love*. New York: Alfred A. Knopf, 1959.

Linton, R. *The Study of Man*. New York: Appleton-Century-Crofts, 1936.

Lumsden, C. J., and Wilson, E. O. *Promethean Fire*. Cambridge, Mass.: Harvard University Press, 1983.

McMillan, Priscilla Johnson. "An Assassin's Portrait." *New Republic*, 187, July 12, pp. 16–18.

Mellen, S. L. *The Evolution of Love*. San Francisco: W. H. Freeman, 1981.

Moore, Molly. "The Dark Side of a Teen Romance." *The Washington Post*, January 7, 1983, pp. A1, A10.

Newsweek. "Answers from Hinckley." Oct. 12, 1981, pp. 50–51.

Peele, Stanton, and Brodsky, Archie. *Love and Addiction*. New York: New American Library, 1976.

Pfeiffer, John. "Teacher's Pet." *Science 83*, June 1983, pp. 100–101.

Pope, Kenneth, and associates. *On Love and Loving*. San Francisco: Jossey-Bass, 1980.

Rosenberg, M. *Conceiving the Self*. New York: Basic Books, 1979.

Russell, Bertrand. *Marriage and Morals*. New York: Garden City Publishers, 1929.

Samuel, D. T. *Love, Liberation and Marriage*. New York: Funk & Wagnalls, 1976.

Shaffer, Ron and Henry, Neil. "Hinckley Pursued Actress for Months, Letter Shows." *The Washington Post*, April 2, 1981, p. A1.

Solomon, R. C. *Love: Emotion, Myth and Metaphor*. Garden City, N.Y.: Anchor/Doubleday, 1981.

Sullivan, H. S. *Conceptions of Modern Psychiatry*. New York: W. W. Norton, 1953.

Swidler, A. "Love and Adulthood in American Culture." In *Themes of Work and Love in Adulthood*, edited by N. J. Smelser and E. H. Erikson. Cambridge, Mass.: Harvard University Press, 1980.

Tannahill, R. *Sex in History*. New York: Stein & Day, 1980.

Tennov, Dorothy. *Love and Limerence*. New York: Stein & Day, 1979.

Waller, W. *The Family: A Dynamic Interpretation*. New York: Cordon Press, 1938.

West, U. *If Love Is the Answer, What Is the Problem?* New York: McGraw-Hill, 1977.

Wilson, E. O. *Sociobiology, the New Synthesis*. Cambridge, Mass.: Harvard University Press, 1975.

Younger, J. T. "Divorce and Feminism: Love Is Not Enough." In *Confronting the Issues: Marriage, the Family and Sex Roles*, edited by Kenneth C. W. Kammeyer, pp. 80–82. Boston: Allyn and Bacon, 1981.

Chapter 4

Barth, F. H. "Marriage Traditions and Customs among Transylvanian Saxons." *East Europe Quarterly* 12 (1978):93–111.

Berscheid, E., Dion, K., Walster, E., and Walster, G. "Physical Attractiveness and Dating Choice: A Test of the Matching Hypothesis." *Journal of Experimental Social Psychology* 7 (1971): 173–189.

Brislin, R. W., and Lewis, S. A. "Dating and Physical Attractiveness: A Replication." *Psychological Reports* 22 (1968):976.

Cook, Mark, and McHenry, Robert. *Sexual Attraction*. New York: Pergamon Press, 1978.

Dion, Karen. "Physical Attractiveness, Sex Roles and Heterosexual Attraction." In *The Bases of Human Sexual Attraction*, edited by Mark Cook, pp. 3–22. New York: Academic Press, 1981.

Dion, K., and Berscheid, E., and Walster, E. "What Is Beautiful Is Good." *Journal of Personality and Social Psychology* 24 (1972):285–290.

Foxman, Sherri. *Classified Love*. New York: McGraw-Hill, 1982.

Goffman, Erving. "On Cooling Out the Mark: Some Aspects of Adaptation to Failure." *Psychiatry* 15 (1952):451–463.

Goldman, W., and Lewis, P. "Beautiful Is Good: Evidence That the Physically Attractive Are More Socially Skilled." *Journal of Experimental Social Psychology* 13 (1977):125–130.

Hall, J. A. "Gender Effects in Decoding Nonverbal Clues." *Psychological Bulletin* 85 (1978):845–857.

Hansen, S. "Dating Choices of High School Students." *Family Coordinator* 26 (1977):133–138.

Hochschild, Arlie R. "Attending to, Codifying and Managing Feelings: Sex Differences in Love." In *Feminist Frontiers: Rethinking Sex, Gender, and Society*, edited by Laurel Richardson and Verta Taylor, pp. 250–262. Reading, Mass.: Addison-Wesley, 1983.

Hoffman, M. L. "Sex Differences in Empathy and Related Behaviors." *Psychological Bulletin* 84 (1977):712–722.

Hudson, J., and Henze, L. "Campus Values in Mate Selection: A Replication." *Journal of Marriage and the Family* 31 (1969):772–779.

Jedlicka, D. "Automated Go-betweens: Mate Selection of Tomorrow?" *Family Relations* 30 (1981):373–376.

Jones, R. L. "Courtship in an Eastern Nepal Community." *Anthropos* 72 (1977):288–299.

Kephart, W. M. *The Family, Society, and the Individual.* 4th ed. Boston: Houghton Mifflin, 1977.

Kleck, R. E., and Rubenstein, C. "Physical Attractiveness, Perceived Attitude Similarity, and Interpersonal Attraction." *Journal of Personality and Social Psychology* 31 (1975):107–114.

Knox, D., and Wilson, K. "Dating Behaviors of University Students." *Family Coordinator* 30 (1981):255–258.

Krucoff, C. "Singles: Love Among the Classifieds." *The Washington Post*, November 4, 1982, p. C5.

Lerner, R. M., and Schroeder, C. "Physique Identification, Preference and Aversion in Kindergarten Children." *Developmental Psychology* 5 (1971a):538.

Lerner, R. M., and Schroeder, C. "Kindergarten Children's Active Vocabulary about Body Build." *Developmental Psychology* 5 (1971b):179.

Merton, R. K. *Social Theory and Social Structure.* New York: The Free Press, 1957.

Miller, A. "Role of Physical Attractiveness in Impression Formation." *Psychonomic Science* 19 (1970):241–243.

Murstein, B. "Physical Attractiveness and Marital Choice." *Journal of Personality and Social Psychology* 22 (1972):8–12.

Rosenblatt, P. C., and Anderson, R. M. "Human Sexuality in Cross-Cultural Perspective." In *The Bases of Human Sexual Attraction,* edited by Mark Cook, pp. 3–22. New York: Academic Press, 1981.

Rubin, Z. "Measurement of Romantic Love." *Journal of Personality and Social Psychology* 16 (1970):265–273.

Rubin, Z., Peplau, L. A., and Hill, C. T. "Loving and Leaving: Sex Differences in Romantic Attachments." *Sex Roles* 7 (1981):821–835.

Saxe, L. "The Ubiquity of Physical Appearance as a Determinant of Social Relationships." In *Love and Attraction,* edited by M. Cook and G. Wilson, pp. 9–13. New York: Pergamon Press, 1979.

Saxton, L. *The Individual, Marriage and the Family.* Belmont, Calif.: Wadsworth, 1977.

Schwartz, P., and Lever, J. "Fear and Loathing at a College Mixer." *Urban Life* 4 (1976):413–431.

Silverman, I. "Physical Attractiveness and Courtship." *Sexual Behavior* 1 (1971):22–25.

U.S. News and World Report. "America's Obsession with Beautiful People." Jan. 11, 1982, pp. 60–61.

Walster, E., Aronson, V., Abrahams, D., and Rottman, L. "Importance of Physical Attractiveness in Dating Behavior." *Journal of Personality and Social Psychology* 4 (1966):508–516.

Chapter 5

Calhoun, A. W. *A Social History of the American Family.* 3 vols. New York: Barnes & Noble Books, 1945.

Chilman, Catherine (ed.). *Adolescent Pregnancy and Childbearing, Findings from Research.* Washington, D.C.: U.S. Government Printing Office, 1980.

DeLamater, John, and MacCorquodale, Patricia. *Premarital Sexuality.* Madison, Wis.: University of Wisconsin Press, 1979.

Furstenberg, Frank F. "The Social Consequences of Teenage Parenthood." In *Teenage Sexuality, Pregnancy and Childbearing,* edited by Frank F. Furstenberg, Richard Lincoln, and Jane Menken. Philadelphia: University of Pennsylvania Press, 1981.

Furstenberg, Frank F., Lincoln, Richard, and Menken, Jane. *Teenage Sexuality, Pregnancy and Childbearing.* Philadelphia: University of Pennsylvania Press, 1981.

Gagnon, John H. *Human Sexualities.* Glenview, Ill.: Scott, Foresman, 1977.

Gagnon, John H., and Simon, William. *Sexual Conduct.* Chicago: Aldine, 1973.

Istvan, Joseph, and Griffitt, William. "Effects of Sexual Experience on Dating Desireability and Marriage Desireability: An Experimental Study." *Journal of Marriage and the Family* 42 (1980):377–385.

Kennedy, Robert E. Jr. *The Irish: Emigration, Marriage, and Fertility.* Berkeley: University of California Press, 1973.

Kinsey, Alfred C., Pomeroy, Wardell B., and Martin, Clyde E. *Sexual Behavior in the Human Male.* Philadelphia: W. B. Saunders, 1948.

Kinsey, Alfred C., Pomeroy, Wardell B., Martin, Clyde E., and Gebhard, Paul H. *Sexual Behavior in the Human Female.* Philadelphia: W. B. Saunders, 1953.

Knox, David, and Wilson, Kenneth. "Dating Behaviors of University Students." *Family Relations* 30 (1981):255–258.

MacCorquodale, Patricia, and DeLamater, John. "Self-Image and Premarital Sexuality." *Jour-*

nal of Marriage and the Family 41 (1979):327–339.

Messenger, John C. *Inis Beag: Isle of Ireland*. New York: Holt, Rinehart & Winston, 1969.

Messenger, John C. "Sex and Repression in an Irish Folk Community." In *Human Sexual Behavior: Variations in the Ethnographic Spectrum*, edited by Donald S. Marshall and Robert C. Suggs. New York: Basic Books, 1971.

Nass, Gilbert D., Libby, Roger W., and Fisher, Mary Pat. *Sexual Choices: An Introduction to Human Sexuality*. Belmont, Calif.: Wadsworth, 1981.

Peillon, Michael. *Contemporary Irish Society: An Introduction*. Dublin, Ireland: Gill and Macmillan, 1982.

Peplau, Letitia, Rubin, Zick, and Hill, Charles T. "Sexual Intimacy in Dating Relationships." *Journal of Social Issues* 33 (1977):86–109.

Presser, Harriett. "The Social and Demographic Consequences of Teenage Childbearing for Urban Women." Final report to Center for Population Research. Bethesda, Maryland: National Institute of Child Health and Human Development (NTIS #PB80–149859), 1980.

Reiss, Ira L. *The Social Context of Premarital Sexual Permissiveness*. New York: Holt, Rinehart & Winston, 1967.

Reiss, Ira L. *Family Systems in America*. New York: Holt, Rinehart & Winston, 1980.

Reiss, Ira L. "Some Observations on Ideology and Sexuality in America." *Journal of Marriage and the Family* 43 (1981):271–283.

Rothman, Ellen K. *Hands and Hearts: A History of Courtship in America*. New York: Basic Books, 1984.

Rothman, Ellen K. "Sex and Self-Control: Middle Class Courtship in America 1770–1870" In *The American Family in Social Historical Perspectives*, 3rd ed., edited by Michael Gordon. New York: St. Martin's Press, 1983.

Rubin, Zick, Peplau, Letitia Anne, and Hill, Charles T. "Loving and Leaving: Sex Differences in Romantic Attachments." *Sex Roles* 7 (1981):832–835.

Smith, Daniel S. "The Dating of the American Sexual Revolution." In *The American Family in Social Historical Perspective*, 2nd ed., edited by Michael Gordon. New York: St. Martins Press, 1978.

Tomasson, Richard. *Iceland: The First New Society*. Minneapolis: University of Minnesota Press, 1980.

Zelnik, Melvin, and Kantner, John F. "Sexual Activity, Contraceptive Use and Pregnancy Among Metropolitan Teenagers: 1971–1979." *Family Planning Perspectives* 12 (1980):230–237.

Zelnik, Melvin, and Shah, Farida K. "First Intercourse Among Young Americans." *Family Planning Perspectives* 15 (1983):64–70.

Chapter 6

Arafat, Ibtiha, and Yorburg, Betty. "On Living Together without Marriage." *The Journal of Sex Research* 9 (1973):97–106.

Cargan, Leonard, and Melko, Matthew. *Singles: Myths and Realities*. Beverly Hills, Calif.: Sage Publications, 1982.

Cherlin, Andrew. "Cohabitation: How the French and Swedes Do It." *Psychology Today*, October 1979, pp. 18–20.

"Cohabiting in Europe." *Society*, May/June 1981, pp. 3–4.

Davis, Alan G., and Strong, Philip M. "Working without a Net: The Bachelor and Social Problems." *The Sociological Review* 25 (1977):109–129.

Festy, Patrick. "Aspects Demographiques de la Formation de la Famille en Europe Occidentale." In *Marriage and Cohabitation in Contemporary Societies*, edited by John M. Eekelaar and Sanford N. Katz, pp. 2–15. Toronto, Canada: Butterworth, 1980.

Glick, Paul C., and Norton, Arthur. "Marrying, Divorcing and Living Together in the U.S. Today." *Population Bulletin*, February 1979 (update), p. 1–41.

Glick, Paul C., and Spanier, Graham B. "Married and Unmarried Cohabitation in the United States." *Journal of Marriage and the Family* 42 (1980):19–30.

Jackson, Patrick G. "On Living Together Unmarried: Awareness Contexts and Social Interaction." *Journal of Family Issues* 4 (1983):35–59.

Jacques, Jeffrey M., and Chason, Karen T. "Cohabitation: Its Impact on Marital Success." *The Family Coordinator* 28 (1979):35–39.

Leonard, Charles (pseudonym). "A Letter from a Father to his Daughter." In *Confronting the Issues: Marriage, the Family and Sex Roles*, edited by Kenneth C. W. Kammeyer, pp. 124–126. Boston: Allyn and Bacon, 1981.

Lewin, Bo. "Unmarried Cohabitation: A Marriage Form in a Changing Society." *Journal of Marriage and the Family* 44 (1982):763–773.

Lyness, Judith L., Lipetz, Milton E., and Davis, Keith E. "Living Together: An Alternative to Marriage." *Journal of Marriage and the Family* 34 (1972):305–311.

Macklin, Eleanor. "Heterosexual Cohabitation among Unmarried Students." *The Family Coordinator* 21 (1972):463–472.

Macklin, Eleanor. "Cohabitation in College: Going Very Steady." *Psychology Today,* November 1974, pp. 53–59.

Macklin, Eleanor. "Nonmarital Heterosexual Cohabitation." *Marriage and Family Review,* March/April 1978, pp. 1–12.

Merit Report, Audits and Surveys. *National Sample Survey.* Storrs, Conn.: The Roper Center, 1982.

Newcomb, Michael, and Bentler, Peter. "Marital Stability and Satisfaction Among Cohabitors." *Journal of Personality Assessment* 44 (1980):147–154.

Peterman, Dan J., Ridley, Carl A. and Anderson, Scott M. "A Comparison of Cohabiting and Noncohabiting College Students." *Journal of Marriage and the Family* 36 (1974):344–354.

Risman, Barbara J., Hill, Charles T., Rubin, Zick, and Peplau, Letitia Ann. "Living Together in College: Implications for Courtship." *Journal of Marriage and the Family* 43 (1981):77–83.

Sanoff, Alvin P., "19 Million Singles: Their Joys and Frustrations." *U.S. News and World Reports,* February 21, 1983, pp. 53–56.

Simenauer, Jacqueline, and Carroll, David. *Singles: The New Americans.* New York: New American Library, 1982.

Spanier, Graham B. "Married and Unmarried Cohabitation in the United States: 1980." *Journal of Marriage and the Family* 45 (1983):277–288.

Stafford, Rebecca, Backman, Elaine, and Dibona, Pamela. "The Division of Labor Among Cohabiting and Married Couples." *Journal of Marriage and the Family* 39 (1977):43–57.

Thornton, Arland, and Freedman, Deborah. "Changing Attitudes Toward Marriage and Single Life." *Family Planning Perspectives* 14 (1982):297–303.

Time/Yankelovich, Skelly and White. *National Survey of Registered Voters.* Storrs, Conn.: The Roper Center, 1982.

Trost, Jan. "Cohabitation Without Marriage in Sweden." In *Marriage and Cohabitation in Contemporary Societies,* edited by John M. Eekelaar and Sanford N. Katz, pp. 16–22. Toronto, Canada: Butterworth, 1980.

U.S. Bureau of the Census. "Marital Status and Living Arrangements." *Current Population Reports,* Series P-20, No. 380. Washington D.C.; U.S. Government Printing Office, 1983.

U.S. Bureau of the Census. *The Statistical Abstract of the United States,* 1985. Washington, D.C.: U.S. Government Printing Office, 1984.

Watson, Roy E. L. "Premarital Cohabitation vs. Traditional Courtship: Their Effects on Subsequent Marital Adjustment." *Family Relations* 32 (1983):139–147.

Chapter 7

Arensberg, Conrad M., and Kimball, Solon T. *Family and Community in Ireland.* Cambridge, Mass.: Harvard University Press, 1940.

Blood, Robert O. *Love Match and Arranged Marriage.* New York: The Free Press, 1967.

Cherlin, Andrew J. *Marriage Divorce Remarriage.* Cambridge, Mass.: Harvard University Press, 1981.

Clair, Bernard E., and Daniele, Anthoney R. *Love Pact: A Layman's Complete Guide to Legal Living Together Agreements.* New York: Grove Press, 1980.

Demos, J. *A Little Commonwealth: Family Life in Plymouth Colony.* New York: Oxford University Press, 1970.

Farber, Bernard. *Family: Organization and Interaction.* San Francisco: Chandler Publishing, 1964.

Furstenberg, Frank. "Industrialization and the American Family: A Look Backward." *American Sociological Review* 31 (1966):326–337.

Gordon, Michael, and Miller, Fandi L. "Going Steady in the 1980s: Exclusive Relationships in Six Connecticut High Schools." Paper presented at the Eastern Sociological Society Meetings, Boston, 1984.

Gottlieb, Beatrice. "The Meaning of Clandestine Marriage." in *Family and Sexuality in French History,* edited by Robert Wheaton and Tamara K. Haveren. Philadelphia: University of Pennsylvania Press, 1980.

Hopkins, Keith. "Brother-Sister Marriage in Roman Egypt." *Journal for Comparative Study of Society and History* 22 (1980):303–354.

Kammeyer, Kenneth C. W. "The Dynamics of Population." *Irish History and Culture: Aspects of a People's Heritage,* edited by Harold Orel, pp. 189–223. Lawrence, Kans.: The University of Kansas Press, 1976.

Levi-Strauss, Claude. "Family." In *Men, Culture, and Society,* edited by Harry L. Shapiro. New York: Oxford University Press, 1956.

Lindholm, Charles, and Lindholm, Cherry. "Marriage as Warfare." *Natural History,* October 1979, pp. 11–20.

McCall, Michael. "Courtship as Social Exchange: Some Historical Comparisons." In *Kinship* and Family Organization, edited by Bernard Farber. New York: John Wiley & Sons, 1966.

Monsarrat, Ann. And the Bride Wore . . . The Story of the White Wedding. New York: Dodd, Mead, 1974.

Outhwaite, R. B. "Introduction: Problems and Perspectives in the History of Marriage." In Marriage and Society: Studies in the Social History of Marriage, edited by R. B. Outhwaite, pp. 1–16. New York: St. Martin's Press, 1981.

Peterman, Dan J., Ridley, Carl A., and Anderson, Scott M. "A Comparison of Cohabiting and Noncohabiting College Students." Journal of Marriage and the Family 36 (1974):344–358.

Petersen, William. Population. 3rd ed. New York: Macmillan, 1975.

Schwartz, Gary, and Merten, Don. Love and Commitment. Beverly Hills, Calif.: Sage Publications, 1980.

Scott, John Finley. The American College Sorority: Its Role in Class and Ethnic Endogamy." American Sociological Review, 30 (1965):514–527.

Thornton, Arland, and Freedman, Deborah. "The Changing American Family." Population Bulletin, October 1983, pp. 3–44.

U.S. Bureau of the Census. Statistical Abstract of the United States, 1985. Wash. D.C.: U.S. Gov't. Printing Office, 1984.

U.S. Bureau of the Census. "Child Support and Alimony, 1981." Current Population Reports, Special Studies, Series P-23, No. 140. Washington, D.C.: U.S. Government Printing Office, 1984.

Wadler, Joyce. "Moon's Marriage of the Masses." The Washington Post, July 2, 1982 D1, D3.

Waller, Willard. The Family: a Dynamic Interpretation. New York: Cordon Press, 1938.

Weitzman, Lenore J. The Marriage Contract: Spouses, Lovers, and the Law. New York: The Free Press, 1981.

Weitzman, Lenore J., Dixon, Carol M., Bair, Joyce Adair, McGinn, Neil, and Robertson, Dena M. "Contracts for Intimate Relationships." Alternative Lifestyles, Vol. 1, August 1978, pp. 303–378.

Wells, J. Gipson. "A Critical Look at Personal Marriage Contracts." The Family Coordinator 25 (1976):33–37.

Chapter 8

Alexander, John W. "Headship in Marriage: Flip of a Coin?" Christianity Today, February 20, 1981, pp. 24–26.

Allen, Craig M. "On the Validity of Relative Validity Studies of 'Final-Say' Measures of Marital Power." Journal of Marriage and the Family 46 (1984):619–629.

Anderson, Stephen A., Russell, Candyce S., and Schumm, Walter R. "Perceived Marital Quality and Family Life Cycle Categories: A Further Analysis." Journal of Marriage and the Family 45 (1983):127–139.

Bahr, Stephen J., Chappell, C. Bradford, and Leigh, Geoffrey K. "Age at Marriage, Role Enactment, Role Consensus, and Marital Satisfaction." Journal of Marriage and Family Living 45 (1983):795–803.

Bem, Sandra and Bem, Daryl. Androgyny, Equality, and Beyond. New York: BMA Audio Cassettes, 1979.

Bierstedt, Robert. "An Analysis of Power." The American Sociological Review 15 (1950):730–738.

Blood, Robert O., and Wolfe, Donald M. Husbands and Wives: The Dynamics of Married Living. New York: The Free Press, 1960.

Bott, Elizabeth. Family and Social Network. London: Tavistock, 1957.

Brandt, John L. Marriage and the Home. Chicago: Laird and Lee, 1892.

Broderick, Carlfred. "How to Rewrite Your Marriage Script So It Works." Redbook, February 1979, p. 21, 154.

Broderick, Carlfred B. Marriage and the Family. 2nd ed. Englewood Cliffs, N.J.: Prentice-Hall, 1984.

Burgess, Ernest W., and Wallin, Paul. Engagement and Marriage. Philadelphia: J. B. Lippincott, 1953.

Burr, Wesley R. "Satisfaction with Various Aspects of Marriage over the Life Cycle." Journal of Marriage and the Family 32 (1970):29–37.

Burr, Wesley R. Theory Construction and the Sociology of the Family. New York: John Wiley & Sons, 1973.

Cadwallader, Mervyn. "Marriage as a Wretched Institution." The Atlantic, November 1966, pp. 62–66.

Chodorow, Nancy. The Reproduction of Mothering: Psychoanalysis and the Sociology of Gender. Berkeley, Calif.: University of California Press, 1978.

Cozby, P. C. "Self-Disclosure: A Literature Review." Psychological Bulletin 79 (1973):73–91.

Cuber, John F., and Harroff, Peggy B. Sex and the Significant Americans: A Study of Sexual Behavior among the Affluent. Baltimore: Penguin Books, 1968.

Davidson, Bernard, Balswick, Jack, and Halverson, Charles. "Affective Self-Disclosure and Marital Adjustment: A Test of Equity Theory." Journal of Marriage and the Family 45 (1983):93–102.

Filsinger, Erik E., and Wilson, Margaret R. "Religiosity, Socioeconomic Rewards, and Family Development: Predictors of Marital Adjustment." *Journal of Marriage and the Family* 46 (1984):663–670.

Gelles, Richard J. "Violence in the Family: A Review of Research in the Seventies." *Journal of Marriage and the Family* 42 (1980):873–885.

Glenn, Norval D., and Weaver, C. N. "The Marital Happiness of Remarried Divorced Persons." *Journal of Marriage and the Family* 39 (1977):331–337.

Glenn, Norval D., & Weaver, C. N. "A Multivariate, Multisurvey Study of Marital Happiness." *Journal of Marriage and the Family* 40 (1978):269–282.

Gordon, Michael. *The American Family: Past, Present and Future.* New York: Random House, 1978.

Hawkins, James L., Weisberg, Carol, and Ray, Dixie W. "Spouse Differences in Communication Style." *Journal of Marriage and the Family* 42 (1980):585–593.

Hendrick, Susan Singer. "Self-Disclosure and Marital Satisfaction." *Journal of Personality and Social Psychology* 40 (1981):1150–1159.

Hill, Reuben. "Decision Making and the Family Life Cycle." In *Social Structure and the Family* edited by E. Shanas and G. F. Streib, pp. 113–139. Englewood Cliffs, N.J.: Prentice-Hall, 1965.

Houseknecht, Sharon K. "Childlessness and Marital Adjustment." *Journal of Marriage and the Family* 41 (1979):259–265.

Jourard, Sidney M. *The Transparent Self.* 2nd ed. New York: Van Nostrand, 1971.

Kenkel, William F. "Influence Differentiation in Family Decision Making." *Sociology and Social Research* 42 (1957):18–25.

Kerckhoff, Alan C. "The Structure of the Conjugal Relationship in Industrial Society." In *Cross-National Family Research,* edited by Marvin B. Sussman and Betty E. Cogswell. Leiden, The Netherlands: E. J. Brill, 1972.

Komarovsky, Mirra. *Blue-Collar Marriage.* New York: Vintage Books, 1962.

Lee, Gary R. "The Effects of Social Networks on the Family." In *Contemporary Theories About the Family,* edited by W. R. Burr, R. Hill, F. I. Nye, and I. L. Reiss. pp. 27–56, New York: The Free Press, 1979.

LeMasters, E. E. "Holy Deadlock: A Study of Unsuccessful Marriages." *The Midwest Sociologist* 21 (1959):86–91.

Lewis, R. A., and Spanier, G. B. "Theorizing about the Quality and Stability of Marriage." In *Contemporary Theories About the Family* edited by W. R. Burr, R. Hill, F. I. Nye and

I. L. Reiss, pp. 268–294. New York: The Free Press, 1979.

Lindholm, Charles, and Lindholm, Cherry. "Marriage as Warfare." *Natural History,* October 1979, pp. 11–20.

Montgomery, Barbara. "The Form and Function of Quality Communication in Marriage." *Family Relations* 30 (1981):21–30.

Norton, Robert. "Measuring Marital Quality: A Critical Look at the Dependent Variable." *Journal of Marriage and the Family* 45 (1983):141–151.

Olson, David H., and Cromwell, Ronald E. "Power in Families." In *Power in Families,* edited by Ronald E. Cromwell and David H. Olson, pp. 3–11. New York: John Wiley & Sons, 1975a.

Olson, David H., and Cromwell, Ronald E. "Methodological Issues in Family Power." In *Power in Families,* edited by Ronald E. Cromwell and David H. Olson, pp. 131–150. New York: John Wiley & Sons, 1975b.

Orden, Susan R., and Bradburn, Norman M. "Dimensions of Marriage Happiness." *American Journal of Sociology* 73 (1968):715–731.

Orthner, Dennis K. "Leisure Activity Patterns and Marital Satisfaction over the Marital Career." *Journal of Marriage and the Family* 37 (1975):91–102.

Pineo, Peter C. "Disenchantment in the Later Years of Marriage." *Marriage and Family Living* 23 (1961):3–11.

Pogrebin, Letty Cottin. *Family Politics: Love and Power on the Imtimate Frontier.* New York: McGraw-Hill, 1983.

Rainwater, Lee. *Family Design: Marital Sexuality, Family Size and Contraception.* Chicago: Aldine, 1965.

Rodman, Hyman. "Marital Power and the Theory of Resources in Cultural Context." *Journal of Comparative Family Studies* 3 (1972):50–67.

Rollins, B. C., and Feldman, H. "Marital Satisfaction over the Family Life Cycle." *Journal of Marriage and the Family* 32 (1970):20–27.

Rollins, B. C., and Galligan, R. "The Developing Child and Marital Satisfaction of Parents." In *Child Influences on Marital and Family Interaction,* edited by R. M. Lerner and G. B. Spanier, pp. 71–105. New York: Academic Press, 1978.

Rossi, Alice. "Gender and Parenthood." *American Sociological Review* 49 (1984):1–19.

Rubin, Lillian B. *Intimate Strangers: Men and Women Together.* New York: Harper & Row, 1983.

Safilios-Rothschild, C. "A Comparison of Power Structure and Marital Satisfaction in Urban Greek and French Families." *Journal of Marriage and the Family* 29 (1967):345–352.

Safilios-Rothschild, C. "Study of Family Power Structure: 1960–1969." *Journal of Marriage and the Family* 32 (1970):539–552.

Satir, Virginia. *Peoplemaking.* Palo Alto, Calif.: Science and Behavior Books, 1972.

Scanzoni, John. "Social Processes and Power in Families." In *Contemporary Theories About the Family* edited by W. R. Burr, R. Hill, F. I. Nye, and I. L. Reiss, Vol. 1, pp. 295–316. New York: The Free Press, 1979.

Scanzoni, John. "Contemporary Marriage Types: A Research Note." *Journal of Family Issues* 1 (1980):125–140.

Schlafly, Phyllis. *The Power of Positive Woman.* New Rochelle, N.Y.: Arlington House, 1977.

Spanier, Graham. "Measuring Dyadic Adjustment: New Scales for Assessing the Quality of Marriage and Similar Dyads." *Journal of Marriage and the Family* 38 (1976):15–28.

Spanier, Graham B., and Lewis, Robert A. "Marital Quality: A Review of the Seventies." *Journal of Marriage and the Family* 42 (1980): 825–839.

Spanier, G. B., Lewis, R. A., and Cole, C. L. "Marital Adjustment over the Family Life Cycle: The Issue of Curvilinearity." Journal of Marriage and the Family 37 (1975):253–275.

Spanier, G. B., Sauer, W., and Larzelere, R. "An Empirical Evaluation of the Life Cycle." *Journal of Marriage and the Family* 41 (1979):27–38.

Straus, Murray, and Steinmetz, Suzanne. *Behind Closed Doors: Violence in the American Family.* New York: Anchor/Doubleday, 1980.

Terman, Lewis M. *Journal of Social Psychology* 6 (1935):143–171.

Turk, J. L., and Bell, N. W. "Measuring Power in Families." *Journal of Marriage and the Family* 34 (1972):215–222.

Udry, J. Richard. *The Social Context of Marriage.* 3rd ed. Philadelphia: J. B. Lippincott, 1974.

Watzlawick, P., Beavin, J., and Jackson, D. *Pragmatics of Human Communication: A Study of Interactional Patterns, Pathologies, and Paradoxes.* New York: W. W. Norton, 1967.

Wikan, Unni. *Behind the Veil in Arabia: Women in Oman.* Baltimore: The Johns Hopkins University Press, 1982.

Winter, D. G. *The Power Motive.* New York: The Free Press, 1973.

Chapter 9

Atwater, Lynn. "Getting Involved: Women's Transition to First Extramarital Sex." *Alternative LifeStyles,* February 1979, pp. 33–68.

Atwater, Lynn. *The Extramarital Connection: Sex, Intimacy and Identity.* New York: Irvington, Publishers, 1982.

Barker-Benfield, G. J. *The Horrors of the Half-Known Life: Male Attitudes Toward Women and Sexuality in Nineteenth-Century America.* New York: Harper & Row, 1976.

Beckwith, Carol. "Niger's Wodaabe: People of the Taboo." *National Georgraphic,* October 1983, pp. 482–509.

Benet, Sula. *Abkhasians: The Long Living People of the Caucasus.* New York: Holt, Rinehart & Winston, 1974.

Blumstein, Philip, and Schwartz, Pepper. *American Couples: Money, Work, Sex.* New York: William Morrow, 1983.

Brissett, Dennis, and Lewis, Lional S. "The Big Toe, Armpits, and Natural Perfume: Notes on the Production of Ecstacy." *Society,* January/February 1979, pp. 63–73.

Geddes, Patrick, and Thompson, Arthur J. *Sex.* New York: Henry Holt and Company, 1914.

Glenn, Norval D., and Weaver, Charles N. "Attitudes Toward Premarital, Extramarital, and Homosexual Relations in the 1970s." *The Journal of Sex Research* 15 (1979):108–118.

Gordon, Michael. "From an Unfortunate Necessity to a Cult of Mutual Orgasm: Sex in American Marital Education Literature, 1830–1940." In *The Sociology of Sex,* edited by James M. Henslin and Edward Sagarin, 2nd ed. New York: Schocken Books, 1978.

Gordon, Michael, and Shankweiler, Penelope. "Different Equals Less: Female Sexuality in Recent Marriage Manuals." *Journal of Marriage and the Family* 33 (1971): 459–466.

Hayes, A. *Sexual Physiology of Women.* Boston: Peabody Medical Press of New York, 1869.

Hunt, Morton. *Sexual Behavior in the 1970s.* Chicago: Playboy Press, 1974.

Kinsey, Alfred C., Pomeroy, Wardell B., and Martin, Clyde E. *Sexual Behavior in the Human Male.* Philadelphia: W. B. Saunders, 1948.

Kinsey, Alfred, Pomeroy, Wardell B., Martin, Clyde E. and Gebhard, Paul H. *Sexual Behavior in the Human Female.* Philadelphia: W. B. Saunders, 1953.

Lewis, Lionel S., and Brissett, Dennis. "Sex as Work: A Study of Avocational Counseling." *Social Problems* 15 (1967):8–18.

Luker, Kristin. "The War Between Women." *Family Planning Perspectives* 16 (1984):105–110.

Mathias, Barbara. "An Affair to Remember. . . . Or to Forget." *The Washington Post,* July 8, 1981, p. C-5.

Maykovich, Minako K. "Attitudes versus Behavior in Extramarital Relations." *Journal of Marriage and the Family* 38 (1976):693–699.

Mintz, Warren. "Open Marriage—A New Style for Couples." In *Confronting the Issues: Marriage, the Family and Sex Roles*, edited by Kenneth C. W. Kammeyer, pp. 326–333. Boston: Allyn and Bacon, 1981.

Morgan, Edmund S. "Colonial Sexuality." In *Procreation or Pleasure?: Sexual Attitudes in American History*, edited by Thomas L. Althers, pp. 5–16. Malabar, Fla.: R. E. Krieger Publishing, 1983.

Napheys, George. *The Physical Life of Woman*. Philadelphia: David McKay, 1869 (republished 1890).

Nass, Gilbert D., Libby, Roger W., and Fisher, Mary Pat. *Sexual Choices: An Introduction to Human Sexuality*. Monterey, Calif.: Wadsworth, 1981.

O'Neill, Nena. *The Marriage Premise*. New York: M. Evans, 1977.

O'Neill, Nena, and O'Neill, George. *Open Marriage*. New York: M. Evans, 1972.

Reiss, Ira L. *Family Systems in America*. 3rd ed. New York: Holt, Rinehart & Winston, 1980.

Richardson, Laurel. *The New Other Woman: Contemporary Single Women in Affairs with Married Men*. New York: The Free Press, 1985.

Robinson, William J. *Woman: Her sex and Love Life*. New York: Eugenics Publishing, 1917 (republished 1929).

Rubin, Lillian Breslow. *Worlds of Pain: Life in the Working Class Family*. New York: Basic Books, 1976.

Shorter, Edward. *A History of Women's Bodies*. New York: Basic Books, 1982.

Tavris, Carol, and Sadd, Susan. *The Redbook Report on Female Sexuality*. New York: Delacorte, 1977.

Trall, R. T. *Sexual Physiology and Hygiene*. New York: Fowler and Wells, 1866 (republished 1897).

Westoff, Charles F. "Coital Frequency and Contraception." *Family Planning Perspectives* 6 (1974):136–141.

Chapter 10

Bachrach, Christine A. "Contraceptive Practice among American Women, 1973–1982." *Family Planning Perspectives* 16, No. 6, Nov./Dec. (1984), pp. 253–259.

Belsky, Jay. "The Determinants of Parenting: A Process Model." *Child Development* 55 (1984):83–96.

Belsky, Jay, and Rovine, Michael. "Social-Network Contract, Family Support, and the Transition to Parenthood." *Journal of Marriage and the Family* 46 (1984):455–462.

Bongaarts, J. "Infertility after Age 30: A False Alarm." *Family Planning Perspectives* 14 (1982):75–78.

Breathnach, Sarah B. "Transitions: The Realities of Parenthood." *The Washington Post*, Feb. 6, 1984, p. C5.

Chico, Nan Paulsen, and Hartley, Shirley Foster. "Widening Choices of Motherhood of the Future." *Psychology of Women Quarterly*, Fall 1981, pp. 12–25.

Churchman, Deborah. "If You Ask Me: There's a Reason for Children." *The Washington Post*, October 16, 1979, p. C5.

Daniels, Pamela, and Weingarten, Kathy. *Sooner or Later: The Timing of Parenthood in Adult Lives*. New York: W. W. Norton, 1982.

Davitz, Lois Leiderman. "Baby Hunger." *McCall's*, November 1981, p. 10.

Doering, S. G., and Entwisle, D. "Preparation During Pregnancy and Ability to Cope with Labor and Delivery." *American Journal of Orthopsychiatry* 45 (1975):825–837.

Dohwrenwend, B., Krasnoff, L., Askenasy, A., and Dohwrenwend, B. "Exemplification of a Method for Scaling Life Events." *Journal of Health and Social Behavior* 19 (1978):205–229.

Ebin, V. "Interpretations of Infertility: The Aowin People of South-west Ghana." In *Ethnography of Fertility and Birth*, edited by Carol P. MacCormack. New York: Academic Press, 1982.

Entwisle, Doris B., and Doering, Susan G. *The First Birth: A Family Turning Point*. Baltimore: The Johns Hopkins University Press, 1981.

Etzioni, Amatai. *Genetic Fix*. New York: Macmillan, 1973.

Friday, Nancy. My Mother/My Self. New York: Dell, 1977.

Glass, Jennifer. "Pre-birth Attitudes and Adjustment to Parenthood: When 'Preparing for the Worst' Helps." *Family Relations* 32 (1983):377–386.

Guiness Book of World Records. Edited by David A. Boehm, New York: Sterling Publishing, 1985.

Hardin, Garrett. "Abortion—or Compulsory Pregnancy?" *Journal of Marriage and the Family* 30 (1968):246–251.

Hartley, Shirley Foster. "Attitudes Toward Reproductive Engineering: An Overview." *Journal of Family Issues* 2 (1981):5–24.

Hendershot, Gerry E., Mosher, William D., and Pratt, William F. "Infertility and Age: An Unresolved Issue." *Family Planning Perspectives* 14 (1982):287–289.

Hilts, Philip. "Human Gender Selection Nears Reality." *The Washington Post*, May 28, 1983, p. A7.

Himes, Norman E. *Medical History of Contraception.* New York: Schocken Books, 1970.

Hoffman, Lois Wladis, and Manis, Jean Denby. "The Value of Children in the United States: A New Approach to the Study of Fertility." *Journal of Marriage and the Family* 41 (1979):583–596.

Hoffman, Lois Wladis, Thornton, Arland, and Manis, Jean Denby. "The Value of Children to Parents in the United States." *Journal of Population* 1 (1978):91–131.

Homans, H. "Pregnancy and Birth as Rites of Passage for Two Groups of Women in Britain." In *Ethnography of Fertility and Birth,* edited by Carol P. MacCormack. New York: Academic Press, 1982.

Houseknecht, Sharon K. "Voluntary Childlessness in the 1980s: A Significant Increase?" *Marriage and Family Review* 5 (1982a):51–69.

Houseknecht, Sharon K. "Voluntary Childlessness: Toward a Theoretical Integration." *Journal of Family Issues* 3 (1982b):459–471.

Intercom. "Delivering the Male: Sperm Separation Method Expected to Produce Higher Ratio of Boys." *Intercom* September 1976, p. 1.

Intercom. "Raising a $200,000 + Child." *Intercom,* November/December 1982, pp. 6–7.

Jaffe, Frederick S., Lindheim, Barbara L. and Lee, Philip R. *Abortion Politics: Private Morality and Public Policy.* New York: McGraw-Hill, 1981.

Kach, Julie A., and McGhee, Paul E. "Adjustment of Early Parenthood: The Role of Accuracy of Preparenthood Experiences." *Journal of Family Issues* 3 (1982):375–388.

Kammeyer, Kenneth C. W., and Ginn, Helen L. *An Introduction to Population.* Chicago, Ill.: The Dorsey Press, 1986.

Kephart, William M. *Extraordinary Groups: The Sociology of Unconventional Life Styles.* New York: St. Martin's Press, 1976.

Kephart, William M. *The Family, Society and the Individual.* 4th ed. Boston: Houghton Mifflin, 1977.

Krucoff, Carol. "The Surrogate Baby Boom." *The Washington Post,* January 25, 1983, p. C5.

LaRossa, Ralph. "The Transition to Parenthood and the Social Reality of Time." *Journal of Marriage and the Family* 45 (1983):579–589.

Lightbourne, Robert, Jr., and Singh, Susheela. "The World Fertility Survey: Charting Global Childbearing." *Population Bulletin,* March 1982, pp. 1–54.

Lowenstein, Douglas, and Lowenstein, Rochelle. "The Baby and Us." *The Washington Post Magazine,* October 16, 1983, pp. 12–13.

Mamdani, Mahmood. *The Myths of Population Control.* New York: Monthly Review Press, 1972.

Masters, William H., and Johnson, Virginia E. *Human Sexual Response.* Boston: Little, Brown, 1966.

Mathews, Jay. " 'Nobel Sperm Bank' Spawns Babies—and Questions." *The Washington Post,* August 3, 1982, p. A5.

Mathews, Jay. "Surrogate Motherhood Becoming an American Growth Industry." *The Washington Post,* January 25, 1983, p. A2.

Maubouche, Sabine. "Life After Death: French Woman Wins Sperm Bank Decision." *The Washington Post,* Aug. 2, 1984, p. B1.

McFalls, Joseph A., Jr. "Frustrated Fertility: A Population Paradox." *Population Bulletin* May 1979, pp. 1–43.

Mohr, James C. *Abortion in America: The Origins and Evolution of National Policy, 1800–1900.* New York: Oxford University Press, 1978.

Mosher, William D., and Bachrach, Christine A. "Childlessness in the United States: Estimates from the National Survey of Family Growth." *Journal of Family Issues* 3 (1982):517–543.

Muncy, Raymond L. *Sex and Marriage in Utopian Communities: 19th Century America.* Bloomington, Ind.: Indiana University Press, 1973.

Nass, Gilbert D., Libby, Roger W., and Fisher, Mary Pat. *Sexual Choices: An Introduction to Sexuality.* Monterey, Calif.: Wadsworth, 1981.

Oakley, Ann. *Becoming a Mother.* New York: Schocken Books, 1980.

Olson, Lawrence. *Costs of Children.* Lexington, Mass.: Lexington Books, 1983.

Pebley, Anne R., and Westoff, Charles F. "Sex Preferences in the United States: 1970 to 1975." *Demography* 19 (1982):177–189.

Pratt, William F., Mosher, William D., Bachrach, Christine A., and Horn, Marjorie C. "Understanding U.S. Fertility." *Population Bulletin,* December 1984, pp. 1–42.

Rinehart, Ward, and Kols, Adrienne, with Moore, Sidney H. "Healthier Mothers and Children Through Family Planning." *Population Reports* (Series J) 12 (1984):J657–J696.

Rubin, Lillian Breslow. *Worlds of Pain: Life in the Working-Class Family.* New York: Basic Books, 1976.

Russell, Cristine. "French Study Finds Decline in Fertility in Women over 30." *The Washington Post,* February 18, 1982, p. A9.

Schwartz, D., and Mayaux, M. J. "Female Fecundity as a Function of Age." *New England Journal of Medicine* 307 (1982):404–406.

Sollie, D., and Miller, B. "The Transition to Parenthood as a Critical Time for Building Family Strengths." In *Family Strengths: Positive Models of Family Life,* edited by N. Stinnet and P. Knaub, pp. 149–169. Lincoln, Neb.: University of Nebraska Press, 1980.

Stockwell, Edward G., and Groat, H. Theodore *World Population: An Introduction to Demography.* New York: Franklin Watts, 1984.

Tierney, John. "Fanisi's Choice." *Science 86.* 7 (1986): 26–42.

Tinsley, B. Parke, R. "Grandparents as Support and Socialization Agents." In *Beyond the Dyad,* edited by M. Lewis and L. Rosenblum. New York: Plenum, 1983.

U.S. Bureau of the Census. *Statistical Abstract of the United States, 1985.* Wash. D.C.: U.S. Gov't. Printing Office, 1984.

Veevers, Jean E. "Voluntary Childlessness: A Review of Issues and Evidence." *Marriage and Family Review* 2 (1979):2–26.

Veevers, Jean E. *Childless by Choice.* Toronto: Butterworth, 1980.

Wilkie, Jane Riblett. "The Trend Toward Delayed Parenthood." *Journal of Marriage and the Family* 43 (1981):583–591.

Williamson, Nancy E. "Sex Preferences, Sex Control, and the Status of Women." *Signs: Journal of Women in Culture and Society* 1 (1976a):847–862.

Williamson, Nancy E. *Sons or Daughters: A Cross-Cultural Survey of Parental Preferences.* Beverly Hills, Calif.: Sage Publications, 1976b.

Williamson, Nancy E. "Boys or Girls? Parents' Preferences and Sex Control." *Population Bulletin,* Jan. 1978, pp. 1–3.

Young, M., and Willmott, P. *Family and Kinship in East London.* London: Penguin, 1964.

Chapter 11

Alba, R. D. "Social Assimilation Among American Catholic National-Origin Groups." *American Sociological Review* 41 (1976):1030–1046.

Alba, R D. "The Twilight of Ethnicity Among American Catholics of European Ancestry." *Annals of the American Academy of Political and Social Science* 454 (1981):86–97.

Alwin, Duane F. "Trends in Parental Socialization Values: Detroit, 1958–1983." *American Journal of Sociology* 90 (1984):359–382.

Ariès, Philippe. *Centuries of Childhood: A Social History of Family Life.* Translated by Robert Baldick. New York: Vintage Books, 1962.

Baruch, Grace K., and Barnett, Rosalind C. "Fathers' Participation in the Care of Their Preschool Children." *Sex Roles* 7 (1981): 1043–1055.

Belsky, Jay, Gilstrap, Bonnie, and Rovine, Michael. "The Pennsylvania Infant and Family Development Project, I: Stability and Change in Mother-Infant and Father-Infant Interaction in a Family Setting at One, Three, and Nine Months." *Child Development* 55 (1984):692–705.

Breathnach, Sarah Ban. "The World According to the Unborn . . . and After." *The Washington Post,* January 10, 1983, p. B5.

Cagan, Elizabeth. "The Positive Parent: Raising Children the Scientific Way." *Social Policy* 10 (1980):40–48.

Campbell, Ernest Q. *Socialization: Culture and Personality.* Dubuque, Iowa: William C. Brown, 1975.

Curtiss, Susan. *Genie: A Psycholinguistic Study of a Modern-day 'Wild Child'.* New York: Academic Press, 1977.

Davis, Kingsley. "Extreme Isolation of a Child." *American Journal of Sociology* 45 (1940):554–565.

Davis, Kingsley. "Final Note on a Case of Extreme Isolation." *American Journal of Sociology* 52 (1947):432–437.

deMause, Lloyd, ed. *The History of Childhood.* New York: The Psychohistory Press, 1974.

"Family Day Care Study." *Children Today,* March/April 1981, pp. 29–30.

Farson, Richard. *Birthrights.* New York: Macmillan, 1974.

Fein, Robert A. "Research on Fathering: Social Policy and an Emergent Perspective." In *Family in Transition,* edited by Arlene S. Skolnick and Jerome H. Skolnick, 4th ed. pp. 463–474. Boston: Little, Brown, 1983.

Fraiberg, Selma. *Every Child's Birthright: In Defense of Mothering.* New York: Basic Books, 1977.

Friedan, Betty. *The Second Stage.* New York: Summit Books, 1981.

Gouldner, Alvin W. "The Norm of Reciprocity." *American Sociological Review* 25 (1960):161–178.

Greeley, Andrew M. *The American Catholic.* New York: Basic Books, 1977.

Illick, Joseph E. "Child-Rearing in Seventeenth-Century England and America." In *The History of Childhood,* edited by Lloyd deMause, pp. 303–350. New York: The Psychohistory Press, 1974.

Kagan, Jerome, Kearsley, Richard B., and Zelazo, Philip R. "The Effects of Infant Day Care on Psychological Development." *Evaluation Quarterly* 1 (1977):109–142.

Kakar, Sudhir. "Childhood in India: Traditional Ideals and Contemporary Reality." *International Social Science Journal* 31 (1979):444–456.

Katsh, Beverly S. "Fathers and Infants: Reported Caregiving and Interaction." *Journal of Family Issues 2 (1981):275–296.*

Kohn, Melvin, L. *Class and Conformity: A Study of Values.* 2nd ed. Chicago: University of Chicago Press, 1977.

Kohn, Melvin L., and Schooler, Carmi. "Class, Occupation and Orientation." *American Sociological Review* 34 (1969):659–678.

Kohn, Melvin L., and Schooler, Carmi. "Occupational Experience and Psychological Functioning." *American Sociological Review* 38 (1973):97–118.

Lamb, Michael, ed. *The Role of the Father in Child Development.* 2nd ed. New York: John Wiley & Sons, 1981.

Langer, William L. "Infanticide: A Historical Survey." *History of Childhood Quarterly: The Journal of Psychohistory* 1 (1973):353–367.

LaRossa, Ralph, and Larossa, M. M. *Transition to Parenthood.* Beverly Hills, Calif.: Sage Publications, 1981.

Mitchell, Juliet. "Women: The Longest Revolution." *New Left Review,* November/December 1966, pp. 11–37.

Neill, A. S. Freedom—Not License! New York: Hart Publishing, 1966.

Norman, Margie. "Substitutes for Mother." *Human Behavior* 7 (1978):17–21.

Parke, R., and Tinsley, B. "The Father's Role in Infancy: Determinants in Caregiving and Play." In *The Role of the Father in Child Development,* edited by Michael Lamb, 2nd ed. New York: John Wiley & Sons, 1981.

Pogrebin, Letty Cottin. "Big Changes in Parenting." *Ms,* February 1982, pp. 41–46.

Pogrebin, Letty Cottin. *Growing Up Free: Raising Your Kids in the 80s.* New York: Bantam, 1981.

Rich, Adrienne. *On Lies, Secrets, and Silence.* New York: W. W. Norton, 1979.

Robertson, Priscilla. "Home as a Nest: Middle Class Childhood in Nineteenth-Century Europe." In *The History of Childhood,* edited by Lloyd deMause, pp. 407–431. New York: The Psychohistory Press, 1974.

Rolph, C. H. "A Backward Glance at the Age of 'Obscenity.' " *Encounter,* June 1969, pp. 19–28.

Rossi, Alice. "Gender and Parenthood." *American Sociological Review* 49 (1984):1–19.

Scarr, Sandra. *Mother Care/Other Care.* New York: Basic Books, 1984.

Scheper-Hughes, Nancy. "Breeding Breaks Out in the Eye of the Cat: Sex Roles, Birth Order and the Irish Double- Bind." *Journal of Comparative Family Studies* 10 (1979):207–226.

Thorne, Barrie. "Feminist Rethinking of the Family: An Overview." in *Rethinking the Family: Some Feminist Questions,* edited by Barrie Thorne and Marilyn Yalom, pp. 1–24. New York: Longman, 1982.

United Nations. General Assembly Resolution 1386 (XIV), November 20, 1959, published in the *Official Records of the General Assembly, Fourteenth Session, Supplement No. 16, 1960,* p. 19.

U.S. Bureau of the Census. *Statistical Abstracts of the United States,* Wash. D.C.: U.S. Gov't. Printing Office, 1985.

Verny, Thomas, with Kelly, John. *The Secret Life of the Unborn Child.* New York: Dell, 1984.

Walzer, John F. "A Period of Ambivalence: Eighteenth-Century Childhood." In *The History of Childhood,* edited by Lloyd deMause, pp. 351–382. New York: The Psychohistory Press, 1974.

Weigand, Johathan. "The Single Father." *Ms,* January 1973, pp. 29–31, 110–111.

Weisner, T. S. "Sibling Interdependence and Child Caretaking: A Cross-Cultural View." In *Sibling Relationships: Their Nature and Significance Across the Lifespan,* edited by M. W. Lamb and B. Sutton-Smith. Hillsdale, N.J.: Lawrence Erlbaum Associates, 1982.

Whitbread, Jane. "Beware of Fraiberg's Apron Strings." *Ms,* August 1978, pp. 35–38.

Whiting, B., and Whiting, J. W. *Children of Six Cultures: A Psycho-Cultural Analysis.* Cambridge, Mass.: Harvard University Press, 1975.

Chapter 12

Aldous, Joan. "From Dual-Earner to Dual-Career Families and Back Again." In *Two Paychecks: Life in Dual-Earner Families,* edited by Joan Aldous, pp. 11–26. Beverly Hills, Calif.: Sage Publications, 1982.

Aldous, Joan, Osmond, Marie W., and Hicks, Mary W. "Men's Work and Men's Families." In *Contemporary Theories About the Family: Research Based Theories,* edited by W. R. Burr, R. Hill, F. I. Nye, and I. L. Reiss, vol. I, pp. 227–256. New York: The Free Press, 1979.

Atkinson, Maxine P., and Boles, Jacqueline. "WASP (Wives as Senior Partners)." *Journal of Marriage and the Family* 46 (1984):861–870.

Berheide, Catherine White. "Women's Work in the Home: Seems Like Old Times." *Marriage and Family Review,* Fall/Winter 1984, pp. 37–55.

Berk, R., and Berk, S. *Labor and Leisure in the Home.* Beverly Hills, Calif.: Sage Publications, 1979.

Bernard, Jessie. "The Good- Provider Role: Its Rise and Fall." *American Psychologist* 36 (1981): 1–12.

Bird, Gloria W., Bird, Gerald A., and Scruggs, Marguerite. "Determinants of Family Task Sharing: A Study of Husbands and Wives." *Journal of Marriage and the Family* 46 (1984):345–355.

Blumstein, Philip, and Schwartz, Pepper. *American Couples: Money, Work, Sex.* New York: William Morrow, 1983.

Bohen, Halcyone H., and Viveros-Long, Ana-maria. *Balancing Jobs and Family Life*. Philadelphia: Temple University Press, 1981.

Coverman, Shelly. "Explaining Husband's Participation in Domestic Labor." *The Sociological Quarterly*, 26 (1985):81–97.

Crittenden, Ann. "We 'Liberated' Mothers Aren't." *The Washington Post*, Feb. 5, 1984, p. D1.

Davis, Kingsley. "Wives and Work: Consequences of the Sex Revolution." *Population and Development Review* 10 (1984):397–417.

Fendrich, Michael. "Wives' Employment and Husbands' Distress: A Meta-analysis and a Replication." *Journal of Marriage and the Family* 46 (1984):871–879.

Ferree, Myra Marx. "Working-Class Jobs: Housework and Paid Work as Sources of Satisfaction." *Social Problems* 23 (1976):431–444.

Ferree, Myra Marx. "The View from Below: Women's Employment and Gender Equality in Working Class Families." *Marriage and Family Review*, 7 (1984): 57–75.

Fowlkes, Martha R. *Behind Every Successful Man: Wives of Medicine and Academe*. New York: Columbia University Press, 1980.

Fuchs, Victor R. *How We Live*. Cambridge, Mass.: Harvard University Press, 1983.

Furstenberg, Frank F., Jr. "Work Experience and Family Life." In *Work and the Quality of Life*, edited by J. O'Toole. Cambridge, Mass.: The MIT Press, 1974.

Geerken, Michael, and Gove, Walter R. *At Home and at Work: The Family's Allocation of Labor.* Beverly Hills, Calif.: Sage Publications, 1983.

Gerstel, Naomi, and Gross, Harriet Engel. "Commuter Marriages: A Review." *Marriage and Family Review*, Summer 1982, pp. 71–93.

Gerstel, Naomi, and Gross, Harriet Engel. *Commuter Marriage*. New York: The Guilford Press, 1984.

Gongla, Patricia A. "Single Parent Families: A Look at Families of Mothers and Children." *Marriage and Family Review*, Summer 1982, pp. 5–27.

Gordon, Michael. *The American Family: Past, Present and Future*. New York: Random House, 1978.

Gove, Walter R., and Geerken, Michael. "The Effect of Children and Employment on the Mental Health of Married Men and Women." *Social Forces* 56 (1977):66–76.

Gove, Walter R., and Peterson, Claire. "An Update of the Literature on Personal and Marital Adjustment: The Effect of Children and the Employment of Wives." *Marriage and Family Review*, Fall/Winter 1980, pp. 63–96.

Hayghe, Howard. "Dual-Earner Families: Their Economic and Demographic Characteris-tics." In *Two Paychecks: Life in Dual-Earner Families*, edited by Joan Aldous, pp. 27–40. Beverly Hills, Calif.: Sage Publications, 1982.

Herzog, Elizabeth, and Sudia, Cecelia E. "Father-less Homes: A Review of Research." *Children* 15 (1968):177–182.

Hess, Beth. "Afterword." *Marriage and Family Review*, Fall/Winter, 1984, pp. 249–252.

Hornung, Carlton A., and McCollough, B. Claire. "Status Relationships in Dual-Employment Marriages: Consequences for Psychological Well-Being." *Journal of Marriage and the Family* 43 (1981):125–141.

Hornung, Carlton A., McCollough, B. Claire, and Sugimoto, Taichi. "Status Relationships in Marriage: Risk Factors in Spouse Abuse." *Journal of Marriage and the Family* 43 (1981):675–692.

Hunt, Janet G., and Hunt, Larry L. "Dual-Career Families: Vanguard of the Future or Residue of the Past?" In *Two Paychecks: Life in Dual-Earner Families*, edited by Joan Aldous, pp. 41–59. Beverly Hills, Calif.: Sage Publications, 1982.

Johnson, Phyllis J. "Divorced Mothers' Management of Responsibilities." *Journal of Family Issues* 4 (1983):83–103.

Kanter, Rosabeth M. *Men and Women of the Corporation*. New York: Basic Books, Inc. Publishers, 1977.

Kessler, Ronald C., and McRae, James A., Jr. "The Effect of Wives' Employment on the Mental Health of Married Men and Women." *American Sociological Review* 47 (1982):216–227.

Komarovsky, Mirra. *The Unemployed Man and His Family.* New York: The Dryden Press, 1940.

Komarovsky, Mirra. *Blue Collar Marriage*. New York: Random House, 1962.

Larson, Jeffry H. "The Effect of Husband's Unemployment on Marital and Family Relations in Blue-Collar Families." *Family Relations* 33 (1984):503–511.

Lerner, Gerda. "The Lady and the Mill Girl: Changes in the Status of Women in the Age of Jackson." *Midcontinent American Studies*, Spring 1969, pp. 5–14.

Locksley, A. "On the Effects of Wives' Employment on Marital Adjustment and Companionship." *Journal of Marriage and the Family* 42 (1980):337–346.

Maret, Elizabeth, and Finlay, Barbara. "The Distribution of Household Labor Among Women in Dual-Earner Families." *Journal of Marriage and the Family* 46 (1984):357–364.

McLanahan, Sara S. "Family Structure and Stress: A Longitudinal Comparison of Two-Parent and Female-Headed Families." *Journal of Marriage and the Family* 45 (1983):347–357.

Moore, Kristin, Spain, Daphne, and Bianchi, Suzanne. "Working Wives and Mothers." *Marriage and Family Review,* Fall/Winter 1984, pp. 77–98.

Nock, Steven L., and Kingston, Paul William. "The Family Work Day." *Journal of Marriage and the Family* 46 (1984):333–343.

Ostrander, Susan A. *Women of the Upper Class.* Philadelphia: Temple University Press, 1984.

Pearce, Diana, and McAdoo, Harriette. *Women and Children: Alone and in Poverty.* Washington, D.C.: National Advisory Council on Economic Opportunity, 1981.

Pearlin, Leonard L. "Sex Roles and Depression." In *Life Span Developmental Psychology: Normative Life Crises,* edited by Nancy Datan and Leon H. Ginsberg. New York: Academic Press, 1975.

Philliber, William W., and Hiller, Dana V. "Relative Occupation Attainments of Spouses and Later Changes in Marriage and Wife's Work Experience." *Journal of Marriage and the Family* 45 (1983):161–170.

Pleck, Joseph H., and Rustad, M. *Husbands and Wives' Time in Family Work and Paid Work in the 1975–1976 Study of Time Use.* Wellesley, Mass.: Wellesley College Center for Research on Women, 1981.

Pleck, Joseph H., and Staines, Graham L. "Work Schedules and Work-Family Conflict." In *Two Paychecks: Life in Dual-Earner Families,* edited by Joan Aldous, pp. 63–87. Beverly Hills, Calif.: Sage Publications, 1982.

Presser, Harriet B., and Cain, Virginia S. "Shift Work Among Dual-Earner Couples with Children." *Science* 219 (1983):876–879.

Radloff, L. "Sex Differences in Depression: The Effect of Occupation and Marital Status." *Sex Roles* 1 (1975):249–265.

Robboy, H. "Work with the Night Worker." In *Social Interaction: Readings in Sociology,* edited by H. Robboy and Candace Clark, 2nd ed. New York: St. Martin's Press, 1983.

Ross, Catherine E., Mirowsky, John, and Huber, Joan. "Dividing Work, Sharing Work, and In-Between: Marriage Patterns and Depression." *American Sociological Review* 48 (1983):809–823.

Rubenstein, Carin. "Real Men Don't Earn Less Than Their Wives." *Psychology Today,* November 1982, pp. 36–41.

Scanzoni, John. "Contemporary Marriage Types." *Journal of Family Issues* 1 (1980):125–140.

Simpson, Ida Harper, and England, Paula. "Conjugal Work Roles and Marital Solidarity." In *Two Paychecks: Life in Dual-Earner Families,* edited by Joan Aldous, pp. 147–171. Beverly Hills, Calif.: Sage Publications, 1982.

Smelser, Neil J. *Social Change in the Industrial Revolution.* Chicago: University of Chicago Press, 1959.

Stein, Peter. "Men in Families." *Marriage and Family Review,* 7 (1984): 143–162.

Szinovacz, Maximiliane E. "Changing Family Roles and Interactions." *Marriage and Family Review,* Fall/Winter 1984, pp. 163–201.

Toffler, Alvin. *The Third Wave.* New York: William Morrow, 1980.

U.S. Bureau of the Census, *The Statistical Abstract of the United States,* 1985. Washington, D.C.: U.S. Government Printing Office, 1984.

Voydanoff, Patricia, and Kelly, Robert F. "Determinants of Work-Related Family Problems Among Employed Parents." *Journal of Marriage and the Family* 46 (1984):881–892.

Welter, Barbara. "The Cult of True Womanhood: 1820–1860." *American Quarterly,* Summer 1966, pp. 151–174.

Wright, J. "Are Working Women Really More Satisfied? Evidence from Several National Surveys." *Journal of Marriage and the Family* 40 (1978):301–313.

Chapter 13

Berkowitz, L. "The Case for Bottling Up Rage." *Psychology Today,* July 1973, pp. 24–31.

Blood, Robert O., and Blood, Margaret. *Marriage.* 3rd ed. New York: The Free Press, 1978.

Blumstein, Philip, and Schwartz, Pepper. *American Couples: Money, Work, Sex.* New York: William Morrow, 1983.

Brandt, Anthony. "Avoiding Couple Karate: Lessons in the Marital Arts." *Psychology Today,* October 1982, pp. 38–43.

Collins, Randall. "A Conflict Theory of Sexual Stratification." *Social Problems* 19 (1971): 3–21.

Coser, L. A. *The Functions of Social Conflict.* New York: The Free Press, 1956.

Crawford, Christina. *Mommie Dearest.* New York: William Morrow, 1978.

Dahrendorf, Ralf. *Class and Class Conflict in an Industrial Society.* London: Routledge & Kegan Paul, 1959.

Denzin, Norman K. "Toward a Phenomenology of Domestic, Family Violence." *American Journal of Sociology* 90 (1984):483–513.

Dobash, R. Emerson, and Dobash, Russell. *Violence Against Women: A Case Against Patriarchy.* New York: The Free Press, 1979.

Elkins, Stanley M. *Slavery: A Problem in American Institutional and Intellectual Life.* Chicago: University of Chicago Press, 1959.

Felson, Richard B. "Aggression and Violence Between Siblings." *Social Psychology Quarterly,* December 1983, pp. 271–285.

Finkelhor, David. *Sexually Victimized Children.* New York: The Free Press, 1979.

Frederick, W. N., and Boriskin, J. A. "The Role of the Child in Abuse: A Review of the Literature." In *Traumatic Abuse and Neglect of Children at Home,* edited by G. J. Williams and J. Money. Baltimore: The Johns Hopkins University Press, 1980.

Fullerton, Gail Putney. *Survival in Marriage.* 2nd ed. Hinsdale, Ill.: The Dryden Press, 1977.

Garbarino, James, and Sherman, Deborah. "High-Risk Neighborhoods and High-Risk Families: The Human Ecology of Child Maltreatment." *Child Development* 51 (1980):188–198.

Gayford, J. J. "Battered Wives." In *International Perspectives on Family Violence,* edited by Richard J. Gelles and Claire Pedrick Cornell, pp. 123–137. Lexington, Mass.: Lexington Books, 1983.

Gelles, Richard J. "Child Abuse as Psychopathology: A Social Critique and Reformulation." *American Journal of Orthopsychiatry* 43 (1973):611–621.

Gelles, Richard J. *The Violent Home.* Beverly Hills, Calif.: Sage Publications, 1974.

Gelles, Richard J., and Straus, Murray A. "Determinants of Violence in the Family: Toward a Theoretical Integration." In *Contemporary Theories About the Family,* edited by W. R. Burr, R. Hill, F. I. Nye and I. L. Reiss, pp. 549–581. New York: The Free Press, 1979.

Gil, O. G. *Violence Against Children: Physical Child Abuse in the United States.* Cambridge, Mass.: Harvard University Press, 1970.

Gordon, Thomas. *Parent Effectiveness Training.* New York: Wyden Books, 1970.

Gottman, John M. *Marital Interaction: Experimental Investigation.* New York: Academic Press, 1979.

Gottman, John M., Markman, Howard, and Notarius, Cliff. "The Topography of Marital Conflict: A Sequential Analysis of Verbal and Nonverbal Behavior." *Journal of Marriage and the Family* 39 (1977):461–477.

Halperin, S. *Helping Maltreated Children: School and Community Involvement.* St. Louis: C. V. Mosby, 1979.

Herman, Judith, and Hirschman, Lisa. "Families at Risk for Father-Daughter Incest." *American Journal of Psychiatry* 138 (1981):967–970.

Kamerman, Sheila B. "Eight Countries: Cross-National Perspectives on Child Abuse and Neglect." In *International Perspectives on Family Violence,* edited by Richard J. Gelles and Claire Pedrick Cornell, pp. 63–71. Lexington, Mass.: Lexington Books, 1983.

Koch, Michael. "Sexual Abuse in Children." *Adolescence* 15 (1980): 643–648.

LaRossa, Ralph. " 'And We Haven't Had Any Problems Since': Conjugal Violence and the Politics of Marriage." In *The Social Causes of Husband-Wife Violence,* edited by Murray A. Straus and Gerald T. Hotaling, pp. 157–175. Minneapolis: University of Minnesota Press, 1980.

Lindholm, Charles, and Lindholm, Cherry. "Marriage as Warfare." *Natural History,* October 1979, pp. 11–20.

Meiselman, Karin C. *Incest.* San Francisco: Jossey-Bass, 1978.

Meyers, Laura. "Battered Wives, Dead Husbands." In *Family in Transition,* edited by Arlene S. Skolnick and Jerome H. Skolnick 4th ed. Boston: Little, Brown, 1983.

Nass, Gilbert D., Libby, Roger W., and Fisher, Mary Pat. *Sexual Choices: An Introduction to Human Sexuality.* Belmont, Calif.: Wadsworth, 1981.

Pagelow, Mildred Daley. *Woman-Battering: Victims and Their Experiences.* Beverly Hills, Calif.: Sage Publications, 1981.

Rush, Florence. *The Best Kept Secret: Sexual Abuse of Children.* New York: McGraw-Hill, 1980.

Scanzoni, John. *Sexual Bargaining: Power Politics in the American Marriage.* Englewood Cliffs, N.J.: Prentice-Hall, 1972.

Scanzoni, Letha Dawson, and Scanzoni, John. *Men, Women, and Change: A Sociology of Marriage and the Family.* New York: McGraw-Hill, 1981.

Skolnick, Arlene. *The Intimate Environment: Exploring Marriage and the Family.* 2nd ed. Boston: Little, Brown, 1978.

Stark, Elizabeth. "Spanking Kids for the Wrong Reasons." *Psychology Today,* January 1985, p. 16.

Stark, Rodney, and McEvoy, James, III. "Middle Class Violence." *Psychology Today,* November 1970, pp. 52–65.

Steinmetz, Suzanne K., and Straus, Murray A. "The Family as Cradle of Violence." *Society,* September/October 1973, pp. 50–58.

Straus, Murray A. "Leveling, Civility, and Violence in the Family." *Journal of Marriage and the Family* 36 (1974):13–29.

Straus, Murray A. "Wife Beating: How Common and Why?" *Victimology: An International Journal* 2 (1977/1978):443–458.

Straus, Murray A. "Victims and Aggressors in Marital Violence." *American Behavioral Scientist* 23 (1980):681–704.

Straus, Murray A., and Hotaling, Gerald T., eds. *The Social Causes of Husband-Wife Violence.*

Minneapolis: University of Minnesota Press, 1980.

Straus, Murray A., Gelles, Richard J., and Steinmetz, Suzanne K. *Behind Closed Doors: Violence in the American Family.* Garden City, N.Y.: Anchor/Doubleday, 1980.

Szinovacz, Maximiliane E. "Using Couple Data as a Methodological Tool: The Case of Marital Violence." *Journal of Marriage and the Family* 45 (1983):633–644.

Taylor, Lesli, and Newberger, Eli H. "Child Abuse in the International Year of the Child." In *International Perspectives on Family Violence*, edited by Richard J. Gelles and Claire Pedrick Cornell, pp. 45–62. Lexington, Mass.: Lexington Books, 1983.

Walker, Lenore. *The Battered Woman.* New York: Harper & Row, 1979.

Watkins, Harriet D., and Bradbard, Marilyn R. "Child Maltreatment: An Overview with Suggestions for Intervention and Research." *Family Relations* 31 (1982):323–333.

Chapter 14

Adams, Bert N. *Kinship in an Urban Setting.* Chicago: Markham, 1968.

Ade-Ridder, Linda, and Brubaker, Timothy H. "The Quality of Long-Term Marriages." In *Family Relationships in Later Life*, edited by Timothy H. Brubaker, pp. 21–30. Beverly Hills, Calif.: Sage Publications, 1983.

Anderson, Trudy B. "Widowhood as a Life Transition: Its Impact on Kinship Ties." *Journal of Marriage and the Family* 46 (1984):105–114.

Atchley, Robert C., and Miller, Sheila J. "Types of Elderly Couples." In *Family Relationships in Later Life*, edited by Timothy H. Brubaker, pp. 77–90. Beverly Hills, Calif.: Sage Publications, 1983.

Baruch, Grace, and Barnett, Rosalind C. "Adult Daughter's Relationships with Their Mothers." *Journal of Marriage and the Family* 45 (1983):601–606.

Bengston, Vern, and Kuypers, J. A. "Generational Differences and the Developmental Stake." *Aging and Human Development* 2 (1971):246–260.

Blau, Zena Smith, Oser, George T., and Stephens, Richard C. "Patterns of Adaptation in Retirement: A Comparative Analysis." In *Coping with Medical Issues: Aging*, edited by Aliza Kolker and Paul I. Ahmed, pp. 119–138. New York: Elsevier, 1982.

Brim, Orville G., Jr. "Theories of the Male Midlife Crisis." *Counseling Psychologist* 6 (1976):2–9.

Brubaker, Timothy H. "Introduction." In *Family Relationships in Later Life*, edited by Timothy H. Brubaker, pp. 9–18. Beverly Hills, Calif.: Sage Publications, 1983.

Bumiller, Elizabeth. "Coming Home." *The Washington Post*, February 16, 1982, pp. B1–B2.

Cheal, David J. "Intergenerational Family Transfers." *The Journal of Marriage and the Family* 45 (1983):805–813.

Cicirelli, Victor G. *Helping Elderly Parents: Role of Adult Children.* Boston: Auburn House, 1981.

Cicirelli, Victor G. "Adult Children and Their Elderly Parents." In *Family Relationships in Later Life*, edited by Timothy H. Brubaker, pp. 31–46. Beverly Hills, Calif.: Sage Publications, 1983.

Farrell, Michael, and Rosenberg, Stanley D. *Men at Midlife.* Boston: Auburn House, 1981.

Fischer, Lucy Rose. "Transitions in the Mother-Daughter Relationship." *Journal of Marriage and the Family* 43 (1981):613–622.

Foote, Audrey. "The Kids Who Won't Leave Home." In *Relationships: The Marriage and Family Reader.* edited by Jeffrey P. Rosenfeld. Glenview, Ill.: Scott, Foresman, 1982. (Originally published in *Atlantic Monthly*, March 1978.)

Friday, Nancy. *My Mother/My Self: The Daughter's Search for Identity.* New York: Dell, 1977.

Frost, Robert. The Poems of Robert Frost. New York: Random House.

Garza, Joseph M., and Dressel, Paula L. "Sexuality and Later-Life Marriages." In *Family Relationships in Later Life*, edited by Timothy H. Brubaker, pp. 91–108. Beverly Hills, Calif.: Sage Publications, 1983.

George, L. K., and Weiler, S. J. "Sexuality in Middle and Late Life." *Archives of General Psychiatry* 38 (1981):919–923.

Gibson, G. "Kin Family Network: Overheralded Structure in Past Conceptualization of Family Functioning." *The Journal of Marriage and the Family* 34 (1972):13–23.

Gilford, Rosalie, and Bengston, Vern. "Measuring Marital Satisfaction in Three Generations: Positive and Negative Dimensions." *Journal of Marriage and the Family* 41 (1979):387–398.

Guttman, D. L. "Individual Adaptation in the Middle Years: Developmental Issues in the Masculine Midlife Crisis." In *Dimensions in Aging: Readings*, edited by J. Hendricks and C. Hendricks. Cambridge, Mass.: Winthrop Pubs., Inc., 1979.

Hagestad, Gunhild O. "Problems and Promises in the Social Psychology of Intergenerational Relations." In *Aging: Stability and Change in* the Family, edited by Robert W. Fogel, Elaine Hatfield, Sara B. Kiesler, and Ethel Shanas, pp. 11–46. New York: Academic Press, 1981.

Hess, Beth, and Waring, J. M. "Parent and Child in later Life: Rethinking the Relationship." In *Child Influences on Marital and Family Interaction: A Life Span Perspective*, edited by R. M. Lerner and G. B. Spanier. New York: Academic Press, 1978.

Hill, Reuben, Foote, Nelson, Aldous, Joan, Carlson, Robert, and MacDonald, Robert. *Family Development in Three Generations.* Cambridge, Mass.: Schenkman, 1970.

Jacques, Elliott. "Death and the Mid-Life Crisis." *International Journal of Psychoanalysis* 46 (1965):502–514.

Kammeyer, Kenneth C. W., and Ginn, Helen L. *An Introduction to Population.* Chicago, Ill.: The Dorsey Press, 1986.

Keating, Norah C., and Cole, Priscilla. "What Do I Do with Him 24 Hours a Day? Changes in the Housewife Role After Retirement." *The Gerontologist* 20 (1980):84–89.

Kinsey, Alfred C., Pomeroy, Wardell B., and Martin, Clyde E. *Sexual Behavior in the Human Male.* Philadelphia: W. B. Saunders, 1948.

Lang, Abigail M., and Brody, Elaine M. "Characteristics of Middle-Aged Daughters and Help to Their Elderly Mothers." *Journal of Marriage and the Family* 45 (1983):193–202.

Lear, M. W. "Is There a Male Menopause?" *New York Times Magazine*, January 28, 1973, pp. 10–11.

Levinson, Daniel J., with Darrow, Charlotte N., Klein, Edward B., Levinson, Maria H., and McKee, Braxton. *The Seasons of a Man's Life.* New York: Ballantine, 1978.

Lowenthal, Marjorie Fiske, and Chiriboga, David. "Transition to the Empty Nest." *Archives of General Psychiatry* 26 (1972):8–14.

Miller, Sheila J. "Will the Real 'Older Woman' Please Stand Up?" In *Social Problems of the Aging: Readings*, edited by Mildred M. Seltzer, Sherry L. Corbett and Robert C. Atchley. Belmont, Calif.: Wadsworth, 1978.

Morgan, Leslie A. "Changes in Family Interaction Following Widowhood." *Journal of Marriage and the Family* 46 (1984):323–331.

Neugarten, Bernice L., ed. *Middle Age and Aging: A Reader in Social Psychology.* Chicago: University of Chicago Press, 1968a.

Neugarten, Bernice L. "Awareness in Middle Age." In *Middle Age and Aging: A Reader in Social Psychology*, edited by Bernice L. Neugarten. Chicago: University of Chicago Press, 1968b.

Neugarten, Bernice L., and Weinstein, K. K. "The Changing American Grandparent." *Journal of Marriage and the Family* 26 (1964):199–204.

Palmore, Erdman. *Social Patterns in Normal Aging: Findings from the Duke Longitudinal Study.* Durham, N.C.: Duke University Press, 1981.

Pedrick-Cornell, Claire, and Gelles, Richard J. "Elder Abuse: The Status of Current Knowledge." *Family Relations* 31 (1982):457–465.

Peterson, J. A., and Payne, B. *Love in the Later Years.* New York: Association Press, 1975.

Pfeiffer, E., Verwoerdt, A., and Wang, H. S. "Sexual Behavior in Middle Life." In *Normal Aging II*, edited by Erdman Palmore. Durham, N.C.: Duke University Press, 1974.

Rathbone-McCuan, Eloise. "Elderly Victims of Family Violence and Neglect." *The Journal of Contemporary Social Work* 61 (1980):296–304.

Roberts, W. L. "Significant Elements in the Relationship of Long- Married Couples." *International Journal of Aging and Human Development* 10 (1980):265–271.

Rubin, Lillian B. *Women of a Certain Age. The Midlife Search for Self.* New York: Harper & Row, 1979.

Shanas, Ethel and Sussman, Marvin B. *Family, Bureaucracy, and the Elderly.* Durham, N.C.: Duke University Press, 1977.

Smelser, N. J., and Halpern, S. "The Historical Triangulation of Family, Economy and Education." In *Turning Points*, edited by J. Demos and J. Boocock. *American Journal of Sociology* 84 (Supplement), 1978.

Smith, Daniel Scott. "Historical Change in the Household Structure of the Elderly in Economically Developed Societies." In *Aging: Stability and Change in the Family*, edited by Robert W. Fogel, Elaine Hatfield, Sara B. Kiesler, and Ethel Shanas, pp. 91–114. New York: Academic Press, 1981.

Spence, Donald, and Lonner, Thomas. "The 'Empty Nest': A Transition Within Motherhood." *The Family Coordinator* 20 (1971):369–375.

Starr, Bernard D., and Weiner, Marcella Bakur. *The Starr-Weiner Report on Sex and Sexuality in the Mature Years.* New York: Stein & Day, 1981.

Steinmetz, Suzanne K., and Amsden, Deborah J. "Dependent Elders, Family Stress, and Abuse." In *Family Relationships in Later Life*, edited by Timothy H. Brubaker, pp. 173–192. Beverly Hills, Calif.: Sage Publications, 1983.

Stoller, Eleanor Palo. "Parental Caregiving by Adult Children." *Journal of Marriage and the Family* 45 (1983):851–858.

Swensen, Clifford H., Eskew, Ron W. and Kohlhepp, Karen A. "Stage of Family Life Cycle, Ego Development, and the Marriage Relationship." *Journal of Marriage and the Family* 43 (1981):841–853.

Szinovacz, Maximiliane E. "Female Retirement: Effects on Spousal Roles and Marital Adjustment." *Journal of Family Issues* 1 (1980):423–440.

Tinsley, Barbara R., and Parke, Ross D. "Grandparents as Support and Socialization Agents." In *Beyond the Dyad*, edited by Michael Lewis, pp. 161–194. New York: Plenum Press, 1984.

Troll, Lillian E. "The Family in Later Life: A Decade in Review." *The Journal of Marriage and the Family* 33 (1971):263–290.

Troll, Lillian E. "Is Parent-Child Conflict What We Mean by the Generation Gap?" *The Family Coordinator* 21 (1972):347–349.

Troll, Lillian E. "Grandparents: The Family Watchdogs." In *Family Relationships in Later Life*, edited by Timothy H. Brubaker, pp. 63–74. Beverly Hills, Calif.: Sage Publications, 1983.

Troll, Lillian E., and Bengston, Vern. "Generations in the Family." In *Contemporary Theories About the Family: Research Based Theories*, edited by W. R. Burr, R. Hill, F. I. Nye and I. L. Reiss, pp. 127–161. New York: The Free Press, 1979.

Troll, Lillian E., Miller, Sheila J., and Atchley, Robert C. *Families in Later Life*. Belmont, Calif.: Wadsworth, 1979.

Turner, Joseph G. "Patterns of Intergenerational Exchange: A Development Approach." *International Journal of Aging and Human Development* 6 (1975):111–115.

U.S. Bureau of the Census. "Marital Status and Living Arrangements." *Current Population Reports*, Series P–20, N. 389, 1983a.

U.S. Bureau of the Census. *The Statistical Abstract of the United States*, 1985. Washington D.C.: U.S. Government Printing Office, 1984.

Wood, V., and Robertson, J. F. *'The Significance of Grandparenthood.'* in *Time, Roles and Self in Old Age*, edited by J. Gubrium. New York: Human Services Press, 1976.

Zube, Margaret. "Changing Behavior and Outlook of Aging Men and Women: Implications for Marriage in the Middle and Later Years." *Family Relations* 31 (1982):147–156.

Chapter 15

Adegboye, R. O. "Divorce and Remarriage among the Sedentary Fulani in the South of Kaduna State in Nigeria." Free paper presented at the XIX International Committee on Family Research Seminar on Divorce and Remarriage, Leuvan, Belgium, 1981.

Albrecht, Stan L., Bahr, Howard M., and Goodman, Kristen L. *Divorce and Remarriage: Problems, Adaptations, and Adjustments*. Westport, Conn.: Greenwood Press, 1983.

Bahr, Stephen J. "An Evaluation of Court Mediation: A Comparison in Divorce Cases with Children." *Journal of Family Issues* 2 (1981):39–60.

Bahr, Stephen J. "Marital Dissolution Laws: Impact of Recent Changes For Women." *Journal of Family Issues* 4 (1983):455–466.

Becker, Gary S. "A Theory of Marriage: Part I." *Journal of Political Economy* 81 (1973):813–846.

Bohannan, Paul. "The Six Stations of Divorce." In *Divorce and After*, edited by Paul Bohannan, pp. 33–62. New York: Anchor Books, 1971.

Booth, Alan, and Edwards, John N. "Age at Marriage and Marital Stability." *Journal of Marriage and the Family* 47 (1985):67–75.

Bumpass, Larry L., and James A. Sweet "Differentials in Marital Instability: 1970." *American Sociological Review* 37 (1972):754–766.

Cherlin, Andrew J., *Marriage, Divorce, Remarriage*. Cambridge, Mass.: Harvard University Press, 1981.

Clingempeel, W. Glenn, and Reppucci, N. Dickon. "Joint Custody after Divorce: Major Issues and Goals for Research." *Psychological Bulletin* 91 (1982):102–127.

Cohen, Ronald. "Brittle Marriage as a Stable System: The Kanuri Case." In *Divorce and After*, edited by Paul Bohannan, pp. 205–239. New York: Anchor Books, 1971.

Coombs, L. C., and Zumeta, Z. "Correlates of Marital Dissolution in a Prospective Fertility Study: A Research Note." *Social Problems*, 18 (1970):92–101.

Cott, Nancy F. "Divorce and the Changing Status of Women in Eighteenth-Century Massachusetts." In *The American Family in Social-Historical Perspective, 3rd ed.* edited by Michael Gordon, pp. 347–371. New York: St. Martin's Press, 1983.

Derdeyn, Andre P., and Scott, Elizabeth. "Joint Custody: A Critical Analysis and Appraisal." *American Journal of Orthopsychiatry* 54 (1984): 199–209.

Dixon, Ruth B., and Weitzman, Lenore J. "Evaluating the Impact of No-Fault Divorce in California." *Family Relations* 29 (1980):297–307.

Furstenberg, Frank F., Jr. *Unplanned Parenthood: The Social Consequences of Teenage Childbearing*. New York: The Free Press, 1976.

Furstenberg, Frank F., Jr. "Premarital Pregnancy and Marital Instability." In *Divorce and Separation: Context, Causes, and Consequences*, edited by George Levinger and Oliver C.

Moles, pp. 83–98. New York: Basic Books, 1979.

Glenn, Norval D., and Supancic, Michael. "The Social and Demographic Correlates of Divorce and Separation in the United States: An Update and Reconsideration." *Journal of Marriage and the Family* 46 (1984):563–575.

Glick, Paul C. *American Families.* New York: John Wiley & Sons, 1957.

Goode, William J. *After Divorce.* New York: The Free Press, 1956.

Gordon, Michael. *The American Family: Past, Present and Future.* New York: Random House, 1978.

Griswold, Robert L. *Family and Divorce in California, 1850–1890: Victorian Illusions and Everyday Realities.* Albany, N.Y.: State University of New York Press, 1982.

Hetherington, E. Mavis, Cox, Martha, and Cox, Roger. "The Aftermath of Divorce." In *Mother-Child, Father-Child Relations*, edited by J. H. Stevens, Jr., and M. Matthew, pp. 146–176. Washington, D.C.: National Association for the Education of Young Children, 1978.

Kammeyer, Kenneth C. W. "The Decline of Divorce in America." Paper presented at the meetings of the Midwest Sociological Society, Des Moines, Iowa, 1981.

Kurdek, L. A., Blisk, D., and Siesky, A. E. "Correlates of Children's Long-Term Adjustment to Their Parents' Divorce." *Developmental Psychology,* 17 (1981):565–579.

Kulka, R. A., and Weingarten, H. "The Long-Term Effects of Parental Divorce in Childhood on Adult Adjustment." *Journal of Social Issues* 35 (1979):50–78.

Lee, Gary R. "Age at Marriage and Marital Satisfaction: A Multivariate Analysis with Implications for Marital Stability." *Journal of Marriage and the Family* 39 (1977):493–504.

Levinger, George. "A Social Psychological Perspective on Marital Dissolution." In *Divorce and Separation: Context, Causes, and Consequences*, edited by George Levinger and Oliver C. Moles, pp. 37–60. New York: Basic Books, 1979.

Levitan, Teresa E. "Children of Divorce: An Introduction." *Journal of Social Issues* 35 (1979):1–25.

Longfellow, Cynthia. "Divorce in Context: Its Impact on Children." In *Divorce and Separation: Context, Causes, and Consequences*, edited by George Levinger and Oliver C. Moles, pp. 287–306. New York: Basic Books, 1979.

Luepnitz, Deborah Anna. *Child Custody.* Lexington, Mass.: D. C. Health, 1982.

Mace, David R., and Mace, Vera. *The Soviet Family.* Garden City, N.Y.: Doubleday, 1963.

McCarthy, James. "A Comparison of the Probability of the Dissolution of First and Second Marriages." *Demography* 15 (1978):345–359.

Menefee, Samuel Pyeatt. *Wives for Sale: An Ethnographic Study of British Popular Divorce.* New York: St Martin's Press, 1981.

Moskoff, William. "Divorce in the USSR." *Journal of Marriage and the Family* 45 (1983):419–425.

National Center for Health Statistics. "Advance Report of Final Divorce Statistics, 1982." *Monthly Vital Statistics Report*, Vol. 33, No. 11, Supp. DHHS Pub. No. (PHS) 85–1120, Public Health Service, 1985.

Norton, Arthur J., and Glick, Paul C. "Marital Instability in America: Past, Present, and Future." In *Divorce and Separation: Context, Causes, and Consequences*, edited by George Levinger and Oliver C. Moles, pp. 6–19. New York: Basic Books, 1979.

Petit, Ellen J., and Bloom, Bernard L. "Whose Decision Was It? The Effects of Initiator Status on Adjustment to Marital Disruption." *Journal of Marriage and the Family* 46 (1984):587–595.

Preston, Samuel, and McDonald, John. "The Incidence of Divorce within Cohorts of American Marriages Contracted Since the Civil War." *Demography* 16 (1979):1–23.

Roman, Mel, and Haddad, William. *The Disposable Parent: The Case for Joint Custody.* New York: Penguin Books, 1978.

Ross, Heather L., and Sawhill, Isabel V. "Marital Instability." In *Framing the Family: Contemporary Portraits*, edited by Bert N. Adams and John L. Campbell, pp. 359–388. Prospect Heights, Ill.: Waveland Press, 1984.

Schoen, R. H., Greenblatt, N., and Mielke, R. B. "California's Experience with Non-Adversary Divorce." *Demography* 12 (1975):223–243.

Seal, K. "A Decade of No-Fault Divorce: What It Has Meant Financially for Women in California." *Family Advocate* 1 (1979):10–15.

Sell, Kenneth D. "Divorce Law Reform and Increasing Divorce Rates." In *Current Issues in Marriage and the Family*, edited by Jipson G. Wells, pp. 290–308. New York: Macmillan, 1979.

South, Scott J. "Economic Conditions and the Divorce Rate: A Time-Series Analysis of the Postwar United States." *Journal of Marriage and the Family* 4 (1985):31–41.

Spanier, Graham B., and Casto, Robert F. "Adjustment to Separation and Divorce: A Qualitative Analysis." In *Divorce and Separation: Context, Causes, and Consequences*, edited by George Levinger and Oliver C. Moles, pp. 211–227. New York: Basic Books, 1979.

Teachman, Jay D. "Early Marriage, Premarital Fertility, and Marital Dissolution: Results for

Blacks and Whites." *Journal of Family Issues* 4 (1983):105–126.

Thornton, Arland. "Marital Instability Differentials and Interactions: Insights from Multivariate Contingency Table Analysis." *Sociology and Social Research* 62 (1978):572–595.

U.S. Bureau of the Census "Marital Status and Living Arrangements: March 1983." *Current Population Reports*, Series P-20, No. 389, 1983.

U.S. Bureau of the Census *Statistical Abstract of the United States, 1985*. Washington, D. C.: U.S. Government Printing Office, 1984.

Wallerstein, Judith S. "Children of Divorce: Preliminary Report of a Ten-Year Follow-up of Young Children." *American Journal of Orthopsychiatry* 54 (1984):444–458.

Wallerstein, Judith S., and Kelly, Joan B. "The Effects of Parental Divorce: The Adolescent Experience." In *The Child in His Family: Children at Psychiatric Risk*, Vol. 3, edited by E. J. Anthony and C. Koupernik. New York: John Wiley & Sons, 1974.

Wallerstein, Judith S., and Kelly, Joan B. "The Effects of Parental Divorce: Experiences of the Preschool Child. *The Journal of the American Academy of Child Psychiatry* 14 (1975):600–616.

Wallerstein, Judith S., and Kelly, Joan B. "Effects of Parental Divorce: Experience of Children in Later Latency." *American Journal of Orthopsychiatry* 46 (1976):256–269.

Wallerstein, Judith S., and Kelly, Joan B. *Surviving the Breakup: How Children and Parents Cope with Divorce*. New York: Basic Books, 1980.

Watson, Mary Ann. "Custody Alternatives: Defining the Best Interests of the Children." *Family Relations* 30 (1981):474–479.

Weed, James A. *National Estimates of Marriage Dissolution and Survivorship*. Washington, D. C.: U.S. Government Printing Office, 1980.

Weiss, Robert S. *Marital Separation*. New York: Basic Books, 1975.

Weiss, Robert S. "Issues in the Adjudication of Custody When Parents Separate." In *Divorce and Separation: Context, Causes, and Consequences*, edited by George Levinger and Oliver C. Moles, pp. 324–336. New York: Basic Books, 1979.

Weitzman, Lenore J. *The Divorce Revolution: The Unexpected Social and Economic Consequences for Women and Children in America*. New York: The Free Press, 1985.

Welch, Charles E., III, and Price-Bonham, Sharon. "A Decade of No-Fault Divorce Revisited: California, Georgia, and Washington." *Journal of Marriage and the Family* 45 (1983):411–418.

Zelnik, Melvin, and Kantner, John F. "Sexual Activity, Contraceptive Use and Pregnancy among Metropolitan Area Teenagers: 1971–1979." *Family Planning Perspectives* 12 (1980):230–237.

Chapter 16

Ahrons, Constance R. "The Binuclear Family: Two Households, One Family." *Alternative Life Styles* 2 (1979):499–515.

Ahrons, Constance R. "The Continuing Coparental Relationship between Divorced Spouses." *American Journal of Orthopsychiatry* 51 (1981):415–428.

Albrecht, Stan L. "Reactions and Adjustments to Divorce: Differences in the Experiences of Males and Females." *Family Relations* 29 (1980):59–68.

Albrecht, Stan L., Bahr, Howard M., and Goodman, Kristen L. *Divorce and Remarriage: Problems, Adaptations, and Adjustments*. Westport, Conn.: Greenwood Press, 1983.

Bohannan, Paul. "The Six Stations of Divorce." In *Divorce and After*, edited by Paul Bohannan, pp. 33–62. Garden City, N.Y.: Anchor Books, 1971a.

Bohannan, Paul. "Divorce Chains, Households of Remarriage, and Multiple Divorces." In *Divorce and After*, edited by Paul Bohannan, pp. 127–139. Garden City, N.Y.: Anchor Books, 1971b.

Cherlin, Andrew J. "Remarriage as an Incomplete Institution." *American Journal of Sociology* 84 (1978):634–650.

Cherlin, Andrew J. *Marriage, Divorce, Remarriage*. Cambridge, Mass.: Harvard University Press, 1981.

Cherlin, Andrew J., and McCarthy, James. "Remarried Couple Households: Data from the June 1980 Current Population Survey." *Journal of Marriage and the Family* 47 (1985):23–30.

Demos, John. *A Little Commonwealth: Family Life in Plymouth Colony*. New York: Oxford University Press, 1970.

Duberman, Lucille. The Reconstituted Family: A Study of Remarried Couples and Their Children. Chicago: Nelson-Hall Publishers, 1975.

Family Relations. Pasley, Kay and Ihinger-Tallman, Marilyn, eds. "Remarriage and Stepparenting: Special Issue," 33 (1984).

Furstenberg, Frank F., Jr. "Recycling the Family: Perspectives for a Neglected Family Form." *Marriage and Family Review*, 2 (1979): 1, 12–22.

Furstenberg, Frank F., Jr., and Spanier, Graham B. *Recycling the Family: Remarriage after Divorce*. Beverly Hills, Calif.: Sage Publications, 1984.

Glenn, Norval. "The Well-Being of Persons Remarried after Divorce." *Journal of Family Issues* 2 (1981):61–75.

Glick, Paul. "Remarriage: Some Recent Changes and Variations." *Journal of Family Issues* 1 (1980):455–478.

Goffman, Erving. *Asylums*. New York: Doubleday, 1961.

Gove, Walter R. "Sex, Marital Status and Mortality." *American Journal of Sociology* 79 (1973):45–67.

Halliday, Terence C. "Remarriage: The More Compleat Institution?" *American Journal of Sociology* 86 (1980):630–635.

Hart, Nicky. *When Marriage Ends: A Study in Status Passage*. London: Tavistock Publications, 1976.

Jacobson, D. S. "The Impact of Marital Separation/Divorce on Children: II. Interparent Hostility and Child Adjustment." *Journal of Divorce* 2 (1978):3–20.

Knaub, Patricia Kain, Hanna, Sharon L. and Stinnett, Nick "Strengths of Remarried Families." *Journal of Divorce* 7(1984):41–55.

Kohen, Janet A., Brown, Carol A., and Feldberg, Roslyn. "Divorced Mothers: The Costs and Benefits of Female Family Control." In *Divorce and Separation: Contexts, Causes, and Consequences*, edited by George Levinger and Oliver C. Moles, pp. 228–245. New York: Basic Books, 1979.

McCarthy, James. "A Comparison of the Probability of Dissolution of First and Second Marriages." *Demography* 15 (1978):345–359.

Mead, Margaret. "Anomalies in American Postdivorce Relationships." In *Divorce and After*, edited by Paul Bohannan, pp. 107–125. Garden City, N.Y.: Anchor Books, 1971.

National Center for Health Statistics. *Advance Report on Final Marriage Statistics, 1982*. Monthly Vital Statistics Report, vol. 34, no. 3, (supplement, June 28). Hyattsville, Md.: National Center for Health Statistics, 1985.

Spanier, Graham B., and Casto, Robert F. "Adjustment to Separation and Divorce: A Qualitative Analysis." In *Divorce and Separation: Context, Causes, and Consequences*, edited by George Levinger and Oliver C. Moles. New York: Basic Books, 1979a.

Spanier, Graham B., and Casto, Robert F. "Adjustment to Separation and Divorce: An Analysis of 50 Cases." *Journal of Divorce* 2 (1979b):241–253.

Thornton, Arland, and Freedman, Deborah. "The Changing American Family." *Population Bulletin*, October 1983, pp. 1–43.

Walker, Kenneth N., and Messinger, Lillian. "Remarriage after Divorce: Dissolution and Reconstruction of Family Boundaries." *Family Process* 18 (1979):185–192.

Wallerstein, Judith S., and Kelly, Joan Berlin. *Surviving Breakup: How Children and Parents Cope with Divorce*. New York: Basic Books, 1980.

Weed, James A. "National Estimates of Marriage Dissolution and Survivorship: United States." *Vital and Health Statistics*, series 3, no. 19. Hyattsville, Md.: National Center for Health Statistics, 1980.

Weiss, Robert S. *Marital Separation*. New York: Basic Books, 1975.

Weiss, Robert S. *Going It Alone: The Family Life and Social Situation of the Single Parent*. New York: Basic Books, 1979a.

Weiss, Robert S. "Growing Up a Little Faster: The Experience of Growing Up in a Single-Parent Household." *Journal of Social Issues* 35 (1979b):97–111.

Weitzman, Lenore J. "Legal Regulation of Marriage: Tradition and Change." *California Law Review* 62 (1974):1169–1288.

Westoff, Leslie A. *The Second Time Around: Remarriage in America* New York: Viking Press, 1977.

White, L. K. "Sex Differentials in the Effect of Remarriage on Global Happiness." *Journal of Marriage and the Family* 41 (1979):869–876.

NAME INDEX *

*This name index is limited to names found in the text. For reference names, see References section immediately preceding Name Index.

SUBJECT INDEX

PHOTO 3.4 p. 75—Christy L. Rosso. PHOTO 3.5 p. 79—David S. Strickler/Click/Chicago, Ltd. CARTOON 3.1 p. 84—Reprinted by permission of the Putnam Publishing Group from HUSBANDS, WIVES & LIVE TOGETHERS by William Hamilton. Copyright © 1976 by William Hamilton. CARTOON 3.2 p. 88—From MONEY SHOULD BE FUN by William Hamilton. Copyright © 1980 by William Hamilton. Reprinted by permission of Houghton Mifflin Company.

Chapter 4

PHOTO 4.1 p. 97—© Gilles Peress/Magnum Photos, Inc. CARTOON 4.1 p. 102—Drawing by Hoff; © 1972 The New Yorker Magazine, Inc. PHOTO 4.2 p. 108—a) Courtesy of The Free Library of Philadelphia Theatre Collection; PHOTO 4.3 p. 108—b) Courtesy of The Free Library of Philadelphia Theatre Collection; PHOTO 4.4 p. 108—c) Philippe Halsman/Magnum Photos, Inc.; PHOTO 4.5 p. 108—d) Courtesy of The George Eastman House Film Stills Collection. PHOTO 4.6 p. 111—© Eric Kroll/Taurus Photos, Inc. PHOTO 4.7 p. 114—Christy L. Rosso.

Chapter 5

PHOTO 5.1 p. 127—Peter Vandermark/Stock, Boston, Inc. PHOTO 5.2 p. 131—© Barbara Alper/Stock, Boston, Inc. CARTOON 5.1 p. 139— © *1974 by William Hamilton. Originally in ANTI-SOCIAL REGISTER published by Chronicle Books, 1974.* PHOTO 5.3 p. 147—Arthur Grace/Stock, Boston, Inc. PHOTO 5.4 p. 149—Frank Siteman. PHOTO 5.5 p. 151—Kenneth C.W. Kammeyer.

Chapter 6

PHOTO 6.1 p. 159—Michael Weisbrot. CARTOON 6.1 p. 179—Drawing by Sauers; © 1984 The New Yorker Magazine, Inc. PHOTO 6.2 p. 175—Michael Weisbrot. PHOTO 6.3 p. 183—Jerry Howard/Positive Images.

Chapter 7

PHOTO 7.1 p. 191—Timothy A. Murphy/ U.S. News & World Report.—PHOTO 7.2 p. 195—David Austen/Stock, Boston, Inc.—PHOTO 7.3 p. 199—Historical Pictures Service, Chicago.—PHOTO 7.4 p. 209—UPI/Bettmann Newsphotos. CARTOON 7.1 p. 218—*Feiffer.* Copyright © 1983, Jules Feiffer. Reprinted with permission of Universal Press Syndicate. All rights reserved.

Chapter 8

PHOTO 8.1 p. 227—© Randy Matusow/Archive Pictures, Inc.—PHOTO 8.2 p. 230—© Erich Hartmann/Magnum Photos, Inc.—PHOTO 8.3 p. 233—David S. Strickler/The Picture Cube. CARTOON 8.1 p. 238—Drawing by Weber; © 1984 The New Yorker Magazine, Inc.—PHOTO 8.4 p. 243—Emilio Mercado/Jeroboam, Inc.

Chapter 9

PHOTO 9.1 p. 263—Christopher S. Johnson/ Stock, Boston, Inc.—PHOTO 9.2 p. 266—Gayle Levee.—PHOTO 9.3 p. 268—Godey's Lady's Book and Magazine, August, 1863.—PHOTO 9.4 p. 272—Christy L. Rosso.—PHOTO 9.5 p. 280—© Andrew Brilliant/The Picture Cube. CARTOON 9.1 p. 285—From MONEY SHOULD BE FUN by William Hamilton. Copyright © 1980 by William Hamilton. Reprinted by permission of Houghton Mifflin Company.

Chapter 10

PHOTO 10.1 p. 297—Lisa Law/Jeroboam, Inc.—PHOTO 10.2 p. 303—Ellis Herwig/The Picture Cube.—PHOTO 10.3 p. 306—Margaret Thompson/The Picture Cube. CARTOON 10.1 p. 309—Drawing by Koren; © 1974 The New Yorker Magazine, Inc.—PHOTO 10.4 p. 311—Mary Ellen Mark/Archive Pictures, Inc.—PHOTO 10.5 p. 314—John Rawle/Stock, Boston, Inc.—PHOTO 10.6 p. 320—Christy L. Rosso.

Chapter 11

PHOTO 11.1 p. 337—© Peter Menzel/Stock, Boston, Inc.—PHOTO 11.2 p. 341—Michael Weisbrot.—PHOTO 11.3 p. 346—Michael Weisbrot.—PHOTO 11.4 p. 353—Anna Kaufman Moon/Stock, Boston, Inc. CARTOON 11.1 p. 359—Drawing by Ziegler; © 1985 The New Yorker Magazine, Inc.

Chapter 12

PHOTO 12.1 p. 369—Frank Siteman/The Picture Cube.—PHOTO 12.2 p. 372—Grandma Moses. *Apple Butter Making.* Copyright © 1982, Grandma Moses Properties Co., New York. CARTOON 12.1 p. 375—From MONEY SHOULD BE FUN by William Hamilton. Copyright © 1980 by William Hamilton. Reprinted by permission of Houghton Mifflin Company.—PHOTO 12.3 p. 380—Brent Jones/Click/Chicago, Ltd.—PHOTO 12.4 p. 381—© Sepp Seitz/Woodfin Camp and Associates.—PHOTO 12.5 p. 385—© Ken Karp/ Omni-Photo Communications, Inc.